SPORT MARKETING

SECOND EDITION

Bernard J. Mullin
Roller Hockey International, Inc.

Stephen Hardy
University of New Hampshire

William A. Sutton
University of Massachusetts-Amherst

Human Kinetics

Library of Congress Cataloging-in-Publication Data

Mullin, Bernard James.
    Sport marketing / Bernard Mullin, Stephen Hardy, William Sutton. -
- 2nd ed.
        p.   cm.
    Includes bibliographical references and index.
    ISBN 0-88011-877-6
    1. Sports--Marketing. I. Hardy, Stephen, 1948-   . II. Sutton,
William Anthony, 1951-   . III. Title.
GV716.M85 2000
796'.06'98--dc21   99-41126
                                                             CIP

ISBN 0-88011-877-6

Acquisitions Editor: Steven W. Pope, PhD; **Developmental Editor:** Katy M. Patterson; **Assistant Editors:** Amanda Ewing and Susan Hagan; **Copyeditor:** Joyce Sexton; **Proofreader:** Erin Cler; **Indexer:** Craig Brown; **Permission Manager:** Heather Munson; **Graphic Designer:** Stuart Cartwright; **Graphic Artist:** Kathleen Boudreau-Fuoss; **Photo Editor:** Clark Brooks; **Cover Designer:** Jack W. Davis; **Photographer (cover):** ©Rob Tringali/SportsChrome USA; **Photographer (interior):** William A. Sutton (except where otherwise noted). Photos on pages 4, 8, 23, 30, 44, 57, 59, 79, 83, 106, 119, 120, 168, 295, 308, 333, 337, 346, 359, 360, 361, and 372 by Tom Roberts; **Illustrator:** Tom Roberts; **Printer:** United Graphics, Inc./Dekker Bookbinding

Printed in the United States of America   10 9 8 7 6 5 4 3 2 1

Human Kinetics

Web site: http://www.humankinetics.com/

United States: Human Kinetics
P.O. Box 5076
Champaign, IL 61825-5076
1-800-747-4457
e-mail: humank@hkusa.com

Canada: Human Kinetics
475 Devonshire Road Unit 100
Windsor, ON N8Y 2L5
1-800-465-7301 (in Canada only)
e-mail: humank@hkcanada.com

Europe: Human Kinetics, P.O. Box IW14
Leeds LS16 6TR, United Kingdom
+44 (0)113-278 1708
e-mail: humank@hkeurope.com

Australia: Human Kinetics
57A Price Avenue
Lower Mitcham, South Australia 5062
(08) 82771555
e-mail: humank@hkaustralia.com

New Zealand: Human Kinetics
P.O. Box 105-231, Auckland Central
09-523-3462
e-mail: humank@hknewz.com

CONTENTS

CONTENTS

CONTENTS

FOREWORD

In 1985, Orlando was already a tourist mecca, but still a small town. So when the NBA began considering the concept of expansion, Miami and Tampa looked like the Sunshine State's best chances for landing a team. But a trip to Orlando planted the seed in my head . . . why not bring professional hoops to the "City Beautiful?" And thus the dream was born—a simple but daunting task—bring professional basketball to a brand new arena in downtown Orlando.

The dream became a reality in April 1987, as the Board of Governors awarded Orlando a new franchise to begin play in 1989. But even with a new arena, a new logo, and new fan support, the work was just beginning. We knew we would have to provide something to watch besides basketball, after all, we were probably not going to win many games the first few seasons.

On top of that, we would be playing our home games in the entertainment capital of the world. In a town with unlimited options, we would face stiff competition for people's entertainment dollars. And since our fans grew up in Fantasyland on the outskirts of Cinderella's castle, we knew that they would expect Disney-quality entertainment.

Our goal was to meet their expectations and our challenge was to exceed them. Every game night, fans would spend two and a half hours in our arena to watch 48 minutes of basketball. For us, this not only presented a challenge, but an incredible opportunity—102 minutes of opportunity, to be exact!

Our dance team would dazzle them, our mascot would amuse them, our Sports Magic Team would entertain them . . . this is what it would take to turn a 48-minute basketball game into a non-stop, fun-filled entertainment experience! In 1989, all the pieces fell into place. Through a backdrop of music, lighting, and pyrotechnics, the Orlando Magic took to the court, and a ball was tipped on a new era in professional sports.

Since this time, we have brought two more professional sports teams to Orlando, each of which drew a new group of fans to the O-rena. In 1995, the Orlando Solar Bears skated into the International Hockey League and all the way to the Turner Cup Finals in their inaugural season. This fast-paced, hard-hitting game offered a cool alternative to basketball through affordable ticket prices and a focus on family entertainment.

"We got next" took Orlando by storm in 1999, when the Orlando Miracle came to town, winning fans (as well as basketball games!) with their competitive play, teamwork, sportsmanship, and heart. The energetic crowd at the O-rena proved that fans of all ages would support a game of high-quality basketball played by women. Affordable ticket prices, interactive game presentation, and fan-friendly players are all essential parts of the Miracle experience.

With each new sport, we have had to find a different way to market the new team to the Orlando community. And let me tell you, it's been fun! Night after night, our staff works behind the scenes to set the stage for some of the greatest athletes in the world. We entertain thousands of fans and provide them with experiences memorable enough to last a lifetime. Throughout the long hours of late-night games or weekend events, our employees stay excited about their jobs knowing that each day will present a challenge that is fresh, unique, and fun!

The authors of Sport Marketing share these same experiences and, through their book, provide you with information and approaches that are relevant in today's sports marketplace. They have included excellent examples of surveys, sales materials, and promotional activities that are actually being used by sports marketing professionals today. This textbook is a valuable tool for those wishing to pursue a career in sports, as well an excellent resource for today's sport marketers as they continue to tackle the challenges of each new day.

I wish you all the opportunity and excitement that a career in sports can bring. Work hard, play hard, and follow your dreams. But most of all . . . love what you are doing!

Pat Williams
Sr. Executive Vice President,
RDV Sports/Orlando Magic

PREFACE

There is only one way to describe the massive changes in the sport world since the first edition of *Sport Marketing* came out in 1993. As the late Harry Caray put it, "*Holy cow!*" In 1993, most people would have thought that the Internet was a spy ring and that a Web page was something they'd find in a Ducks Unlimited newsletter. Few fans outside of the skating world had heard of Nancy or Tonya. If someone used the term "big-time basketball," it meant the NBA or the "Dream Team," not a women's league (let alone two of them). Most fans still considered NASCAR a redneck, good-old-boys enterprise, fit for the backwaters of the Old South. Ice hockey seemed better suited to the frozen tundra. Finally, some die-hard soccer fans were predicting a few sellouts for the 1994 World Cup games played in the United States, but most pundits expected lukewarm interest, especially if the U.S. team didn't advance.

Now in 1999, a Web page is a standard marketing tool for any sport organization. Marketing executives throughout the sport world get their industry news through online services such as Sports Business Daily or "SBRnet." Nancy and Tonya's skating showdown in Lillehammer was a media frenzy that resulted in the sixth highest rated prime-time television show *ever*. Skating shows are now a key element of network sport strategy. The NBA jumped into the "big-time" market for women's pro basketball with the WNBA, which for two years anyway had big-time competition from the American Basketball League. In 1999, NASCAR seemed to be everywhere, selling out huge new speedways in the likes of Loudon, New Hampshire, not far from White Mountain ski areas; NASCAR has perhaps been the biggest success story over the past several years. The sport's "big three" companies—Speedway Motorsports, International Speedway Corporation, and Penske Motorsports—are publicly traded on Wall Street and are hot items. Lauri Wils of Speedway was justified in bubbling to *Street and Smith's Sports Business Journal* that, "we're now in *Forbes*, we're now in *Fortune*, we're now in *Kiplinger's Personal Finance*." But if NASCAR has moved to Wall Street, ice hockey has ventured into the Deep South with a vengeance. Better yet, in the topsy-turvy world of sport marketing, the NHL and NASCAR have linked up to help promote each other's sport in new markets. The Nashville Predators can count on top country stars to attend their games. Finally, the 1994 World Cup succeeded beyond everyone's expectations, but that was only a warm-up compared to the mania surrounding the Women's World Cup of 1999.[1]

Of course, some things haven't changed much. The competition for the sport and entertainment dollar is as heavy as ever. Sport marketing has continued to be a competitive business, involving as much front office strategy, risk, discipline, and energy as are shown by the players and coaches who figure so prominently in the public's imagination. For instance, VISA and American Express slugged it out like boxers in their 1994 Winter Olympics ads; some might say their battle was worthy of a medal. But the stakes were higher. As an official Olympic sponsor, VISA reminded viewers that if they were going to Lillehammer, they'd better take their VISA card "because the Olympics don't take American Express." American Express could not use the term Olympics, but they might as well have. They bought time on CBS, the

Olympics network, and responded with clever images of Norway and Lillehammer, emphasizing the fact that a visa was not necessary for travel to this friendly country. The International Olympic Committee was outraged at the obvious "ambush marketing" and promised much harsher policing for sponsors of the Atlanta Games.

Meanwhile, Nike, one of the inventors of such clever ads (remember their 1984 "I Love LA" campaign?), struggled to maintain its lofty perch as an industry leader. Public pressure mounted on Nike's overseas manufacturing plants, with college students leading the way in protests against "sweatshop" labor. In fact, by 1999 all the "givens" of the shoe-player-sport triangle, so well developed by Nike, Michael Jordan, and the NBA, were crumbling in the face of a weak market of sneakers and players. Michael Jordan had retired, no one could replace him, and shoe companies backed away from throwing money at players. In 1995, Reebok had had 130 NBA players signed to lucrative contracts. In 1999, the expected number was 30. Nike was also trimming back its endorsement contracts. Lagging sales and profits were one reason. But the investment in athletes—once a given in the view of every high draft choice—no longer made sense in the marketplace. Howe Burch of Fila USA echoed the thoughts of many disgruntled fans: "Kids aren't as inspired by athletes any more." One of the sport industry's "golden geese" (the others being television and corporate sponsors) had suddenly stopped laying so many eggs.[2]

As academics, we have been studying changes in the sport industry for over 25 years, since long before *Forbes* and *Fortune* began to take sport seriously with regular coverage. When we started out as graduate students in the early 1970s, few scholars were willing to accept sport as a serious topic of study. Now leading academics in marketing, management, law, and economics (to name only a few disciplines) are rushing headlong into contracts for books on sport. We have both followed and helped to build this growing body of literature.

More important, each of us has also worked inside the industry, trying to make sense of the ways that fans, players, coaches, the media, equipment companies, and others interact to make the game tick. We have planned, administered, or consulted on literally thousands of events in just about every sport considered mainstream, and at just about every level. This book emanates from our own fusion of experience as academics and practitioners. We have written a survey that we hope is as useful for the classroom student as for the athletics director of a college or high school, the general manager of a fitness club, or the marketer of a professional franchise.

We have tried to balance theoretical models with case studies from the rinks, fields, courts, slopes, gyms, tracks, and sundry other venues that make up the sport marketplace. If theory is the skeleton that gives structure to thinking, then case studies put meat on the bones. While our examples are almost all from the United States, we hope that much of our thinking will be of benefit to sport marketers in other countries.

The second edition of *Sport Marketing* is much expanded and is built upon an almost completely new database, both from new academic journals like *Sport Marketing Quarterly* and from new industry serials like *Sports Business Daily*. The first part of the book—chapters 1 and 2—provides an overview of the sport market and of sport marketing, as an area of study and as a process. Chapters 3 through 6 consider critical areas and steps of preliminary market research and market segmentation—critical to overcoming a tendency to equate promotions with marketing. Marketing begins and ends with knowing the consumer's needs and wants; chapters 3 through 6 provide that essential perspective. Chapters 7 through 15 explore the nuts and bolts of marketing plans: the five Ps of sport marketing—product, price, promotion, place, and public relations. To this part of the book we have added three entirely new chapters—on selling, on merchandising (by Dan Covell), and on electronic media (by Tim Ashwell). The last three chapters address some important elements of control and evaluation; these chapters include a new one on legal issues (by Lisa Pike Masteralexis) and a "Nostradamus" chapter suggesting (with the help of a few experts) where we think the field will go in the next century.

ACKNOWLEDGMENTS

Our chapter notes acknowledge the sources we have used. In addition, however, we offer special acknowledgments to a number of people. The first is Philip Kotler, a scholar whose classic surveys on marketing management inspired us decades ago, and continue to influence the way we have structured this book. On the practitioner side, Bill Veeck, the great baseball magnate, looms large in our belief that everyday sport consumers have more good marketing ideas than any hundred "experts" and their summit meetings. Matt Levine, the father of modern sport marketing in the 1970s, has continued to lead the field of ideas in his executive capacity with the San Jose Sharks. We owe additional debt to Pat Williams of the Orlando Magic for his inspiration and ability to put into practice many of the concepts discussed in this book. We also thank Dan Covell, Tim Ashwell, and Lisa Pike Masteralexis for their chapter contributions, and Eric Krupa for his advice on improving sections of chapter 9.

Many people helped us obtain, organize, and develop materials for the book, including Martha Shattuck, a gifted M.B.A. student at UNH; Ed Saunders and Joe Bertagna at Hockey East; Jeffrey Pollack, Abe Madkour, Shelly Finkel and the staff at the *Sports Business Daily* (now an essential resource for anyone trying to make sense of the sport industry); Shawn Hunter at the Phoenix Coyotes; Vic Gregovits and Kathy Guy at the Pittsburgh Pirates; Alycen McAuley, Mitch Wheeler and Harry Campbell at Marketing Associates International; David Ball and John Brody at Major League Baseball Properties; Lisa Weinzetl at the Pittsburgh Steelers; Steve Swetoha at RDV Sports; Jim Kahler and Nathaniel Tilton at the Cleveland Cavs; Rick Welts, formerly at NBA Properties; John Rooney, a pioneer in sports geography; Ayala Deutsch at the NBA; Dick Bresciani and Larry Cancro at the Boston Red Sox; Dan Dumais at Coed Sportswear; Dot Sheehan at the University of New Hampshire; Dave Synowka at Robert Morris College; Charlie Eshbach at the Portland Sea Dogs; Bill Miller and Jill Greenfield at the NHL; Gregg Hanrahan at the United Center; Lisa Kovlakas at ESPN; Jerry Solomon at P.S. Star Games; Will Rudd at the NCAA; June Levy at SRDS; Carol Swartz and Susan Deckard at Goodyear; Tina Grutsch at Fleishman/Hillard; Ann Reynolds of ISL; and Alan Freidman and Sean Brenner of Team Marketing Report. We would also like to acknowledge the contributions of Jan Ori and Pamela Levine who helped develop some of the diagrams and figures in the text.

We also want to thank our excellent editors at Human Kinetics: Steve Pope, Katy Patterson, Heather Munson, and Amanda Ewing. Steve worked hard to get us on track; Katy and her staff kept us there. We appreciate their efforts.

In our capacities as sport administrators and consultants, we have worked with hundreds of dedicated executives, coaches, sports information directors, and marketers who have inspired us with their energy. As academics, we want to thank and salute our students over the years at the University of Washington, Robert Morris College, Ohio State University, the University of Massachusetts, and the University of New Hampshire. They have challenged, stretched, and indulged our thinking on all of the topics in this book. To all of these old and recent colleagues, we dedicate this book in hopes that we can convey to our readers their wisdom, their enthusiasm, and their wonder for learning.

CREDITS

APPENDIX

NCAA Championship Patron Questionnaire: Reprinted, by permission, from NCAA Championship Patron Questionnaire.

FIGURES

Figure 10.2: Copyright 1985, Lexis Law Publishing. Reprinted with permission from *Successful Sport Management* by Guy Lewis and Herb Appenzeller. Lexis Law Publishing Charlottesville, VA (800)446-3410. All Rights Reserved.

Figure 11.5: Organizational chart reprinted, by permission, from San Francisco Giants.

Figure 12.1: Reprinted, by permission, from *IEG Sponsorship Report*, 1999 (Chicago: IEG, Inc.).

Figure 12.5: Reprinted, by permission, from R.G. Hagstrom, 1998, *The NASCAR way: The business that drives the sport* (New York: Wiley), 50.

Figure 12.6: Reprinted, by permission, from *IEG Sponsorship Report*, 1999 (Chicago: IEG, Inc.).

PHOTOS

Page 1: Photo of Bill Veeck by Brace Photo.

Page 12 : Photo by Bill Sutton. Mascots appear courtesy of University of Massachusetts and Pittsfield Mets.

Page 14: Photo by Hockey East / Monty Rand Studios.

Page 31: Brochure reprinted, by permission, from WNBA. 1997.

Page 35: Reprinted, by permission, from NCAA. NCAA Hockey Championship Audience Demographics. 1998.

Page 37: © 1999 Joe Robbins.

Page 46: Photo of Jeff Gordon by Sue Deckard courtesy of Goodyear.

Page 52: Reprinted, by permission, from *The Sports Business Daily*, a publication of Street & Smith's Sports Group.

Page 64: Reprinted, by permission, from *Atlas of American Sport* (New York: McMillan) 1992.

Page 65: Mary Langenfeld Photo.

Page 72: Photo by Hockey East / Monty Rand Studios.

Page 102: Photo of Jane Blalock courtesy of The Jane Blalock Company.

Page 108: Photo of female fans by Christopher A. Enstrom.

Page 124: Photo of Bill Sutton, Dave Synowka, Vic Gregovits, and Pirate intern at Fantasy camp by Dave Arrigo / Pittsburgh Pirates.

Page126: Photo of Red Sox ticket dated April 20, 1998 reprinted by permission from Boston Red Sox.

Page 133: T-shirt reprinted, by permission, from *Power of a Woman* catalog. Copyright Coed Sportswear, Inc.; T-shirt reprinted, by permission, from *180 Degrees* catalog. Copyright Coed Sportswear, Inc.: T-shirt reprinted, by permission, from *Power of a Woman* catalog. Copyright Coed Sportswear, Inc.

Page 136: University of New Hampshire 1998-99 hockey pocket schedule reprinted, by permission, from University of New Hampshire.

Page 158: Golden State Warriors logo reprinted, with permission, from NBA Properties, Inc.; Golden State Warriors logo reprinted, with permission, from NBA Properties, Inc.

Page 159: Villanova University logo reprinted, by permission, from Collegiate Licensing Company and Villanova University; St. John's University logo reprinted, by permission, from Collegiate Licensing Company and St. John's University.

Page 178-179: Portland Sea Dogs 1999 ticket brochure reprinted, by permission, from Portland Sea Dogs.

Pgae 184: Beanie Babies are registered trademarks of Ty Inc. Glory is a registered trademark of Ty Inc. All photographs are used by permission of Ty Inc. Major League Baseball and Minor League Baseball trademarks and copyrights are used with permission of Major League Baseball Properties, Inc.

Page 188: Hockey puck ticket advertisement reprinted, by permission, from Phoenix Coyotes.

Page 190: Photo of soccer player and empty sign reprinted, by permission, from Imadgine Video Systems USA; Photo of soccer player and signage reprinted, by permission, from Imadgine Video Systems USA.

Page 198: Pirate bus reprinted, by permission, from Pittsburgh Pirates.

Page 202: Major League Baseball and Minor League Baseball trademarks and copyrights are used with permission of Major League Baseball Properties, Inc.

Page 204: Pirates' promotional events flyer reprinted, by permission, from Pittsburgh Pirates.

Page 211: Pirates' open house flyer reprinted, by permission, from Pittsburgh Pirates.

Page 232: Compadres Reward System chart reprinted, by permission, from San Diego Padres and Major League Baseball.

Page 233: Compadres Club Application reprinted, by permission, from San Diego Padres and Major League Baseball.

Page 241: Pirates' Open House photo reprinted, by permission, from Pittsburgh Pirates.

Page 243: Hockey 101 brochure reprinted, by permission, from Phoenix Coyotes.

Page 244: Family Nights advertisement reprinted, by permission, from Los Angeles Kings.

Page 283: NHL Breakout brochure reprinted, by permission, from National Hockey League.

Page 286: United Center map reprinted, by permission, from United Center Joint Venture, all rights reserved.

Page 289: Photo of model suite reprinted courtesy of Pittsburgh Steelers.

Page 296: Photo of NBA store reprinted, by permission, from NBA Photos, a division of NBA Entertainment, Inc.

Page 303: Photo of ESPN plaza by Ray Martin reprinted, by permission, from ESPN, Inc.

Page 306: Photo of production truck by Scott Clarke reprinted, by permission, from ESPN, Inc.

Page 313: Red Sox Web page reprinted, by permission, from Boston Red Sox. Photo reprinted, by permission, from Bill Horsman.

Page 321: Your team, our town sign reprinted, by permission, from Pittsburgh Pirates.

Page 322: Copyright, photo by Bob Donaldson/*Pittsburgh Post-Gazette* 1998 all rights reserved. Reprinted with permission.

Page 334: Photo courtesy of Jim Bouton.

Page 338: Photo by Rebecca Crist.

Page 348: © SportsChrome East/West.

Page 379: Photo of male fans by Rebecca Crist.

Page 381: Photo of fans at game by Christopher A. Enstrom.

TABLES

Table 3.2: Adapted from *Miller Lite Report on American Attitudes Towards Sports*, 1983 (p.27) by the Miller Brewing Company, 1983. Milwaukee: Author. Copyright 1983 by the Miller Brewing Company. Reprinted with permission.

Table 3.6: Adapted, by permission, from "What do the children play? Top three growing youth sports," 1997, *The Sports Business Daily* 15 Sept. 1997: 15. *The Sports Business Daily* is a publication of Street & Smith's Sports Group.

Table 3.7: Reprinted from the 1999 edition of *The Lifestyle Market Analyst*, published by SRDS with data supplied by Polk.

Table 3.8: Adapted, by permission, from "Sports sponsometer: Soccer interest and sponsor awareness," 1997, *The Sports Business Daily* 2 April 1997: 15. *The Sports Business Daily* is a publication of Street & Smith's Sports Group.

Table 3.9: Reprinted, by permission, from "U.S. soccer participation, 1995-96," *NCAA News* 19 May 1997: 2.

Table 4.2: Adapted, by permission, from "Sports sponsometer: Targeting the female sports audience," 1997, *The Sports Business Daily* 8 Oct. 1997: 16. *The Sports Business Daily* is a publication of Street & Smith's Sports Group.

Table 4.4: Reprinted from the 1999 edition of *The Lifestyle Market Analyst*, published by SRDS with data supplied by Polk.

Table 6.1: Adapted, by permission, from "ESPN Chilton sports poll: Gauging interest meter," 1997, *The Sports Business Daily* 15 Aug. 1997: 15. *The Sports Business Daily* is a publication of Street & Smith's Sports Group.

Table 16.1: Adapted, by permission, from "ESPN Chilton sports poll: Are purchasing decisions based on brand?" 1998, *The Sports Business Daily* 24 July 1998: 16. *The Sports Business Daily* is a publication of Street & Smith's Sports Group.

THE SPECIAL NATURE OF SPORT MARKETING

OBJECTIVES

1. To understand the market forces that create the need for enlightened marketing strategies in the sport industry.

2. To understand the obstacles to clear marketing strategy in sport.

3. To recognize the components of the sport product and of the sport industry.

4. To recognize the factors that make sport marketing a unique enterprise.

THE "DIVINE" WORLD OF SPORT

In October 1997, as the Chicago Bulls battled five other international pro league winners in the McDonald's Championship in the Palais Omnisports de Bercy, the Eiffel Tower yielded its icon status to Michael Jordan. The French prime minister joined some 27,000 fans and 1,000 journalists to worship the player some call "His Airness." One fawning journalist asked "l'idole" if he was, in fact, divine. Jordan responded that he was embarrassed at the question. He was a player: "I try to entertain for two hours and then let people go home to their lives . . . I could never consider myself a god." Maybe not, but as National Basketball Association (NBA) Commissioner David Stern recognized, "He's the most famous athlete of his time, and perhaps, with Muhammad Ali, of any time." Whether he was a god or merely a mortal, Michael Jordan was a sport product of divine proportions. His talent, his competitiveness, and his charisma had also supported the international marketing strategies of two other sport giants—Nike and David Stern's NBA.[1]

Although entrepreneurs have been selling sport for centuries, rational systems of marketing sport are relatively new. In this chapter, we discuss the need to employ modern marketing principles in the sport domain. We examine the sport industry trends of growth and competition that heighten the need for scientific, professional approaches to sport marketing. We consider examples of lingering "marketing myopia" in sport, as well as signs of progress. Next, we consider the components of the sport product and of the sport industry. Finally, we outline the numerous features that in combination make sport marketing a unique area of inquiry and application.

SPORTS GO GLOBAL; SO DOES THE COMPETITION

If Michael Jordan was a worldwide sporting god in 1997, then David Stern was the high priest of the religion of basketball, presiding over a far-flung, international temple inappropriately called the National Basketball Association. When Stern became commissioner in 1984 (he had been NBA general counsel since 1978), the NBA was a struggling enterprise, despite stars like Magic Johnson and Larry Bird. Teams were playing in arenas at less than two-thirds capacity, NBA merchandise sales were only about $15 million, network television coverage was limited, and corporate sponsors were scared off, in large part because of a poor public image resulting from drug scandals and labor strife. As one NBA executive recalled in a 1991 profile of Stern: "If you had thirty minutes with a prospective sponsor, your first 20 minutes were spent trying to convince him that the players weren't all on drugs."[2]

Even before his elevation to the commissionership, Stern had laid the foundation for the NBA to become the most successful brand name in sport. He did it by recognizing and utilizing standard tools of marketing. He knew, among other things, that product recognition required a more expansive television package. In turn, the broadcast networks demanded a more stable product with a cleaner image. That meant getting owners and players to agree on several fundamental issues, including revenue sharing, salary caps, and tougher drug testing. As a Spalding executive concluded, "A good marketing guy knows that he has to get the product right before marketing it. That's what Stern did with basketball."[3]

Once he had accomplished this, Stern began packaging NBA products in a host of forms, including television, videotape, radio, and assorted merchandise. Equally important, he pressed hard for an international NBA presence, starting with season-opening league games in Tokyo in 1990. The 1992 "Dream Team" Olympic venture and the McDonald's Open followed. By 1997, the NBA was the most recognized sport brand in the world. Some examples of the sweeping expansion of NBA "believers" around the globe:[1]

➤ NBA Entertainment was sending a range of programs, including "NBA Inside Stuff," "Game of the Week," "NBA Jam," and "NBA Action," to viewers in over 170 countries. Rights fees varied with ability to pay. China got the programming for free, so almost all of China's television households (250 million) watched NBA programs.

➤ In 1995-1996, fans in Europe, Australia, and Hong Kong joined their North American counterparts in voting for All-Stars via the World Wide Web. The NBA's official Web site, NBA.com, provided language options in English, Spanish, French, and Italian. The result: 35 percent of traffic on the site came from outside the United States.

➤ By 1997, the NBA was selling nearly $500 million in merchandise outside the United States. Youngsters in the Dominican Republic were shedding their baseball cleats in favor of Nike or Reebok sneakers and official NBA jerseys. Many spent a month's wages in order to look like Michael or Shaq. Said Hugo Lopez Morrobel, sports editor of *Listin Diario,* the largest daily in this baseball-rich nation: "The NBA is el maximo here right now."

➤ From Tokyo to Moscow, kids were abandoning national heroes and embracing NBA stars. As Vasya Katargin put it in 1994, shortly after the Russian team gave Dream Team II a serious run at the World Championships: "No one wants to be Yevgeny Kissurin. Everyone wants to be Charles Barkley."

Marketing in today's complex sport marketplace requires Bill Veeck's timeless creativity and customer satisfaction, as well as the latest technology.

In 1997, the NBA was on top of the world. Of course, as the Parisians recognized, the NBA's rise to glory rested in large part on the sturdy back of Michael Jordan. David Stern also knew that Michael himself was the product of a special moment, when corporate giants like Nike, McDonald's, and Coca-Cola joined hands with expanding television technologies to create megastars and megasports. In Stern's words, "Michael Jordan came along at the same time that sports marketing developed. . . . There will never be a growth spurt like that again."[5]

ANOTHER GOLDEN AGE OF SPORT?

In fact, sport marketing has a long history, dating back to promoters in ancient Greece and Rome. There have been many "golden ages" and growth spurts. David Stern has thousands of predecessors, including the legendary Bill Veeck, one of the most imaginative sport entrepreneurs of the past century, and the most creative marketer in the history of baseball (see photo). Boxing had Tex Rickard, who made a name in the first quarter of this century promoting boxing matches with the likes of Jack Johnson and Jack Dempsey. He later ran sports at Madison Square Garden, where the press referred to his young hockey franchise as Tex's "Rangers." In 1928, he was asked by a pundit, "What do you regard as the secret to your success as a promoter—what psychological impulse guides you?" Rickard answered quickly: "It's no secret. By merely reading the newspapers most anybody can tell what the public wants to see."[6]

During the last decade, it appeared that sport marketers gave the public what they wanted to see—and hear and play. On the surface, the 1990s seemed to be another golden age of sport, much like the 1920s and 1950s. Some examples:[7]

➤ Economists at Georgia Tech estimated that the 1995 total U.S. domestic sport consumption and investment amounted to a whopping $151.9 billion, making the sport industry the nation's 11th largest—more than twice the size of the auto repair services and parking industries (see table 1.1).

Table 1.1 WHERE DO SPORTS RANK?

Some of the top 25 U.S. industry rankings based on 1995 estimated gross domestic product

Rank	Industry	Size in billions of dollars
1	Real estate	850.0
2	Retail trade	639.9
4	Health service	443.4
5	Construction	277.6
8	Utilities	205.3
11	Sports	152.0
15	Insurance carriers	115.4
18	Legal services	100.5
25	Auto repair, services, parking	60.5

From Alfie Meek, *Sport Marketing Quarterly*, 6,4 (December 1997).

➤ From 1996 to 1997, financial values of the 113 major league teams (NBA, National Hockey League [NHL], Major League Baseball [MLB], National Football League [NFL]) appreciated 18 percent, according to *Financial World*, even though operating income was down.

➤ The Super Bowl continued to cement its position as one of America's modern commercial "holidays." Most of the top 10 television ratings winners have been Super Bowls. A worldwide audience annually marked its calendar for the orgy of nachos, dips, football, and advertisements. By November of 1997, NBC had sold all of its ad time for Super Bowl XXXII, at an average rate of $1.3 million for a 30-second spot. Anheuser-Busch, PepsiCo, Nike, American Express, and Disney were among the corporate giants lined up to pour their dollars and their products over the mass audience.

➤ Once viewed as a "regional" sport, ice hockey seemed to be breaking out all over the country. Pro franchises existed in Arizona and Florida. When the University of Nebraska at Omaha opened season-ticket sales for its new men's hockey team, slated to begin play some 17 months later, all 6,200 season tickets were sold in just over two weeks. Hockey has experienced spectacular increases among girls and women. In December of 1997, the U.S. women's national team played a televised prime-time game against Canada, in a warm-up to the Nagano Olympics, where they became America's most positive story. Their gold medal success spawned talk of a women's professional league.

During the 1990s, a number of traditionally news- and business-oriented magazines and papers began to incorporate sports news into their regular formats.

➤ Interest in sport for women and girls surged among players and fans alike. At some schools, like the Universities of Tennessee and Maine, the women's basketball team regularly outdrew the men's. The National Collegiate Athletic Association (NCAA) Champion "Lady Vols" averaged 14,000 fans per game, better than the averages for six different NBA teams! The market for women's basketball was so ripe that 1997 saw not one but two pro leagues carving up the map and competing for talent. Many of the women's fans were men. At the same time, the NFL fan base had shifted its gender ratio during the decade, from 33 to 43 percent female.

➤ *Fortune, Forbes, Business Week,* and the *Wall Street Journal* began to cover the sport beat on a regular basis, something unheard of two decades earlier. The *New York Times* finally succumbed to the rage for sport news and began a stand-alone sport section, seven days a week. Sport, it seems, was finally among "All the News That's Fit To Print."

➤ Hollywood continued to expand its sport interests, making a range of films from acclaimed documentaries like *Hoop Dreams* to lukewarm comedies like *Tin Cup*. Despite the range of quality, the public embraced celluloid sport. The 1997 video release of *Jerry Maguire*, Cameron Crowe's take on the world of sports agents, set a weekend record with almost 3 million copies rented and 3.5 million sold.

➤ In 1996, sport programming made up 2,100 hours of time on the four major networks. That amounted to 40 hours per week, 52 weeks of the year, just on the networks. With the growth of sport channels on cable—from Classic Sports to Speed and the Golf Channel—the hard-core fan could watch sports 24 hours a day, all year round. Sponsors were delighted with the prospects and funneled more than a billion dollars in ad revenue to cable sports alone.

A TROUBLED GOLDEN AGE

With this huge increase in media exposure and public interest, we might expect sport marketing to have become progressively easier in the last few decades. In fact, the opposite is true. Public interest spawned militant unions, higher salaries, and spoiled players who seemed to be spiraling out of anyone's control. And that was just the start of the marketing problems.

CRACKS IN THE NATIONAL BASKETBALL ASSOCIATION'S ARMOR?

No one knew this better than David Stern. Shortly after the McDonald's Open in Paris, cracks appeared in the NBA's armor, many of them caused by fan and media hostility toward high-priced athletes and high-priced tickets. The lightning rod for criticism was a talented but troubled star named Latrell Sprewell of the Golden State Warriors. Sprewell, in the middle of a $32 million contract, allegedly slugged and choked his coach at a practice. He was quickly fired by his team and banished for a year by David Stern himself. An arbitrator soon reduced the punishment, which triggered an avalanche of commentary on talk radio and Web sites. Media critics wondered if the glorious ride on top was over for the NBA. Jack McCallum of *Sports Illustrated* wrote a feature opinion directed at the league office. He reminded Stern that too many stars were either acting up, playing poorly, or sitting out with various "ailments." League attendance was down. Some teams were just plain stinky (to use the Celtics owner's own descriptor). To make matters even worse, McCallum reminded Stern that "Michael says he's quitting." After another championship ring in 1998 and a nasty lockout, Michael Jordan announced his retirement in January 1999. It appeared that David Stern had big troubles with his product—shades of 1982.[8]

Some pundits claimed that the backlash was racial. The NBA's core product revolved around skilled players, 80 percent of whom, like Sprewell and Michael Jordan, were black. Were the NBA's so-called troubles part of a larger national angst over race? Rob Parker of *Newsday* didn't think so. It wasn't Sprewell; it was the league itself. "It's simple," said Parker. "Too much expansion has eroded the talent level, making many games both uncompetitive and boring to watch." With average ticket prices over $40 each in 1997, Parker saw the fans as rational consumers: "Fans seem to be deciding that the game they have been brainwashed to believe is fantastic, simply isn't anymore." The NBA will surely survive its current challenges, but they clearly represent how volatile the sports marketplace can be.[9]

BASEBALL'S WOES AND HOPES

If David Stern's NBA was on a 1990s roller coaster, so was MLB, as just a few facts suggest:[10]

➤ A 1997 Harris poll (table 1.2) suggested that baseball's popularity had slipped dramatically in a decade.

➤ The major leagues seemed to drift. A long, bitter strike had canceled the 1994 World Series (world wars had not done that), the owners had hatched a disastrous television plan called the Baseball Network, and there was no real commissioner (until August 1998); but prices, like player salaries, kept spiraling upward. Although

Table 1.2 TOP FIVE FAVORITE SPORTS—1985–1997

Sport	1985	1992	1994	1997
Pro football	24%	28%	24%	28%
Baseball	23%	21%	17%	17%
Pro basketball	6%	8%	11%	13%
College basketball	6%	8%	8%	6%
College football	10%	7%`	7%	10%

From *Sports Business Daily*, 17 November 1997, p. 16. Excerpted from Harris poll survey of adults, asking their "favorite sport."

MLB announced that 1997 attendance had climbed to 63.1 million, that figure was still 7 million below the high-water mark of 1993. In 1998, despite the home run heroics of Mark McGwire and Sammy Sosa, close division races, and higher television ratings, average attendance still lagged behind pre-strike levels.

➤ Fan interest was highly unsettled. Minor leagues appeared to be booming, but sales of minor league merchandise continued to slip from their 1994 high of $60 million. Sales in 1996 were down to $33.7 million. Youth baseball thrived in places, but Americans were fixated on the "problems" of baseball. On the eve of the 1997 play-offs, 58 percent of respondents in a *New York Times* poll said they were "not interested" in baseball. An Associated Press poll in August 1998 suggested that even the assault on Ruth and Maris had less impact than met the eye. Among a national, adult sample, 62 percent said "I don't pay much attention to baseball."

➤ In March 1988, Reebok announced that it was cutting back on its MLB investments. While it would retain a stable of stars (such as Mo Vaughan), it would no longer flood the dugouts with redeemable certificates. The reason, said Reebok: "a lackluster athletic shoe market, particularly for baseball cleats."

➤ For a sport steeped in tradition, there was further bad news: attendance at the Hall of Fame in Cooperstown was down 33 percent since the strike.

If the 1980s had been boom years for baseball, would history point to the 1990s as the swan song for the national pastime?

THE COMPETITIVE MARKETPLACE

Baseball "troubles" must be seen in light of a sport marketplace that shows both steady growth and cutthroat competition. As table 1.3 illustrates, Americans have expanded their consumption of "recreation," of which spectator sports are just a part. In 1985, recreation accounted for 6.1 percent of total personal consumption. By 1994, that percentage had jumped to 8.3 percent. "Recreation," at least, was getting a bigger piece of the consumption pie. The statistics were not so good, however, for spectator sports, which have seen a steady decline as a percentage of total recreation expenditures (from 3.9 percent in 1970 to 1.3 percent in 1994). And where is the recreation dollar going? As table 1.3 suggests, "commercial participant amusements" (e.g., bowling, skating, and golf) have held a steady proportion while video and audio goods, including computers, have skyrocketed—from 6.6 percent to almost one quarter of all recreation expenditures.[11]

One might argue that sports simply can't expand like VCRs and computers. Sports require an infrastructure of fields and stadiums, which are slow to develop. A person won't shell out $800 for golf clubs if she has no place to play. All this is

Table 1.3 SPECTATOR SPORTS, AMUSEMENTS, AND THE CONSUMPTION "PIE" IN BILLIONS OF REAL (1992) DOLLARS

Product or Service	1970	1980	1985	1990	1994
Total recreation expenditure	93.8	159.7	215	291.8	369.9
as % of total personal consumption	4.3	5.3	6.1	7.1	8.3
Spectator sports admissions	3.7	4.5	4.8	4.8	4.9
as % of total recreation expenditure	3.9	2.8	2.2	1.6	1.3
Commercial participant amusements	7.7	15.3	20.0	24.9	32.9
as % of total recreation expenditure	8.2	9.5	9.3	8.5	8.8
Video, audio, computer equipment	6.2	12.7	24.7	47.9	89.0
as % of total recreation expenditure	6.6	7.9	11.4	16.4	24.0

From U.S. Dept. of Commerce, *Statistical Abstract of the United States*, 1996, Table 401, p. 252.

true; there are some long-standing brakes on the growth of the sport market. But that is not the whole answer. There is great competition for the discretionary dollar, from outside and inside the sport industry.

COMPETITION WITHIN SPORTS

Competition within professional team sports has increased with the addition (and frequent failure) of rival leagues and with the ongoing expansion of playing seasons. For over a century, entrepreneurs and investors have jostled for market space. Professional baseball's troubles are internal these days, but the game's history is punctuated by a number of wars among rival leagues, the last threat being the Continental League in the early 1960s. Football took center stage in the 1960s with the rivalry between the American and the National Football Leagues. The World Football League and the U.S. Football League followed in the 1970s and 1980s; and things may not be quiet on the pro football front today. In early 1998, NBC (which had lost its American Football Conference broadcast rights in a bidding war with CBS) announced negotiations with TBS for a new pro football league—to go head-to-head against the NFL. The most interesting market battle, however, was in women's pro basketball, where the Women's National Basketball Association (WNBA) and the American Basketball League (ABL) offered consumers alternative visions of a "big league," at least until the ABL dissolved in early 1999.

Competition extends well beyond that of any one industry segment. Data from the *Statistical Abstract of the United States* (table 1.4) suggest that some activities may prosper at the expense of others.

These data do not mean that horse-race fanatics suddenly shifted their dollars to golf, or that tennis players stopped playing on clay courts to watch women's basketball on other courts. But the marketplace shows evidence of competition. There will be winners and losers, at both the "big-time" and the "grassroots" levels. For instance, in early 1998, McDonald's announced that it was ending its long partnership with the NFL and expanding its relationship with the NBA. McDonald's Senior Vice President for Marketing Brad Bell simply concluded that the NBA allowed him to "penetrate a wider base of fans," since there was "a wider base of the kid and youth market actually playing" basketball than there was playing football.

Along similar lines, kids were not responding to the star endorsers the way they had in the 1980s and early 1990s. Shoe companies began to cancel their deals. As Luke Cyphers of the *New York Daily News* argued, "Too many sports products, leagues and teams" were "chasing too few dollars." As experts analyzed FILA's decision to end its endorsement deal with baseball star Derek Jeter, Cyphers concluded: "While no one is putting a going-out-of-business sign on the NFL, the NBA or even the Florida Marlins, the sports world has found out it is not immune from supply and demand."

In some markets, heavy competition among sport enterprises exacerbated the law of supply and demand. In 1998-1999, Buffalo had seven minor league franchises— indoor soccer and lacrosse, roller hockey, arena football, men's and women's baseball, and outdoor soccer—competing for fans along with the Bills, the Sabres, and a half-dozen colleges and universities. One team administrator summed up the reality: "I think there's a market for us. It's just a matter of swaying people to spend their

Table 1.4 CHANGING FORTUNES OF SELECTED SPORTS

Sport product	1990	1994	% change
Public golf course receipts (in billions)	2.2	3.2	45.4
NCAA men's basketball attendance (in millions)	28.7	28.3	−1.3
NCAA women's basketball attendance (in millions)	2.7	4.5	66.6
Horse-race attendance (in millions)	63.8	42.0	−34.1
Tennis equipment sales (in millions)	287.0	257.0	−10.4

From U.S. Census Bureau, *Statistical Abstract of the United States*, 1996, Table 412, p. 257.

While youth soccer participation is at an all-time high, attendance at professional soccer leagues has not followed suit.

entertainment dollar with us."[12]

Even the "hot" sport of soccer shows how complicated the sport market is. While American youth soccer participation has boomed beyond even Pele's wildest dreams, that has not ensured a market for elite-level competition. On the eve of the 1994 World Cup, hosted by the United States, 73 percent of adult respondents to a Harris poll said they had heard of the World Cup, but 56 percent also said they were not interested in watching a single game on television. World Cup attendance and ratings exceeded expectations, however, and investors lined up to buy into Major League Soccer, the latest American attempt at a pro league. The inaugural season enjoyed better-than-projected attendance and television ratings. Unfortunately, attendance slumped 10 percent in 1997. In early 1998, however, the finals of the CONCACAF Gold Cup Championships in the Los Angeles Coliseum drew a crowd of 91,255. Was America finally ready to join the world in its love affair with professional soccer? Maybe and maybe not.[13]

The market for sport can't be taken for granted, even at the youth level. For example, the Center for the Study of Sport in Society (located at Northeastern University) found that while 80 to 90 percent of suburban Boston youth played at least one sport, the rate dropped dramatically—to an estimated 30 percent—for youth in the city of Boston itself. The Center's Art Taylor noted that 30 percent looked good compared to Detroit's estimated 10 percent. The low rates were not just a product of apathy. The inner cities had relatively few people or companies promoting sports for kids, especially girls. Boston's Mayor Thomas Menino responded by organizing the Youth Sports Congress to search for solutions.[14]

SPORT MARKETING DEFINED

As the needs and demographic makeup of sport consumers have become more complex, and as competition for the spectator and participant dollar has increased, the demand for professional marketing has also grown. Racquet or golf clubs, professional teams, small colleges, high schools, and youth programs have all looked for a better way to attract and maintain consumers. Among other things, they know that they compete for time and money with a host of rivals, including malls, mega-movie complexes, Internet providers, music/concerts, and museums.[15]

Today's marketers clearly need a rational, coherent system that can match sport consumers with sport products. We may call this sport marketing—but what is sport marketing? Unfortunately, the concept is still quite loose. The term "sports marketing" was coined by *Advertising Age* in 1978 to describe the activities of consumer and industrial product and service marketers who were increasingly using sport as a promotional vehicle. Even a casual television viewer cannot help noticing the use of sport images and personalities to sell beer, cars, and a whole range of other products.[16]

This sense of the term, however, is extremely limited in that it fails to recognize the dominant portion of sport marketing, which is the marketing of sport products, events, and services. This text will recognize two components in sport marketing: marketing *of* sport and marketing *through* sport.

A professional team or a racquet club engages in the former; a brewery or an auto dealer employs the latter. Although most of this book addresses the marketing *of* sport, we also consider (especially in chapter 12) the corporate sponsor, who markets *through* sport.

Another confusing element is use of the term sports (plural) marketing rather than sport (singular) marketing. "Sports" marketing connotes an industry of diverse and uncoordinated segments that have little commonality. Certainly each segment of the sport industry does operate independently and with minimal sharing of managerial practice. However, if standardized management and marketing practice is ever to come to the sport industry, then at some point we need to conceptualize industry segments as a homogeneous entity. In the chapters that follow, we hope first to provide a general theory of sport marketing across all segments, and then to supplement this theory with marketing issues peculiar to separate segments.

Given these notions about the sport industry and marketing, we offer the following definition of sport marketing, adapted from a standard definition of general marketing:

> *Sport marketing consists of all activities designed to meet the needs and wants of sport consumers through exchange processes. Sport marketing has developed two major thrusts: the marketing of sport products and services directly to consumers of sport, and marketing of other consumer and industrial products or services through the use of sport promotions.*

As we shall see, the terms "sport consumers" and "sport consumption" entail many types of involvement with sport, including playing, officiating, watching, listening, reading, and collecting.[17]

MARKETING MYOPIA IN SPORT

If sport marketing ideally consists of activities designed to meet the wants and needs of sport consumers, then historically the industry has been guilty of what Theodore Levitt called "marketing myopia," or "a lack of foresight in marketing ventures." Some of the standard symptoms of myopia include the following:[18]

➢ A focus on producing and selling goods and services rather than identifying and satisfying the needs and wants of consumers and their markets. Spencer Garrett, part owner and general manager of the successful Pierpont Racquet Club, recognized a problem that plagues many sport teams: "There are industry people who still focus on closing the sale. Membership [we can add "fan"] retention is where the future of the industry lies, so selling has to focus on benefits to the potential member." Selling is a critical component of marketing, but it is not the end-all.[19]

➢ The belief that winning absolves all other sins. Longtime Buffalo Bills owner, Ralph Wilson, expressed this sentiment recently as he questioned some expenditures. "You go about marketing by winning," he insisted. "That's how you do it. A couple years ago we spent $700,000 on television, advertising the Bills, and we didn't sell five tickets. . . . This is sort of an anomaly, this marketing. Everybody gets carried away with it."[20]

➢ Confusion between promotions and marketing. Promotion—including advertising and special events—is only part of a marketing mix or strategy. Many fail to see the difference. For instance, in 1993 the *NCAA News* ran a feature story entitled "Professional Marketing Finds Its Way into College Basketball." The article hardly described "professional marketing"—only the influx into college arenas of promotional tactics like NBA-style laser shows, cheerleaders, and half-time shows. Said Jim Harrick, UCLA coach at the time: "In the past, UCLA has had a history of its game being its main attraction. Marketing has become a great asset." Good promotions can certainly be the "sizzle" that sells the "steak," but promotions must be part of an integrated strategy that begins with knowing consumer wants and needs.[21]

➤ A short-sighted focus on quick-return investments like sponsorships rather than long-term investments in research and in relationship marketing. This is especially true at the professional levels, where escalating salaries have prompted front offices to focus resources on selling corporate signage, often at the expense of building a large database around small groups, families, and individual ticket buyers.[22]

Although some organizations have shifted their perspectives, marketing myopia is still a widespread affliction in many industry segments. This shows up in the continued emphasis on sales and promotions and in the continued lag in the number of professionally-trained marketers.

THE SLOW GROWTH OF THE PROFESSION

Marketing myopia also slowed the sport industry's development of professional marketing staff. Brilliant legends like Tex Rickard or Bill Veeck learned their craft in the school of hard knocks—there was no formal training for their job. They were called "promoters"; many of their colleagues were called "press agents." They were considered hucksters. As late as the 1980s, it was unusual to find a collegiate athletics program that had any staff member whose title contained the word *marketing*. This is slowly changing. Recent data from 291 NCAA Division I and II programs showed that "63% of the administrators in charge of sport marketing were employed full-time in that activity." Further, 20 percent of the positions were designated "sport marketing." Hundreds of universities around the world run degree programs with some amount of focus on sport marketing. In addition, a number of professional groups, such as the National Association of Collegiate Marketing Administrators, exist today. At the industry's executive end, annual conferences and symposiums focus on marketing issues—the International Sports Summit and the Super Show, among others.[23]

On the other hand, "professional" sport marketers have a way to go before they enjoy salaries commensurate with their skills and responsibilities. Annual surveys by *Team Marketing Report*, a standard industry newsletter, paint a sobering picture, as outlined briefly in table 1.5. Directors of marketing at the professional and collegiate ranks averaged about nine years of experience by 1997, yet their salaries were closer to those of entry-level computer programmers. Much of this stemmed from a "supply-and-demand" mentality among executives, who are flooded with resumes from sport fanatics willing to work for free. Low salaries and long hours have created high levels of frustration. The 1996 *Team Marketing Report* survey showed that 37 percent of the marketing staff in the minor leagues were applying for new jobs. Collegiate professionals were applying at a 31 percent rate, while major league marketing staffs appeared to be more stable, with 16 percent applying for other jobs.

THE LACK OF MARKET RESEARCH

While lately even the casual sport consumer has been surveyed at games, in clubs, or in malls,

Table 1.5 *TEAM MARKETING REPORT*—SALARY SURVEY RESULTS 1992, 1996, 1998			
Occupation	Average salary by year		
	1992	1996	1998
Major league VP of marketing	122,500	114,444	120,250
Major league director of marketing	70,124	76,785	NA
"Secondary" league director of marketing	39,827	37,031	45,000
Collegiate director of marketing	33,353	36,346	38,500

From *Team Marketing Report*, October 1992, 6; May 1997, 7; June 1998, 6, 7.

much of the research is myopic, lacking any "sportsense." For instance, as we discuss in chapter 5, the sport venue requires special considera–tions on sampling. Simply handing out surveys at the front door will not do the trick. Further, questions on sport "participation" require much more clarity than one normally sees in an average survey. Does playing one round of golf per year—with someone else's clubs—make a person a "golfer"? Some surveys have suggested this sort of thing. Most important is the lingering need for sport executives to invest in well-designed research that includes qualitative methods (e.g., in-depth interviews), not simply quick, sloppy surveys.

Research failures exist at all levels. For instance, it appears that the NFL did no research when it let Nashville play the 1997 season in Memphis, a long-standing rival city whose residents were not about to support a carpetbagging franchise. Attendance was an embarrassment. Dallas Cowboys owner Jerry Jones was candid enough to admit the NFL's hubris: "I wish we'd done our homework more. . . . We could have better identified the unique mentality between Memphis and Nashville." Some colleges and universities also operate without research. A recent study of NCAA Division I and II programs suggested that only 32 percent conduct fan surveys at home games. The authors have experienced firsthand some of the frustrations in selling research to executives. One pro team administrator delivered completed, machine-readable surveys to us in four Hefty trash bags! Myopia can't get much worse.[24]

POOR SALES TECHNIQUES

Although many sport firms have equated sales and promotions with marketing, few have even invested in the sales effort. Historically, sales have been driven by quota and commissions mentalities, with little emphasis on training, on tactics, or on sales as part of the larger marketing strategy.

For instance, why do so many tennis, racquetball, fitness, and health clubs still hire part-time students to work as control-desk personnel and double as sales staff? Don't the owners realize that their destiny (and financial stability) is in inexperienced hands? In all but a few clubs, desk personnel are the primary consumer contact (on the phone, at the front desk, and for walk-in prospects). It seems incomprehensible that a business that is subject to high customer turnover, fads, and trends would overlook such a critical marketing function; yet it clearly has done so in the past, in part because of absentee ownership and in part because untrained managers have been hired from the ranks of former participants and coaches. However, with increased competition and stabilized demand, professional marketing is a must for survival.

SOME SIGNS OF PROMISE

Despite lingering myopia, the last 10 years have seen many encouraging signs of "professional" approaches to sport marketing. Among them:[25]

➤ As already noted, a greater number of formal organizations are providing information, training, and professional identity to men and women in the field. See appendix A for an extensive list.

➤ Industry leaders like the NCAA are publicly discussing their marketing plans and strategies. In recent years, the NCAA has had the very active Special Committee to Study Marketing, Licensing, and Promotional Activities (see photo on page 12). Along similar lines, horse racing's track owners, breeders, and events managers recently formed a new trade association, the National Thoroughbred Racing Association. After admitting to past "complacence," they pooled $20 million for a

In the last decade, colleges and universities have sharpened their promotional skills in order to attract a wider audience.

professional marketing operation, to be headed by Tim Smith, a seasoned veteran of Professional Golfers' Association (PGA) and Olympics marketing programs.

➤ Organizations such as the Women's Sports Foundation are providing marketing primers to grassroots organizations that become involved in events such as National Girls and Women in Sports Day. The National Soccer Coaches Association and the magazine *Soccer America* combined to produce a similar primer, entitled *How to Market College Soccer.* Such primers not only help ensure event success, but also expose more grassroots coordinators to a professional marketing mentality. There's no need to reinvent the wheel.

➤ More organizations, like the Philadelphia Eagles, are employing a professional sales staff that enjoys an ongoing training and planning program. For firms that want outside help, there are now consultants like Rob Cornilles, whose Game Face Marketing company and its sales seminars are in high demand.

➤ A number of new journals and magazines, such as *Team Marketing Report, Sport Marketing Quarterly, Street and Smith's Sports Business Journal, Sports Business Daily,* and the *Journal of Sport Management* provide forums for sharing research reports and convention calendars.

THE UNIQUENESS OF SPORT: PRODUCT, MARKET, FINANCE, AND PROMOTION

Overcoming sport marketing myopia requires an appreciation of this special domain of human experience. This book, in fact, rests on a simple premise: that humans view sport as a "special" experience or as having a special place in their lives, and that marketers must approach sport differently than they do used cars, donuts, or tax advice. This is not to say that attitudes or principles do not overlap to some extent. Much of the marketing process is similar, and some of the sharpest industry minds—like Matt Levine of the San Jose Sharks and Dick Lipsey of Sports Business Research Net (SBRnet), the industry's biggest online database—came from a packaged-goods background. Both of these men, however, invested a great deal of time in learning about the special nature of the sport business. Distinct features of the sport domain appear in the following areas, which we discuss here: product, market, finance, and promotion.

As we hope to convey, sport is different. While to some extent one can argue that "marketing is marketing," the field is littered with the carcasses of firms (and people) who treated tennis, golf, and basketball as if they were the latest fashion design or tooth whitener.

THE SPORT PRODUCT

A product can be described generally as "any bundle or combination of qualities, processes, and capabilities (goods, services, and/or ideas) that a buyer expects will deliver want satisfaction." A peculiar bundling distinguishes the sport product, including at least the following elements:[26]

➤ Playful competition, typically in some game form

➤ A separation from "normal" space and time

➤ Regulation by special rules

➤ Physical prowess and physical training

➤ Special facilities and special equipment

Figure 1.1 illustrates the importance that this special bundling has for the sport product. At its core, the sport product offers the consumer some basic need such as health, entertainment, sociability, or achievement. Of course, many other products may offer the same core benefit. The sport marketer must understand why a consumer chooses to satisfy a given want or need by purchasing a sport product rather than some other type of product. Why do some people seek achievement in sport while others prefer to raise prize tomatoes? Although research on such a question is sparse, we may assume that the preference relates partially to the generic product components of sport: emphasis on physical activity that is regulated in special game forms. At the same time, the golfers among this "sport" group might scorn tennis, and vice versa. The tennis players may be split into groups who prefer public courts and those who prefer private club membership. One can recognize the complex dynamics behind each level of segmentation (considered in later chapters). The fundamental point, however, is that the sport product is unique.

Additional elements of the basic sport product—the game or event—make it unusual. Some of these elements reflect the nature of sport as a "service":[27]

➤ An intangible, ephemeral, experiential, and subjective nature. Sports are expressions of our humanity; they can't be bottled like tonic water. Even tangible elements like equipment have little meaning outside the game or the event. Few products are open to such a wide array of interpretations by consumers. What each consumer sees in a sport is quite subjective, making it extremely difficult for the sport marketer to ensure a high probability of consumer satisfaction. As baseball executive Peter Bavasi once said: "Marketing baseball isn't the same as selling soap or bread. You're selling a memory, an illusion." Each fan and each active participant create a different illusion. Each round of golf, each tennis match, each softball game brings a different experience. It is difficult to "sell" the benefits of consuming sport because they are hard to pinpoint or describe.[28]

➤ Simultaneous production and consumption. Sports are perishable commodities. As events, they must be presold, and there are no inventories. Sport consumers are typically also producers; they help create the game or event that they simultaneously consume (see photo on page 14). Although videotapes or newspaper accounts extend product life in a different form, the original event is fleeting. No marketer can sell a seat for yesterday's game, yesterday's ski-lift ticket, or last night's 10 P.M. time slot on court

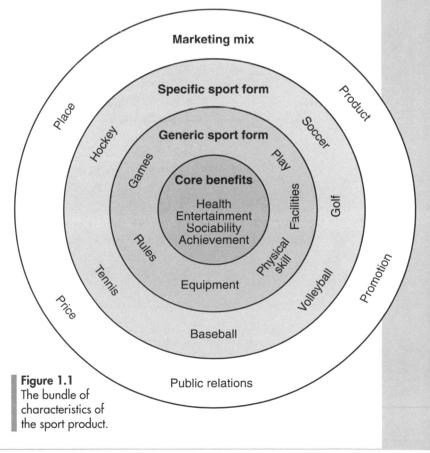

Figure 1.1
The bundle of characteristics of the sport product.

number 1. Day-of-game sales alone are not sufficient, because inclement weather or some other factor may diminish gate sales. Preselling, especially of season-ticket programs or yearly memberships, guarantees a minimum revenue.

➤ Dependence on social facilitation. The loneliness of the long-distance runner notwithstanding, sport usually occurs in a public setting. Enjoyment of sport—as player or fan—is almost always a function of interaction with other people. Typically, less than 2 percent of those attending collegiate and professional sport events attend by themselves. Only a few sports, such as running, can be undertaken by a single person. And who watches the Super Bowl alone? Consequently, sport marketers need to recognize the central role of social facilitation.

At sports events, like the Hockey East Championship tournament, fans are consumers, but they also contribute to producing the event.

➤ Inconsistency and unpredictability. A baseball game played today will be different from next week's game even if the starting lineups are the same. Numerous factors such as weather, injuries, momentum, rivalries, and crowd response create the logic of "On any given day. . . ." Who can predict a no-hitter, or a dog of a game, or the sudden squall on a mountain? Unpredictability is one of the lures of sport, but it makes the marketer's job more complex. New York Mets Marketing Vice President Michael Aronin, who previously spent 13 years with Clairol, put it this way: "Before, I had control of the product, I could design it the way I wanted it to be. Here the product changes every day and you've got to adapt quickly to the changes."[29]

➤ Core-product control beyond marketer's hands. As Aronin suggested, most sport marketers have little control of their core product—the game itself. General managers make trades. Leagues make schedules and game rules. Although there are clear cases of core-product decisions with an eye on marketing (in baseball, one such decision was the designated-hitter rule to create more offense), these decisions are still typically made by coaches and administrators whose agendas are often the game's "purity" or "equalizing offense and defense." For sport team marketers this means selling the "sizzle" as much as the "steak." For Boston Marathon managers, it means selling T-shirts, collector's-item lithographs, and special Marathon-label wine. Only one person finishes first, but everyone can have a "winning" memento.[30]

THE SPORT MARKET

Some special features of the sport market include the following:

➤ Many sport organizations simultaneously compete and cooperate. Few sport organizations can exist in isolation. Professional, intercollegiate, and interscholastic sports require other franchises and schools in order to have meaningful competition. The same is true for private or amateur sport clubs.

➤ Product salience and strong personal identification lead many sport consumers to consider themselves experts. The "expert mentality" was clearly revealed over a decade ago in a national survey. Among the respondents, 52 percent said "yes" when asked, "Do you think you could play for a professional team if you practiced?"; 74 percent said "yes" when asked, "Do you think that you could do a better job of officiating than most officials?"; 51 percent said "yes" to the question, "Do you think that you could do a better job of coaching than the average coach?" No other business is viewed so simplistically and with such personal identification by its consumers.[31]

➤ Demand tends to fluctuate widely. Athletic club members crowd facilities during winter "prime-time" hours and then trade their indoor sports for something else in the summer, when they crowd public tennis courts or golf courses. Each sport form tends to have an annual life cycle, and spectator sport fans are especially prone to quick changes in interest. Season openers bring high hopes and high demand; but midseason slumps, injuries, or weak competition may kill ticket sales.

➤ Sport has an almost universal appeal and pervades all elements of life (see photo). While there is clearly a "Western" sport tradition, there is also clearly a wide world of sport. What appear to be simple games—soccer, hockey, or basketball—link easily to other facets of our humanity, for better and worse:

Eating and drinking. From the Wheaties box to the Bud Light Penguin, sport images are part of the consumption experience. Clearly the "couch potato" is typically watching sports while munching and slurping. Sport brands such as ESPN have moved into the restaurant business in order to exploit this widespread association.

Sex. The sexuality in sport has not involved only men leering at gymnasts and figure skaters. As early as 1975, the Golden State Warriors appealed to female fans with ad campaigns like "We've got five men in shorts who can go all night." While gender stereotypes and homophobia still abound in the sport world, the marketplace is much more open and complex than ever before. Women soccer players are now embraced as athletes while male soccer players are pursued as sex symbols.[32]

Religion. For many people, sports don't open the gates to Sybaris but to salvation. According to sport philosopher Michael Novak, sport has many quasi-religious properties, such as ceremonies, asceticism, sacred grounds, and symbols. In some cases, sport seems to transcend religious differences. For example, when the Iranian soccer team qualified for the 1998 World Cup, celebrations in the streets of Tehran joined fundamentalist clerics with liberal university students in ways unimagined in a nation torn within itself over religion, politics, and economics. For that moment, the only ideology that mattered was winning soccer games. Said one engineer, struck by the flow of alcohol (forbidden in Islam), "Not in our wildest dreams would we have thought that people could be acting out this way."[33]

Sport has the ability to transcend all social and cultural categories.

SPORT FINANCE

The financing of sport encompasses special features:

➤ It is difficult to price the individual sport product unit by traditional job costing. For example, it is virtually impossible for the sport marketer to allocate fixed and operating costs to the individual ticket or membership. How can one account for the "possible" use of an usher, an instructor, an attendant, or a shower? Further, the marginal cost of providing an additional product unit is typically small.

Therefore, pricing the sport product is often based on the marketer's sense of consumer demand—for certain seats, for certain times of day, for certain privileges.

➤ The price of the sport product itself is invariably quite small in comparison to the total cost paid by the consumer. As we shall see in chapter 9, marketers must recognize the "hidden" costs of sports. The cost of tickets to a ball game may be only one third of a family's total costs, which include travel, parking, hot dogs, drinks, and merchandise—all perhaps controlled by someone other than the team hosting the event.

➤ Indirect revenues are frequently greater than direct operating revenues. Because consumers are (and should be) cost sensitive, income from fans or club members is often not enough to cover total expenses, especially debt service to the shiny, high-tech facilities that consumers demand. In pro sports, the strain is magnified by undisciplined owners who have driven player salaries so high. The direct income-expense gap has focused more attention on media and sponsor revenues. The quest for television and signage extends to all levels and segments of the sport industry, in part because the money is there. A good example is the NCAA, which signed an eight-year deal in 1994 with CBS—$1.75 billion for men's basketball tournament rights. This revenue alone accounts for over 80 percent of the NCAA's annual operating budget. In 1996, television income of $95.6 million represented 30 percent of the PGA Tour's total revenues.[34]

SPORT PROMOTION

Promoting sport is not as easy as it seems, despite widespread media attention:

➤ *The widespread media exposure is a double-edged sword.* Unlike a hardware store, sport teams get "free" promotions daily, in the newspapers, on the radio, and on television. Cases in point:[35]

In 1997, the *Chicago Sun-Times* and the *Chicago Tribune* published 6,259 articles mentioning Bill Clinton, the elected president and the "leader of the free world." Michael Jordan was mentioned in 4,173 articles.

A recent economic impact study by Price/McNabb (North Carolina) estimated that the University of Tennessee-Chattanooga men's basketball team generated $22 million of free media exposure through its 1997 Sweet Sixteen run. At a time of great competition in college admissions, any president or trustee would take notice. On the one hand, this exposure is a blessing, particularly for financially strapped programs at the grass roots. At the same time, free exposure can lead to laziness, arrogance, and amnesia toward fans.

➤ *Media and sponsors emphasize "celebrities."* Sport marketers—as we shall see in chapter 15—work hard to shape their organization's image. This becomes problematic with so much sponsor and media attention focused on a few celebrities, whose expanded egos can lead to wholesale problems inside and out of the locker room.

THE CHANGING SHAPE OF THE SPORT INDUSTRY

Every industry has some discernible shape or form, defined by the ways in which organizations align. Sport is no different. Theorists refer to these shapes or forms as models. At the same time, any model is a snapshot frozen in time. All industries change their shape. In this final section, we offer a model for understanding the shape of the current industry, as well as a description of the consolidation that is creating important changes in the ways products are produced and distributed to sport consumers.

A MODEL OF THE SPORT INDUSTRY

Several valuable models outline various "segments" of the sport industry. Naturally, any model is to some degree arbitrary. Older models of sport, for instance, stressed a distinct line between professional and amateur organizations. In the last 20 years, however, amateurism has eroded in sport. The Olympics, once the bastion of strict amateurism, are now open to professionals in most sports, depending on the eligibility codes of the various international sports federations. So the old models of the sport industry—cut along "amateur-professional" lines—make little sense these days. In our model of the industry, segments correspond to the organizations' primary marketing functions:

➤ *To provide "packaged" events to spectators at the venue or via the mass media.*

> Professional team sport franchises
>
> Professional tours such as golf and tennis
>
> Arenas, stadiums, coliseums
>
> Racetracks

All of these entities have a common, primary objective: to create an event their target consumers will buy, either live or via the media.

➤ *To provide facilities, equipment, and programming to players, who then produce the game form.*

> College or high school intramurals
>
> Country clubs, resorts, marinas
>
> Commercial facilities (e.g., racquet clubs and bowling alleys)
>
> Corporate, industrial, or military recreation
>
> Camps (e.g., Five-Star Basketball)
>
> Public and nonprofit agencies (e.g., YMCAs, YWCAs, and parks)
>
> Sporting goods companies (Nike, Adidas)
>
> Board game and video game companies (Rotisserie Baseball, Sega)

Although some of these organizations also host "packaged" events with an eye on spectator ticket sales, their primary objective ends with players playing the sport. When these organizations run events for spectator revenue, they often simply host a governing body that runs the event. This is normal, for instance, when golf clubs host a PGA or Ladies Professional Golf Association event.

➤ *To provide "packaged" games or events for spectators as well as facilities, equipment, and programming for players.*

> Intercollegiate athletics
>
> Interscholastic athletics

College and high school athletics programs continue to walk a tightrope between their "amateur/educational" functions and their bottom-line needs to aggressively promote revenues to pay for their programs.

➤ *To provide general administrative support, control, and publicity to other sport organizations and people.*

> Regulatory agencies, leagues, or conferences
>
> Sport media

- Sport sponsors

- Agents

- Management, research, and consulting groups

This segment has seen enormous growth in the last decade. New leagues and governing bodies have grown with the increase in television and sponsor revenues. Likewise, new consulting and research services have jumped into the expanding marketplace.

CONSOLIDATION: A MAJOR FORCE OF CHANGE

The model just described helps to explain how certain organizations share common missions and objectives, which help to shape the industry as a whole. Like most industries, however, sport is dynamic. The American economy has seen many cycles of "merger mania" and consolidation. In the late 1800s, cutthroat capitalist competition led to huge monopolies and trusts in steel, railroads, processed foods, and oil. Not to be outdone, some National League baseball owners hatched a plan in 1901 to consolidate ownership into a central trust that would control salaries and redistribute players every season, to ensure better competition. Although this revolution failed aborning, it stands as a prototype for ownership structure in recent leagues such as Major League Soccer and the WNBA.

The Sherman Antitrust Act has limited some of this process, but American enterprise is still quite "free." In the last few years, conglomerates have risen across the sport landscape. This has been especially evident in four areas: 1) the team-media connection, 2) sporting goods, 3) skiing, and 4) talent or events agencies.

Media Teams

One hundred years ago, the big businesses in sport were breweries and trolley companies. Both had something to gain from the connection. Fans drink beer and they need a way to get to the game. Over the last two decades, the trend has been toward media/entertainment conglomerates that see sport as the product of choice for just about any desired audience. If earlier decades had great team rivalries (Packers-Bears, Red Sox-Yankees) or player rivalries (Magic-Larry), the 1990s have yielded to corporation or owner rivalries. The big three rivals are these:[36]

Eisner/Disney. Michael Eisner's Disney empire extends in all directions through the sport world. At the major league level, there are the NHL Mighty Ducks and the MLB Anaheim Angels. Of course, teams need television. No problem for Disney, which owns Capital Cities, which owns both ABC and ESPN. Not satisfied with television, Disney purchased Starwave Corporation, the Internet-product company started by Microsoft cofounder Paul Allen. On the facilities front, Disney has opened a World Sports Center in Orlando. It is now the home of the Harlem Globetrotters and the Amateur Athletic Union.

Murdoch/FOX. In the battle for big-time sports, Rupert Murdoch is the sworn enemy of Disney. Murdoch's News Corp. is a major force in worldwide news and television. His Fox Network shook up the American television landscape with "The Simpsons" and "NFL Football" (wrestled from CBS). When Disney bought ESPN, the dominant sport cable channel, Murdoch countered with his FOX Sportsnet strategy (outlined in chapter 14). When Disney began *ESPN: The Magazine* to challenge Time Warner's *Sports Illustrated,* Murdoch announced plans for a "Fox Sports NFL '98 Preview" insert in sport magazines published by the Peterson Co. Finally, there is the question of competing teams. The central battlefield is Los Angeles, where Murdoch's latest acquisition, the Dodgers, will fight for ratings against Disney's Angels.

Turner/Time Warner. With Ted Turner, it's personal. He just doesn't like Rupert Murdoch. Turner is one of the great entrepreneurs in television history. His TBS superstation proved that sports and reruns could make money nationwide, even if the schedule was packed with Turner's Atlanta Braves and Hawks. His CNN succeeded beyond everyone's expectations. When Turner could not buy his way into competition with Disney and Murdoch, he sold to Time Warner, which now had several major sport properties to feature along with Bugs Bunny.

Sporting Goods

Mergers are an old story in this business. In the late 1800s, the Spalding Company became the force in the industry by gobbling up rivals. For much of this century, sporting goods were dominated by the "big four": Spalding, MacGregor, Rawlings, and Wilson. Everyone knows today's powerhouse—Nike. But the real news is the return of Adidas, which Nike knocked off the map in the 1980s. Their bitter war includes acquisition strategies. For instance, Nike purchased Bauer to move into the ice hockey market. Adidas purchased Salomom for skiing, prompting rumors that Nike would buy Rossignol.

At the retail level, chains of both full-line (Sports Authority) and specialty (Sneaker Stadium) stores have grabbed more and more market share. A 1997 report from the National Sporting Goods Association showed that sales in chains of 10 or more stores had increased from 21 percent of all sales in 1982 to 46 percent in 1992. By the end of the 1990s, sales for these chains exceeded 60 percent of all retail sporting goods sales.[37]

The Ski Industry

In 1961, there were about 1,000 American ski resorts, most of them small, family-run enterprises. By 1996, the number had dropped to 519. There is little room for the Mom-and-Pop ski area; the costs for snowmaking, grooming, ultrafast lifts, and plush restaurants or chalets are too steep. "Build it and they will come" has a different meaning in skiing. In 1998, six companies owned 50 of the top 75 resorts. The biggest conglomerate is American Skiing Company (ASC), owned by Les Otten; it has purchased eight major resorts in four years, from Killington in Vermont to The Canyons in Utah. Stock in ASC is traded on Wall Street. In the fall of 1997, Otten sent a direct-mail packet, including a credit card called "The Edge" (worth discounts at any ASC resort), to thousands of consumers around the country. Said Michael Berry of the National Ski Areas Association: "The small guys, to be very honest with you, are working hard to stay in business." Berry's implied question was "Could they manage to stay in business?"[38]

Marketing Players and Events

Except in boxing, agents are a recent phenomenon in the sport world, created by the rise of unions and television. The biggest company is International Management Group (IMG), founded and run by Mark McCormack, who built an empire starting with Arnold Palmer and Jack Nicklaus. Talent from IMG is now everywhere, even at the Vatican (IMG has promoted recent papal tours). Rival firms such as ProServ and Advantage International offered limited competition to IMG—until recently. In 1997, a new conglomerate called the Marquee Group began to shake up the landscape, buying ProServ, ProServ Television, and QBQ Entertainment. In May 1998, another, SFX Entertainment, purchased David Falk's F.A.M.E., home of Michael Jordan. Next, SFX bought the Marquee Group. While there might always be a niche for a maverick like Hollywood's Jerry Maguire, a few giant firms appeared to be cornering the market for the most lucrative sport talent.[39]

Is Bigger Better?

The sport business, like most of its counterparts, has never been a pure enterprise. Cheats and swindlers have operated openly for centuries. Beer barons have owned franchises solely to sell their watery suds to thirsty patrons on hot summer days.

Radio and television announcers have often been hand-picked shills. While today's executives are more polished, do the more complex connections of these new corporate behemoths create unacceptable conflicts of interest? Some think so. For instance, in April 1998, Chris Berman of ESPN flew out to Anaheim for the Angels' opening-day festivities. Unfortunately, he wasn't on assignment for ESPN's SportsCenter. He was a promoter for Disney and Michael Eisner, referring to the conglomerate as "we." One sportswriter correctly referred to Berman as an "on-field carnival barker."[40]

Can the public ever believe that ESPN—so righteous in its attacks on corruption in sport—will be objective in reporting on the Disney empire? And what about the growing conflicts of the agent/marketing/events firms like IMG or the Marquee Group? When IMG produces a made-for-television golf, tennis, or skating event, filled with its own stable of athletes (who may or may not receive guaranteed appearance fees), can this be legitimately promoted as a "competition"? Most of the public recognizes that professional wrestling is phony. In the new world of conglomerate sports, wrestling may not be alone.

WRAP-UP

Sport is a distinct enterprise. It cannot be marketed like soap or tax advice. A sport marketer is asked to market a product that is unpredictable, inconsistent, and open to subjective interpretation. The marketer must undertake this task in a highly competitive marketplace with a much lower promotional budget than those of similarly sized organizations in other industries. Finally, the sport marketer must do all this with only limited direct control over the product mix. On the bright side, the media are anxious to give wide exposure to the general product, and many opportunities exist to generate revenue through associations with business and industry.

ACTIVITIES

1. List three reasons for the great need for better sport marketing.
2. Define marketing myopia; give three examples in the sport industry.
3. On the basis of figure 1.1, discuss how two golf players might consume very different products in terms of benefits, sport forms, or marketing mix.
4. Find the names of four sport organizations from a major newspaper to illustrate each segment of the industry identified in this chapter.
5. Discuss the three elements of sport that you believe most contribute to the uniqueness of sport marketing.

CHAPTER

2

MARKETING MANAGEMENT IN SPORT: AN OVERVIEW

OBJECTIVES

1. To recognize the interacting components of the marketing management process.

2. To appreciate the core elements of market analysis, product concept, and product position.

3. To understand the distinctions among the five Ps of sport marketing: product, price, place, promotion, and public relations.

A HOT SPORT HITS THE ROCKS

Beach volleyball was one of the hot sports at the 1996 Atlanta Olympic Games. Hopes were high for men's and women's professional circuits. By 1998, however, both the Association of Volleyball Professionals (AVP, men) and the Women's Professional Volleyball Association (WPVA) appeared to be headed for the large morgue of defunct sports leagues. The WPVA dissolved itself, and the AVP was in debt and disarray. Players and promoters were at odds over who was to blame for all the red ink. Terry Lefton of *Brandweek* concluded that "while sponsors and organizers still express confidence in beach volleyball as a sport marketing property, the organizations putting on the tours are either wounded, dead, or on their last legs." The causes were manifold, but Lefton stressed the marketing problem. The players would not allow "consistent, marketing-minded leadership." In other words, beach volleyball lacked a vision and a plan that players, promoters, and sponsors could all embrace.[1]

Consistent, marketing-minded leadership—complete with a vision and a plan—is a necessity in today's competitive environment. For the high school athletic director, the racquet club manager, or the commissioner of a professional league, absence of this type of leadership is a sure ticket to disaster. In this chapter, we will lay out the basic elements required for consistent, marketing-minded leadership. We refer to these elements as the marketing management process, a process that combines both strategy (the big picture) and tactics (the details of a plan). Subsequent chapters in this book flesh out the various tactical steps in the marketing management process. This chapter places each step in the broader perspective of strategy.

SPORT STRATEGY IS MORE THAN LOCKER-ROOM TALK

Unlike the AVP and the WPVA, the NBA and Nike became industry leaders in the 1990s with clear strategies to develop and position their products in the marketplace of consumer needs. While Nike and the NBA both face their own challenges to retain prominence and profitability, their success came from carefully developed visions and plans—game plans, to use a sport term. In fact, most successful organizations have taken key pages from the game plans of successful coaches who have always evaluated their own talent, carefully scouted their opponents, and developed their tactics and playbooks accordingly. In simple terms, that is the essence of strategy, and it's spread from the locker rooms to the front offices of the sport industry. In its simplest sense, strategy entails setting long-term goals and developing plans to achieve those goals. This requires a continual analysis of the environment and the organization. The challenges of today's marketplace have forced sport executives to think much more strategically, as shown in the following examples from tennis, track, and golf.[2]

TENNIS

In 1960, American tennis had 5.6 million "participants" (people playing at least once per year). By 1974, tennis was booming with 34 million participants. Then came the "big slump" downward to 13 million in 1985 (see figure 2.1). By 1995, tennis was still only half as popular as it had been 20 years before. If the grass roots of tennis were suffering, professional tennis had mixed symptoms. Corporations were pouring more sponsor dollars into major events like the U.S. Open—held at the new $245 million Arthur Ashe complex in Flushing Meadows, New York. But television ratings were dwindling, from a 4.4 in 1991 to a 2.5 in 1996 (one rating point equals 1 percent of households with televisions). Men's tennis at least did not seem to have the star

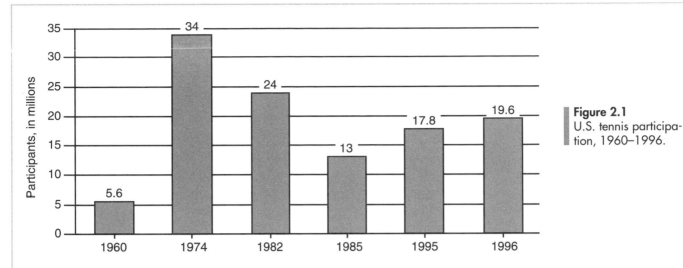

Figure 2.1
U.S. tennis participation, 1960–1996.

power or "hipness" of basketball. Two major 1997 U.S. Open sponsors, Heineken and International Business Machines (IBM), built their television spots around John McEnroe, who had long since moved to the announcing booth. Could you imagine their focusing NFL ads on Terry Bradshaw?

The problems in tennis were recognized in 1995 when the Tennis Industry Association, or TIA (a trade association), announced a strategic "Initiative to Grow the Game" from the grassroots level upward. As Brad Patterson, TIA executive director put it, each tournament, manufacturer, club, association, and pro tour had been marketing itself; "The fact is that nobody was marketing tennis." Tennis, in effect, had lost its position to aerobics, in-line skating, basketball, and other competitors. In 1997-1998, the United States Tennis Association and the TIA developed a range of programs under the banner "Play Tennis America," which included free clinics, free equipment, and organized leagues for all ages. As Patterson reminded his colleagues, "What was missing was that we were not telling people to come out and play tennis." The TIA's $7.5 million Image Campaign in key markets aimed to rid the sport of its elitist image. Tennis has a long way to go, but at least it has begun to pursue an integrated strategy.[3]

Track and field captures the public's attention primarily during the Olympics.

TRACK AND FIELD

Every four years, track and field takes center stage at the Olympics. Some athletes, like Florence Griffith Joyner ("Flo-Jo") become household names the world over. But aside from watching the Olympics and a few marathons, the general public takes little notice of the sport and its athletes. Although the grassroots base of runners seems solid (30 million self-described runners, 7.8 million entrants in road races, and over 1 million high school participants), there is a sense of crisis in the sport. Statistics from the National Federation of State High School Associations have indicated a downward spiral in squad sizes. At the collegiate and world-class levels, some critics have lamented an invasion of foreign athletes. In 1998, some road races began offering special prizes for

"American" runners. This looked like veiled racism to some, for the "foreigners" were often from Africa.

In 1997, Craig Mashback, the new chief executive officer of USA Track & Field (the national governing body), admitted that his sport had "lost its place in the American consciousness." His answer was a three-point strategy that would

> ➤ marshal the sport's main assets—its participants at all levels, not just the Olympic team;

> ➤ liven up the product by cutting the long delays at meets, improving the venues of meets, and staging exciting challenges such as existed in the 1960s when the mile and high jump records were under constant assault by the likes of Herb Elliott, Jim Beatty, Jim Ryan, John Thomas, Valery Brumel, and Dick Fosbury;

> ➤ work harder on exposure and image, for instance by tackling "the drug issue head on."

In 1998, Mashback announced that USA Track & Field would have a network television package of major events, a cable package of road races, *Inside Track* magazine, and a celebrity-driven rock show that would take track into the land of MTV. It sounded a great deal like an emulation of the NBA. Would it work for track? Time will tell. Like tennis, Mashback and track have a long way to go, but at least they have begun to articulate a strategy. They might be wise to take some clues from the legendary Fred Lebow, who skillfully led the New York City Marathon from a nothing event of 126 starters in 1970 to an international, televised "happening" with 16,005 starters in 1980.[4]

GOLF

In 1997, the golf establishment announced a similar campaign called "The First Tee," which aimed to develop hundreds of new golf facilities around the country in the next decade. Former President George Bush agreed to serve as honorary chairman of the initiative; the PGA Tour, the United States Golf Association, the Ladies Professional Golf Association, the Professional Golfers' Association of America, and the Augusta National Golf Club all joined the partnership, collectively committing over $5 million per year. Their effort stemmed from a simple conclusion that the game of golf was limited only by the availability of facilities. Tiger Woods might excite millions, but millions couldn't take up the game without available, affordable facilities.[5]

Tennis, track, and golf leaders began to realize that marketing their sport required broad, integrated effort—a campaign that would transcend old divisions between amateurs and professionals, between grass roots and elites, and between manufacturers and governing bodies.

IMPLEMENTING A SPORT MARKETING PROGRAM: STRATEGY AND TACTICS EQUAL THE GAME PLAN

The elements of marketing strategy can be conceptualized in models; marketing theorist Philip Kotler has called one model the Marketing Management Process (MMP). We have blended Kotler's model with others (see figure 2.2). Our version of the MMP is both a step-by-step process and a way of thinking. As some of our chapter exercises suggest, the MMP can be used to develop a marketing plan. But the marketing plan must be integrated into an organization's larger strategic plan that includes finance, asset management, resource allocation, and personnel management, among other elements. The MMP is the backbone of marketing; it emphasizes interdependencies at all stages.[6]

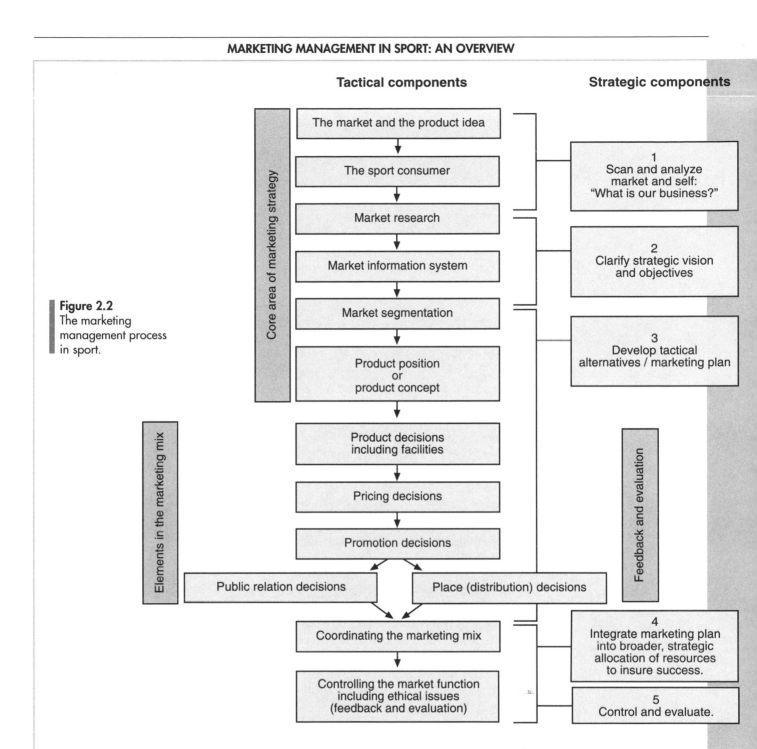

Figure 2.2
The marketing management process in sport.

Although subsequent chapters examine in greater detail the MMP steps (e.g., research, product development, pricing, and promotion), a brief introduction is important here if only to emphasize that decision making is an ongoing, circular process. There is really no off-season in the business world of sport.

As figure 2.2 suggests, a marketing plan aligns tactical details and operations (like pricing) with broader organizational strategy (like setting profit goals). To use a sport metaphor, tactics are the offensive and defensive plays or sets, used for various situations, that collectively make up a strategic game plan for victory. The game plan provides a broad direction to the coach or quarterback who will pick the specific tactics to be used during the game itself. This chapter will introduce that important blend of strategy and tactics.

The strategic steps of the MMP, and their relation to the remaining book chapters, are as follows:

1. Analyze the market and the organization (chapters 3-5, 18)
2. Clarify mission and objectives (chapter 6)
3. Develop marketing mix and plan (chapters 7-15)
4. Integrate marketing plan into broader organizational strategy (chapter 16)
5. Control and evaluate all elements of plan (chapters 16, 17)

Strategic Step One:
ANALYZE THE MARKET AND THE ORGANIZATION

THE SWOT ANALYSIS

All strategy begins with an understanding of the environment and your place within it. As executives in tennis, golf, and track realized, you must know where you are before you can decide where you want to go or how to get there. Knowing where you are requires a knowledge of consumers and their behavior (chapters 3, 4), which in turn requires careful research and development of a marketing information system (MIS; see chapter 5) that supplies timely, accurate, and usable data to decision makers. As we will explain, the elements of the MIS range from magazine clippings to vast computer databases.

Step One often includes what is called a SWOT analysis, a careful analysis of the Strengths and Weaknesses of the organization as well as the Opportunities and Threats in the marketplace or beyond. The SWOT analysis relies on the MIS and reinforces its importance. Marketers must understand their industry and their business, or they are doomed. For a historical case study via the SWOT approach, see the case study on "Lucky Les" Harrison, who was not able to adapt to changes in the marketplace. Later in this chapter, we will consider some "megatrends" in the sport industry and offer some tips on culling trends from fads.

Ideally, the SWOT analysis involves a broad range of constituents in the organization. Narrowly crafted, "top-down" planning, whether farmed out to consultants or not, rarely succeeds because few workers are willing to buy into the effort. Knowing your organization means paying close attention to what Peter Drucker has called the "theory of the business," which he defines as assumptions about the environment, the organizational mission, and the core competencies needed to accomplish the mission. Managers must be sure that the "theory" is realistic and widely understood.[7]

MARKETING INFORMATION SYSTEMS

The elements of an effective MIS can range from a sophisticated, expensive, computerized database to scraps of paper shoved in a coat pocket. In the end, what counts most is the information that infiltrates the decision maker's brain. As we discuss in chapter 5, information can be internal (e.g., a list of season-ticket holders) or external (e.g., regional demographics). Marketers can use readily available secondary data (e.g., compilations in the *Statistical Abstract of the United States*) or develop their own primary research studies (e.g., a fan survey). In the last two decades, the sport industry has seen more large-scale syndicated research, which customers buy from firms like Nielsen, R.O.I., or ESPN/Chilton. Syndicated sport studies began in the 1970s with the work of Dick Lipsey, who now operates the SportsBusiness Research Net, the largest online database in the business. For a list of some standard sources of industry data (magazines and newsletters, hard-copy and online sources), see appendix A at the back of this book. The marketer must use all available information to be sure that any plan is realistic. Consumer tastes change, competitors change, technology changes. Any of these changes may require an alteration in the marketing plan. Some examples:[8]

➤ Athletic club manager Marla Chavetz has built a strong clientele by knowing her consumers. For instance, member surveys showed that a large number of older members had orthopedic problems and that asthma was far more prevalent than anticipated. Chavetz responded with clearer guidelines on dealing with knee and shoulder rehabs as well as working with people who had asthma. Says Chavetz, "The whole point is to identify your client's needs and to develop programming to meet those needs."

➤ The NFL employs the services of USAData, a market research firm, to better understand the consumers in NFL markets—for example, favorite sports to watch on television, leisure-time activities, and car-purchasing habits. The information, gleaned from telephone and booklet surveys, is used to develop sponsorships, among other things.

Case Study

"Lucky Les" Harrison's Rochester Royals: The Challenge of the Market's Full-Court Press

Basketball, and the NBA, have dominated the imagination of sport marketers in the last decade. Despite the antics of petulant players, the NBA has been a showcase for successful strategies in packaging merchandise, personalities, and athletic skill. An NBA franchise has been the hallmark of a "world-class" city. The glitz of "Showtime," however, has its roots in the dusty armories and small auditoriums of places like Rochester, New York, where the Sacramento Kings were born in 1945—as the Rochester Royals. The Royals' early success and ultimate failure provide enduring lessons in the difficulties of shaping strategy to fit the changing market.

The Royals' founder was a local star named Lester "Lucky Les" Harrison, who played and managed a number of teams in the loose, semiprofessional associations of the 1920s and 1930s. In 1945, Les and his brother bought a franchise in the National Basketball League (NBL), the only real "pro" league of the day. Cost of the franchise: $25,000. The newly christened Rochester Royals played in the NBL's Eastern Division with the Fort Wayne Zollner Pistons (yes, the very same Pistons), the Youngstown Bears, and the Cleveland Allmen Transfers. The team names and locations reflected the small-market, company-team, industrial-league base of the NBL. Still,

the NBL had the country's best pro players. It was "the" big league.

The times were changing swiftly, though. In 1946, big-arena owners in New York, Boston, Chicago, Detroit, Cleveland, Philadelphia, Pittsburgh, Providence, St. Louis, Toronto, and Washington formed the Basketball Association of America (BAA). Their main purpose was to fill arena dates not taken by their hockey teams in the NHL or the American Hockey League. Their first president was Maurice Podoloff, who also ran the American Hockey League. Franchises in the "upstart" league cost only $1000 to begin with, but the BAA had high hopes. Although neither side admitted it, another sport war was on, just as a war was on In pro football between the NFL and the All-American Football Conference. There would be winners and losers in the struggle between the bigger and smaller markets. Only the shrewd, the ruthless, and the lucky would survive.

The Rochester Royals began with a bang—NBL play-off championships in 1945-1946 and 1946-1947. They constantly sold out Edgerton Park Sports Arena (approximately 4000 seats). In 1948, they jumped the NBL ship to the BAA, joining three other talent-laden defectors (Minneapolis, Indianapolis, and Fort Wayne). It seemed to be the right move, as the BAA won the brief league war before reorganizing as the NBA in 1949. Unfortunately, the rise of the NBA and its big-market franchises spelled long-range doom for the Rochester Royals. By 1956-1957, despite an NBA title in 1951 and rising attendance at the 8000-seat War Memorial (opened in 1955), the Royals were mired in red ink. Their six-year average loss of over $21,000 was the third worst in the league (the league's best annual profit average for 1951-1957 was the Knicks' $89,000, but most teams lost money). In April 1957, Les Harrison packed his team up and moved to Cincinnati, hoping for better profits.

What had gone wrong for a franchise that was the talk of the town in the postwar years? As Hall of Famer Red Holtzman (a Royal player from 1945 to 1953) recalled of those years: "Anyone who was anyone came to our games. It was go to the game and dinner afterward—a Rochester Saturday night ritual. . . ." How can one reconcile that memory with Les Harrison's bitter recollection to historian Donald Fisher: "They didn't realize what a good thing they had here. That's all. They didn't realize it."

In fact, one can view the Royals' demise as a good case study in marketing strategy (or the lack of it). Although the rise of the BAA and its large-market teams might have tilted the playing field, the Royals did not read the strategic environment well. Beyond this, in the clear hindsight of history that Les Harrison did not have, the Royals blundered in some basic areas of sales and promotions. This becomes clearer if we examine their organizational strengths and weaknesses as well as the environmental opportunities and threats.[9]

Organizational Strengths

Les Harrison was a major strength for the Royals. He was a local hoops legend. He knew the town and its culture; he had a good feel for the type of team that would sell in Rochester, even to the extent of signing Italian and Jewish players who could attract their ethnic communities. Further, the Royals were Harrison's sole interest. They were his love affair, not his ego trip. His well-crafted postwar teams had outstanding winning percentages, with play-off championships to boot. Those Royals played to constant sellouts in Edgerton Park Arena. Despite the arena's limited size, the team averaged over 100,000 in annual attendance for league play, an excellent mark for the time.

Environmental Opportunities

The Royals made two major "positioning" decisions during these years. Both appeared to make great sense in light of a changing environment. The first was the jump in 1948 from the NBL to the BAA. Sport history has always worked to the advantage of "big-market" leagues. And most interleague wars end with mergers (think of the World Hockey Association-NHL or the NBA-American Basketball Association in the 1970s) whereby a few of the "losing" league's teams merge into the "winning" league. Les Harrison saw the handwriting on the wall in 1948. As Donald Fisher succinctly concluded, "They not only would be bringing new big-city opponents into Rochester, but they were joining a more commercialized business association." The move into the bigger league naturally required a move into a larger arena. Harrison was not alone in promoting the need for a new facility; Rochester boosters of all stripes pushed for it. "Big-league" teams in a "big-league" arena were proof of a "big-league" city. Thus the move in 1955 into the new 8000-seat War Memorial was a logical step in repositioning the team and the city.

Environmental Threats

The move to the BAA seemed logical in 1948. What was the alternative—to stay in the "small-time" league? At the same time, the BAA's structure was hazardous for a franchise like the Royals. For one thing, the BAA prohibited its teams from playing an exhibition schedule. Exhibition matches, against anyone who could draw a crowd, had long been a staple of professional basketball and football. But the BAA owners wanted to upgrade the game's image, so exhibitions were out. Only league play was allowed for league teams. This rule especially hurt teams with small arenas who needed to maximize the number of paydays. Worse yet, the BAA rules stipulated that all gate receipts would reside with the home team. This was a killer for the small-arena teams. What good was it to play the Knicks regularly if you couldn't get a piece of their gate, and your gate was already maximized?

Two other threats loomed in the social and cultural environment that transformed much of American life in the 1950s: suburbanization and television. Both were uppercuts to the chin of clubs like the Royals. The history of pro basketball was tied to urban neighborhoods and ethnic communities. Les Harrison's Royals were but a generation removed from the days when a "pro" game was the opener for a neighborhood dance on the very same floor. The postwar Royals captured attention as the "city's" team only so long as fans lived and pursued their leisure in the "city." What would happen when the fan base started to move to suburban areas? Some of those nights out at Royals games would be spent building ties to new neighborhoods and communities, at Parent-Teacher Association meetings, at Scouts, or the YMCA. Or— the family might all sit at night in front of the new television set and watch the likes of Milton Berle. Les Harrison himself recalled that "when TV itself came in, we operated on Tuesday and Saturday nights. Milton Berle put us out of business on Tuesday. And then on Saturday with Sid Caesar and Imogene Coca—they put us out of business."

Organizational Weaknesses

It wasn't just "outside" threats that killed the Royals. In hindsight, they made a major tactical error in their marketing. They killed themselves with sellouts. How can that be? Simple. A team that sells out its arena with season tickets can never hatch a new generation of committed attenders, especially if television becomes an option. The "live" game has special attractions that television cannot match. But fans must be introduced to the live event. If they can't get in the doors, they can never cultivate a taste for "being there."

Bobby Wanzer, Royals player and longtime Rochester resident, sensed this when he talked to historian Donald Fisher four decades later. "In the beginning," Wanzer noted, the Royals "were in demand" with "a lot of season-ticket holders." Success had a downside, however, as Wanzer realized: "We couldn't build any new fans because we were sold out . . . after a while people stopped trying to get tickets." Fan frustrations were aggravated by rumors that the Harrison brothers took advantage of the high demand by scalping their own tickets.

And so, a number of factors piled up on the Royals. The season-ticket sellouts reduced the flow of the fan "escalator" (discussed later) that might have moved once-a-year fans (e.g., on a birthday) into five-game-a-year fans, and moderate fans into season-ticket holders. The limitations of Edgerton Park Arena, the BAA's restrictive policy on exhibitions, and its lack of revenue sharing all meant that even sellouts could not provide the revenues Rochester needed to compete with teams from New York or Boston.

By 1955, when the team moved into a bigger arena, the roster was no longer filled with young stars, and Harrison's need to pinch pennies made it hard to attract replacements. In 1956, Bill Russell announced that he would sign with the Globetrotters before he would play in a place like Rochester. Harrison made a deal with Boston's owner, Walter Brown. The Royals would pass on drafting Russell (the Celts had the next pick) if Brown would give Harrison his ice show for two weeks a year. Hard pressed for cash, Harrison had to look at the short term. Two weeks of an ice show was more valuable than Bill Russell. Two years later, the Royals were in Cincinnati.

SPORT MEGATRENDS INTO THE MILLENNIUM

Marketing strategy is not an easy game, especially when the environment is rapidly changing, as it was in the 1950s. Les Harrison is not alone among sport entrepreneurs who lost such a chess match. The last two letters of SWOT refer to a constant scanning of the environment, a search for trends and clues about the future. Of course, there is a big difference between recognizing trends (more of a historical analysis) and forecasting the future. Some trends—like population growth and demographic shifts—have real predictive power. Consumer tastes are a different matter. Take automobile styles, for instance. In the late 1970s, the trend was toward smaller, fuel-efficient cars. No one predicted the surge of demand two decades later for tanklike, gas-guzzling sport utility vehicles. Just ask the executives who banked on continued demand for minivans! Forecasting is an art, not a science. A rigid faith in forecasts has led many an executive, in the words of *American Demographics,* to "plan for a future that never arrives, while a different future passes them by." With this caution in mind, we next offer a few sport megatrends that should carry into the next millennium.[10]

Women's Sports Continue to Crest

In 1970, 1 in 27 girls played on high school teams. By 1996, the ratio was 1 in 3. The reason is simple: Title IX. And the Title IX generation is coming of age, with marketing implications that we will examine throughout the book. Most casual fans are aware of the enormous interest in women's basketball, but the potential exists in all sports. Take the case of ice hockey:[11]

➤ In 1991, USA Hockey had 5,533 registered female players. By 1997, the number was almost 21,000.

➤ In 1998, the NHL estimated that 45 percent of NHL game attendees were female.

➤ A Fox/TMG poll taken after the Nagano Olympics indicated that over 80 percent of the people who watched the U.S. women's hockey team were either somewhat or very likely to watch a women's hockey game in the near future.

➤ Equipment manufacturers have begun to make hockey gear designed for girls and women. For instance, Louisville's pants for women have wider hips, a narrower waist, and more pelvic protection than the men's version. CCM's women's "Tack" brand skate is narrower through the heel.

Back to the Grass Roots

Women and girls both forged and reflected important links across sport levels—from the grass roots to the elite professionals (see photo). Women seemed to be throwbacks to an earlier age of unspoiled athletes who played for the love of the game and not

Interest in women's basketball is only the beginning of the growing popularity of women's sports.

for the next deal. Sponsors noticed this as they sought to spend their dollars more effectively. As the millennium approached, sponsors began to invest more heavily in grassroots sports. Wendy's and General Motors are two examples. In 1998, Wendy's signed a $1 million partnership with the North Carolina High School Athletic Association, whereby it will become a presenting sponsor of the association's 11 championships. The grassroots presence made great sense for Wendy's, which has 196 locations in the state. General Motors has also reached out, leveraging its $3.5 million WNBA sponsorship well beyond commercials during WNBA telecasts; WNBA players will represent General Motors at local schools, charitable events, and shopping centers. Said one Buick executive: "It's a great opportunity to connect with people."[12]

The Interactive Digital Revolution

The move to grassroots marketing is part of a larger interactive trend. In the 1970s, with network television executives seeming to wield enormous influence over sports schedules and rules, some pundits predicted the rise of "studio" sports. Why would fans bother to go to the stadium when they could see better on television? Fans would become couch potatoes, inert dupes for the latest network package of sports slop. That is not what happened. Consider these examples:[13]

➤ The cellular phone has turned millions of "drive-time" commuters into celebrity callers on radio stations like WFAN in New York or WIN in Philadelphia. In some cases, sport call-in shows have influenced player trades and contracts.

➤ Sport Web sites have come to dominate the Internet. The NFL's 1997 site, Superbowl.com, generated more than 8 million "hits," leading IBM to pay $1 million for the sole sponsor rights to the 1998 version. By May 1998, a million people per day were logging into the Quokka Sports Web site, www.whitbread.com, to enjoy a "virtual sail" with crew members on the nine boats competing in the Whitbread Round the World Race. The video and audio effects were so staggering that Quokka President Alan Ramadan could justifiably call his Web site an experience in "total immersion sports."

The digital revolution and other communications breakthroughs of the last decade have heightened fan involvement. As with radio in the 1920s and television in the 1950s, technology has unleashed (rather than shackled) fan activism.

The Rise of the Sports Mall

Although sport consumers have the Internet on which to get "up close and personal," the desire for hands-on, one-stop shopping has resulted in a new phenomenon—the sports mall. Historians can find prototypes of the sports mall concept in the pro shops at golf clubs and arenas, or in the shopping mall built as part of the Hartford Civic Center in the 1970s. By 2000, however, we will see giant developments that consolidate a range of sport consumption, including virtual arcades, halls of fame, big-box stores like MVP Sports for merchandise and equipment, medical and rehab centers, and playing venues of all sizes and types. We will discuss these further in chapter 13. For now, some evidence:

➤ Several pro franchises have developed new practice facilities in joint ventures with hospitals and health care providers. The Boston Celtics broke ground in 1998 for a $30 million training and wellness center funded in large part by a metropolitan health conglomerate called CareGroup. In October 1997, the Philadelphia Eagles announced a 25-year deal with NovaCare. In both cases, the teams get massive new facilities and offices and medical and rehabilitative care, while the providers get recognized "name" affiliation in the growing sports medicine marketplace. When Johnny or Janie sprains an ankle, the theory goes, won't the child want to see the "Celtics" doctors and get rehabilitated at the "Celtics" facility? The public may not care to discriminate between hospitals, but they sure know their sport teams.[14]

The WNBA has given women's basketball a bona fide, big-time league.

➤ In May 1998, the NFL announced plans to build NFLX interactive entertainment centers in 7 to 10 cities, starting with New York, San Francisco, Orlando, and Boston. Like a large part of the sports mall concept, this initiative grew out of the NFL's fan "Experience" shows at Super Bowl venues. The assumption is that fans (especially the young) can get "close" to the game through interactive exhibits, games, and even the odd "real" player who stops by. The "NFL Experience" is affordable and, more important, available to fans who cannot get a game ticket. The NFLX centers will simply be more permanent sites that include restaurants, entertainment areas, retail shops, and museums.[15]

The Drive to "Brand"

One purpose of the sports mall is to promote a sport product brand—NBA, NFL, NHL, NCAA, and the like. The drive toward brand marketing explains a great deal of the industry consolidation we described in chapter 1. Disney, for instance, bought ABC and ESPN largely because it saw ESPN as a hot brand. In May of 1998, Disney even hinted at a name change from "Monday Night Football" to "ESPN's Monday Night Football on ABC." The name was ridiculous to those who didn't appreciate the power of brand names. We will look at product branding more in chapter 7; but for now, consider a few examples:

➤ In 1998, the National Association for Stock Car Auto Racing (NASCAR) began planning a series of "brand" concerts in partnership with TNN (the Nashville

Network) and CBS. The concerts, tentatively called "The NASCAR Summer Music Festival," would bring country music talent—and the NASCAR name brand—to markets outside the core southeastern area. And TNN, CBS, and network affiliates would tie into shows based on concert (and race event?) highlights, with abundant exposure opportunities for NASCAR's corporate sponsors.[16]

➤ In 1998, the horse-racing industry, historically a patchwork of independent track owners, breeders, jockeys, and trainers, jumped on the branding bandwagon by creating the National Thoroughbred Racing Association (NTRA). A $15 million advertising campaign and plans for a clearly defined race "tour" beyond the Triple Crown promised to give horses and tracks the kind of name and brand recognition enjoyed by—you guessed it—NASCAR. Said new NTRA Executive Director Tim Smith, "The fan is going to see something that is easier to follow, something that generates a story line, with horses that fans can follow from race to race."[17]

More Ambush Marketing?

In 1998, a post-Nagano Olympics survey of 512 consumers revealed that 55 percent incorrectly named Pepsi as an official Olympic sponsor. One reason for the confusion was the practice of "ambush marketing," in which a nonsponsor corporation's ads create the image of sponsorship without using any official logos or symbols reserved for a sponsor. In 1998, for instance, Wendy's ran ads with a hockey theme during the Olympics, even though McDonald's was the official sponsor.

As more sport organizations and athletes push their brands in the marketplace, will this further confuse consumers? If Shaquille O'Neal endorses Pepsi on television wearing a gold and purple uniform (without "Lakers" on it), will consumers remember that another cola is the Lakers' "official" sponsor? The sorting of multiple sponsorships is an escalating problem, especially in professional team sports where leagues, players, teams, and venues are all looking to push their brands.[18]

CULLING THE FADS FROM THE TRENDS

As marketers scan the environment, some trends jump out quite clearly. The rise of aerobics in the 1980s is a good example. Even the casual observer could see this. Nike, on the other hand, was slow to respond to aerobics and lost that huge market to Reebok. Sport history, however, is also punctuated with lots of fads that lit up the skies for a few years, then fizzled. Examples are the roller skating craze of the 1860s, the bicycle boom of the 1890s, and the miniature golf mania of 1920s. So how can the marketer distinguish between a solid trend and a short-term fad? Recently, consultant Martin Letscher suggested a few simple questions that can help:

➤ Does the new development fit with other basic lifestyle trends or changes in the consumer world?

➤ How varied, immediate, and important are the benefits associated with the new development?

➤ Can the product or service be personalized or modified to meet individual needs?

➤ Is it a trend in itself or merely the manifestation of a larger trend?

➤ Has the new development been adopted by key consumers who drive change?

➤ Is the new development supported by changes in unrelated or surprising areas?

Using these questions, Letscher has distinguished the trend of in-line skating from the fad of billiards and pool. Although both activities enjoyed booms from 1992 to 1995, especially in the percentage growth of "frequent" participants (in-line skating, over 250 percent; billiards/pool, over 200 percent), there are key differences. First, in-line skating flows with a larger trend toward fitness and individualism. In-line skating is flexible: skaters can pursue fitness or recreation, alone or in groups. This is not the case for billiards and pool, which have grown as part of an expanded "entertainment" mix in food courts, restaurants, and assorted activity centers. Pool and billiards are not flexible. While they will always enjoy a stable base of partici-pants, Letscher does not foresee a continued escalation of frequent players.[19]

Time alone will be the judge of Letscher's prognosis, but his questions provide an effective framework for analysis. In an industry in which racquetball is hot one year and fly-fishing the next, in which changing tastes in color create wild swings in merchandise from bright pastels to earth tones or teal and black, the marketer must be careful to distinguish fads from trends.

Strategic Step Two:
CLARIFY YOUR MISSION, GOALS, AND OBJECTIVES

AFTER THE SWOT ANALYSIS

After a SWOT analysis, it may be necessary to adjust the organizational mission and steer a slightly or drastically different course. Nike, for instance, expanded its mission in the last 15 years from its original focus on designing and marketing running shoes. Part of the reason was the lesson Nike learned from missing the aerobics market. By the mid-1990s, Nike had expanded into equipment of all sorts, including ice hockey equipment. With its many successful ties to athletes and events, the company even dabbled in the marketing and agent business. In 1990, Nike felt it could do anything in the sport marketplace. In 2000, the company may see itself and the marketplace quite differently.[20]

Like all organizations, Nike must constantly assess the realism of its "theory of the business"—what Peter Drucker called the assumptions about (a) the environment, (b) the organizational mission, and (c) the core competencies needed to accomplish the mission. Some key triggers for testing these assumptions can be seen in the following box:[21]

> When you achieve original goals
> When something prevents goal attainment
> When you think you know your consumers well
> When you don't think you know your consumers well
> When you sustain rapid growth
> When growth is unexpectedly slow
> When you are surprised by success
> When you are surprised by failure
> When a competitor enjoys unexpected success or failure
> When the environment is changing quickly
> When you haven't seriously questioned your assumptions in two years

A reassessment of goals and objectives will emerge from the environmental analysis. Although people sometimes interchange the terms goals and objectives, goals are typically broad statements while objectives provide more detailed, usually quantified targets. For example, in 1994, the Denver Grizzlies Professional Hockey Club, a highly successful member of the International Hockey League, developed the following goals in its "Community Relations Plan":[22]

1. To create high awareness/visibility for Grizzlies in the community—we want positive publicity for all the programs in which we are involved. (It is not enough for us to do these programs; people have to see pictures, read about us or see our involvement on TV).
2. To generate goodwill and positive feelings about the Grizzlies in all areas of the community.
3. To develop new programs and support existing programs, which encourage youth participation in ice hockey and street hockey.
4. To identify quality organizations and provide them with Grizzlies tickets to be distributed to 100,000 underprivileged, handicapped or at-risk youths throughout our market areas.

These goals clarify direction in a number of ways. First, they call for publicity that will be measured in media exposure. Specific objectives might be exposure in a certain number of newspaper column inches or features on the evening television news. Second, the goals require goodwill in all areas of the community, measured perhaps by surveys in Denver's various inner-city neighborhoods and suburbs. As the fourth goal suggests, the Grizzlies did not want to be only the team of upscale, professional families. They wanted to be a team for all of Denver. With goals and objectives in place, the Grizzlies moved to the next step: preparing plans to get them to their target goals.

Strategic Step Three:
DEVELOP A MARKETING PLAN

With mission and objectives in place, it is time for the marketer to develop a plan at both the broad (strategic) and specific (tactical) levels. This requires a return to the MIS to identify the consumer segments we are targeting (the way the Grizzlies identified inner-city neighborhoods as a specific segment for one of their programs). One of the most important ways for sport marketers to segment consumers is by their position on the escalator of involvement, a concept we will examine later in this section. After identifying target segments, the marketer must develop products; prices; distribution systems; promotions; and public relations, media, and sponsorship programs that will ensure successful attainment of objectives and mission. These functions make up the core of this book—chapters 6 through 15.

DETERMINING KEY TARGETS: MARKET SEGMENTATION

People are different. That goes without saying. Some sport businesses (e.g., personal training services) treat every consumer as an individual, creating a program tailored to individual needs and capabilities. This is not practical or profitable in all situations. The Portland Sea Dogs, for instance, may tailor ticket plans for corporate sponsors, but they do not have the staff or the resources to approach each person in southern Maine with an individual message. At the same time, the Sea Dogs have more than one message for more than one target market. They recognize market segments in which consumers are grouped into clusters of similar characteristics. Marketing theorists have typically considered several bases for segmentation, which we discuss in detail in chapter 6:

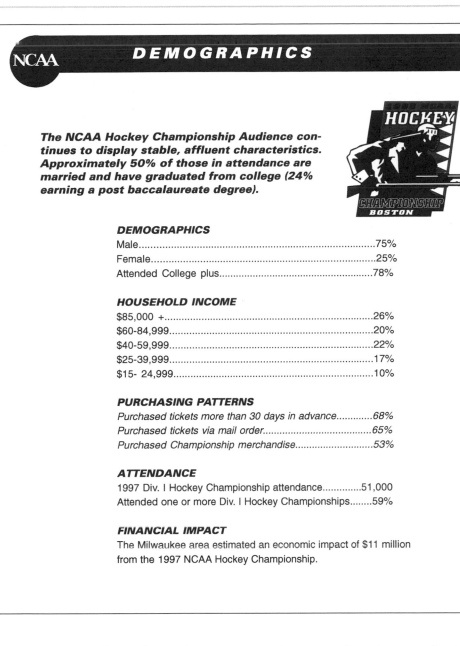

The NCAA Hockey Championship Audience continues to display stable, affluent characteristics. Approximately 50% of those in attendance are married and have graduated from college (24% earning a post baccalaureate degree).

DEMOGRAPHICS
Male...75%
Female...25%
Attended College plus...78%

HOUSEHOLD INCOME
$85,000 +...26%
$60-84,999...20%
$40-59,999...22%
$25-39,999...17%
$15- 24,999..10%

PURCHASING PATTERNS
Purchased tickets more than 30 days in advance.............68%
Purchased tickets via mail order.......................................65%
Purchased Championship merchandise............................53%

ATTENDANCE
1997 Div. I Hockey Championship attendance..............51,000
Attended one or more Div. I Hockey Championships........59%

FINANCIAL IMPACT
The Milwaukee area estimated an economic impact of $11 million
from the 1997 NCAA Hockey Championship.

The NCAA has invested considerable research efforts into developing a sense of its tournament brands and their audiences, in this case men's hockey.

➤ Demographic information—age, sex, income, education, profession (see above)

➤ Geomarket information—location of residence, by zip code

➤ Psychographic information—lifestyle factors such as activities, interests, and opinions

➤ Product usage rate—attendance or activity frequency, or size of donation

➤ Product benefits—product attributes or benefits that are most important to the consumer, and consumers' perceptions regarding the major benefits of the product and its competitors

Obviously, any segmentation strategy relies on the MIS to distinguish marketable clusters. Although marketing theorists differ on definitions, some clusters may be called niches—small groups of consumers who share special, often unfulfilled needs or interests. One might view Rotisserie Baseball (initially at least) as a niche market of statistics-hungry baseball fanatics who relished any chance to argue about player talent and trades, and were willing to spend hours doing so. These days, such sport consumers appear to make up more than a niche.

Marketing information system databases also create the potential for something closer to individual marketing strategies. This is sometimes called relationship marketing. For instance, a database of information on season-ticket holders would allow a marketer to send birthday greetings along with information on special events (like concerts) or special group deals (for the children's birthdays).[23]

DEVELOPING YOUR MARKET: THE ESCALATOR CONCEPT

User segments are especially important in the sport business, for they constitute the sport consumer escalator (see figure 2.3)—perhaps the most important concept in this book. We discuss the escalator from many angles in the chapters that follow, but for now a simple explanation will do. The escalator is a graphic representation of consumer movement to higher levels of involvement in a sport, as a player or a fan. In the 1970s, Dick Lipsey began national, syndicated research on the sporting goods

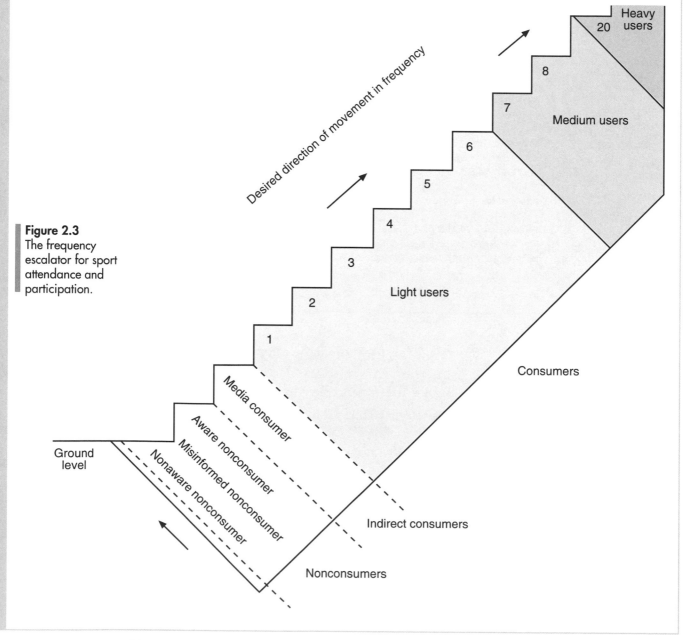

Figure 2.3
The frequency escalator for sport attendance and participation.

business. These studies, one of which is now the annual National Sporting Goods Association survey, uncovered some important elements of the sport escalator, including the fact that new participants represented a minor portion of total purchases (from 5 to 12 percent of dollars and from 10 to 20 percent of units sold). It became clear that sport participants moved up an escalator of involvement and that the vast majority of equipment buyers were already playing the sport, looking for ways to improve.

For team sport marketers, the escalator is crucial, in part because fan surveys indicate clear intentions to move up the escalator. For instance, fans who currently attend three games per year typically indicate their intention to attend five to six games the next year. The key is to create a marketing plan—with an array of elements and tactics—that can satisfy the needs of various consumer clusters and thereby move user groups up the escalator. At the same time, even a casual fan knows that great numbers of consumers can fall off the escalator at any time. Nike and Reebok have seen serious sales dips, in part because sports have lost their luster as a fashion statement in the youth market. More "earthy" shoes, like the ones Timberland makes, have become trendy. Similarly, fan defections can become hemorrhages for many reasons beyond a long losing streak.[24]

PRODUCT DEVELOPMENT AND POSITIONING

One way to move consumers up the escalator is to design, redesign, and promote products to capture special "space" in target consumers' minds. This is sometimes called "positioning." The concept was promoted in the 1980s by two advertising executives whose book title captured their argument: *Positioning: The Battle for Your Mind*. Their basic mantra was simple: "Positioning is not what you do to a product. Positioning is what you do to the mind of the prospect. That is, you position the product in the mind of the prospect." As we discuss in chapter 7, product positioning is not simply a matter of advertising; it also involves research, development, and design. Baseball redesigned its basic product with the designated hitter, largely to reposition itself as a more exciting and offensive sport in the face of football's smashing popularity in the 1960s. Ice hockey has clamped down on the worst of its street-fighting image with tough rules against the "third man in" and against leaving the bench during a fight.[25]

Once pigeon-holed as a blue-collar sport, NASCAR is now enjoying widespread popularity.

There are many "positions" to occupy in the sport industry. Take the notion of "big-league" sport. It is a fluid marketplace. In the past, many viewed NASCAR as blue-collar entertainment for Southern "Bubbas" and their women. If that was ever true, it surely is no longer, as NASCAR has become the hottest "big-league" sport for the high-class corporate suits, male or female. One way NASCAR shifted its position was with new, modern megatracks, complete with hundreds of corporate boxes (see photo).

While NASCAR aspired to corporate embrace, Major League Soccer (MLS) Commissioner Doug Logan has looked to position his league as an alternative to the corporate-conglomerate glitz of his higher-profile counterparts. Logan articulated his position at the start of the 1998 season: an amalgam of soccer purists, young soccer players (and their moms, no doubt), Hispanics, and the disenfranchised fan (especially the baseball fan) "who reads his newspaper back to front" and is "tired of the players." Emphasizing MLS as an alternative, Logan threw down the gauntlet at the "big" leagues and their emphasis on corporate revenues: "The biggest piece of garbage in American sports is the luxury box, with its couches faced away from the field . . . with everybody eating sushi."[26]

Successful athletic clubs have also expanded their product concepts. As Spencer Garrett argues, a tennis club member will have a hard time justifying her investment if she thinks only in terms of playing time. "If cost-per-play is the driving mechanism for members, they're not going to be satisfied." In Garrett's view, members are renting space with a full range of amenities. In these terms, $20 per hour is a good investment.[27]

Finally, the city of Lancaster, California, completely repositioned its entire city image by upgrading an athletic facility. This is an old story at the big-league level—build a big, new stadium and you can get a big-league franchise that will make you a big-league city. It is also a very debatable formula. Lancaster had another idea: become one of America's major venues for softball tournaments. With a clear vision, Lancaster expanded the city park to include six high-quality diamonds to go with assorted tennis courts, soccer fields, basketball, and volleyball courts. With a new logo and promotional campaign called "BIG SIX," Lancaster increased its number of softball tournament days from 27 in 1994 to over 75 in 1996. In 1998, the BIG SIX will host the American Softball Association's Men's Class D National Tournament. Unlike a pro franchise, national tournaments quite obviously attract revenue—in hotel and restaurant fees and taxes, for instance—from well outside the area. It is not as if local residents simply choose to spend money on a softball game rather than a movie. With a careful strategy, Lancaster repositioned itself in both the sport and revenue maps.[28]

THE FIVE Ps IN THE SPORT MARKETING MIX

The product is often referred to as one of marketing's "four Ps":

> ➤ Product (development and positioning)

> ➤ Price

> ➤ Place (or product distribution)

> ➤ Promotion (personal selling, advertising, special events)

Because sport enjoys so much media attention, we treat public relations (usually considered part of promotion) as a separate P.

> ➤ Public relations

In a service-oriented industry like sport, all the Ps are influenced by how well employees interact with consumers—we could call this "process management." We will see how critical process management is to the running of any promotion. For instance, if stadium personnel are surly to fans looking to exchange "giveaway" T-shirts (often for a different size), those fans—who might well be at their only game of the year—might fall off the escalator in the belief that the stadium is a hostile place to bring a family.

Strategic Step Four:
INTEGRATE MARKETING PLAN INTO BROADER, STRATEGIC ALLOCATION OF RESOURCES THAT ENSURE SUCCESS

After developing the five Ps—product, place, price, promotion, public relations—into a plan for action, the marketer must ensure that higher executives support it.

There is nothing worse for a marketer than to develop an imaginative, "can't-miss" plan that fails because it lacks support at a higher level. College athletics staff face this problem often. Surefire plans for promoting a bigger fan base in women's sports linger on the shelf because the limited funds go into promoting the traditional "revenue" sports (usually men's sports) that have historically helped to fund everyone else. Even though shifting money to a promotion of women's sports might result in a greater revenue yield, the risks seem too great. This is almost a self-fulfilling prophesy. Successful marketers make sure they have support as they move along, so Step Four must be ongoing.

Once adopted, a strategy may require some changes in personnel or in the organizational structure. The historical studies of Harvard's Alfred Chandler demonstrate that successful organizations design and redesign themselves around their strategies, not the other way around. In Chandler's words, "Structure follows strategy." The alert executive has an eye on environmental changes that might require restructuring. Quick changes can be traumatic. A good example is the 1998 sponsor contract between Coca-Cola and the NFL. Coke walked away from its huge leaguewide sponsorship, leaving individual clubs with greater control and autonomy in making sponsor deals in the soft-drink category. Alan Friedman, editor of the influential *Team Marketing Report*, immediately saw the implications. "While NFL clubs have upgraded their front office marketing talent over the last few years, some clubs still don't have executives with full-time sponsorship-development and service responsibility." In the new world of sponsorships, restructuring would be a priority.[29]

COORDINATING THE MARKETING EFFORT

An effective marketing plan will carefully blend all the Ps into a portfolio of activities that move a range of consumer clusters up the escalator. An enlightened school, college, or professional sport program will blend several of the Ps into packages differing in cost and benefits, promoted with different messages, and targeted at different segments or even niches. For a college program, this might mean special plans for students, area families, distant alums, and corporate sponsors. This requires careful coordination of efforts, with broad support from the athletic director, coaches, players, sport information personnel, facilities managers, and the ticket office. Marketing is not the work of just a few people.

A lack of coordination can dump fans off the escalator like a series of waterfalls. This is what happened to the Kansas City Wizards of MLS. Average attendance had slipped from 12,900 in 1996 to 8661 by July 1997. The MLS commissioner emphasized, "There are no excuses. Kansas City has a terrific team that plays in a great stadium in a town that prides itself on its sports teams." No excuses except for what one local reporter called "marketing blunders" and gaffes, including unwarranted price hikes and unclear tinkering with the team's name and logo, which muddled any attempts at a brand image and hindered merchandise sales.[30]

Strategic Step Five:
CONTROL AND EVALUATE THE PLAN'S IMPLEMENTATION

Step Five is another ongoing step. It makes little sense to wait for the end of the season to see if you're in last place!

If consumer satisfaction is an objective for any organization, then marketing is everyone's business. As any coach who hopes to recruit a top-quality athlete knows, the relationship between product quality (a top-notch team) and the sport facility (the stadium or field house) is crucial. Similarly, a highly effective promotional campaign can only do so much if the product does not deliver that which is promised. As many teams have learned the hard way, it's risky business to promise a championship. Ultimately, success in marketing is determined only through the consumer's eyes. It is a simple equation:

Consumer Satisfaction = Product Benefits – Costs

While marketers must control their own budgets and costs, their more important "control" function is to ensure customer satisfaction. This means monitoring and evaluating indicators of satisfaction, benefits, and cost. We will address these in greater detail in chapter 5, but consider here a few examples of possible indicators:

SATISFACTION	Attendance
	Ticket or member renewal rates
BENEFITS	Food quality
	Access to and speed of parking
COSTS	Time spent in parking lot after game
	Beer spilled on children by drunken fan
	Embarrassment caused by surly usher

There are other issues to consider, including ethical principles. At the turn of the century, for instance, white baseball audiences enjoyed the antics of black "mascots," who cavorted between innings like clowns and kneeled near the on-deck circle so their white bosses could rub their wooly heads for good luck. Such were the mores of Jim Crow America. No major league team would consider this acceptable entertainment today, and more than 2000 colleges and universities have dropped Native American nicknames. Yet, some major college and professional teams have resisted and continue to employ Native American team names and images (see photo).

Many sports mascots are controversial, particularly those that resonate with the disrespect and racism projected on Native American tribes throughout U.S. history.

Any evaluation system in the MMP must consider social responsibility. Chapter 17 examines some key legal issues in sport marketing. Beyond the legal, there are ethical dimensions to any marketing plan or decision, and there are numerous frameworks for ethical decisions—in business, in marketing, in sport, or in any domain of activity. We haven't found anything better than Laura Nash's simple framework of 12 questions, "Ethics Without the Sermon," (see next page) to consider when confronting a problem.[31]

In 1998, sport ethics seemed focused on Nike's labor practices in the developing countries in Asia. Was Nike exploiting labor with wages clearly unacceptable by American standards? Or, as Nike argued, was the company creating economic opportunities with wages in keeping with local standards? There were more issues, to be sure, and Nike was not alone in trying to justify its management and marketing decisions. Take the University of Memphis, for example. In 1998, Athletic Director

"ETHICS WITHOUT THE SERMON"

1. Have you defined the problem accurately?
2. How would you define the problem if you stood on the other side of the fence?
3. How did this situation occur in the first place?
4. To whom and to what do you give your loyalty?
5. What is your intention?
6. How does this intention compare with probable results?
7. Whom could your decision or action injure?
8. Will you discuss this with affected parties before making the decision?
9. Will your position be valid over the long run?
10. Could you disclose your decision or action without qualm?
11. What is the symbolic potential of your action if understood? If misunderstood?
12. Under what conditions would you make exceptions?

R.C. Johnson had apparently approved a golf outing for the "Tiger Clubs," the major fund-raising entities for the university's athletics. The problem was the golf-outing sponsor, the Horseshoe Casino, which paid Johnson $10,000 to underwrite the "Tiger Clubs/Horseshoe Casino Spring Fling." The sponsor choice upset a number of boosters, and soon the *Memphis Commercial Appeal* picked up the story. The criticism was obvious. At a time when campus gambling had reached epidemic proportions and the NCAA had created anti-gambling policies, how could U of M justify a booster outing formally sponsored by a casino? R.C. Johnson had lots of explaining to do, and hard decisions to make. Should he dump the event? the sponsor? Hindsight is always easy, but Johnson might well have benefited from asking himself some of Laura Nash's critical questions.[32]

WRAP-UP

Sport organizations clearly face many unique challenges and demands, not all of which they can best meet with frenzied marketing action. Many challenges require considerable thought and a well-planned response. Yet the majority of demands do have comparatively simply solutions once all the data are put together. In the 1990s and beyond, sport will continue to be unique, but it will follow one principle experienced without modification in all industries: those sport organizations most likely to succeed will be the ones that have the best handle on the marketplace. Such a handle comes only with the development, analysis, and integration of every function of marketing. In the following chapters, we will consider all these steps in much greater detail.

ACTIVITIES

1. Define the Ps of the sport marketing mix.
2. Find evidence of a sport organization that does an excellent job of recognizing market trends and adjusting its strategy accordingly. How does the organization refashion its product concept and reposition its product?
3. Describe a new product concept that you think would meet unfilled consumer needs in your favorite sport.

4. List the market or consumer segments that most clearly relate to a tennis or golf club near you.

5. From the stories or ads in any newspaper sport section, try to find examples of the five Ps of the marketing mix.

6. Consider the case of the American Basketball League (ABL) versus the WNBA— one of the more interesting contests of sport marketing strategy in the late 1990s, at least until the ABL declared bankruptcy in 1999. Make a table that compares elements of the leagues' strategies. For instance, the leagues made clear choices on "placing" their products. The ABL played during the "traditional" basketball season, while the WNBA played during the summer. Their media packages also differed. What about their products, including player talent and rules? How were they different? And their promotion via ad campaigns? Think of all the ways that the leagues differed in the Ps of marketing. Was the WNBA's marketing strategy a key component of its victory over the ABL? Sources include "One on One," *Sports Illustrated for Women*, fall 1997, 70-71; and Rachel Sherman, "Twice as Nice," *Athletic Business*, July 1997, 42-46.

YOUR MARKETING PLAN

The first step in this project is to choose (or create) an organization for which you will develop a marketing plan. Your ultimate goal is to prepare a 20- to 30-page plan that helps the organization attain strategic objectives. This plan should become an item in your personal portfolio. Is there an organization that you aspire to work in? Do you have an idea for a sport product that will fill some existing consumer needs or wants?

1. Identify resources for internal and external scanning.
2. Identify the three most important market trends affecting your firm or product.
3. Begin to define your "business" and your product.

CHAPTER 3

STUDIES OF SPORT CONSUMERS

OBJECTIVES

1. To recognize the many questions that sport marketers must ask about their consumers.

2. To appreciate the many different sources available for analysis.

3. To understand the strengths and weaknesses in many published studies of sport consumers.

GOLF CONSUMERS LOOK BETTER THAN PAR FOR THE COURSE

Golf course development became big corporate business in the 1990s. One thousand new courses opened between 1992 and 1997 (18.8 percent growth)—a time when the number of golfers and rounds golfed remained flat. High-profile players like Jack Nicklaus and Arnold Palmer moved their golf companies into high gear for designing courses as well as clubs. Was it folly? Hardly. Even though the market of golf players stayed flat in the 1990s, the demographics looked good for golf's future. Baby boomers were starting to near retirement age. And the baby boom "echo" promised an expanding bubble of young Americans who might be sold on the game. More than a third of new golfers were women, representing an even greater market. Golf developers felt comfortable investing an average of $9 million on a new course because they felt they knew the market of existing and potential golf consumers. They liked what they saw.[1]

Women golfers represent more than a third of new golfers.

As we noted in chapter 1, the marketing concept begins and ends with the consumer. The marketer of any commodity—golf, grain, or gasoline—needs to understand who might be interested in buying her product; therefore, the intelligent marketer constantly seeks to answer a series of questions:

> ➤ Who are my consumers—past, present, and future—in terms of both demographics (age, sex, income) and psychographics (attitudes, opinions, lifestyles)?

> ➤ Where do my consumers reside? Where do they work? How do they travel to and from the places where they consume my product?

> ➤ Where, when, and how have my consumers been exposed to my product and its advertising?

> ➤ How and why did they become involved with my product?

> ➤ If they have been committed to my product, why?

This chapter provides an orientation to existing studies on the first general question, namely, who is the sport consumer? Specifically, we will discuss the profiles of sport consumers that have emerged in published studies. Chapter 4 explores the literature on the other questions listed. Chapter 5 outlines the ways that marketers in any sport organization can conduct their own research on consumers. As the case study on NASCAR suggests, there are many reasons for knowing your consumers.

➤ TYPES OF SPORT CONSUMER STUDIES

There is no foolproof profile of the "average" player or sport fan, nationwide or worldwide. There are simply too many variables. At the same time, many clubs, equipment companies, teams, and governing bodies (like NASCAR) have conducted

Case Study

It Pays to Know Your Consumers—Just Ask NASCAR

Since the early days when bootleggers made a buck on backwoods dirt tracks, NASCAR has come a long way. In the late 1990s it was transforming itself into the most glamorous sport to take fire in the 20th century. The NASCAR fan was no longer just an old boy in bib overalls chewing Red Man; perhaps the biggest fans were the chief executive officers of major corporations like General Mills, Kodak, and Anheuser-Busch. Or even Thorn Apple Valley, a sausage maker that had committed $15 million for three years to sponsor a car on the Winston Cup circuit—NASCAR's marquee events. Corporate executives like Thorn Apple Valley's Joel Dorfman knew that a NASCAR sponsorship provided exposure he could get in no other sport—to a growing and very loyal audience. In two months of sponsorship, Dorfman saw his products getting shelf space. "We're already getting authorization for our product," he said, "with retailers who weren't interested in us at all before." Seventy Fortune 500 companies saw similar benefits in NASCAR. In 1998 alone, NASCAR banked about $475 million in sponsorships (of the more than $1 billion in auto racing). No other sport came close to this level.[2]

What was behind all of this corporate interest? Simple: a very attractive consumer profile that NASCAR carefully promoted. Some statistics:

➢ From 1991 to 1996, NASCAR attendance (6.1 million for Winston Cup races in 1997) grew 65.5 percent. In the same period, the NBA grew by 16.9 percent, MLB by 5.8 percent, the NHL by 38.1 percent, and the NFL (with little room to grow) by only 5.6 percent.

➢ Among NASCAR fans, 38 percent were female, 65 percent owned homes, 29 percent earned over $50,000 annually, 53 percent were professionals, and best of all, 78 percent used credit cards.

NASCAR fans know Jeff Gordon, but NASCAR knows, just as well, its consumers and their interests.

➢ A 1994 study suggested that 71 percent of NASCAR fans bought NASCAR products. Compare this to the sponsor brand loyalty of golf fans (47 percent), tennis fans (52 percent), or fans of the so-called big three—the NFL, NBA, and MLB (36-38 percent). Best of all, 40 percent of NASCAR fans said they would switch brands to a product that became a NASCAR sponsor.

While other studies suggested that NASCAR fans were not quite as loyal as the 1994 data portrayed, corporate sponsors were not quibbling. Said Jim Andrews, vice president of International Events Group (IEG), Inc., a sponsor research group: "NASCAR has done a very good job of getting the word out—whether it be perception or reality—that their fans are the most brand-loyal fans." Brian France, NASCAR's marketing vice president, echoed the opinion: "We can talk sponsorships all we want, but the core of our business always gets back to the fans." Or, we might conclude, knowing who your fans are.

enough research to feel comfortable about knowing their consumers. Further, a number of research organizations—increasingly over the last decade—have analyzed America's involvement in sport. This research offers a rich database for study. Because the topics and purposes of these studies are so varied, we have chosen to provide an overview of their utility to the sport marketer rather than a synthesis of their contents. Many of the sources we discuss are listed in appendix A for easy reference.

There are many ways to categorize these sport consumer studies. For instance, information can be reported in many forms:

➤ Published newsletters, such as the *NCAA News,* which provides periodic excerpts from its annual participation survey

➤ Internet databases, such as the Sports Business Research Net (SBRnet), which contains archives of multiple studies, including the annual participation report of the National Sporting Goods Association

➤ Public documents such as the annual *Statistical Abstract of the United States,* published by the U.S. Census Bureau, which includes a large section on recreation and leisure

We could group consumer studies in several ways:

➤ By industry segment (sporting goods, high school athletics)

➤ By sport

➤ By consumer demographics (men, women, people who are elderly)

➤ By consumer activity (spending on equipment, watching on television, participation)

We organize this chapter simply by the frequency and scope of the sport consumer study. We suggest that the research on sport consumers is either "irregular" or "annual/periodic" in frequency, and either "specific" or "general" in the scope of industry segments or populations it considers. We will discuss results from the studies listed in table 3.1, simply as examples of sport consumer studies.

Table 3.1 SOME SPORT CONSUMER STUDIES

Scope of segment/ population	Frequency of research	
	Irregular: (hit-or-miss)	Regular: (monthly, annual, biannual)
Limited	Creighton soccer Volvo tennis	NCAA, NFSHSA IEG *Sponsorship Reports*
Broad	Miller Lite *Sports Illustrated*	NSGA, SGMA American Sports Data *Lifestyle Market Analyst*

IRREGULAR, LIMITED STUDIES

Irregular, limited studies are typically commissioned by a team, a league, or a sponsor. They are not part of a scheduled research program; often they are one-shot deals. They tend to focus on consumer demographics (e.g., age, income), media or product consumption (e.g., favorite television station or fast food), and some attitudes (e.g., rating of concessions). Although most of them are proprietary and remain unpublished, some are printed and distributed in an effort to attract sponsors. In 1995, for example, Creighton University and Bozell Advertising Worldwide collaborated on developing and distributing a fan survey that considered fan demographics, attendance rates, media habits, attitudes toward Creighton, and purchase of Creighton merchandise. Economic impact studies are another common type of irregular study. These are usually linked to the promotion of a facility or an event, in part to justify public support. In 1991, for example, Jewell Productions commissioned both Yale University's School of Organization and Management and National Demographics and Lifestyles, Inc. to analyze the Volvo International Pro Tennis Tournament's fan profile and economic impact on the surrounding community.[3]

IRREGULAR, BROAD STUDIES

Studies of broad, particularly national, populations can require significant investments of time and money. In the sport world, corporations with sport interests have occasionally funded such research. In the late 1970s, for instance, Perrier Waters commissioned the Harris Poll to examine the sport and fitness activities of American adults. It was a logical study for Perrier, which had an eye on the growing interest in healthy living, including consumption of nonalcoholic beverages. The Harris Poll, which already employed national probability samples, was likewise a logical partner. Among other things, the Perrier Study considered activity levels by age, income, gender, and region. Results suggested that "high actives" (those who spent 360 minutes per week on vigorous activity) tended to be males under 35 who had higher incomes and lived in suburbs in the Midwest or the West.[4]

A few years later, Miller Brewing sponsored a national study of American involvement in and attitudes toward sport. The results contained interesting information on age-group interests. Aging did not mean withdrawal from sport involvement. For example, although the survey indicated that older people (especially those over age 50) attended fewer events, the results also showed very little drop-off in interest in sport as one grows older (table 3.2). People retain their interest through television, radio, reading, and conversation. The question for the marketer is why this interest does not translate into more active forms of involvement. We will offer some suggestions in the next chapter.

REGULAR, LIMITED STUDIES

Because they are snapshots of a brief moment in time, even the best irregularly conducted studies are limited in value. They can't help the marketer discover emerging trends in the ever changing environment. As we discuss in chapter 5, an effective marketing information system must include regular, consistent studies of questions that allow for trend analysis.

Fortunately, we can learn about large-scale trends in the surveys and reports of organizations such as the NCAA and the National Federation of State High School Associations (NFHSA), which publish annual statistics on participation. Although these reports deal with particular populations, they go back several decades and are widely reproduced. Excerpts are available on the organizations' Web sites, as well as in the sport industry's standard directory, the *Sports Market Place*, published annually by Franklin Covey (see listings in appendix A).

Table 3.3 offers some statistics culled from the annual NCAA participation survey, which considers the number of athletes on NCAA eligibility rosters. Obviously, this is a very special sample, but given the centrality of collegiate athletics in the American sport market, the data can suggest important trends. While inclusion on an eligibility roster does not mean that an athlete played in every (or any) game (some might suffer season-ending injuries), we still may assume that each athlete on such a roster has high levels of commitment and involvement. As we look at the data for soccer, basketball, and tennis, we note that over a 10-year period, participation in all these sports increased, for both men and women. Some of this growth resulted from an

Table 3.2 MILLER SPORT FAN INDEX BY AGE GROUP

Age group	% nonfans	% low-moderate fans	% high-moderate fans	% avid fans
14–17	7	37	33	23
18–24	12	39	27	22
25–34	12	40	30	18
35–49	10	32	40	18
50–64	12	36	34	18
65+	12	34	38	16

Adapted from *Miller Lite Report on American Attitudes Towards Sports, 1983* (p. 27) by the Miller Brewing Company, 1983, Milwaukee: Author. Copyright 1983 by the Miller Brewing Company. Reprinted with permission.

Table 3.3 GROWTH OF PARTICIPATION IN SELECTED NCAA SPORTS, 1987–1997

Sport	1987–1988	1993–1994	1996–1997	% Change 1987–1997
Soccer				
Women	5,602	9,446	14,829	164.7
Men	13,603	15,021	17,053	25.3
Basketball				
Women	10,147	11,710	13,392	31.9
Men	12,041	13,350	15,141	25.7
Tennis				
Women	7,088	7,356	8,223	16
Men	7,525	7,530	7,999	6.2

From *NCAA News*, 15 August 1990; 15 February 1995; 27 April 1998.

SPORT MARKETING

increase in NCAA membership. Even more telling are relative rates of change, especially the explosive growth of women's soccer.

Athletes are not the only "participants" tracked in regular, narrow studies. Several organizations cover trends in corporate sponsorships. One is IEG, Inc., whose *IEG Sponsorship Report* is standard reading at the top industry levels. As we emphasize in chapter 12, corporate sponsors are a special segment of sport consumers, whose objectives include not only entertainment but also exposure. Several companies track sponsor success in gaining exposure and recognition. One is Joyce Julius and Associates, whose *Sponsors Report* is a popular subscription-based publication. Another is Lou Harris & Associates, whose "Harris Ad Track" results are regularly published in *USA Today.* The ad track simply conveys consumer responses to major ad campaigns like Nike's 1997 series of Tiger Woods promotions.[5]

REGULAR, BROAD STUDIES

The first regular, broad-based study on sport consumers began during the 1970s. While working for Audits & Surveys, Dick Lipsey (who also began the *Sports Market Place* and the SBRnet) introduced a syndicated study, using a national probability sample, that measured participation and purchasing habits related to specific types of sports equipment. The study was repeated for 11 years, funded by subscribers such as Nike, Spalding, Reebok, and Rawlings. One important discovery was that new participants accounted for only a small percentage of sporting goods purchases (10-20 percent of units; 5-12 percent of dollars). The industry, however, had been emphasizing "come-on" equipment targeted to new participants at low cost and low profit. Obviously, the strategy needed adjustment to focus on higher levels of the escalator. Most consumers were looking to move up.[6]

In 1985, the National Sporting Goods Association (NSGA), the trade association for retailers, purchased another Lipsey research project. It is now the annual NSGA Sports Participation study, a widely cited and highly respected trend analysis. The NSGA study includes not only participation, but also equipment purchases, for a national sample of people aged seven or older. The NSGA data are obviously based more broadly than the NCAA or NFSHSA data. As table 3.4 indicates, however, some trends run parallel. For instance, the soccer base is growing at the fastest rate, and tennis looks shaky.

The NSGA survey is complemented by annual data from the Sporting Goods Manufacturers Association (SGMA), which among other things looks at equipment sales. Continuing our comparison, we see in table 3.5 that basketball, soccer, and tennis all experienced small growth in equipment sales from 1995 to 1996. Once again, however, the tennis market looks worse than "soft" (an industry euphemism for weak) if we compare 1996 to 1993.

Both the NSGA and the SGMA dig deeply into the question "Who plays what?" The organizations' national studies are broken down by age, gender, race, income, and residence, among other variables. Both organizations have used the services of American Sports Data, Inc. (ASD), one of the major research firms in the business. American Sports Data employs a national probability sample of 15,000 households who complete an annual four-page mail survey. Consistent methodology yields the most valid trend data. Both the NSGA and the SGMA have much at stake in tracking trends, especially

Table 3.4 1995–1996 SPORT PARTICIPATION TRENDS AMONG AMERICANS AGED 7 AND UP

Sport	Total participants 1996 (in millions)	% change 1995–1996
Basketball	33.3	+10.6
Soccer	13.9	+15.6
Tennis	11.5	−8.8

From *Spring 1998 Sports Market Place,* 1728. Based on NSGA Annual Participation Study.

Table 3.5 EQUIPMENT SALES FOR BASKETBALL, SOCCER, AND TENNIS (WHOLESALE VALUE IN MILLIONS $)

Sport	1996 Sales	1995 Sales	1993 Sales
Basketball	150	148	136
Soccer	200	185	155
Tennis	240	235	300

From *Spring 1998 Sports Market Place,* 1821.

48

among youth who might not appear in either NFSHSA or NCAA data. In the early 1990s, for example, the ASD sample showed that traditional sports were not where the action was. As table 3.6 shows, the three hottest activities for ages 6 to 17 were in-line skating, mountain biking, and free-weight training. In each case, the sample consisted of youth who par-

Table 3.6 HOTTEST ACTIVITIES FOR YOUTH, AGES 6–17

Activity	Days/Year Frequency	1992 Market (000)	1996 Market (000)	% gain 1992–1996
In-line skating	25+ days	1,893	7,890	+316.8
Mountain biking	52+ days	362	761	+110.2
Free weights	100+ days	958	1,461	+52.5

From *Sports Business Daily* 9/15/97: p. 15. From SGMA/American Sports Data Surveys.

ticipated "frequently" (defined as 25 or more days per year for in-line skaters, 52 days or more per year for mountain biking, and 100 days or more for weight lifters).[7]

A number of firms do similar research on long-term lifestyle trends with large, national samples. The Simmons Market Research Bureau, Nielsen Sports Marketing Service, USA Data, and Mediamark Research are just a few. Their services, although beyond some budgets, allow marketers to dig below surface trends to segment sport consumers in many ways, as we will discuss in chapter 6.

INDEXING SPORT CONSUMERS

National studies can also offer comparisons from one market to another and from any market to the national sample. These comparisons typically appear in the form of an index. An index simply compares the demographic or lifestyle level of a sub-sample to that of the national sample. An example of indexing may be found in the *Lifestyle Market Analyst*, a standard reference that examines demographics and lifestyles in 210 metropolitan areas of the United States.

Lifestyles are divided into seven categories, one of which is "Sports, Fitness, and Health." Indexing allows the researcher to make some interesting analyses. For instance, the 1999 edition devoted four pages to tables analyzing American households who golfed regularly.

As table 3.7 shows, 17.8 percent of golf-

Table 3.7 SAMPLE PROFILE OF GOLFING U.S. HOUSEHOLDS

Household characteristic	% of total golfing households	Index*
Have income of $100,000 or more	17.8	187
Regularly use credit card for travel/entertainment	19.3	152
Regularly watch sports on TV	58	149
Snow ski frequently	16.1	194

*Index = 100 equals national average of the household characteristic.

Source: SRDS, *1999 Lifestyle Market Analyst* (Des Plains, IL: 1999): 778-779.

ing households earn over $100,000 annually. This yields an index of 187, or 87 percent higher than the national average. Thus we see that golfing households are 87 percent more likely to earn $100,000 or more, are 52 percent more likely to use a credit card for travel and entertainment, 49 percent more likely to watch sports on TV, and 94 percent more likely to snow ski frequently. This is just a tiny fraction of the analysis offered by such frequent and broad consumer studies.

READING SPORT CONSUMER STUDIES

The most important step for the researcher is to recognize the limitations of any study. As we discuss in chapter 5, all market research is limited by time and resources. Researchers make choices about many elements, including the following:

> Definitions—What constitutes a "fan" or a "participant"?

> Methodologies—Interviews? Observations? By phone? By mail? At an event?

> Sampling—A random sample of the whole population? Several random samples grouped or "stratified" by some criterion (e.g., ticket type)?

Anyone trying to make sense out of published studies must consider all these questions.

DEFINITIONS

Definitions are especially important. For instance, 1997 and 1998 saw many references to a golf "boom" in the wake of Tiger Woods's phenomenal start on the PGA Tour. In some respects there was a boom. The industry newsletter *IEG Sponsorship Report* indicated that the corporate world had spent $600 million on golf sponsorships in 1997—double the level for 1990. Some data suggested that the stage had been set for Tiger Woods. The National Golf Foundation, a trade association, had shown American spending on golf at the $15.1 billion level for 1994, almost double the 1986 level of $7.8 billion. Finally, over 1,300 new courses had opened in the mid-1990s alone. But the "boom" did not look so strong in another area—participation. The National Golf Foundation estimated that 24.7 million people aged 12 or above had played one round of golf in 1996, which was a decrease from the 1991 level of 24.8 million. Were golf course investors ill-advised? Not necessarily, since "one-time play" might not be a good gauge of golf participation. In other words, perhaps fewer people played just one round of golf and more people played multiple rounds.[8]

Defining Involvement and Commitment

The golf "boom" raises key questions about defining two critical aspects of sport consumption—involvement and commitment (see photos). We will consider these concepts again in chapter 4, but we cannot emphasize their importance enough. Among other things, they underlie the logic of the escalator (refer back to figure 2.3).

Fans express their commitment by wearing their team's colors while attending games.

As the escalator suggests, even simple awareness is a form of involvement. So is "interest," a frequently measured aspect of sport consumption. Take, for instance, data in table 3.8, from a 1996 survey by Sponsorship Research International that looked at soccer interest among Americans. These data were culled from 12,000 interviews, with the results segmented by age and gender.

At first glance, table 3.8 conveys some sobering news about the American soccer market. Some 80 percent of the sample had either "low" or no interest in soccer, across all categories except the 18- to 24-year-old age group, which we already saw represented in the NCAA data. And even among this "youth" market, so long proclaimed as the future of soccer, almost three quarters were in the low- or no-interest category.

Table 3.8	SOCCER INTEREST (IN %) IN AMERICA, BY AGE AND GENDER					
			Age		Gender	
Interest	Total	18–24	25–54	55+	Male	Female
High	6.8	12.1	5.7	6.4	7.1	6.5
Medium	11.3	15.6	10.6	10.8	12.6	10.1
Low	19.7	21.3	20.3	18.0	23.9	15.9
Not at all	61.4	50.9	63.1	62.7	55.7	66.6

From Sponsorship Research International, reported in *Sports Business Daily*, 2 April 1997.

Does this mean that the soccer boom is a giant fiction? Not at all. Among other things, a suburban-focused sample might provide much higher interest levels. More importantly, interest is only one measure of involvement. What about participation? Perhaps a very high percentage of the interested people will move up the escalator of involvement and become participants. In fact, recent statistics from the Soccer Industry Council and the SGMA suggest that the soccer boom has continued. As table 3.9 shows, participation in soccer is continuing to grow. Total participation grew almost 8 percent from 1995 to 1996, with a 34 percent increase in the adult (18+) category. Obviously kids are not abandoning the game as they get older.

Defining Participation

Table 3.9 emphasizes another critical aspect of sport consumer studies—defining "participation." The 18.1 million soccer participants in 1996 are people who played at least once a year. This is a fairly typical use of the term "participant," but it has obvious limitations. It can be helpful in tracking long-term interest, but it has little to do with marketing the sport. The categories "Frequent," "Core," and "Aficionado" are far more telling because they reflect movement up the escalator. If we look more closely at rates of change at different levels of the escalator, the picture for soccer appears mixed. For instance, the rate of increase of aficionados was greater (8.1 percent) than that of the overall base of participants (7.7). That is good news; soccer wants to see more consumers at higher levels of interest and commitment. On the other hand, the growth rates for frequent and core participants were slower than that of the overall base. And these data show that overall female participation actually declined, in sharp contrast to the NCAA statistics considering only players on NCAA teams.[9]

Table 3.9 U.S. SOCCER PARTICIPATION, 1995–1996			
Category	1995 in millions	1996 in millions	% Increase 1995–1996
Total participants	16.8	18.1	7.7
Male	9.5	10.9	14.7
Female	7.3	7.2	–1.3
Under 18	13.3	13.4	0.7
18 and over	3.5	4.7	34.2
"Frequent": 25 or more days per year	7.3	7.7	5.4
"Core": 52 or more days per year	3.2	3.2	0.0
"Aficionados": Soccer is favorite activity	3.7	4	8.1

From *NCAA News*, 19 May 1997, 2; 2.

These statistics provide a very limited snapshot—one year's rate of change. Their real importance lies in their more precise approach to defining participation. In developing or interpreting research, sport marketers must take great care to remember a key question:

How will I define . . .

Casual or careless use of definitions will severely limit the utility of any statistics. Take, for example, the 1997 poll commissioned by MLB to examine fan support for league realignment—a very controversial issue. The poll—of 801 "fans" aged 16 or older—supposedly represented the vast population of the baseball nation. When the Associated Press people looked more carefully at the sample, however, they discovered that 70 percent of the sample were not aware that MLB was considering realignment. Worse yet, 44 percent had never heard of the expansion Diamondbacks or Devil Rays, and 13 percent had never heard of the Colorado Rockies. Almost half of the sample planned to attend only one game or no games during the season. As the Associated Press concluded, these were "casual fans at best": hardly the type of "fan" worth making realignment decisions over.[10]

MULTIPLE MEASURES

The most effective research on the sport consumer employs clearly defined, multiple measures of involvement and commitment. As our data have suggested, there are many ways to measure sport consumption. Playing is but one index, and even here one can separate "real" playing from "virtual" playing on a video game. There is also watching at an event or on television, listening on the radio, or reading in the sport section of the newspaper. Moreover, people are consuming sport when they buy equipment—even if they don't use what they buy. After all, how many stationary bicycles now stand idle, with daily use as a clothes hanger? Marketers must consider multiple measures when writing or reading sport consumer research.[11]

CONSISTENT SAMPLES AND METHODS

Even regularly produced studies occasionally alter the samples or methods of record keeping. Thus a trend in participation may be a result of changes in record keeping and not in participation at all. For instance, beginning in 1979, the NFSHSA discontinued collecting participation data from Canadian schools and from junior high schools. This makes it very difficult to analyze trends that began before 1979. Along methodological lines, in 1994 the Simmons Market Research Bureau changed its approach to measuring consumer reading habits (for instance, Simmons can tell you what magazines skiers read regularly). This effectively created a fault line in Simmons's data. As one publishing executive put it, "The name is the same, Simmons. Otherwise, you're dealing with a new company." An unaware researcher would risk grave errors by tracking trends across the fault line.[12]

REPRESENTATIVE SAMPLES

We will discuss sampling more thoroughly in chapter 5; its importance cannot be stressed enough. Although the intent is often to represent the broader population, few studies can reach an entire population. Errors in sampling can distort results, regardless of numerical "significance." The classic sampling error occurred in the 1936 presidential election, when the magazine *Literary Digest* predicted a victory for Alf Landon over Franklin Roosevelt. The prediction rested on the results of a survey of readers. Unfortunately, readers of *Literary Digest* tended to be educated, relatively well-off Republicans; the sample was therefore stacked for Landon. Roosevelt won in a landslide.

Sport consumer studies have had their share of sampling errors. In fact, ASD began its own syndicated national study in 1984 in response to a belief that existing studies were grossly underestimating the size of the sporting goods market. President of ASD, Harvey Lauer, identified two reasons for sampling errors in existing studies: (1) a focus on participants, when many purchases (especially of running shoes) were by nonparticipants; (2) underrepresentation of under-18 youth and of young singles. In part, ASD built its study to correct these errors.[13]

WRAP-UP

We have offered an introduction to the many sources of information available to the sport marketer. Several sources, such as the Simmons, Harris, Nielsen, and Census Bureau reports, are rather standard fare for any product marketer. Others are specific to the sport industry. Many of the regular, broad studies are syndicated, or available for a price. The marketer may find excerpted information by reading such periodicals as *Marketing News, Business Week, Advertising Age,* and *Amusement Business,* all of which devote sections to the sport industry. In addition, an increasing number of periodicals deal specifically with sport business issues, including *Team Marketing Report, Sport Marketing Quarterly, Street and Smith's Sports Business Journal, Sports Business Daily (SBD),* and *Athletic Business,* to name just a few. The *SBD* is especially valuable because it compiles and edits stories from a vast range of sources. It is an essential resource for serious executives and researchers. Finally, there are growing numbers of Internet sources, led by the SBRnet. All contain information on recent studies of the sport consumer. (For more sources, see appendix A.)

Although source material is abundant, the marketer must use it judiciously. Most studies are difficult to compare because they use different measures of participation, involvement, social status, and lifestyle. The marketer must also look very carefully at methodologies. Some studies have rather limited samples; others include highly leading questions. For instance, one upstart professional league commissioned a "study" of "fans" in that sport. But even a casual researcher could quickly see that too many questions in the survey led the subjects to make statements unfavorable to the established rival league, which the sponsor of the study was about to sue. If the marketer analyzes studies carefully, however, she should better appreciate and understand the consumers of her own sport product. While gathering information on who her consumers are likely to be, given national trends, she must also ponder the more difficult question of why a person would want to buy or consume her product. This question moves her into the general realm of consumer behavior, a topic we discuss in the next chapter.

ACTIVITIES

1. What standard questions must a sport marketer ask about consumers?

2. Take an hour in the library to discover and list all the available sources on consumers of your favorite sport. Try to categorize these sources (e.g., by frequency and scope, by medium of publication).

3. Analyze two of these sources and suggest how you might improve their strength.

4. Provide examples of research that differs according to scope of the populations or sports analyzed.

YOUR MARKETING PLAN

You have picked an organization, considered your "theory of the business" and your mission, conducted a SWOT analysis (strengths, weaknesses, opportunities, threats), and set some objectives. To some extent, you should have already considered your consumers. But after reading this chapter, you might refine some of your thinking. Use some of the data sources described in the chapter (or listed in the appendix) to develop a clearer picture of your consumers. How will you define "involvement," "commitment," or "participation"? Can you identify special segments of consumers?

CHAPTER

4

PERSPECTIVES IN SPORT CONSUMER BEHAVIOR

OBJECTIVES

1. To recognize the differences among socialization, involvement, and commitment for sport consumers.

2. To understand the various individual and environmental factors that shape consumer involvement and commitment in sport.

3. To understand the decision process for sport consumers.

IF YOU BUILD IT, WHY WILL THEY COME?

In 1994, an estimated 50,000 people, some from thousands of miles away, visited an Iowa cornfield. Along the way, they may have picked up a flyer from the local Chamber of Commerce. The headline read, "Is this Heaven? Dyersville, Iowa, Where Dreams Come True." The destination? Don Lansing's baseball field, featured in the hit movie *Field of Dreams*. Why would 50,000 pilgrims trek to a con- verted cornfield that was just part of Hollywood's dreamland? Well, we could just as easily ask why thousands buy tennis racquets, golf clubs, bicycles, and fishing rods that they hardly use. Or why others pay $1500 for a courtside NBA seat. Or why others train daily like Navy SEALs so they can punish their bodies in grueling "Ironman" triathlons. The answers are as numerous as the people involved.[1]

We have looked in various ways at who the sport consumer is. In this chapter, we will examine why people consume sport. To that end, we will consider sport consumers within the larger context of general consumer behavior, including various factors that help to explain how people are socialized into involvement in or commitment to sport. Although innumerable studies, theories, and models attempt to get into the mind of the consumer, we may characterize the factors that influence behavior as either environmental or individual. Environmental factors may include significant others such as family, peers, and coaches; social and cultural norms; social class structure; race and gender relations; climatic and geographic conditions; market behavior of firms in the sport industry; and sport opportunity structure. Individual factors include one's self-concept, stage in the life or family cycle, physical characteristics, learning, perceptions, motivations, and attitudes, as well as the complex process of consumer decision making itself. In this chapter, we will consider each of these factors in turn.[2]

SOCIALIZATION, INVOLVEMENT, AND COMMITMENT

Environmental and individual factors influence how and to what extent people become involved with and committed to sport. Think about your own sport activities, whether as a child, a youth, or an adult. Something or somebody got you interested, somehow, in an activity. Perhaps it was a trip to watch a game, an afternoon playing with a parent or friend, or a television broadcast of a championship. A trigger of interest prompted your involvement and perhaps your socialization in a sport.

Sociologists typically consider socialization to be the process by which individuals assimilate and develop the skills, knowledge, attitudes, and other "equipment" necessary to perform various social roles. As depicted in figure 4.1, this involves two-way interaction between the individual and the environment. Socialization, in turn, demands some kind of involvement, in our case with sport.[3] Involvement takes one of three basic forms:

➤ *Behavioral* involvement: the hands-on "doing." This includes playing at practice or in competition; it also includes the activities of fans at a game (or at home), watching and listening and rooting.

➤ *Cognitive* involvement: the acquisition of information and knowledge about a sport. Players sitting through a chalk talk, and fans at a Boosters Club meeting listening to the coach explain how last week's game plan worked so well, both exemplify cognitive involvement. Magazines, newspapers, game programs, radio, and television are key media of cognitive involvement for consumers eager to know more about a sport.

➤ *Affective* involvement: the attitudes, feelings, and emotions that a consumer has toward an activity. Pep rallies and pregame locker-room talks are standard fare for affective involvement. But so too are the best advertisements. Just think of any Nike ad. Like them or not, these ads stir the emotions about a sport (or about Nike).

Commitment refers to frequency, duration, and intensity of involvement in a sport, or the willingness to expend money, time, and energy in a pattern of sport involvement. Movement up the escalator normally indicates a deeper commitment. For some sports, like tennis and golf, the levels can be dramatic. For instance, a random sample of 468 fans at the 1991 Men's Clay Court Tennis Championships displayed the following types and levels of tennis involvement:

➤ 89 percent were tennis players.

➤ 45.7 percent rated their own skills as "intermediate."

➤ 42.1 percent rated their own skills as "advanced intermediate."

➤ 71.8 percent rated tennis as "favorite" participant sport.

➤ 52.9 percent rated tennis as "most frequent" sport attended.

➤ 39.6 percent rated tennis as "most frequent" sport viewed on television.

➤ 75.5 percent owned a $100 to $199 racquet.

➤ 27.8 percent owned a $200+ racquet.

A fan who attends tennis competitions is likely to have a strong personal commitment to the sport.

These were highly committed consumers, spending considerable time, money, and energy on the sport of tennis.[4]

The marketer must clearly understand the types of involvement and commitment that consumers represent. The season-ticket holder who subscribes to *Sporting News*, attends every game, fills in a scorecard, and roots with great emotion is obviously different from the father who brings his child to one game to satisfy a sense of parental duty. A similar distinction exists between club members who use many amenities at a facility, and use them often, versus those who don't. The member who swims, plays racquetball, regularly attends aerobics, and brings children to the club's child-care program is far more likely to rejoin than the member who occasionally comes alone to ride a stationary bike. The committed player, fan, or member thinks more, feels more, and does more. Nurturing the committed consumer is a key goal.[5]

Obviously, environmental and individual factors constantly interact. Although individuals are influenced by their environment, they are also capable of reshaping the social, physical, and cultural landscape around them. If this were not so, life would be static. Change is part of existence in politics, in art, in music, and in sport. For this reason, the sport marketer must understand the complex dynamics that shape consumers. The model in figure 4.1 depicts the interaction that determines the outcomes of importance to this chapter: socialization, involvement, and commitment in sport. For example, the proprietors of a summer hockey camp must develop the marketing mix that will match the wants and needs of potential consumers. In order to do so, the proprietors rely on and become a part of this socialization process in sport.

For instance, our hockey camp entrepreneurs must base their marketing mix on their assessment of demand. Do the regional values and norms support hockey to the extent that kids want summer instruction? This may in part relate to climatic conditions; one expects more demand in northern regions. But at the same time, a hockey hotbed like Huntsville, Alabama, may defy climatic trends. A few fanatics may devote much of their lives to promoting a nontraditional sport in a given area and thereby alter local or regional values—and in turn alter consumer attitudes toward the activity. At the same time, potential consumers who have developed a desire to play hockey may lack opportunities to participate because of economic hardship or racial or gender discrimination.

Although marketers adjust or develop the marketing mix for their hockey camp, potential consumers find that a host of individual factors affect their socialization, involvement, and commitment in relation to hockey. Some parents may perceive hockey as a brawling, violent sport that their children should avoid. Some children may be motivated to play hockey because they feel it will "toughen" them. Other children may believe that only big people can play hockey successfully. Such individual and environmental factors will play a part in the decision-making process between parent and child on the question of attending a hockey camp. As figure 4.1 suggests, consumer decision making is the processing of all the knowledge, feelings, and behaviors (both individual and environmental) that results in increased (or decreased) involvement in or commitment to sport. Players and fans alike are constantly making decisions that move them up, down, or off the escalator!

Like all models, figure 4.1 is a picture of a complex process, not a formula that guarantees understanding and correct decisions. This figure should serve to remind the marketer of all the factors to sift through in order to understand and develop consumer interest, involvement, and commitment.

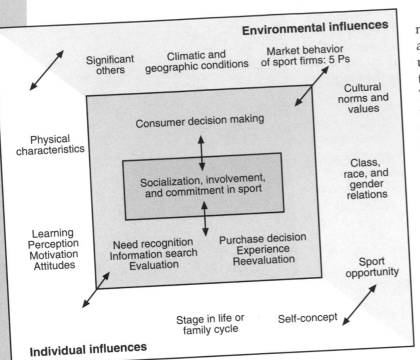

Figure 4.1 Consumer behavior in sport.

ENVIRONMENTAL FACTORS

Consumers are surrounded by a host of factors that may influence their decisions about sport involvement. As we consider some of the more prominent factors, we stress again the constant interaction between and among them.

SIGNIFICANT OTHERS

Much of a person's socialization into sport roles occurs through interaction with significant others, who may actively shape patterns of involvement or who may act as role models. Some of the most important are family members, coaches, teachers, and peers. While these are personal relations, consumers may also have impersonal, distant "reference groups" that are also significant.[6]

Parents play a vital role in introducing children to sport. In the 1980s, a national sample of parents showed the following:

➤ About 75 percent almost always or often encouraged their children to participate.

➤ About 72 percent encouraged their children to practice their skills away from the game.

➤ Only 6 percent encouraged their children to spend less time playing sports.

Nothing suggests that things have changed—for better or worse.[7]

Peers and friends are also important. In fact, some studies of female athletes have indicated that peers are more significant than family in encouraging participation through adulthood. Studies of health or athletic club members have also demonstrated the importance of the peer network; 61 percent of one national sample said they first became aware of their clubs from friends or colleagues. Further, friends were the single most important factor in getting a person to try the club's offerings; advertising and special promotions had far less impact. These results parallel general consumer behavior. For instance, a 1997 study by the Yankelovich Monitor showed the following responses from American consumers:

Parents play a significant role in their children's sport participation.

➤ 40 percent said that advice from friends had a strong influence on buying behavior.

➤ 57 percent considered advice from a friend or relative a good reason to try a new grocery brand.

➤ 60 percent said they seek advice from friends when considering products they know little about.

Sport is no exception: pals have power.[8] At the same time, consumers have reference groups, heroes, or role models who may be distant and impersonal but nonetheless important. "I want to be like Mike" has worked as an ad campaign for Gatorade because it rings true across America. But Michael Jordan is just one of many distant models or reference groups. For sixth graders in any middle school, it could also be the seemingly Olympian "cool kids" in the eighth grade. Or for many adolescents, it may be the "cool kids" on MTV, who influence both school and sport fashions. As we shall see in chapters 7 and 12, teams, leagues, and corporate sponsors have much at stake in making particular athletes central to consumer reference groups.[9]

CULTURAL NORMS AND VALUES

Significant others tend to convey the beliefs, attitudes, and behaviors that typify their own cultural settings. In a society's broader framework, however, there are many alternative cultures, subcultures, and countercultures that may nurture different lifestyles. This is as true in sport as it is in all areas of living; if not for the dynamics of culture, society would not change over time. A stagnant society would greatly affect sport. Consider, for example, that as late as the 1920s, many American communities outlawed organized sports on Sunday. Can you imagine being arrested for golfing on a Sunday? That is unthinkable today, yet at the turn of the century it happened with some regularity in American cities where cultural groups fought over secularism and the Sabbath. And 40 years ago, who would have predicted that the 1995 Minnesota high school hockey championship sellout of Aldrich Arena in St.

Paul was for girls' hockey? Or that the star hockey team at the 1998 Olympics was a women's team?[10]

America may have some dominant, long-lasting values about sport, including notions of character building, discipline, fitness, and competition—all of which parallel the values of free-enterprise capitalism. These values certainly motivate people to consume sports. At the same time, one can find alternative norms and values. "Slackers" offer new styles of character and discipline in the X Games. Skateboarding and rollerblading appeal to adolescents who value creativity and freedom over adult-directed regimens. Skateboarding will hardly destroy baseball or football. Yet it would be instructive to understand better the values of this special subculture, just as it would for cross-country skiers, field hockey players, and fans of jai alai—all of whom may be outside the mainstream of the dominant sports creed.[11]

There are also probable differences in regional values, despite the sweep of television. The Boston Celtics and Bruins, for instance, have been very slow to adopt the glitzy promotions that fill most NBA and NHL arenas—laser shows, strobe lights, smoky and thunderous introductions, cheerleaders, and dancing mascots. These are the very same promotions that have helped build hockey markets in places like Charleston, South Carolina, and Lafayette Parish, Louisiana. So far, they haven't flown in staid old Boston. But if the Bruins or Celtics want to attract young families, in the age of MTV, how long can they hold out? Says Pat Williams, the Orlando Magic's longtime promotional wizard: "This is a huge, huge dilemma for New England. Is conservative New England capable of handling this all at once? Or do you ease into it?" In 1997, North Dakota's Carlisle Cereal eased into brisk sales and profits based on alternative values. Carlisle's Hometown Stars brand featured box-cover pictures of local teams, not major leaguers. The prime market was small towns, where local heroes still loom large in the public's eye. Whether on Boston's mythical parquet floor or in the cramped gym of Hoosierville, alternative norms and values still exist. Cultural values and norms influence how and to what level different people get involved in different sports.[12]

CLASS, RACE, AND GENDER RELATIONS

Cultural differences often stem from differences in power and influence within a general social structure. Some groups have easier access to rewards and prestige, which may include sport. Americans may believe that sport is an egalitarian and democratic institution; the historical and sociological record indicates something else. The marketer must recognize the difference.

Class

The influence of social class is sometimes subtle. There is little consensus among researchers on exactly what constitutes social class distinctions or how to assess a person's class rank. For some, class is a function of income, education, or occupation. For others, it is a matter of inherited prestige and status, which derive from residence and lifestyle. Numerous scales attempt to describe various strata in the class system. It is clear, though, that differences in class standing relate to differences in lifestyle, including sports involvement.

This complexity is especially acute among many middle-class Americans, to which may be added some people from traditional working-class jobs, such as plumbers and carpenters. Most of these people consider themselves to be middle class, and many of them have household incomes that are similar to their white-collar counterparts. However, there are also important differences. "White-collar" middle-class people may spend money on tennis and golf, while their "blue-collar" counterparts may choose to invest in bowling and hunting. In this case, there is a serious difference between purchasing power and purchase behavior.[13]

Table 4.1 offers several simple dimensions by which social class groups have historically diverged in their sports life. For example, elite sports like polo, the hunt, and golf, have required great expanses of open space that often are not available to those with lower incomes. Middle-class groups, especially from within the white-collar, managerial segments, have

Table 4.1 SOME HISTORICAL DIMENSIONS OF SPORT, CLASS, AND STATUS

Class	Space	Use of body	Ethos
Upper, elite	Usually expansive (golf, polo, hunt)	Expressive	Exclusivity
Middle	Rationally defined (baseball, football)	Instrumental	Discipline, respectability
Working	Limited by circumstance (boxing, dog-fighting)	Expressive	Replicate life conditions of struggle, violence, chance

Source: D. Booth and J. Loy, "Sport, Status, and Style," *Sport History Review* 30 (1999): 1–26.

flocked to sports like football and baseball, where space has been carefully designed and rationalized. Working-class sports like boxing or dog fighting (still alive although illegal) grew in confined areas. Even basketball began in small armories, gymnasiums, and multipurpose auditoriums.

The reasons why certain sports link with certain classes remain somewhat obscure and in need of research. Some activities appeal to the upper ranks because of their esoteric and historically exclusive nature. Golf, polo, and yachting are examples of what Thorstein Veblen called "conspicuous consumption"—clear expressions of wealth and privilege, particularly through membership in exclusive clubs.

At the other end are what some sociologists have called "prole sports," working-class or proletarian activities like roller derby, motorcycle racing, or demolition derby. Such sports, with their speed, machinery, and danger, may be ways in which members of this social class express the peculiar regimentation of their work worlds.

While both elites and workers have focused on expressive uses of their bodies in sport, the middle class has tended to use sport as an instrument for achieving the disciplined life so ingrained in the American corporate lifestyle. Hard work, sacrifice, teamwork, and precision, so closely tied to football and baseball, dominate the ethos of middle-class sport.[14]

Of course, life can't be put into boxes. The complexities of history usually confound simple models. Auto racing, especially NASCAR, is a good example. It is a "prole sport" that started on dirt tracks; it is now produced on highly rationalized, modern tracks for the highest levels of the American elite who sit in glassy boxes above the crowd. Indeed, there are some indications that the major team sports are provoking elements of class struggle. Bigger and gaudier skyboxes, expanded areas of expensive club seats, and endless rounds of price hikes seem to indicate to the everyday fan that America's teams have been transformed into a private club for everyday corporate suits. We will return to this issue in chapters 6, 9, and 13. The marketer must recognize the complexity of the American class structure.

Race

Race relations have a similar impact on patterns of sport involvement, particularly among people of color. Although it is clear that African Americans are represented in all categories of social class, it is equally clear that they have endured continued racial discrimination resulting in overrepresentation in urban areas and in low-income, low-education categories. Researchers are less clear on whether African Americans demonstrate substantially different consumption patterns from other groups. In the case of sport consumption, however, even a casual observer can see the dominance of black athletes in basketball, football, and track, as well as their underrepresentation in hockey, golf, and tennis (despite the prominence of Tiger Woods and Venus and Serena Williams). At the same time, there is little evidence that patterns of black sport involvement have any basis in "race," which is itself more a social than a natural construction. Rather, blacks appear to excel in certain sports because these sports are available through school and recreation programs and appear as viable avenues to status and achievement.[15]

Race is the enduring American conundrum, especially in the sport marketplace. The American public generally embraces the notion that Jackie Robinson opened doors of opportunity, and that the integration of baseball helped spur a revolution in civil rights. And there is no denying Muhammad Ali and Michael Jordan a place in the all-time pantheon of American heroes. On the other hand, economists have amassed quantitative evidence of consumer discrimination against black athletes:

> Two studies on the market for baseball cards suggest that white players are valued more highly than minority players of equal productivity.

> A study of revenues and racial composition at 42 NCAA Division I basketball programs concluded that "on average, a team replacing a black player with a white player of equal skill gains in excess of $100,000 in annual gate receipts, providing a strong incentive for college basketball programs to discriminate against black recruits."

> A study of 259 local NBA broadcasts concluded that a team's local ratings went up .4 points (about 5,800 homes in the Minneapolis market) for every additional 10 minutes of playing time given to a white player.

While these studies must be read with caution for context, samples, and significance, they suggest clearly that race still matters.[16]

Gender

Gender relations cut across both class and race. Although historically women have been denied opportunities to participate in most sports, that has changed considerably in the last three decades, largely because of Title IX. In 1971, only 1 in 27 high school girls played sports. By 1996, the ratio was 1 in 3. The increases in college sports have been equally dramatic, although in both high school and college sports the ratios have not changed much in the last several years.

The development of female athletics has been a long struggle involving not only legal challenges to the established, male-dominated structure of competitive athletics in schools and colleges, but also general assaults on cultural values that equate aggressive, physical activities with masculinity. Given such conditions, it is not surprising that researchers discovered peer groups to have a greater importance for female athletes than for their male counterparts.[17]

Women also are a major force among spectators, across a host of "big-time" sports. Recent fan surveys have shown that females make up over 40 percent of the fan base in football, indoor soccer, and auto racing. Data from Sponsorship Research International, USA (see table 4.2) show widespread female interest at "medium to strong" levels for the Olympics, the NFL, ice skating, and gymnastics. With the arrival of the American Basketball League and the WNBA, women had two professional leagues of their own—let alone the booming interest in women's collegiate basketball, which fueled record-breaking levels of attendance and television ratings.[18]

Women's sports have clearly come of age, raising some critical questions for marketers. For instance, will women's interests in sport products parallel those of males, or do women, regardless of skill levels, derive different satisfactions from sport involvement? Early studies of sports television viewing—dominated by

Table 4.2 SPORTS INTEREST AMONG A NATIONAL SAMPLE OF 6000 FEMALES

Sport	Percentage by age reporting an interest of 5 or higher on a 10-point scale		
	18–34	35–54	55+
Olympic Games	69	71	65
NFL	65	53	46
Ice skating	57	62	69
Gymnastics	56	57	57

From SRi USA, reported in *SBD* 8 October 1997: 16.

traditional "male" sports—showed interesting differences between male and female viewers:

> ➤ Men were more emotionally involved in viewing.
> ➤ Men engaged in pregame rituals to "pump up" for the game.
> ➤ Women were more likely to watch sports because others were watching.
> ➤ Women were more likely to work while they watched.

We need much more research on the notion of a gender divide in fan interests and behaviors. One suspects that the results would differ for mixed audiences of the WNBA or the Winter Olympics.[19]

Women's high brand loyalty is good news for new professional leagues. For instance, WNBA merchandise sold briskly to female customers in the league's inaugural season. Said one consultant, "Women who perhaps had never entered a sports store are now looking for WNBA team merchandise." This made WNBA sponsors quite happy, especially Sears, which saw merchandise orders double in a month.[20]

Finally, the commercial success of women's spectator sports—whether basketball, figure skating, gymnastics, volleyball, tennis, or golf—raises questions about the sport product. Women's sports appear to offer alternative visions of what sport is or can be. We will return to this in chapter 6. Sport still may be the altar for many male rituals, but females have carved out their own cults, with huge numbers of converts, many of whom are male.[21]

Gender, race, class, ethnicity, and region are all part of the swirl of culture in American life. Their effects on consumer behavior are multiple, interrelated, complex, and critically important. As one writer concluded, "Although no one expects every marketer to be an anthropologist, sociologist, or ethnologist, we need to learn how the cultural issues of language, religion, family patterns, gender roles, education, and aspirations affect consumer behavior patterns." This is certainly true in the sport world.[22]

CLIMATIC AND GEOGRAPHIC CONDITIONS

Although revolutions in travel and communications have diminished some of the regional variations in sport consumption, there are still some differences based on climate and topography. For instance, few hockey players are produced outside the northern regions. Within the North, Minnesota and Massachusetts dominate the production of players. Similarly, the mountainous areas of New England and the West produce far more world-class skiers than other parts of the country. The dry sun and long coast of California spawned both surfing and skateboarding. Geographer John Rooney recently identified eleven distinct "regions" of sport involvement, from the "Eastern Cradle" to the "Pigskin Cult" of the deep South to the "Pacific Cornucopia" of surfing, skiing, and just about everything else (see map on page 64). Historians have begun to look at the history of southern approaches to sports, including hunting, auto racing, and baseball. While regional sport cultures demand much greater analysis, clearly climate and topography have played important roles.[23]

MARKET BEHAVIOR OF SPORT FIRMS

The behavior of sport firms has important ramifications for consumer involvement. As subsequent chapters outline in detail, these market activities revolve around product, place (distribution), price, promotion, and public relations—the five Ps of sport marketing. It is clear, for instance, that the vast distribution of sport events via television has had a major effect on enlarging the base of consumers for

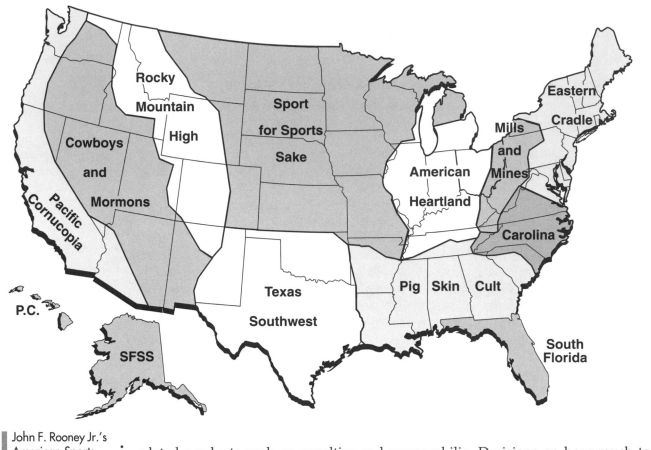

John F. Rooney Jr.'s American Sports Regions.

related products such as novelties and memorabilia. Decisions on how much to televise are part of any team's marketing strategy. Similarly, decisions on club membership fees and promotional campaigns may make or break a consumer's decision to join.

New sports typically depend on the marketing behavior of existing suppliers. Snowboarding is a good case in point. In the early 1990s, many ski resorts viewed snowboarding as an intrusive, dangerous, slope-wrecking activity for young, show-off "slackers." Snowboarders were either prohibited, crowded onto limited runs, or forced to pass safety and courtesy tests (which many skiers could also use). By the mid-1990s, however, most ski resorts recognized that snowboarding represented the major hope for industry growth. *American Demographics* even predicted that by 2012, snowboarders would outnumber skiers. Market behavior changed dramatically, with resorts developing special areas and events for snowboarders, coupled with aggressive promotions about being snowboarder friendly. The new market behavior probably hastened the day of the snowboard majority.[24]

Sport involvement

	High	Low
High	Country-club set	Busy professionals
Low	Playground basketball groups	People who are elderly, sick, or disabled

Sport opportunity structure

Figure 4.2
The sport involvement/opportunity structure grid.

THE SPORT OPPORTUNITY STRUCTURE

When we consider the array of environmental factors that influence consumer behavior in sport, we can see how complicated the marketer's task really is. This is why segmentation strategies (considered in chapter 6) are so important. They help to categorize consumer groups by some of the important and perceptible environmental (and also individual) factors related to involvement in and commitment to sport.

Ultimately, environmental factors combine to create various sport opportunity structures that may vary from social group to social group. The sport marketer may develop a market grid that assesses various locales and groups along the dimensions of involvement and opportunity structure. Figure 4.2 provides a simple grid that the marketer might use for crude sorting.

The "country club set" is taking advantage of opportunity and is active. At the other extreme are people who are "elderly, sick, or infirm" who have little opportunity and little involvement. Although all groups deserve attention for different social, ethical, or economic reasons, the marketer is apt to concentrate on the "playground groups" or the "busy professionals." Both groups indicate much about consumer behavior in sport: one group is quite involved despite a lack of opportunity, whereas the other has the economic ability to participate but shows low involvement.

In fact, the inner-city "playground" group has been the target of many special promotions. The NHL, the Boston Bruins, and some other local groups began the SCORE BOSTON program in 1996, aimed at providing more opportunities for inner-city kids to learn ice hockey. The Ladies Professional Golf Association (LPGA), the PGA, and the United States Tennis Association (USTA) have similar programs to boost inner-city interest in golf and tennis. Such programs are praiseworthy, but they also require long-term commitments of resources. Only time will judge commitment and success.[25]

Proprietors of ski resorts now court the business of the growing numbers of snowboarders, a population once considered a nuisance.

INDIVIDUAL FACTORS

Environmental factors swirl constantly around the consumer, but individual or internal factors influence the way the individual interacts and makes sense of that larger world. Among the important factors are self-concept, stage in the life cycle, physical characteristics, the learning process, perception, motivation, and attitudes. We will look at how these may affect involvement in and commitment to sport.

SELF-CONCEPT

Every beginning golfer has felt the sting of self-consciousness after dribbling a 40-yard drive off a crowded first tee. All people hold certain cognitions or beliefs about themselves; these cognitions are not simply the self-view (self-image) but are a rather complex set of interacting perceptions. The most complete theory of self-concept suggests that we have more than self-images (ways in which we view ourselves); we also have images of how we think others view us (perceived or apparent selves), images of how we would like to be (desired or ideal selves), and images of how we interact with particularly important reference groups (reference-group selves). The proponents of this theory suggest that there is also a fifth image, namely the real self—what we truly are and never will know, because no mortal ever sees this "true" image.[26]

All of these "selves" make up the self-concept, a fundamental part of motivation into (or out of) sport. For some time, psychologists have known that a positive self-concept spurs greater involvement and commitment. This is why the best coaching manuals stress positive and constructive reinforcement, especially for kids. At the same time, what adult would return for lessons from a golf pro who regularly said, "You stink at golf; don't waste your time with your lousy swing!" One can find traces of the self-concept throughout the industry. For instance, a 1991 study of 10,000 youth, aged 10 to 18, revealed three major groups of sport participants, according to similarities in motivation. All had links to self-concept:

> ➤ 40 percent participated "for the image."

> ➤ 35 percent participated "to improve self."

> ➤ 25 percent participated "because of pressure."

Kids are obviously building or protecting their self-image as they make decisions about sport involvement. This goes beyond the playing. One of the mid-1990s apparel trends was the "attitude" T-shirt, best represented by the Coed Naked and No Fear brands. These shirts were statements about the wearer's self-concept:

"Coed Naked tennis. It's in . . . it's out . . . it's over!"

"If you can't win, don't play."

"You let up, you lose."

As we shall see in chapter 6, the marketer can segment consumers on the basis of lifestyles and values that relate strongly to the self-concept and associated consumption behaviors. For instance, research indicates that "inner-directed" people—those who seek to fulfill personal needs and self-image—are nearly twice as likely to exercise as "outer-directed" people, who are more concerned with what others think.[27]

STAGE IN LIFE OR FAMILY CYCLE

The self-concept is a dynamic entity, often changing as a person interacts with the environment. One path of self-development is the life course or the family cycle. Each of us passes through a series of stages that often correspond to transitions in our values, identities, feelings of competence, and attitudes. These transitions, in turn, may have a profound effect on our sport involvement and commitment, even as sport may be an important ingredient in our quest for identity at any stage.

The prominent leisure researcher John Kelly has outlined stages of the life course that have particular relevance to our topic (see table 4.3). These stages, of course, vary from person to person, and much more research is needed on their effects. For instance, some data suggest that the "youth" period is especially important in fan development. Recent research by NFL Properties indicated that 43 percent of fans claimed to have become fans of a particular sport by the age of 8. And 60 percent said they had become fans by age 11. This is a staggering number.[28]

Table 4.4, taken from the 1999 *Lifestyle Market Analyst*, offers another glimpse. Using an index that compares each life course segment to a total national average, we can see some clear effects of life stage on golf involvement. Since golf partici-

Table 4.3 EFFECTS OF LIFE STAGE ON SPORT INVOLVEMENT
Stage in life course/Possible effects on sport involvement
Preparation periods
Youth—Sport activities may be an important part of peer group identity.
Courtship—New relationships and sexual identities either reinforce or conflict with existing patterns of involvement.
Establishment periods
Singles—Sports and active lifestyles are currently a central part of the "singles" set.
Marriage—Great adjustment is possible with the arrival of children. As children grow, a couple may continue independent involvement, develop integrated family activities, or be controlled by children's activities.
Maturity—With the launching of children, there is more time and independence for new or renewed involvements.
Reintegration periods
Retirement—More free time and fixed income may force adjustments; spouses may pursue joint or individual activities.
Singles—Death of a spouse may require shift out of certain group activities.

From Kelly (1982, pp. 133–156). See Kelly.[28]

pation is not clearly gauged, we can assume a base only of regular golfers, those who golf at least three times per month. Notice the effects. Golfing households are between 4 and 46 percent more likely to be married/no kid households than the overall population. Yet single golfing households are largely underrepresented (indexes below 100) compared to the total population. There seems to be some link between marital status and golfing.

There has been even less research on how sport may influence the life course. For instance, conventional wisdom long ago created the archetype of the "football widow," abandoned by her fanatic spouse who regularly rendezvoused with his mistress (the team) at the stadium or in front of the television. When ESPN launched 24-hour sports, one wag claimed that the only beneficiaries would be divorce lawyers! Despite such impressions, one research study of 399 adults in Indianapolis and Los Angeles concluded that televised sports played a "generally positive, albeit small role in marital life."[29]

Table 4.4 GOLF INVOLVEMENT BY STAGE IN FAMILY LIFE COURSE

Stage in family life course of household head, by marriage/age/ kids in home	% of total U.S. "Golfing" households	Index*
Single, 18–34, no kids	11	102
Single, 35–44, no kids	5.1	85
Single, 45–64, no kids	6.4	70
Single, 65+, no kids	4.0	48
Married, 18–34, no kids	6.0	146
Married, 35–44, no kids	3.8	119
Married, 45–64, no kids	15.5	120
Married, 65+, no kids	10.6	104
Single, kids of any age	5.6	59
Married, kids under 13	18.2	128
Married, kids age 13–18	13.7	119

*Index = 100 equals national average rate of participation at each life cycle stage.

Source: SRDS, *1999 Lifestyle Market Analyst* (Des Plains, IL: 1999): 778.

PHYSICAL CHARACTERISTICS

Physical characteristics and abilities, both real and perceived, play a major role in sport consumer behavior. This is logical because the core sport product is a physical activity that often requires strength, endurance, and flexibility. Consequently, body types and demonstrations of physical skill are closely linked to consumer self-concepts and decisions about sport involvement. One need only think of the typical advertisement for an athletic club, which portrays not the normal citizen of the republic but rather a male or female deity of physical culture, glistening in shorts or a leotard, offering the promise of a similar physique. Such allures appeal to the consumer's ideal self; they are powerful stuff, perhaps as likely to scare off as to attract members.

Worse yet, there is still little programming for people who are physically disabled or even those who are just less capable. Youth sport programs tend to advance those who are already superior at the expense of those who need attention. Prospects are bleaker for people who are elderly; few programs exist. In programs that do exist, potential consumers may be alienated by feelings that they do not have the physical capabilities to enjoy sports. Although the Americans with Disabilities Act has opened doors for both participants and spectators, the thresholds are still hard to cross. In 1998, when Casey Martin, a golfer who is physically disabled, successfully challenged the PGA Tour rules prohibiting the use of carts, many traditionalists suggested that Armageddon was just around the corner. Sports are still very much the province of people who are able-bodied and not those who are physically challenged.

LEARNING

Although some physical characteristics are inherited, many are learned. A person learns to be a competent or skilled athlete despite initial awkwardness. A person also may learn to become a couch potato, content to enjoy the performances of elite athletes in competition on television. Both types of consumers play prominent roles in the sport industry, and who is to say one is "better" or "healthier" than the other? In both cases, however, learning plays a major role in behavior.

A formal definition of learning is "the acquisition of new responses to behavioral cues in the environment, occurring as the result of reinforcement."[30] This definition includes several components common to learning theories. The first component encompasses drives or arousal mechanisms that cause an individual to act; the desire for esteem is an example. The second includes cues or environmental stimuli that may trigger an individual drive. Advertisements for luxury cars during televised golf tournaments are good examples of cues that attempt to trigger esteem drives. The third component includes reinforcements or outcomes (usually positive rewards) that serve to reduce the drive. The golf fan who purchases a Cadillac may (or may not) learn the connections between lifestyle and esteem.

Several areas of learning theory have special relevance to the sport marketer. For example, cognitive, affective, and behavioral types of involvement correspond to the hierarchy of effects sometimes used to describe consumer purchase behavior. The basic hierarchy suggests that consumers first process information about a product (cognitive involvement), normally through advertising. If additional messages succeed, consumers next develop a new feeling about the product (affective involvement), which may in turn lead them to buy the product or purchase it (behavioral involvement). This hierarchy is displayed as

Learn → Feel → Do.

One way or another, product knowledge is an important variable in consumer behavior. Knowledge links to involvement and commitment in an endless loop. Anyone who has ever been bitten by the "golf bug" understands this. The more you play, the more you want to learn about the game and its nuances. The more you learn, the more you want to play.

The same is true for sport fans. One recent study of minor league hockey fans showed that hockey knowledge—measured by a set of simple questions (e.g., "What does icing mean?")—accounted for over 12 percent of the variance in games attended. All things being equal, the more fans knew about hockey, the more they attended. On the one hand, this is just common sense. But then consider how little effort many organizations put into teaching their consumers about their sport the way ESPN has taught the X Games (see case study).[31] The "Guide to the X Games" was an excellent primer. Even a casual reader would feel empowered with the information.[32]

Some researchers suggest that the standard hierarchy "Learn → Feel → Do" may not apply to services, which are intangible and therefore less conducive to initial cognitive messages about product, price, and the like. This is certainly true for many sport products, which often involve intricate physical activities. In sports, consumers may be more responsive to information that triggers their emotions about an overall experience, even if the initial image is limited in its detail. Consumers may be willing to act on such information, try the sport product, and then learn more about it after the trial. In sport, then, the hierarchy may be more like

Feel → Do → Learn.

This is certainly the approach of most Nike ads, which look to stir emotions before anything else. So did the NBA and its merchandise sponsors when they placed a 12-page insert in the 1997 *Sports Illustrated* NBA preview edition. The pictures—of a diverse set of young men and women in NBA apparel—expressed the fantasies that many fans pursue through "official" merchandise. One woman, clad in a Rockets jacket, looked dreamily across the seats of a trolley car as she considered her playing

Case Study

"Teaching" the X Games

The sport market has never been static. Sports run hot and cold. Some sports, like gander pulling, die off, and new sports continue to pop up. In the 1980s, stunt bikes, skateboards, rollerblades, and snowboards spawned a host of activities and competitions that became associated with the "slackers" of the so-called Generation X. The profile was a perfect match for ESPN2, which wanted to reach the same children of MTV. Voila! The X Games were born. In many respects "made for television," the X Games required some consumer learning, especially of the basics—"What are the X Games?"

ESPN used aggressive teaching tools such as television ads and an Internet site. In 1998, three years into the games, ESPN was still helping consumers learn the basics, for instance putting a 20-page magazine insert into *Rolling Stone,* a perfect medium for reaching the target audience. The insert included basic information on all the events, which ran from bicycle stunts to sportclimbing, wakeboarding, and street luge. Exquisite visuals were surrounded by text on "the point," or the rules; "the tools," or the equipment; and "the names," or the prominent contestants.

---

ability and knowledge. "When Charles Barkley points into the crowd, he's pointing at me" was among the fantasies reported in her caption. She was the mentor, Barkley the student. The ad was a perfect expression of

Feel ➔ Do ➔ Learn.[33]

Some activities, on the other hand, demand a hierarchy of

Do ➔ Feel and Learn.

Rollerblading, skiing, surfing, and other speed/skill sports may be among such activities. In 1997, Rollerblade, Inc. looked to drive a shake-out in the cluttered market of in-line skating. The prime strategy was a grassroots effort to get more people to try its product. This included giving free lessons in New York City parks and giving thousands of free pairs of rollerblades to public schools. Rollerblade, Inc. recognized the long history of American sport: there is no better promoter than a national corps of physical education teachers offering millions of kids lessons in Do ➔ Feel and Learn.

In an age of interactivity, the most progressive organizations use exhibits, "fan zones" like the NCAA's "Hoop City Web site," and Web sites to promote all three elements of the learning hierarchy. We shall look more closely at these programs in chapters 7, 10, 13, and 14.[34]

PERCEPTION

Learning requires the consumer to use perception, which may be defined as the process by which a person scans, gathers, assesses, and interprets information in the environment. Although perception employs the five senses, it involves far more. Perception depends on the characteristics of the person, situation, or thing perceived (stimulus factors) and also the characteristics of the perceiver (individual factors). A roaring crowd may be an exhilarating and uplifting experience for a knowledgeable fan but a threatening mob to someone else. Our perceptions, then, are something of a filter, influenced by our values, attitudes, needs, and expectations. This filter contributes to selective exposure, selective distortion, and selective retention of the innumerable stimuli that confront us daily.[35]

Consumers and prospective consumers are constantly filtering and interpreting cues about sport products vis-a-vis their self-concepts. Failure to provide congruent and consonant images to consumers will typically reduce involvement. This is why high-priced perfume companies keep their products out of discount stores. The place of purchase enhances the perception of quality. Sport marketers must be particularly sensitive to a number of perceptual issues, including the following:

➤ *Facility cleanliness.* Long ago, Bill Veeck realized that clean bathrooms were critical to attracting women and families to the ballpark. But not all men love a mess. "Club dirty" is a prime reason for quitting an athletic club.

➤ *Exposure to violence.* This perception can work both ways, as shown in ice hockey. Some fans love a good brawl; others abhor the goons. The NHL continues to walk a fine line, with Commissioner Gary Bettman trying to distinguish between goonism and a "spontaneous altercation." Can the casual fan—a target market if the NHL wants to grow on television—tell the difference? Worse than television violence is the fear of rowdy, drunken fans. No parent wants to expose children to that form of "entertainment." Some clubs have responded with no-alcohol family zones.

➤ *Risk of injury or embarrassment.* Sport consumers take many risks, to their health and their egos. Studies by Reebok showed that "injury prevention" is second only to "fit and comfort" in consumer decisions about running shoes. Perceptions of high risk turn many people away from active participation. Few people are willing to look like a fool on a ski slope or a treadmill. And how many are turned off by the ads suggesting that only "hardbodies" frequent the athletic club?

➤ *Waste of time, money, effort.* As we will see in chapter 9, consumer costs include far more than the event ticket, the lift ticket, or the greens fee. In an age focused on "quality time," every choice is a risk. As figure 4.3 suggests, consumers create their own perceptual space maps that help them assess choices in terms of effort and risk.[36]

In our visual, electronic age of slick images and sound bites, advertising campaigns are the primary means of reaching consumers. Most ads try to overcome, even reshape perceptions in order to reposition their product in the consumer's mind. We will look at ads more closely in chapter 10, but we conclude here with the thought that today's flood of ads creates perceptual clutter for most sport consumers. Thus the question in our sidebar: Can you sort through the clutter?

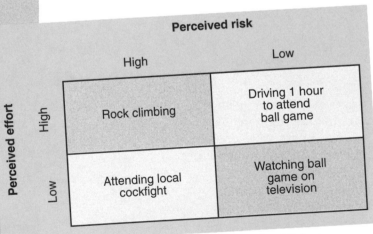

Figure 4.3
The risk-effort grid.

MOTIVATION

Amid a constant swirl of stimuli, can we identify any individual "triggers" of sport involvement? According to motivation theory, environmental stimuli may activate the drive to satisfy an underlying need. Theorists like Abraham Maslow, Henry Murray, and David McClelland have outlined elaborate models explaining how physiological, psychological, and social needs influence human behavior; their categories have clearly shown up in contemporary sport research. At the same time, historians have outlined a number of "long residual" factors that have motivated involvement in sport across vast extents of time and space. These are among the more prominent:[38]

Can You Sort Through the Clutter?

Many sport organizations have recently flooded the media with new, slick slogans designed to reshape consumer perceptions. With so many such slogans floating around, it is easy to get confused. Recent research by NFL Properties showed that only 56 percent of the people surveyed correctly associated a new slogan with the NFL.[37] As we will see in chapters 10 and 12, recognition and recall are standard measures of successful ad campaigns. Try your luck at this matching test. Have you been sorting through the perceptual clutter?

1. "Feel the Power"	A.	NTRA
2. "We Got Next"	B.	NBA
3. "I Can"	C.	USTA
4. "Go Baby Go"	D.	NFL
5. "The Power of One"	E.	Football Network
6. "I Love This Game"	F.	WNBA
7. "Get in the Game"	G.	Nike
8. "Enough Is Never Enough"	H.	NCAA football
9. "The Coolest Game"	I.	LPGA
10. "Hey We Can Play"	J.	NHL

Your score:	Tells you:
9-10	You're ready for SportsCenter.
7-8	Not bad, but not quite prime-time material.
5-6	Change your magazine subscriptions.
2-4	You're watching too much Weather Channel.
0-1	It's time to think about another career.

[Answers: 1-D, 2-F, 3-G, 4-A, 5-H, 6-B, 7-C, 8-E, 9-J, 10-I]

Achievement. The notion of winning does matter, for players and fans. In one USTA survey, serious players listed winning as a major reason for playing. Likewise, numerous studies show that fans tend to "bask in reflected glory" when their team wins.

Craft. Winning isn't all that counts. For many, developing or enjoying physical skill prompts sport interest. "Learning a new skill" typically ranks high among reasons people list for playing. And the chance to watch a star display great skill brings a crowd to any game.

Affiliation or community. "To be with friends" is a common reason people give for any sport involvement, as indicated in studies of tennis participation, athletic club membership, and fan motivations (see photo on page 72). Fan communities have existed for thousands of years, represented in the Roman "factions" of blues, greens, reds, and whites who passionately rooted for their color in the chariot races. Their

Fans and teams often create rituals of community, such as at the University of New Hampshire, where students throw a dead fish on the ice after their team's first goal.

modern counterparts may wear official merchandise, but the motives are the same. Research has clearly shown that few fans (1-3 percent) attend games alone.

Health and fitness. This is an obvious motive for club membership and equipment purchase. Even golfers can argue that a "good walk spoiled" beats watching television.

Fun and festival. Humans have a long history of framing their games with circles of spectators and fun-lovers, who exchange money for sight lines, food, and merchandise. What is big-time football without the tailgating? For similar reasons, most new venues contain a concourse, which is the locus of fun and festival. Perhaps the most visible symbol of festival is the team mascot, now almost a necessity.

Eros. Evidence is clear that many players and fans have erotic motives. There is a certain sexual attraction to sweaty bodies in motion, not all of which are clad in tights or a leotard. In 1975, the Golden State Warriors ran a promotional campaign to attract female fans. The tag line: "We've got five men in shorts who can go all night." Recent Pay-Per-View promos for Oscar De La Hoya included female voice-overs saying, "You know, Oscar, I could sit around and watch you sweat all night. And that's exactly what I'm gonna do." A recent study of Florida Gator fans showed that they were more aroused at football action shots than at patently erotic photographs. The erotic motive is still somewhat taboo as an academic subject; it demands much more attention.

Although motivations are elusive and difficult to quantify, they will remain essential constructs for understanding consumer behavior in sport.

ATTITUDES

One of the long-term results of perceptions, learning, and involvement is the growth of attitudes, defined by Kotler as "a person's enduring favorable or unfavorable cognitive evaluations, emotional feelings, and action tendencies toward some object or idea."[39]

People have many attitudes about sport. As we saw earlier, some collective attitudes may become dominant in a given culture. Individual or collective, attitudes often affect sport involvement. Several studies have demonstrated that fans' attitudes toward teams influence their perceptions of enjoyment in watching pro football games. And according to an assessment of the literature on physical activity, an estimated 10 percent of the population may be "intransigent" in their nonexercise behavior. They will probably never become exercisers, and we may assume that they have overwhelmingly negative attitudes toward exercise.[40]

But positive attitudes toward sport and exercise don't always trigger "positive" behavior. Die-hard fans don't always attend games; hard-core players don't always get to the club to practice. In 1993, for instance, Prince Manufacturing conducted a national poll on attitudes toward tennis. The survey's main angle and results were summarized in a press release: "More than 7 out of 10 Americans think that playing sports is a good way to meet someone for romance with 8 out of 10 rallying to tennis to make love connections." According to the survey results, sports (at 70 percent) ranked higher on the "love-o-dometer" than bars (41 percent), movies (31 percent), or video dating services (27 percent). Unfortunately for Prince and the tennis industry, the "love-connection" attitude has not translated into involvement.[41]

Marketers naturally try to cultivate positive attitudes toward their products. As we shall explore in detail, the marketing mix should be an integrated set of tools that

Building Positive Attitudes With Reciprocity

In one way or another, we all are both consumers and marketers on a regular basis. Among our families, our friends, our work associates, and our teammates, we give and take information, counsel, humor, and criticism. In the best of conditions we enjoy sharing relationships. That sharing can be called reciprocity, which can take many forms:

You help me, I'll help you.

You listen to me, I'll listen to you.

You give me a gift, I'll give you one.

Marketers of all types have learned the importance of reciprocity. Todd Crossett's seminal study of the LPGA outlined the basic rules of reciprocity that make or break positive attitudes between players and fans. Players may be "gifted" with skill, but the gift means little without genuine fan appreciation. On the pro golf tour, fans interact with players more intimately than in most other sport venues. Crossett showed how sincere reciprocity builds strong bonds between players and fans. He also conveyed how fragile the bonds can be.

Player accessibility, through autograph sessions and community appearances or service, is a powerful vehicle for reciprocity. Professional team sports have suffered from an erosion of this relationship, with plenty of insincerity and surliness on both sides. With greedy agents and players, it is difficult to nurture reconnections, but marketers should keep trying. College athletics provide better opportunities. More programs should take cues from the University of New Hampshire's 1998 national champion women's ice hockey team, which regularly holds postgame autograph sessions to build bonds with its fans. To some degree, every game should be a "fan fest."

There are other forms of reciprocity. The San Diego Padres developed a successful "Compadres" program, which the Padres' Don Johnson says operates on the basis of "golden rule marketing." "Our assumption," said Johnson, "is that if we take care of the fan, the fan will take care of us." Club membership (free to any fan) includes a bar-coded card that fans "swipe" at a kiosk inside the park, thereby accumulating points for every game they attend. The more points, the more rewards.

Similarly, the AA Baseball Portland Sea Dogs built April and May attendance with their "Adopt a Sea Dog" program, a simple partnership in which 18 local schools adopted a player, who visited the school and gave a motivational talk. In return, the entire school "family"—teachers, students, parents, staff—got a group rate for a game in May. At the game, the school groups participated in various game-day events.

There are many avenues for developing genuine reciprocity, some of which we will explore. At the same time, there are too many examples of ruptured reciprocity, which can spawn a generation of negative attitudes. Gypsy franchises and callous owners may be souring professional sport fans as much as the boorish behavior of player-felons. In a Los Angeles Times survey, 59 percent of respondents said that having an NFL team in the area was not important to them. Such attitudes led U.S. News and World Report to run a cover story entitled "Big League Troubles."

Reciprocity is as easily ruptured as nurtured. But its importance is certain. As Crossett so clearly articulated: "The path to success in sport is paved with gifts."[42]

meet consumer needs, thus creating positive attitudes and moving consumers up the involvement escalator. One avenue is the notion of reciprocity (see sidebar).

DECISION MAKING FOR SPORT INVOLVEMENT

Given the array of factors this chapter has presented, one can appreciate the difficulty of establishing a standard and rational process by which consumers make

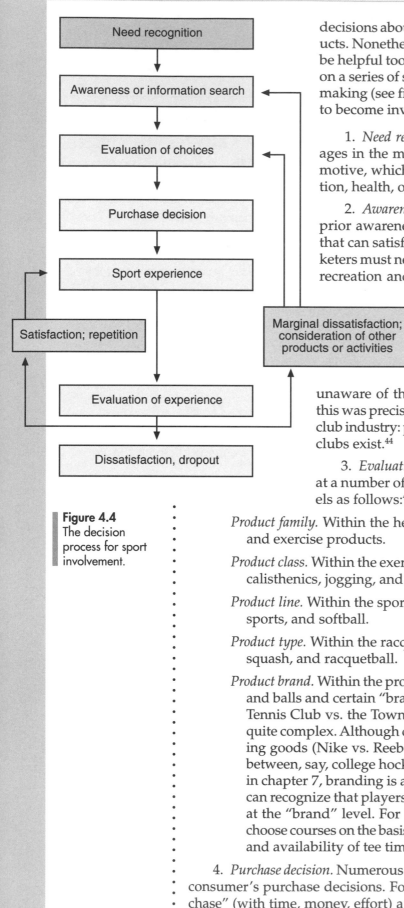

Figure 4.4
The decision process for sport involvement.

decisions about becoming or staying involved with sport products. Nonetheless, such models, even if they are imperfect, can be helpful tools for marketers. We offer one such model, based on a series of steps generally seen as part of consumer decision making (see figure 4.4). As displayed, the consumer's decision to become involved in sport includes several stages:[43]

1. *Need recognition.* Any number of cues, particularly images in the mass media, may trigger the arousal of a need or motive, which may be related to achievement, esteem, affiliation, health, or other sport motives.

2. *Awareness or information search.* The consumer may have prior awareness of, or may seek information about, products that can satisfy aroused needs. This is a critical stage that marketers must never underestimate. Countless studies of outdoor recreation and sport involvement point to the importance of information about distance to site, time to travel, and beauty of site. Given the consumer's "filter" of perceptions, the marketer cannot make any assumptions about the accuracy of the consumer's perceptions. Worse yet is the possibility that consumers are unaware of the product. One well-known study showed that this was precisely the problem facing the sports/racquet/health club industry: potential club members were unaware that nearby clubs exist.[44]

3. *Evaluation of choices.* Consumers make product choices at a number of levels. Philip Kotler has distinguished these levels as follows:[45]

Product family. Within the health and fitness industry are nutrition products and exercise products.

Product class. Within the exercise family are classes of products such as sports, calisthenics, jogging, and walking.

Product line. Within the sport class are lines of products such as golf, racquet sports, and softball.

Product type. Within the racquet sports line are product types such as tennis, squash, and racquetball.

Product brand. Within the product type of tennis are certain brands of racquets and balls and certain "brands" of facilities and experiences (e.g., the Eagle Tennis Club vs. the Town Courts). The "brand" level of sport products is quite complex. Although consumers consider "brand" differences in sporting goods (Nike vs. Reebok), they are less conscious of brand differences between, say, college hockey and minor league hockey. As we will discuss in chapter 7, branding is a hot issue across the sport industry. For now, we can recognize that players and fans sort through loads of information even at the "brand" level. For instance, research has shown that active golfers choose courses on the basis of 17 different attributes, including course length and availability of tee times.[46]

4. *Purchase decision.* Numerous questions demand research concerning the sport consumer's purchase decisions. For instance, to what extent are decisions to "purchase" (with time, money, effort) a sport experience planned and calculated or un-

planned and impulsive? How far in advance are decisions made? Numerous studies of sport fans indicate that a majority—especially in baseball, basketball, and hockey—make purchase decisions only a few days before the event. "Walk-up" fans and season-ticket holders obviously require different messages, as we will discuss in chapters 10 and 11.

5. *Sport experience.* As Chubb and Chubb have suggested, this stage may include a period of anticipation after one has made the decision (thinking about the ski trip a month before it is to occur), a period of preparation (waxing and mounting the skis the night before), travel to the site of the experience, the main experience, and travel from the main experience.[47]

6. *Evaluation of experience.* An effective illustration of evaluation is the consumer-satisfaction equation:

Satisfaction = Benefits − Cost

Satisfaction can relate to social experience, self-concept, skill, or reliability, for example. Benefits relate to characteristics like quantity and duration. Costs can include money, time, ego, and effort. In the end, benefits must outweigh costs.

Marketers attempt to maximize satisfaction through the various elements in the marketing mix. But consumers continue to filter the stimuli around them. They can develop positive or negative attitudes for a host of reasons. One of the most important is the consumer's assessment of competence, as a player or a fan. Has the experience enhanced the person's sense of competence and self-worth? Has it strengthened his or her identity as a golfer, a skier, an exerciser, a fan? The answer has a major influence on subsequent behavior.[48]

7. *Postevaluation behavior.* After evaluating, the consumer has three basic choices:

➤ If satisfied, to repeat the experience, and perhaps build an identity or affinity with the activity. Fans of NASCAR reflect high levels of satisfaction, which spill over into brand loyalty to NASCAR sponsors.[49]

➤ If dissatisfied, to abandon the activity.

➤ If marginally satisfied or dissatisfied, to reevaluate information and decisions about product choices at various levels (family, class, line, type, and brand).

These loops require much more attention from sport marketers. For instance, although information is increasingly available on youth sport dropouts, we know relatively little about adult dropouts.

WRAP-UP

In this chapter we have examined some of the theories that may indicate why people consume sport. Specifically, we have considered the literature on sport consumers within the larger context of general consumer behavior. We have discussed various factors that help to explain the process whereby people are socialized into involvement in or commitment to sport. We have seen that factors influencing behavior may be either environmental or individual. Environmental factors include significant others; cultural norms and values; class, race, and gender relations; climatic and geographic conditions; market behavior of sport firms; and society, culture, and the sport opportunity structure. Individual factors include self-concept, stage in life or family cycle, physical characteristics, learning and involvement, perception, motivation, and attitudes.

We have been able to provide only a brief introduction to some of the components in the vastly complex area of consumer behavior. Further research is sorely needed before marketers can build theories for decision making. In the next chapter, we will provide some information on how the marketer should conduct such research.

1. Define socialization, involvement, and commitment in sport consumer behavior.

2. Describe the most logical indicators of commitment for the following sport consumers: (a) Montreal Canadiens fans, (b) members of a local gymnastics club.

3. Discuss which environmental factors most influenced your involvement in your favorite sport.

4. Why is it likely that the normal "hierarchy of effects" (learn—feel—do) is less applicable with sport consumers than with consumers of detergent?

5. Find a magazine ad for a sport product or team. Analyze how, in your opinion, the ad is trying to influence consumer perceptions of the product.

6. List the steps in the decision-making process for sport consumers. Reconstruct your most recent decision to attend a major sport event. How did your experience compare to the decision-making model?

YOUR MARKETING PLAN

Chapters 3, 4, and 5 all concern research on sport consumers. This chapter has outlined many of the factors that influence how people become involved in and committed to sport. As you conduct research on the current and possible consumers for your product, event, or organization, pay close attention to the most prominent environmental and individual factors that influence their behavior. This analysis should, in turn, influence your decisions about product development, pricing, promotion, distribution (place), and public relations.

C H A P T E R
5

THE ROLE OF RESEARCH IN SPORT MARKETING

OBJECTIVES

1. To appreciate the components and the importance of a marketing information system.

2. To understand the various research methodologies and approaches most commonly utilized in sport marketing.

3. To recognize internal data sources available to sport organizations.

Asking the Right Questions

In some cases it's not what you know, but what you don't know. Several years ago, the LPGA hired Bill Sutton to assess consumer reactions to a proposed new merchandise line by conducting focus groups on-site at LPGA Tour events. Bill was excited about the opportunity to assess, firsthand, the consumers' reaction to the products he had to show them. He randomly selected 10 participants from among the crowd attending the tournament and arranged to meet them later that afternoon at the entrance to a room in the clubhouse where the focus group would meet.

He greeted people as they entered, provided each person with a name tag, and offered refreshments. He watched as the participants milled around the room and touched and admired the merchandise. This, at least so it seemed, would be a rather easy task with a clear-cut resolution. Fifteen minutes later Bill realized how wrong he was.

After people had assumed their places at the table, Bill identified himself and explained what they would be doing that afternoon. He then asked people to introduce themselves and explain their level of interest and involvement in the sport of golf. He was interrupted by Stan, a man in his early sixties who wanted to know whether he could ask a question

before the session began. Bill replied, "Sure, Stan, what would you like to ask?" Stan asked the simplest—yet the most central—question. A researcher in most cases assumes that a participant understands the topic to be discussed. But Stan said, "I'm not sure what the LPGA is—can you tell me what it is?" Before Bill could answer, seven other participants indicated that they did not understand what the LPGA was and would really like to know.

Realizing the importance of the question, Bill began to answer, knowing that the group would never talk about merchandise that afternoon. The results? In short, the merchandise program was delayed several years, and another initiative was designed and developed: the LPGA Fan Village, a fan reception and interactive area, located at selected LPGA events (and later sold as a sponsorship to Target) to help the LPGA communicate its mission and purpose to fans attending its events. The hope was that a better understanding might increase the level of fan involvement and also the number of fans of the LPGA. In two short years, this project has been an enormous success, and the Fan Village, now sponsored by Target, includes an area devoted to the new LPGA merchandise line.

Bill Sutton's research with LPGA helped spawn the idea of the Fan Village.

Chapter 2 introduced the marketing information system (MIS) as an integral part of the marketing process. Chapters 3 and 4 also stressed the need for research to determine who consumers are and why they become involved with or drop out of sport. This chapter provides information about how to establish and maintain an effective MIS. Specifically, we will consider the characteristics of an MIS and the key questions to ask when one is gathering data about the general market, individual consumers, and competitors. We will also provide an overview of internal and external data sources and primary research techniques, including designs and approaches for sample surveys. Finally, we will discuss common problems in sport marketing research as well as applications of the MIS in the marketing process.

AN INFORMATION-BASED APPROACH TO MARKETING SPORT

Basic data for effective marketing decision making are essential to any organization regardless of its size or scope. Such data are especially crucial to sport organizations because fan and participant trends appear to change so rapidly. Those who market sport products need to gather information systematically and continuously. Rather than taking a reactive approach to communicating with their target markets, which in today's highly competitive entertainment marketplace is often too late to prevent defection by the consumer, sport marketers must take a proactive approach. An updated and monitored MIS system that is used to communicate regularly with the consumer is an excellent example of being proactive.

An MIS system can be as simple as a system of index cards or as complex as a fully integrated database stored on a computer and available to all personnel via network servers. Obviously there are many alternatives between these two extremes, and just where an organization chooses to stand depends upon the following factors:

➤ The size and geographic dispersion of the market for the organization's product or service: the larger and more geographically dispersed the market, the larger and more complex the MIS.

➤ The availability of data on consumers and potential consumers: the more data available, the larger the MIS.

➤ The budget allocated to developing and maintaining the MIS: the larger the budget, the more sophisticated the MIS.

➤ The organizational leadership style and vision: the more the organization encourages employees to be creative and seek new approaches and solutions, and the more it focuses on the future, the greater the likelihood that MIS resources and training will be available to more individuals, expanding the size and role of the MIS and its support components.

Whether the choice is an index card system or a computerized system does not affect the type of data that the organization must collect or the analysis and manipulations it performs with the data.

Computerized systems provide many advantages over manual systems: greater volumes of data can be stored and analyzed; the data can be analyzed much more quickly and accurately; multiple departments throughout the organization can access the data simultaneously; and data from various sources can be integrated and compared.

The problem with noncomputerized systems is that they require many hours of tedious work—often a deterrent to all but the most ardent of sport managers. With

Computerized marketing information systems have a number of significant advantages over manual systems.

the continuous decline in prices of personal computers and software programs, even the smallest organization can afford computer-based systems that have sufficient memory capacity to handle the records of thousands of customers. Because of the low cost of hardware and of database and word-processing software, the capital outlay is easily justified, particularly when the computer can be used for other management functions such as accounting, inventory control, desktop publishing, web pages, and so on. Some sport organizations, particularly collegiate and professional ones, are able to "trade" their goods and services to a computer supplier for hardware, software, and often expertise. But although the advantages of a computer-based MIS are significant, as they permit generation of much more powerful marketing data and hence development of more sophisticated marketing strategies, maintaining index files or other paper-based systems is still worth the effort. Even for the sport entrepreneur working in the smallest of organizations, the payback is considerable.

The San Diego Padres' Compadres program is an excellent example of an effective data-based marketing effort.

Case Study

Don Johnson and the Compadres Program—An Example of Data-Based Marketing

Don Johnson, then vice president of marketing for the San Diego Padres, and Brook Govan, Compadres Club manager, created the Compadres program to monitor fan attendance and to encourage and provide incentives for more frequent attendance. Club membership is free to any fan. To become a member, a fan simply completes an application, which is actually a 10-question lifestyle survey. After completing the application, the fan receives an attractive bar-coded membership card that functions as a tracking mechanism to monitor future attendance. Compadres Club members receive points for their attendance by "swiping" their membership card at an electronic kiosk inside the stadium. Each game is worth three points, with selected games worth four or five points. In the way it works, the program is similar to a frequent-flier program—the more games you attend, the higher the level of the prize. (Please note that the Compadres program is an excellent example of the concept of reciprocity as discussed in chapter 4.)

However, the database created from the membership information provides the Padres with a target group for ticket plans, special events, and merchandise. The likelihood of selling a ticket plan to someone in this database is greater than the norm because those in the database have already demonstrated knowledge of and interest in the product through their previous attendance. In fact, by monitoring fans' attendance, the Padres are in a position to suggest a ticket plan that reflects a fan's current level of interest in the team. The database can also be used to identify club members who have not attended very frequently, giving the Padres staff an opportunity to contact such fans to determine whether there is a problem and to demonstrate that the Padres are a caring and concerned organization that hopes they will return to the ballpark.[1]

CHARACTERISTICS OF AN IDEAL MARKETING INFORMATION SYSTEM

While opinions may vary as to what elements should be included in an ideal MIS system, the following characteristics are generally accepted as important elements for any sport-related organization.

An MIS should have the following characteristics:

➤ It must be centralized; an organization needs to have all its data located in one system.

➤ The various databases (consumer files, accounting records, and sales records) need to be fully integrated so that data from multiple sources can be contrasted or merged when appropriate.

➤ The marketer (and other users) must be able to retrieve data in a form (tables, reports, charts) that can be used for decision making.

➤ The MIS must allow for multiple users and simultaneous multiple access.

Only if all four of these conditions are met does an MIS reach its full potential. Beyond these conditions, however, marketers and managers must agree on how data will be used in decision making. To reach such an agreement, marketers and managers must identify questions such as those outlined in figure 5.1.[2]

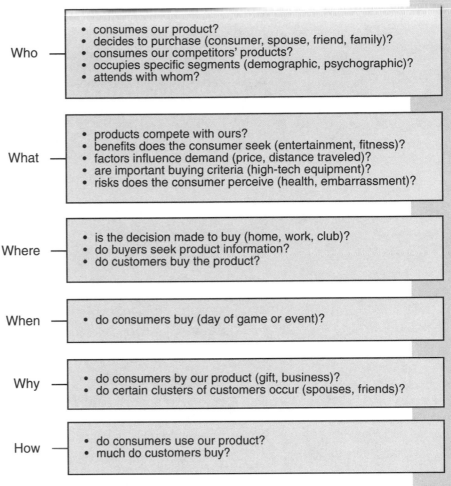

Who
• consumes our product?
• decides to purchase (consumer, spouse, friend, family)?
• consumes our competitors' products?
• occupies specific segments (demographic, psychographic)?
• attends with whom?

What
• products compete with ours?
• benefits does the consumer seek (entertainment, fitness)?
• factors influence demand (price, distance traveled)?
• are important buying criteria (high-tech equipment)?
• risks does the consumer perceive (health, embarrassment)?

Where
• is the decision made to buy (home, work, club)?
• do buyers seek product information?
• do customers buy the product?

When
• do consumers buy (day of game or event)?

Why
• do consumers by our product (gift, business)?
• do certain clusters of customers occur (spouses, friends)?

How
• do consumers use our product?
• much do customers buy?

Figure 5.1 Marketing questions for sport organizations.

These are standard questions that appear in various forms in most types of market research. They may serve as useful prompts in helping the marketer determine the answer to the all-important question: What do you hope to discover in your market research?[3] The resulting information can be categorized into three main sets: general market data, (aggregate, analysis), data on individual consumers, and data on competitors.

GENERAL MARKET DATA

First the marketer needs to define the extent of her market area. A concept used in the retail industry is that of the "critical trading radius." The critical trading radius was initially conceived as a system of concentric circles of mileage, with the facility location as the center and 5-, 7-, and 10-mile radii as milestones. Because of the variance in traffic congestion and in some cases the absence of a direct route, the concept has been redefined as a series of radii based on customer traveling time to the sport facility rather than straight mileage.

The size of the critical trading area varies with the segment of the sport industry. A commercial fitness facility has a 20-minute driving-time radius within which 80 to 85 percent of the members and potential members reside or work; a retail sporting goods store in an urban or suburban area has a trading area similar to that of the fitness facility. In rural areas, the radius naturally expands. The trading radius also increases as the degree of competition decreases. For a professional sport team, an intercollegiate athletic event, or an event at a coliseum, stadium, or arena, up to 80 percent of the market resides within a one-hour driving- or traveling-time radius (longer for weekend events). For a small ski resort near a population area, the radius will be an hour or less. For a large, popular ski resort or a sport/entertainment destination resort such as Hilton Head Island in South Carolina or Disney World in Orlando, Florida, the trading area is unlimited and virtually global. The concept of traveling time rather than straight mileage reflects more accurately the decision criteria for a consumer and consequently predicts potential demand more precisely.

The critical data to be kept on hand concerning the nature and extent of the market area are as follows:

➤ *Size of the market (total number of individuals living or working within the critical trading area).* This indicates whether the market is big enough to support the sport product.

➤ *The demographics of individuals residing or working in the critical trading radius.* Specifically, the major factors entail a breakdown by age, gender, income, ethnicity, or other variables relevant to the profile of target consumers. From these data, the marketer is able to predict the total market potential. When industry averages are available, marketers can predict quite accurately the total demand for a particular product. For example, for many years the bowling industry has had the demand standard of one bowling alley for every 10,000 people. At the same time, studies such as those described in chapter 3 (e.g., Simmons Annual Survey) can indicate whether an area's income, age, or gender composition matches national profiles for bowling.

➤ *The purchase behaviors and consumption patterns of those residing and/or working within the market.* Data on the spending patterns of consumers help the marketer determine potential market demand. Marketers have found demographics extremely useful in determining the profile of potential consumers, yet demographics have their limitations. For example, a 35-year-old, college-educated, white professional male who lives in Iowa is simply not the same "animal" to a marketer as the similarly profiled individual who lives in New York City. The major difference is lifestyle characteristics, which are called *psychographics* and are usually captured through studies of attitudes, interests, and opinions. Psychographic studies tend to be expensive, and they are difficult to undertake. Soliciting psychographic data requires a great deal of effort, and respondents are not always forthcoming in offering opinions and attitudes. Consequently, many marketing decisions are made in the absence of such research.

When no hard demographic data are available, or when the data bear no relationship to the product being marketed, it is essential that the marketer perform at least a "quick-and-dirty" pulse check of consumer attitudes about key product attributes. An example of this process might be a verbal sampling of opinions of participants in a road race about certain aspects of the race's total organization, registration process, marketing, course layout, and goody bag. Or for a more comprehensive study, the marketer might ask individuals to complete surveys on their attitudes concerning several brands or models of running shoes. First the marketer can ask respondents to identify product attributes such as price, tread design, color, and weight that are critical in their choices of shoes. Next they can rate each shoe on each attribute identified. From these data the marketer can develop a strong idea of product attributes that influence and help determine product choice. The marketer can also "guesstimate" the strengths and weaknesses of the product according to consumer perception and, similarly, develop some general ideas about the competition's strengths and weaknesses.

➤ *The level of spectatorship or participation in a sport broken down by demographic categories.* This identifies the profile of the target consumer of any given sport. The marketer designs all promotional strategies and advertising media choices to reach a target market segment. For example, to create awareness about the WNBA, the league utilized the Lifetime Network (a cable station that attracts a high percentage of female viewers) to televise a portion of its games, hoping to attract the female market.

➤ *Data on future trends.* No organization can exist without considering the future. The ability to project future trends may be even more critical in sport than in other industries. Sport continues to operate in a highly volatile marketplace: fads are coming and going; labor agreements are constantly being modified; sponsorship agreements, entertainment expenses, and charitable contributions relating to sport are under government review; and the growth and impact of technology offer both solutions and problems. With sport trends apparently running in seven-year cycles, no aspect of the industry can be taken for granted or viewed as insulated from change.

Perhaps the most vivid illustration of such change is the fitness club industry. The majority of facilities in this industry segment started in the eastern United States in the 1960s as indoor tennis clubs. New trends developed in California and spread east as clubs added bars and lounges, weight rooms (free weights and later Nautilus-type equipment), racquetball courts, aerobic dance studios, cardiovascular fitness centers, pools, saunas, pro shops, and day-care centers. The more sophisticated clubs have now moved into injury rehabilitation, stress management, diet and nutrition classes, cardiovascular screening, family fitness programs, and complete child care and programming. Few other industries have experienced such marked changes so quickly, yet it is clear that evolutions in this segment of the sport industry still have some way to go! Although other sport industry segments have not altered their concepts quite as drastically, changes in the marketplace for their products have been equally volatile.[4]

There is an old saying that all of marketing boils down to how well you know the market. There can be little doubt that knowledge of the market is critical to marketing success, even if other important factors affect success.

DATA ON INDIVIDUAL CONSUMERS

Ideally, the marketer has the names, addresses, and phone numbers (ideally, fax numbers and e-mail addresses where applicable) of all of his consumers so that he can communicate with them directly. In the case of private clubs, season-ticket holders, subscriber services, and the like, these data are part of a registration purchase, and the records form a consumer file for each account. A large portion of these data can also become part of the organizational database and can be imported or exported as the need arises. Comprehensive databases can be easily updated and monitored as a regular business practice. While it is a common and accepted practice to gather information at the time of purchase/registration, people often miss numerous opportunities to add to the database. For example, professional sport franchises that qualify for postseason play often return unfilled ticket applications containing the names and addresses of potential ticket purchasers who should be added to the database. At golf events, it is common for major corporate sponsors to offer prize drawings as an incentive to capture the names of potential consumers. While the sponsor capitalizes on this opportunity, in many cases event managers fail to secure the information from the sponsors to use in their own marketing efforts for the

Fitness clubs today have expanded to become resource centers where members do everything from rehabilitate injuries to learn about nutrition and stress management.

following year. Retail establishments that ask for the zip code of consumers making purchases should also be capturing their names and addresses.

The data on existing customers that are most critical to marketing decision making are as follows:

Names, addresses, and phone numbers of consumers—to be used for communication, correspondence, and direct mailings and telemarketing.

Frequency of purchase/attendance, use of product type and quantity of product purchases, and dates of purchasing/attendance—to be used for tracking usage frequency, targeting low-frequency users, and upgrading existing customers from lower-priced products or options to higher-priced products or options.

Method of payment, location where product was purchased, and lead time—used to determine price, distribution outlets, promotional effectiveness, and lead time in promoting events and ticket distribution.

Media utilized/source of awareness (i.e., the media source that generated the customer)—used to determine promotional effectiveness, advertising reach and effectiveness, targeting of appropriate consumers, and appropriate media outlets.

The pattern of consumption—to determine, for example, whether the consumer consumes alone or with family or friends, or what the consumer does before, during, or after consuming the sport. This information is extremely valuable in strategic market planning, particularly in answering the following questions: What promotional items/offers should be considered? Is a particular event day more likely to attract families, couples, business groups, or children? What types of concessions are most popular? What type of music should be played during the event? Should the marketer promote more to the father, mother, single female, child?

In short, the marketer's goal in establishing an MIS is threefold. A marketer should be able to identify consumers by name, be able to communicate with them on a regular basis through a variety of media, and be able to discern the variances in consumer buying and utilization patterns by creating segments of the total user universe.

There are many ways to integrate an effective MIS system into current operational practices and procedures. ProFile, an inexpensive, easy-to-use program, provides a format for creating a variety of database files that the organization can use effectively for a variety of tasks.

DATA ON COMPETITORS

The MIS should contain up-to-date information on competitors, including price lists, product lines, promotional strategies, and possibly a description of services as well as comparisons among all similar organizations. A competitor can generally be defined as an organization offering similar products or services whose critical trading radius overlaps more than 25 percent of the marketer's own trading radius. Usually this means that the competitor's facility or retail outlet will be located within a 30-minute traveling time of the marketer's own facility.

In the fitness club industry, it is common to have all new employees visit competing facilities as part of their orientation. During this visit, they critique the competitor for strengths and weaknesses. This practice is also common in a variety of other sport venues and operations. For example, salespeople from one retail outlet visit a competitor's store and ask questions, observe customer interaction, critique product placement and other logistical issues, and so on. Professional sport franchises often conduct similar research in cities with multiple franchises, a practice

ProFile: An Effective MIS System for Managing and Using Data to Aggressively Market Products and Services

ProFile, developed as a joint venture by Audience Analysts, the NBA's Cleveland Cavaliers, and Field Information Systems (FIS), is a data-based marketing tool that gathers data, collects and organizes the data according to relevant organizational needs, analyzes the data, and reports the data in both narrative and graph or table formats. According to Michael McCreary of FIS, "ProFile can track consumer be- havior, preferences, and other key information relat- ing to the consumer. The customer file is created by the user, and can include any types of information that the organization wishes to track." Applications for a professional sport franchise, collegiate athletic department, or health club or other commercial en- terprise that keeps records might include any or all of the following functions:

- ➤ Analyze ticket-plan holders by type of ticket plan or by seating location
- ➤ Profile donors to athletic programs demographically
- ➤ Target consumers for sales, promotions, and special events
- ➤ Conduct periodic database surveys
- ➤ Monitor product utilization, attendance, and the like
- ➤ Target appropriate households for direct-mail campaigns
- ➤ Market other events at the same venue, such as concerts, to select database groups based on their musical or entertainment interests, interests in other sports, age, and number of family members

ProFile is an inexpensive (less than $300) com- puter program that requires limited computer knowl- edge and runs on either a personal computer or a network system equipped with Windows, 8 mega- bytes of memory, and 12 megabytes of hard-drive space.

that is effective because the various franchises often serve the exact same customers. Another way to obtain this type of information is to hire "mystery shoppers" who visit the operations of competitors and report on their experience.

DATA SOURCES FOR A MARKETING INFORMATION SYSTEM

Once the marketer understands the important questions to ask in creating an MIS, she must grapple with data sources to answer them. The two major sources of data are internal sources and external sources. *Internal* refers to within-organization in- formation, and *external* refers to information from outside the company. This chap- ter addresses methods by which these data can be generated, stored, retrieved, and used to maximum effect at minimum cost. Figure 5.2 illustrates the sources and pro- cesses at work in an effective MIS.

As the model suggests, information emanates from the marketplace of consum- ers and nonconsumers through either internal or external sources, which the organi- zation must effectively manage. Given the potentially vast array of information sources, marketers must integrate the material in ways that enable effective strategic planning and decision making. Such planning and decision making result in the overall product that enters the marketplace for consumer and nonconsumer reaction.

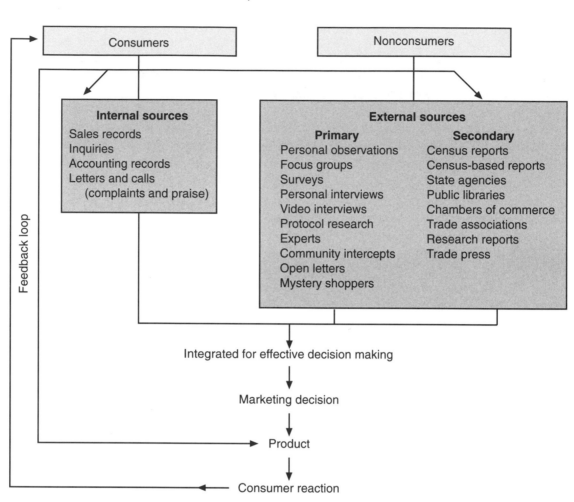

Figure 5.2 A basic design for a marketing information system.

The feedback loop is essential for measuring the effect of a marketing decision on the general population. It is also important for measuring how the population perceives a marketing decision. Let's turn to the two basic types of sources: internal and external.

INTERNAL DATA SOURCES

Often, most of the data needed for principal decisions in marketing are gathered in the normal day-to-day operation of the business. Most organizations have opportunities to use internal sources of data for much of their marketing information. Unfortunately, organizations often overlook and underuse these sources. A brief review will suggest the potential benefits of use of internal sources.

Sales Records Every "charge" or "check" sale identifies the customer's name and possibly his or her address—information that should be recorded before payments and checks are processed. If possible, the sales staff should record a code number that describes the sale; this will be most useful later. This information can be used to extend special offers to previous customers before announcement of sales to the general public, as well as in other marketing efforts designed to make the customer feel special. We will discuss this aspect in greater detail in chapter 11. Additional names can be generated from lists of participants in contests, drawings, program registrations, catalogue lists, and the like.

Inquiries Requests for play-off tickets contain names and addresses. Even telephone inquiries are a good source of potential customers. The marketer may offer incentives such as free or discounted items to induce people to inquire about the product (and thus provide their names). Addresses on fan mail requesting autographs should also be added to a marketer's database. In addition, requests for catalogues and any other consumer- or organization-initiated information should be integrated into the master database.

Accounting Records Accounting records contain names that should be placed on mailing lists for direct promotional mailings. Season-ticket holders, corporate sponsors, and companies supplying the organization with goods and services may feel obligated to buy tickets, merchandise, memberships, and so on.

Letters and Phone Calls of Complaint or Praise Positive and negative letters and phone calls merit attention and follow-up. The name of the writer or caller should be recorded in the database, and a list of complaints and compliments should be compiled and monitored over time.

All these types of data (from sales records, inquiries, accounting records, letters, etc.), when integrated, form the internal data system. For ease of retrieval, they should be stored as separate computer files that can be merged when the need arises. In the majority of cases, the cost of not having such data is much greater than the cost of maintaining the data.

EXTERNAL DATA SOURCES

External data sources, those originating outside the organization, may be categorized as either secondary or primary. Secondary sources contain data that are already published or compiled. Primary sources are studies or surveys that the organization initiates directly with consumers, competitors, or other organizations.

Secondary Data Sources

We cited some of the standard secondary sources on the sport industry in chapter 3 when we discussed the sport consumer. But many other sources are worth investigating.[5]

Census Reports Census reports are a basic source of statistical information that is primarily demographic (e.g., income, age, marital status, education, size of household). Census reports are published by both federal and state agencies and are available from any Department of Commerce office.

Census-Based Demographic Reports Two valuable sources that regularly extrapolate information from census data are the *Rand McNally Commercial Atlas and Marketing Guide* (Skokie, IL: Rand McNally) and a publication of National Demographics and Lifestyles, *Lifestyle Market Analyst* (Wilmette, IL: Standard Rate and Data Service). Both provide general demographic information on most metropolitan areas—data that the marketer can use as the basis for comparisons.

State Agencies Agencies such as state departments of recreation often have state and local data on sport consumption as well as an inventory of state facilities and programs.

Public Libraries Libraries can provide historical information on businesses and organizations in the community.

Chambers of Commerce Chambers of commerce usually employ research directors or contract externally for research relating to the local business environment. This service may be free to chamber members and may be available to nonmembers for a fee.

Trade Associations Trade associations exist to help businesses in a given field, and often provide extremely useful information on that industry to their membership.

Whether an association will release information to nonmembers depends on the industry. The sporting goods industry has a variety of trade associations that vary in their pursuit of data and their willingness to share data. The single best reference for addresses and phone numbers of sport organizations, including trade organizations, is *Sport Marketplace,* published annually by Franklin-Covey.

Professional (Syndicated) Research Services   These companies are in the business of providing information: A.C. Nielsen, Simmons Market Research Bureau, American Sports Data, Inc., Joyce Julius and Associates, Team Marketing Report, Audience Analysts, and Performance Research. Research services have their own regular surveys and reports that are available for sale. Special and customized projects can be more expensive.

Trade and Scholarly Press   Trade and scholarly publications can be important not only because their advertising space is designed to target a market segment, but also because they reveal collective experience as well as competitor information. These publications also reveal trends in other areas. Examples of trade publications are *Sporting Goods Directory, Sporting Goods Dealer, Team Marketing Report, Amusement Business,* and *Marketing News.* A large group of publications concern professional sports. Each commissioner's office provides some information to individual clubs. Information on collegiate athletics comes from *NCAA News, Athletic Administration, Athletic Management,* and *Athletic Business.* Two research journals, *Journal of Sport Management* and *Sport Marketing Quarterly,* contain excellent material and resources.

Primary Data Sources

Unless the marketer is in an industry that has sophisticated market research programs performed by trade organizations, she will invariably need some specific market segment information. In the majority of cases, this will come from primary market research—that is, research that the organization has originated (from either internal or external sources). The standard methods of primary market data collection are personal observation and surveys, including questionnaires and interviews. Before discussing each of these methods, we should first examine the rationale for conducting primary market research.

The Importance of Primary Market Research to the Marketing Information System

There are a number of excellent reasons for conducting surveys, most of which relate to gathering knowledge to improve marketing performance:

> **Communicate** with the target market

> **Assess** your position in the market

> **Establish** a demographic profile of the audience

> **Initiate** data-based marketing efforts

> **Benchmark** and evaluate operational elements

> **Gather** information essential for sponsorship renewal and/or solicitation of new sponsors, or for determining reaction to new concepts, products, or services

Communicating With the Target Market   A survey provides a vehicle for two-way communication between the team and its supporters. The team asks questions and the supporter responds. For this reason, it is essential in any survey to provide the fan with a general question, such as "If you could give any message to the team president/ownership, what would that message be?" This type of question provides an "open door" for fans to communicate whatever they feel is important to the team management. Input from the fan might be in the form of a suggestion, a complaint, or even praise. The most important thing to remember is that in conducting a survey, you have asked the questions that were important to you and if the goal is really to create a two-way dialogue, you must show the same courtesy to the fan.

Assessing Your Position in the Market   A team can use a survey to get an idea of how respondents view it in relation to other entertainment options available to them. Do they enjoy attending your basketball game more than they enjoy attending a soccer game, and if so why? This type of research will provide insight into the importance and effectiveness of entertainment and promotions—and possibly concessions as well as the overall experience of attending.

Establishing a Demographic Profile of the Audience   Successful marketers must know not only their target market, but also the actual market they are attracting. If, for example, the team is approaching a sponsor who wishes to have access to young men between the ages of 18 and 24, the team should be able to verify that this audience is in fact attending the games. Survey research can provide this documentation. The following categories are commonly used to generate a demographic profile:

- ➢ Age
- ➢ Marital status
- ➢ Gender
- ➢ Household income
- ➢ Educational background
- ➢ Postal code
- ➢ Size and composition of household

This information is essential not only in the preparation of sponsorship proposals, but also for the purpose of selecting the proper radio station to use for advertising or the correct postal codes for direct-mail efforts.

Initiating Data-Based Marketing Efforts   Registration forms such as those commonly used for ticket purchasing can easily be modified to function also as a survey. Because these information forms contain names and addresses, they can be used to initiate or expand data-based marketing efforts. For example, a season-ticket holder registration form, which normally contains information relating to the purchaser such as name, address, and number and location of tickets, can also ask for the names of spouse and children, their birth dates, preferred radio station, and the like. The database of information from this "mini-survey" can then be used in future marketing campaigns for tickets to other sports, summer sport camps, children's clinics, and so on. These data can also be provided to sponsors for their marketing purposes.

Benchmarking and Evaluating Operational Elements   In services marketing, customer satisfaction is a crucial element. Sport provides a service: entertainment. In providing this entertainment—especially since the marketer does not control the on-field product and cannot guarantee the performance and end result of the product—the sport team must provide quality product extensions. Product extensions are elements relating to the fan's entertainment experience such as concessions, parking, music, halftime entertainment, clean rest rooms, ushers, merchandise for sale, and tailgating areas. It is essential for marketers to evaluate these product extensions to ensure that they incorporate everything possible to ensure fan satisfaction. Once the initial survey has established the ratings or "benchmark," one can evaluate these same elements the next year against the benchmark to determine if, in the mind of the ticket purchaser, the situation has improved.

Gathering Information for Sponsorship Activities   While surveys are generally designed to enable the organization to be responsive, they can also play a valuable role in helping the organization become proactive. Such a proactive role could entail evaluating ticket holders as a group in relation to the products or services offered by current or potential sponsors. According to Wood Selig, associate athletic director for external affairs at the University of Virginia:

In our surveys, we ask a core of questions to be utilized for our current sponsors and to help in future sales efforts. These questions include items such as favorite fast food restaurant, number of nights spent in a hotel last month, etc. We can then use this information to demonstrate to a McDonald's that they are the preferred fast food restaurant among our respondents and therefore they are reaching their target market. If say the results show that Pizza Hut, a current sponsor is not faring well, then we can work with Pizza Hut to create some opportunities to help improve their status. We also try to be future focused in our surveys as they relate to sponsors. If perhaps we are looking to add a car dealer, we could ask our respondents via the survey if they are planning to purchase or lease a new vehicle in the next 12 months. We can then use the results to help a car dealer justify why they should become involved with the University of Virginia Athletic program and how they can benefit from that association.[6]

A number of firms specialize in generating sponsorship-related data. These firms provide general trend data, or for a fee they will conduct research specifically for a particular organization or event. Sponsorship Research International is an example of such a firm.

Sponsorship Research International

London-based Sponsorship Research International (SRi), a division of ISL Consulting, is among the leading sport marketing research and consulting firms in the world. A comprehensive agency, SRi provides a variety of services employing a number of research methodologies. It offers an interesting array of research options, including the following:

➤ *Sports Monitor:* A detailed international sport survey focusing on 37 core sports in terms of participation, spectatorship, and television viewership. The image of each sport is rated on 10 criteria, including "dynamic," "prestigious," "competitive," "healthy," and "modern."

➤ *Sponsorship Selection Research:* A service designed to provide corporations with a list of suitable sponsorship options that fit corporate objectives, competitors' activities, seasonality, and cost.

➤ *Sponsortest:* A service that measures the awareness of sponsors within major sports and specific events. Awareness is tracked among the general population as well as among fans of the particular sports and subscriber's target markets.

➤ *Sports Image Database:* An interactive computer database comprising image information on 36 sports across seven major countries. The database provides sponsors subscribing to the service with a series of "best-fit" analyses such as which sports provide the best match between the sport and the company's profile, brand image, or target market. An organization can also use the information to look at the image profile of a particular sport across any combination of countries and demographic groups.

➤ *Media Evaluation Research:* Research that examines corporate sponsorship/brand exposure over television and print media sources. Media coverage such as news articles and stories, photographs, video footage and so forth are analyzed for the purpose of calculating a cost per impression (the value of such coverage if it were purchased and how many people would see the coverage). A ratio of cost to number of impressions generated is figured, which helps in determining the value and suitability of the event or sporting activity being analyzed.

Types of Primary Market Research Utilized in Sport

Because of its nature and variety, the sport product lends itself to a number of research methodologies for the organization to consider and ultimately select. Examining these methods provides insight into their aims and benefits.

Personal Observation   Many managers perform unstructured research of their own; informal talks with friends, employees, and customers are usually the rule. Although these "surveys" are unstructured, they do have some value. For years, Hall of Famer and baseball owner, the late Bill Veeck, maintained that the only way to understand the real desires of baseball fans was to mingle with them in the stadium and watch how they interacted not only with the game on the field, but also with the activities and people around them. Veeck's success with promotions stemmed in large part from his personal knowledge of fan behavior. Such grassroots involvement by executives has been linked to some of the Japanese breakthroughs in international marketing.

The observational method allows people in the market to act "naturally"—that is, of course, if the observer remains undiscovered, as Bill Veeck obviously could not. But the kind of information observers can obtain is limited; while they can observe behavior, they cannot find out income and home address, for example. For these and other reasons, marketers tend to rely on direct questioning of consumers.[7]

Focus Groups   Research using focus groups is highly individualized, not mass oriented like a paper survey. A focus group usually consists of 10 to 12 participants chosen because of one or more common characteristics; for example, they may be season-ticket holders, males between the ages of 18 and 24, or former players. A moderator, usually someone from outside the organization but familiar with the sport product, serves as a facilitator. A focus group usually lasts between one and a half and two hours and concentrates on two to three predetermined issues. Focus groups are often used in conjunction with survey research. Sometimes they are conducted before a survey is administered to help develop the survey instrument. They can also be used subsequently to a survey for the purpose of testing the findings or assessing response to proposed changes or new programs.

Surveys and Questionnaires   There are several situations in which a sport marketer would want to conduct a structured market survey:

When considering the launch of a new product or service or a major revision of an existing product or service

When dealing with a highly volatile (changeable-elastic) market

When considering a revision of a pricing structure across stadium or arena seats; considering revamping price differentials between various products or seating areas; or changing the product line, item, or mix (of particular note in today's marketplace, this refers to priority-seating programs, personal seat licenses, club seat programs, etc.)

On-site, computerized surveys are attractive to fans and can provide instant feedback to marketers.

The major instrument of structured research is invariably a formal survey instrument known as a questionnaire. The following sections present guidelines on conducting questionnaires.

On-Site Surveys   On-site surveys or audience audits are highly effective for determining the attitudes and feelings of individuals actually attending games. One can distribute the survey as people enter the game or when they are in their seats. Several factors affect the response rate: (1) whether or not people have a pen or pencil, (2) whether they bother to return the surveys, and (3) whether they receive a small token in exchange for their time. Experience shows that the most effective method is to distribute the surveys to people in their seats before the game or at halftime, give them a logoed pen as a gift for their time, and remain in the stands to collect the surveys. This generally provides a completed-survey return of over 80 percent. See appendix B for an example of an on-site survey.

In conducting on-site surveys, the surveyor must consider and address several aspects in order to guarantee accuracy and protect against bias. One of these is frequency. Surveys must be conducted often enough to ensure against biases like day of the week, opponent or attraction, starting time, presence of a promotion, or (in the case of team sports) "halos" caused by circumstances such as a winning streak. It is also important that the complexity of the survey fit the situation. Because of the likelihood that respondents may become distracted as a result of their surroundings, survey content should be simple.

Mail Surveys   Organizations most commonly use mail surveys to survey a consumer group that has been identified through records or other types of lists. Obviously, having correct addresses for the target market is key to a successful mail survey. For this reason, the most common targets for mail surveys are health club members, season-ticket holders who own one or more tickets and have completed an application that the team has on record, and registrants from past events or purchasers of past goods or services. Other targets might include a particular postal code (for a mass mailing) or people who have purchased their tickets with credit cards, thereby providing the information needed for the mailing.

Because the obligation is with the addressee, to complete and return the survey, response rates are significantly lower than with other forms of research. Depending on the size of the population receiving the mail survey, a response rate of 20 percent or greater is acknowledged as acceptable. One key point to remember in utilizing a mail survey is that since the respondent is "out of touch" with the source of the survey, the instrument should be simple and should not contain questions that could be interpreted more than one way. For example, a question such as "When is your preferred starting time for Pittsburgh Pirate games?" assumes that there is little or no difference between weekdays and weekends. Past research and practices have shown that there are significant differences. Thus the question would need to be divided into two parts—weekdays and weekends—or asked as two distinct questions to ensure that the reader understands the intent. See appendix B for an example of a mail survey.

Telephone Surveys Similar to mail surveys, telephone surveys are more efficient if one can identify an appropriate target group. While random-dialing programs are available, telephone surveys are most effective when the intent is to contact a specific group.

Telephone surveys are highly applicable across the general population if they are used to measure awareness, particularly relating to publicity or advertising. For example, if the team is announcing a ticket campaign or offering sport clinics for youth, and has been advertising and publicizing this information, a telephone survey can confirm whether this knowledge is reaching the market and which channels are most effective.

Telephone surveys are cost efficient and can be performed from one central location, or at subsites throughout the country if the interest is in a national sample. Because of people's work habits and family obligations, most surveying is done in the evening or on weekends. The practices of telephone solicitation and telemarketing are negatively impacting the success of telephone surveys because of the increasing numbers of uninitiated calls coming to households throughout the United States and Canada. People are using unlisted phone numbers and caller ID systems in part to limit access to members of the household.

Computerized Surveys Computerization has given us the opportunity to improve on the survey process. Through computerization the surveyor can create an interactive, self-directed survey methodology. Computerization also eliminates data-entry costs and the lag time between gathering and analyzing the data. DelWilber & Associates was one of the first firms to advocate this technology, naming their version Rapid Audience Profile System (RAPS). A major advantage of computerization is the ability to create "branches" within the questionnaire that are triggered on the basis of a response to a previous question. For example, an automotive company sponsoring an event may wish to know the likelihood of car-purchasing behavior among its audience. Thus a question might be "Do you plan on leasing or purchasing a new vehicle within the next 6 months?" Respondents who answer "no" continue down the main path of the questionnaire; those who answer "yes" can be directed to a branch of the questionnaire that might include one or more questions specifically related to this anticipated purchase. Sample branch questions might be "Which automobile manufacturers are you considering? Will this be a purchase or lease? Manufacturer of your current vehicle?" This branching ability provides a significant advantage over traditional paper surveys.

Another major advantage of this technology-based approach to market research is the turnaround time. Traditional research methods include time for data entry—a process in which the data gathered during the research are coded and entered into a computer program for analysis (usually SPSS or similar programs that allow analysis and segmentation of the information according to how the organization wishes to view it). Computer-based programs such as RAPS and TEAM (Team & Event Assessment Model, developed at the University of Massachusetts) eliminate the data-entry step and enable the researcher to review the results within minutes after completing the data collection. This can be particularly important because it permits the event or organization to make timely changes or improvements in areas identified by the respondents. The main disadvantages of this method are the following:

> Limitation of possible sample size because of the number of computers available

> Computer literacy of the potential respondent (touch-screen technology, allowing the individual to touch a designated area of the screen to enter a response, can alleviate some computer fear or lack of experience)

> Reading speed and comprehension level, which will influence the time necessary to complete the survey

> Computer failure, power outages, or related concerns

Personal Interviews   Another popular and commonly used survey approach is the personal interview. People are generally willing to be questioned, and they are often flattered to be asked their opinion and to participate in a survey. Interviewing offers several advantages:

> The interviewer can provide clarification if the respondent does not understand what is being asked.

> The interviewer can probe to find out more detailed information.

> It is easy to record comments and observations.

The greatest danger in personal interviewing is that the interviewer may deliberately or inadvertently "lead" the respondent to answer the question in a certain way. Leading usually occurs because of facial expressions, changes in intonation, nods of approval, and the like.

Video Interviews   Video interviews are usually four to six minutes in length and are often recorded at the game or event. The purpose of a video interview is to provide not only the response to the question, but also the facial expressions, animation, and emotion associated with the response.[8] Video interviews are a form of qualitative research in that they not only elicit answers to questions but also offer an opportunity to find out why the respondent provided a particular answer. Video interviews are most effective when used in concert with a written survey. A method related to video interviewing is an ethnographic approach that involves videotaping consumer behavior at sporting events to provide a permanent record of learned behaviors that don't necessarily emerge during the survey process[9], either because the question doesn't provoke the emotional response or because the question isn't asked at all. In the sport setting, use of video can have significant value for observing community relations activities, interaction with mascots, retail operations, concessions areas, and so forth.

Community Intercepts   One of the most effective yet least utilized forms of research is the community intercept. Researchers use community intercepts to identify any barriers that people perceive to exist (correctly or incorrectly) so that the team can address them through its marketing efforts. Simply stated, in addition to asking why people are attending (on-site surveys), community intercepts allow one to ask why people aren't attending. The community intercept can also be used to document media patterns, gain reaction to new concepts, and compare the subject of the survey (e.g., a team, health club, venue) to its area competition.[10] See appendix B for an example of a community intercept.

Community intercepts are usually conducted as interviews, but can, depending on the venue and type of audience, be administered as a pass-out survey similar to the on-site survey described earlier. In sport, community intercepts usually occur at places (other than at the actual event or game addressed in the research) where people socialize or pursue leisure activities. Such locations could include, among others, sports bars, fitness centers, and theaters and movie complexes. The community intercept elicits perceptions and misperceptions that exist about the sport organization in the community as a whole—the community including people who may have attended a game as well as those who may not have. Both viewpoints are essential to assessing the status of marketing initiatives and future planning. If attendance is to increase, current attendees must attend more frequently; but in addition, a percentage of those who have not previously attended must also attend.

Protocol Research   One of the emerging methods of consumer research involves a type of interview process known as "protocol research." This entails getting the consumer to answer certain questions while she is in the process of decision making. Although protocol research has been validated as a method of understanding the general approaches to decision making (it is the foundation of cybernetics), consumer and marketing researchers have not used it extensively. As John O'Shaughnessey notes in his book, *Why People Buy,* organizations should find ways to have the consumers think aloud at various times: (a) before they buy (anticipatory account), (b) during their purchase (contemporaneous account), and (c) after they have bought (retrospective account).

When enough of these protocols have been recorded, certain patterns may emerge.[11] For example, protocol research may indicate that people may not consider corporate sponsorships before they purchase, or that teens tend to purchase athletic footwear in malls where they have at least three purchasing options to consider.

Panel of Experts   The panel of experts survey method is not used as much as it should be. It is comparatively simple to put together a group of experts in any industry. One of the most successful methods employing experts is called the "delphi method." With this method, experts individually rank certain questions concerning the issue; the group then sees the collective (averaged) findings, and some discussion follows. The experts then vote again, and the process is repeated until there is a general consensus on a particular issue. Experts are often used to predict trends in sales of sporting goods equipment, to judge the effectiveness of certain promotions, and to gauge trends in club memberships, to name but a few areas. The overall effect, in most cases, is a quite accurate prediction.[12]

In sport, consumer panels are more common than expert panels. In this research process, consumers are selected for the panel because of their history or experience in purchasing the products or services of interest. These panels are selected from a database that is either purchased from an outside source or derived from the records of the entity initiating the research. The individuals are then contacted regarding their willingness to serve over a specific period of time, often two to three years. Thus consumer panels usually serve in longitudinal studies performed to measure behavior patterns and trends over time. This is a particularly valuable approach as new products and concepts enter the marketplace or as new ad campaigns promote these products and services.

Respondents on such panels usually receive compensation and may also receive the products under consideration for trial use and feedback. Consumer panels are usually very successful, in part because the participants feel special in having access to information and products before the general public does, and in part because use of these panels is cost efficient for the manufacturer or supplier.[13]

Internet and Web Site Surveys   A newer methodology that is becoming more popular in terms of adaptation and utilization is the Internet or Web site survey. The ease of designing a web page complete with a survey instrument, the almost overnight results, and the absence of cost and staff time are very attractive factors. The number of Internet users has been growing rapidly; according to a recent study, an estimated

23 percent of people aged 16 and older in the United States and Canada reported that they had used the Internet in the past month.[14] However, at least two major considerations come into play with this research approach. First, Internet respondents may not be random; they are choosing or self-selecting themselves to complete the survey. At present, Internet users are primarily male, hold management positions, are over the age of 18, and live in affluent households.[15] This creates a sample bias because this group may not be representative of the group the cyberresearcher is interested in.

In relation to sport, this methodology may be most useful for conducting informal polls such as attitude opinion surveys. However, if the sport organization can document through other types of surveys and research that the majority of its consumers have online access and use it regularly, this type of research may prove to be an efficient and timely way to gather data. Each organization must make its own determination about how valuable this research source might be in relation to its goals.[16]

The Open Letter   One of the simplest and most economical ways to learn about the consumers of your product or service could be to simply invite customers to write to you. Researchers who ask people to write are opening the door for communication—hence the term "open letter."[17] Letters of this type might indicate what is on the mind of the consumer, possibly complaints, praise, suggestions for improvement. Open letters are valuable because they provide the words and convey the feelings of the consumer; but because they might not arrive in sufficient quantity, they should be used as an addition to other forms of research that are both more quantifiable and more reliable in terms of sample size. The open-letter format may also be adapted to fax, 1-800 phone messages, e-mail, and so on.

The Mystery Shopper   According to noted sport marketer Jon Spoelstra, the most valuable information emerges via personal experience and observation.[18] Although it is incumbent upon management to occasionally "survey" the premises, interacting with patrons and noting consumer behaviors and operational weaknesses, surveying and observing may not be enough for a comprehensive assessment of all event operations. Likewise, the visual presence of management is sure to inspire the unfriendliest of employees, thereby adversely affecting any opportunity for capturing the "true" service encounter between the event patron and staff. Enter the mystery patron, aka secret shopper. In the technique known as the mystery shopper, an individual who works for an organization is hired to observe employees and operations in the same organization or that of a competitor and to compile a report. This approach is becoming more popular in sport settings because of the high levels of interaction with customers.

Mystery shoppers look and act like ordinary customers, and their job is to evaluate the service and attention the ordinary customer receives. Mystery shopping has been used for many years in marketing research to evaluate customer satisfaction and employee performance and satisfaction, as well as for other purposes requiring a dispassionate and unobtrusive data collector.[19] In the sport setting, an approach based on personal observation would require mystery shoppers to visit the workout floor, bleacher seats, concession stands, ticket outlets, pro shops, or wherever they might gather information about consumers, products, and the distribution system that brings them together.[20] The mystery patron audit can generate valuable feedback on such details as employee knowledge and performance, facility cleanliness, waiting time, concessions quality, and security.[21]

Integration of Primary Data Sources

To be truly effective and to develop a valid, inclusive, and comprehensive organizational "picture" through research, managers are now finding it best to integrate several of the methodologies discussed in this chapter instead of relying on just one approach. Integrating qualitative (e.g., focus groups) with quantitative practices (e.g., a mail survey) is more likely to provide the manager with not only statistics but also the rationale as to respondents' answers.

One might think of a benchmark market research study as one that employs a number of the methods described in this chapter. An example of such a study is an analysis sponsored by the United States Tennis Association and the Tennis Industry Council. Entitled Why People Play, the study addressed some key questions for an industry that has seen declining participation rates and interest in general. These were the questions that the marketers centered their research on:

- Who plays tennis? How often? Why?
- Why do players quit and why do many return/rejoin?
- What are the perceptions of players, ex-players, and nonplayers?
- What are the barriers to participation?
- What can the industry do about these barriers and perceptions?

In addressing these questions, the research team conducted a three-phase study. Phase 1 involved a series of personal interviews with groups of "tennis experts," including manufacturers, retailers, members of trade and professional associations, publishers, club owners, and corporate sponsors. The interviews helped the researchers develop initial hypotheses and identify factors related to the questions at hand. Phase 2 consisted of 11 focus-group discussions throughout the country, involving mixtures of players, ex-players, and nonplayers. These discussions allowed the researchers to refine the earlier hypotheses and gain a sense of relevant factors, especially those involving attitudes, behaviors, and motivations. Phase 3 was a telephone survey, based on a refinement of Phases 1 and 2 and conducted with a random stratified national sample of 1,200 people that included 600 players, 300 ex-players, and 300 nonplayers. Although, of course, no study is perfect, this study had a methodologically balanced design.[22]

COMMON PROBLEMS IN SPORT MARKETING RESEARCH

The researcher must be aware of a number of common problems in marketing research that are not necessarily unique to the sport industry but are relevant nevertheless. Close attention to these areas is necessary to ensure the effectiveness of the MIS. These are some questions that researchers commonly face:

- How many people should I survey to be accurate?
- How dependable are my findings?
- Where should demographic questions be placed in a survey?
- How can I be assured of a random population for the survey?

Marketers address these questions with appropriate sampling and questionnaire design techniques.

SAMPLING

Typically, one cannot collect data from all fans, all club members, or all users. The purpose of sampling is to allow researchers to make generalizations about a population based on a scientifically selected subset of that population. A sample therefore is intended to become a microcosm of a larger universe.[23] For this reason, researchers must always be concerned with the representativeness of the sample. They must ask and answer the following questions:

Table 5.1 MINIMUM SAMPLE SIZES FOR SMALL POPULATIONS

Population Size (N)	Sample size with a 5% margin of error and 95% confidence level	Sample size with a 5% margin of error and 99% confidence level
500	218	250
1,000	278	399
1,500	306	460
2,000	323	498
3,000	341	544
5,000	357	586
10,000	370	622
20,000	377	642
50,000	382	655
100,000	383	659

See Rea and Parker.[24]

> *What is the structure of the population to be surveyed?* If the population is a homogenous group, then a simple random-sample survey (see table 5.1) can be used. If the population is not homogenous (it is segmented), then a random stratified sample survey is required (the proportion of each segment in the total population is represented in the sample population). A good example is the on-site survey in figure 5.3: fans are segmented by the type of seat (general admission, reserved, etc.) that they purchased. Therefore, the research team ensured that the sample in the study approximated the overall attendance segmentation by seat type.

> *How can randomness be ensured?* This is a particular problem with on-site surveys and audience audits. If a researcher gives a questionnaire to every person passing through the gate, she might not get the stratified sample that she intended. It may be necessary to make assumptions that persons in aisle seats have a certain randomness; or distributing surveys in concession areas may ensure a higher degree of randomness.

> *How reliable should the results be?* Before marketers say "100 percent," they must realize that reliability involves a cost-accuracy trade-off. A marketer who just wants a general idea should survey friends, customers, and fellow suppliers to get a feel for the market. If predictive reliability is required, then it is necessary to use a sufficiently large, random sample. Such a survey must use a well-planned questionnaire administered by trained researchers. The larger the sample, the more predictive the results. For example, to state the results with a 95 percent level of confidence (meaning that in 95 cases out of 100 this is expected) may require a sample size of at least 400, but to state the results with a 99 percent level of confidence (in 99 cases out of 100 this is expected) may require a sample size of almost 800. However, as sample size increases, so do the survey, interviewer, and processing costs.[24] This is the trade-off in market research.

DESIGNING THE QUESTIONNAIRE

These are important points to remember in designing the questionnaire itself:[25]

> The questionnaire should contain only questions for which the marketer really needs answers.

> The marketer should have a feel for the kind of answer he expects to get and should also know what he will do with each answer (how he will interpret each response).

> Simple, objective, precoded questions (with responses provided or scales) are easier to interpret and analyze than open-ended questions.

> Demographic questions (age, income, etc.) should come at the end of the questionnaire. In an interview process, these same questions might be printed on a card for the respondent to fill in so that it is not necessary to ask the questions aloud.

> Similar and related questions should be grouped together on the basis of topic areas. Such questions should be in a logical sequence and should flow from general to specific.

➤ When the questionnaire uses precoded or semantic differentials (i.e., asks subjects to choose between opposite positions, such as good-bad, enjoyable-not enjoyable), it should not present a large number of these questions in sequence, as some respondents may become bored with the questions and begin answering them without reading or thinking about them.

➤ The marketer should use semantic differentiation with care when asking attitudinal questions. (Many respondents will not have thought in terms of these topics and questions and hence may be forced into erroneous responses.) In many cases, and time permitting, there is value in following up these questions with the question "Why?" This not only provides the rationale for the response but also ensures that the respondent has understood and thought about the question.

➤ The questions should be free of ambiguities.

➤ Each question should have a distinct purpose. Often times, though, it takes more than one question to generate the data needed to make a decision. Questions may be interrelated and may be initiated from the responses of previous questions.

➤ As a survey is a form of communication, it is often a good practice to offer the respondent a final open-ended response to the organization directing the research. This ensures that the communication process is two-way and that the researcher is not missing any issues of substance. This question might be stated, "Are there any issues that were not covered in the survey that you would like to address and discuss? If so, please list and explain your feelings regarding these issues."

ANALYZING SURVEY DATA

Undoubtedly the greatest advantage in using precoded (forced choice) responses is that the data are easily input into a data-entry/analysis program. The ideal (and most commonly used) computer program for data entry and analysis is SPSS/PC+, a sophisticated and multifaceted program with a thorough tutorial on use of the package as well as on certain basic statistical procedures. The system is menu driven, featuring context-sensitive help screens. Cross tabulations (analysis of responses through examining the response by variable segmentation—e.g., female season-ticket holders, youth aged 14-18) are produced efficiently and quickly. Add-on packages to produce graphic interpretations and presentations are also available. Overall, SPSS/PC+ is a comprehensive system, capable of performing for both the professional statistician and the less experienced researcher.[26]

WRAP-UP

The MIS links the market and the marketer and is therefore the lifeline of marketing. Perhaps the factors most critical to marketing success are (a) the marketer's ability to collect accurate and timely information about consumers and potential consumers and (b) to use this data to create marketing plans specifically targeted to meet the needs of specific consumer groups (known as target market segments). Marketing-mix decisions must be based on accurate and comprehensive data on the market, the competition, the way the market views the product, the pricing structure, and the promotional messages transmitted about the product. Simply stated, anything short of a complete MIS leaves the door open for competition to erode the organization's product position and stature and to eat into its market share.

The marketer can select from a wide variety of options for collecting the data needed to generate the appropriate information. There is no one way of collecting data that is best for all organizations. The organization needs to determine what its marketing priorities are and what information it needs in order to proceed with market planning. It then needs to determine the most efficient method to accurately gather the data on its consumers, potential consumers, and competition.

The data generated in the MIS show the marketer that not all consumers think the same way or have the same needs or wants that they expect the product to fulfill. The recognition that consumers have different aspirations, needs, or wants, and the grouping together of consumers based on certain characteristics common to a group, constitute what is called market segmentation. The process of dividing consumers into several target market segments is essential to any marketing strategy development. We turn to that process in the next chapter.

ACTIVITIES

1. What is the goal of an effective MIS system?
2. What is the essential difference between qualitative and quantitative research?
3. Design an effective 20-item questionnaire focusing on attendance and enjoyment issues as they relate to attending collegiate women's basketball games.
4. Identify a minimum of five secondary data sources that could provide information about trends relating to youth sport.
5. Visit a local health or fitness center. Determine the types of organizational records that the center has available. Ask how these records are used in terms of marketing efforts. Do they effectively generate a consumer profile? If not, what other types of information need to be solicited to generate an effective consumer profile?
6. In this chapter we discussed the San Diego Padres Compadres program. Are there similar frequent-attender or frequent-user programs in your community? If so, how are they monitored and utilized? If not, how could such a program be utilized or implemented in your community or region?

YOUR MARKETING PLAN

In examining the organization that you previously selected as the focus for your marketing plan, identify the areas on which you will need additional data (from both primary and secondary sources) before setting realistic objectives and determining strategies and tactics. What are the most effective ways to secure such information? What part will research play as you asses the effectiveness of your marketing plan?

C H A P T E R

6

MARKET SEGMENTATION

OBJECTIVES

1. To appreciate the central role of segmentation in the marketing process.

2. To recognize the standard bases of market segmentation in sport.

Women Learn to "Putt for Dough"

In 1997, surveys by the National Golf Foundation suggested that 5.7 million women made up 22 percent of the American golf market. Their average age was 42, average household income $66,000, and average annual golf spending $649. There was one more, critical statistic: 40 percent of all women golfers held managerial, professional, or administrative positions. This was a large group of people (over 2 million) for whom golf might have great business as well as leisure value. After all, male executives had long fostered the ethos of making deals on the fairways. Jane Blalock, a New England Sports Hall of Fame golfer, knew her sport held the same potential for women, if only they got a little help. The Gillette Company saw similar prospects, and a partnership developed—the LPGA Golf Clinics for Women, promoted and run by the Jane Blalock Company. In 1998, the clinics ran in a 14-city tour, with hundreds of women registered at each site, paying $225 for a day learning the craft of golf. Blalock neatly summarized her vision: "Women miss out on a lot of quality time with clients when they can't go out on the course at the sales meeting. We want to break down the barriers and intimidation many women feel about the game."[1]

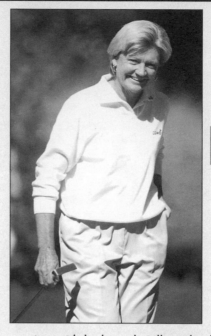

Jane Blalock, leading the way in women's golf.

Jane Blalock and Gillette had researched the market. They recognized the links between sport, lifestyle, and a clearly defined group of people. Their product was designed to satisfy unmet needs of that group. In short, they had employed a segmentation strategy.

The ability to segment a market is made possible by the kind of market research we discussed in chapter 5. In this chapter, we will explain segmentation, its centrality to the marketing process, and its feasibility. Then we will look at the common bases for segmenting the sport market: state of being (demographics), state of mind (psychographics), product usage, and product benefits.

WHAT IS MARKET SEGMENTATION?

Market segmentation is a key concept in this text because it creates the bridge between managerial analysis and managerial action. It provides a conceptual framework upon which a sport marketer builds promotional strategies.

In simple terms, market segmentation is the process of dividing a large, heterogeneous market into more homogeneous groups of people, who have similar wants, needs, or demographic profiles, to whom a product may be targeted. The Jane Blalock Company, for instance, does not target its clinics at all golfers, or even all female golfers. Instead, the focus is the female executive golfer. Such segmentation is basic to most successful marketing efforts throughout the world. Even within the massive global marketing strategies of corporate giants like McDonald's and Coke, there is a recognition that consumers in Germany are different from consumers in Japan. If technology has made the world smaller, it has not homogenized the world's cultures. Neither has television created a "mass mentality" within a nation of television viewers like the United States. Indeed, the dozens of channels now available on any cable television system reflect the fragmentation of the marketplace.[2]

The sport marketplace is just as segmented. As chapters 3 and 4 indicate, there is no single profile of the sport consumer. The consumer profile varies by sport, by place of residence, by life situation, and by a host of other factors. One thing is clear, however; segmentation rules. Sport television provides clear evidence. Twenty years ago, the "broadcast" networks dominated sport television. Sport junkies (a very important segment of men) had little choice in their viewing. Then came HBO and ESPN, cable networks that began to widen the choices. ESPN especially wagered its program schedule (and its corporate life) on the sport junkies to whom the old networks had appealed a few times per week. In recent years, "narrowcasting" has spawned even more clearly defined segment strategies, like the Golf Channel, which grew in four years from under a million subscribers to a projected 24 million homes in 1998. The patrons at Jane Blalock's clinics can continue their education at all hours of the day on the Golf Channel, which may begin producing its own golf game show ("Alex—I'd like 'Bobby Jones' for $500").[3]

Given the competitiveness of the sport market and the intangible nature of most sport products, market segmentation is both logical and necessary. A product is nothing more than a "bundle of benefits." The deeply committed fan may want special privileges that come with a season ticket (newsletter, access to autographs), whereas the infrequent fan may need a telephone or Internet ticket-ordering system that reduces anxieties and hassles over ticket purchase. The young executive who uses a racquet club on a frequent basis may require a club that provides laundry service. Another member may prefer fewer amenities for lower fees. Segmentation, then, is designed to maximize consumer satisfaction; yet it is also a marketing tactic to maximize market demand. Thus segmentation should not be carried to the point beyond which it no longer provides meaningful returns. The New York Islanders might maximize attendance by individualizing ticket packages to suit the desires of every fan. That would not be feasible. The Islanders, then, identify and target segments they can reach.

IDENTIFIABILITY, ACCESSIBILITY, RESPONSIVENESS

Several issues are important in choosing whether to segment a market—identifiability, accessibility, and responsiveness of potential segments.[4]

First, a marketer must ask, can the segment be identified or measured in terms of its size and purchasing power? The marketer may make this determination using the kind of research discussed in chapter 5. At the same time, some segments may be difficult or prohibitively expensive to identify. For instance, professional baseball clubs did not spend time in 1998 trying to determine the size or strength of the market for a Beanie Baby promotion. The raging success in other markets was enough for them to go with a gut instinct that Beanie Babies were hot everywhere, at least for the moment. A golf course developer, however, would want to research a local or regional market before making a $9 million investment.

Second, can the marketer access the segment? Is it possible to gain access to these groups of consumers individually without upsetting marketing efforts aimed at other segments? Our Beanie Baby promoters had no problem with this in the hot summer of 1998. A few weeks of promotional ads brought out more than enough Beanie Baby collectors. Things are not so easy, however, for a state high school association trying to promote its championship games, especially in "minor" sports. The time between play-off rounds is often short, upsets happen with regularity, and fan bases are segmented by community identity. It is not feasible for most state associations to prepare special contingency plans for each team that might advance. Hence, campaigns tend to be broad-based promotions of high school sports.

Finally, the marketer must ask, will the segment be responsive? Two questions need to be answered here. The first is whether the product will match the wants of the chosen segment. The second concerns the significance of the segment. Is it worthwhile (given segment size and response) to break down product characteristics and promotional efforts sufficiently to reach a segment?

The marketer must address all of these factors in deciding whether to segment and to what extent.

SEGMENT OR NICHE?

You may sometimes hear the term "niche strategy"; it is not quite the same as segmentation. Marketing theorists distinguish segments from niches largely on the basis of size and competition. Segments are large but also prone to competition. Consider, for instance, adult, male football fans. Colleges and pro leagues compete for this audience, at live gates, on television, and with merchandise. A niche may be smaller (perhaps even Jane Blalock's golfers), but typically, larger firms ignore a niche. In sport marketing, niches have also been distinguished from segments on the basis of sport specificity. Niches arise from the sport market; segments are imposed on the sport market. For example, the Sled Dogs Company developed its product in the early 1990s—a mini-ski and boot combination—with an eye on a part of the existing in-line skater population. Specifically, it targeted skaters (most of whom are young) who had no winter activity. "Sled Dogs" were simply a way to skate on snow. The niche started in a group within sport: in-line skaters, who had no winter counterpart. Unfortunately for the Sled Dogs Company, much of this niche market has since adopted snowboarding, in part because ski resorts recognized the same market potential and began embracing snowboard "shredders."

As we shall see in chapter 14, niche marketers have used the Internet aggressively. On the other hand, the massive online bookseller, Amazon.com, has shown that the World Wide Web can work equally well for mass marketing.

"Niches" or "segments"? Much of the distinction is semantic, especially within the sport industry, where many firms exist in a single-sport domain. In both cases, however, the key questions of identification, accessibility, and responsiveness remain.[5]

FOUR BASES OF SEGMENTATION

Market segments are formed upon the basis of differentials in consumer wants and desires; that is, segments derive from consumer satisfaction. Four bases are commonly used for segmentation, each of which rests on an assumption that homogeneity in one variable may relate to homogeneity in wants and desires. The four common bases are:

> ➤ the consumer's state of being (demographics),
> ➤ the consumer's state of mind (psychographics),
> ➤ product usage, and
> ➤ product benefits.

Typically, marketers employ cross sections of segments—middle-income Hispanic families in a baseball team's metropolitan market, or affluent and "active" older persons who live within 30 minutes of a particular athletic club. The following sections, then, must be understood to represent very fluid categories.

STATE-OF-BEING SEGMENTATION

State-of-being segmentation includes the following dimensions, which are generally easier to measure than state-of-mind or product benefits:

Geography

Income

Age

Gender

Race/Ethnicity

Sexual Orientation

Geography

There are several clear dimensions of geographic segmentation in sport:

Proximity rules. A simple survey of participants will typically support the long-recognized relationship between proximity and activity or involvement. Basically, the closer a person lives to a sport facility, the more likely she is to become involved with activities there.

Know your geoclusters. Good internal marketing data from ticket applications, membership inquiries, and similar sources often reveal "geoclusters" of consumers who are especially important. Abundant software is available to help with mapping. All the marketer needs are consumer zip codes to go with other data—types of purchases (season tickets? full membership?), frequency of participation, income, and so on. Mapping allows the marketer to see whether certain suburbs or neighborhoods are especially prone to a certain product. Those areas can be targeted for special campaigns, especially direct mail.[6]

The value of outer rims. Some consumer clusters may come from considerable distances. These represent "outer-rim" markets that can repay extraordinary attention in terms of advertising, promotions, radio, or television networking. Outer rims in sport date at least as far back as the rise of radio broadcasts. Midwest major league teams like the St. Louis Cardinals developed fan bases at great distances, nurtured largely by radio. Outer-rim markets are logical targets for group sales and special events. But in football, with relatively few home games, outer rims mean season tickets. In the summer of 1998, the San Diego Chargers spent several hundred thousand dollars on an ad campaign in the Los Angeles area. When the Rams and the Raiders deserted, L.A. was left without an NFL team. In effect, it became a potential "outer-rim" market for the Chargers. First the Chargers had to seek an exemption from the NFL rule that prohibits marketing outside a franchise's 75-mile radius. That was no problem. Second, and more difficult, the Chargers had to reach a market of fans who desired an affiliation with a team up to 160 miles away (for those in the north of Los Angeles County). The Seattle Seahawks had long maintained an outer rim of Alaskan fans, over 1,000 miles from the Kingdome. But, then, Alaska had never had an NFL franchise.[7]

Income

Geoclustering matches income with residence and, presumably, lifestyle. While a certain income is no guarantee of a particular lifestyle, it is frequently a central index. National Football League football can demand high television-rights fees because it delivers males with relatively high disposable incomes. Golf does not draw as many, but its income profile is even better. That's why luxury car companies advertise during golf telecasts. Some sports are even more closely tied to high incomes—take polo. In fact, polo is so valuable that in May 1998, the Polo Ralph Lauren Company sued the U.S. Polo Association's magazine, insisting that it drop the name "Polo." The Lauren Company, which obtained a 1985 trademark for the term "polo," complained that *Polo* magazine was now overstepping its bounds, focusing "not on equestrian sports but on sophisticated fashions and elegant lifestyles." We might ask, was there ever a difference in the world of polo?[8]

Table 6.1 PERCENTAGE OF AGE GROUP "AT LEAST SOMEWHAT INTERESTED" IN SUPER BOWL OR KENTUCKY DERBY

Age	Super Bowl	Kentucky Derby
12–17	78.0	7.8
18–24	72.9	9.4
25–34	66.0	22.0
35–44	70.4	19.6
45–54	61.9	33.6
55–64	57.2	30.5
65+	52.1	36.8

From *Sports Business Daily*, 8/15/97, p. 15.

Age

The old notion of the "generation gap" contains obvious truth—the young have different tastes and lifestyles from their parents, who in turn diverged from their own parents. Marketers talk about "cohorts" rather than generations (e.g., the Depression cohort, the baby boomer cohort). Musical tastes, sexual mores, approaches to debt or savings, and fashion sense are but a few of the cohort touchstones. In some cases, we may include sporting tastes. For instance, table 6.1 shows some results of an ESPN/Chilton poll of 1,000 Americans in 1997. It suggests that while age has some negative affect on Super Bowl interest, the January extravaganza is clearly an intercohort experience. On the other hand, horse racing has good reason to launch a massive promotional campaign targeted at a younger audience.[9]

Youth have been a target of sport promotions for over a century, often with the idea of building character through baseball, or basketball, or just about any sport. In the early 20th century the "sports curriculum" swept gymnastics and calisthenics to the background of the burgeoning physical education programs in American public schools. After World War II, organized youth leagues exploded in the suburbs, first in baseball and then across a broad range of sports. Starting ages drifted downward, so that today, "under-8 travel" teams are the norm.

But registration does not ensure commitment. In fact, American youth appear less and less committed to mainstream modes of fitness, exercise, and sport, at least as measured in national surveys. For instance, the federal Centers for Disease Control found significant reductions in the exercise profile of teenagers between 1984 and 1994. Young people may not be interested in their parents' sports.[10] Sport firms have responded in several ways:

Get 'em to the action to do—feel—learn. Baseball in particular has recognized the need for special efforts to get kids on the escalator. The logic of nurturing fans at a young age is accentuated in MLB because of the long strike in 1994-1995, which dropped many longtime fans off the escalator. In luring kids back, the Anaheim Angels started letting them run the bases on Sunday games. The Oakland Athletics dropped ticket prices to 98 cents for kids 14 and under. Also, the first 100 kids were allowed onto the field to get players' autographs.[11]

Repackage the product for youth. A number of bowling alleys have begun to create late-night, weekend slots devoted to the youth of Generation X. Using tag lines like "Extreme Bowling" or "Rock 'n' Bowl," proprietors transform their premises with night-glow balls, strobe lights, and heavy-metal music. Bowling is not alone. While special "youth-sized" equipment has been a longtime staple in golf, one manufacturer—Dead on Sports—touted a 1998 line for "grunge" golfers. This included clubs with a skull and crossbones on the shaft and the phrase "kill it" on the heel. With less drastic adjustments, *Sports Illustrated* launched *SI for Kids.* By 1997, circulation was 950,000. As the case study on NASCAR suggests, however, "youth" campaigns often raise special ethical issues.[12]

Youth sport participation increased steadily throughout the 20th century.

The senior or "maturity" market is another target for special marketing plans. As the baby boomers grow older, they bring their vast cohort into another life/family stage. In the next quarter century, the over-50 market will grow by 75 percent, the under-50 market by only 1 percent. Increasingly, baby boomers will move from their "family" stages to empty-nest and single stages. More research is needed on the sporting attitudes, lifestyles, and subsegments of this maturing market, but the implications are obvious for sport marketers from the major leagues to the local athletic club. A recent article in *Athletic Business* offered some valuable questions for any marketer to ask about plans proposed for this segment:

> Does the program speak to aging's possibilities, as opposed to its limitations?
>
> Does the program have motivated leadership?
>
> Is the program user-friendly?[14]

Gender

As sport marketers have recognized the importance of a "female" market, they have discovered two distinct facets to segmentation strategies. First, women and girls are a special group of consumers with special needs and wants. Second, women's and girls' sports are a special type of product, with benefits distinct from those in men's and boys' sports. The first is appropriately considered demographic segmentation. The second is really benefits segmentation, considered later in the chapter.

Sport firms have recognized women as a special segment for over a century. For the most part, however, marketing strategies focused on rather glib visions of the "fair sex"—very white, relatively affluent, and limited in capabilities. Bicycle companies made V-shaped women's frames to avoid criticism that cy-

• Special concession stands and FanFest contests are part of marketing strategies to attract young fans.

Case Study

The Ethics of "NASCAR for KIDS"?

Like most sport organizations, NASCAR has aggressively targeted the family and youth markets. Said NASCAR's Director of Communications Worldwide John Griffin: "We're going after youth as a whole. We want to continue in our direction of becoming more of a white-collar sport, where it's mom, dad and the kids sitting around the TV and rooting for their favorite driver on Sunday. We're going after urban youth as much as any other youth." The youth campaign has included NASCAR toys, games, theme

parks, and cafes. A NASCAR cartoon show was in the planning stages in 1998. And there was already a NASCAR Barbie doll. This was all logical, but NASCAR had to make one major alteration in these youth and family products. It had to cut out the tobacco references that are so prominent in the wider NASCAR image. The NASCAR Barbie might have a Pennzoil patch, but no Winston.

But one must wonder: what will the cartoon characters compete for, if not the Winston Cup? And when Mommy and Daddy take the kids to the live event, how can they prevent them from seeing the clear link between the NASCAR and the Winston brands? The NASCAR people walk a tightrope on this. They must continually ask several of Laura Nash's 12 questions:

"What is your intention?"

"How does your intention compare with probable results?"

"What is the symbolic potential of your action if understood? If misunderstood?"

One R.J. Reynolds executive offered some answers about his company's intentions with its NASCAR affiliation: "This isn't about getting anyone—regardless of their age—to smoke. It's about trying to convert and switch adult smokers to our product." A jaundiced public might think otherwise.[13]

cling forced women into unladylike positions. Golf and tennis firms made smaller racquets and clubs for women. Baseball teams promoted "ladies' days" in order to elevate the image of their crowds. This was segmentation, but it was a far cry from Jane Blalock's intent. The women's sport market is no longer an afterthought to the "real" market for men (but see the sidebar, "A Backlash Coming?"). Title IX and Billie Jean King ushered in a new era that is now coming of age. The female fan base for the dominant men's sports is nearing equity—43 percent in the case of the NFL.

The words of Sara Levinson, president of NFL Properties, capture the widespread desire to win with women: "Women are of critical importance to us. They control the TV dial on Sunday afternoons and decide what sport their kids will get involved in. We have to make these gate-keepers comfortable." Levinson could have added that women purchase 70 percent of all NFL-licensed merchandise. In hopes of expansion, the NFL launched a series of seminars in 1997 in 10 cities. The tag line was "Football 101." For a nominal fee, women could hear presentations on equipment, rules, and tactics. In Pittsburgh, the class also toured the locker room and practiced plays on the field. Some students viewed football in the same way that Jane Blalock views golf. Susan Gray, a shipping clerk from Irving, Texas, said she came to the Cowboys' clinic because she no longer wanted to get left out of football talk at the office: "It might be nice to know the difference between a running back and a wide receiver."

Female fans are a growing presence at both men's and women's sporting events.

Other women were not amused, including Jeanne Clark, a former national board member of the National Organization for Women. In Clark's view, "Football 101 sounded like long-ago stories in teen girl magazines, warning the football novices that a little inside knowledge of quarterbacks and linebackers was necessary if you wanted to catch that handsome football hero." Concluded Clark, "They're making a lot of gender assumptions that are unwarranted."[15]

The female sport consumer market will only grow stronger, with more professional leagues, more specialized equipment, more magazines, and television networks that recognize special interests, wants, and needs. More firms, like Stars and Strategies (marketing) and Moving Comfort (running wear), are run by and for women. Regardless of a marketer's gender, however, there is little return in a patronizing message or a one-shot, low-budget program. As Donna Lopiano, Executive Director of the Women's Sports Foundation, concludes: "Selling to women is different from selling to men."[16]

Is a Backlash Coming?

Women have made great strides in sport, but in many ways they are still objects in a male-dominated game—whether as consumers to target or as athletes to ogle. Says Mariah Burton Nelson, author of *The Stronger Women Get, the More Men Love Football:* "Sport constitutes the only large cultural institution where men and women are (sometimes) justifiably segregated according to gender. It is one of the few remaining endeavors where male muscle matters." And males still have plenty of muscle. Olympic telecasts may prove to be a testing ground. For over a decade, the networks have moved away from hard sport coverage in the Olympics. The stories are increasingly "up close and personal" looks at the athletes' private lives and especially their tribulations. It is sport as soap opera, and for a good reason. Prime-time ratings are driven by women, who appear to prefer more of the personal, less of the agonal.

This has not been good news to Anheuser-Busch, which saw almost a 50 percent decline from 1994 to 1998 in the Olympic viewing by males aged 25 to 54. Said Tony Ponturo, Anheuser-Busch's vice president for corporate media and sport marketing, "You have to make sure women are intrigued with the Olympics. But we're now concerned that the pendulum is so far over the 21- to 34-year-old male is saying that 'you're not talking to me anymore.'" Ponturo suggested that Anheuser-Busch might ask NBC to guarantee an audience of young men when it negotiates its advertising for the Sydney Games of 2000.[17]

Race and Ethnicity

American history has been heavily influenced by enduring struggles between natives and immigrants, between races and ethnic groups. The nation's motto—e pluribus unum ("out of many, one")—captures part of this ethos. Opinions still diverge on whether the motto represents an achievement or a goal. Battles over bilingual education reflect opposition on the emphasis: the "unum" or the "pluribus." And minority groups increasingly challenge the right of white, "European" immigrants to control the definitions of the American "unum."

Cultural diversity is both the American strength and the American conundrum. In some ways, the sport world has provided the most vivid theater for this struggle. Jack Johnson, Joe Dimaggio, Eddie Gottlieb, Althea Gibson, and Roberto Clemente are just a few names that represent millions of athletes, promoters, and fans for whom sport has been a touchstone of racial and ethnic tensions. While the dominant leagues, teams, and clubs have gradually opened their doors to qualified athletes, they have been slower to pursue minority fans. That is changing, however, in response to the obvious. Americans of African, Asian, and Hispanic descent represent a quarter of the population. They represent important consumer bases that demand diligent respect, not benign neglect.

African Americans, for instance, are way underrepresented as fans of professional and collegiate sports. Data for 1994 from Simmons Market Research Bureau indicated that blacks made up only 6 percent of professional baseball attendees and only 8.8 percent of pro football attendees. Given the high proportion of black players in these sports, the attendance rates reflect marketing failures, particularly a lack of segmentation strategies.[18] The Hispanic market has been more aggressively pursued, perhaps because it is the fastest growing minority segment, projected to represent one quarter of all Americans by 2050.

The success of Spanish language media has prompted even greater attention among sport marketers. For instance, during the 1998 World Cup Finals, Univision, the top Spanish language network in the United States, easily outdrew ESPN in the ratings race—850,000 households per game versus 670,000. Hispanic Americans have an even hungrier appetite for baseball, fueled in part by the more than 150 major leaguers who were born in Spanish-speaking countries.

Sport marketers are beginning to recognize several important principles for success in reaching minority segments:[19]

Utilize minority firms, individuals, and icons. In 1998 the St. Louis Cardinals engaged FPM/Fuse, a minority-owned ad agency, to create a campaign aimed at attracting more black fans to Busch Stadium. With good reason. Although the St. Louis metropolitan area is 17.4 percent black, and although the Cardinals have enjoyed Hall of Fame careers from a host of African Americans including Bob Gibson and Ozzie Smith, black attendance has lagged behind—making up between 1 and 3 percent of all fans for over a decade. The FPM/Fuse $100,000 campaign used bus, billboard, and radio ads featuring black players like outfielder Brian Jordan, who says, "God gave me the ability. My parents gave me the opportunity. Everything else I earned." Clifford Franklin, FPM/Fuse partner, expressed the gist of the campaign message as "hard work, dedication, and focus." Although only time will test the effectiveness of this campaign, it was widely hailed as a prototype for success.[20]

Recognize diversity and change within minority groups. Major League Soccer franchises have been very active in addressing their Hispanic fan base. For good reason: Hispanics accounted for 23 percent of all Major League Soccer fans in 1998. But the rapidly evolving Hispanic population will require changes in strategy. Says consultant Dean Bonham: "The Hispanic market is lower- to middle-income right now, but can be described as a soccer-educated demographic with spendable income that's growing at a very rapid rate." The message was not lost on the Long Beach Ice Dogs of the International Hockey League, who targeted Latinos under 35 with ads on Spanish radio and in Spanish newspapers. The first effort, in February 1998, yielded more than double the average attendance (although there were no statistics on fan ethnicity).[21]

Recognize minority consumer loyalty. In the summer of 1998, Street and Smith Publishers announced a new annual football "preview" magazine: *Street and Smith's Black College Football.* The prospectus ad for this joint effort with the Historically Black Collegiate Coalition noted some of the superstars who had played at HBCUs (historically black colleges and universities), including Jerry Rice and Walter Payton. But it also emphasized that "black college sporting events are attended by more African Americans than any other type of sporting event in the country."[22]

The Gay and Lesbian Market

Historically taboo markets in the sport world, gays and lesbians continue to struggle for recognition, opportunity, and understanding. The success of the Gay Games, however, may both reflect and project a more positive turn. Sponsors of the 1994 Gay Games, like AT&T and Miller Brewing Company, enjoyed high (33 percent) recall rates among attendees. Three quarters of attendees said they were "very likely" to attend the 1998 games. These high levels of commitment, coupled with high income and education profiles, led *American Demographics* to label the gay and lesbian market "an untapped goldmine."[23]

STATE-OF-MIND SEGMENTATION

State-of-mind segmentation assumes that consumers may be divided by personality traits; by lifestyle characteristics such as attitudes, interests, and opinions; and by preferences and perceptions. The most noteworthy approach to state-of-mind segmentation has been developed by the Stanford Research Institute (SRI). Called the Values and Life Style (VALS) typology, it assumes that attitudes, opinions, desires, needs, and other psychological dimensions collectively govern daily behavior. In 1989, SRI revised its system into eight segments of the adult population, based on resources and orientations to action, status, and principle. These were the VALS 2 categories:[24]

Actualizers	Fulfilleds
Achievers	Experiencers
Believers	Strivers
Makers	Strugglers

Although one study of exercisers showed a relationship between earlier VALS categories and exercise ("inner-directed" people exercised at twice the rate of "outer-directed" people), we are not aware of recent studies of sport consumers using VALS 2 as a base. The possibilities of state-of-mind segmentation, however, are intriguing. For instance, Discovery Communications, which runs the Learning Channel and the Discovery Channel, uncovered eight segments among its viewers. The "Machos," who composed 12 percent of viewers, were 76 percent male, largely blue-collar, average in income, and oriented toward "action" programming, including sports and war. In contrast, the 15 percent of viewers who were "Scholars" were 54 percent female, urbane, upscale, and prone to programming in archeology, history, and anthropology. Discovery Communications can use the knowledge to create and promote programming for the various segments. We might project similar segments among ice hockey fans—"Rumblers" who revel in aggressive hitting and fighting and "Aesthetes" who focus on skill, craft, and grace.[25]

PRODUCT USAGE SEGMENTATION

We know that product usage segmentation is also quite significant. Here, marketers have concentrated on the "heavy half," or heavy users of the product. In many markets, the so-called 80-20 rule applies, according to which 80 percent of market consumption comes from only 20 percent of the consumers. Sensitivity to marketing-mix factors has been shown to vary significantly with product use. In sport, we have long been cognizant of the various usage patterns (e.g., the season-ticket holder vs. the single-ticket purchaser). This is true across most sports, for players and fans alike. Research on the women's 1990s golf market, for example, showed that "occasional" golfers (1-7 rounds per year) made up over 50 percent of all the golfers but accounted for only 12 percent of the total rounds played. Meanwhile, "avid" golfers (25+ rounds per year) accounted for 64 percent of total rounds played. Along similar lines, the "light"-fan segment of one MLB club made up an estimated 43 percent of 1990 total attendees (different people attending), but only 19 percent of total tickets sold. "Heavy" fans accounted for only 14.4 percent of the attendees, but almost 30 percent of tickets sold. Whether the sport is golf, tennis, or weight lifting, the "heavy-half" rule seems to apply.[26]

Table 6.2 illustrates varying consumption-rate groups that can be identified for various sport products. Although heavy users may return greater immediate dividends, the sport marketer must aim to satisfy the needs of each group as much as possible to ensure a steady stream of light, medium, and heavy users, because the light user of today may be the medium user of tomorrow and the heavy user of next year. Chapters 10 and 11 will address the need for special promotions for different user groups. [27]

Table 6.2 USER SEGMENTS AND ESTIMATED ATTENDANCE IMPACT ON A MAJOR LEAGUE BASEBALL CLUB—1976, 1990

Segment	Number of games	Year	Percentage of people	Estimated percentage of attendance
Heavy	11+	1976	4.2	20.4
		1990	14.4	29.6
Medium	3–10	1976	29.4	45.5
		1990	42.7	51.1
Light	1–2	1976	66.4	34.1
		1990	42.9	19.3

Breadth \ Frequency	High frequency (>10 times/month)	Medium frequency (5-9 times/month)	Low frequency (1-4 times/month)
High breadth (>3 activities)	"Denizens": read game stories daily; attend five games/month; buy programs; watch all away games on TV		
Medium breadth (2-3 activities)		"Growlers": Share miniplan; wear Bruins hat; watch weekly telecast	
Low breadth (1 activity)			"Cubs": Watch big game on TV

Figure 6.1
Sample frequency/breadth grid for Bruins fan.

There are several summary points about usage segmentation we want to emphasize:

➤ Not all consumers consume at the same rate.

➤ The levels of consumption (e.g., heavy, medium, and light) vary from sport to sport, so the relative importance of usage rates (in terms of total attendance/participation) differs from sport to sport.

➤ The levels of consumption are likely to vary from age group to age group. Thus sport spectatorship and consumption show a life-cycle pattern.

➤ It is essential that the sport marketer maintain opportunities for consumers to consume at many usage levels. That is, the marketer should not sell all of a court club's "contract" time to a few people, or should not depend too heavily on season-ticket sales and thus exclude the occasional user. This mistake cost the Rochester Royals dearly, as we read in chapter 2.

This latter problem is well known to the Boston Bruins, who were sold out for many years primarily through season-ticket sales. Once Bobby Orr left and fan interest declined, there were no light users and few medium users to replace the "defecting" season-ticket holders. Sport organizations (especially clubs, camps, and YMCA/YWCAs) must also segment use in terms of breadth of activities, that is, offer a number of different sport programs and products. In this case, the notion of a heavy user should include number of activities as well as frequency of participation. Indeed, a strategy that aims for breadth of activities may provide the club with a buffer to prevent members from becoming bored and burned out and thus from defecting. Such organizations might want to develop a grid to visualize segmentation along the dimensions of breadth and frequency. Internal marketing data, as discussed in chapter 5, can be placed within the grid. Figure 6.1 provides a sample grid for a hypothetical "Bruins" fan base. Only three cells are filled in here, but the concept of such a grid is the important point. For instance, "denizens" are clearly committed in breadth and frequency; they are the hard-core fans. On the opposite end, "cubs" represent the bottom of the involved-fan base. They are highly prone to falling off the escalator and may well turn their attention to another sport before they actually attend a game. Such a frequency/breadth grid with all the cells filled in would provide the basis for promotional campaigns.

BENEFITS SEGMENTATION

Sport marketers have adopted benefits segmentation in many ways. The most easily illustrated applications are in the sporting goods industry. Take athletic shoes. The competitive runner who logs over 60 miles per week seeks the product benefits of support, shock reduction, and long wear; the intermediate tennis player seeks sound grip and comfort; and the casual sneaker purchaser is just looking for a light and fashionable shoe to use as regular footwear. Each purchaser is looking for totally different benefits and will be best served by totally different shoes.

The motivational factors discussed in chapter 4 provide insights into the benefits sought by sport consumers. Affiliation, achievement, status, health, and fitness, in various forms and configurations, are certainly related to benefits that consumers perceive from sport consumption. Team marketers, for instance, know that season-ticket holders expect exclusive benefits such as access to inside information (often via newsletters) or special events (autograph sessions). Groups, on the other hand, look for scoreboard recognition, on-site liaisons, discounts, and team promotional materials to drum up interest. The NFL in 1997 defined its "six core equities" (with sample symbols) as follows:

> Action/Power: hitting, circus catches, the NFL shield

> History/Tradition: leaves, NFL legends, tailgating

> Thrill/Release: fans/players laughing, screaming

> Teamwork/Competition: the "steel curtain" defense of the Pittsburgh Steelers Super Bowl champions

> Authenticity: the pigskin, muddy field, blood

> Unifying Force: groups of fans, teams

These "core equities" may be viewed as core benefits, to be cultivated in live events, broadcasts, videos, programs, and merchandise. [28]

The steady rise of high-performance, commercialized women's team sports (e.g., college and pro basketball, international soccer and ice hockey) appears to be a case in alternative benefits more than demographics. To be sure, fan research does suggest that women's team sports fans represent a wider age range than their male counterparts. And the generally lower prices are more attractive to families. But the strong male base—40 percent for the WNBA—belies notions that women's sports are a "chick thing." More likely, most fans enjoy a game that is distinctly different (e.g., "below the rim"), played by athletes who appear more articulate, more accessible, and yes, more like role models, than the men. Women's sports are evolving rapidly; time will test the margins of these product differences. At present, however, they serve as an excellent example of benefits segmentation. [29]

WRAP-UP

Segmentation is truly central to the notion of knowing one's consumers, for segmentation recognizes that consumers vary along a number of dimensions that the marketer may use to form the basis of specialized strategies. Therefore the marketing information system should be keyed in to the notion of segmentation, and research should examine the possible bases for meaningful segmentation of the marketplace. Whether segmentation makes the most sense in terms of geography, demographics, usage, benefits, or some combination will depend on the marketer's knowledge and feel for the market. Indeed it makes sense to pursue a relational approach to segmentation. That is, consumer segments distinguished by "benefits sought" should be evaluated for any internal homogeneity on the basis of demographics, psychographics, or usage. Discoveries of such relationships will provide fruitful insight for improved communication with such target segments. In any case, however, the decision maker must recognize that people can and must be distinguished. Whether the business is pro basketball, high school lacrosse, or public parks and recreation, it is hard to consider any plan a marketing plan if it doesn't incorporate some aspect of segmentation. [30]

ACTIVITIES

1. Define segmentation. Describe the differences among segment identification, segment access, and segment responsiveness. Think of examples in the sport world of segments that might be identifiable but not accessible or responsive.

2. What are the basic components of state-of-being segmentation? Give examples of the state-of-being segments most important to your local college women's basketball team.

3. Define state-of-mind segmentation. Try to find an ad for a sport product or team that appeals to a state-of-mind segment.

4. Explain why the heavy-user segment is so important to sport marketers. Use table 6.2 to explain.

5. How would you relate the notion of benefits segmentation to the discussion of motivation in chapter 4? List and compare the benefits of attending MLB and playing golf at the nearest public golf course.

YOUR MARKETING PLAN

Can you define the core benefits of your product(s)? Will any of these benefits link to consumer segments defined by demographics, psychographics, or product usage? You should begin to clarify, at the least, the product usage segments in your consumer base. Try to fill in a frequency/breadth grid for your consumer base. Use figure 6.1 as a guide.

THE SPORT PRODUCT

OBJECTIVES

1. To recognize the elements of the sport product that contribute to its uniqueness in the wider market-place of goods and services.

2. To learn the process involved in product development as well as its relation to the concept of the product life cycle.

3. To understand product positioning, product image, product branding, and their roles in successful sport marketing.

"If You Can Play Soccer Indoors, Why Not Football?"

"It's the best two hours and 10 minutes of football you'll ever see," claimed Jack Youngblood, an NFL star in his days with the L.A. Rams. Was this the West Coast Offense run to perfection by Steve Young and the 49ers? Not quite. In 1998, Jack Youngblood was president of the Orlando Predators, which was decidedly not an NFL franchise. Their game was played indoors, with eight players per team and no punting. There were narrow, extended goal posts surrounded by netting to keep errant kicks and passes in play; there were full pads; and—best of all—there were hockey boards to bounce opponents into. It was Arena Football, the new AFL, the brainchild of Jim Foster, who had conceived the product in 1981 after watching indoor soccer. "I turned to my friend," recalled Foster, "and said if you can play soccer indoors, why not football?"

It took boundless energy, his life savings, and six years of experiments before Foster saw the AFL's birth in 1987 as a four-team league with a deal for ESPN coverage. Foster's product concept had several key dimensions:

➢ Football's basic form adapted to arenas

➢ League controls on franchise costs (i.e., salaries) to keep ticket prices attractive

to football fans who could not afford the NFL

➢ A spring/summer season that would tap both the infinite cravings of football fanatics and the arenas' desire to book dates when their anchor tenants (hockey and basketball) were off-season

Foster's formula worked. The 1987 season saw an average attendance of 12,600. Television ratings were respectable. And the next decade proved that the new product was much more than a fad. By 1998, the AFL was attracting deep-pocket investors who drove franchise values to unheard-of heights. In May 1998, the NFL owners approved a change in policy that would allow ownership of an AFL franchise. Tom Benson of the New Orleans Saints immediately bought a franchise. In 1999, the NFL entered into a formal marketing agreement with Arena Football that included the NFL's option to buy up to 49.9 percent of the indoor league. National Football League Commissioner Paul Tagliabue said, "Our goal is to support football at all levels." The Associated Press reported that "AFL teams that once went for $500,000 now have a price tag of close to $5 million."[1]

As discussed previously, sport products are bundles of benefits. Jim Foster is one of many entrepreneurs who have designed a new sport product that offers benefits to satisfy consumer wants and needs. In this chapter on the sport product, we begin to delve into the marketing mix, or the five Ps of sport marketing—product, price, promotion, place, and public relations. First, we review the elements that make the sport product unique. These include the event, the ticket, the organization, the facility, and equipment and apparel, to name a few. Next, we discuss the intricacies of developing products, including the concepts of line, item, and mix; procedures for launching new products; and the product life cycle. Finally, we examine "positioning" and "branding," the most critical parts of contemporary product development.

WHAT IS THE SPORT PRODUCT?

The sport product is a complex package of the tangible and the intangible. Hear the word "golf" and you think of little, dimpled balls and oversized, "metal" woods that are, in different ways, standardized. They are tangible elements of the golf product. But the "golf" experience is hardly standardized: it can be total frustration for the occasional duffer and total infatuation for the addicted. It is no different in any other sport, since all sports depend on human performance. As we discussed in chapter 1, this makes the marketer's job challenging in several respects:[2]

➤ *The sport product is inconsistent from consumption to consumption.* Today's friendly racquetball game is totally different from last week's game against the same opponent, even though all the elements—time, court, skill, equipment—appear unchanged. For the fan or for the participant, it is the uncertainty and the spontaneity of the sport product that make it attractive. As Fox Sports President David Hill concluded, "If there's one great thing about sports, it's that it's unscripted. And the guy in the white hat doesn't always get to kiss the horse. Sports is the last frontier of reality in television."[3]

➤ *The "core" game or performance is just one element of a larger ensemble.* Players or fans rarely consume the game, event, or contest in isolation. The sport "experience" includes the atmosphere of the venue, the equipment, the apparel, the music, the concessions, and the pre- and postgame festival. All of these elements extend the sport product beyond the contest itself, for players and fans alike. In some cases, the contest is almost secondary. Satellite television and the Internet, with their instantaneous, worldwide reach, have prompted an increase in sport events that exist less for their intrinsic value and more for their ability to deliver product extensions. One industry executive expressed the widespread belief that more events would "be created purely to sell specific brands and products such as shoes and apparel. Events will be the integrated marketing sales engine of the future." A casual look at the Olympics, the Super Bowl, or the Extreme Games suggests that this future has been slowly arriving for some time.[4]

➤ *The marketer typically has little control over the core product and consequently must focus efforts on product extensions.* Marketers cannot control the contest, especially the winning and the losing. Don Canham, longtime and successful athletic director at the University of Michigan, knew this well. His advice almost 25 years ago still rings true: "We do not market that Michigan football is Number 1, because next year we may not be! Instead we market a Fall weekend in Ann Arbor." Canham knew that as a marketer he had little control over the contest. Instead, he created and promoted a more comprehensive experience, with more benefits for more consumers. In sport marketing, winning is not the only thing![5]

THE SPORT PRODUCT: ITS CORE AND EXTENSIONS

As figure 7.1 suggests (see page 118), the sport product is both an integrated ensemble and a bunch of components with lives of their own. At the core is the "event experience," composed of four components:

Game form (rules/techniques)

Players

Equipment

Venue

Whether we consider a friendly game of three-on-three on a hot asphalt court or a Cleveland Cavs game in the lush surroundings of Gund Arena, we will find the common features of game, player, equipment, and venue. Everything else builds on these components. Take the game of golf. Even though the duffer has a different experience from the scratch golfer, the particular nature of rules/techniques, equipment, and venue joins the two players and distinguishes golf from tennis. Moreover, it is the "playing out" of rules/techniques, equipment, and venue that makes sport products distinct from all other products. As the sidebar on fair play suggests, there is much at stake in controlling how the game is played.

As figure 7.1 also suggests, the event experience may include an abundance of supplements. These are the things that move us from the playground to Gund Arena:

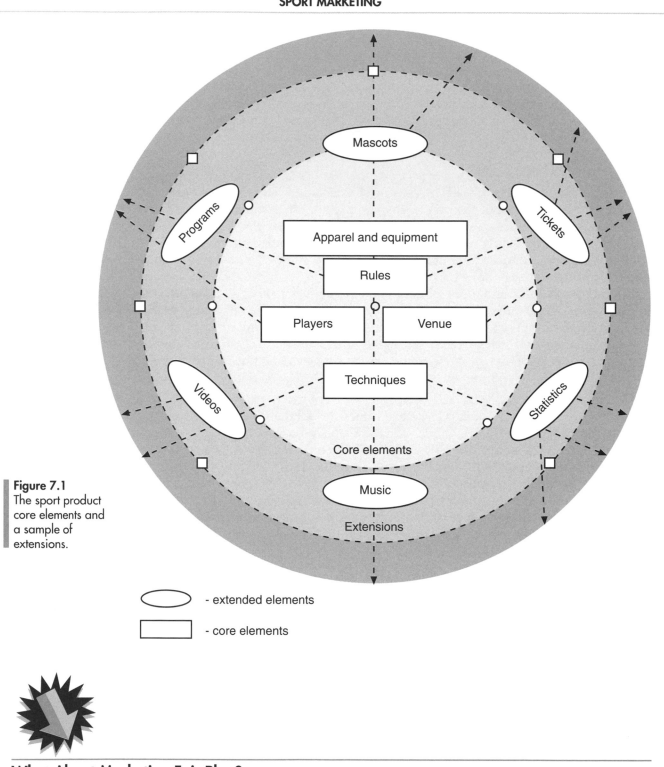

Figure 7.1
The sport product core elements and a sample of extensions.

- extended elements
- core elements

What About Marketing Fair Play?

Sport events are very much a matter of winners and losers. There is no getting around this. The simplicity of recognizing a win or a loss is the factor that makes events and athletes such rallying points for passionate interest. On the other hand, any game requires some boundaries of fair play. After all, we normally don't equate "cheaters" with "winners." Notions of

fair play have marked sport events as far back as the ancient Greeks, who certainly treasured winning as much as any civilization. In the last century, the Anglo-American sport tradition repackaged fair play as "sportsmanship" (a term that betrays the strong links between sport and "old boys"). Whatever the name, the notion seems to be under siege. If fair play is central to the value of any event, we must be concerned about increases in violent behavior at all levels. Fights and brawls in the "big leagues" may be spilling over, as seen in recent reports in the *NCAA News:*

➤ In February 1998, spectators cheered as a New York high school hockey player was hauled off in handcuffs for assaulting a referee.

➤ In October 1997, a California youth football coach assaulted and repeatedly kicked a referee. His grievance? The referee had flagged one of the coach's players for unsportsmanlike conduct.

➤ In December 1997, a mob of Alabama high school football fans attacked two officials. Just prior to the melee, the game's announcer had berated the officials over the public address system, taunting them and complaining that they "needed to go back to school."

No marketer can guarantee fair play and friendly crowds. On the other hand, marketers may demand a measure of fair play in the mix of any promotion. Marketers may also work with the event staff to improve crowd decorum. There can be a fine line between nurturing entertainment and degrading fair play. Should ushers prevent fans from waving papers and towels to unnerve a player at the foul line? This may depend on the level of competition. Should a college marketer pursue a deal with an auto body shop that wants to sponsor the "toughest collision" at each home hockey game? This sounds innocent enough, but what if the sponsor runs newspaper and television promos that juxtapose pictures of tough hockey hits and auto wrecks? What is the message to fans? What is the message to families who have lost children in "tough collisions"? We go back to three of Laura Nash's questions in "Ethics Without the Sermon":

What message do hockey sponsors send to fans when they emphasize the "exciting" tough hits and collisions?

➤ What is your intention?

➤ How does this intention compare with probable results?

➤ What is the symbolic potential of your action if understood? If misunderstood?

Ethics require both principles and common sense. So do marketing and maintaining sport products with enduring value.[6]

tickets, programs, video, music, memorabilia, and mascots. A supplement is simply a product component that enhances the value (and the price) of an event experience. At the same time, any product component—from the player to the mascot—can also become a product extension, with a life (and sales) beyond an event or even a season of events. Some examples:

➤ Late in the 1998 MLB season, Mark McGwire and Sammy Sosa changed the nature of every game they played in, boosting attendance, television ratings, and general interest. It was a special boon for rival hosts, who stood to double or triple average attendance. Only Beanie Baby giveaways had similar effects. At the same time, the players' celebrity value extended well beyond any event. As he approached the Babe Ruth and Roger Maris records, McGwire appeared on television interviews wearing a cap from the Abbey Seal Restaurant in Orange County, California. Immediately, the restaurant's owners said they were "inundated with calls from coast to coast and overseas"; anything with McGwire's identity was now an extension of the home run record chase, a hot commodity.[7]

➤ Uniform designs and colors have been part of the sport event for centuries. Fans in the ancient Roman stadiums cheered for chariot drivers of particular stable colors—red, white, green, blue. Many of today's teams are known by their colors. Say "the Crimson" around Boston and most fans will think of Harvard. Say "Crimson Tide" south of the Mason-Dixon line and any football fan will think of Bear Bryant and Alabama. In the 1990s, uniform design became part of broader strategies that extended the event into everyday apparel. Every major league team expanded its properties division to oversee the careful development and sale of merchandise, including "official" team jerseys. Among other things, this meant that two basic uniforms—home and away—were no longer enough. Teams developed "secondary" home and away uniforms. Some were retro and some were avant-garde, but they shared a logic. If big-league players showcased new uniforms at the live event, plenty of people would buy replicas at their local department store.

➤ The San Diego Chicken became a major sport figure in the late 1970s. The comic mascot livened up the sport crowd at any venue willing to book him. Pro and college teams took note and created their own mascots as elements that transferred an event into "showtime." In 1994, Dave Raymond, the longtime alter ego of the Philadelphia Phillies' "Phanatic," decided to go out on his own. He created a mascot-for-hire called "Sport," who could assume any team's identity and guarantee a crowd-pleasing performance. But Sport was not limited to sports; he was happy to extend his special "event" experience to conventions, trade shows, and hospitals.[8]

| Grace and power are two appealing features of basketball.

THE GAME

As we noted in chapter 1, sport always contains some kind of game form that includes rules and techniques. Each sport has its own special features that may make it especially attractive to certain consumers. For instance, basketball has speed, agility, physical contact, power, and grace. If James Naismith—who invented the game in 1891—could see the Bulls play today, however, he would be surprised at the radical changes in his product. Senda Berenson, who quickly adapted Naismith's game for women, would be even more surprised at a WNBA game. Of course, game forms change all the time. Players invent new moves (see sidebar), and rules committees tinker with this or that as they work to balance offense and defense. Three classic basketball examples are the 24-second shot clock, the three-point line, and the goaltending rule.

One might argue that changes in rules and techniques are comparable to design changes in any consumer product; sort of like making a tastier, low-fat potato chip or a faster computer modem: changes are made to satisfy consumer wants and needs. To some extent this is true. The college football rules committee first allowed forward passing in 1906 with a clear eye on public opinion about the deadly nature of the "mass" game. Likewise, American League owners approved the designated hitter in 1973 in an effort to jack interest and attendance; National League owners, with higher average attendance and more new ballparks, felt no such urgency.

On the other hand, most changes in rules and techniques revolve around attempts to gain or balance competitive advantage. The everyday consumer is a secondary interest. A clear example is the recent change in Indiana high school basketball. In 1996, the Indiana High School Athletic Association (IHSAA) ended the

Can "Moves" Be Patented?

Skill, craft, and "moves" have always been a central attraction to the sport consumer. Kids model the actions of more established players—a sibling, a local school hero, or a professional star. Movies extended the audience for the special skills of elite athletes. Kids in Walla Walla could see Babe Ruth's swing, Helen Wills's volleys, and Joe Louis's jabs. Television multiplied the images and the modeling. It became easier for athletes to see and learn the latest "moves" and innovations. Dick Fosbury's "flop" quickly changed the face of high jumping. Icky Woods's "Icky shuffle" set off a national storm of end-zone celebrations. Jimmy Connors and Chris Evert changed the game of tennis with their patented two-fisted backhand strokes.

Fans and broadcasters have long discussed the "patented" moves of this or that player. Now, patent attorneys at the New York firm of Pennie & Edmonds have suggested that "patented" moves can really be patented. Why shouldn't Kareem Abdul-Jabbar have protected his "skyhook," says F. Scott Kieff: "What we find remarkable is that this is viewed as remarkable." In the view of these attorneys, Dick Fosbury should have received royalties from those who copied his revolutionary move. Coaches who dream up distinctly new tactics (the "West Coast Offense" perhaps?) would get some income from copycats, a notorious breed in football.

But is any sport move, technique, or team play ever really original? Would sport patents lead to a cadre of new patent protectors who would monitor games around the country, ensuring that no one took a free ride with a hook shot, a two-fisted backhand, or a postscore celebration? We will examine some of these issues in chapter 17.[10]

---

long-standing "single-class" approach to its annual championship. For two years at least, there would be no Davids slaying Goliaths as the movie *Hoosiers* so poignantly depicted. There would be four classes of competition, which supporters claimed would mean fairer competition and more trophies. Unfortunately, the fans didn't quite see it that way. Tournament attendance in 1998 was down 6 percent for girls and 21 percent for boys. Television ratings were down, and overall revenue dipped to its lowest level in 18 years. The IHSAA appointed a citizen's advisory council to develop a survey that will help determine whether the rule remains. Better late than never; the IHSAA's reaction underscores the lesson that sports can't market themselves.[9]

STAR POWER

The most memorable event experiences build drama from the playing surface outward. Players and coaches are the keys, as all successful promoters learned from the likes of Tex Rickard and Christy Walsh. These architects of the "golden age" of sport of the 1920s recognized the need to accentuate the struggles of hero against villain or mind against muscle. Their strategy was simple—star power. Babe Ruth, Jack Dempsey, Knute Rockne, Bobby Jones, Helen Wills: these are the names we remember and associate with that fabulous era.

In some respects, things have not changed much in the last 75 years; the drama of sport still requires star power. On the other hand, today's players and coaches are extended beyond the event far more than their predecessors. Players still provide most of the script in sport. The NBA rose from its near-ashes state of the late 1970s on the backs of stars like Larry Bird and Magic Johnson. Michael Jordan took the league into the stratosphere. Venus and Serena Williams, along with several other young, flashy players, have recently made the Women's Tennis Association (WTA) Tour a very hot product. Sportswriter Mike Lupica captured Venus Williams's attraction: "From the beaded braids on her head to the way she carries herself on the court [she] makes you come into the stadium instead of walking the other way. If she is on television, she jumps out of your set." Some coaches have the same effect. Bill Parcells is one of them. When he left New England for the New York Jets, his presence alone helped boost ad sales 20 percent for televised Jets' games. Star talent, or its absence, can make or break entire leagues. Just as Joe Namath may have saved the American Football League in the mid-1960s, the absence of household names has been, in the words of one racing writer, the "malady that plagues" both the Indy Racing League (IRL) and the Championship Auto Racing Teams (CART). For some time, they have slumped into the shadows of their star-studded cousin NASCAR.[11]

The NASCAR drivers demonstrate how stars extend the product beyond the event. As we will discuss in depth in chapter 12, drivers and athletes help non-sport sponsors reach the sport audience of educated, affluent, energetic men, women, and families. It is also a two-way street. Legions of NASCAR fans know that Dale Jarrett endorses White Rain shampoo and Jeff Gordon endorses Pepsi. But every time White Rain or Pepsi uses a NASCAR image in a promo, the company also promotes NASCAR as a sport. In 1997, Dale Earnhardt earned $3.6 million from racing and $15.5 million in endorsements, almost a 5 to 1 ratio of extended value. Tiger Woods's ratio was almost 12 to 1, with $2.1 million earned on the PGA Tour and $24 million in endorsements.[12]

Although women have made progress in this area, they still face problems of limited media exposure. In 1997, Monica Seles topped the list of female athlete endorsers, with $6 million. It was not surprising that 7 of the top 19 endorsers were either WTA players or figure skaters, that is, were in sports that enjoyed relatively high television coverage.[13]

Sport stars have come and gone over the last century, bringing various amounts of value to the core and extended product. Then there is Michael Jordan, who redefined the notion of player as product. Beginning with the Air Jordan shoe that brought Nike out of its mid-1980s doldrums, Jordan has demonstrated a Midas touch like no other athlete before him. In June 1998, *Fortune* magazine added up the "Jordan effect" on gate receipts, television revenues, merchandise sales, endorsements, and even his agent's business. The total value: "just about" $10 billion. While most professional athletes want to be like Mike, very few can hope to combine the skills, the championship results, the looks, and the engaging persona that have made Jordan the poster boy of 1990s capitalism. Even the most brilliant strategists at International Management Group or the Marquee Group can't ensure success, and the market is quick to dump a loser. For instance, Hideki Irabu aroused great expectations when he joined the New York Yankees in 1997. One New York publisher reportedly offered him $2.5 million for a book. The deal died with his poor performance, which reduced him from a hero to a David Letterman punching bag. And Shaquille O'Neal, for all his talent and charisma, may have overextended himself, especially into several movie flops. With no championship rings on his fingers, O'Neal seemed to be losing his appeal in 1998, when Reebok parted ways with the man they once felt could challenge Nike's Michael Jordan.[14]

Although neither agents nor teams can control all elements of players' or coaches' performances or behavior, the last decade has seen greater efforts to enhance their interpersonal skills. One example was the Corel WTA Tour and the United States Tennis Association, which co-promoted a 1997 media skills training program for players. An even better investment is the NCAA Champs/Life Skills Program for Division I athletes. This is a comprehensive educational program that covers not only communication skills but also such issues as substance abuse, eating disorders, and stress management.[15]

EQUIPMENT AND APPAREL

As we noted earlier, sport equipment might be considered part of the "core" product for any participant. No sport is played today without equipment, much of it increasingly "high tech" (see sidebar). Sport equipment purchases in 1995 made up almost half the $152 billion "gross domestic sport product." But equipment can also be an extension of the core-event experience. A glove, a stick, or a hat is a tangible touchstone for the memory of a game or a match—for players and fans alike. And as we discussed in chapter 4, sport merchandise is a critical part of the learning process in any sport. For over a century, player cards have introduced youngsters to the lore of sport information and statistics. Sport-related T-shirts, jackets, and ball caps became a badge of personal identity in the 1980s and 1990s, as any parent or teacher knows well. (For more detail on merchandising, see chapter 8.)

Authentic sport memorabilia have made their way into the fancy auctions once devoted to high art. In 1992, Leland's auction house sold the infamous (to Red Sox fans) "Bill Buckner ball" to actor Charlie Sheen for $92,500. In 1996, Leland's was chosen to auction off the bricks and seats of the old Boston Garden. Consumers gravitated to some special place of memories. Some dead stars even had agents. In the mid-1990s, Curtis Management Group protected the rights to images of Babe Ruth and 51 other sport heroes. In 1995, the centennial of Ruth's birth, his licensed products and royalties were expected to generate over $25 million for his estate. Merchandise even resurrected dead franchises. When Snoop Doggy Dog wore a Springfield Indians hockey jersey in his hit 1995 video "Gin and Juice," sales jumped 500 percent, vaulting the Indians to third place in American Hockey League merchandise sales. It didn't matter that the Indians franchise had died in 1994 or that the jersey design was over a decade old. Retro was in.[16]

Technology Drives the Game

Equipment innovations have continually pressed the boundaries of sport performance. Pole-vaulting moved through distinct chapters as poles evolved from bamboo to metal to fiberglass. The plastic helmet and the face mask revolutionized blocking and tackling in football. Inventors and manufacturers continually seek the new product that will sweep the market. Some innovations are controversial, such as "square grooving" or "spring-like effect" in golf clubs—innovations that have pitted manufacturers against the United States Golf Association, sometimes into litigation. Governing bodies typically react to innovations that appear to affect the integrity of playing skill, safety, or competitive fairness. In the fall of 1997, for example, the International Ski Federation banned the racing suits worn by Picabo Street and others because they had been developed from technology that was unavailable to competitors.

Other innovations are clearly marked for non-competitive situations. In 1998, the hottest new product was the Rawlings "Radar" baseball that could clock the speed of a pitch covering 60 feet, six inches. Introduced in April, the ball enjoyed over 100,000 sales by summer. Rawlings executives licked their chops at the thought of Christmas sales. At $34.99, the ball was priced as more than a novelty that could answer sandlot arguments about who had the better arm. Major leaguer Tom Glavine saw potential for pitchers on rehab who could work on their own without the benefit of $1200 radar guns. "There could be a place for it," said Glavine. The sport industry radar screen shows many more high-tech products on the horizon, ready to create more profits for manufacturers and more tension for rule makers.[17]

NOVELTIES AND FANTASIES

The 1990s saw an acceleration of products designed largely to extend the core experience. Sport toys and novelties had certainly existed before, but not as clearly tied to integrated marketing strategies. In 1997, the NBA along with Mattel, and the NFL along with Hasbro, entered into major deals for toy lines. The NBA had a Barbie Doll line, with the WNBA slated to follow. The NFL launched a "Pro Action Athlete" collectible line; NASCAR had driver figurines. By the summer of 1998, the focus was on Beanie Baby promotional giveaways. They were as hot as McGwire and Sosa.

The NASCAR teams integrated their novelties backward—into recycling old tires, which fans happily buy for $5-10 each. Said one consumer about his purchase: "I'm going to keep it on my floor at home, next to my bed. You know, so that I can see it first thing in the morning when I wake up."[18]

Then there are the fan fests, fantasy camps, and cruises, which have developed for two simple reasons. The first reason is the meteoric rise of tickets, concessions, and parking at big-league events. The standard event in any sport gets less and less accessible to the majority of potential consumers. If fewer people can afford to get on the consumer escalator, how can they sample the sport product "up close and personal"? At the same time, even the most committed consumers want to learn, feel, and do more. Fan fests, fantasy camps, and cruises were the answer, with free or low-cost fests at the entry level and high-cost cruises or camps for consumers willing to pay for closer contact with past or present-day players. The intent behind all these products was clearly expressed when the LPGA announced the new LPGA Fan Village in 1997. The 2400-square-foot multimedia entertainment and information center—sponsored by Target Stores—would travel with the tour. At the village, fans could enjoy

- fan-player photo opportunities,

- rules and technique seminars,

- health and fitness forums,

- club-fitting and hitting areas,

- a pictorial time line of LPGA highlights, and

- video and computer displays.

As LPGA Commissioner Jim Ritts concluded, the Fan Village was a "fun and entertaining way to satisfy our fans' appetite to get closer to the realness of our players and to learn more about our organization." The NFL, NHL, NBA, NCAA, and

Fans of all kinds, even authors, can have a major league experience at a fantasy camp. Bill Sutton (far right) with (from left) Dave "The Plumber" Synowka, Scott Fruehan (Robert Morris College), and Vic Gregovits (Vice President of marketing for the Pirates).

Dave Arrigo/Pittsburgh Pirates.

MLB have the same objectives at their fan fests. Individual franchises have jumped on the concept. The Buffalo Bills, for example, set up a "Bills Experience" before each home game.[19]

THE VENUE

All sports have a venue, a field, a facility as part of the product package. We will look more closely at the sport "place" in chapter 13, but it is clear that teams and franchises are closely aligned with their venues, which are the cauldrons of powerful memory and community. As historian Bruce Kuklick noted in his monograph on Philadelphia's Shibe Park, "Meaning and the items that bear it are fragile. The meanings accrue over time in their visible embodiments, artifacts like Shibe Park. Memories do not exist in the mind's isolation but are connected to objects and stored in them." A fan's identity, particularly in a large city, often resides in the stories or the recollections that link people and events with a place. A place like Shibe Park offered special rituals that fused Irish or Italians into "Philadelphians." The same may be true for any venue. The fear of losing this distinct identity agitated critics of the "cookie-cutter" stadiums that sprang up in the 1970s. The newer "retro" parks like Camden Yards seem to represent a swing back to Kuklick's sense of a distinct community place—a modernized version of Wrigley Field. At the same time, however, in the new ballparks, the fans are more segregated than ever according to their ability to pay for high-priced loges, club seats, and skyboxes.[20]

Venues provide structure to more than "community." As we discussed in chapter 4, venues define the frames of game/spectacle/festival. In some arenas—Boston's Fleet Center, for example—the concourse-festival frame lies outside the arena of seats. Fans who have milled around between periods, buying concessions and mingling in groups, must reenter the spectacle through tunnels. In other venues, the concourse offers direct sight lines to the action. Camden Yards is a case in point. Similarly, Hadlock Field in Portland, Maine, offers a group picnic area along the right-field line. Here festival and spectacle are combined inside the park. For most football fans, festival means tailgating in a parking lot. Regardless of the sport, however, the venue is a crucial part of the product, for players and fans alike.[21]

In the contentious world of professional sport, owners sometimes insult their venues worse than they impugn their players at arbitration. The New York Islanders took this to the extreme in September 1998. Embroiled in a battle with the Spectacor Management Group, which managed the Nassau Coliseum, the Islanders greeted their season-ticket holders with a letter that included a warning about the safety of the coliseum's sound system. The Islanders claimed that Spectacor would not let them inspect the hoists thoroughly. A final promise to protect fans and players from "any conditions we believe to be unsafe" was hardly reassuring.[22]

PERSONNEL AND PROCESS

If the core sport product is a performance or an event, then successful marketing depends on the people who process the product. A.J. Magrath argues persuasively that personnel and process are additional Ps in the marketing mix. Any fan who has gone to numerous "giveaways" at sport events knows the frustration of receiving the wrong size or of being told, "Sorry, we're all out . . . we didn't expect so many fans today." The actions of a surly attendant or the hopelessness of a botched promotion can never be replaced or repaired. The consumer cannot return or exchange the experience. In the consumer's eyes, personnel and process are inextricably linked to the product.[23]

Charles L. Martin's research on customer relations in bowling centers led him to coin a telling phrase: *All sports are "contact" sports.* The consumer simply cannot access the product without contacting personnel in the sport organization. An intrinsically fine core product may be destroyed by lackluster personnel or process performance. Martin found that both highly and lightly involved bowlers rated "courteous personnel" among the most important attributes of a bowling center. Bernie Mullin recognized this in his work with the Pittsburgh Pirates and the Colorado Rockies. His inspiration was the "guest-centered" philosophy of Disneyland and Disney World. Martin, Mullin, and the Disney enterprises offer some simple tips to any sport organization:

> Emphasize common courtesy, especially sincere "thank-yous," even when making change.

> Make "extratransactional" encounters with customers, beyond what they normally expect. This shows extra concern for their satisfaction.

> Be proactive. Offer assistance before being asked. Work to solve problems immediately. Treat consumers as if they were guests in your home.

> Increase complaints. Encourage consumers to speak their mind. In the language of Disney, "Ask the guests what they want . . . then give it to them." Only then will the organization know how to satisfy the consumer.

> Develop a theme and a consistent ethos of service that cascade through the venue—in signage, color, cleanliness, personnel appearance, and a tenacious belief that all consumers have "special needs."

> Incorporate personnel procedures and training into company policy.

Little things do matter. Roving concierges who can supply binoculars, cell phones, or even reservations for a postgame dinner will become more common in the next decade. The various processes involving sport personnel—ticket-taking, front desk management, locker-room attending, concessions operations, skills instruction, and field maintenance—are essential features of the product. They cannot be overlooked or taken for granted. As we noted in chapter 4, the "golden rule" may be expressed in a word: *reciprocity.*[24]

THE TICKET AND OTHER PRINT MATERIALS

Few people realize the full value of a ticket to an event. The obvious uses are to provide a receipt, to guide people to their seats, and to communicate the terms and conditions of purchase. Statements of limited liability are standard these days. But these mundane applications are just the tip of the iceberg in terms of marketing potential. The ticket can clearly be used both as a promotional tool and as a source of revenue. Many minor league baseball teams use the ticket as an advertising medium. Other organizations have been quick to use it for a promotional tie-in—having drawings of ticket numbers for prizes, for example, or printing redeemable coupons (often for fast food) on the back of the ticket. Tickets often carry prestige (not to mention scalping value) that turn them into souvenirs (see photo). In 1994, World Cup tickets included an embedded hologram that made counterfeiting much more difficult.

The value of ticket access is reflected in the rise of personal seat licenses—onetime payments for the right to buy season tickets in a particular seat. Personal seat licenses have become a standard way to fund new stadiums. At the same time, turning seats into quasi-private property can backfire. In 1995, the Denver Broncos announced that season-ticket accounts could be transferred only to family members. They changed their minds in 1997 after being hit with a $35 million class action suit.[25]

Other print materials can extend the product. Programs are one example. Besides including player, coach, or game profiles and statistics, rules, and records,

A ticket, especially if it contains the photo of a star in a special uniform, can be a collectible product unto itself.

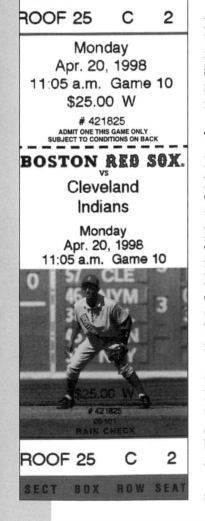

programs can include lucky numbers, used for special prize drawings. And like tick-ets, programs can be tailored for big events, with added features that make them collectibles. Teams, clubs, and leagues can also publish magazines and newsletters. Few sport organizations in North America match the reach of Manchester United, whose magazine can be purchased at newsstands all over Britain; NASCAR, with its magazine *Inside NASCAR,* may be one of them. Many groups have high-quality se-rials that circulate to members and season-ticket holders. The *NCAA News,* a tabloid weekly, is available at a nominal price to the general public.[26]

ELECTRONIC PRODUCTS

The *NCAA News* began in the 1960s; by the 1990s, standard print circulation was no longer enough to ensure connecting with key target segments. The *NCAA News* went online at the association's Web site, www.ncaa.org. We will examine Internet mar-keting along with radio and television more closely in chapter 14. Sport events and heroes have benefited from innovations in communications since the late 1840s, when New York newspapers began printing telegraph dispatches of bare-knuckle prize-fights. Motion pictures, radio, and television each brought new opportunities (and problems). At this point we simply emphasize Internet sport as part of a larger de-velopment in electronic and digital products. Some examples:

➤ Sports Simulation Inc. has developed "John Davidson's Hockey Challenge," a $47,000 virtual game designed for use wherever there is room for the 18-foot-long simulator. Shooters challenge Dominik Hasek, whose image responds on the 12-by-10-foot screen according to extensive computer programming of 299 video clips that Davidson, Hasek, and Sports Simulation filmed in 1998. The simulator's artificial intelligence allows even the youngest novice a chance to score on the "Dominator."[27]

➤ In 1998, MLB Properties and Donruss introduced a series of CD-ROM player cards for $21.99 apiece. The New England Patriots opened a Web site—www.patriots.tripod.com—that allowed fans to pull down and trade "virtual col-lectibles" like team marks and pictures, in license-protected bundles that could be traded but not altered. Some could be limited editions that might rise in "value" with a player's performance. Such products give a whole new meaning to the notion of "trading" card.[28]

➤ While music and sport have been linked since the 1910s ("Take Me Out to the Ball Game"), the late 1990s saw more aggressive connections. A long marriage between NASCAR and Nashville was formalized with compilations, such as "NASCAR: Runnin' Wide Open," that featured songs by Billy Ray Cyrus, Rick Trevino, and even Kyle Petty. The Marquee Group purchased Alphabet City Music Productions, whose products included in-venue music videos tailored to rally fans of client franchises. In 1997, Alphabet's special-edition Chicago Bulls CD sold over 300,000 copies.[29]

Wherever there was new technology in the 1990s, there also seemed to be a new sport product. While marketers must not trade taste for technology (see sidebar), there is no question that technology is helping to drive the sport market.

THE ORGANIZATION

Ultimately, all of the product elements can add value to the individual team, club, league, or association. That is the ultimate objective of a careful marketing strategy. Players, equipment, venues, merchandise, books, movies, and Web sites can all com-bine in the consumer's mind as representations of a particular organization. This is why all major leagues have divisions called "Properties" or "Enterprises." Integrated product strategies yield values through synergy, meaning that the whole is more

Are There Penalties for Bad Taste?

High technology is now an expectation for fans in college and professional sport venues. Laser lights, high-energy music clips, instant replays on the big screen—for a $50 ticket, we expect no less. But high-tech packaging does not always prove that the medium is the message. Some messages are so outrageous that we wonder "What could they have been thinking?" Two examples:

➤ In November 1997, the San Jose Sharks crossed the line with their music playlist. In two separate games against teams with African American players, the events crew played the pop song "Dirty White Boy" after a black player was sent to the penalty box. The public uproar forced Sharks Vice President Malcolm Bordelon to admit, "Mistakes. Embarrassing mistakes."

➤ In 1998, ads for the new NFL video game called "NFL Xtreme" promised that "after the coin toss, anything goes. . . . It's a helmet-popping, trash-talking, late-hitting free-for-all." *Sports Illustrated* correctly asked, "How can the league come down on cheap-shot artists and hotheads while also endorsing this video?" One NFL executive responded that it was, after all, only a "fantasy game" that was "consistent with how to get the attention of the upper-teen and early-20s market."

"Entertainment" is a clear objective underlying any sport product. But Laura Nash reminds us of at least one other obligation with her question, "Whom could your decision or action injure?"[30]

than just the sum of the parts. This is why professional franchise values continue to escalate despite salary pressures and fan antagonisms. Sometimes we gasp at franchise selling prices—$530 million for the NFL expansion Cleveland Browns or Rupert Murdoch's proposed $1 billion for the English Premier League's Manchester United. But if we begin to add up all the values associated with the core- and extended-product elements, these selling prices make more sense.[31]

The same perspective is needed with recreation and athletic clubs. Spencer Garrett, general manager of the Pierpont Racquet Club of Ventura, California, argued a decade ago that club owners had to form a partnership in the minds of their members. As Garrett insisted, most members would have a hard time justifying their investment on a simple cost-per-play basis. They must recognize that each visit is a rental of the whole club and all of its amenities: a hard match on a quality court, a hot sauna, friendly exchange in a clean locker room, a snack in the lounge, a tip on racquet maintenance in the pro shop. Thus the member pays for a whole ensemble of activities characterized in a word—"club."[32]

KEY ISSUES: DIFFERENTIATION, DEVELOPMENT, POSITIONING, BRANDING

Spencer Garrett articulated a central, ongoing struggle for all managers and marketers—ensuring that their product is conceived, packaged, and positioned in a way that resonates in the minds of their consumers. If consumers don't recognize the club, the team, the player, the event, or the equipment as meeting their needs, then marketing becomes a one-way drive to oblivion. Like all successful coaches who must tinker with their lineups and their strategies, marketers must continuously revise, delete, and add elements to their comprehensive product. Unlike coaches, however, marketers must consider their consumers and their competitors simultaneously. Whether the product is new, established, or old, the challenge is ever present—make the product distinctive and attractive in your consumers' minds. Some examples:

➤ Nike's image battles. The Nike "Swoosh" is as recognizable today as Mickey Mouse or McDonald's golden arches. Despite recent dips in sales and profits, Nike still looms as a dominant force in the wide world of sport. As Nike's Phil Knight is the first to recognize, however, getting to the top and staying there require constant reinvention and reconfiguration. In the early 1980s, for instance, Nike was temporarily toppled from preeminence by Reebok, which captured the fast swelling aerobics market. As Knight recalled later, "We made an aerobics shoe that was functionally superior to Reebok's, but we missed the styling. Reebok's shoe was sleek and attractive, while ours was sturdy and clunky." Nike survived and then thrived by repackaging and reconfiguring its products to include style as well as performance. Moreover, Nike began to use aggressive television ads to focus consumer attention on this shift. In Knight's words, "Our advertising tried to link consumers to the Nike brand though the emotions of sports and fitness. We show competition, determination, achievement, fun, and even the spiritual rewards of participating in these activities." Nike ads have succeeded because of these emotions. But Nike's foreign manufacturing and labor practices have stirred equally strong emotions, forcing Knight to admit in May 1998 that "the Nike product has become synonymous with slave wages, forced overtime and arbitrary abuse." This was a distinction that Nike could do without.[33]

➤ The repackaging of Anna Kournikova. Players sometimes reform themselves, for many reasons. As he aged and his waistline expanded, George Foreman carefully revised his image from fierce to friendly. Tennis star Anna Kournikova seemed to make a parallel move in 1998 when she abruptly changed agents, from International Management Group to Advantage International. A fierce competitor, ranked number 14 in the world, Kournikova was better known for her baby doll looks and pinup poses in *Rolling Stone. Sports Illustrated* claimed that two Fortune 500 companies had "backed off deals with Kournikova because of her racy image." Advantage International president Phil de Picciotto appeared to outline the new packaging strategy when he argued that "her tennis is what makes her attractive." Time will tell whether the teenager can make the adjustment quickly enough for corporate America.[34]

➤ The competition between the ABL and WNBA. In 1997, women's professional basketball provided sport fans with two new products—the ABL and the WNBA. The league "war" revisited product battles that had dotted the sport landscape back as far as the 1880s when the American Association challenged the National League's choke-hold on big-time baseball. Issues included the following:

> *Markets and venues.* The ABL played in mid-sized markets and venues, like Columbus (Ohio) and Richmond (Virginia). The WNBA played in the big-market venues of the "parent" franchises—New York, Los Angeles, Cleveland, Phoenix.

> *Star appeal.* Both leagues pushed for star talent. The WNBA had the best-known players (Lisa Leslie, Rebecca Lobo, and Sheryl Swoopes), but the ABL grabbed eight of the 1996 Olympic team members.

> *Television.* What counted most here was NBA leverage, as the WNBA enjoyed secure television packages with NBC and ESPN while the ABL got limited exposure on BET and regional sport channels.

> *Season of play.* The ABL played in the "traditional" period (October to February) whereas the WNBA played a summer schedule.

The choices were clear, for players and fans. It was almost David against Goliath, except that David was offering higher average salaries than Goliath. And that was the rub. Without the clout of big markets and big media, the ABL strained to stay afloat with a higher payroll than its rival had. In early 1999, the ABL declared bankruptcy; however, the brief league war will be remembered for providing one of the starker product contrasts in sport history.[35]

DIFFERENTIATING SPORT PRODUCTS

The WNBA and the ABL pressed their product distinctions to the public in 1997. Gary Cavelli, the ABL's founder, hammered away at the WNBA for relegating women to secondary status with a summer season that was little more than a filler for NBA arenas. But the public didn't seem to care. If the ABL was to survive, it would not be on the basis of its playing season. As the ABL case suggests, marketers must constantly evaluate and reevaluate their products, especially as they exist in consumers' minds. Philip Kotler has defined differentiation as "the act of designing a set of meaningful differences to distinguish the company's offering from competitors' offerings." Sport products can be differentiated on the basis of any or all of the elements we have discussed. Many people, for instance, see women's basketball as more of a "team" game, requiring more precision passing, and men's basketball more of a one-on-one, above-the-rim, slam-dunk game.[36]

Marketers must use their knowledge and imagination to recognize the ways in which their products may be distinct in the consumer's mind. As a simple exercise, take a standard LPGA event compared to a standard NFL event. How are they different? Table 7.1 offers some possibilities.

The nature of the game, the way fans are framed around players, their proximity to players, and their chances of interaction with players all help to distinguish pro football from tour golf. Any and all of these could be helpful in developing surveys and promotions that might clarify important distinctions for other sport products. Marketers are limited only by their imagination.

PRODUCT DEVELOPMENT

Marketers must continuously develop the product. This may include deleting, revising, or adding any one or more of the elements that make up the comprehensive bundle of benefits. Product development includes two standard steps:

1. Generation of ideas
2. Screening of ideas, which includes refinement of the product concept, market and business analysis, development of actual product, market testing, and commercialization

An excellent example of a brilliant development strategy was the introduction by hockey's San Jose Sharks of their colors and marks in the early 1990s, largely

Table 7.1	SPORT PRODUCT DIFFERENTIATION: THE LPGA AND THE NFL	
Element	LPGA	NFL
Game form	High skill, slow pace	High skill, high pace
Framing of fans around players	Clustered around course; fans can move with players	Uniframe, determined by venue seating; little or no movement by fans
Proximity to action	Very close	Distant
Chances of exchange with players	High	Low

under the leadership of Matt Levine, long regarded as the "father of modern sport marketing." A small task force developed a list of key criteria to be used in name selection. These criteria included clarity, regional links, brevity, and graphic potential. With the name "Sharks" in the forefront of their minds, the team held a name sweepstakes to generate even more ideas, as well as interest. More than 2300 different names came in, with the name "Sharks" running second to "Blades," which was never seriously considered because of its gang implications.

With a name and an image under design, the next step was colors. Here the Sharks used a number of steps, including "bypass" interviews with 800 season-ticket depositors who rated various color schemes, and consultations with expert designers such as L.L. Bean. The final product was a raging success—teal and black colors that accentuated a cartoon-like "Sharkie" who was crunching a hockey stick. In 1992, after one year of public distribution, sales of San Jose Sharks merchandise had reached $125 million. By the end of 1994, the Sharks were the number-one seller of NHL merchandise. In the ever changing market of popular taste, however, Sharks merchandise sales drifted downward, so that by 1997, they ranked 21st in the NHL. Other teams had jumped on the Sharks' innovations and had redesigned their uniforms. By 1998, the Sharks were back at the drawing boards.[37]

Product innovations often walk a fine line between success and failure (see sidebar on Coed Sportswear on page 132). In the end, of course, it is consumers who determine the results. Theories of innovation suggest that consumers grapple with five perceptual issues as they decide whether to adopt a product innovation. These are (1) relative advantage of the new product over old preferences, (2) complexity or difficulty in adoption and use, (3) compatibility with consumer values, (4) divisibility into smaller trial portions, and (5) communicability of benefits. Researchers studying a small sample of Cleveland Cavalier fans (who had attended at least one game) in the Akron-Canton area found that all five issues came into play when the Cavs moved from the Richfield Coliseum near Akron to the new Gund Arena in downtown Cleveland:

> *Relative advantage.* The greater travel distance often outweighed the benefits of the beautiful new arena.
> *Complexity.* Issues of distance, time, parking, and safety might be too daunting.
> *Compatibility.* Of the women sampled, 91 percent said they rarely or never visited downtown Cleveland.
> *Divisibility.* Some fans could not link higher ticket prices to the benefits of a new facility.
> *Communicability.* Aggressive ad campaigns did not register with some fans; one respondent was not even aware of the new arena.

The Cavs did address these issues in the promotional campaign associated with their move, and the success of the Gund Arena supports the Cavs' move to downtown Cleveland. The research results listed, however, reinforce the virtues of careful planning for all product innovations.[38]

PRODUCT POSITION

The elements in any sport product should contribute to a coherent image; product development should not be pursued haphazardly. Further, the sport organization must get this image across to the consumer. In cases in which all elements of the product provide the same message, the image is clear and distinct. A major factor influencing the reception of this image is consumer perception. As the Cleveland Cavs study suggests, consumer perceptions may be selective and inconsistent. Just

Coed Sportswear: The Vagaries of T-Shirt Development

Dan Dumais, Marketing Director, Coed Sportswear

Coed Sportswear shot up like a meteor in the early 1990s with its irreverent "Coed Naked" line. Sales jumped from $1 million in 1991 to $24 million in 1994. But the young owners of the company, based in Newfields, New Hampshire, realized that the T-shirt business was volatile. Although the "Coed Naked" line was hot today, it would inevitably cool down. New product lines were needed. In 1995, Coed developed a new line of shirts that focused on the "emerging/fringe" market so well captured by the X Games. In 1996, the company followed up with another line, this time aimed at female athletes. Each new product was developed through a parallel process in which the company took six basic steps:

1. Recognized a market trend.

   1995—Extreme sport equipment sales were rising fast; music videos were using extreme images.

   1996—The strong team sport legacy of Title IX was projecting into the big time—in the Olympics, in pro leagues, and on television.

2. Recognized that the increase in segment participation would increase demand for segment-related goods, including imprinted apparel.

3. Researched the market to see whether the imprinted category was being addressed, contacted retailers and sales reps, attended trade shows, and did competitor shopping.

   1995—Most imprinted "extreme" apparel was very basic and simple, promoting the brand name of a hard-goods company (e.g., Burton). Shirts were bought largely in surf shops and from hard-goods suppliers.

   1996—Although there were imprinted shirts with female athlete themes, the competition was not strong, and the shirts were purchased primarily in sporting goods stores and department stores. In both years, the Coed people concluded that their creativity and track record in production, supply, and service warranted a move into the targeted segment.

4. Developed a trademark/brand name through brainstorming, trademark research, and trademark filing.

   1995—Selected "180 degrees from anywhere" mark, which the firm already owned.

   1996—Filed for "Power of a Woman" mark in the United States and Canada.

5. Developed and designed product, brainstorming ideas for images and getting feedback from target consumers and sales reps.

   1995—Obtained feedback from surfers and skaters at their points of usage.

   1996—Obtained feedback from females of all ages—some athletes, some non-athletes.

6. Launched new product line.

Coed felt good about both products when they were launched. The products were innovative and attractive. But the results were dramatically different. The "Power of a Woman" line received enormous market support, including requests that Coed develop a parallel line for girls. Coed happily developed the "Power of a Girl" line (see photo). These lines, especially the "Power of a Girl," are currently selling successfully at over 3000 retail locations nationwide. In contrast, "180 degrees from anywhere" got mediocre to poor results, leading to the discontinuation of the line. Coed's follow-up analysis uncovered four reasons for the poor reception of the "180 degrees from anywhere" shirts:

➤ Mainstream retailers/buyers were more conservative than expected in taking on "extreme" products.

➤ Many retailers/buyers felt it was too early to run "extreme" products.

➤ Extreme sport enthusiasts were committed to buying T-shirts that were tied to hard-goods brand names.

➤ Extreme sport enthusiasts did not shop in "mainstream" sporting goods and department store chains.

Coed Sportswear employs a standard development process for its T-shirt lines.

think of the prospects if the sport organization is also inconsistent in the images it sends out!

The bottom line is the product's position in the minds of the target consumers. Marketing campaigns often focus on "positioning" or "repositioning" the product in consumer minds. Positioning strategy, however, is especially tough in the sport industry, where media images are so public and where they are beyond the control of team and league marketers. Ice hockey provides a good example: What is pro hockey's core—skill or violence?

As professional hockey has expanded beyond Canada and the American "Rust Belt," the game has continually wrestled with its sense of self. For at least a century, hockey has tried to balance speed and skill with violent hitting and tight checking. What has made pro hockey different from any other sport, however, is its longtime embrace of bare-knuckle fighting. No other professional sport allows fighting with such relative impunity (a five-minute penalty). Hockey is also the fastest sport of all, in which quick moves and elusiveness still allow smaller players like Wayne Gretzky and Paul Kariya to excel. Hockey has found it hard to balance the images of bloody mayhem and graceful playmaking. In 1993, for instance, the NHL ran a $1.7 million national television ad campaign, tagged "Share the Glory": it highlighted, in the words of one NHL team executive, "what the game really is—speed, finesse, grace, and style—as opposed to the perception that we're the World Wrestling Federation of the sports world." But not all pro franchises shared this sense of the game, especially minor league teams in southern markets. In 1997, for instance, the Winston-Salem Ice Hawks filled their sales campaign with radio spots promising "the return of workingman's hockey . . . I'm talking about body-crashing, puck-screaming, helmet-cracking, gloves-dropping *American hockey.*" In 1998, the struggling New York Islanders decided that skill and grace wouldn't sell. Their sales campaign used "Fighting Without Ear Biting" as a tag line. Fans at all levels of the escalator were left to reconcile the images.[39]

The battle for positioning occurs at all levels, in all sports. In the late 1990s, two sports—horse racing and bowling—mounted multimillion-dollar campaigns to reposition their products, especially in the minds of younger consumers. Along similar lines, urban universities with NCAA Division I programs must develop strategies to distinguish their programs from the rising number of pro teams in basketball, hockey, baseball, and lacrosse. And if high school sports are to remain solvent, their administrators must emulate Novi, Michigan, athletic director John Fundukian, whose annual "Athletics Highlights" bulletin focuses attention on the distinct contributions of high school athletics to the local community. Among other things, Fundukian has emphasized statistics showing the relation between participation and academic performance.[40]

The Product-Space Map

Positioning strategies can benefit from the use of perceptual space maps, which are formed by asking consumers to rank certain product attributes. The critical attributes vary from product to product and from sport to sport, but the following example illustrates the principle (see Figure 7.2). Suppose the University of Durham wanted to conceptualize the position of its very successful women's ice hockey team in the minds of local (25-mile radius) consumers, including students at the university. The U of D women's team draws only 300 to 400 fans per game, at low prices, while the less successful men's hockey team nearly sells out every game, at triple the price. Many factors drive the attendance levels, but the athletics marketers want to get a better sense of where women's hockey fits in the minds of current and potential fans.

To do this, they would develop a survey (such as those described in chapter 5) to administer at athletic events on campus and at local malls. On the survey, they might ask consumers to indicate their levels of attendance/involvement in a number of activities, including U of D events. They also might ask consumers to indicate their perception of the *cost* (time and money) and the *excitement/action* levels in the same activities. The levels are rated on a 10-point scale. Using the results, the marketers could construct a product-space map that suggests the relative positions of these activities along the dimensions of *cost* and *excitement/action*.

The results might look like those in figure 7.2. Note that U of D women's ice hockey had an "overall" position that in the minds of area consumers reflected low cost but also low action. Respondents saw the games as more exciting than watching television, but much less exciting than high school basketball. But suppose the marketers also noticed, when they looked at the U of D women's hockey position among consumers who indicated a high interest/involvement in women's hockey, that the

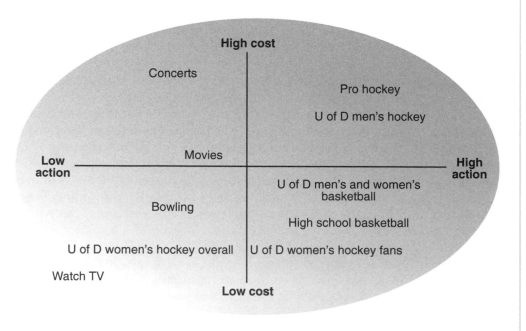

Figure 7.2
Product space map of U of D women's ice hockey.

position was dramatically different (that of "fans"). This result would be even more significant if higher interest/involvement in other activities (say bowling) didn't have the same effect on increasing perception of excitement/action. It would indicate that U of D women's hockey had real upside potential for a shift in image and position. Women's hockey might simply need more aggressive promotion of its excitement and action.

Product-space maps can also be useful in conceptualizing market segments. The U of D research might include demographic information that reveals different market segments for women's hockey. For instance, U of D students will likely perceive women's hockey as a low-cost product since their ID cards get them into all games for free. Older people outside a five-mile radius, however, may mistakenly believe that U of D women's hockey costs as much as U of D men's hockey. Here is a segment worth addressing, since research shows that women's athletics generally attract a wider age range of fans than men's athletics.[41]

Images and Marks

In the last few years, many teams and leagues have tried to reposition their products through a redesign of their logos and "marks" (the general term for images and names associated with a product). New Jersey Nets Executive Vice President for Sales and Marketing Leo Ehrline explained that redesigning marks and colors amounted to a "fresh start" for the Nets. No longer would they spend all their advertising dollars "marketing the other stars of the NBA" by running ads of Michael Jordan or Shaq. Those dollars would go to product redesign. In 1998, 50 percent of the advertising budget focused on "image-building alone." (In the wake of the 1998 lockout, the percentage would doubtless increase.)

Like the Nets, many teams have discovered that new colors, logos, and marks help attract new corporate partners and sell more merchandise. This includes both the invention and the protection of these properties. For instance, the NCAA has become more aggressive about protecting the use of the word mark "Final Four," which is trademarked for use only with the NCAA Division I men's basketball tournament. Other NCAA Championships must now develop their own marks. Some have become creative. The Division I men's and women's soccer championship committees developed a "Name the Game" promotion with Nabisco. Fans who enter the top three names will receive trips, shopping sprees, and soccer balls. "Name the Game" or "Name the Team" contests are not new, but they will get more play in a decade of greater image awareness. Companies such as SME Design and THINK New Ideas, which work with teams, leagues, and universities to reposition and redevelop images, will have a higher public profile. See chapter 8 for a more detailed examination of redesigning marks.[42]

BRANDS AND BRANDING

For many years, coaches, writers, and fans have discussed certain "brands" of play—the Notre Dame brand of football, the Montreal Canadiens brand of hockey. In recent years, the concept of "branding" has swept the sport industry. Branding is both a means and an end to product differentiation. Brands can be created or retained in the names, marks, designs, or images of any one or more of the product elements described in this chapter. Nike successfully built its overall brand (the Swoosh) as well as special product brands (Air Jordan). Phil Knight explained how Wieden & Kennedy helped to build the special image of the Nike brand that was so hot in the late 1980s and early 1990s: "They spend countless hours trying to figure out what the product is, what the message is, what the theme is, what the athletes are all about, what emotion is involved. They try to extract something that's meaningful, an honest message that is true to who we are."[43]

In the late 1990s the king of sport branding was ESPN, whose parent corporation, Disney, pushed the ESPN brand as a major weapon in its marketplace showdown with Fox and Time Warner. ESPN brand products included the following:

ESPN flagship network with its SportsCenter core

ESPN2 and ESPN News cable networks

ESPN Radio

ESPN Sports Zone Web site

ESPN Espy Awards show

ESPN magazine

ESPN CDs and video games

ESPN Zone restaurants

The successful men's and women's hockey teams at University of New Hampshire are branded together on these combined pocket schedules.

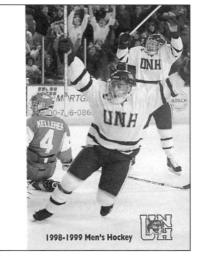

1998-1999 Women's Hockey

1998-1999 Men's Hockey

ESPN, like Nike, was very conscious about building brand equity, a crucial concept for sport marketers. On its face, brand equity is a relatively simple concept: the added value, or equity, that a certain product has by virtue of its brand name. Coca-Cola, Disney, and ESPN are good examples. Put their name or image on a product and it is worth more than a generic product of similar quality. Why? Because Coke, Disney, and ESPN have spent a great deal of time and money building brand equity.

Several components of brand equity have special interest to sport marketers, especially in events, where the "product" is usually an intangible perception or memory:

Name recognition or awareness

Strong mental/emotional associations

Perceived brand quality

Strong customer loyalty

Marketers can build brand equity through any of the various product elements. The following are some examples:

➤ *Tangible product extensions/merchandise.* This is an essential strategy for marketers of teams, events, facilities, and activities. The "Fenway Frank" hot dog is an example of a successful product extension associated with the Boston Red Sox.

➤ *Star players/coaches.* Michael Jordan is a brand unto himself, but teams often use celebrity figures in their ad campaigns. Both the New England Patriots and the New York Jets have used Bill Parcells to drive brand equity. He has paid off in both cases in season-ticket sales alone. Both the ABL and the WNBA pursued star players in order to increase their brand equity. On the other hand, the use of a single figure can be dangerous. A star player can be injured or, worse, can hold out for a better contract. A coach can be fired early in a season, which happened to Maury Wills of the Seattle Mariners just a few months after he was featured as the cover figure in the Mariners' preseason promotions.

➤ *Distinct patents/trademarks.* Nike's Swoosh.

➤ *History and tradition.* Augusta National, "The Masters," the green jacket.

➤ *Festival and spectacle.* At some venues, the halftime show or the pep band is as important to the overall product value as the game itself. The dotting of the "i" by an honored band member when the Ohio State University marching band performs its "Script Ohio," spelling out Ohio in script on the field during home football halftime shows, is a signature that contributes to Ohio State University band equity.

"Building the brand" has been the buzzword of marketing strategy in the late-1990s sport industry. There is no sign that this will change in the next decade.[44]

PRODUCT AND BRAND CYCLES

Product and brand strategies must consider various stages in the life of any product, product element, or brand. Some theorists have referred to these stages as the product life cycle, with several standard stages:

Introduction

Growth

Maturity

Decline

Other theorists have attacked the notion of a standard life cycle as an unsupported concept that, in the worst scenarios, could become a self-fulfilling prophecy whereby managers would reduce support for a product because it had reached its "decline" stage. Sport products vary in the actual shape of their developmental and life cycles. The following are speculations about sport product life cycles:

➤ Game forms that enjoy any kind of maturity seem to be resistant to decline. Baseball's popularity hit a low in the 1960s and early 1970s, rebounded in the 1980s, and now must rebound from the strike of 1994; similarly, NBA and NHL attendance have been down periodically. Both Arena Football and women's professional basketball have moved beyond the introduction stage. What will their growth curves look like? Similarly, NASCAR had a long, flat maturity. The last few years have seen a huge spike of "rejuvenation."

➤ Teams and franchises have much more volatile and unpredictable cycles than those of their overall sport. Team and franchise cycles are more subject to owner or management whims, economic downturns, and labor issues.

➤ Equipment cycles appear more technology driven than apparel cycles.

➤ Apparel cycles blend the more stable trends in game forms with wide fluctuations of fashion.

The concepts of product or brand life and competitive cycles deserve much greater attention from researchers. There may well be discernible trends of importance to practicing marketers.[45]

WRAP-UP

In this chapter, we have begun our investigation of the marketing mix, or the five Ps of sport marketing—product, price, promotion, place, and public relations. We have reviewed the features that make the sport product unique and have outlined its various components. These include the game or event and its stars, equipment and apparel, novelties and fantasies, the venue, personnel and process, the ticket, electronic and digital products, and finally the organization itself. We also discussed the intricacies of product development, including developing new products, positioning, branding, and the product life cycle.

As much as possible, products must be shaped to meet the needs and wants of the consumers targeted in prior research. In the next chapter, we look at a particularly important product area—merchandising.

ACTIVITIES

1. Investigate the Web site of your favorite sport organization. List the various product components (as discussed in this chapter) that you find on the Web site.

2. Try your hand at a new product image for the merchandise of your favorite sport organization. What are the key elements of this image that you think will make it attractive to consumers? How will you protect your product's value? Use ideas from readings (note page numbers).

3. Prepare an outline that shows at least three dimensions on which brand image differs between Nike, World Wrestling Federation, and the WNBA.

YOUR MARKETING PLAN

Briefly outline a new digital, virtual, or interactive product (not a Web site) for your organization. Create a product-space map, like the one in figure 7.2, that indicates where your product can be positioned in a competitive marketplace.

C H A P T E R

8

LICENSED AND BRANDED MERCHANDISE

OBJECTIVES

1. To understand the structure of the licensor-licensee relationship.

2. To recognize the various components of the licensing industry.

3. To understand the growth and importance of licensing for revenue generation, the development of organizational brand equity, and the promotion of fan identification.

4. To identify the impact of product styles and trends and of competition on the licensing industry.

BY DAN COVELL

Mad Hatters

Lids, a retail outlet that sells only licensed and branded headwear, has become the largest retailer of hats in the United States. Lids was created in the fall of 1992 by two college students who opened a small kiosk in a Boston-area mall. Lids has grown to over 300 stores in the United States and is looking next to expand internationally, first in Puerto Rico. Approximately 50 percent of sales are of licensed product (New Era's "Diamond Collection," the line of caps worn on the field by MLB teams, sells well during baseball season), approximately 50 percent branded (Nike, Kangol, and Stussy are top sellers). Retail sales for 1996 were $27.5 million (2 million caps annually), with projections to reach $59.4 million in 1997. This growth rate of 116.8 percent makes Lids the second fastest growing chain by sales in the United States.[1]

One of the strengths of Lids is that the company sells only hats. Another is that "We keep track of what customers want," according to a local store manager, Ken Roberts, "and that feedback goes from managers to the district office." The decisions on which products will be distributed to local stores are made by personnel in the company home office in Westwood, Massachusetts; but to keep in touch with consumers and their needs, local store managers have the autonomy to order a specific item if they feel it can be sold, and they are consulted on proposed product samples at regular sales meetings. Because of its position as the leader in headwear sales, Lids also has the ability to work closely with both branded and licensed manufacturers on designing merchandise. This arrangement gives Lids priority on the sale of new products, as well as exclusivity on certain products. The company is also considering the release of its own brand of headwear to capitalize on its leadership in the retail market, and expects the market to shift more toward branded merchandise in the future.[2]

In this chapter, we consider what licensing is and how it works for the sport organization and the licensee. We also look at recent trends in licensed-product revenues and at the licensing process for various types of sport organizations and for the manufacturers. Finally, we examine some aspects of the retail segment of the licensing industry and consider several current merchandising issues and trends.

WHAT IS A LICENSED PRODUCT?

Think of a pen, notebook, clock, lamp, or pennant that bears the name or logo of your school, or of another popular collegiate sport team, or of your favorite professional sport team. Or think of a jersey emblazoned with the name and number of your favorite player, or a jersey just like the one worn by your favorite team. These are all licensed products—not manufactured by leagues, teams, or schools, but rather by independent companies under an agreement with a sport entity.

Licensing is "a contractual method of developing and exploiting intellectual property by transferring rights of use to third parties without the transfer of ownership."[3] The "third parties" in this instance are the licensees, the companies that manufacture these products. Licensees include a wide variety of sport product companies; some are well-known firms such as apparel and sporting goods manufacturers Adidas, Nike, Converse, Reebok, and Champion. Licensed-product manufacturers also include electronics and video game manufacturers such as Electronic Arts, Nintendo, Sega, and Sony; trading card companies such as Topps and Upper Deck; and smaller, lesser-known companies like Bev Key of Canada (maker of beverage openers), Sportscast (maker of ceiling fans, lamps, and switch plate covers), and Diana Home Fashions (maker of pot holders, oven mitts, and two- and three-piece diaper sets). All these companies hold licenses to manufacture and sell products bearing the logos and marks of professional and amateur sport entities.

"Intellectual property" refers to the names and logos of sport organizations. To be claimed as property, these names and logos must be registered with the U.S. Patent and Trademark Office in Arlington, Virginia. Once this process is completed, the names and logos become trademarks of the organization. A trademark is defined under the Federal Trademark Act of 1946, commonly referred to as the Lanham Act, as "any word, name, symbol, or device or combination thereof adopted and used by a manufacturer or merchant to identify his goods and distinguish them from those manufactured or sold by others."[4] The law defines trademark infringement as the reproduction, counterfeiting, copying, or imitation in commerce of a registered mark, and bars companies that do not pay for the right to use these trademarks from manufacturing products bearing those marks. Only the owner of a mark may apply for federal registration. The application must include a drawing of the mark, a written description of the mark, identification of the goods and services for which the registration is sought, and explanation of the basis for filing.[5] Sport organizations "transfer the right of use" of their names, marks, and logos to other companies so that these companies may use them in producing products for sale.

WHAT MAKES LICENSING WORK?

Baseball historian Warren Goldstein wrote of the importance of the impact of team uniforms on fans in the late 1800s, noting that many early baseball teams (such as the Cincinnati Red Stockings) got their nicknames from their distinctive apparel and that "uniforms served as expressions of club sentiment, of fraternal feeling and pride."[6] However, Goldstein also noted that these uniforms created a sense of apartness and defined who was a player and who was not.

As identified in chapter 1, a fundamental canon of sport marketing is that the sport product is distinct from most mainstream products partly because it is intangible and experiential. Also, sport marketers understand that most sport fans and followers are highly vested consumers and are more strongly drawn to their favorite team than they are to, say, their favorite toothpaste. In addition, many fans and participants are drawn to sport because of its social aspect, and enjoy being able to build personal affiliations based on attending events, following a team, or participating in a sport or activity. It is these three factors that define the licensing industry. Since so much of what is called a sport experience is intangible, the ability to buy, display, or wear a product that attempts to capture or to rekindle a sport experience is an alluring prospect for these highly vested sport followers.

Buying a licensed product allows fans to "take the experience home" after an event; or in some cases the product is a substitute for or adjunct to experiencing an event. In addition, using, wearing, or displaying these products indicates to others that the user is a fan; thus the person exhibits support of and involvement with the sport organization and also, the user hopes, his or her affiliation with that organization. Using or displaying the product is an attempt to breach the barriers between players and fans. Fans may not be able to play like their sport heroes, but licensed products allow them in a sense to possess a hero's raiment and bask more fully in a reflected identification. Such products also allow users to transmit their affiliation to others who might share it, thereby building a sense of a social community of fans. A notable example is the fans of NASCAR, who through the display of licensed products exhibit their allegiance not only to their favorite drivers, but also to their favorite brand of car. An observer at Darlington Raceway in South Carolina recommended that a first-time attendee purchase such a licensed product before the race, as the act "will save you from having to answer, for the next three hours, the same question over and over: who's your favorite driver?"[7]

In addition, as player movement in professional sport organizations increases due to increased contractual freedoms, ownership of licensed products may serve as

This in-store advertisement is an example of New Era's point-of-sale promotion for its line of caps worn by Major League baseball teams.

a more permanent bond between organizations and fans; for as players hop from club to club, fans increasingly follow organizations rather than particular organizational personnel. The purchase and use of licensed merchandise reinforce this organizational support independent of specific team members.

The licensing process enables sport organizations that understand these marketing factors to increase revenues with very little risk; it also enables licensees to capitalize on these same factors to generate brand recognition of and interest in their products. Consider that Huffy Sports of Waukesha, Wisconsin—the NBA's exclusive recreational-use backboards licensee—sold 3 million such items with NBA team and league logos in 1996. These backboards, complete with mesh nets in matching team colors, allow the NBA to establish team and league awareness among consumers with a strong interest in basketball,[8] and also to get the word out without having to get into the backboard-manufacturing business.

How does licensing work, and how does the licensee hope to benefit? In addition to paying the licensor an initial, one-time licensing fee, licensees take on the production issues and the assumed risk by manufacturing the product; they then pay a fee to the licensor, called a "royalty," for the use of specific trademarks on specific products. Royalty fees, which generally range from 6 to 10 percent, are based on gross sales at wholesale costs.[9] (Wholesale costs are those paid by the retailer, as opposed to the price paid by consumers.) Licensees are able to use licenses to enter new markets and to boost sales of existing products by utilizing the established images and popularity of sport teams. Huffy is banking on the idea that a fan of a particular NBA team will be more likely to purchase the Huffy product, the one that has the logo and colors of that team, than the product of an unlicensed competitor. In 1998, the companies with the most licensed-product sales included Starter (with wholesale sales totaling $300 million), Pro Player ($213 million), Logo Athletic ($200 million), and New Era ($107 million).[10]

Although many licensing relationships are positive, licensing agreements are not a sure bet for manufacturers. Regardless of the sophistication and effectiveness of a sport organization's licensing program, teams that win tend to sell the most licensed merchandise. This element, on-field success, which as noted in earlier chapters the sport marketer cannot control, also serves to complicate the licensing process. Competition throughout the licensing industry is fierce. Leagues compete against leagues for fan purchases, and licensees within leagues compete against each other and against licensees from other leagues. Licensees constantly produce new products in an attempt to capture more market share, driving competitors to do likewise.

Another risk, as in any fashion-based industry, is that trends can come and go almost overnight, leaving a licensee out in the cold. What is hot today can easily be out tomorrow. In the late 1990s, MLB and its main headwear licensee, New Era, experienced a sales boom with the release of MLB team caps in alternative colors. Celebrities, star musicians and rappers, and regular fans alike donned orange New York Yankee caps, lime green Atlanta Braves caps, and gold Los Angeles Dodger caps. Other licensees quickly followed suit, with manufacturers creating similarly newly hued jerseys and jackets. Will these items find their way into the backs of closets across America, next to earth shoes and leisure suits? From the history of the fashion industry we might expect so.

Starter, formerly a major licensee for many leagues and sport organizations, has fallen on hard times because of poor product-design decisions and increased competition from companies such as Adidas and Puma that are seeking to establish their niche in the licensing market. Although Starter established itself through its licensing efforts, it lost its creative niche in product and never established a positive independent brand image. As a result of these problems, the company posted a loss of $27.8 million in 1997, with higher losses in 1998. Starter filed for chapter 11 bankruptcy protection in April 1999. However, upon hearing of Starter's fate, many other companies expressed to professional sport leagues an interest in picking up Starter's licensing agreements.[11]

Many of these same competitive components impact the retail industry as well. According to Peter McGrath, vice president of the Children's Division of national retail chain J.C. Penney, "There is a continuing love of sports in the United States, and carrying [sport] product provides a way to bring those who love sports to our stores."[12] McGrath is hoping that the passion consumers harbor for sport organizations will translate into increased sales for J.C. Penney. However, the licensed-product retail industry is just as volatile, for as companies like Lids expand and thrive, other retailers will, like Starter, wither and die.

LICENSED-PRODUCT REVENUES

Revenues from licensed-product sales have become a significant part of the sport industry in a relatively short period of time. Sutton et al. noted that winning records and seasons, as well as affiliation with other fans and the team organization, influence fans to purchase licensed products. Consequently, as noted previously, millions of consumers purchase licensed-product items to show support for and demonstrate affiliation with sport entities.[13] To counteract ever increasing expenditures such as rising player salaries, sport organizations have recently embraced these factors as they seek to prime revenue sources, and have examined their licensing efforts in order to maximize revenues. Gone are the days when sport organizations—run by owners who viewed their holdings as the hobby of a sporting gentleman and who could control player salaries—were loathe to promote the sale and use of licensed products, seeing this as a seedy commercialization of the game. In the mid-1950s, for example, New York Yankees General Manager George Weiss, who viewed Yankee garb as equivalent to "the pope's vestments," said, "Do you think I want every kid in this city walking around with a Yankee cap?"[14]

This search for increased revenues has shattered the perceptions of that era and has led sport organizations to mirror the actions of the retail clothing industry in looking to create diverse product offerings for their many potential customers. The following statistics underscore the growth of the licensed-product industry and provide evidence of effects of these actions:

> ➤ Retail sales of licensed sport products in the United States have accelerated during the 1990s: 1990, $5.3 billion; 1995, $10.4 billion; 1996, $13.8 billion.[15]

> ➤ Retail sales of sport logo clothing in the United States reached $3.03 billion in 1996, a 13 percent increase over 1995.[16]

> ➤ According to a June 1997 poll conducted by ESPN and Chilton, 51.1 percent of all sport fans had purchased sport logo clothing within the past three months.[17]

> ➤ A total of $10.9 billion was spent on collegiate, NFL, MLB, NBA, and NHL items in 1996—a 4.8 percent increase over 1995.[18]

Other factors are involved in the increased focus on the potential of the licensed-product market. As just mentioned, while some fans may want a lime green Atlanta Braves cap, others seek to express their association in more traditional or more understated ways. This has led to a diversification in product offerings to reach all fan segments. Also, because of the rising cost of attending games and events, direct experience and interaction with sport organizations—especially professional sport leagues such as the NFL, NBA, NHL, and MLB—have become increasingly less affordable for many potential fans. As more and more fans, especially younger fans and families with children (a crucial component in building a future fan base) find it financially burdensome to attend events, licensed products become a more tangible and more affordable way to build and demonstrate affiliation and association with the organization and with fellow fans.

THE LICENSING PROCESS

In this section, we consider the steps that sport organizations take in developing a licensing program. We then look at the licensing programs of the professional sport leagues (usually administered by a for-profit branch of the league), as well as those of other types of sport organizations such as the United States Olympic Committee and the smaller professional leagues.

SPORT ORGANIZATIONS

To capitalize on the benefits of licensing, the sport organization developing a licensing program needs to take several steps:

1. Conduct a trademark search. After creating affiliated marks and logos, the organization should perform a trademark search to determine whether a conflicting mark exists. To ascertain whether there is a conflict, the Patent and Trademark Office determines whether a likelihood of confusion exists (whether consumers would be likely to associate the good or service of one party with that of another as a result of the use of the marks). In order for there to be a conflict with an existing mark, the marks need not be identical, just substantially similar. Trademark searches are performed for a small fee by certain specified Patent and Trademark Depository Libraries throughout the United States. The term of a federal trademark is 10 years, with 10-year renewal terms. Between the 5th and 6th year after the date of initial registration, the registrant must file an affidavit setting forth certain information to keep the registration alive. If no affidavit is filed, the registration is canceled.[19]

2. Devise a process for screening prospective licensees.

3. Devise a process for policing the marketplace for trademark infringement.

THE APPROACH OF PROFESSIONAL SPORT LEAGUES

In professional sport leagues, licensing programs are administered by a for-profit branch of the league, generally known as the Properties Division. Properties divisions approve licensees, police trademark infringement, and distribute licensing revenues equally among league franchises. Properties divisions usually handle marketing and sponsorship efforts as well.

The NFL was the first professional league to develop a properties component, in 1963, under the leadership of then-Commissioner Alvin "Pete" Rozelle. The first licenses were granted to the Topps Company, a trading card manufacturer,[20] and Sport Specialties. David Warsaw, the founder of Sport Specialties, had worked with Chicago Bears owner George Halas in the 1930s in selling Bears merchandise, and later developed licensing agreements with the Los Angeles Dodgers and the then

Los Angeles Rams.[21] Sport Specialties, now a subsidiary of Nike, provides player sideline headwear for several NFL teams. National Football League Properties grossed over $124,000 the first year, and the league then began to expand licensing activities aggressively.[22] By the late 1970s, each NFL team's licensing share was believed to be nearly half a million dollars annually. Today, NFL Properties generates $250 million annually in sponsorship sales and licensing royalties, and has agreements with 275 licensees that generated retail sales of over $3 billion in 1997.

Major League Baseball created its properties division in 1966, although many teams that had strong local sales were reluctant to give up their licensing rights to the league. Major League Baseball has 400 licensing agreements, and in 1977 had retail sales of $2.1 billion. In addition, MLB handles associated licensing duties for minor league and Negro League properties. "Professional Baseball—The Minor Leagues" is MLB Properties' licensing program for 160 minor league clubs, with minor league retail sales reaching over $50 million dollars annually.[23] National Hockey League Enterprises began formal league-governed licensing in 1969, has agreements with 250 licensees, and generated retail sales of approximately $1 billion in 1997. National Basketball Association Properties initiated activities in 1982.[24] Major League Soccer retail sales totaled between $20 and $30 million in 1996, the league's inaugural season.

An examination of NBA Properties' licensing component provides insight into the structure of a league's licensing operations. National Basketball Association Properties has agreements with approximately 150 licensees, half of which are apparel manufacturers. Licensing operations are coordinated by a vice president and general manager of consumer products, who is responsible for overseeing four departments: sales, marketing programs, apparel licensing, and non-apparel licensing. A separate quality-control department has final approval powers over all products and graphics. The league also serves as licensing agent for the WNBA, NBC Sports, and USA Basketball. The following is an outline of the general mission of each segment:

Sales: Has responsibility for providing a liaison with retailers for sales and retail promotions; oversees shipment of products.

Marketing program: Oversees development and implementation of retail promotions, produces merchandise catalogues, and coordinates trade show activities.

Apparel licensing: Coordinates licensing agreements and designs for the following product lines: on-court and courtside authentics, headwear, youth clothing, adult clothing, activewear, outerwear.

Non-apparel licensing: Coordinates licensing agreements and designs for non-clothing product lines, including school supplies, home furnishings, electronics and video games, sporting goods, toys and games, publishing, collectibles, and trading cards.

The NBA has no set fee for royalty payments by licensees. The scale ranges from 6 percent for low-margin sporting goods to 20 percent for certain apparel items. National Basketball Association Properties retains a portion of these royalties to be reinvested in the licensing operations, but forwards most of the funds back to the clubs.[25]

League properties divisions also create mechanisms to police the marketplace for unauthorized use of marks and logos. The unauthorized use of a mark is illegal, but U.S. and international counterfeit-merchandise sales total $200 billion annually nonetheless. According to William Edwards, an assistant U.S. attorney, the maximum penalty for violating trademark rights via the sales of counterfeit merchandise is a 10-year prison term.[26] Licensors actively police the marketplace to stop the sale of unauthorized merchandise, and leagues and independent companies use internal legal departments and publicity campaigns in the mainstream media. These entities also cooperate among themselves, as demonstrated by the formation of CAPS (Coalition to Advance the Protection of Sports Logos). The coalition was formed in 1992 to conduct criminal and civil seizures of counterfeit merchandise and campaigns for stricter anticounterfeiting legislation. Since its inception, the organization has confiscated unauthorized merchandise and equipment valued in excess of $62 million.[27]

The keys to success for league-based licensing programs are as follows:

➤ Coordination of efforts among many licensees, as ownership of team trademarks by the league provides greater value to licensees (who need to go to only one source to access all league marks[28]) and provides potential product-licensing exclusivity.

➤ Increased quality control over approved merchandise.

➤ Easier national distribution of product. League programs also effectively segment the national market for licensed sport products by emphasizing the varied colors, logos, and uniforms of league teams in specific local markets.

➤ Increased and effectively coordinated enforcement of trademark infringement by nonlicensed manufacturers.

The primary criticism of league-based programs by some franchises, most notably by the NFL's Dallas Cowboys owner/general manager Jerry Jones and MLB's New York Yankees owner George Steinbrenner, is equal royalty-revenue distribution. As it is now, the top-selling clubs get the same share of revenues as the worst-selling clubs (although in the NHL, individual teams keep all money earned on their products sold within a 75-mile radius of their city).[29] These owners argue that their clubs should not be forced to subsidize less desirable properties through the equal division of sales revenues. If the sale of Cowboys merchandise accounted for 25 percent of all 1996 NFL sales,[30] Jones might argue that he should get 25 percent ($825 million) of that $3.3 billion.

Supporters of this system would counter Jones's claim by noting that one of the main reasons for the NFL's success as a league is precisely this type of revenue sharing, which is evidenced more strongly in the league's equal distribution of broadcast revenue. This allows "small-market" teams such as the Green Bay Packers to compete with Jones's Cowboys, creating a better overall product by allowing for more equitable competition. Such revenue sharing creates a better overall product—NFL football—that in the long run permits the league to demand more in overall revenue.

LICENSING PROGRAMS OF OTHER SPORT ORGANIZATIONS

Many other sport organizations, including the United States Olympic Committee (USOC) and the United States Tennis Association, also act as licensors to generate income and awareness. Section 110 of the Amateur Sports Act of 1978 grants the USOC the right to prohibit the unauthorized use of the word "olympic" for trade purposes.[31] The USOC Licensing Program returns 82.7 percent of proceeds from sales of Olympic merchandise back to athletes through funding of training programs and through athlete grants and services. Licensees of the USOC include Champion and Mattel; other licensees such as Marker, Ltd. and Duofold produced items specifically for winter sport enthusiasts to boost interest in the 1998 Winter Games in Nagano, Japan.

A major limitation of Olympic licensing is that even with the recently adopted staggered two-year cycle for the Summer and Winter Olympics, USOC-licensed products tend to sell only in and around the period of time of the games. Said the USOC's

John Krimsky: "Ultimately, the goal is to have an ongoing mass presence. There's a lot of untapped consumer segments and distribution channels. We intend to find them." Another reason for the limited interest is that some national governing bodies, such as USA Basketball, are not part of the USOC program, so licensees must contract separately with them. Additionally, local Olympic organizing committees, such as the Atlanta Centennial Olympic Committee, also operate independent licensing programs, which in 1996 outsold USOC products substantially. In response to this, the USOC and the organizing committee for the 2002 Winter Games in Salt Lake City will join forces for licensing approval and administration.[32]

LICENSING AGENCIES

Some smaller professional leagues, tournaments, and events hire independent companies to run their licensing operations. Brian P. Hakan & Associates, for example, runs licensing operations for the Arena Football League, the National Lacrosse League, the United States Figure Skating Association, the East Coast Hockey League, and Roller Hockey International. The independent companies serve as intermediaries for smaller leagues that lack the resources to maintain effective licensing operations, and work for a percentage (as high as 35 percent) of gross revenues from retail sales. These organizations operate much like league properties divisions and implement many of the same protocols.

MANUFACTURERS

In this section, we take a look at the licensing process from the manufacturer's point of view. Before manufacturing a licensed product, a company seeking to produce the product needs to adopt the following procedures:

1. Assess its marketplace to determine the consumer and retail interest in a prospective licensed product or line of products.
2. Contact potential licensors to establish licensing agreements. Under such agreements, licensees pay teams and leagues a one-time fee for the right to manufacture products bearing team and school names, nicknames, colors, and logos.

As already noted, the range of companies that hold licensing agreements with sport entities is vast and varied. Licensees with significant marketing clout and experience are looking to use sport as a promotional vehicle in many ways, such as through advertising at contests and venues, during broadcasts, and at associated events. Shoe and apparel companies such as Fila, Nike, and Adidas, which have developed strong independent brand identities, are now leveraging this strength and are breaking into the licensed-product market. Nike, after a long history of independence, recently became a licensee of the NFL, NHL, and the NBA. Nike has the obligation to provide league uniforms in exchange for the right to manufacture authentic and replica uniforms and other apparel lines in an effort to increase overall annual corporate sales to $12 billion by 2000.[33] Adidas has plans to become the next big licensee, backed by a worldwide marketing budget of $270 million.[34] Leagues are interested in the considerable marketing clout of these shoe and apparel companies, believing that these companies can help them market the league as they market their own products.

Other entities looking to expand into licensing include media conglomerates such as Time Warner and Disney. Under the credo that "sports is entertainment," Time Warner has created WB Sports, a sport apparel and footwear brand that combines the familiar Warner Brothers logo with the likenesses of famous professional athletes. The brand will be highlighted at the Warner Brothers Studio stores, which number more than 150, and will be promoted via athlete ribbon-cutting ceremonies. "Any entertainment company who wants to break into sports will have to be authentic, and create a foundation with leagues, players, or grassroots programs to give credibility to the brand," says Jeff Sofka, who heads up the program for Integrated Sport International, the independent marketing firm coordinating the project.[35] Warner Brothers understands that licensing brings a level of fan identification to its sport line that would be more difficult to establish through athlete affiliation.

In addition, licensed companies also benefit from ambush-marketing techniques. One such company is Ebbets Field Flannels, Inc. of Seattle, Washington, an apparel company founded by Jerry Cohen in 1986 that specializes in the sale and manufacture of historically accurate old-time uniforms, caps, and jackets. Cohen, who was first a fan of the game, wrote: "I used to buy baseball card sets to see the uniforms. There was something about those old flannels. Something about the way they looked." Cohen turned this interest into a merchandise business because, as he says, "to my delight, I found out other people feel the same."[36] Ebbets Field manufactures and sells licensed apparel of former Negro League teams, as well as replicas of uniforms formerly worn by current major and minor league baseball and hockey franchises. But the company's original business, which continues today, is the selling of items of defunct major and minor league and Negro League baseball and football teams, such as the Brooklyn Tip Tops, Oakland Larks, Newark Tornadoes, and Seattle Bombers, for which trademarks either never existed or have expired. Such works need not be licensed, and no royalties need be paid to trademark holders. Ebbets Field uses its ambush and official status interchangeably to sell product, thereby legitimizing the ambushing process.

However, nonlicensed "ambushing" manufacturers can realize the same brand awareness sought by licensees by entering into endorsement deals with individual athletes. Before its recent entry into the licensed market through agreements with many of the prominent North American professional leagues, Nike specialized in this approach, epitomized by its endorsement use of baseball star Ken Griffey Jr. and the "Griffey for President" advertising campaign in 1996 (see photo). Nike used Griffey Jr. in ads to project an affiliation with MLB without going through the process of obtaining a license and having to pay MLB royalties. Nike went to great lengths to define this affiliation, as some of the television ads for the "campaign" portrayed the Mariner Moose, the mascot of the Seattle Mariners (Griffey Jr.'s team), as Griffey Jr.'s running mate. In the mind of the consumer, associations such as these seem very logical. This form of "perception marketing" has long been a Nike trademark and has proven highly successful. In fact, this ad campaign was so effective that many fans actually believed Griffey Jr. was running for president. Nike has since become a licensee for MLB.

PLAYERS' UNIONS

Players' unions also administer licensing programs to increase revenues for their players and the union itself. These revenues can be a significant source of income. The same principles that boost licensing as a significant revenue source for sport organizations—making the sport product more tangible and allowing users to exhibit support for and involvement with the organization and other fans—also apply to union licensing programs. In these licensing efforts, however, players seek to create brand awareness not as much through the established recognition of and interest in team colors and logos, but more through fan identification with particular athletes or groups of athletes.

As with sport organizations whose licensed-product sales lag because of losing records, licensing linked to individual players and player groups is vulnerable to player performance, and in some cases, player behavioral factors. Since Albert

Spalding used his own playing expertise to promote his company's line of sporting goods, player-endorsed products have relied on favorable fan perceptions of player expertise to assuage consumer doubts and reinforce the decision-making process. However, just as fans might buy a sport shoe to "be like Mike," they will also be unlikely to make a purchase if they do not want to emulate or do not like an endorsing player. If a player's on-field performance or off-field behavior is suspect, this will reflect directly on the ability of that player to impact licensed-product sales. As noted in the preceding chapter, these aspects complicate the licensing process for players' unions because such factors are not controllable.

To promote the generation of additional revenues, union properties divisions not only establish licensee agreements separately from leagues, but also license jointly with leagues and share revenue with leagues for trading cards, electronics and video games, and associated memorabilia sales. The MLB Players Association was the first to enter into such an agreement, in the late 1960s, when then-Executive Director Marvin Miller entered into a two-year, $120,000 pact with Coca-Cola to permit the beverage manufacturer to put players' likenesses on bottle caps. Such royalties helped fund the emerging union's organizing activities. Miller also negotiated a comprehensive agreement with trading card manufacturer Topps Company in 1968. Topps was permitted to continue manufacturing trading

Nike's "Griffey in '96" van at the 1996 MLB All-Star Game in Philadelphia was one component of a successful ambushing campaign made by Nike.

The National Football League Players Association

Players, Inc., an organization within the National Football League Players Association (NFLPA) that has a staff of 16 headquartered in Washington, DC, represents agreements with nearly 3000 current and former NFL players and with nearly 100 licensees. Licensing activities, which generate $30 million annually, relate to traditional apparel and nonapparel items as well as special events, music and video productions, and a players' golf association. According to the NFLPA, when a player signs an NFLPA group-licensing form or assigns his group-licensing rights to the NFLPA through his NFL player contract, he gives the NFLPA the exclusive right to use his name, likeness, voice, facsimile signature, photograph, picture, and biographical information in licensed-product programs involving six or more players.[38]

Licensees also are free to act independently of union properties divisions and to negotiate separate endorsement agreements with players to wear their products and appear in ads; an example is the $200,000 deal between Logo Athletic and Dallas Cowboys quarterback Troy Aikman.[39] In 1995, the NFLPA opted to give each eligible active NFL player a royalty payment, on an equal-share basis, of 37 percent of Players, Inc. revenue. Players who participate in any program involving 35 or fewer players receive additional royalty payments on retail products sold on a national basis. There are also increased payments for players who are singly depicted in posters, special programs, point-of-sale materials, print and television ads, and packaging. Some programs involve as few as 12 players, others the entire membership.[40]

cards bearing player likenesses for double the players' previous yearly fees (from $125 to $250); the company paid the union 8 percent on annual sales up to $4 million, and 10 percent on all subsequent sales. The first year of the contract earned the MLB Players Association about $320,000.[37] Refer to the sidebar to learn about the NFL's players' association.

LICENSING IN INDIVIDUAL PROFESSIONAL SPORTS

Whereas players' unions handle the bulk of licensing agreements in professional team sports, athletes in individual professional sports, through their agents and advisors, usually handle licensing agreements on their own. While this makes it more difficult for lesser-known individuals to obtain licensing money, the potential exists (as with commercial endorsements) for highly recognizable individuals to earn significant licensing revenue over which they have more control than do most professional team sport athletes. Nowhere is this more true than for well-known drivers on the increasingly popular NASCAR racing circuit; the top drivers earn more in licensing than from their racing salaries or winnings. Dale Earnhardt, who is known as "the Michael Jordan of stock car racing" and who reportedly accounts for 40 percent of NASCAR licensing sales, recently sold his licensing company for $30 million. The company, Sports Image, Inc., has annual sales of close to $50 million. Earnhardt retained royalty rights from future sales. The most popular products for NASCAR licensees include apparel, die-cast cars, and trading cards.[41]

COLLEGIATE LICENSING

In 1924, sportswriter Francis Wallace noted that while walking down New York City's Fifth Avenue, one could spy in the shops displays in the colors of Notre Dame, Army, Yale, Harvard, and Princeton—and walking up Broadway one could see "neckties advertised in the colors of the same schools—the aristocracy of the gridiron."[42] This early example of ambush marketing indicates that even then, retailers understood that fan identification with sport organizations could increase sales. Formalized licensing agreements were slow to emerge, although in 1947 Walt Disney agreed to let the University of Oregon use Disney's Donald Duck image for its mascot.[43] From these embryonic beginnings, the collegiate licensing industry was born. It has since grown into an industry that takes in a billion dollars annually.

The University of California-Los Angeles (UCLA) is generally considered the first school to enter into a licensing agreement with a manufacturer: its bookstore granted a license to a watch manufacturer in 1973. The NCAA formed its properties division to license championship merchandise in 1975, but does not administer licensing programs for member schools. The NCAA earned $17.2 million in royalties in 1997-1998.[44]

Collegiate licensed-product sales to retailers have a couple of distinct strengths. First, the selling season is longer, as colleges field different teams each season and do not experience the off-season down periods that professional leagues do. Additionally, the regional product diversification and coverage are greater, as college athletic programs exist everywhere throughout the country, not just in select cities with a large population base. In most regions, such as the Southeast, collegiate products sell well all year-round; for example, Garnet and Gold, a retail outlet dedicated to selling only Florida State University merchandise, has four stores in Tallahassee alone.[45]

KEY POINTS IN COLLEGIATE LICENSING

After many years of unrestricted use of the sport logos and trademarks of educational institutions by manufacturers and retailers, schools began to register their trademarks, which prevented companies from using them without paying royalties. In 1982, several schools challenged the notion that school marks belonged in the public domain when the University of Pittsburgh, Ohio State University, DePaul University, and UCLA sued Champion Products for using their marks without permission. According to Alexander, in the case of *University of Pittsburgh v. Champion Products, Inc.*, the university failed to show that Champion owed it retroactive payments for the sale of products, but the sides settled out of court to assure future royalty agreements.[46]

Significant revenue growth began in the late 1980s. Although collegiate athletic programs do not have the player salary concerns of other sport organizations, other expenditures and decreasing institutional funding—along with the pressure to make each athletic department financially self-sufficient—have motivated collegiate athletic departments to capitalize on the vested interests of their fans to increase licensing revenues. Nearly 300 schools now have established licensing programs. Except in certain circumstances, institutional licensing revenue is retained in institutional general funds.

TO JOIN OR NOT TO JOIN?

According to Mazzeo et al., 41 percent of Division IA schools, including Notre Dame, Southern California, Ohio State, and Texas, administer their own licensing programs.[47] The remainder of Division IA schools give independent licensing agencies the authority to run these programs. The benefit of self-maintenance is that schools can retain a greater portion of sales revenues. However, a 1993 study showed that nearly half of all independent college licensing directors spent less than 10 percent of their time on licensing issues—which underscores the fact that these schools are far from realizing their full licensing-revenue potential.[48]

The remainder of Division IA and IAA schools, like smaller pro leagues, enlist the services of independent licensing companies to manage their programs. These independent organizations also administer the licensing programs of several Division I conferences and football bowl games. The major companies are the Collegiate Licensing Company (CLC), which acts on behalf of nearly 160 colleges and universities, as well as collegiate bowls and conferences; Licensing Resource Group; and the Black College Licensing Company, founded in 1991 as a subsidiary of the Drew Pearson Companies, serving traditionally African American colleges with their licensing programs. These companies are paid a portion of the royalties (usually 50 percent) as their administrative fee. For the school, the advantages of using an independent licensing company include the greater opportunity for national distribution of products, exposure to a greater number of licensees, increased expertise in sales and design, and broader trademark enforcement protection, along with the ability to keep departmental expenses low. Kelley of CLC puts it this way: "We have a knowledge of what's going on in the industry as a whole, the strengths of individual schools and conferences. A new company may be looking to get a license from UConn and St. John's in the Northeast, but could also sell their product in other areas as well. Each area has an environment of its own. We know the segments of the market."[49]

As discussed in the sidebar, CLC handles clients such as Alabama, Arizona, Brigham Young, Connecticut, Duke, Illinois, Maryland, Nebraska, Penn State, Tulane, Big XII Conference, Nokia Sugar Bowl, Jerry Tarkanian, and NCAA Championships. Some Licensing Resource Group clients are Arizona State, Kansas, Northwestern, Providence, the U.S. Naval Academy, and Washington State.

SELLING YOUR SOLES

Footwear companies that also manufacture apparel (or have agreements with apparel manufacturers) have begun to look to highly visible Division IA athletic departments to serve as marketing vehicles. These companies, including FILA, Nike,

The Collegiate Licensing Company

In lieu of a professional sport league model that would supply a higher degree of licensing standardization and organization,[50] CLC has become the most significant force in collegiate licensing. Headquartered in Atlanta, the company was founded in 1983 by Bill Battle, who had first established licensing agreements with Paul "Bear" Bryant, the longtime University of Alabama head football coach, in 1981. The company has 50 full-time employees, and company operations are divided into four departments:

Accounting—Accounts for and allocates all monies on behalf of CLC.

Legal and Enforcement—Enforces trademark rights of member schools, registers marks, and approves contracts.

Licensing Administration—Handles quality control, artwork approval, product approval, renewals, and customer service for manufacturers. Licensing coordinators handle specific manufacturers based on the type of product produced.

Marketing—Conducts activities through four divisions:

➤ Promotions/Special Products—Handles promotional licensing and attracting new business.

➤ Public Relations—Disseminates information to the industry via press releases, newsletters, brochures, and advertisements.

➤ Retail Marketing—Works with retailers and manufacturers to develop local, regional, and national promotions and programs to assist retailers in marketing products and attracting customers.

➤ University Services—Handles the day-to-day management of each school account. Assists with local enforcement issues and the development of school-based marketing programs.[51]

The CLC also has joined forces with Players, Inc. for the creation of the jointly licensed "Heroes of the Gridiron" program. Because NCAA restrictions do not permit schools to use the pictures and likenesses of current players to sell merchandise, this program presents products featuring current NFL players in conjunction with their collegiate institutions. Such efforts between organizations, referred to as "cross-licensing," allow two or more organizations to benefit from the ability to reach shared markets and to increase fan identification. In this case, the program can help boost visibility for Players, Inc. and union members in areas that have no local NFL team,[52] and can also help CLC and its membership expand product line and related revenues (see photo).

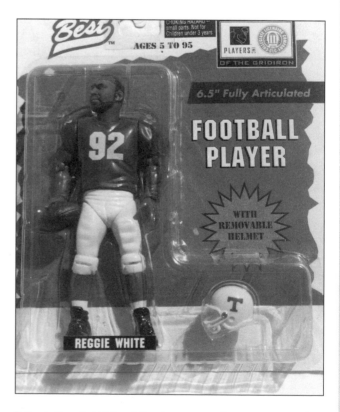

Best's Reggie White doll in University of Tennessee regalia is a clear example of cross-licensing.

Reebok, and Converse, have made their mark in the collegiate licensing world via institution-wide shoe and apparel contracts.

Two examples of this type of agreement involve Nike and two prominent Division IA schools. In 1997, Nike inked separate agreements with the University of North Carolina and the University of Colorado. North Carolina will receive $7.1 million and equipment and apparel through 2001, including a $400,000 annual donation to the chancellor's academic enhancement fund, and $200,000 a year to be shared for one men's and one women's basketball tour. Nike receives licensed-apparel sales and advertising rights, eight season tickets each for football and men's and women's basketball, and tickets to postseason tournaments and bowl games.[53]

That same year, Nike and the University of Colorado agreed to a six-year, $6 million equipment and apparel contract, which will also pay the school more money based on the football team's performance. If the football team wins the Big XII Conference title, the university earns an additional $10,000; if the team wins the national title, it gets another $100,000. A men's basketball national title would earn the university $200,000, a women's national title $50,000. Nike receives licensed-apparel sales and advertising rights, as well as permission to redesign the university's logo. Said Colorado Athletic Director Dick Tharp: "You don't sell your integrity or the university's in making a deal [but] you can, in fact, balance the opportunity of gaining sponsorship and taking advantage of the dollars involved without selling the soul of the institution."[54]

Although licensors have quality control over the images on licensed products, they do not control all operations of the licensees. Licensees, as independent businesses, conduct their business as they see fit. Nike has received significant negative publicity for its business practices in Vietnam, where local managers treated workers harshly and made them run laps around factories if they were found wearing non-Nike products.[55] While Nike—as the industry leader—has borne the brunt of public criticisms for such actions and certainly cannot be excused for these draconian measures, the fact remains that nearly every clothing and footwear manufacturer that assembles products outside the United States (and free from U.S. labor laws) is guilty of some degree of improper labor exploitation, ranging from using child labor to paying (by U.S. standards) paltry wages.

It is not uncommon for these widespread questionable industry practices of licensees to reflect poorly on licensors as well. Colleges and universities are especially susceptible to this sort of scrutiny, given the heightened politicization of educational communities and institutional educational missions, which are occasionally intensified by a school's religious affiliation. When the University of Wisconsin made public its licensing agreement with Reebok, certain personnel at the university questioned Reebok's business practices and labor relations with Southeast Asian manufacturers, claiming that Reebok shoe assemblers in Indonesia received only $2.45 per day. Some took the position stated in a petition circulated by a group of professors: "If the University of Wisconsin advertises a firm like Reebok, it accepts the conditions under which Reebok profits." The agreement also contained a clause stating that university employees would not disparage Reebok; but after a campus outcry, the clause was omitted from the contract.[56]

In response to this sort of criticism, many schools have published a code of conduct for all licensees. Notre Dame, affiliated with the Congregatio a Sancta Cruce order of the Roman Catholic Church and particularly susceptible to such criticisms given its combined status as a religious institution and a perennial football power, has composed this type of code. The code states that the school is "committed to conducting its business affairs in a socially responsible manner consistent with its religious and educational mission" and stipulates that licensees must meet the university's stated standards for legal and environmental compliance, ethical principles, and employment practices.[57]

RETAIL

The retail segment of the licensing industry is big business; sales at sporting goods and licensed-product outlet stores totaled $1.5 billion in 1996.[58] It may surprise some to learn that in 1997, while the highest-profile demographic for sport fans is males ages 18 to 45, females own as much sport apparel as males, and 40 percent of all sport apparel dollars were spent on women's apparel (compared to 36 percent on men's and 24 percent on children's).[59]

In response to these trends, the NFL and NBA are experimenting actively with product trials in attempting to develop strategic, controlled growth that moves away from a unisex look and toward products specifically designed for women. The NBA is using the WNBA as a vehicle to promote licensed products for women, primarily with the on-court merchandise manufactured by Champion,[60] as well as to extend the selling season of NBA-associated merchandise to a year-round calendar (as the WNBA plays only from June to August).

To help generate sales, the retailers, licensors, and licensees are continuing to create new and innovative products, stores, and selling methods. The following are some tips for licensing retailers:

Stock a variety of team- and player-identified items. Mark Sage, director and group manager of sales for NBA Properties, recommends that for optimum sales, retailers should seek to "create a mix of local and key nationally popular team- and player-identified items."[61]

Recognize the appeal of sideline apparel. Jim Connelly of the NFL commented, "You can't walk down the street looking like Joe Torre, in pinstripes, and you can't walk down the street in Armani, like [New York Knicks head coach] Jeff Van Gundy, unless you're rich, but you can wear exactly what [Green Bay Packers head coach] Ray Rhodes wears on the sidelines."[62] This perspective also underscores the importance of fan identification in driving the sales of licensed products.

Target youth. According to Tom O'Grady, NBA Properties creative director, "Kids are a little bit less worried about the performance of the team [than adults] and more into fashion."[63] Targeting youth also serves to establish the future fan base of a sport organization; and youth are a group that are less likely to be able to afford the increasingly expensive main sport organization product, the event itself.

Maintain a good mix of products. The recommended mix of products includes

- ➤ authentics (sideline/courtside merchandise, regular and alternate uniforms)—especially those for children and infants and toddlers;
- ➤ embroidered fleece;
- ➤ fashion outerwear (such as reversible jackets); and
- ➤ windbreakers

Cultivate the seasonal approach. Leagues should work with retailers to gear associated promotional efforts to coincide with the opening of regular-season league play, as well as holidays and back-to-school purchase windows. The NFL has created strong marketing programs targeted toward specific segments of the NFL fan base to prod sales (including "Pledge Allegiance," "Feel the Power," and "Play Football") with a corresponding emphasis on merchandise sales, as well as nearly 200 retail promotional efforts. The Play Football campaign promotes youth participation; its tie-ins with merchandise and retail promotions are scheduled during the high-volume back-to-school (June to September) and Christmas purchase times. "Punt, Pass and Kick," a football skills competition for children, also helps the NFL attract youth consumers.

Continue developing specialty stores and purchasing areas. Specialty outlets and space allocations are used to reinforce brand awareness and affiliation for licensees, licensors, and retailers. Firms like Jon Greenberg and Associates, serving as design consultants, assist in constructing such areas for retailers like Bradley's Major League Clubhouse Stores, Bob's Stores, and the Finish Line—the latter a retail chain dedicated to sport footwear and branded merchandise sales (see photo).[64]

CURRENT MERCHANDISING ISSUES AND TRENDS

As noted earlier, the industry has enjoyed robust growth over the past decade, with sales nearly doubling since 1990. Manufacturers, particularly of apparel, found that they could increase earnings by expanding and diversifying merchandise offerings. The increased number of retail stores that sell only licensed merchandise (estimated at 450 stores in 1997) and collectibles has served to create additional retail outlets for this merchandise and to promote additional growth in this area. Retail expansion has had an especially significant impact in collegiate licensing product distribution. Until the early 1980s, roughly 80 percent of collegiate sales took place in college bookstores. Today, that figure has dropped to 20 percent.[65]

Finish Line stores, found in many malls, specialize in sport footwear and branded merchandise.

However, the growth trend has slowed recently. Overall sales increased by only 1.5 percent in 1994, fell slightly in 1995, and recovered in 1996 and 1997 to post modest gains over 1994 figures. See table 8.1 for a summary of the growth of licensed-product sales (in billions) from 1993 to 1997.

Some of the reasons for the sales plateau include recent and continued professional-league labor strife. Such friction, specifically the 1994 player strike in MLB and subsequent cancellation of postseason play, the threatened union decertification in the NBA in 1995 and the subsequent lockout of players by NBA owners in 1998-1999, and a similar player lockout by NHL management in 1995, have served to dampen fan enthusiasm about professional sport. This in turn negatively impacts purchasing of licensed merchandise.

Sluggish recent growth can also be attributed to the extended period of rising sales from 1990 to 1995, which resulted in an oversupply of product with too many licensed vendors trying to push too much merchandise to too many retail outlets. This led to an oversupply of inventory and in turn smaller purchases by retailers. The increased competition for retail sales and floor space from major branded sport product manufacturers, larger fashion brands (such as Nautica and Calvin Klein), and smaller fashion manufacturers (such as No Fear, Mossimo, and Stussy) has also cut into licensed sales. The NFL has proven to be the most resilient during this market contraction, with 1996 sales of $3.3 billion topping its 1995 mark of $3.15 billion. The NFL has not had significant labor unrest within the last decade, and has fought the retail slumps experienced by other leagues by streamlining its base of licensees and retaining its strongest companies.

Table 8.1	U.S. RETAIL LICENSED-PRODUCT SALES (IN BILLIONS)				
League	1993	1994	1995	1996	1997
MLB	$2.4	$2.5	$1.7	$1.8	$1.9
NBA	$2.1	$2.5	$2.6	$2.6	$2.6
NFL	$2.6	$3.0	$3.15	$3.1	$3.0
NHL	$ .8	$1.0	$1.0	$1.0	$1.2

Taken from the May/June 1997 issue of *Team Licensing Business*. Refer to note 66.

Other concerns of retailers include similarity in distribution of products among retail outlets, the overdevelopment of new products, and complaints that licensees meet the orders of large retailers before meeting those of smaller specialty stores. The advent of new leagues, such as Major League Soccer, has served to create additional sales but is further crowding an already packed market.

THE ADVENT OF BRANDED APPAREL

Items that carry only the logo and marks of the manufacturer are referred to as branded products. The popularity of branded products has grown substantially in recent years, and this has cut into the demand for licensed products. Joe Gately of the retail chain FootAction USA offers this perspective: "Our licensing business is shrinking in terms of percent of total over the last few years. Right now, we only carry licensed products in about 60 percent of our stores due to poor category performance and space limitations."[67]

There are several reasons for the growth in popularity of branded apparel. High-profile companies such as Nike have made their mark, so to speak, based on their efforts to foster strong sport consumer identification not with a particular team, sport, or athlete (Michael Jordan notwithstanding), but rather with what sport consumers perceive the company itself to stand for. Through its creative and innovative advertising and product development, Nike, much like a professional team, has developed a significant base of followers who identify with the image that Nike has chosen to promote—a culture of athletic excellence based on individual performance and participation.

The success of Nike in this area has given rise to many imitators, mostly apparel and shoe companies looking to cash in using the Nike model. This has served to reinforce the market for branded merchandise through intercompany competition and has made the notion of wearing (and swearing allegiance to) a brand rather than a team socially acceptable to sport consumers. This shift in identification and purchasing has enabled apparel and shoe manufacturers with established brand identities of their own (independent of licensing agreements) to sell their own branded products independent of licensed marks. These firms include established fashion apparel companies such as Tommy Hilfiger, David Chu, Liz Claiborne, Donna Karan, and Ralph Lauren, but also some, such as Champion, Adidas, and Reebok, that have substantial investments in the licensed market.

Brand marketing has become a significant source of focus for these companies. Some maintain a commitment to licensing; but Roberto Mueller, former president of Reebok and head of his own marketing company, sees it another way: "A company that is just in sports licensing simply can't compete in terms of brand recognition with Nike and Reebok."[68] A heavy reliance on licensing can be risky for manufacturers, as we have noted in discussing the recent sales plateau. Because of these risks, many companies have sought to develop strong brand identification for their own products without a connection to other sport organizations. For example, Starter's reliance on licensing served to limit the company's sales in the competitive apparel market and contributed to its demise.

As companies switch their focus from licensed to branded merchandise to establish their own brand identities rather than using licensed marks and logos for that purpose, licensors may see reductions in fees and royalties.

INTERNATIONAL SALES

As noted in chapter 1, marketers in sport organizations have an advantage over their mainstream counterparts because of the universal appeal of sport. As sales figures continue to indicate that domestic markets have less potential for growth, licensors and licensees alike are looking toward international markets. This focus has become sharper as trade barriers continue to fall across the globe, making international trade and distribution easier than ever. Foreign exhibition and regular-season games have been used successfully to prompt local interest in league merchandise. Major League Baseball opened its MLB Clubhouse Shop in Tokyo in 1996[69] to build on the emergence of Japanese players in the United States. The San Diego Padres, who played regular-season games in Monterrey, Mexico, in 1997 and 1999, opened a retail store in Tijuana[70] to capitalize on increased interest and purchasing power of nearby Mexican residents. The NFL has utilized NFL Europe, arrangements with the Canadian Football League, and exhibition games in Japan, Mexico, and Europe to further its sales and brand awareness.

The NHL, with its large percentage of European players and a first-ever two-week midseason break to allow league players to participate in Olympic competition in Nagano in 1998, has sought to actively leverage this in combination with the USOC, the NHL Players Association, and USA Hockey. Adapting the league's "Coolest Game" theme in the "Coolest Game in Nagano" program, NHL Enterprises has gained permission from the USOC to use the Olympic rings in sales and promotions, and will market the program to both domestic and international consumers.[71] This cross-licensing effort expands the reach of both organizations.

National Hockey League Enterprises categorizes its European consumers into two segments. One group is Scandinavian, composed of Finns and Swedes who follow native players and their current teams; among this group the Maple Leafs and Flyers sell best. The other is the rest of Europe, where sales are motivated by fashion. Ducks, Blackhawks, Penguins, Sharks, and Kings merchandise is most popular in this segment.[72]

United States licensed-product manufacturers are purchasing foreign companies not only to market their products overseas, but also to capitalize on the growth in sales of indigenous licensed products. Russell Corporation's purchase of Dutch and British firms allowed it to make use of those companies' established product-distribution lines in Europe, to produce Russell products to capitalize on locally popular sports, and to cultivate stronger relationships with European retailers.[73]

NEW AND REDESIGNED LOGOS, MARKS, AND UNIFORMS

In 1991, the NHL's San Jose Sharks became that league's top seller for licensed merchandise, yet the team hadn't played a single game. The team's distinctive logo, depicting a shark biting through a hockey stick, combined with the then-innovative teal and black color scheme, served as a collective epiphany to the licensing industry: new and innovative can sell. Soon thereafter, the NHL's Anaheim Mighty Ducks introduced their Disney-designed mark, described by Ducks marketing staff member Bob Scichli as "a combination between Jason from *Friday the Thirteenth* and Donald Duck."[74] Although as already noted, teams that win tend to sell the most merchandise, a number of teams, leagues, colleges, and manufacturers realized that sales could be boosted through logo introduction and redesign, uniform redesign and diversification, and secondary and commemorative logos and marks. Subsequently, in a 32-month period (January 1995-August 1997), nearly 25 major league teams unveiled significantly redesigned logos and uniforms (almost 25 percent of all clubs in the four major leagues), including the Anaheim Angels, Denver Broncos, Golden State Warriors (see both old and new logos on page 158), and Vancouver Canucks. The introduction of alternate logos and uniform components—such as a third jersey and home, road, and alternate hats—has also served to increase sales. All new and redesigned logos and marks must have final approval by the creative departments of league properties divisions.

The fact that the new MLB expansion teams (the Arizona Diamondbacks and the Tampa Bay Devil Rays) have not enjoyed the rousing success that the Sharks and the Mighty Ducks experienced may indicate that their color schemes (which both include black and teal, as well as purple and other accent colors) have lost their original panache. The difference in success may also point to other factors: the newness of the Sharks' and the Mighty Ducks' looks in relation to the majority of logos and marks at the time of introduction, the inability of any new product to register that same level of retail verve, and also the general cooling in the overall licensed-product market.

Many minor league baseball teams have also discovered the power of the new or redesigned logo. In 1994-1995 alone, 139 clubs changed their logo, nickname, or both.[75] Clubs such as the Portland (Maine) Sea Dogs (the Class AA Eastern League affiliate of the Florida Marlins), the Lansing (Michigan) Lugnuts (the Class A Midwest League affiliate of the Chicago Cubs), the Chattanooga (Tennessee) Lookouts (the Cincinnati Reds' Class AA Southern League affiliate), and the Rancho Cucamonga (California) Quakes (the San Diego Padres' Class A affiliate in the California League) all enjoy high national sales and distribution because of innovative logos and color schemes. The Wichita (Kansas) Wranglers (the Kansas City Royals' AA Texas League entry) redesigned in October 1994, with assistance from MLB's creative division. The club then sold $15,000 worth of new-logo merchandise over the Christmas season, 10 times what it had done during the previous holiday period. Minor league clubs generally get a royalty of 9 percent on sales from licensees, with New Era Company, the official cap manufacturer for MLB, the largest licensee.[76]

There have been cases of consumer backlash against these new looks, however, as the New York Islanders discovered in 1995 when they dropped their original logo and uniforms for a new look that featured a slicker-clad sailor grasping the helm of a ship. Surprisingly, new marks and color schemes are often not tested through consumer research, so initial negative responses are quite common. Both opposition and Islander fans who either disliked the new look, or had an emotional connection with the old (which harkened back to the team's Stanley Cup victories in the 1980s), publicly mocked the logo with "We want fish sticks" chants at Islander games—connecting the sailor with the logo of Gorton's, a processed food company that specializes in packaged frozen fish dinners. The club resurrected the original logo for the 1997-1998 season. In 1997, fans of the venerable Montreal Canadiens franchise were disturbed to learn that their club planned to introduce a third jersey and alter a uniform look that had remained essentially the same since 1916. In response, Dave Haney, the NHL Enterprises staffer responsible for the third-jersey program, stated that creation of any new design "requires a certain responsibility for Original Six teams, their marketability is their tradition."[77]

Many colleges and universities have also undergone image changes through uniform redesign. Iowa State, Maryland, UCLA, Utah State, St. John's, Virginia, and Villanova are among the schools that have seen licensing revenues jump after significant logo redesigns, with accompanying uniform changes for high-visibility sports like football and men's and women's basketball. (See the new St. John's and Villanova logos on page 159.) After the release of its redesigned logo in 1994, Villanova saw its licensing profits jump to $200,000 annually, although some schools (as in the case of the Islanders) also suffer from student, alumnus, and consumer

The old logo (top) for the Golden State Warriors was significantly updated along with numerous other teams' logos in the 32 months between January 1995 and August 1997.

backlash when a new logo or mascot is introduced. This occurred when Lehigh University in Pennsylvania changed from the "Engineers" (a tribute to the school's traditionally strong engineering and science programs) to the Mountain Hawks. Said one student: "I haven't bought any Mountain Hawks stuff, and I don't plan to." At American University, students criticized school administrators for instituting a design change without any student consultation or input.[78]

This boom in the industry has also led to the development of design firms that specialize in sport logo and mark redesign. As the licensed-product market has expanded and diversified, sport entities now look to utilize numerous logos and marks, referred to as a "family." Because most sport organizations have little expertise in visual design, they turn to design companies to create and render logos and marks for them. Sean Michael Edwards Design (SMED), Inc. of New York City has carved its niche in the industry by specializing in working with professional and collegiate sport entities to create new and innovative logos and trademarks. The company charges between $40,000 and $100,000 to create a comprehensive family of primary and secondary marks and logos. In the case of Villanova University, the school's athletic department sought SMED's help to update its image and attract a younger demographic to its merchandise, and was looking to boost its annual licensing revenues from $35,000 to $200,000.[80] Sean Michael Edwards has also formed a partnership with CLC to allow CLC-aligned schools access to SMED resources. When schools consult with CLC about a possible redesign, CLC refers the school to SMED. One pitfall of utilizing a company that has created multiple logos and marks is that many of the looks tend to be similar, robbing a sport property of the ability to stand out in an increasingly crowded and competitive marketplace.

The new logos for Villanova and St. John's were designed by Sean Michael Edwards design.

The Tampa Bay Buccaneers Redesign

In 1996, the Tampa Bay Buccaneers finished with a record of 6-10—the 14th consecutive losing campaign since a 5-4 finish during the strike-shortened 1982 season. The franchise, initially owned by local millionaire Hugh Culverhouse, began play in the NFL in 1976 and didn't win a game until near the end of its second full season. The Bucs (or the "Yucs," a well-earned epithet coined after years of futility) had become the NFL's synonym for ineptitude. The team color scheme (primary color, orange; secondary color, red) and logo (a dandyish befeathered pirate with a knife clenched gingerly between his teeth) embodied the franchise's feebleness. Hugh Culverhouse's wife had chosen the color scheme and logo before the team began play in 1976. The design weaknesses, coupled with the team's consistently poor on-field performance, left Bucs merchandise sales perennially at the

bottom of the NFL licensed-product standings (28th in 1996).

The Bucs' marketing staff long held to the party line that the design was fine; the team just needed to win. But after Malcolm Glazier took over as owner in 1995, and after years of losses and lost revenue due to poor sales, a new design and color scheme were introduced in the 1997 season. The Bucs trashed the old look in favor of two new primary colors (pewter and red), the addition of black as a secondary color, and the relegation of orange to secondary status. Gone also is the Erroll Flynn look-alike in favor of a red flag with skull and crossbones. In keeping with the redesign trend, a family of marks and secondary logos was also introduced.

Said one longtime Bucs fan: "I didn't like the orange I'm not sure about the new colors, but I think they needed a new start." Said Bucs coach Tony Dungy: "I think its great for the fans [but] Hall of Fame players help make uniforms look good."[79]

For the Buccaneers, the changing of logos and colors brought no risk. No positive associations were attached to their former scheme. However, teams that change looks just to prime licensed-product sales must consider carefully how fans will react to the removal of the visual symbols to which they may be strongly attached.

WRAP-UP

Licensed-product merchandise has become a significant part of today's sport marketplace. Sport entities seeking to maximize revenues must understand fully the potential impact a strong licensing program can make. For sport marketers, licensed-product sales are an integral way for fans to demonstrate their affiliation with a sport entity; they also provide an excellent vehicle through which the sport entity can create an unpaid method of advertising. Nothing speaks more clearly about a person's emotional connection with a team than his or her desire to become affiliated with that team. Clothing styles are a transmitted code that can impart meanings of identity, gender, status, and sexuality.[81] Licensed-product apparel communicates at each of these levels. Men and women who love sport, but who are not big, fast, or strong enough to participate on the field or court, can bond with their team and its players through licensed products. "I may not be good enough to play in the big-time," a fan reasons, "but I can buy an authentic jersey with the name of my favorite player." This is as close as many of us will ever get.

ACTIVITIES

1. What advantages does licensing provide to sport entities? To licensees?

2. Describe the steps involved in the licensing process. What are the components of licensing agreements?

3. If you were a collegiate athletic director, would you opt for an independent licensing program, or would you enlist the services of a licensing company? Why?

4. Describe the difference between a licensed and a branded product. What recent trends have affected the sales for each?

5. What are some of the reasons that sport entities choose to redesign logos and color schemes? What are the risks involved in these decisions?

C H A P T E R

9

PRICING
STRATEGIES

OBJECTIVES

1. To understand core issues of price versus cost, price and value, and the setting of pricing objectives.

2. To understand the four main pricing practices used in the sport industry.

3. To recognize the special factors that influence any pricing strategy.

"Prices Send Gallery Gods to the Penalty Box"

When Bobby Orr led Boston's "Big, Bad Bruins" to the Stanley Cup in 1970, the celebration may have been loudest in Boston Garden's upper balcony, the home of the famous "Gallery Gods." As vocal as they were knowledgeable, the Gallery Gods represented the everyday, working-class fan. Orr's winning goal was payback for 29 years of loyal, Cup-less rooting, often for cellar-dwelling teams. Unfortunately, loyalty became an endangered ethos when professional sport entered the age of free agents and corporate suits. Higher payrolls for players and administrators meant only one thing—higher ticket prices—especially in pro hockey, which lacked a strong national television package. By 1998, Bruins ticket prices in the new Fleet Center were the highest in the NHL. The cheapest price for an "upper-bowl" seat was $24, on a season basis. The same seat on a single-game basis cost $29. In the "lower bowl," where the elevation didn't induce nosebleeds, the seats were $60 per game.

The higher prices meant fewer Gallery Gods like Roger Naples, a 77-year-old Bruins die-hard. After the price hike, the 780 remaining Gallery Gods pooled their money into 300 season tickets. In effect, escalating prices had shoved some of the most committed Bruins fans down the escalator of involvement. Higher prices and a few mediocre teams drove attendance levels well below capacity, to about 15,000 per game in the 17,565-seat Fleet Center. The season-ticket base dropped 30 percent, from about 16,000 in 1995-1996 to around 10,500 in 1997-1998.

In April 1998, the Bruins announced a dramatic $9.50 (39.5 percent) decrease in prices for 7500 upper-bowl seats. Not all prices went down, however; 5000 lower-bowl seats went up by $5 (8.3 percent). The "Robin Hood" strategy sat well with Roger Naples, who offered a common reaction: "Hey, they're the rich people. Take it from them. . . . Lemme tell ya, it was the best move they ever made. . . . I think you'll see a lot of the Gods come back and buy seats again." Matt Brennan, Bruins director of ticket operations, corroborated Naples's common sense. "Generally speaking," said Brennan, "it's gone over very well. One of the nice things is, some of the people who dropped their season tickets . . . they're coming back." Roger Naples figured that the average guy could now go to three or four games per year instead of one, maybe even taking "a couple of kids." The frivolous fan might even splurge on a "$2.50 hot dog or a $4.75 beer." That is where Roger Naples drew the line. "Not me," he swore. "At those prices, I have my beer after the game."[1]

Roger Naples understood some fundamental principles in pricing sports. For one thing, while price drives consumer perceptions of product value, consumers also have limits on total costs. For another, marketers must be very clear on the objectives of their pricing strategy. The Bruins made a clear statement with their 1998 "Robin Hood" strategy. They were also responding to supply and demand.

In this chapter, we consider the notion of market demand. We also outline traditional pricing strategies such as break-even, cost-plus, and their variants. Finally, we consider special factors in sport pricing such as penetration and skimming, lead time, user-segmentation pricing, time- and place-segmentation pricing, and the role of pricing in public relations and promotions.

THE BASICS OF PRICING

Marketers must recognize the vast range of product elements that requires pricing. In the sport world, these include the following:

- Hard or soft goods (equipment or apparel)
- Tickets
- Memberships
- Concessions
- Information (magazine, cable subscriptions)
- Signage

Marketers must consider the location of signage when determining price.

These elements are priced according to a range of variables, including location, image, and time.

Price is a critical element in the marketing mix, for a number of reasons. First, price can be most readily changed. Second, in certain market conditions (specifically, where demand is elastic), it is one of the most effective tools. Third, price is highly visible; hence changes are easily communicated, resulting in possible changes in consumer perceptions. Finally, price is never far from the consumer's mind.

CORE ISSUES

The core issues in any pricing situation are cost, value, and objectives. Remember our central equation:

Satisfaction = Benefit – Cost

Cost is the most visible and often most compelling part of the equation. In a recent survey, female golfers listed the following factors (by percentage) as "important" in decisions about purchasing equipment:

PRICE	76 percent
VALUE	54 percent
BRAND REPUTATION	29 percent
SELECTION VARIETY	27 percent
SERVICE	17 percent

This is probably not far from the results one would get from Roger Naples and the other Gallery Gods as they consider ticket purchases. Price, as we said, is never far from the consumer's mind.[2]

COST VERSUS PRICE

As Roger Naples recognized, the price of a ticket does not represent the real "cost" of attendance, which would include travel, parking, and concessions (that is, if Roger buys a hot dog and a beer at the game). The difference between a marketer's sense of "price" and a consumer's sense of "cost" holds true in most forms of sport involvement. For instance, the real "cost" of golfing includes at least the following:

- Purchase or rental of clubs, bag, and shoes
- Balls, tees, glove
- Cart (pull or ride)
- Greens fees
- Travel
- "19th hole"

Golfers might pay a range of prices for these elements according to certain values, for example:

- Tee time availability
- Course difficulty
- Aesthetic appeal

Skiers face even greater total costs for their experience. For instance, the Michigan Ski Industries Association estimated that in the 1994-1995 season, the average adult skier spent $114.60 per day, in the following proportions:

RETAIL	26 percent
ENTERTAINMENT	10 percent
LODGING	18 percent
TRANSPORTATION	9 percent
TICKETS	17 percent
SKI RENTAL	4 percent
FOOD	14 percent
LESSONS	2 percent

The obvious point is that marketers must appreciate total "cost" from the consumer's perspective, which often includes elements priced by three or four different providers.[3]

In the team sport industry, this approach to cost was first championed by Team Marketing Report, a leading industry newsletter. Since 1991, Team Marketing Report has tracked the "Fan Cost Index" (FCI) for every team in MLB, the NBA, the NFL, and the NHL. The FCI includes the following price elements for a family of four:

- Four "average-price" tickets
- Two small draft beers
- Four small soft drinks
- Four hot dogs
- Parking for one car
- Two game programs
- Two adult-size caps

In 1997, for example, the NHL average FCI was $228.39. The Pittsburgh Penguins had the highest average ticket price ($53.87), but ranked fifth in the FCI at $267.47. The Boston Bruins, second on average ticket price ($53.56), took the cake for highest FCI at $295.25. The Edmonton Oilers had the lowest average ticket ($25.50) and the lowest FCI ($150.40). The NHL average ticket was $40.64.[4]

Team Marketing Report's annual "Fan Cost Index"—now widely distributed via other publications such as USA Today—has been an invaluable service to fans and marketers alike, even if some teams have objected to the formula. In 1997, for instance, the Boston Red Sox distributed a one-page press release claiming that the FCI (the Red Sox ranked second in MLB) did not factor in stadium size, availability of parking, cost of living, or special discounts. According to the Red Sox, if you took only the price of the best 33,871 seats (Fenway Park's capacity) in each MLB stadium, the Red Sox would look much better. *Team Marketing Report* Editor Sean Brenner responded that this argument entirely missed the point of the FCI, which is meant to be a relative measure. Fans will make up their own minds about the cost of living, availability of parking, and number of seats. After all, Fenway Park's coziness and limited seating can also increase demand for tickets. Other leagues and media outlets have adopted the logic of the FCI—ticket prices alone do not tell an accurate story.[5]

VALUE AND PRICE

A higher price—or higher total cost—is not a categorical evil to consumers. Consumers often perceive a higher price to indicate higher quality; conversely, lower prices often suggest lower quality. This seems especially true with hard goods like sports equipment. But the relationship is extensive. In 1996, for example, CBS/Fox Sports Marketing reported on consumer research into the optimum pricing of sport videos. The ideal price point was $14.98. Consumers were hesitant to pay more. On the other hand, consumers felt that lower prices reflected lower quality.[6]

Numerous teams and leagues have learned the hard way about the price-value relationship. The Women's Professional Basketball League (WBL) failed for many reasons, but price/value was one of them. For the WBL, the NBA was an obvious basis of comparison. The WBL marketers clearly wanted to avoid a price so low as to suggest an inferior product, yet the WBL's fan demographics, facilities, and low product recognition precluded prices near the NBA range. They found themselves in a Catch-22. Low prices suggested low quality, which reinforced low prices, which . . . ad infinitum.

As collegiate women's programs have grown in stature, they have correctly begun to charge admission to events that had been free. Fans have discovered quickly that women's sports are worth the ticket price. These perceptions are critical to the marketing effort. Women's programs have become more aggressive about equating their prices (and total fan costs) to particular values, such as accessible and articulate athletes who enjoy higher graduation rates than their male counterparts. To many fans, this is a value worth paying for.

Consumer perceptions somehow link price (and total cost) with value. Marketers must recognize this and attempt to explain the connection. Product values may include these elements:

Convenience

Aesthetics

Cleanliness, comfort, security

Availability

Durability

These are just a few of the elements of value. Like total costs, value lives in the mind of the consumer. It is the marketer's job to understand consumer perceptions of cost and value and to price accordingly.[7]

PRICING OBJECTIVES

While sport marketers must consider consumer perceptions of cost and value, they must also consider their organization's objectives when setting product prices. Depending on the nature of the organization (private versus public, profit versus nonprofit), the marketer may be influenced by some of the following examples of objectives:

- Efficient use of resources (personnel, space)
- Fairness (consumers' ability to pay)
- Maximum participation opportunities
- Positive user attitudes/image
- Maximum product exposure and distribution
- Profits
- Survival

The push and pull of various objectives can lead to interesting pricing schemes. In the fall of 1997, for example, club seats for the NHL's Washington Caps and the NBA's Washington Wizards had a ticket face value of $48. This seemed like odd arithmetic, since club seats were sold only on a season basis, at $3500 apiece: $3500 divided by 41 games should equal $85.37 for each ticket, not $48. The *Washington Post* quickly discovered the most probable objective behind the pricing. If the new MCI Center—home to the Caps and the Wizards—hoped to market the club seats to corporations and lobbyists, the face value of the ticket could not exceed the U.S. Senate's $49.99 limit on gifts to senators or their staffers![8]

STANDARD APPROACHES TO PRICING

There are several standard approaches to pricing that operate to varying degrees in the sport industry. In most cases, a common set of factors comes into play. These factors include the following:[9]

- ➤ Production costs.
- ➤ Market conditions—namely, the supply and demand for a product that will, to some extent, define the market price. This relates to the consumer's sense of product value, the levels of product brand equity, and the availability of alternatives.
- ➤ Competitors' prices—not just of similar products, but also of any other products competing for the same consumer dollar (e.g., movies or a few drinks in a bar might well compete with an evening at a baseball game).
- ➤ Organizational objectives, including profit and distribution targets.
- ➤ Product or event frequency—MLB tickets cost less than NFL tickets in large part because MLB teams play 81 home games whereas NFL teams play 10.

BREAK-EVEN ANALYSIS

There are two main elements of cost: fixed costs (FC) and variable costs (VC). Fixed costs, often referred to as overhead, consist of fundamentals such as stadium rental, taxes, and office equipment. Variable costs vary with output and include costs such as wages, material costs, and cost of food and drinks at concessions. An example of a break-even analysis for production and sale of soccer balls unfolds as follows given that FC + VC (per unit quantity produced) equals total cost (TC):[10]

XYZ Soccer Ball Manufacturers have the following cost:

$$FC = \$100,000$$

$$VC = \$11.50 \text{ per ball}$$

$$TC = FC + VC \text{ (per unit quantity produced)}$$

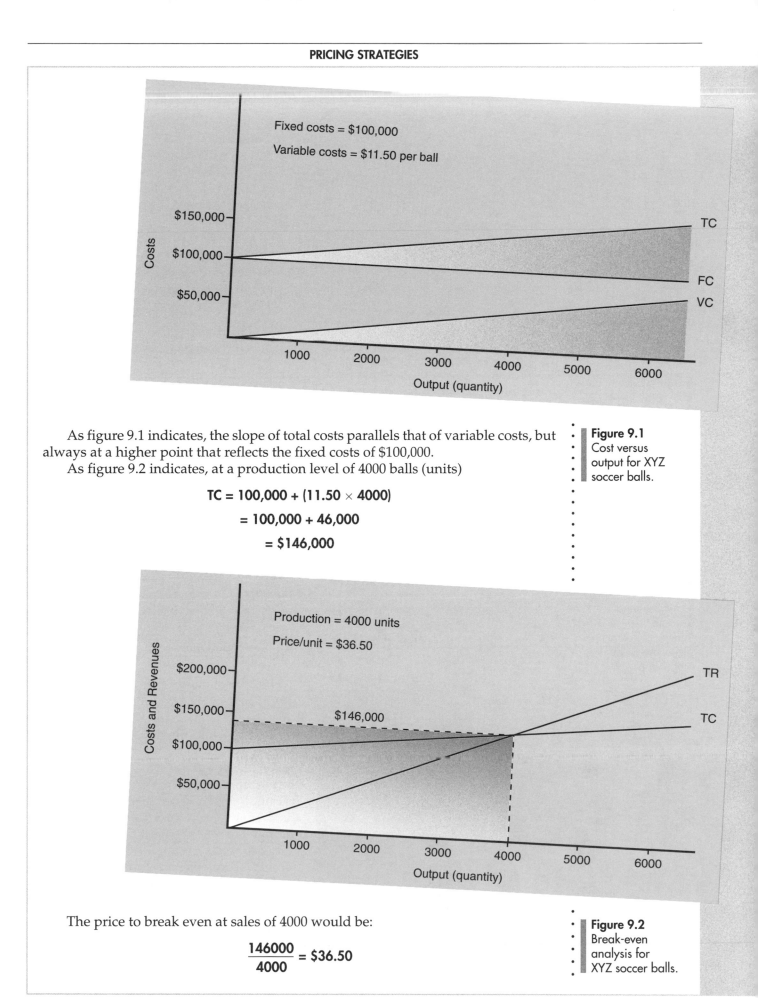

As figure 9.1 indicates, the slope of total costs parallels that of variable costs, but always at a higher point that reflects the fixed costs of $100,000.

As figure 9.2 indicates, at a production level of 4000 balls (units)

TC = 100,000 + (11.50 × 4000)

= 100,000 + 46,000

= $146,000

Figure 9.1
Cost versus output for XYZ soccer balls.

The price to break even at sales of 4000 would be:

$$\frac{146000}{4000} = \$36.50$$

Figure 9.2
Break-even analysis for XYZ soccer balls.

Although most firms will not price their product at just a break-even level, the analysis is instructive in several key areas.

First, as shown in figure 9.3, fixed cost per ball decreases as output increases (i.e., overhead allocated to each ball decreases as more balls are produced).

A second key concept in a break-even analysis is that of *contribution* (toward paying off fixed costs). The contribution margin equals the selling price (SP) in excess of variable costs per unit.

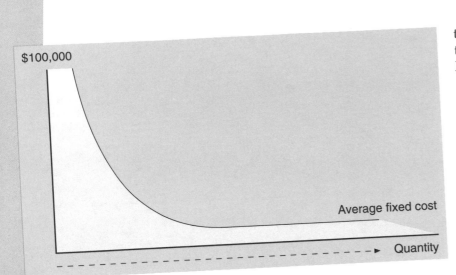

Figure 9.3 Average fixed cost per ball.

During off-peak hours, a fitness club manager would be wise to lower prices to encourage attendance.

$$\text{Contribution} = \text{SP} - \text{VC}$$

From our previous example for XYZ Soccer Ball Manufacturers, we can determine the contribution for each ball sold as follows:

$$\text{SP} = \$36.50$$

$$\text{VC} = \$11.50$$

$$\text{Contribution} = \$25.00$$

This analysis tells us how much each ball is *contributing* toward paying off the *overhead* of operating the ball-manufacturing business. Contribution also provides an easy way to calculate the break-even point. The break-even point is the point at which all fixed costs associated with producing a product are covered through sales of the product.

$$\text{Break-Even Point} = \frac{\text{FC}}{\text{Contribution}}$$

$$\text{FC} = 100,000$$

$$\text{Break-Even Point} = \frac{\$100,000}{25} = 4000 \text{ units}$$

The importance of break-even analysis to sport marketers lies in the implications it has for off-peak pricing in court clubs, health clubs, hockey rinks, and the like. During off-peak hours, when courts would remain idle at full price, a manager should charge anything above variable cost. Pricing slow periods in this manner allows the manager to soak up overhead costs through the receipt of additional revenues that otherwise would not have been received. The business could not remain in operation for the long run if all time periods were priced in this manner, but any contribution to overhead is good policy as long as people do not begin to switch from more costly peak hours.

Publicly sponsored sport programs often price their services using a variant of break-even pricing. In this case, on the philosophy that fixed costs (especially fields and facilities) are paid for by taxpayers, programmers will try to recapture only variable costs. An example is the Smallville Recreation Department's two-week summer camp. The camp is run on Smallville's existing fields and facilities. Therefore, the price must cover the variable costs of

> counselors, lifeguards, and other program leaders, plus any fringe benefits (at 25 percent of wages); and

> supplies and materials used to run the programs (balls, transportation, snacks, shirts).

If the camp accommodates 80 youth and if safety policies call for a total of six personnel, the variable costs might look like this:

(a) 6 leaders at $7 per hour × 6 hours per day × 10 days = $2520

(b) Fringe benefits = 25 percent of (a) = $630

(c) Supplies = $1600

Total variable costs = $4750

With 80 campers, the price would be $4750 ÷ 80 = $59+ per camper.

If the Smallville Recreation Department budget is in a squeeze, the programmers may be forced to recapture some of their overhead costs as they price the camp. This would contribute to the costs of overall administration, facilities, and maintenance. In this case, the department may decide to recapture for overhead 10 percent of variable costs. Continuing our scenario, total costs would be increased by 10 percent, or by $475. Therefore the price per camper would be

$$\frac{\$4750}{80} + \frac{\$475}{80} = \$5225 = \$65 \text{ per camper}$$

Although the philosophy and objectives of the public program require slight adjustments, the pricing principles are the same as for the XYZ Soccer Ball Manufacturers.[11]

In the soccer ball example, variable costs are represented as having a constant increase as output increases. Due to economies and diseconomies of scale, the actual situation does not conform to this simplistic model, but rather looks more like the model in figure 9.4.

Economies of scale often accrue from such things as bulk-rate discounts on materials or higher attendance levels that result in more efficient use of stadium personnel. Diseconomies of scale can occur when an organization becomes so large that communication breaks down or personnel become overloaded. This results in a less efficient, more costly operation.

In figure 9.4, the profit maximization point exists at the point where the largest gap occurs between total

Figure 9.4
Realistic break-even analysis. TR = total revenue; TC = total cost; VC = variable costs; FC = fixed costs.

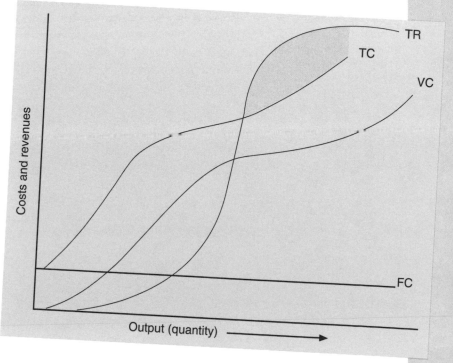

revenue (TR) and total cost (TC). The following chart continues the XYZ Soccer Ball Manufacturers example:

Soccer Ball Units Produced	FC ($)	VC ($ Per Ball)
0-10,000	100,000	10
10,001-19,999	100,000	8

9000 produced: TC = $100,000 + $90,000 = $190,000

9001 produced: TC = $100,000 + $90,010 = $190,010

The additional cost of producing one unit is defined as the marginal cost (MC), which in this example is $10. Similarly, the change in revenue (marginal revenue, MR) can be calculated. Not surprisingly, the change in revenue at any level of sales will be exactly equal to the selling price. Therefore:

MC = VC per unit for the last unit produced

MR = selling price (SP) of last unit sold

Marginal revenue tells us how much additional (extra) revenue we receive from the last unit sold. Marginal cost tells us how much additional (extra) cost we have incurred by producing that last unit sold.

Given that fixed costs, by definition, do not change with output, variable-cost changes (marginal cost) are the only cost changes we experience when we change production output levels (up to existing capacity levels). Hence:

MR – MC = change in profits, or

MR – MC = marginal profit (MP)

It should be obvious, then, that at any sales level the marginal revenue (selling price) less the marginal cost (variable cost) will be the contribution. As we pay off overhead we approach breakeven. Hence, we contribute to breakeven and to profits and reduce the amount of loss. Once all overheads are covered, we break even (at this point, contribution equals overheads).

Beyond the break-even point, each unit sold contributes (adds) to profit. If the straight-line break-even analysis were true, we would add to profit ad infinitum. Of course, it is not true. Instead, we find that in order to sell more of a product, we usually have to drop price. Hence, marginal revenue decreases. In figure 9.5, the plotted line called the marginal revenue curve is sloping downward. This is actually the demand curve for the product. Similarly, the marginal cost curve drops to show economies of scale, but eventually rises to show diseconomies of scale. Hence the marginal cost curve is U-shaped.

As long as marginal revenue is greater than marginal cost, the producer is adding to profit. As soon as marginal cost is greater than marginal revenue, the producer detracts from profit. Thus, as figure 9.5 shows, the point of maximum profit (profit maximization) is the point at which marginal cost equals marginal revenue, because all possible additions to profit have been made.[12]

Figure 9.5
Profit maximization point. TR = total revenue; TC = total cost; MC = marginal cost; MR = marginal revenue.

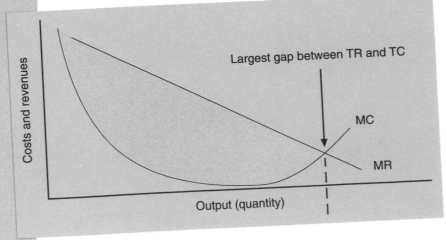

Largest gap between TR and TC

MC

MR

Costs and revenues

Output (quantity)

COST-PLUS PRICING

The cost-plus method of pricing is also common in the sport industry. This method uses the following simple formula: costs plus a desired profit equal price. In order for this system to be effective, accurate information on both fixed and variable costs must be available.

To illustrate this method we can use an example involving the concessions operation of an intercollegiate athletics program. Suppose the director decides to run her overall concessions pricing on a cost plus 40 percent basis. She might begin with hot dogs, a fast selling item, and mark them up by 100 percent. Thus, hot dogs will sell for twice their cost. Markups may vary for other products—cola at 400 percent, programs at 200 percent, novelties at 10 percent, and so on—so that the total return is 40 percent.

Athletic clubs may use a form of cost-plus pricing to determine member fees. In this case the manager carefully estimates the total fixed and operating costs to support the desired number of members. For example, Club X projects 900 members, and its management estimates total costs for one year to be $500,000. To maintain a profit margin of $100,000, which requires an overall revenue target of $600,000, the club will have to charge as follows:

$$\frac{\$600,000}{900} = \$666 \text{ per member}$$

This fee, of course represents an average. Tennis members may pay more than fitness-only members; individuals will pay less than families; pay-as-you-go members may pay more or less than members who pay monthly dues, depending on their club usage. Thus management will have pricing flexibility as long as membership fees average out to $666.[13]

Break-even analysis, cost-plus analysis, and their variations are valuable tools for the sport marketer. At the least, they can provide some baselines against which to develop pricing strategies. Further, the same concepts may be helpful in pricing sponsorships. A sponsor might be asked to pay for the total cost of an event, the variable costs, or the break-even cost difference between revenues and expenses.[14]

WHAT THE MARKET WILL BEAR

The most common approach to pricing sport products is to take "what the market will bear." This approach is largely based on experience and comparisons. The Boston Bruins, for instance, will learn from their repricing experience. Other hockey clubs may also consider the Bruins example if they move to bigger, more modern venues. The "market" approach to pricing can result in radical adjustments, especially when one is pricing new products or when a team suffers a losing streak. Some examples:

➤ After signing Tiger Woods to a lucrative contract, Nike hoped that a "Nike Tiger Woods" line of golf shoes would replicate the success of Air Jordan basketball shoes—high demand and high prices. They were wrong. The market did not support the new shoes, which bore a price tag of $225. By fall 1998, Nike introduced a second line of Tiger Woods shoes, with a new price of $160. Golfweek magazine claimed that the price reduction was a "direct response to retailer and consumer outrage."[15]

➤ In the 1980s, the Seattle Seahawks had 55,000 season-ticket holders. The waiting list was 30,000. Heady times for any franchise—except that the high proportion of season tickets meant that few people could begin at the low end of the escalator. Worse yet, the high demand provided no incentives, and shortsighted marketing saw only a gravy train or a "deep well" (see sidebar on permanent seat licenses). By 1996, poor field performance and arrogant ownership pushed season-ticket sales down to 37,000. To fill the empty seats, the Seahawks began to offer more $10 seats.

Pricing based on what the market will bear represents the dominant approach among sport teams—from high school to the pros.[16]

CAPITATION PRICING

Capitation pricing—or offering a price "per head" or per person—is a concept that some fitness clubs have borrowed from the health care providers they target for group rates. Capitation pricing is typically used on a group basis. A good example is the one-year contract signed in 1995 between Albuquerque's New Mexico Sports

Permanent Seat Licenses: A Recent "Deep Well" for Sport Managers

Ever since baseball became an avowedly capitalist enterprise, with the founding of the National League in 1876, sport managers have looked to discover "deep wells" of revenue, including the following:

Tickets

Concessions

Stadium signage

Radio and television rights

Expansion-franchise fees

Public subsidies for stadiums

A casual look at history suggests that managers and owners have pumped each well as dry as possible—with higher prices and fees—and then have continued to search for new ones. In 1968, the Dallas Cowboys (quite appropriately) discovered a deep well as they developed a financing package for their new stadium. They floated bonded seat options, priced between $300 and $1000, that gave the bondholder first rights to buy Cowboy season tickets. This appears to have been the first time that a team required fans to pay a fee for the right to buy a ticket. College football programs grabbed the idea in the 1980s with priority-seating plans. Under this arrangement, season tickets in the most desirable sections of the stadium (often between the 40-yard lines) were available only to friends or boosters who donated money to the athletics department.

In the mid-1990s, the frenzy to attract or retain NFL franchises spawned a related deep well called the permanent or personal seat license—the PSL. Like its Texas Stadium forebear, the PSL was an instrument of stadium financing. The NFL's Carolina Panthers, using a strategy developed by Max Muhleman for the Charlotte Hornets of the NBA, built their new $247.7 million Charlotte stadium with $90 million from PSLs. They promoted PSLs as necessary to build a stadium that would attract an NFL franchise. With a range of PSL prices and an effective publicity campaign, the Panthers succeeded in tapping a well without alienating their market of fans. Others have not been so successful. The Oakland Raiders attempted to sell personal seat licenses that had a 10-year life, after which the Raiders would sell them again. This plan resulted in low sales and heavy criticism for the Raiders, who already suffered from a greedy image.

The PSL (whether "permanent" or "personal") has become a fixture in stadium and arena deals. Offering a new price challenge to team owners and managers, PSLs clearly present a new "cost" to the fan. Some analysts fear that owners will become reckless in forcing this new "well tap" on ticket holders in old stadiums. In the summer of 1998, the *Wall Street Journal* described an "uproar" over PSLs that they predicted would lead to "angry fans and empty seats."[17]

and Wellness Centers and the 150-employee New Mexico Heart Institute. The contract gave all the Institute employees a "membership" at a total cost that equaled the price of 33 individual memberships. This bulk rate meant a capitation of $10 per employee, which created a high perceived value for the New Mexico Heart Institute. At the same time, the New Mexico Sports and Wellness Centers estimated that only 22 percent (or 33) of the 150 employees would actually use their facilities. While the actual number of regular users turned out to be 40, the capitation represented only a modest "group" discount that, in turn, created a bulk-revenue stream. Capitation may be a useful approach for any sport organization seeking to maximize use of a seatless facility—a museum or a hall of fame, for example.[18]

SPECIAL FACTORS

There are several additional factors to consider in pricing, regardless of which approach one employs. These include market demand, lead time, user segmentation, "smoothing," and the actions of competitors.

MARKET DEMAND

In pricing strategies, economic market conditions play an essential role, whether one is pricing equipment, club memberships, or tickets (something ticket scalpers know better than anyone, as shown in the sidebar on page 174). The concept underlying economics and price setting is elasticity of demand. Note the following formula:

$$\text{Elasticity of demand} = \frac{\text{Percentage change in quantity demanded}}{\text{Percentage change in price}}$$

This concept is a measure of how sensitive a market is to price change. An inelastic demand occurs when a given percentage change in price results in a smaller percentage change in quantity. An elastic demand exists when a given percentage change in price results in a larger percentage change in quantity. Unitary demand exists when a given percentage change in price results in an equal percentage change in quantity. Figure 9.6 details this concept graphically.[19]

With the inelastic curve, as we can see, a price increase of $2.00, or 33 percent, leads to a decrease in quantity demanded of only 3.2 percent (from 6200 to 6000 attendees). It is obvious that a manager here can increase prices and revenues at the same time. In fact, that is one way of looking at inelastic demand. Changes in revenue will parallel changes in price, in either direction. The opposite would be true with an elastic curve. Here the same 33 percent price increase would result in a reduction of attendees from 12,000 to 6000—a 50 percent decrease. With unitary demand, the price rise would be equaled by the percentage reduction in attendance, 33 percent, resulting in no change in revenues.

In the sport industry, we are faced with a constantly changing demand curve that includes elastic, inelastic, and unitary components. Figure 9.7 on page 174 illustrates how this curve might potentially look.

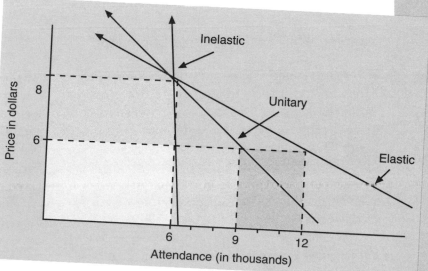

Figure 9.6 Elasticity of demand.

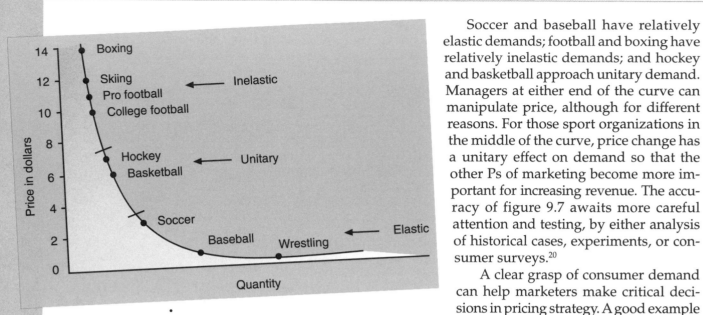

Figure 9.7
The spectator sport industry demand curve.

Soccer and baseball have relatively elastic demands; football and boxing have relatively inelastic demands; and hockey and basketball approach unitary demand. Managers at either end of the curve can manipulate price, although for different reasons. For those sport organizations in the middle of the curve, price change has a unitary effect on demand so that the other Ps of marketing become more important for increasing revenue. The accuracy of figure 9.7 awaits more careful attention and testing, by either analysis of historical cases, experiments, or consumer surveys.[20]

A clear grasp of consumer demand can help marketers make critical decisions in pricing strategy. A good example is the choice between penetration and skim pricing. *Penetration pricing* is pricing in the lower range of expected prices, in the belief that an elastic market exists and that the lower price will increase the quantity purchased. *Skim pricing* is pricing high in the expected range of prices, in the belief that demand is price inelastic. In this case, the higher price charged will generate more revenue. Goods may also be priced above skim price. These are overpriced luxury or prestige products. Goods priced below penetration price are classified as salvage or bargain priced and can be perceived as cheap. Sometimes a good is overproduced and then must be dumped at such bargain prices.

Scalping: The "Last Bastion of Capitalism"

Ticket brokers and scalpers may be the purest practitioners of market pricing. As a recent article in *Sports Illustrated* suggests, "ticket guys" (as scalpers call themselves) have enjoyed a wider market as sport events have grown in status. A $275 face-value Super Bowl ticket can sell on the street for as high as $1350. A four-day badge to the Masters can fetch over $2000. As one "broker" puts it, face value is "a meaningless term."

Of course, in an enterprise as speculative as trying to guess the value of next year's orange crop, there are no surefire winners. When a team starts losing, ticket values can drop faster than television ratings. Take the Washington Redskins. With a decade of play-off appearances from 1982 to 1992, the Redskins built a huge demand for seats; as of 1998, they still had 40,000 people on a waiting list for season tickets. But a move to a new stadium with 25,000 more seats, coupled with several dismal years on the field, left ticket brokers and scalpers watching their investments drip onto the sidewalks in front of Jack Kent Cooke Stadium. A club-level seat for the November 1998 game against the Philadelphia Eagles had a face value of $125. It was selling on game day for $60.

There is actually a governing body of ticket speculators, the National Association of Ticket Brokers, that claims to have 200 members. Whether working as a broker out of an office or as a scalper hawking on the streets, such "ticket guys" buy and sell blocks of tickets with a hopeful eye on higher demand at the right time. The laws on ticket speculation and scalping vary from state to state, so some ticket guys must keep one eye on the police while the other eye is on the ever shifting market of supply and demand.[21]

Because price is synonymous with value, managers do not like to lower prices or let fans in free because this may act to cheapen the product's image. In place of lowering price, most sport marketers will use non-price promotions such as bat nights, cap days, or jacket nights, or entertainment events like postgame fireworks, to attract additional consumers. These promotions act to lower in the consumer's mind the perceived cost of an event while not cheapening the product image by reducing the ticket price.

The pricing of product extensions (souvenirs, concessions, parking, etc.) is also very important in the sport area because of their large impact on profitability. Very often, visible extensions such as hot dogs and beer will be occasionally discounted. The discounts are aimed at increasing the volume of these products so that overall profitability is increased. It is also believed that sales of other items will increase in this situation.

LEAD TIME

In pricing sports, another important factor to be considered is the lead time required for purchase. The average amount of time between ticket purchase and the date of the event typically decreases as the price for the event decreases. This means that an event like an MLB game sees much higher day-of-game sales and impulse buying because ticket prices per game in MLB are lower than, for instance, those for an NBA basketball game. The use of a toll-free number to purchase tickets has been proven very effective in reaching these last-minute-decision consumers in circumstances in which impulse buying is heavy. Day-of-game advertising also becomes more effective in this situation. As we will also discuss in chapter 14, direct sales via Web sites has helped to reduce the lead-time effect as well.

Improving ease of purchase can be one way of offsetting some of the impact of price increases. For instance, in the late 1980s, the hockey program at the University of Illinois at Chicago enjoyed a one-year, 56 percent increase in average attendance that management attributed in part to allowing customers to charge tickets to their credit cards.[22]

USER SEGMENTATION

The concept of user segmentation is a valuable one in sport pricing. Based on his extensive experience in spectator sports, Matt Levine argued some years ago that corporate season-ticket holders, group-ticket purchasers, and single- or repeat-purchase patrons each have different reactions to price increases. Corporate season-ticket holders, said Levine, "are not significantly influenced by orderly and reasoned price increases as long as preferential seating is assured." Group purchasers typically have preset price ranges in mind before pursuing tickets. As Levine cautioned, "*Be* in that range or be *out* of the group business." Single- or repeat-purchase patrons are the most susceptible to defection because of price increases.[23]

As Levine noted, groups are a special user segment, and they are quite hotly pursued by sport marketers today. Encouraging groups is a particularly effective way of attracting new consumers. Typically marketers will reduce ticket prices according to the size of the group. Thus a football program might offer group discounts in the $10 ticket section as follows:

$10	single ticket	$8	51-100 tickets
$9	20-50 tickets	$7	100+ tickets

While group discounts are sound policy, it is not wise to offer such discounts in the most expensive ticket zone. Patrons who pay the top prices expect a degree of exclusivity.[24]

College athletic programs typically employ a basic user-segmentation pricing strategy in their reduced prices for student tickets. Here, the successful programs trade off potential revenue for fervent and boisterous student support. Typically, from 10 to 20+ percent of stadium seats are sold to students at a discount, often representing a significant loss in potential gate receipts.[25]

In a similar fashion, public recreation agencies will often segment users, and user fees, on the basis of ability to pay. Thus senior, low-income, or nonprofit groups will pay less than higher-income or commercial groups. Typically, children enjoy lower charges at recreation facilities, which is a standard practice in need of closer thought. In fact, children often cost more to service in terms of supervision and damages.[26]

Athletic clubs have become more sensitive to user segments in their pricing strategies. This has led to "unbundling," or breaking a full-time, full-service membership into packages of restricted access, such as Monday-Wednesday-Friday only. This may be the best vehicle for attracting older people, families, and "deconditioned" defectors who do not want to invest high monthly full-service dues for facilities they may not get around to using. In this case, clubs may have to trade off secure cash flow for market expansion.[27]

Sport teams unbundled their season tickets in the 1980s with mini-plans that targeted user segments between the single-game consumer and the season-ticket holder. Rarely does one find a drastic and bare choice between the full-season and the single-game ticket. Except in pro football, wide-ranging menus are the order of the day. This is especially true in baseball: baseball fans can typically purchase plans for a full season, a half season, a set of midweek nights, or a set of weekends or can buy the increasingly popular "Flex book" of coupons redeemable for any combination of available tickets. In 1998, the mini-plan was alive and well, especially in baseball. For instance, the San Francisco Giants expected to sell about 15,000 "six packs"—six games for the price of five, with the bonus game a clash with the Dodgers. The Giants built their mini-plan on research showing that about one third of their fans came from outside the metropolitan Bay Area. Said Giants Vice President of Communications Bob Rose: "This stretches out people who usually do two or three games a year."[28]

TIME AND PLACE "SMOOTHING"

Club managers often unbundle their memberships by time, typically "prime" versus "non-prime." In this case the proposition is simple. Any revenues generated by renting courts when they would otherwise be empty act as a contribution to overhead costs even if the additional revenues do not fully cover costs. Prime-time hours are most often booked up. Non-prime hours have slack usage. By charging different prices during the two periods, managers hope to equalize demand during peak and nonpeak hours. The pricing scheme must indicate to the consumer that there are real savings for using non-prime hours. In management terms, this is called "smoothing" demand. One must be careful, of course, that any smoothing strategy does not siphon too much demand from the higher-priced, prime-time or prime-place service.

We see the most obvious use of place segmentation or smoothing in price scales of stadiums and arenas. Proximity, line of sight, and demand are usually the key factors in "scaling the house." Some prime locations are obvious, such as courtside in any NBA venue. In May 1998, the New York Knicks announced that courtside-seat prices would rise to $1,350 per game, which would amount to $58,050 for a season. At the other end of the scale, the least expensive seat for a Knicks game would be $22 per game. Ticket scales reveal the influence of demand in facilities that house more than one anchor (or principal) tenant. For instance, the same upper-bowl seat in the Fleet Center cost $10 for a 1995-1996 Boston Celtics game and $29 for a Bruins game. A few poor seasons without Larry Bird, coupled with the move to a bigger facility, and the Celtics' streak of 664 sellouts was quickly over. Demand was still high for the choice seats; it was nonexistent for those in the top rim. Vice President for Marketing Stuart Layne summed up the pricing strategy: "What we are trying to do now is price by demand."[29]

Another example of price/place smoothing is seen in signage deals. Field-side or courtside signage, especially on the "TV side" of a venue, sells for more money because it generates more exposures of the buyer's name. In 1996, for example, the Colorado Avalanche began selling three categories of dasherboard signage—$50,000, $110,000, and $135,000—based on their determination of the visibility to fans at home and in the venue.[30]

RESPONDING TO COMPETITORS

Shifts in market demand for a firm's products are often the result of a competitor's actions. This is a constant part of life in the retail world, as any sporting goods dealer knows. In the fall of 1998, for example, Venator (formerly Woolworth) began slashing prices of Nike, Adidas, and Timberland shoes at its Foot Locker franchises—in some cases over 30 percent. One Wall Street analyst referred to the "breadth of discounting" as "amazing"; it was also an obvious response to sluggish back-to-school sales. Not only did this put pressure on other retailers to cut their prices; it also diminished the perceived value of all name-brand shoes. Alan Cohen, chief executive officer of Finish Line stores, was not happy: "For a primary retailer to denigrate these brands is a travesty and a tragedy." Of course, Cohen didn't have to follow suit and slash his prices, but he obviously felt the squeeze.[31]

Foot Locker and Finish Line operate in several markets at once. They must respond to local conditions, yet their products are produced and promoted by international corporations; and their competitors include mail-order and Internet retailers who know no boundaries, have less overhead, and can offer the same products at a lower margin. The conditions are different for teams and franchises whose products are distinct in their market (e.g., Nebraska Cornhusker football) and whose "competitors" exist at a more generic level (e.g., televised sports of any kind). Athletic club owners have yet another set of conditions: they typically face strong local competitors with similar products and services (e.g., the local YMCA or the town recreation league).

In all of these cases, however, marketers must identify who their competitors really are, monitor competitor activities (including pricing) that affect market demand, and prepare alternative tactics to meet competitor actions. Typically, the tactics involve price, quality, or some combination of the two: that is, (a) raising or lowering price and/or (b) raising or lowering the actual or the perceived quality of the product.

While there is no magic formula for reading the market and responding to competitors' pricing, it is obvious that planning will beat simple reacting.[32]

WRITING ABOUT PRICE AND VALUE

Brochures are often a key element in marketing sport products—from tickets to merchandise and memberships. Brochures are especially critical to teams and clubs. Most brochures fold up to mailing size, and they come in all colors and layouts. The most effective ones, however, contain key elements that link price with value. We see these elements clearly in the brochure below of the highly successful Portland Sea Dogs (AA baseball).

The following elements in this brochure link price with value:

A clear image of the venue and its ticket locations.

A clear table of discounts, if they are part of the plan. The Sea Dogs' brochure is aimed at individuals and groups rather than potential season-ticket holders, but notice the table emphasizing the discounts for groups, children, and seniors.

A focus on value-added. Notice the paragraphs on amenities like the Portland Room or the Kids Club. Note also how the calendar indicates the promotions for each game.

A calendar, if lead time is an issue. For the Sea Dogs' brochure, a calendar is essential, since the infrequently attending individual or group typically plans dates well in advance and often must coordinate with others.

Whether marketing tickets or memberships, the key is to communicate value as well as cost.

▶ REMEMBER THE ESCALATOR! PRICING, PUBLIC RELATIONS, AND PROMOTIONS

Ticket brochures must clarify price, cost, and benefits as successfully as the Portland Sea Dogs' brochure.

Longtime sport consumers, like Roger Naples and his colleagues among the Gallery Gods, have seen players and owners come and go. One thing they can count on, however, is higher prices and higher costs. Some wonder if fans have reached their

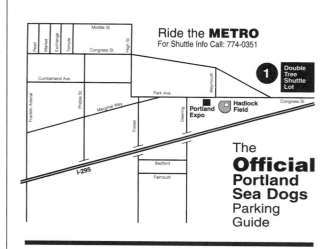

Ride the METRO
For Shuttle Info Call: 774-0351

The
Official
Portland
Sea Dogs
Parking
Guide

KIDS CLUB INFORMATION

The Sea Dogs Kids Club provides a unique way for children to be a special part of the Sea Dogs' experience. Benefits for members include: a specially designed T-shirt, membership card, commemorative certificate, a welcome letter from Slugger, admission to six Kids Club games during the season, entrance into special Kids Club raffles, an invitation to a Kids Club only autograph session, and many more!! These benefits have a value of more than $30.00, but it only costs $15.00 to join. For more information stop by the Sea Dogs' gift shop or call 874-9300.

WEBSITE INFORMATION

Want to keep up with all the Sea Dogs' information? Bookmark our Website www.portlandseadogs.com on your computer. Our Website has information on tickets, players, our schedule and much, much, more. Surf the Web with Slugger and keep yourself tied into Sea Dogs Nation.

www.portlandseadogs.com

DIRECTIONS TO HADLOCK FIELD

From the south
From Interstate 295 - take exit 5 (Congress Street)
Merge onto Congress Street - stay left.
Make a left at the first set of lights (St. John St.)
Stay right - Merge onto Park Avenue
Hadlock Field will be directly in front of you.

From the north
From Interstate 295 - Take exit 6A (Forest Ave. South)
right at the first set of lights - (go thru Deering Oaks Park)
Take a right onto Park Avenue - go approx. 1/2 mile
The stadium is just past the Expo building on your right.

Gates open 1 1/2 hours before game time.

TICKET PRICES
DON'T BE SHUT OUT!! ORDER YOUR TICKETS EARLY
Picnics • Birthday Parties • Sky Box Rentals

INDIVIDUAL GAME PRICES

	Adult	Child (16 and under) Senior (62 and over)
Box (Sold Out)	$6.00	$5.00
Reserved	$5.00	$4.00
General Admission	$4.00	$2.00

DISCOUNTED GROUP RATES*

Adults	General Admission	Reserved
Group 20-999	$3.50	$4.00
Group 1000+	$3.00	N/A
Child/Senior	**General Admission**	**Reserved**
Group 20-999	$1.50	$4.00
Group 1000+	$1.00	N/A

* Some restrictions apply to group rates on weekends.

GROUP SALES

Want to bring your group to a Sea Dogs' game? We offer groups discounts on orders of 20 tickets or more to an individual event. The ideal, inexpensive outing for groups to come together and enjoy the excitement of Portland Sea Dogs' Baseball. Sea Dogs' group rates are also a great way to entertain customers or clients who you want to come back to your organization in the future. Whatever the occasion, a Sea Dogs' group outing is a great solution to all of your entertaining needs. Call the Sea Dogs' Ticket Office before your game sells out! CALL 879-9500 TODAY!

PORTLAND ROOM

For groups of 30 people, the Portland Room at Hadlock Field provides the good combination of gathering with friends or co-workers before a game to eat and enjoy watching the game together afterwards. The Portland Room is a function room located in the concourse at Hadlock Field, which is ideal for pre-game meetings, dinners, or ceremonies. When game time rolls around, move into the stands and sit in your FIELD LEVEL BOX SEATS. What better way to watch a game than from the field level? Prices start at $15.00 per person and vary with meal choice. CALL 874-9300 AND BOOK YOUR DATE TODAY !!

DATE	OPPONENT	TIME	PROMOTION
Thursday, June 3	Akron	6:00pm	United States Air Force Drill Team Demonstration Pre-game on-field demonstration by uniformed members of the United States Air Force. also...WRKO and WZAN drive time talk show host Howie Carr will broadcast LIVE from Hadlock Field.
Saturday, June 5	Akron	1:00pm	Babe Ruth Baseball Day All six area Babe Ruth League teams will play in an exhibition immediately after the Sea Dogs take on the Aeros.
Sunday, June 6	Akron	1:00pm	Most Improved Student Day #5
Thursday, June 10	New Britain	12:00pm	Business Person's Special #2 Special noon start time. Quaker Oats Day Free granola bar for all fans as they leave the park.
Wednesday, June 23	**Harrisburg**	**7:00pm**	**Dairy Queen, WMTW & Oldies 100.0 present "SkyyDog USA & Rockin' Ray" bring their canine acrobat show to Hadlock Field.**
Thursday, June 24	Harrisburg	7:00pm	Delta Airlines Night One lucky fan will win two round trip tickets anywhere Delta Airlines flies.
Friday, June 25	Bowie	6:00pm	Shop 'N Save & WJBQ Fantastic Fireworks Night
Monday, July 5	Trenton	6:00pm	Dairy Queen post-game fireworks show
Wednesday, July 7	Trenton	12:00pm	Parks & Recreation Day #1
Thursday, July 8	Trenton	7:00pm	IHOP Blueberry Night
Sunday, July 11	Norwich	4:00pm	Maine Baseball Hall of Fame Day Pre-game ceremony where we will introduce the Class of '99.
Monday, July 12	Norwich	12:00pm	Parks & Recreation Day #2
Thursday, July 15	Binghamton	7:00pm	Governor's Council on Physical Fitness Night Pre-game gymnastics demonstration.
Friday, July 16	Binghamton	7:00pm	Oxford Hills Night
Friday, July 23	New Haven	7:00pm	BIC Poster Night Free team photo/poster to the first 3,000 fans to enter the park.
Sunday, July 25	New Haven	4:00pm	WYNZ Oldies 100.9 Camera Day After the game, come out on the field to take a picture of your favorite Sea Dog. Don't forget your camera! Family Literacy Day
Tuesday, August 3	Norwich	7:00pm	Slugger's Buddies Night Before the Sea Dogs play, watch Slugger and his friends play a three "inning" kickball game.
Wednesday, August 4	Norwich	12:00pm	Parks & Recreation Day #3
Saturday, August 7	Trenton	7:00pm	70's Night CN Brown/Citgo tie-dyed jersey auction for Muscular Dystrophy.
Thursday, August 12	**Erie**	**7:00pm**	**Mercy Hospital, WMTW & WPOR present "The Blue Brothers"**
Friday, August 13	Erie	7:00pm	Friday the 13th Halloween Night Fans should wear their best costumes and we'll have a "ghoulishly" good time throughout the game.
Tuesday, August 17	**Altoona**	**7:00pm**	**Dairy Queen, WMTW & WMGX present "The Famous Chicken"**
Wednesday, August 18	Altoona	12:00pm	Parks & Recreation Day #4
Saturday, August 28	New Haven	7:00pm	Oakhurst Dairy presents "The Better Bones Tour" Game long display with bone-health awareness, info and tests.
Friday, September 3	New Britain	6:00pm	Shop 'N Save & WHOM Fantastic Fireworks Night
Saturday, September 4	New Britain	7:00pm	Speed Pitch "Reliever of the Year" Pre-game "pitch-off," on the field, for our Speed Pitch game champions throughout the season.
Sunday, September 5	New Britain	4:00pm	"Field of Dreams" Fan Appreciation Day
Monday, September 6	New Britain	1:00pm	Labor Day

SkyyDog USA & Rockin' Ray

The Blues Brothers

The Famous Chicken

THIS SCHEDULE IS SUBJECT TO CHANGE - FOR MORE INFORMATION CALL THE SEA DOGS BOX OFFICE AT 207-879-9500

KidSpeak™ A Voice For Kids Sponsored by Brigham's

What is KidSpeak?

KidSpeak is an exciting initiative sponsored by the folks at Brigham's Ice Cream. It was developed to give kids a voice through interactive surveys, newsletters, programs and sponsorship for solving real-world problems. If you are between the ages of 8 and 18, you can become a kidSpeak member. It's your chance to speak out and make a difference both locally and globally.

How do I get involved?

All you have to do is fill out this form and drop it in the mail. After we receive your form, KidSpeak information will be mailed to you. It's free!

Anything else I should know?

If you and your class are interested in getting involved, let us know. We can come and talk to your class about KidSpeak and bring along some Brigham's ice cream for a treat!

Name _____
Address _____
City _____ State ____ Zip ____
Phone# _____ Date of Birth __/__/__
School _____

Mail to: Brigham's Inc. c/o KidSpeak, 30 Mill St., Arlington, MA 02476
1-800-880-1121 • www.brighams.com

PORTLAND Sea Dogs

Brigham's Birthday Parties
for more info call 1-207-879-9500

Brigham's

limit. In July 1998, *U.S. News and World Report* ran the cover story "Big League Troubles." Was the bubble finally bursting? Economist Andrew Zimbalist captured a common sentiment: "The middle-income and lower-income fans are being priced out of the game."[33]

Everywhere sport consumers turned, there seemed to be an arrogant executive wrenching up their costs. Some examples:

➤ The PGA of America announced that golf fans would have to pay a nonrefundable $5 fee in order to enter a lottery for 1999 Ryder Cup tickets. Organizational officials claimed that the "entry fee" was needed to cover telemarketing and ticket-processing costs, although this sounded lame in light of ticket demand. Within a week, 30,000 people had applied for the 10,000 (of 30,000 total) tickets available to the public. The *Boston Globe's* "Consumer Beat" columnists accused the PGA of running an "illegal lottery."[34]

➤ After what their own president called a "disappointing" and "least successful season," the Anaheim Mighty Ducks raised ticket prices for the fifth straight year. Worse yet, President Tony Tavares bluntly announced that he "made no apologies" for the increases. *Orange County Register* columnist Randy Youngman didn't see it the same way. He found Tavares's attitude "nonchalant and unapologetic" and "particularly galling." In a nutshell, it was "typical Disney arrogance."[35]

➤ After agreeing to pay the NFL $600 million per year for the rights to Thursday and Sunday night games, ESPN announced plans to hike its fees to cable operators by 20 percent. Cable executives expected similar hikes over the eight-year length of ESPN's deal with the NFL. In the end, who would pay? The local consumer, through higher monthly cable fees.[36]

An arrogant tone in announcing price hikes is a sure way to push consumers off the escalator. Fortunately, there are plenty of alternative models. A campaign run by the Pittsburgh Penguins in May of 1987 is a good example of mixed success in this regard. The Penguins, who had missed the NHL play-offs for five consecutive years, announced an average season-ticket price increase of roughly 15 percent. To reduce public indignation, the club added a special "playoff or payoff" provision for all fans who purchased their tickets by July 1 of that year. Under the plan, these fans would receive a $1 per game ticket refund if the Penguins did not make the play-offs. The Pens wanted to demonstrate special value to their loyal fans. Although the policy assuaged some of the negative feelings among fans, and although it may have helped sales, the Penguins failed to make the 1988 play-offs. The payoff was considerable.[37]

While few sport organizations can be expected to go to these extremes, most try to add a message about value to any communications on price. This is especially true for sporting goods retailers who must price their products higher than the department stores and discounters. As Craig Koenig of the Koenig Sporting Goods chain explained, the best policy is to emphasize quality, value, range, and expertise to the 70 percent of consumers who are concerned about these things in addition to price. To these consumers, said Koenig, "Price is important but not the key element. They are most interested in value so we work very hard to make sure customers perceive Koenig's as offering value."[38]

At times, especially in new venues, sport franchises misjudge the desirability of seat locations or even of overall demand. A weak team performance can exacerbate the problems. If a price reduction is necessary, one might as well be up front about it. The Carolina Hurricanes of the NHL took this route when they slashed most single-game tickets by $10 after a dismal performance on and off the ice in 1997-1998. Hurricane owner Peter Karmanos announced the price reductions by saying, "We admit that we priced the tickets too high. We are begging for forgiveness and putting our money where our mouth is."[39]

WRAP-UP

As we have noted, the majority of sport pricing decisions are based on what the market will bear; prices are set in relation to what the organization believes the consumer is willing to pay for the product. It may seem that to some extent, sport managers have a captive market. If you are not prepared to pay the price to see Denver Broncos NFL football, then you will not see it live. However, the Broncos and similar clubs do not compete for the entertainment dollar only with other NFL teams. There are several substitutes for NFL football in the Denver area. Among them are college hockey, professional baseball, movies, restaurants, and other forms of entertainment. All these activities compete for the consumer entertainment dollar.

Sports are truly a complex product. In making pricing decisions, the sport organization must consider the cost and availability of substitute products. The sport manager must try to determine how much this sport really competes with other forms of entertainment, as well as how people view it in comparison to the other forms. Good demographic information on sport consumers can tell a great deal about a product's competition. Similarly, surveys can tell a great deal about how much the public values the product and how elastic or inelastic demand may be. On the basis of demand, competitors' actions, and other factors, the organization can create a pricing strategy that meets its objectives. While the marketer can take many approaches to pricing, there is no substitute for knowing the market.

ACTIVITIES

1. Explain the differences among the following pricing strategies: break-even, cost-plus, capitation, time and place smoothing, skim, and penetration. Find examples of each in a sport setting.

2. Explain the difference between a marketer's view of "price" and a consumer's view of "cost." Create a "cost index" for your favorite sport activity (as either a fan or a player).

3. Consumers associate price with value. Assume you are the new marketing director of a franchise with a history of selling discount tickets. The new owners have mandated no more ticket discounting. Create a strategy to overcome negative consumer responses to this new policy.

4. Find a recent example of a sport organization that encountered very negative publicity for a pricing move. How would you have done things differently?

5. Define market demand. Try to find a sport example that demonstrates how price can reveal elasticity or inelasticity of demand.

YOUR MARKETING PLAN

Carefully articulate the objectives that will control the pricing strategies for your organization. Then map out pricing strategies for your primary products—be they events, memberships, or hard or soft goods. Consider how you will approach the various segments of your consumers, as well as how you will respond to competitors or to uncertain demand.

PROMOTIONS

OBJECTIVES

1. To recognize the complexity of promotion with respect to the various forms it can assume as part of the marketing mix.

2. To identify integral elements of promotion and the various approaches used in advertising.

3. To understand promotion in a historical context and consider how that context has evolved as a result of the importance of media and sponsorship relationships.

4. To recognize the key characteristics of effective promotional programs and campaigns aimed at expanding existing consumer bases and at increasing the frequency of consumption.

Beanie Babies—The End or the Means?

What is the number-one draw in sport? According to *Sports Illustrated* columnist Rick Reilly, it just might be Beanie Babies.[1] Although Reilly argues this in a light-hearted, tongue-in-cheek essay, he may not be far from the truth. Interest in the product ensued from a 1997 promotion in which the Chicago Cubs had two Beanie Baby giveaway days and attracted crowds of 37,958 and 38,849. Not quite convinced? On May 12, 1998, David Wells was the starting pitcher for the Yankees and drew 16,606. On May 17, less than one week later, Wells pitched again, aided by the presence of the Ty Beanie Baby Valentino the Bear; the crowd was 49,820. The result—a perfect game, a happy crowd, and a place in Cooperstown for Valentino along with some memorabilia from Wells.

Consider the following. There were 16 promotional dates involving authentic Beanie Babies during the 1998 MLB season: the Yankees, Cubs, and Cardinals each offered two such dates. During the 1998 season, the 12 teams using Ty Beanie Babies realized an average gain of 37.4 percent at the gate. The number is particularly significant given that all these promotions were on weekends when attendance is traditionally strongest.[2] Other clubs such as the Boston Red Sox and Pittsburgh Pirates offered similar promotions without authentic Ty Beanie Babies because they wished to promote their own characters.[3]

The MLB All-Star Game, held on July 7 at Denver's Coors Field, also featured a Beanie Baby giveaway (see photo). This was not needed to increase attendance at the All-Star Game, but perhaps to draw attention to upcoming promotional nights at other parks throughout the country. Everyone attending the game received Ty's Glory, a red, white, and blue bear. The result: scalpers offered as much as $500 to fans leaving the game. Recently, the 1998 version of the Chicago White Sox, performing below the expectations of their ticket purchasing public, attracted their largest crowd of the year—32,929 for a Beanie Babies giveaway day.[4]

■ Beanie Babies—the top promotion in sports?

This chapter focuses primarily on advertising and the premise of promotion. Publicity in sport, and its inherent elements of public relations, media relations, and community relations, are addressed in depth in chapter 15. The sales process, including personal selling, is examined in detail in chapter 11. In this chapter, after discussing how these basic activities apply to promotion, we consider their potential for moving consumers up the escalator of increasing involvement.[5]

THE CATCH-ALL "P": PROMOTION

Promotion, another of the Ps in sport marketing, is a catch-all category for any one of numerous activities designed to stimulate consumer interest in, awareness of, and purchase of the product. Basically, promotion involves the vehicles through which the marketer conveys information about product, place, and price. More importantly, promotion is a critical mechanism for positioning a product and its image in the mind of the consumer. Promotion concentrates on "selling" the product; without sales, a company will not be in operation very long. Although selling does not equal marketing, it is a vital component.

The marketing term *promotion* includes the following forms of marketing activity:

> *Advertising:* any paid, nonpersonal (not directed to individuals), clearly sponsored message conveyed through the media

> *Personal selling:* any face-to-face presentation in which the seller has an opportunity to persuade the consumer

> *Publicity:* any form of exposure in the media not paid for by the beneficiary or within the beneficiary's control or influence

> *Sales promotion:* a wide variety of activities including displays, trade shows, sampling, coupons, premium items, exhibitions, and performances

To be successful, promotional efforts should follow the **AIDA** approach. That is, such efforts should include the following steps:

Increase awareness **(A)**

Attract interest **(I)**

Arouse desire **(D)**

Initiate action **(A)**

ADVERTISING

As with all promotion, the core of advertising is effective communication. That is, advertising is a communication process and is subject to the same problems as any other communication process. A major problem in advertising is perceptual distortion, which occurs when the receiver of a message interprets it differently from the way the sender intended. This phenomenon can cause misunderstanding of advertising messages, which may prevent marketers from reaching advertising goals. Thus, in terms of advertising and other promotional activities, the sport marketer must operate under the axiom that *perception is reality*. In other words, the sport marketer must attempt to ensure that the message is targeted and that it is clearly specific so that the receiver comprehends it. If this doesn't happen, the sport marketer will have to work to address the misperception and correct it—because for the consumer, this misperception has become fact.

Multipurpose athletic and fitness clubs have recognized the need to communicate to a target market that may want the same things—better appearance, conditioning, and health—but with varying degrees of intensity. Thus the advertising message must not be limited to beautiful bodies sweating to "feel the burn." Such messages suggest too much agony and single-minded purpose for whole segments of the market who fall into the categories of "deconditioned" and "dropout." For some, the perception might be that they are not in condition to join a fitness club or that more pain than enjoyment is involved. The fitness industry has worked diligently to create advertising campaigns that present images combining fitness, sociability, achievement, fun, and togetherness (family orientation). Perceptual distortion cannot be completely eliminated, but through attention to message construction, the marketer can reduce the amount of distortion.[6]

WHAT SHOULD ADVERTISING ACCOMPLISH?

According to Batra, Myers, and Aaker,[7] an advertising message can have a variety of effects upon the receiver or intended audience. An advertising message can

create awareness,

communicate information about attributes and benefits,

develop or change an image or personality,

associate a brand with feelings and emotions,

create norm groups, and

precipitate behavior.

Sport shares many of these same advertising goals. News releases and press conferences, very common in sport, are utilized to create awareness about new developments such as personnel moves, product innovations, upcoming promotional events, or special events and activities. The LPGA Fan Village, discussed in chapters 5 and 7, provides an excellent illustration of how a press release can create awareness about innovations. In a January 1997 news release, the LPGA and Target announced the creation of the Target-sponsored LPGA Fan Village, a 2400-square-foot on-site fan entertainment and information center. The news release had three functions: to create awareness, to communicate information about the attributes and benefits of this project as it related to the fans, and to associate a brand (Target) with feelings and emotions:

Primary features of the LPGA Fan Village Presented by Target include: player autograph sessions, special fan-player photo opportunities, rules and instruction seminars, health and fitness forums, a club-fitting and hitting area, video presentations, computer information, a captivating 60-foot long pictorial time line that tells the LPGA story, and the ability to purchase merchandise from the LPGA's newly-launched Authentic LPGA Collection. Fans are also able to watch, and at times participate in, live television and radio broadcasts from the LPGA Fan Village Presented by Target.[8]

Assessing advertising effectiveness entails a number of key considerations:

➤ *Wasted circulation.* One problem in advertising is wasted circulation, which occurs when advertising reaches consumers not within the target market of the organization. This happens to some degree in almost all campaigns—but how can the marketer keep it to a minimum? As stated earlier, a good starting point is the delineation of the target market; an organization must know whom it is trying to reach. If an organization has good geographic, demographic, and psychographic information on its target markets, then it can choose media placements that will maximize exposure to the target market and minimize wasted effort.

➤ *Cost per exposure.* Another issue related to media selection is cost per exposure, which is merely the measure of cost required to reach one consumer through the various media under consideration. Using cost per exposure data along with target market profiles, an organization can reach the greatest number of people within its target market at the lowest cost.

➤ *Determining the creative approach.* After all media and cost decisions have been made, the creative part of advertising begins. One starting point for developing an effective creative strategy is called the knock-knock scenario. The scenario begins with a knock-knock on the door. The door opens. The person behind the door frowns. The salesperson says, "You should buy this product because it makes your life easier [better, more fun, more exciting, etc.]." The person opens the door and says, "Come on in and show me." And the salesperson is on his or her way to making a sale.[9] Some marketing questions and issues must be addressed via the creative component. What is the goal of the ad? What is its message?

➤ *Measurement.* Assuming that a creative campaign is under way, how will the organization measure its effectiveness? Organizations spend a great deal of money on advertising, but much less on finding out how well advertising works, mainly because of the difficulties inherent in measuring the effectiveness of ads. A traditional method of evaluating ads is to measure sales response in the period following an advertising campaign that has been aimed at immediate sales, but this method has several limitations. The first is the problem of the time lag. How long does it take for an ad to be effective? Are current sales the result of yesterday's ads, last week's ads, or the ads placed six months ago? No one can answer these questions. Another problem is that all advertising may not be aimed at immediate sales; some advertising may have an effect over a longer time period. How can an organization take this into account? These two limitations must be addressed if one is to use sales results to measure advertising effectiveness.

There are other ways to evaluate the effectiveness of advertising. One is to offer a discount if the consumer brings in the ad (in sport this is usually a clipped print ad, but it can also be a soft-drink can from a sponsor involved in the promotion); a simple count of the ads redeemed provides some measure of the effect of the campaign. Other methods include recall and recognition tests, as used by Stotler and Johnson in a study of stadium advertising,[10] and scannable cards that document attendance, purchases, and other transactions appropriate to the sport venue.

Ultimately, running a successful ad campaign relies on two basic elements: knowing the product and knowing the consumers. Ads are simply a means of communicating information about the product or service to the consumer.

ADVERTISING AGENCIES

One issue facing sport marketers is that of determining when to attempt to do the work themselves, or "in-house," and when to employ an advertising agency. All advertisers, by definition, use some form of media to accomplish organizational objectives.[11] Depending upon the size and type of the organization wishing to use an advertising campaign, it may be necessary to employ an advertising agency to help in developing the ad and in working directly with media outlets to disseminate the message. The advertising agency is usually involved in making the creative decisions (decisions about how the message is conveyed) and the media decisions (about which form[s] of media to utilize). In many cases, the advertising agency not only designs the campaign, but also selects the media and purchases the media time (electronic) and space (print). To ensure that the advertising message is targeted to the proper market segments, and through the channels with the highest potential for impact, the advertising agency may also employ a research firm to conduct consumer research or may purchase existing research reports.

Experts suggest that an organization take the following seven steps before employing an advertising agency:

➤ Have a comprehensive marketing plan in place, or ensure that the advertising agency will help you create a comprehensive marketing plan—not just a media plan.

➤ Make sure the agency is interested in your organization's success—not just in winning awards, but in increasing sales and revenue.

➤ Choose an agency that has comprehensive marketing skills; advertising is only one element of marketing. Sales promotion and public relations are essential as well.

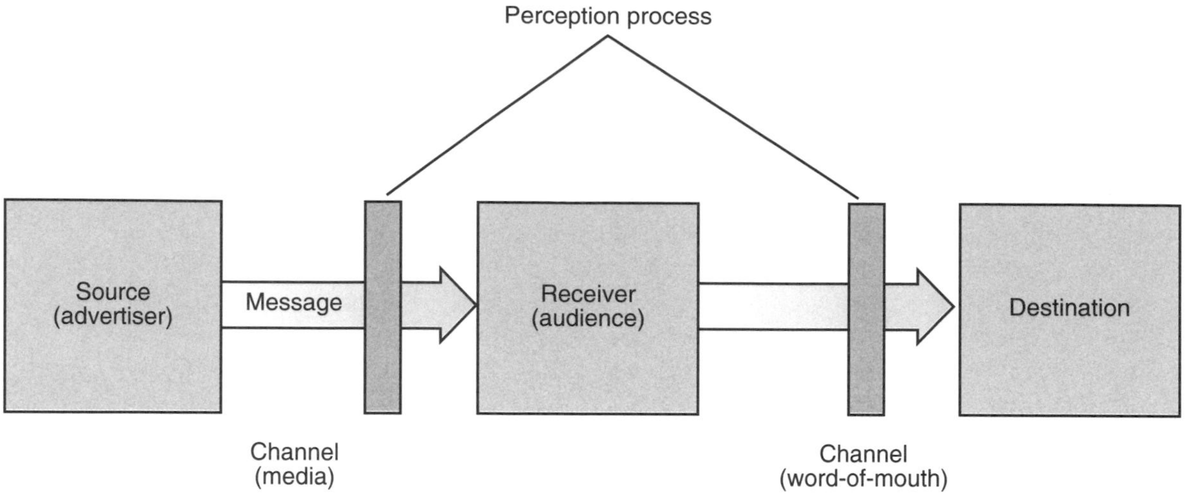

Figure 10.1 Batra, Myers, and Aaker model of the advertising communication system.

- ➢ Determine the target market and how to reach them efficiently. Mass advertising may be desirable at some point, but a targeted approach is the essential first step.
- ➢ Find out who will be handling your account. What are their experiences? Relationships? Style?
- ➢ Make sure that all written copy is customer centered.
- ➢ Select an agency that views itself as a partner in your business. The agency personnel should feel as though their stake is in your success, not in the popularity of the advertising.[12]

THE ADVERTISING COMMUNICATION PROCESS

Figure 10.1 shows the Batra, Myers, and Aaker model of the advertising communication system. Advertising communication always involves a perception process and four of the elements shown in the model: the source, a message, a communication channel, and a receiver (note that the receiver can also become a source by talking to friends or associates—this is referred to as word-of-mouth communication).[13]

Source—Can be defined as the originator of the message. There are a number of types of "sources" in the context of advertising, especially in the area of sport. For example, the NBA is a source of advertising in disseminating its message—"I love this game." The Cleveland Cavs, an NBA team, can also be a source for their own advertising message—"Ya gotta be there." As another example, Nike might disseminate a brand message that can also be associated with Foot Locker, a retailer of the Nike brand.

The Phoenix Coyotes have found that advertising vehicles such as the puck pictured below are effective channels to communicate their message to their audience.

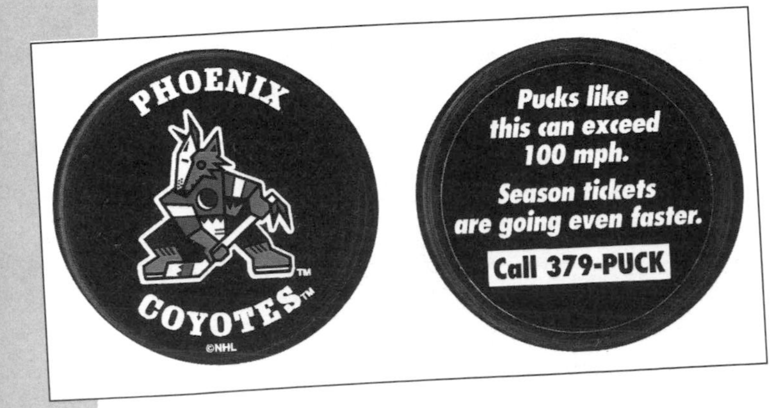

Message—Can be defined as both the content and the execution of the message. In practice, it is the actuality of what the receiver of the message has perceived.

Channel—Refers to one or more kinds of media, such as Internet, radio, television, newspapers, magazines, billboards (fixed and movable), point-of-purchase displays, signage, logo placement (on scoreboards and other sport-related properties such as dasherboards, in-ice, racing cars, uniforms, message boards, premium items, game programs, and so on), virtual signage, and special events (see photo).

Receiver—Commonly refers to the target market. This is the intended audience for the message. The receivers (or audience), as in the case of any target market, usually share certain demographic or psychographic characteristics. In the context of sport marketing, these characteristics may include type of tickets owned, zip code, past purchasing history, children living in the household, past or current sport interest or affiliation, and demographic segmentation such as age or income.

Destination—In many cases the message doesn't end with the receiver because the receiver may continue to disseminate the message via word of mouth, personal contact, thus becoming a source. This is especially true in the case of sport, which because of its emphasis and place within society elicits significantly more interest and coverage (media) than most other topics. Proprietary research conducted for MLB's FanFest and for the Pittsburgh Pirates indicates that a significant portion (over 20 percent) of fans attending a promotional event, or a game with a promotional event, find out about the event from a family member or friend.[14]

ADVERTISING MEDIUMS FOR SPORT

We have examined the advertising message model and what advertising hopes to accomplish. A sport organization must decide which form or forms of media to use in an advertising campaign. In the following section, we examine the various advertising mediums most commonly utilized in sport. Some are common to all forms of advertising, while some are best suited to sport or unique to sport; each has its own set of advantages and disadvantages.

SIGNAGE

Signage includes printed messages or logos identifying a sponsor or event on any of the following types of materials: banners, street-pole attachments, billboards (fixed or movable), scoreboards, electronic message boards, posters, and dasherboards or rink boards. It also includes impressions such as in-ice or on-field messages, rotational courtside messages, on-field or on-court logos, and virtual signage (superimposed on blank stadium walls and playing surfaces but visible on television).[15] The definition of signage has also been expanded to include logo placement opportunities. Logo placement opportunities are most commonly found on racing cars (of all types); racing boats; driver uniforms; professional golfers' caps and shirts; and professional tennis players' caps, headbands, and rackets. In some cases, the name of the sponsor is also the name of the team, as in English football (soccer) or Italian basketball (i.e., Benetton Basket, the 1997 Italian League Champions).

Although signage conveys a message, it is not a spoken, scripted, or consistent message. The message that signage conveys is more accurately described as an impression: the message is received and acted upon based on the awareness and feelings of the receiver with regard to the sender. Because of the high amount of clutter (number of advertising messages and impressions) in American society, many messages or impressions are not received, as the intended audience has built up an immunity, that is, has become so accustomed to advertising messages that they do not stand out. As sport marketers have become more and more reliant upon advertising revenue from sponsors wishing to communicate to their audiences, they have had to search for new ideas and creative concepts and placements for these messages. Several studies have shown that creative placement results in higher recognition and reception of the message. Stotlar and Johnson concluded in a 1989 study that advertising messages that were part of the game—for example, placed on or in front of the scorer's table—were more effective than other placements.[16] Pope and Voges found that automobile manufacturers wishing to increasing product awareness were effective in achieving the objective utilizing on-site displays and vehicle and equipment signage.[17]

Exposure to corporate names and logos at sport venues can increase product awareness and may subsequently lead to loyal product consumption by spectators.[18] This potential for consumption of sponsor products and services plays a key role in the level of creativity and ingenuity we find in sport advertising. A joint effort by the International Hockey League, Champion Consultants Inc., and two International Hockey League member teams (the Chicago Wolves and the Detroit Vipers) recently resulted in an innovative ad placement. The Net Advertising Plan provides signage that is incorporated into the goal net in hockey games. The advertising message is clearly visible on television and in photographs but not to the players, nor does it obscure the view of the goal judge and the officials. The message utilized a Powerade logo (most goalies drink Powerade during the game and most fans associate the drink with goalies). The Powerade logo, placed at the bottom of the net, appears to be moving whenever the goalie or the net moves.[19]

Signage is often one element of an integrated sponsorship purchase. It may be the most important element of the sponsorship for some companies and just a "value-added component" for others (i.e., not the core benefit but a benefit of secondary value or importance). For example, Shell Oil entered into a sponsorship agreement with baseball's St. Louis Cardinals that focused on teaching fans to keep score. The Shell Oil logo was displayed throughout the season on the Cardinals' matrix scoreboard along with instructions on how to score each play. Given that the Cardinals average over 20,000 fans per game for 81 games and that a baseball game contains a minimum of 27 plays, the Shell logo is guaranteed to generate an absolute minimum of 43,740,000 impressions per season. As Shell has the second most identifiable logo in the world, according to Shell marketer Harry Dunn, logo recognition is not the the key element of this sponsorship. Driving traffic to Shell stations is the primary objective, so Shell also distributed 500,000 scorecards through its local stations. The signage will create awareness and recognition and hopefully generate traffic and sales at the local stations.[20]

Virtual advertising provides a way to digitally insert an advertising message via television (top) without that message appearing in the actual venue (bottom).

Signage is one medium that can be enhanced and expanded via the new technologies and media at our disposal. In its simplest application, virtual signage creates an image unseen by fans at the game but crystal clear to television audiences. With added bells and whistles, virtual signage allows for constant updating of images and placement of logos where an actual sign might distract participants, such as the middle of a tennis court. Most importantly, it allows advertisers to target their message to a particular geographic audience. While viewers in the United States may see an ad for Coors, Canadian audiences can be looking at a sign for Molson. This technology has already been used for the international broadcast of the Super Bowl, with Coca-Cola as a lead sponsor.

Im*ad*gine Video Systems, headquartered in Amsterdam with offices in Norwalk (Connecticut) and Paris, is the world leader in the relatively new but quickly growing virtual electronic imaging industry. The company is jointly owned by the ISL Group, one of the world's leading sport marketing companies, and Orad, an Israeli technology company.

According to ISL's Ann Reynolds, Im*ad*gine offers enhanced brand exposure and increased consumer retention of event signage on television by

➤ increasing the total available space for signage and allowing the insertion of signage where no signage exists (see photos);

> ➤ broadcasting of multiple brand messages from each billboard to targeted geographic locations and audience groups;

> ➤ creation of more interesting signage designs (use of three dimensions, animation; increased size);

> ➤ providing multiple-language broadcasts of the brand messages;

> ➤ allowing prohibited product advertisement at certain events; and

> ➤ providing tailored exposure packages with price differentiation based upon advertising timing.[21]

In September 1998, the World Wrestling Federation (WWF) began inserting sponsor logos directly into the wrestling ring, charging 46 percent of the rate for equivalent spot advertising. Major League Soccer and its partners ESPN and ABC have negotiated a virtual-signage clause into their six-year agreement.[22] Can Augusta's fairways, the NBA's center court, the NFL end zones, Fenway's "Green Monster," and the NHL's goal areas be far behind?

ENDORSEMENTS

Brooks has incorporated the work of McCracken and of Friedman and Friedman in defining a celebrity athlete endorser as a well-known celebrity athlete who uses his or her fame to help a company sell or enhance the image of the company, products, or brands.[23] According to McCracken, a celebrity athlete can assume one product endorsement style or a combination of several styles. These are (a) the explicit mode (I endorse this product), (b) the implicit mode (I use this product), (c) the imperative mode (you should use this product), and (d) the co-present mode (in which the athlete merely appears in some setting with the product).[24]

According to Burt Sugar, the first recorded instance of a modern athlete's leasing his name (to endorse a sport product) occurred on September 1, 1905, when Honus Wagner (later enshrined as one of the first four members of the Baseball Hall of Fame) of the Pittsburgh Pirates gave the J.F. Hillerich & Son Company permission to use his name on its Louisville Slugger bats for a consideration of $75. Other athletes, such as Ty Cobb and Babe Ruth, soon began to endorse products for payment.[25] The earliest endorsements involved sport-related products, and some of the most effective endorsements today are of sport-related products (e.g., Michael Jordan for Nike).[26]

The growing popularity of pro football, basketball, baseball, golf, tennis, and motor sports has led to the proliferation of the sport celebrity. Brand identity has become one of the primary reasons that advertisers so closely link their products with sport; fans seem to identify as closely with the sponsor as with the sport itself. Michael Jordan popularized Nike's Air Jordan shoe. After leading his team to a Super Bowl victory, quarterback Joe Montana responded to a commentator's question about what he was going to do next by exclaiming, "I'm going to Disney World." And NASCAR joined with Kellogg's to promote the Winston Cup auto racing series on the backs of 20 million cereal boxes.[27]

Tables 10.1 and 10.2 on page 192 are compilations of various celebrity-rating services that provide some rationale for the varying frequencies with which celebrity athletes appear.

The trustworthiness and influence of Michael Jordan are evidenced by his total endorsement value (in excess of $40 million and growing). One example of Jordan's endorsements is his multimillion dollar contract with Rayovac (batteries). According to *Sports Marketing Letter*, Rayovac believes that using Jordan could reduce to nearly zero the time it will take to educate consumers—especially single-use battery purchasers—on the advantages of its new product. Rayovac's product is the only rechargeable alkaline on the market. As opposed to one long-life use for a regular

Table 10.1 THE TOP 10 ATHLETE ENDORSERS

Most appealing (a)	Most recognized	Most influential/trusted (b)	Most controversial (b)	Highest total endorsements (c)
Tiger Woods	O.J. Simpson	Michael Jordan	Dennis Rodman	Michael Jordan ($40 million)
Michael Jordan	Magic Johnson	Shaquille O'Neal	Michael Irvin	Tiger Woods ($25 million)
Grant Hill	Michael Jordan	Joe Montana	John Daly	Shaquille O'Neal ($23 million)
Dennis Rodman	Muhammad Ali	Tiger Woods	Daryl Strawberry	Arnold Palmer ($19.2 million)
Ken Griffey Jr.	Mike Tyson	Cal Ripken Jr.	Mike Tyson	Grant Hill ($18 million)
Troy Aikman	Joe Montana	Troy Aikman	Jennifer Capriati	Andre Agassi ($17 million)
Scottie Pippen	Nancy Kerrigan	Steve Young	Albert Belle	Jack Nicklaus ($16 million)
George Foreman	Tonya Harding	Ken Griffey Jr.	Pete Rose	Joe Montana ($12 million)
Bonnie Blair	Joe Namath	Dan Marino	Derrick Coleman	Ken Griffey Jr. ($6 million)
Joe Montana	Hank Aaron	Wayne Gretzky	O.J. Simpson	Deion Sanders ($6 million)

From the *Wall Street Journal*. See Brooks and Harris.[28] (a) *Burns Sports Celebrity Services*, April 1997. (b) *Sports Media Index, American Sports Data*, February 1997. (c) "The Ten Most Wanted Spokesperson Survey," *Sports Marketing Newsletter*, August 1997.

Table 10.2 TOP FEMALE ENDORSERS

Athlete	Sport	Endorsements (in millions)
Monica Seles	Tennis	$6
Steffi Graf	Tennis	$5
Martina Hingis	Tennis	$3
Kristi Yamaguchi	Figure skating	$3
Anna Kournikova	Tennis	$2
Tara Lipinski	Figure skating	$2
Picabo Street	Skiing	$2
Venus Williams	Tennis	$2

From the *Los Angeles Times*. See "Top Female Endorsers."[29]

disposable alkaline, the Rayovac product gives as many as 11 long-life uses. So why do they need Jordan?

Jordan, the company believes, will grab instant attention and instant recognition for the battery. Also, the imagery is a tight fit. Expect to see advertising themed on Jordan and the product as "the best of their kind," "the greatest ever," and the like. And who is a better choice to endorse a renewable battery than a superstar whose basketball career has proven to be renewable?[30]

"Since the days of Babe Ruth and Joe Dimaggio, people have known that athletes pulled in attention in some fashion."[31] As we enter the millennium, many industry experts feel that Jordan stands alone and that perhaps investing in athletes as endorsers might not be the most prudent course of action to sell product. According to Keith Daly, senior vice president and general manager at the FootAction USA sneaker chain, "Very few athletes have the kind of national presence that can stimulate the demand for products in all stores. Michael is the only guy who has the ability to sell shoes year in and year out." This lack of a national presence (or an international presence in some cases) is compounded by the recent rash of highly publicized negative incidents involving such high-profile player/endorsers as Latrell Sprewell, Dennis Rodman, Allen Iverson, and Charles Barkley. Nike Chairman Phil Knight feels that this "sports negativism" was a factor in Nike's recent 20 percent drop in quarterly earnings. Bob McGee of *Sporting Goods Intelligence* agrees with

Knight, confirming the obvious: that consumer backlash against sneaker endorsements intensifies when an athlete chokes his coach or kicks a photographer in the groin.[32]

One way to lessen the risk in using celebrity athletes as endorsers is to tie their compensation into product sales by offering them stock options. Dan Marino has an equity share in LaRussa Italian foods; Michael Jordan and Cal Ripken have an equity relationship with Oakley sunglasses; and Tiger Woods received stock for his involvement in the Official All Star Cafe.[33] In a less traditional approach, some clever marketers have hit upon another solution to control the behavior, and hence the image of their endorsers—make sure they're dead. Advances in video technology and computer imaging have permitted companies like Dirt Devil, Mercedes-Benz, and Coors to "resurrect" such cinema and television stars as Fred Astaire, Ed Sullivan, and John Wayne. Why use dead celebrities? There are several reasons. First, "Dead celebrities allow advertisers to tap into feelings of nostalgia about times spent gathered around the television watching classic shows—an emotion that reverberates with baby boomers in particular." Second, with dead celebrities—who can no longer get arrested or offend consumers—advertisers know what they are getting. Latching on to celebrities like Dennis Rodman can prove embarrassing to advertisers. "With dead celebrities, their qualities are known," said Tom Cordner, creative director of Team One Advertising. "They can't get you in trouble. They're a safe bet."[34]

Sport marketers have embraced this tactic as well. ESPN's flattering movie of Ty Cobb was heavily used to promote the 1998 baseball season. Jackie Robinson appeared on Wheaties boxes and commemorative Coca-Cola bottles; he was thanked by famous current athletes in a Nike commercial, and Robinson's estate was projected to earn millions of dollars in endorsement fees—all after he had been dead for 25 years.[35] Given the reception and success of this type of advertising, will we soon see Babe Ruth pitching hot dogs or endorsing beer, or perhaps Babe Didrickson promoting the attributes of golf equipment? Stay tuned.

PRINT MEDIA

Print media is the inclusive term used to refer to newspapers, magazines, brochures, posters, programs, point-of-purchase displays, and direct mail. Among all forms of print media, newspapers have several clear-cut advantages. They are timely because they are published daily. Day-of-game, membership-promotion, or special sales advertising can be placed in a newspaper with only short advance notice. Compared to electronic media such as television, newspaper advertising is lower in cost. Sport and business sections seem to be the preferred spots for ad placements geared to attracting sport consumers,[36] although the lifestyle-type sections and weekend special sections are also excellent placement areas. Magazines have the advantages of very high quality print and color reproduction. However, they are usually published weekly or monthly, and they can be rather expensive.

Posters offer the organization a degree of control, because the organization can determine where and when to distribute them. They can also be self-financing: the organization can sell advertising space on the posters in order to pay for the printing and materials. High school and collegiate athletic programs often utilize posters listing schedules and upcoming promotions and special events to promote their various athletic teams. One limitation of posters is that they are limited to an "immediate area of exposure impact" dependent upon attraction and traffic flow.

Game or *event programs* can pay for themselves and can even generate a profit, in many cases, through the sale of advertising space. The program itself, with its photographs, stories, and statistics, promotes the organization or event and serves as an excellent public relations tool. Host Communications, based in Louisville, Kentucky, is one of the industry leaders in the game/event program marketplace.

Posters and programs may also be part of a *point-of-purchase* (POP) promotion—a promotional activity that takes place at the moment of purchase. Retailers have relied for years on POP promotions. For example, a sporting goods store may offer an instant rebate through a couponing program at the store to encourage the purchase of a specific brand of athletic footwear during the customer's visit. Utilizing POPs is often referred to as reminder advertising. Reminder advertising works in several ways. It can enhance the top-of-mind awareness of the brand, thus increasing the probability that the consumer includes the brand on the shopping list or purchases it as an impulse item. Additionally, it can enforce the key elements of the national advertising campaign at the point of purchase.[37]

Direct-mail advertising is used widely in the sport industry. Its major advantage is that it reaches only the people the organization wants to reach, which minimizes spending on circulating a message to people who have little interest in the contents. Organizations often promote season tickets, partial ticket plans, and single-game tickets through direct mail. One common approach in selling tickets is to cultivate leads from credit card purchases and to develop a direct-mail piece, such as a ticket-plan brochure, to mail to the card-holders. This results in a highly targeted direct mail campaign because the target audience has already demonstrated a familiarity with and interest in the product.[38]

When designing any print materials, the sport marketer should consider the following guidelines:

> The headline must flag down the target reader and pull him or her into the text about the product, offering a reward for reading on.

> Since most people reading print ads never read beyond the headline, it is also crucial that the headline and the visual component complement each other so well, and "tell the story" so clearly, that someone who looks only at the headline and the visual can "get the message" without having to read a word of the body copy.

> The body copy should be detailed and specific, should support the headline, and should be readable and interesting.[39]

Research has shown that people recall information better when it is presented both pictorially and verbally;[40] for this reason, sport marketers should carefully design and utilize images to convey their message. Advertisements describing upcoming promotional items, or brochures describing facility renovations, should contain photographs and artist's renderings whenever possible.

BROADCAST (ELECTRONIC) MEDIA

In this section, we consider radio, television, scoreboards, and public address systems. Chapter 14 deals with the creation and management of broadcast networks for event distribution. All are critical mediums for reaching today's consumer. Scoreboards (which can also be classified as signage for external advertisers) and public address systems represent internal advertising mediums; they cost virtually nothing and offer effective reach to a target market that through its presence in the venue has demonstrated interest in and ability to purchase the product. Scoreboards and public address systems can perform a variety of functions. They can be utilized to sell announcements or provide message space for local businesses; to announce future games, other venue events, special events, or promotional activities; and to recognize groups in attendance in order to encourage them to attend again.[41]

Radio Radio provides an audio message that can be powerful, and radio can be relatively inexpensive. Major League Baseball teams offer 30-second advertising spots for a season-long ad campaign that runs for as little as $200 per spot (Kansas City) to as much as $1700 (Los Angeles Dodgers).[42]

Good copy read by an announcer with a following, backed up by the appropriate "action," noise, or music, can take us to the game or club. Radio plays to the imagination and lets us hear what we wish while letting our minds create a "picture" that may be based upon past memories, hopeful expectations, or perhaps just wishful thinking. As each radio station (and format type) has its own audience, sport organizations can choose a particular format on the basis of its compatibility with their own target market.

In an ethnically diverse country such as the United States, radio also permits sport organizations to offer broadcasts and advertising opportunities in languages other than English. This enables some organizations, particularly those located in south Florida, the Southwest, California, and New York, to reach out to their fans. The trend to broadcast in Spanish could become more mainstream over the next 10 years as the Hispanic population continues to grow. This fact has not been lost on the San Diego Padres, a team located less than 25 miles from Mexico, within a metropolitan area that is home to more than 600,000 Hispanics. Spanish-language broadcasts also provide additional sponsorship and advertising opportunities, according to Don Johnson, the Padres' vice president of marketing: "Because many of our sponsors also have Hispanic marketing departments, they have additional advertising budgets. Miller Brewing Co. is the U.S. domestic beer sponsor for the Padres, while Tecate is the Hispanic domestic beer sponsor. Some of the sponsors we've signed would not be here if it wasn't for the Hispanic broadcasts. It's really opened the door for a lot of new opportunities."[43]

Some sport organizations, particularly minor professional leagues and some college programs, may be too small or too limited in geographic appeal to attract radio advertisers. In such cases, it can be advisable to sell advertising space on a league- or conference-wide basis. For example, the University of Oregon, Oregon State University, Washington State University, and the University of Washington formed a partnership to offer opportunities at all four schools when they learned from the Northwest Ford dealers that an all-inclusive package better fit the dealers' needs and their advertising budget. This combined approach lets the Northwest Ford dealers share the advertising costs and also reap the benefits of a much broader geographic market than they could afford as individual firms.[44]

One of the fears of sport marketers is that sport radio and game broadcasts skew to an older audience. As this perception would also limit the universe of potential radio advertisers, it merits attention and a search for a possible solution. The Philadelphia Phillies have discovered a unique way to attack this perception and hopefully increase younger listenership. According to John Brazer, manager of promotions for the Phillies, "We found out that mostly adults listened to our games on the radio and when we looked at our programming, we found that most of the features were targeted at adults with almost nothing for children." Thus the Phillies will try to make their broadcasts more kid-friendly through features such as a roving reporter who will report live from remote parts of the stadium, like the bull pen and dugout. The features will run during the first three innings of the games so that kids can hear them before they go to sleep.[45] In the long run, the hope is to create a new generation of listeners who will continue as adults, enhancing the radio-rights and advertising revenue potential.

Although radio has its benefits as compared to television, most notably cost, nothing compares to television in advertising reach and the ability to convey to a mass audience the attributes of an advertiser's product or service. Television has grown in a relatively short time from the three national networks and the Public Broadcast System to four major networks—and arguably 20 or more national networks, in view of their availability to mass audiences through cable or satellite broadcasts.

Television   Television reaches the largest number of people, and it conveys sight and sound. The consumer can watch Mark McGwire hit a mammoth home run or see the fans do the "wave"—and can hear the crack of the bat or the roar of the crowd. Although television coverage—particularly of events such as the Olympics and the Super Bowl—can be expensive, advertisers have found this medium to be a critical element of their marketing mix.

Just as a story can be told in several ways, audio and visual elements can be combined to produce several types of television commercials. Television commercials can incorporate the following types of structures:

Story line—Telling a story. The message has a beginning, middle, and end.

Problem-solution—Presenting the viewer with a problem to be solved and the sponsor's product as the solution to that problem.

Chronology—Delivering the message through a series of related scenes. Facts and events are presented sequentially as they occurred.

Special effects—Achieving memorability through the use of some striking device, such as an unusual musical sound or pictorial technique.

Testimonial—Advertising by word of mouth. A well-known figure—or an unknown man in the street—vouches for the value of the product.

Satire—Using sophisticated wit to point out human foibles. This form is generally produced in an exaggerated style, perhaps as parody.

Spokesperson—Using an on-camera announcer who attempts to sell via personal, intimate selling, or perhaps via the hard sell.

Demonstration—Using some sort of physical apparatus to demonstrate the product's effectiveness.

Suspense—Telling a story, as with the story-line approach, but incorporating a high level of drama into the buildup of curiosity and suspense until the ending.

Slice-of-life—Beginning with a person needing to make a decision or in a situation requiring a solution. This approach then shows how the solution has worked.

Analogy—Instead of presenting a direct message about the product, conveying the message through comparison with something else.

Fantasy—Using caricatures or special effects to create fantasy surrounding the product and product use.

Personality—Relying on an actor or actress rather than an announcer to deliver the message. The actor plays a character who talks about the product, reacts to its use, or demonstrates its use or enjoyment.[46]

The NBA's Seattle Supersonics combined the fantasy, story-line, and personality approaches, using members of the team instead of actors to win five Clio awards for their advertising campaign "Coming to Your Home." This campaign featured video of Sonics players and coach George Karl showing up unannounced in unlikely places throughout the community. "Coming to Your Home" sent the message that the Sonics were televising 56 games on free or cable television, moving away from the pay-TV package they'd offered in previous years. At the same time, the campaign provided a link between the Sonics players and the community. The ads were shot using video instead of film to achieve the feel of a home movie, emphasizing the intimacy and spontaneity of the moment.[47]

The use of sport and its celebrities or stars to advertise other products via television has become part of our everyday life. The success of the Miller Lite campaign (see case study) and the popularity of a Coke commercial starring future NFL Hall of Famer "Mean" Joe Greene—a commercial so loved it became a movie[48]—testify to how effective these types of commercials can be. *USA Today's* "Ad Track" (table 10.3) lists the most effective sport-themed television advertising campaigns since 1995.

In the late 1990s, television advertising has begun to move away from the widespread use of athletes and to embrace the "everyday athlete" and "weekend

Table 10.3 EFFECTIVE SPORT-THEMED TELEVISION ADVERTISING CAMPAIGNS

Advertiser/Year	Athletes	Percentage of public perceiving the ad to be effective
McDonald's/1995	Michael Jordan, Larry Bird, Charles Barkley	47
Taco Bell/1995	Shaquille O'Neal, Hakeem Olajuwon	42
Nike/1997	Tiger Woods	40
Nike/1996	Anfernee Hardaway, Michael Jordan	39
Nike/1995	Drew Bledsoe, Marshall Faulk	34
McDonald's/1995	Dan Marino, Emmitt Smith, Drew Bledsoe, Barry Sanders	32
Nike/1998	Gary Payton, Kevin Garnett, Jason Kidd	29
Sprite/1995	Grant Hill	29
VISA/1996	Hakeem Olajuwon	27
Mountain Dew/1998	Michael Johnson	26
Reebok/1996	Emmitt Smith	23
Right Guard/1997	Scottie Pippen, Charles Barkley	23
American Express/1997–98	Tiger Woods	22

Case Study

The Miller Lite Campaign

Beer companies have relied upon sport as an ingredient in their marketing brew since time immemorial, and almost always successfully. In 1973-1974, Miller decided to test a series of commercials with "virgin" spokespersons because the feeling was that an actor would come across as just another actor endorsing a product, possibly lessening the commercial's believability. Subscribing to both the governmental and voluntary codes holding that active athletes could not endorse alcoholic beverages (because doing so would imply that alcohol increases their physical prowess), Miller opted for ex-athletes and characters who exuded machismo. After successful testing and a warm response in terms of sales, the commercials went national in 1975, with the theme "Everything you always wanted in a beer. And less."

McCann-Erikson, Miller's agency, assembled 34 characters—the highest use-of-athlete quotient in the history of sport advertising. They included former NFL stars Dick Butkus, Bubba Smith, Nick Buoniconti, and Deacon Jones; former NBA star Wilt Chamberlain; former NHL stars Jacques Plante and Boom-Boom Geoffrion (who discussed the attributes of the beer in French); and original New York Met "Marvelous" Marv Throneberry.

The commercials not only worked artistically, they worked commercially. In a marketplace where a six-pack of beer was suddenly cheaper than Coke, Miller Lite took the almost nonexistent category of light beer up to 2.5 million barrels in its first year of national distribution. By 1976, sales had doubled to 5 million barrels; and in 1977, by the best estimates available, it had more than doubled again to 12.5 million barrels, or between 8 and 10 percent of the beer market.

With the commercial, called by some a Madison Avenue production and by others a stroke of genius, Miller Lite had created the low-calorie market much as Xerox had created the photocopier market. And the success story behind the success story of Miller Lite has been their effective use of sport and sport stars.[49, 50]

warrior" types. Reebok and Nike are slashing their athlete endorser budgets in favor of showing everyday people in their athletic pursuits. One company, Lamkin Corp. of San Diego, a manufacturer of leather golf club grips, went so far as to parody Nike's famous "I am Tiger Woods" ad with its own "I am in the woods" campaign—an attempt to relate more to the average golfer and suggest a cure for a problem. The ad shows a series of hapless duffers whacking ball after ball into thick shrubbery and moaning, "I'm in the woods." The advertised cure, naturally, is a new leather Lamkin grip.[51] New Nike and Reebok commercials depict everyday people running, playing basketball, or rollerblading. The advertising message? Our products are for everyone, not just elite athletes.

Not all sport-related commercials are effective, and some can alienate viewers—the exact opposite of the commercial's purpose. Take the case of Nike in the 1996 Summer Olympics. With ads costing up to $700,000 for a 30-second prime-time spot, Nike elected to show a commercial that included a scene of a runner throwing up. While Nike's intent was to display the gritty realism of sport competition, the ad generated hundreds of letters from consumers outraged by the spot.[52]

Moveable billboards have proven to be a successful promo vehicle.

BILLBOARDS, BLIMPS, AND BUSES

Outdoor ads placed on billboards, on movable trailers, or on buses can provide a highly visible message, depending upon location and the duration of placement. Price varies according to location, number, and length, but this excellent form of advertisement can be relatively inexpensive compared to television. Fixed billboards can remain in place over a long period of time, providing repeated exposure and thus reinforcement of the message. Fixed-billboard locations can also be utilized for "teaser campaigns" that start out by posing a question and subsequently present the answer a little at a time.

Billboards mounted on trailers and driven throughout the marketplace have become commonplace at large special events such as All-Star Games and Olympic festivals (see top photo).

The purpose of a movable billboard is two-fold. The basic purpose is to draw attention to the event and the message of the advertiser. A second aim is to expose more people to the message than would ordinarily be the case as a billboard moves throughout a city, on highways, and within other high-traffic locations.

The Pirates have turned public transportation into advertising opportunities.

Other effective promotional devices are bus cards, placards on the exterior of buses, and "take-one" boxes, sometimes containing team schedules or ticket applications, that are placed in buses, trains, or taxi cabs. Some teams, such as the Phoenix Suns and the Pittsburgh Pirates, have actually utilized entire buses to display a promotional message (see bottom photo).

Blimps and small planes trailing advertising banners are also very popular forms of outdoor advertising. Companies such as Budweiser, Fuji, and Goodyear have highly visible blimps that travel to major sporting events. The Goodyear blimp, probably the most famous of these ships, provides aerial views that are integrated into the television coverage in ABC's "Monday Night Football."

NEW MEDIA—THE INTERNET

One of the most rapidly growing advertising mediums is the Internet. Accessed via billions of personal and business computers located throughout the world, sport marketers can use a number of approaches to capitalize on the availability of this resource to reach this huge global audience. Professional and collegiate sport organizations commonly use the Internet to advertise; to sell subscriptions, tickets, merchandise, and memorabilia; to broadcast or "cybercast" games in real time; or to provide summaries of events.[53]

The Seattle Supersonics claim that their Internet home page is one of the NBA's most frequently visited Web sites. But they, like most teams, have found that companies accustomed to buying signage, television, radio, and print advertising are still wary of Web site advertising.

So, Full House Sports and Entertainment, which handles the business operations of the Sonics, created an Internet advertising package with some of those traditional advertising components built in. The team hopes that packaging media, signage, and promotions along with Web advertising elements (to which companies will have an easier time assigning real value) will encourage advertisers to at least test the Sonics' Web site. "The bottom line is that nobody really knows what the value [of Web site advertising] is," said Doug Ramsey, director of corporate sponsorship and broadcast for Full House.

Full House has set a price of $50,000 for a one-year Sonics' Internet advertising package. As part of this agreement, Full House will create a sweepstakes or promotion for each month of the season to focus on a different Internet advertiser. For example, the organization might accept entries online for an airline trip to a Sonics' away game to support Southwest Airlines, one of the two sponsors that have advertised on the site in the past.

According to Ramsey, the package was created because the organization is making a concerted effort not to use Web site advertising as a free add-on to sponsors. "We see the Web site as another complete leg to sponsorship," Ramsey said. "And we were concerned we weren't going to maximize its value . . . especially because media tends to get less expensive over time."[54]

PROMOTIONAL CONCEPTS AND PRACTICES

The remainder of this chapter will deal with promotional concepts and practices in the sport industry. As previously noted, we will examine sales strategies and techniques in chapter 11; but the concepts and practices discussed in this section do have sales implications and applications. To explain how promotional concepts and practices have evolved in the United States, we will begin by examining the birth and development of promotional activities in sport.

Some of the greatest promoters in American history were involved in the promotion of sport and entertainment activities. P.T. Barnum, Albert Spalding, C.C. Pyle, Tex Rickard, Abe Saperstein, Rube Foster, J.W. Wilkinson, Ned Irish, Bill Veeck, Charlie Finley, Evel Knieval, Don King, Mike Veeck, Madonna, Howard Stern, and even Dennis Rodman are just a few of the innovative minds that sought to promote their products (or themselves) in most imaginative ways.

THE HALLMARK EVENT

A "hallmark event," as Ritchie defines it, is a major one-time event (or recurring events) of limited duration, developed primarily to enhance the awareness, appeal, and profitability of a tourism destination in the short and/or long term. Such events rely for their success on uniqueness, status, or timely significance to create interest and attract attention.[56]

Decade	Activity
1850s	First intercollegiate athletic event—crew—between Harvard and Yale, held in New Hampshire and sponsored by a railroad to promote its line and a new vacation route to prospective fans.
1880s	Albert G. Spalding publishes the *Spalding Baseball Guide*, an instructional piece that in reality was an attempt to create and expand the marketing for his products by teaching people how to use them. Spalding becomes the "official baseball" of the National League and promotion of the ball as "official" through the Spalding catalogue and through retailers begins.
1900s	First recorded instance of an athlete lending his name—Honus Wagner—to endorse a product, Louisville Slugger (bats), for payment ($75).
	The Doubleday legend (that Doubleday invented baseball) is created to position baseball as a uniquely American game.
	Ty Cobb and Honus Wagner promote Coca-Cola as "The Great National Drink of the Great National Game."
	Bull Durham (smoking tobacco) begins buying outfield signage and offering a prize to any player who hits the sign with a batted ball during the course of a game. This led to an increase in stadium signage and the utilization of this medium to promote products.
1910s	Tex Rickard creates "spectacle" in boxing through promoting the purse (displays of the prize money) to the public, creating public interest and free media coverage prior to the actual event.
	First sport award given for the purpose of product publicity; Chalmers Motor Car Co. donates a car to the MLB batting champion.
1920s	The role of the sport agent as a promoter begins to emerge as Christy Walsh represents Babe Ruth in his non-Yankee contracts.
	Red Grange and C.C. (Cash & Carry) Pyle team up to use a superstar to promote the new NFL and give it credibility.
	William Veeck Sr., wanting to introduce baseball to a new segment of fans (and children), begins broadcasting Chicago Cubs games on the radio.
1930s	The Kansas City Monarchs of the Negro Leagues develop a portable lighting system to enable them not only to play their games at night but also to "barnstorm" and take their game to various cities throughout the United States; concept was so successful that for six years the Monarchs elected not to join the Negro National League, preferring to barnstorm.
	Night baseball is introduced in the major leagues in Cincinnati.
1940s	The tobacco industry becomes more involved in the game of baseball—Chesterfield cigarette signs become a functioning part of the scoreboard in baseball parks with the "h" being lit to signify a hit and the "e" being lit to signify an error.
	First nationally televised World Series.
1950s	Bill Veeck introduces "Bat Day"—the first of many giveaway days featuring premium items, very commonplace today.
	The debut of *Sports Illustrated*.
1960s	International Management Group founded by Mark McCormack, initially as a vehicle to represent Arnold Palmer—now the largest sport marketing agency in the world.
	Signing and marketing of Joe Namath by the New York Jets and the American Football League (AFL)—once again the credibility of an interest in a superstar promotes an entire league.
	First Super Bowl between the NFL and the AFL; success of this venture coupled with the Sports Broadcasting Act led to the merger and growth of what is arguably America's *real* national pastime.
1970s	*Ball Four*, by then New York Yankee Jim Bouton, is published; the first book that portrayed athletes as real people with real problems and behaviors.
	Miller Lite embarks upon a national advertising campaign utilizing past sport figures (34 of them); the largest quotient in the history of sports advertising.
	ESPN begins broadcasting as the first 24-hour per day sport television network.
1980s	The commercial success of the 1984 Los Angeles Olympics organized by Peter Ueberroth; Olympics proving that corporate sponsorship can make the Olympic Games a profitable enterprise.
	The first collegiate bowl game sells its naming rights—the USF&G Sugar Bowl.
	The arrival and marketing of Michael "Air" Jordan—perhaps along with Muhammad Ali the most recognizable sport personality in the world.

Decade	Activity
1990s	The emergence of women's professional team sports—basketball (American Basketball League and WNBA) along with fast-pitch softball and soccer.
	The World League of American Football (now NFL-Europe) premiers to capitalize upon European interest in American sports as well as to provide opportunities for satellite television and merchandising sales.
	Direct TV and Primestar home satellite television services are offered along with packages such as the NFL Sunday Ticket, which permits viewers not only to follow their favorite team regardless of where they live but to follow every team. MLB, NBA, NHL, Major League Soccer, WNBA, and NCAA soon follow suit.
	Fox becomes the fourth national network, using its purchase of NFL television rights and broadcasting schedule to promote its programming, Fox Sports Net; a syndication of regional sport networks soon follows.
	Grassroots marketing through the creation of interactive fan festivals, aimed at fans in markets hosting All-Star games and the Super Bowls, begins. MLB's FanFest, NBA Jam Session, NHL FANtasy, and the NCAA Hoop City are initiated to entertain fans in host cities while at the same time providing a platform for their sponsors to interface with the public.

See G.E. White and B. Sugar.[55]

These hallmark events promote not only the destination, but also the activity as well as the organizations associated with or responsible for the event. Successful hallmark event staging also serves to promote the destination as attractive or the group as qualified or suitable for hosting other similar hallmark-type events.[57] For example, in the late 1990s, the city of San Antonio, Texas, hosted such hallmark events as the NBA All-Star weekend (All-Star Game and Jam Session), the NCAA Final Four, and the Builders Square Alamo Bowl (an annual event). Because of its success with these events, San Antonio was also selected to host the NCAA women's Final Four in 2002 and the men's Final Four in 2004; the city is also under consideration to host the Pan-American Games.

Many leagues, teams, and other sport-related organizations create hallmark or special events to promote their sport or activity to interested publics. They do this with the aim of strengthening or expanding existing relationships or initiating and cultivating new relationships and growing the overall base of support. Each of the three major sport leagues has such an event. The NBA has the NBA Jam Session in February in conjunction with its All-Star Game; the NHL offers the NHL FANtasy in conjunction with its All-Star Game in January; MLB offers MLB FanFest (see photo on page 202) at its All-Star Game in July. Finally, the NFL offers the NFL Experience during Super Bowl week in January. The NCAA offers Hoop City at its annual men's and women's Final Four championships, while major Division I collegiate conferences, such as the Southeastern Conference, have similar promotional events during their conference championships. These events serve as effective promotional vehicles by:

➤ promoting the host organization to the general public,

➤ promoting the sponsors of the event (and their products),

➤ promoting the sport in general,

➤ promoting the event itself as a revenue-generating opportunity,

➤ attracting significant media interest and coverage, and

➤ promoting the destination as a site for tourism and future hallmark events.

FanFests were a major event story in the 1990s.

INTERNET SITES AND WEB PAGES

As technology has evolved, particularly in relation to the media, so has the opportunity for fans to identify with teams and players.[58] Technological developments have also given fans who don't live near their teams more opportunity to maintain or increase their affiliation. Internet sites and Web pages meet these needs and at the same time serve as promotional vehicles. The Internet, and specifically an organization's Web site, promote the organization by providing information that was not as readily available in the past. This information can include any or all of the following elements:

Organizational history

Schedule of events, games, activities

Biographical information on players, performers

Links to related Web sites or pages (in the case of a league, links to sites of all member teams)[59]

Ticket-purchasing options[60]

Merchandise sales opportunities (cyberstores)

Chat rooms and availability of e-mail with players, broadcasters, management, or front office personnel

Statistics

Fan pages

Newspapers or other publications

Video or audio clips of game action or highlights

SALES PROMOTIONS

Sales promotions, which can take the form of price-oriented or non-price-oriented tactics, are an essential part of any sport organization's marketing strategy. In general, non-price promotions include special events, giveaway items, and other tangible incentives, whereas price-oriented promotions involve discounting or other price-related manipulations. Although research suggests that many fans are attracted to price discounts, price promotions may be dangerous if they cheapen the image of the product. Organizations normally use price promotions only when they are facing an elastic demand schedule. Giveaways of the basic product should be avoided because they may indicate to the consumer that the product is not worth anything and because they can infuriate customers who have already purchased the product. Such ideas as two-for-one nights, half-price nights, and family nights can be effective promotions.

The Pittsburgh Pirates, for example, with 81 home dates and an average crowd of approximately 19,000, have more than enough inventory to offer a price promotion. They have teamed with area grocer Giant Eagle to offer half-price nights on selected Wednesday evening games throughout the season. Fans can purchase any available seat for half price upon presenting their Giant Eagle Advantage Card. Although the promotion has been effective in increasing the size of the crowd on the selected dates, the Pirates have also noticed that fans use the promotion primarily to purchase higher-priced seats. The Pirates hope that these fans will become accustomed to the better locations and become interested in purchasing these same seats on nonpromotional nights, or perhaps in becoming mini-plan holders—thus moving up the escalator—in the new stadium.

When relying on sponsors to help underwrite the cost of a sales promotion or to provide a revenue stream, the organization must realize that the promotion needs to work for everyone: the fan, the organization, and the sponsor. For example, the Class A (baseball) Piedmont Boll Weevils, located in North Carolina, recently teamed with Dr. Pepper on a ticket-redemption program that could result in redemption of as many as 1 million tickets no cost to the fan. Dr. Pepper was seeking to promote its lesser-known soft-drink brand, Sun Drop. Dr. Pepper entered into an agreement with the Boll Weevils to provide up to 1 million logoed soft-drink cans that could each be redeemed for one free admission to one of six preselected Boll Weevil games during the 1998 season. The Boll Weevils received a cash payment of $5,000 and the exposure of the soft-drink cans. Sun Drop received the affiliation with the Boll Weevils and access to their target market of teenagers, while the fans received free admission to one or more games in exchange for purchasing the product—a promotional win-win-win situation.[61]

Unfortunately, it's easy to get carried away in the spirit of promoting. Markdowns, contests, sponsorships, sweepstakes, holiday sales, special events, open houses, and the like are often initiated with little thought of the desired long-term outcome. This is especially true in sport. When one examines the long list of promotions that baseball teams might offer during the course of the season (see schedule on page 204), it becomes readily apparent that sales promotions should be designed with the concept of reverse planning in mind. By reverse planning, we mean that you need to determine what it is you wish to accomplish in the long run and then strategically plan initiatives and activities that will help achieve this specified goal.

Price promotions involve some type of discount, rebate, or other financial incentive in relation to the product or service purchased. According to Donald Ziccardi,

> *Sales promotion strategies have become the quick fix for companies desperate for customers, fanatically assembled to adjust for economic swings, fashion trends, calendar shifts, and the weather, without taking into account the overall marketing plan. However, there are long-term effects on the company's image and on customers. For one, sales promotion activities can overshadow the advertising efforts instead of reinforcing them. Secondly, customers have been conditioned to shop only when there is a promotion. A price break, or a storewide sale, could trigger a big sales gain, but then the company could suffer a huge falloff the very next day.[62]*

In sport, one negative effect is that attendance is traditionally down for the event immediately following a promotion. If a promotion does nothing more than induce people to attend one game instead of another, then it is not effective. This pattern indicates that fans are "cherry picking"—attending games only when there is a promotion. When cherry picking occurs, the value of a sales promotion is minimal unless the promotional item is sponsored by someone other than the sport organization.

As previously mentioned, non-price promotions include giveaway items or premiums, fireworks nights, autograph days, and so on. The late Bill Veeck, owner of the Cleveland Indians, St. Louis Browns, and Chicago White Sox, was the master of the non-price promotion. Veeck, the inventor of Bat Day, recognized the importance of attracting new fans by implementing special theme days such as ladies' days and A-student days. Veeck utilized fireworks, had roving entertainers, gave away orchids and other premiums, and practiced a promotional philosophy that said

1998 PROMOTIONAL EVENTS

What Baseball's All About.   For Tickets and Information, call 321-BUCS or 1-800-BUY-BUCS

Date	Event	Opponent	
Fri, May 29	Freezer Mug Night #1/Bucco Bash	MON	7:05
Sat, May 30	Beach Towel Night /Beach Party Sandcastle Night	MON	7:05
Sun, May 31	Kid's Sunglasses Day/Pittsburgh Zoo Day	MON	1:35
Wed, June 3	Half-Price Night	NY	7:05
Fri, June 5	Fireworks Night/Bucco Bash/Singles Night	MIN	7:05
Sat, June 6	Autograph Party	MIN	7:05
Sun, June 7	Kid's T-Shirt Day	MIN	1:35
Fri, June 12	Bucco Bash – 70's Bash & Salute to Cheese	MIL	7:05
Sat, June 13	Road Cap Night /Latin & Caribbean Festival	MIL	7:05
Sun, June 14	Kid's Socks Day	MIL	1:35
Mon, June 22	Giant Eagle Advantage Card® Night	CWS	7:05
Wed, July 1	Giant Eagle Advantage Card® Night	DET	7:05
Thur, July 2	Fireworks Night	DET	7:05
Fri, July 10	Bucco Bash/Singles Night	PHI	7:05
Sat, July 11	Freezer Mug Night #2 / Polish Festival	PHI	7:05
Sun, July 12	Camera Day	PHI	1:35
Wed, July 15	Half-Price Night	CHI	7:05
Fri, July 24	Instant Vacation Night/Bucco Bash	ATL	7:05
Sat, July 25	Golf Umbrella Night	ATL	7:05
Sun, July 26	Kids Watch Day/Nickelodeon Day	ATL	1:35
Fri, July 31	Fireworks Night/Bucco Bash	HOU	7:05
Sat, Aug. 1	Kids Wristband Day (new date)	HOU	1:05
Sun, Aug. 2	Kids Shoelaces Day	HOU	1:35
Tue, Aug. 4	Giant Eagle Advantage Card® Night	COL	7:05
Wed, Aug. 19	Half-Price Night	LA	7:05
Fri, Aug. 21	Bucco Bash/Singles Night	CIN	7:05
Sat, Aug. 22	Alternate Cap Night	STL	7:05
Sun, Aug. 23	Kids Backpack Day/Kids Switch Day	STL	1:35
Tue, Sept. 1	Giant Eagle Advantage Card® Night	ARI	7:05
Wed, Sept. 2	Half Price Night	ARI	7:05
Fri, Sept. 4	Parrot Bean Bag Doll Night/Bucco Bash	CHI	7:05
Sat, Sept. 5	Fireworks Night/Wedding Night	CHI	7:05
Sun, Sept. 6	Parrot Birthday Party / Kids Parrot Cap Day	CHI	1:35
Fri, Sept. 18	Bucco Bash – Country Jamboree	HOU	7:05
Sat, Sept. 19	Greek Festival	HOU	7:05
Sun, Sept. 20	Fan Appreciation Day	HOU	1:35

ALL FANS WOMEN 18 & OVER
FANS 15 & OVER KIDS 14 & UNDER

FIREWORKS NIGHTS
- Friday, June 5
- Thursday, July 2
- Friday, July 31
- Saturday, Sept. 5

BUCCO BASH
Every Friday Night is a Bucco Bash, with a pre-game (5-7pm) party featuring food, live music and entertainment at Gate A.

KIDS DAYS
Every Sunday is a Kids Day, with clowns, facepainters, and kids entertainers.

DRESS YOUR KID HEAD-TO-TOE
The Pirates are offering eight kids (14 & younger) giveaway days this season — attend them all and you can dress your youngster in Bucs apparel from head to toe.

PARROT BEAN BAG DOLL
Just Added!!
Friday, Sept. 4, 7:05pm
All fans in attendance will receive a limited-edition Pirate Parrot Bean Bag Doll!

> The Pirates' promotional schedule is full of special events that are crucial elements in a marketing strategy.

"Every day was Mardi Gras and every fan was king."[63] Veeck recognized the need to market something other than the core product, realizing that you cannot always field a winning team but must provide entertainment every day. Thus, he pioneered non-price promotions in sport to help placate fans whose team might not be winning, to keep them interested in coming out to the park.

A problem with giveaway days is that depending upon the premium item, they may hinder souvenir or concession sales. The marketer must attempt to measure how much sales these giveaways create versus how much they eliminate. Thus, to avoid an adverse effect on souvenir sales, a cap day should involve a cap that does not resemble those sold at the stadium. The cap for the Pittsburgh Pirates' 1999 Cap Day is a replica of the 1979 Pirate cap, which is not sold at the merchandise stands. The same consideration applies to giving away or discounting food items. For instance, a promotional staple in minor league baseball is 10-cent hot dog night. This promotion is usually underwritten by a sponsor, in most cases jointly by the stadium concessions company and its hot dog supplier. While the club loses out on the sale of hot dogs, the higher attendance, coupled with parking fees and soda and beer sales, more than makes up for the loss.

A concessions-related promotion held in the 1970s has gone into the annals as one of the most ill-conceived promotional events in the history of sport, namely Ten-Cent Beer Night at Cleveland's Municipal Stadium on June 4, 1974. The result of that particular promotion? As one might have expected, drunken, unruly fans stormed the field during the game, which was ultimately forfeited to the visiting Texas Rangers.[64]

Timing is another key element in the planning of promotions for sport organizations. The concept of timing includes day of the week, opponent, starting time, time of the season, and time between scheduled promotions. The sport marketer must determine whether it is better to schedule a promotion against a better draw or a weaker draw. A better draw is an opponent that the consumer perceives as an attractive or effectively performing team, or an opponent with a "superstar" who attracts significant media attention and hype. In 1998, Mark McGwire and Sammy Sosa were in hot pursuit of Roger Maris's record of 61 home runs in a season. Thus, they attracted significant interest on the road, even though their teams were not performing up to expectations. Promotions scheduled on nights when they were playing might attract an even larger crowd than normal. Perhaps a team is scheduled to host the Atlanta Braves over a weekend; scheduling the promotional activity on a weekend usually results in higher-than-average attendance. Teams such as Notre Dame (football), the Dallas Cowboys, the Chicago Bulls (when Michael Jordan was playing), the New York Yankees, and the University of North Carolina (basketball) would constitute examples of good draws. For an illustration of scheduling promotional activities, see the case study on the following page.

Table 10.4 on page 208 depicts some of the most successful promotional activities used throughout MLB during the 1998 season.[65]

PROMOTIONAL COMPONENTS

The proper way to utilize sales promotion is to design and conduct balanced and creative sales promotional activities. An effective promotional campaign consists of the right type of activities conducted at the appropriate time, appealing to the target market.[66] In this section, we briefly describe and give examples of some program activities.

The Theme   In developing the theme or creative component of a promotion, one needs to ask and answer a number of questions before developing an effective creative strategy. Table 10.5 on page 209 lists the questions to ask and indicates the reasons for asking them. While this may seem like a function of advertising rather than promotions, it is an issue that promotional planning should address each year.

Most marketing themes that are effective are short, simple, and easily understood. Coca-Cola's "Always the Real Thing" is a very simple message: all other products are not the real thing but instead are imitations and are inferior to the real thing. The aim of Nike's former theme, "Just Do It," as well as of the current theme, "I Can," is to fit almost any situation and almost any target market: with these shoes, you can do whatever activity you wish, or perhaps none at all. "Just Do It" and "I Can" do not suggest the value of any sport or athlete over another. These messages emphasize participation, without implying serious competition or belittling low-key recreational activity.

205

Case Study

Scheduling Promotions

Vince Cazetta, U.S. Military Academy (Army)

Sport marketing professionals in the collegiate ranks are often faced with a dilemma regarding event promotional activities. On one hand, the coach would like to have every game promoted; on the other hand, the sponsor wants to be tied to an event promotion that will generate the greatest number of impressions. As a collegiate sport marketer, how do you satisfy both the coach and the sponsor? It has worked well at the U.S. Military Academy to use a promotional game matrix that we created.

Saturday afternoon or evening, and Sunday afternoon. Unfavorable days are those days with the least chance to attract potential spectators—essentially Sunday evening through Friday afternoon. Of course there are exceptions, notably holidays, which often fall on Monday, and days on which games are being televised.

➢ *Opponents.* Identifying an opponent as favorable or unfavorable is not necessarily based upon the opponent's win-loss record. A favorable opponent could be a school with a storied tradition in one sport, say football, that is therefore perceived to be a "name" and successful in all sports (e.g., Notre Dame). Another factor is name recognition. For example, Marshall University would not be considered a favorable opponent even though it has won numerous Division 1AA championships in the 1990s. However, a Yale football team that went 2-9 last year would be labeled a favorable opponent because of its regional appeal and storied tradition. The third factor in determining the classification of an opponent is the number of alumni and fans living within a 90-mile driving radius of your school. For example, Wake Forest University in Winston-Salem, North Carolina, with fewer than 1000 alums and fans living within a 90-mile radius of West Point, is considered an unfavorable opponent; Rutgers in Piscataway, New Jersey, with thousands of fans and alumni living in the area, would be considered a favorable opponent.

		Opponent	
		Favorable	**Unfavorable**
Day	**Favorable**	FF (Southern Mississippi)	FU (Miami and Tulane)
	Unfavorable	UF	UU

The promotional game matrix includes two primary factors. The left column of the matrix presents the first factor, the day and time during the week when the event takes place. The top row of the matrix shows the second factor, the opponent. These factors are classified as favorable or unfavorable based upon the following conditions:

➢ *Days.* Favorable days are identified as those days and game starting times with the best chance to attract the potential spectator, mainly Friday evening,

Now that we have defined our classification of days and opponents, we can develop our matrix. Favorable days and opponents will be graded "F," whereas unfavorable days and opponents will be graded "U." Consider the 1998 Army football schedule:

September 12 Miami of Ohio

September 19 Cincinnati

October 17 Southern Mississippi

November 7 Air Force

November 14 Tulane

For evaluating favorable versus unfavorable days, this particular football model is ideal because all Army football games are played on Saturday afternoons. Since all five games are on favorable days, each would be labeled an "F" with regard to day. However, if the Army versus Air Force game were scheduled on a Thursday night instead, the day of that game would be considered unfavorable, a "U."

When you are evaluating favorable versus unfavorable opponents, it is often helpful to weigh the pros and cons of your opponent by analyzing the positive and negative impact of the conditions previously discussed. Thus, opponents with more positives than negatives would receive a positive rating. For example, Miami would receive a "U" rating based upon the following considerations:

- Miami is annually one of the top teams in the Mid-American Conference.
- Army is undefeated at 0-0.
- Early September daylight makes for favorable postgame tailgating conditions.
- Miami is a small private school with few fans and alums living in the 90-mile radius.
- The game is too close to Labor Day and family vacations.
- Fall foliage is not even close to peak.
- Miami is not a team that has television appearances (in this market).
- Fans are not sure whether the opponent is Miami of Ohio or Miami of Florida.

On the other hand, Southern Mississippi would receive an "F" rating:

- Southern Mississippi is the defending Conference USA champion.
- Tailgating weather is at its prime with average temperature in the 60s.
- Foliage is at its peak in the Hudson Valley.
- Southern Mississippi has a history of television appearances and plays name opponents.
- Homecoming—U.S. Military Academy classes of '78, '83, '88, and '93 are returning for the game.
- This is the only home game in October—research indicates that October is the most popular month to attend an Army football game.
- Few fans or alumni live in the 90-mile radius.
- Win-loss record of team

Tulane would also receive a "U" rating:

- Tulane might be competing for the Conference USA championship.
- Weather is poor for tailgating (temperature in the 40s).
- Foliage is gone—trees are bare.
- Few Tulane fans or alums live in the 90-mile radius.
- Win-loss record of team

After the days of the events and the opponents have been classified as favorable or unfavorable, the dates and the opponents are entered in the appropriate box in the matrix.

Games labeled "FF," that is, those on a favorable day with a favorable opponent (Southern Mississippi), need very little promotional support. Games labeled "FU" (on a favorable day but with an unfavorable opponent—Miami and Tulane) or "UF" (featuring a favorable opponent on an unfavorable day) will need promotional assistance.

Table 10.4 1998 MAJOR LEAGUE BASEBALL'S MOST EFFECTIVE PROMOTIONS

Rank	Promotion	Ranked in Terms of Percentage Attendance Increase % Increase	Number of fans
1	Beanie Baby	37.4	9175
2	Beach towel	26.4	7779
3	Umbrella	20.1	5330
4	Coupon	20.0	5249
5	Baseball cap	19.9	5370
6	Fireworks	19.1	3998
7	Hat (not baseball cap)	17.3	4822
8	Bat	15.0	4177
9	Heritage/Family Days	14.9	3116
10	Beanbag toy	14.4	4453
11	Schedule magnet	13.8	1079
12	Shirt	13.3	3774
13	Helmet	13.1	3573
14	Fan appreciation	12.1	3535
15	Camera day	11.3	1847
16	Photo	11.1	1985
17	$1 concessions	9.2	1572
18	Business people	8.9	1987
19	Growth chart	8.6	490
20	Backpack	8.0	2468

Note: Increase is calculated by comparing all teams' average attendance in comparison with attendance on all promotional dates.

Whenever possible, the theme should capitalize on unique aspects of the product or the marketplace. When moving from Winnipeg to Phoenix, the NHL Jets changed their name to the Coyotes—an image more in tune with the desert environs surrounding Phoenix. The name and location change provided the Phoenix franchise with a marketing theme capitalizing on the new home—"Experience the Coolest game in the desert."[68]

When selecting a theme, or a name, the marketer should try to ensure that the theme cannot be turned against the organization. Prior to their emergence as a baseball power in the mid-1990s, the Cleveland Indians were a woeful collection of poor performers with little interest and identification outside of their own market. The marketing department in the early 1990s hit upon the theme "The Tribe—This is *your* team." When team performance was even worse than expected, the theme was turned into a joke: The Tribe—This is *your* team—who else would want them? While this kind of reaction is not common, the sidebar by Chad McEvoy illustrates that perhaps themes should be limited and in some cases omitted.

Product Sampling An effective method for getting new products off the ground is to distribute samples to the public. The beauty of sampling is the lack of risk to the customer. When there is no charge, people will try almost anything. Gatorade is a company that has long emphasized sampling. Gatorade maintains a presence at thousands of sport venues throughout the United States and Canada where it utilizes sampling to test consumer reaction to new flavors, to introduce product, and to explain why Gatorade is important. Gatorade maintains a high presence at events such

Table 10.5 QUESTIONS TO BE ANSWERED WHEN FORMULATING A CREATIVE COMPONENT

Question	Rationale
What does this customer want?	Identify the target market; understand what they think and why; know what they value; have documentation of their purchasing habits.
Does our product fit the consumer?	Does the consumer understand the product? How does the perception of the consumer differ from the reality of the product?
How will the competition affect our objectives?	Know and understand the competition, how it operates and its objectives. Whom does the consumer consider as a competitor?
What is the competitive consumer benefit?	What is the statement of benefit the consumer expects from a brand? From an organization? The benefit to the consumer must be clearly stated.
How will marketing communication make the benefit believable to the consumer?	There must be persuasive communication that gently, subtly, credibly convinces the consumer that the product and its benefits are worthwhile and superior to those of other similar products in the marketplace.
What should be the personality of the brand?	The personality must give the brand a life and soul with which the consumer can easily identify. It should differentiate the brand from the competition.
How will the consumer define the product?	How is the message positioned in the mind of the consumer? Is best because it was first? Is it more contemporary? Longer lasting? Fun?
What are the main communication and action objectives?	What action should the consumer take as a result of the message? Do we expect the consumer to call for information? To go directly to a retailer?
What contact points (mediums) should be used to reach the consumer?	What is the best communication strategy to reach the target market? Direct mail? Television? Telemarketing? Open house?

See Schultz, Tannebaum, and Allison.[67]

When Your Marketing Theme Comes Back to Haunt You

Chad McEvoy, Iowa State University

"A Tradition of Excellence," "Refuse to Lose," "A Gathering Storm." Collegiate and professional sport teams use themes and slogans such as these to create excitement among fans for the upcoming season. For an organization with a winning tradition such as the University of Nebraska football program, a theme usually seeks to unify the team and its fans in the quest for a championship. For teams that have been less successful in the past, a theme tied to performance can spell disaster. A theme such as "A Gathering Storm" can come back to haunt the marketer especially if the team flops: by midseason the media may refer to the theme with regard to the possible firing of the head coach.

One of the unique aspects of sport marketing is the fact that the marketer often has little or no control over the core product; rather it is the coaches and general managers who are responsible for assembling the core product by drafting, recruiting, and trading for players and then coaching and developing them to perform at their peak abilities. Marketers cannot assume that their team will be the best in the majors or the worst. Anything can happen over the course of a season. If the 1997 World Champion Florida Marlins has used a theme such as "The Dynasty Begins" for their 1998 campaign, the media might have twisted it into "The Dynasty Tumbles" or "The Dynasty Collapses" after the Marlins had sold or traded most of their stars in an effort to lower the payroll and become more profitable.

In creating a campaign theme, the marketer must decide whether to emphasize winning or whether to stress product extensions such as game atmosphere. According to Greg Gerlach, director of marketing for men's athletics at the University of Minnesota, "Our marketing themes are not in any way associated with performance. We do not promise anything in that regard."

Other teams do not use themes or slogans in their marketing campaigns. Iowa State University elected not to utilize a theme in marketing its 1998 football season. With just six victories over the past four seasons, fans had become somewhat cynical about themes encouraging them to believe that a winning football program was on the way. According to Mary Zeigler, director of athletic marketing at Iowa State,

"We've had our themes come back to haunt us too many times in recent years. Our fans know what they're getting at a Cyclone game and make their decisions whether or not to buy tickets accordingly."

The marketer must carefully consider issues such as these and the risk inherent in any type of implied promise. A theme promising a successful season should be used only if the marketer is absolutely sure the team will win. A theme hyping the product extensions is much less risky. In any case, it is important to utilize market research, and focus groups in particular, to assess public reaction and opinion with respect to potential marketing themes before initiating a marketing campaign.

as marathons, triathlons, and volleyball tournaments and in other settings where the potential consumer is active and building a thirst.

Reebok is another company that uses sampling. Reebok has taken to the streets with a van and trailer setup to encourage consumers to try on the new DMX athletic shoes (see photo).

At these Reebok locations there are no salespeople—just "shoe techs" who explain the shoe and provide demonstration models for the consumer to try on. This more nontraditional type of sampling is also becoming prevalent in larger sporting goods stores, which may utilize court surfaces or running tracks to enable the customer to really sample the product.

As in most sampling situations, use of discount coupons or sales in conjunction with the sampling opportunity can prove highly effective.

The Open House   The open house is similar to the free trial offered in sampling, but is geared toward attracting people to a facility such as a fitness club or YMCA to encourage them to join activity-based sport programs. Promotional activities similar to the open house can also be used to interest consumers in purchasing products like ticket plans for spectator games or events.

Fitness clubs realize that in order for them to sell a membership, prospective purchasers need to "experience" the club before determining whether or not it is right for them. This experience often takes the form of a free visit or trial membership (usually one week) and comes complete with an orientation and personal consultation. Often a YMCA or fitness club will schedule a one-day or a one-week open house that enables prospective members to sample not only the facilities and equipment but also the programming—aerobics, child care, sport leagues, and so forth.

On the spectator-sport side, the Pittsburgh Pirates held an open house in March 1998 to give fans a behind-the-scenes look at what happens during the course of a baseball game (see schedule on page 211).

The day's activities included guided tours of the dugouts, bull pens, announcer's booth, and scoreboard animation area; an opportunity to meet former players and

Marketing efforts such as the Reebok van are designed to provide interaction between the product and the consumer in a non-retail environment.

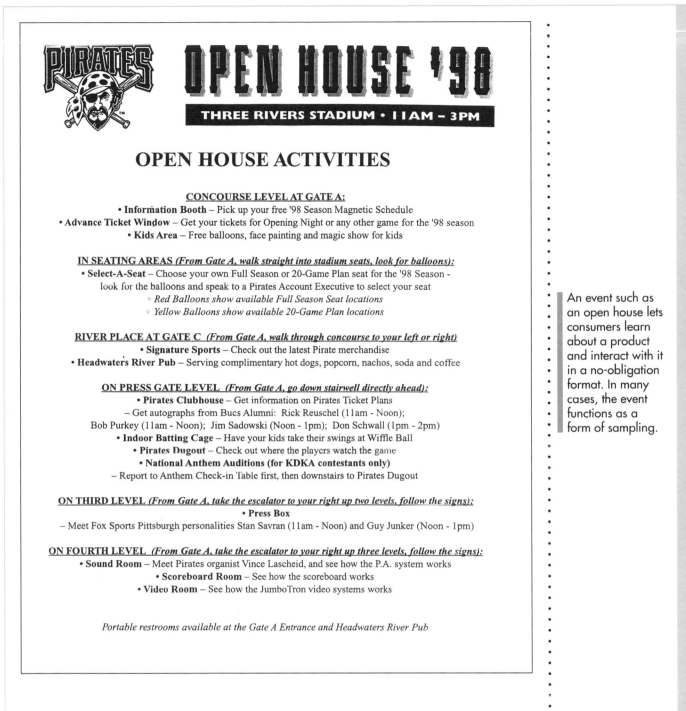

OPEN HOUSE ACTIVITIES

CONCOURSE LEVEL AT GATE A:
• **Information Booth** – Pick up your free '98 Season Magnetic Schedule
• **Advance Ticket Window** – Get your tickets for Opening Night or any other game for the '98 season
• **Kids Area** – Free balloons, face painting and magic show for kids

IN SEATING AREAS *(From Gate A, walk straight into stadium seats, look for balloons):*
• **Select-A-Seat** – Choose your own Full Season or 20-Game Plan seat for the '98 Season -
look for the balloons and speak to a Pirates Account Executive to select your seat
  ◦ *Red Balloons show available Full Season Seat locations*
  ◦ *Yellow Balloons show available 20-Game Plan locations*

RIVER PLACE AT GATE C *(From Gate A, walk through concourse to your left or right)*
• **Signature Sports** – Check out the latest Pirate merchandise
• **Headwaters River Pub** – Serving complimentary hot dogs, popcorn, nachos, soda and coffee

ON PRESS GATE LEVEL *(From Gate A, go down stairwell directly ahead):*
• **Pirates Clubhouse** – Get information on Pirates Ticket Plans
– Get autographs from Bucs Alumni: Rick Reuschel (11am - Noon);
Bob Purkey (11am - Noon); Jim Sadowski (Noon - 1pm); Don Schwall (1pm - 2pm)
• **Indoor Batting Cage** – Have your kids take their swings at Wiffle Ball
• **Pirates Dugout** – Check out where the players watch the game
• **National Anthem Auditions (for KDKA contestants only)**
– Report to Anthem Check-in Table first, then downstairs to Pirates Dugout

ON THIRD LEVEL *(From Gate A, take the escalator to your right up two levels, follow the signs):*
• **Press Box**
– Meet Fox Sports Pittsburgh personalities Stan Savran (11am - Noon) and Guy Junker (Noon - 1pm)

ON FOURTH LEVEL *(From Gate A, take the escalator to your right up three levels, follow the signs):*
• **Sound Room** – Meet Pirates organist Vince Lascheid, and see how the P.A. system works
• **Scoreboard Room** – See how the scoreboard works
• **Video Room** – See how the JumboTron video systems works

Portable restrooms available at the Gate A Entrance and Headwaters River Pub

An event such as an open house lets consumers learn about a product and interact with it in a no-obligation format. In many cases, the event functions as a form of sampling.

the mascot; and also an opportunity to see what seats were available for the 1998 season and to personally select seats. Everyone received free hot dogs and other baseball-type fare.

Coupons Coupons are a popular and accepted promotional strategy, but they must be appropriate to the image and style of the organization. In some cases, people may perceive couponing as a move that cheapens the organization's image and reflects desperation to get sales—particularly if the organization has no history of offering coupons. Fitness clubs offering two memberships for the price of one, or free memberships for payment of a maintenance fee, are sometimes perceived to be in this situation.

All coupons are in some form of print (even Internet coupons usually must be downloaded and printed before they can be presented). In sport, the most popular types of coupons appear in newspapers or in booklets sold as discount coupon book-lets (typically referred to as an "Entertainment Book") that are available in most large American cities and feature two-for-one dining and entertainment offers. One of the more popular coupon ads used by spectator sport organizations targets the family and features the approach "all this for one low price." These coupons, usu-ally found in a newspaper, can be clipped and presented at the box office. They present an offer—usually a price promotion—that may include four game tickets, four hot dogs, four soft drinks, popcorn, and usually parking or a game program for a price between $39 and $79, depending upon the level of the organization.

In many cases, the coupon is for certain games only, and the organization may have selected the games by opponent or by day of the week. This type of offer is usually extended for opponents described as weaker draws and for less attractive game days (usually Monday through Thursday), although some teams may elect to offer this type of promotion on Friday evening or Saturday afternoon.

Bundling Bundling is the practice of offering additional amenities or benefits if the consumer purchases the product or service in a package. In some cases, the product is discounted so that the bundling actually results in a cash savings. Consumers may, for example, be able to purchase a three-year fitness club membership at a discounted rate along with free personal training sessions or classes. A professional sport team may elect to discount the cost per game in a ticket plan or may "bundle in" parking privileges, free statistics sheets, a lounge area for certain levels of ticket holders, and so forth. The NBA's Cleveland Cavs offer their club-seat holders such benefits as 15 general admission tickets to a game during the season at no extra cost, membership benefits at two area golf clubs, a special lounge area to use before and after the game and at halftime, and waitperson service in their seat location.[69]

Contests and Sweepstakes Contests and sweepstakes add glamour, glitz, excite-ment, and fun to the promotional mix. Although most sport patrons don't expect to win, it is often an interesting promotional strategy to offer fans the possibility of winning or of watching someone else compete in a contest. In the mid-1990s, Coca-Cola and the NFL offered a promotional contest, "Monsters of the Gridiron," that included a grand prize but also featured numerous opportunities to win product from Coca-Cola or merchandise from the NFL. Designed to spur the sale of Coca-Cola while providing an association with the NFL and featuring the "personalities" of some NFL players, this contest was popular and successful. In late September and October (to tie in to Halloween), purchasers of Coca-Cola found a 900 number on the inside of the bottle cap; when they called the number, they received a message from one of the "NFL Monsters" that would also inform them if they were a winner.

On the level of the local team, contests such as cash scrambles are utilized for entertainment purposes and for promotion of a sponsor. In cash scrambles, the par-ticipants grab as much cash as they can in a limited amount of time while providing entertainment for the fans in the stands.

Premiums and Redemptions Organizations use premiums and redemptions to attract new consumers and also to encourage greater frequency on the part of exist-ing consumers. A premium item can sometimes be combined with a special event to achieve better results. On Saturday, May 30, 1998, the Pittsburgh Pirates utilized a beach towel as a premium item, coupons to an area water park, and a beach party outside the stadium (complete with music, 240 tons of sand, and virtual surfing); they attracted a crowd of 38,149 fans. This was 20,000 more fans than the average attendance for a Pirate game; but more interestingly, 10,675 fans were walk-ups, having decided to attend that day and purchasing their ticket upon arriving. Ac-cording to Pirates Vice President Vic Gregovits, "What we're trying to do is to take a premium item—which will always embellish the crowd—and make it a whole themed event."[70]

At MLB's FanFest in Denver, title sponsor Pinnacle Brands, a trading card manufacturer, combines premiums and redemptions. When visiting the Pinnacle booth, consumers get one free package of trading cards and learn that if they purchase four more packages (sold by merchants on-site), they can redeem the five wrappers and receive a free collectible, a limited-edition trading card not available anywhere else.

To increase consumer attendance at baseball games, the Oakland Athletics pioneered a thematic promotion, called "Year of the Uniform," that involved premium items. The promotion encouraged consumers to attend multiple (six) Oakland A games by providing a different clothing-item premium (sponsored by Adidas) to members of the target market (those under age 14) at each designated game. One game featured a cap, another a jersey, another wristbands, and so on. This was a promotion geared to a target market and designed to increase frequency of attendance (a move related to the concept of the frequency escalator described later in this chapter). This promotion, introduced in the early 1980s, is still successful for a number of teams. Using the theme "Dress Your Kid from Head to Toe," the Pittsburgh Pirates had eight kid-targeted giveaway dates during the 1999 season.[71]

Astute marketers will utilize premium items that expand their product distribution beyond the game or event and create impressions year-round if possible. Current NCAA Director of Marketing, Licensing and Promotions Dennis Cryder, who at one time worked for the Kansas City Royals, was very deliberate in considering the types of promotional premiums he would distribute when he was with the Royals. He selected premiums with a high "residual distribution," such as ski caps and school notebooks; this meant that the image and message—not to mention the number of impressions—of Royals baseball would resurface regularly throughout the year.[72]

Street Promotion   A number of footwear companies, most notably Nike, Reebok, and Adidas, have taken to the streets to showcase and promote their products by putting them in the hands of perceived leaders who can influence sales and set trends. "Taking to the streets" includes the Reebok van, the Nike Hummer, and other visible signs of the companies' presence, but also much more. It involves interaction through activities, but mainly just through conversation—getting to know people and what they're about so that the companies can design appropriate products and communicate with consumers effectively.

Because apparel trends begin in big cities, understanding the urban youth market as well as targeting it effectively is the secret to fortune in the athletic footwear business. Reebok employs Khari Streeter and DeMane Davis to keep in touch with the target market by hanging out with young people and their friends in the entertainment industry. Streeter and Davis have served as creative directors for a Reebok television ad starring Allen Iverson, and according to Streeter, they "bring Reebok a legitimate point of view" from the streets.[73]

Generation X, the baby boomer "echo," the ".Com generation," and Generation Y are all categories for segments of today's youth that marketers find attractive but in some cases difficult to reach. The values of these groups sometimes reflect the values of the late 1960s and early 1970s. For example, some of these segments have referred to a new technology used by Reebok as "*techorganic*—combining breathable natural fabrics with protective synthetics; and fashion fabrics that mix synthetics with all-natural fibers."[74]

Consider the rationale of Lea, a 23-year-old design assistant living in New York City, for her purchase of a pair of Adidas shoes: "I bought these Adidas shoes because they're totally vegan [do not consume or wear or support any animal or animal by-products]—I know Adidas didn't even think about it, maybe don't even care. But they have no leather on them—all synthetic. And they look good too."[75] Is this what Adidas had in mind when planning the marketing strategy for the shoes?

An aim of street promotions is to reach not only vegans, but also hip-hoppers and other pop segments. Contact with the street could provide a marketer with knowledge that among some groups the word "extreme" isn't cool: it's a word used by "ordinaries" to describe activities outside their range of interests. How can marketers avoid mistakes resulting from lack of knowledge about their potential consumers? It's important to get the help of members of the target segments in designing promotional strategies. Specialty agencies such as Sputnik can help traditional companies reach target markets that are difficult to contact.

THE ULTIMATE GOAL: MOVING CONSUMERS UP THE ESCALATOR

The ultimate goal of promotion in sport is to increase awareness and interest and subsequently consumption of the products or services. When launching a new sport product, such as the NHL's latest additions, the Nashville Predators or the Columbus Blue Jackets, the marketer has little choice but to attract first-time (new) consumers. It is understandable that in such a situation sport marketers will expend the majority of their efforts on mass media advertising to attract a broad market base. However, once the product is off and rolling, many forget to change their approach and become locked into the "new-consumer" mentality. Yet the data show that the more mature a sport organization is, the lower the impact of new consumers on total attendance or participation figures. This is the case not just in terms of new consumers as a percentage of existing consumers, but also in terms of attendance frequencies of new consumers versus "old" consumers. The impact of new consumers is often minimal and short lived. For example, competition for a championship often attracts a number of "new fans," but in reality it is the increased attendance of old consumers or "core attendees" that dictates the long-term financial viability of the franchise. The "new-consumer" myopia is perhaps acceptable for sport industry segments in which total demand is low, such as professional soccer, or for some professional baseball markets, such as Montreal. However, it is in these very sports that high supply of the product (a baseball franchise could have an inventory of 4,050,000 [81 games × 50,000 seats] during the course of a season) creates considerable room for increased attendance frequency on the part of existing customers.

This myopia is not limited to spectator sport; in fact, it is endemic to most segments of the sport industry. Perhaps the only explanation for this widespread ignorance within sport marketing is the limited amount of market research conducted by sport organizations in general, and the low priority given to research in the budgeting process and the strategic plan. Any research data on attendance or participation frequency of sport consumers will reveal that the 80-20 rule (i.e., 80 percent of all goods consumed in a particular category are consumed by 20 percent of all persons consuming the product) does not apply to all sport segments. The impact of the so-called heavy, medium, and light users will vary greatly from sport to sport.

The intelligent approach to sport promotion is to bring consumers progressively up a gradient of involvement and commitment. Bill Giles of the Philadelphia Phillies called this the "staircase approach" (figure 10.2); the marketer attempts to move the fan up the stairs so that a light user becomes a medium user and potentially a heavy user.[76]

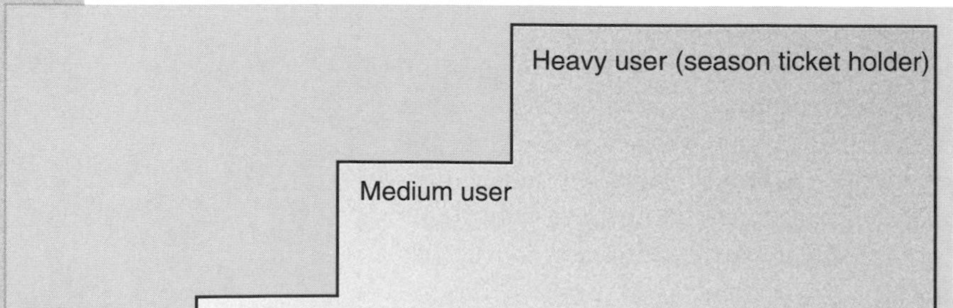

Figure 10.2 The staircase approach to sport marketing.

THE STAIRCASE VERSUS THE ESCALATOR

Although the staircase is similar in concept to the escalator and provides an excellent foundation, it has limitations. First, it assumes that each step in the process entails a distinct and perhaps difficult movement. Second, it implies that all light users are on the same step. Observation of attendance frequency distribution shows that neither assumption is true. Sport consumers are distributed in terms of their attendance or participation frequency across a continuum that runs from 1 through N, where N is the maximum number of events, games, or contests that consumers can attend (or of days on which they can consume the product). The N in professional sport varies greatly; for example, the NFL has 8 home dates, the NBA 40, and MLB 81. The N for other sport industry segments also varies greatly, from the approximately 240 days that a Vermont ski resort could be open to the 360 days that a typical YMCA/YWCA or fitness center could be open. In fact, the frequency distribution is better represented by an escalator, which has many steps that all appear to run into one another. The step between a heavy-light user and a light-medium user is just one extra game attended or one more visit to a ski slope.

Thus the distribution of existing consumers is a continuous series of steps on an escalator that runs from 1 through N. However, before the consumer gets into the ranks of the existing consumers, he or she passes through several stages. Bill Giles used the generic term "nonconsumer," but there are several forms of nonconsumption. Research suggests that as many as 50 percent of all people who consider themselves sport fans have never attended a game.[77] We can therefore construct three levels of the consumer hierarchy:

> *The nonaware nonconsumer* is unaware of the existence of the sport product and consequently does not attend.

> *The aware nonconsumer* is aware of the sport product but does not choose to attend. Presumably the product does not offer the benefits this person is looking for, or this person has no need for this type of product.

> *The media consumer* is aware of the sport product and does not consume directly (by purchasing it from the organization) but does consume indirectly through the media. This type of consumption is not limited to spectator sports but is also seen in participant sports that receive media exposure.

Recent research[78] using community intercept methodology[79], which involves interviewing the general population about their attitudes and perceptions with regard to their local sport teams (professional and collegiate), has enabled us to expand the nonconsumer category to include another level:

> *The misinformed nonconsumer* is aware of the product and wishes to consume directly but does not do so because of misinformation or misperception. The misinformation usually relates to the cost of attending, availability of tickets, or safety concerns. Often the source of the misinformation is word of mouth from friends or relatives. The misinformed consumer usually consumes the product indirectly through the media.

Figure 10.3 on page 216 shows the escalator with these lower levels of consumers. The promotional effort and expense required to move consumers up the escalator are usually considerably less than those required to move nonconsumers onto the escalator to begin direct consumption. But more importantly, response is likely to be considerably greater from existing consumers than from an unaware or disinterested public, unless the existing customers are already satiated.

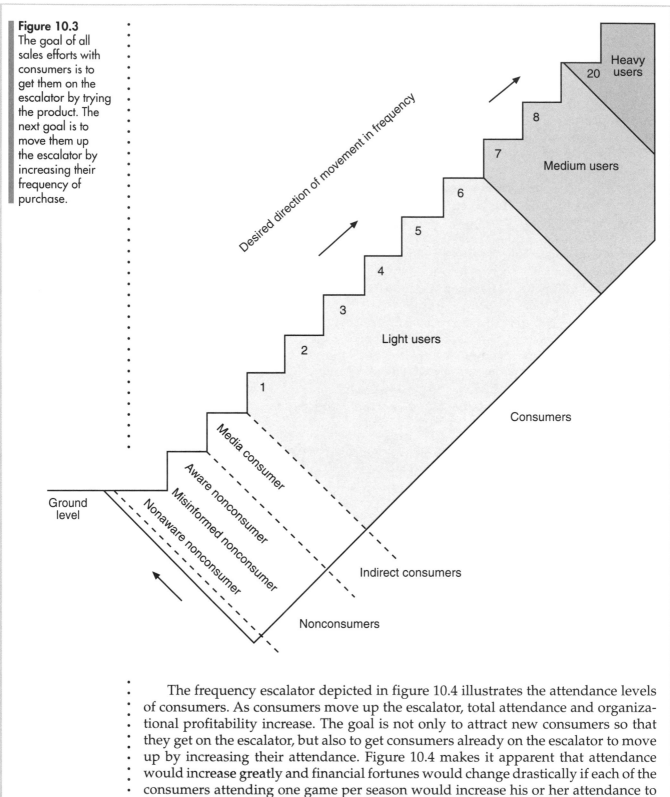

Figure 10.3 The goal of all sales efforts with consumers is to get them on the escalator by trying the product. The next goal is to move them up the escalator by increasing their frequency of purchase.

The frequency escalator depicted in figure 10.4 illustrates the attendance levels of consumers. As consumers move up the escalator, total attendance and organizational profitability increase. The goal is not only to attract new consumers so that they get on the escalator, but also to get consumers already on the escalator to move up by increasing their attendance. Figure 10.4 makes it apparent that attendance would increase greatly and financial fortunes would change drastically if each of the consumers attending one game per season would increase his or her attendance to two games per season.

Further support for the approach of targeting existing consumers comes from the well-known fact that existing satisfied customers are an organization's best salespeople. For most segments of the sport industry, 70 percent of all consumers are referred by word of mouth from existing customers. Marketers have a high stake in keeping current consumers active and satisfied. Indeed, promotional efforts should focus initially on moving existing customers up the escalator.

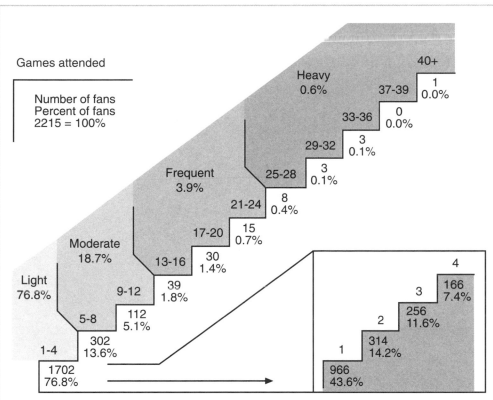

Figure 10.4
A frequency escalator showing fan attendance analysis for a play-off qualifying NBA team. All figures are rounded.

THE PROMOTIONAL PLANNING MODEL

Obviously, marketers of new products or new organizations, or those moving into new markets face a different situation. Beyond this, the most sophisticated campaigns target both existing and potential consumers, concentrating more heavily on current users. Figure 10.5, showing the promotional progression planning model, is a framework for such a campaign (see page 218).

In order for promotions to be effective, they must be arranged and directed. Promotions such as giveaways, all-inclusive one-price nights, and discounts, as well as events such as fireworks, concerts, and other forms of entertainment, have an audience—but it is a limited audience. Promotional strategies must be developed with the entire range of attenders in mind: first-time attenders, parents bringing children, price-conscious attenders, partial plan holders, mini-plan holders, season-ticket holders (personal and corporate), and attenders not participating in any plan or package. The importance of addressing all stages of the escalator is brought home by the situation of the Orlando Magic. The Magic, a team that offered only full-season tickets—thus having all heavy users—has faced some challenges in terms of ticket sales after the free-agency movement of Shaquille O'Neal, injuries to star player Anfernee "Penny" Hardaway, and poor performance on the court. A team that once enjoyed near or full sellouts for all of its games has found itself without any medium-level users to move up the escalator. The team thus faces the task—difficult at best—of almost instantly attracting media consumers toward becoming heavy users.

Level One: Non-Pattern Attenders/Light Users

The consumers on the first level may be classified as having no established attendance pattern (first-timers, people with free tickets, spontaneous attenders, bargain hunters, giveaway collectors such as those who come for Beanie Babies, and so on). These people are motivated to attend by a variety of factors including opponent, weather, day of the week, giveaways/special events/discounts, team performance, and opportunity for social interaction with friends, co-workers, or relatives. Interest

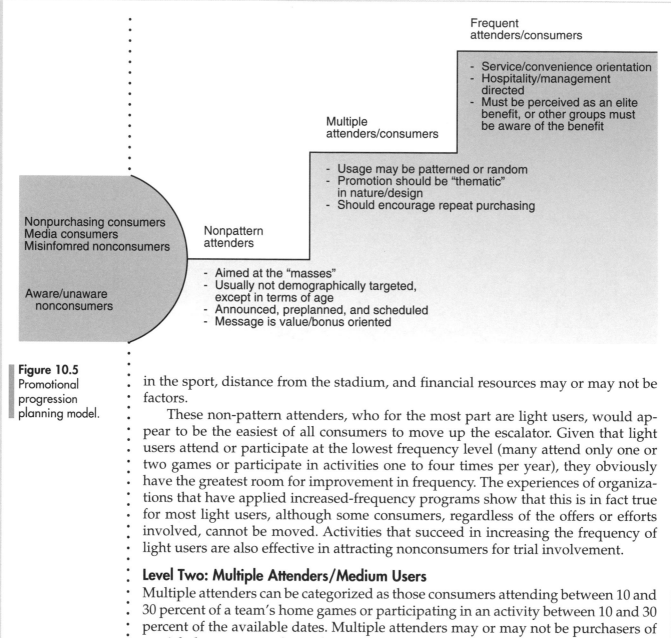

Frequent
attenders/consumers

- Service/convenience orientation
- Hospitality/management
  directed
- Must be perceived as an elite
  benefit, or other groups must
  be aware of the benefit

Multiple
attenders/consumers

- Usage may be patterned or random
- Promotion should be "thematic"
  in nature/design
- Should encourage repeat purchasing

Nonpurchasing consumers
Media consumers
Misinfomred nonconsumers

Nonpattern
attenders

Aware/unaware
nonconsumers

- Aimed at the "masses"
- Usually not demographically targeted,
  except in terms of age
- Announced, preplanned, and scheduled
- Message is value/bonus oriented

Figure 10.5
Promotional
progression
planning model.

in the sport, distance from the stadium, and financial resources may or may not be factors.

These non-pattern attenders, who for the most part are light users, would appear to be the easiest of all consumers to move up the escalator. Given that light users attend or participate at the lowest frequency level (many attend only one or two games or participate in activities one to four times per year), they obviously have the greatest room for improvement in frequency. The experiences of organizations that have applied increased-frequency programs show that this is in fact true for most light users, although some consumers, regardless of the offers or efforts involved, cannot be moved. Activities that succeed in increasing the frequency of light users are also effective in attracting nonconsumers for trial involvement.

Level Two: Multiple Attenders/Medium Users

Multiple attenders can be categorized as those consumers attending between 10 and 30 percent of a team's home games or participating in an activity between 10 and 30 percent of the available dates. Multiple attenders may or may not be purchasers of partial plans or mini-plans. There are several reasons for non-plan ownership. Some consumers may be unaware that such plans exist; others have time commitments or work schedules that would not easily accommodate a plan with set dates. Still others, because of availability of seats at the ballpark or the number of golf courses in the area, for example, perceive no advantage to having such a plan—availability outstrips demand.

Plans offered to these consumers to increase (and stabilize) their frequencies should utilize a menu approach to attract interest and break down reasons for not purchasing. This means offering several options at different price points and with different benefits.

Level Three: Frequent Attenders/Heavy Users

Frequent attenders include half-season plan holders, full-season ticket holders, club-seat purchasers, and luxury-suite holders. In terms of participation, this group would include the membership at a golf, tennis, or fitness facility and the season-pass holders at a ski resort, for example. Promotional strategies aimed at this level must include all of the benefits and opportunities offered to light and medium users, but must also include one or more elements perceived as attractive and elite (not available to consumers at lower levels). Such strategies usually emphasize customer service, hospitality, comfort, convenience, location, priority, increased communication, interaction, and special discounts on related product extensions. This approach not only attracts medium users toward becoming heavy users, but also retains heavy users and decreases reasons for defection (decreasing involvement at one level and dropping to another level, or dropping off the escalator entirely). The benefits of being a heavy user need to be promoted to both light and medium users so that they understand the value of moving up the escalator—and hopefully to convey the fact that they are missing out on something of value.

Defectors—Descending the Escalator

Regardless of the product or service offered, there will be consumers who have overpurchased or overcommitted to an opportunity. These consumers then seek to downgrade their involvement or commitment or to terminate it. Organizations must give careful attention to developing programs to attract consumers to the various levels without "cannibalizing" consumers from higher levels.

In the following chapter on sales, we will offer specific programs to attract consumers to each of these levels; we'll discuss how to retain and move them up the escalator and how to prevent them from defecting.

WRAP-UP

Promotion is a commonly used term in sport marketing. For most, promotion includes advertising, personal selling, publicity, and sales promotion. At the core of promotion is communication—the attempt by an organization or entity to reach its audience. To be effective, the promotional activity must cut through the clutter of the marketplace, inform and persuade the targeted recipient of the message, and hopefully initiate some type of action on the part of the recipient. Advertising through a variety of traditional mediums and new media, and also via personal selling through endorsements, is evolving and changing as a result of technological innovations and the ineffectiveness of past practices. This evolution will continue, and new techniques and practices such as use of the Internet and street marketing will be judged on their effectiveness to deliver the appropriate demographic.

Promotional activities are a valuable strategy to attract new consumers as well as to increase the frequency (participating, purchasing, attending) of current consumers. In determining how to implement such activities, the reverse planning process—knowing what you want to achieve through the promotion—is an essential organizational approach.

Promotional activities, which can take the form of price-oriented efforts such as discounting and packaging, or non-price efforts through the implementation of giveaways and the creation of special events, are an essential part of attracting consumers and increasing their frequency or volume. The theory of the consumer escalator suggests that promotions should be a coherent package in which the aim is to ensure a balance between the light, medium, and heavy users.

Because the repeat user is the lifeblood of the sport organization, investing extensive time and money in an effort to attract one-time patrons is a questionable strategy. Even if a sponsor underwrites the cost of a giveaway, the marketer must consider the resources (staff, time, advertising) spent on attracting consumers who may be nothing more than "cherry pickers." Obviously, any strategy should include attempts to attract non-users—but should not neglect any groups currently on the escalator, who typically provide the bulk of all product consumption. Ultimately, each organization must determine the ideal balance in its promotional strategy. Tactics will include some combination of advertising, personal selling, public relations, and sales promotions. However, successful strategies will recognize the tendency for many consumers to move up an escalator of consumption. Although large numbers may jump off at any point, into the vast recesses of defection, a sound strategy will maintain a steady flow of patrons moving upward.

ACTIVITIES

1. Interview 15-20 students at your institution to determine the most effective way of reaching them (i.e., communicating a message). After identifying the best methods, determine how your athletic department should attempt to communicate with students (both on and off campus) with regard to attending athletic events.

2. Using the same audience as in activity 1, determine whether price or non-price promotional activities would be more effective in attracting college students to athletic events (note that this point may be moot on your campus if students are admitted free to all athletic events).

3. When watching television over the next two weeks, keep an advertising journal and classify each advertisement that you see according to the list of structures for television commercials on page 196. Which commercial type was the most prevalent? Which commercial ad type was the most effective? Why?

4. Identify five athletes who you feel could become effective endorsers. Select a product for each and explain why that individual would be an effective endorser for that product.

5. Using a product or service of your choosing, conduct some research activities in order to profile the consumer group and construct a frequency escalator for that product or service. Develop a series of strategies to change light consumers to medium consumers, and medium consumers to heavy consumers.

YOUR MARKETING PLAN

One of the greatest challenges in marketing is communicating your message to your intended audience. How will advertising and promotional activities help you disseminate your message to your intended target market? How will these same activities be used to initiate action on the part of your intended target market? How will these approaches change after six months? After two years?

SALES: MANAGEMENT AND APPLICATIONS

OBJECTIVES

1. To define what sales is and its role in marketing.
2. To provide an overview of the various sales methodologies utilized in sport.
3. To illustrate, through the use of examples, some successful real-life sales applications.
4. To show the importance of customer service in the sales process.

The Buyer Is Always Right?

Rupert Murdoch, Fox media mogul and owner of the Los Angeles Dodgers, agreed in 1998 to pay $1 billion for England's Manchester United soccer club. Can any property be worth that much? How will he ever recoup his investment? Was it Murdoch's intent to buy one of the top and best-known soccer clubs in the world? Or was he merely competing with his rivals in sport broadcasting, attempting to capture sport programming by owning the teams and leagues they broadcast? Recent developments in sport such as this have shown that the price of the product may not make sense to the general public but makes good business sense to the buyer.

Disney, Time Warner, and numerous other broadcasting conglomerates are buying up premier sport properties for prices that astound the general public. The 1998 rumor mill had the New York Yankees, arguably the jewel of American sport, being sold to Cablevision for a price between $500 million and $1 billion. Cablevision was entering its final year of a 12-year $486 million deal for exclusive cable rights to the New York Yankees. If Cablevision owned the Yankees, as it did the New York Knicks and New York Rangers, it would be able to design and market sponsorships for all three teams that could also be packaged to give a sponsor year-round exposure on MSG Network. In addition, MSG could put together interesting subscription offers and combinations for its fans in New York, as well as for those throughout the United States and beyond who purchase their sport programming via satellite. In determining whether or not to sell and for how much, the owner or seller of a product must understand its immediate short-term benefits for the buyer, as well as the possibilities for packaging and using that product in effect to create other products for sale. Fox, Time Warner, and Disney not only have "read the book" but have rewritten it.[1]

Sales is the "lifeblood" of any sport organization. Whether it be of tickets, media rights, sponsorships, signage, advertising, luxury suites, or any of the sport products, sales accounts for the majority, if not all, of the revenue.

According to Ron Seaver, founder of the National Sports Forum, "Nothing happens until somebody sells something."[2] Unfortunately, the word "sales" or the term "salesperson" usually conjures up images of "hucksters"—individuals using guile and persuasion to talk customers into buying products they might not want at prices they sometimes can't afford. In this chapter, we will attempt to change this perception by exploring the various sales methodologies the sport industry uses; distinguish between product-oriented and customer-oriented sales; and examine the concept of "aftermarketing," or what should happen after the sale to ensure that the purchase is a win-win situation for both the seller (the sport organization) and the purchaser (the sport consumer). This emphasis on relationship marketing (building long-term relationships that grow) and lifetime value (the true measure of a consumer's value to the organization over time) will illustrate the value of the sales process to a sport organization and the professionalism of the sales approaches utilized in this industry.

As we have discussed earlier in this book, sport marketing differs from marketing in a variety of ways. One difference is the presence of emotion. This is also the case for the sales aspect of sport marketing. In sport, the sales process may involve an emotional element that may be, but usually is not, an element of the majority of sales taking place throughout the world every day. This emotional element can be either an aid or a hindrance, usually depending on the public perception of the sport product at that time. Take, for instance, the San Diego Padres. In September 1998, the Padres had clinched their division and a play-off spot in the National League Championship series. During the 1998 season, both ticket demand and attendance were very high. However, five short years before, people had ridiculed and vilified the team for trading away its best players, and demand for tickets had been nonexistent.

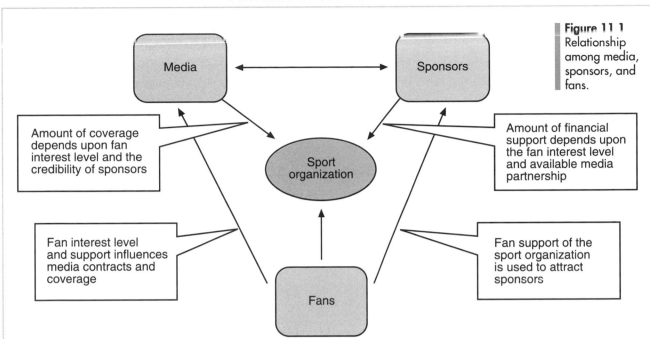

Figure 11.1
Relationship
among media,
sponsors, and
fans.

The emotion at that time dictated that the product had little value, whereas in 1998, emotion dictated that the product was very desirable. After the 1998 season, a number of personnel changes took place, again negatively impacting the quality of the team. Will emotion once again alter demand for a team that performed in last year's World Series?

This chapter will address the types of sales strategies and tactics most commonly employed in the sport industry. We will illustrate these strategies and tactics through examples and insight from expert practitioners from a number of organizations. We will accomplish this primarily within the context of tickets or sponsorship.

Figure 11.1 depicts a critical relationship among the media, sponsors, and fans. This relationship is essentially symbiotic, because the three elements feed off each other to create the types of conditions that attract additional fans.

Media provides the amount of coverage according to the interest accorded the sport by the fans. It is also influenced by the credibility afforded the sport or organization by its sponsors. *Sponsors* provide financial support for the sport or organization based on fan support. The more fans, the more impressions and interaction among sponsors, product, and fans (target market). *Fans* and their support of the sport organization are used to attract sponsors. Their level of interest and support influences media contracts and coverage.

Hall of Famer Yogi Berra once said, "Nobody goes there anymore it's too crowded."[2] In his inimitable style, Yogi captured the goal of any event marketer, to create a crowd—because a crowd attracts a crowd. The game or the venue must become the place to be. The crowd is important because it provides credibility to people in the media, who then deem the event worthy of coverage and attention. The media coverage and interest function to create value for the sponsors, who rationalize their costs on a cost per exposure basis. The larger the crowd, the more exposures and the more cost effective for the sponsors. In the words of many sport marketers, the goal is to put "meat in the seats." This is accomplished through sales.

SALES DEFINED

Sales is the revenue-producing element of the marketing process. In the strictest sense of the word, selling is the process of moving goods and services from the hands of those who produce them into the hands of those who will benefit most from their use.[4] It usually involves the application of persuasive skills and may be supported by print, audio, or video messages designed to promote the product or its brand as essential, the best, or desirable. In some cases, the salesperson might be able to afford the consumer the opportunity to sample or experience the service or product.

In this chapter, we will define and explain sales by referring to famed sport marketer Mark McCormack, founder and chairman of IMG (International Management Group)—arguably the world's leading sport marketing and athlete-management organization. As McCormack explains, selling consists of

> ➤ the process of identifying customers,

> ➤ getting through to them,

> ➤ increasing their awareness and interest in your product or service, and

> ➤ persuading them to act on that interest.[5]

One can also explain sales as *customer performance:* when a customer purchases your product, he or she performs the act of buying.[6] In sport, four main factors cause customers to perform or to fail to perform:

> ➤ *Quality:* How well is the product or service performing? The win-loss record of the 1998 New York Yankees is an example.

> ➤ *Quantity:* In what number is the product sold—for example, 1 unit, 10 units? An individual might purchase a mini-plan for the WNBA Cleveland Rockers that includes 5 games rather than a full-season ticket, which includes more than 15 games.

> ➤ *Time:* Does the consumer have the time to consume the product? For example, family obligations, work schedule, and everyday life might dictate that he or she does not. To make the purchase of a golf membership worthwhile, for example, the individual usually must average 45 or more rounds of golf per year.

> ➤ *Cost:* Cost relates not only to the overall cost, but also to such aspects as payment options and value received for the purchase price. Many fitness clubs position the cost of membership as cost per day: Isn't your health worth 74 cents a day?

Getting the customer to perform, and retaining that customer, will dictate how successful a salesperson or a sport organization really is and how viable the future of the person or the organization will be.

WHAT MAKES A GOOD SALESPERSON?

Are salespersons born or made? The debate has raged for centuries. In the opinion of experts, the naturally born salesperson is a myth; salespersons are made, not born.[7] People usually learn the skills needed to be successful through developing good listening skills, being comfortable speaking to strangers, and having an aggressive attitude in the context of wanting to succeed. These traits are generally learned and developed through experience and modeling; and over time, they form another critical element in a successful salesperson, confidence. These are the qualities Mark McCormack looks for in salespersons in his sport marketing agency:

> ➤ Belief in the product

> ➤ Belief in yourself

> ➤ Seeing a lot of people (sales-call volume)

> ➤ Timing

➤ Listening to the customer (but realizing that what the customer wants is not necessarily what she is telling you)

➤ A sense of humor

➤ Knocking on old doors

➤ Asking everyone to buy

➤ Following up after the sale with the same aggressiveness you demonstrated before the sale

➤ Common sense[8]

WHAT IS A GOOD SALES-ORIENTED ORGANIZATIONAL STRUCTURE?

The organizational structure and style of the organization form a key element in determining the overall success and impact of the sales department's efforts. Organizational structure and style include the following:

➤ *The reporting structure* (whom you report to—your immediate supervisor) in an organization.

➤ *The relationships between departments* that are integral in the sales process. For example, in structuring any organization involved in the sale of tickets, the relationship between the box office manager and the ticket-sales department is critical because of possible offers and incentives and the subsequent redemption of those offers.

➤ *The organizational style/philosophy* with regard to producing support materials (e.g., brochures, direct-mail pieces, advertising) utilized in the sales process.

➤ *The sales developmental process within the department.* Most sales departments begin their salespeople in entry-level type sales. In sport, this often involves starting salespersons in telemarketing (discussed later in this chapter) and letting them progress according to performance. The typical sales-development progression begins with telemarketing and leads to group sales, then to season-ticket sales, and finally on to corporate sales, which often involves sponsorships and other high-priced products such as luxury suites. According to sport sales consultant Jack Mielke, organizations should establish separate and distinct departments for ticket and sponsorship sales and divide ticket sales into season, group, corporate, and telemarketing.[9] Obviously this depends on the size and scope of the organization, but it is a good practice—similar to the approach used in professional fundraising—to produce specialists who become experts in that particular area.

➤ *Determining the composition of the sales force and compensation mix for the sales staff.* In this process, one determines the number of full-time sales staff, the number of part-time sales staff (if any), the use of outside sales services (usually a telemarketing agency), and the way sales personnel will be compensated. Compensation is usually a combination of salary and commission (a percentage of the sales generated). Commission percentages vary according to the salary/commission ratio and the product being sold, and according to whether the sale is a new sale or a renewal.

Vic Gregovits, Pittsburgh Pirates vice president of marketing and broadcasting, began his career in sales and has worked in a sales capacity for more than 10 years with teams such as the Cleveland Cavs, Cleveland Indians, Philadelphia Eagles, and now the Pittsburgh Pirates. According to Gregovits, managing a sales team is an ongoing process that involves daily attention to the activities at hand. Gregovits discusses his approach in the following sidebar on page 226.

Because of multiple franchise ownership or involvement in a variety of enterprises by ownership, some sales staffs are multitask oriented. The NBA/WNBA relationship is one of the more common examples of multitask sales staff. Steve Swetoha

Developing and Managing a Sales Department

Vic Gregovits, Vice President, Marketing and Broadcasting, Pittsburgh Pirates

When developing and managing a sales staff, you must continually evaluate the structure of the staffing and also the individual members of the staff. As part of my evaluation process, I ask the following questions:

➤ Have the sales staff been properly trained?

➤ Do the sales staff have the resources they need to accomplish the established goals?

➤ What are the strengths and weaknesses of the sales team or its individual members?

➤ How can the various personalities and styles of the individual members be used to complement each other and benefit the team as a whole?

➤ Is an attractive incentive structure (i.e., commissions and bonuses) in place that will motivate the salesperson to achieve his or her individual goals?

An examination of each of these questions will provide some insight into the management and evaluative process that I employ.

Have the sales staff been properly trained?

A manager must ensure that the sales staff are intimately knowledgeable about the product that they are selling. Knowledge and confidence go hand in hand. If salespersons know all aspects of the product, they will feel confident that they can fully present the product to the customer and answer any questions the customer may have.

Another very important part of training is role-playing. We use role-playing for familiarizing the sales staff with possible scenarios that they may encounter and for rehearsing their presentations. It is important that the sales personnel have an opportunity to play both roles, that of the salesperson and that of the consumer; this ensures that they understand the process from both sides. After the role-play-

ing, I recommend holding a group discussion to share the perceptions of the sales team about the activities.

Do the sales staff have the resources they need to accomplish the established goals?

When a salesperson makes a sales call, he or she must have all the tools necessary to make this presentation impressive, memorable, and effective. It is my responsibility to make sure that the sales personnel have the appropriate literature (brochures, order forms, diagrams, and so forth) to support the product they are selling. However, as with my earlier point, the salesperson must have detailed knowledge about the product. One way to effectively evaluate whether the sales staff have the tools and training that they need is to periodically accompany them on sales calls.

What are the strengths and weaknesses of the sales team or its individual members?

When you are trying to identify the strengths and weaknesses of a salesperson, you need to analyze his or her techniques. You can accomplish this, as I have already said, by going on sales calls with each team member or, in telemarketing situations, listening to team members' phone solicitations to verify that they are asking the right questions. Going over sales reports is another way to review performance. By reviewing the sales reports, the manager can assess whether the salesperson is stronger at selling one type of product over another, "up-selling" or upgrading consumers to higher product levels, renewing current customers, and so on. By determining which type of package a salesperson sells most often, you can identify his or her strengths and weaknesses. Someone who concentrates on upgrading or renewing packages may have a strength in customer relations and up-selling while possibly exhibiting a weakness in "cold calling" or initiating new sales. Someone who concentrates on new sales may have a weakness in postsales account service. It is important to have a good mix of personalities and styles to balance the sales staff.

How can the various personalities and styles of the individual members be used to complement one another and benefit the team as a whole?

Once you have determined the strengths and weaknesses of your staff, you should structure your department to maximize individual strengths. This may mean allocating certain people to concentrate on selling the products they know best. This will make the entire staff very efficient. However, it is important that you also help these individuals overcome their weaknesses. You do not want to stereotype people with regard to their sales skills. As a manager, you must continue to help each person grow and broaden his or her skills. Individual goals should refer to both the strengths and the weaknesses of the salesperson.

Is an effective incentive structure (i.e., commissions and bonuses) in place that will motivate salespersons to achieve their individual goals and the team goals, thus rewarding them financially?

The incentive structure should be developed with three things in mind: team goals, individual sales staff goals, and a fair commission structure. The team goals specify the budgetary numbers that the team as a

unit needs to achieve. The individual sales goals add up to the team goals. The object is to motivate the individuals to achieve their own targets, which in turn achieves the team goal. Two things, commissions and competition, should provide the motivation. The commission structure motivates by functioning as an immediate reward for the sale. The competition acts as an incentive, through recognition and peer pressure, to sell more. Monthly sales contests with monetary rewards create not only competition and peer recognition, but also additional compensation and gratification. It is also a good idea to have a trophy or some visible token (special parking space, opportunity to travel with the team, and so on) for the winner to display. Besides serving as a constant reminder for the winner of last month's performance, this is a source of motivation to the other competitors and a reminder of what they are capable of achieving.

The underlying factor in all of these areas is fairness. Fairness is critical in managing a sales force. Be accessible to all your team members, and be encouraging and empathetic to their needs and desires. Goals are achieved by a team, and effective management of that team ensures a realistic chance of achieving or exceeding expectations and goals.

---

of RDV Sports, the parent company of the Orlando Magic and Orlando Miracles, offers some insight regarding managing such an enterprise in the case study on page 228.

WHAT IS A GOOD SALES-ORIENTED STRUCTURE?

Figure 11.2 (on page 229) depicts a possible organizational structure for a marketing department in a professional sport franchise—and specifically, how the ticket-sales department could be structured. As we have previously mentioned, the relationship between ticket sales and the box office is essential, but so are other relationships such as that between Management Information Services and ticket sales. This relation is critical because of the practice of data-based marketing (discussed later in this chapter), which would require the MIS personnel to provide segments of the database to the sales department for use as leads (names of potential consumers who through some action or activity have indicated an interest in or ability to purchase the product) or for the purpose of conducting a mailing or similar activity. Similar relationships are necessary for providing tickets to sponsors as part of their packages, to community relations personnel for use in their efforts, and also to the promotions department.

WHAT DO I HAVE TO SELL?

Sales inventory refers to the products available to the sales staff to market, promote, and sell through the sales methodologies described in this chapter. Table 11.1 (on page 229) lists a category, such as naming rights, and indicates the inventories within this category that can be sold.

Case Study

Managing an Integrated Sales Force—Three Similar But Distinct Products

Steve Swetoha, Director of Ticket Sales, RDV Sports

As the director of ticket sales for the Orlando Magic, the Orlando Solar Bears, and our new WNBA franchise, it is my responsibility to maintain and, more importantly, increase ticket-sales revenue. While we are ultimately judged on the end result, it is the process that we hope will enable us to reach the organizational revenue expectations.

Since I joined RDV Sports (the parent company of the three franchises under discussion) some four months ago, one of my first priorities has been to examine and evaluate the current sales staff and sales approaches. My previous experience with the Pittsburgh Penguins (1985-1994) gave me the opportunity to simultaneously manage sales for three different sport teams (hockey, soccer and Arena Football), so the challenges and expectations were not new to me as I assumed this position. In essence, I began by implementing a five-step process enabling me to assess where we stood and where we needed to be.

Step One: Evaluating. As we evaluated our sales strategies for the three teams, it was our feeling that we would have one distinct sales force for the Solar Bears (hockey) and another sales force that would combine on efforts to sell the Magic and the WNBA (basketball). Thus we would have a staff of five or six concentrating on hockey and a basketball staff of six to nine people that could "cross over" from season to season.

Step Two: Hiring. We employ an aggressive recruiting process to attract potential salespeople nationally. To do this we have utilized sport industry contacts not only in basketball and hockey, but also in sport (and non-sport) in general. As this step is critical in achieving our sales goals, we have spent many hours interviewing and checking personal and professional references. If at all possible, we ask our contacts to recommend people who can sell and who have demonstrated success in the field of sales. This provides us with a known commodity in terms of performance and shortens the learning curve—the time

it will take before new personnel are able to begin the sales process and start generating revenue.

Step Three: Training. Orientation and training are key elements in the preparation and development of our sales staff. Too often, organizations "throw" young, inexperienced individuals into telemarketing or sales calls without preparing them for what lies ahead. Salespeople's presentation skills, along with knowledge of and belief in the product, are key components in developing a successful sales team. Without ongoing training and development, an organization runs the risk of turnover and a less-than-successful sales team. Sales personnel undergo an initial comprehensive training period before beginning to sell, and they participate in ongoing seminars and workshops to further define and develop their skills base.

Step Four: Resources. A sales staff must be properly equipped with the right tools to be successful in ticket sales. This translates into computers, software, and sales materials (brochures, videos, diagrams, etc.) that support and relate to well thought out marketing and advertising campaigns. At RDV Sports, we make sure not only that our personnel have what they need, but also that they can employ these resources thoughtfully and creatively to achieve their objectives.

Step Five: Implementation. After selecting, hiring, training, and equipping our staff, it is time to put them to work and implement our sales campaign. At this point I am responsible for motivating my staff to ensure that they are aggressively attacking the marketplace and selling our products. I have the responsibility to follow up and meet with all personnel weekly to review their accomplishments, discuss problems or challenges they have faced, and consider what the organization can do to help them become more productive.

Once we have completed these steps, I continue to gather data and feedback and reinitiate the evaluation process.

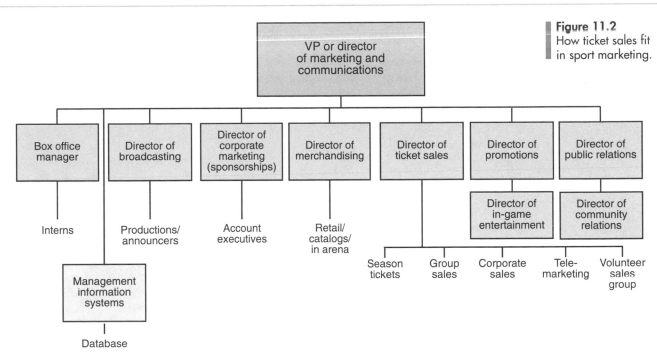

Figure 11.2
How ticket sales fit in sport marketing.

DIRECT DATA-BASED SPORT MARKETING

Direct marketing is an interactive system of marketing that uses one or more advertising media to effect a measurable response and/or transaction at any location. All forms of direct marketing, such as direct mail and telemarketing, involve the use or creation of a database.[10] Simply stated, data-based marketing involves the collection of information about past consumers, current consumers, and potential consumers. This information can come from membership records, lists of past purchasers, credit card slips, surveys, contests, and so forth. The organization uses the information to construct a database (as discussed in chapter 5) that can be segmented according to its needs. Regardless of the sales approach or process that the sport organization is

Table 11.1   INVENTORIES—WHAT DO I HAVE TO SELL?

Naming rights	Electronic inventory	Signage inventory	Print inventory
Arena/Stadium	Television	Dasher, score, matrix,	Game program
Practice facility	Radio	and message boards	Media guide
Team	Web page	Marquees	Newsletters
		Floor/field/ice	Ticket backs
		Medallions	Ticket envelopes
		Concourse	Scorecards/roster sheets
		Blimps	Faxes
		Turnstiles	

Tickets and hospitality inventory	Promotions inventory	Community programs	Miscellaneous inventory
VIP parking	Premium items	School assemblies	Fantasy camps
Stadium/Arena clubs	On-floor promotions	Camps, clinics	Off-season cruises, trips
Season tickets	Diamond Vision	Awards, banquets	with players
Club seats, suites, PSLs	(or similar brand)	Kick-off luncheons/dinners	Road trips
Group tickets	Contests	Golf tournaments	
Parties/Special events	Pre-/Post-game		
	entertainment		

using, some type of database is necessary to generate leads.[11] Table 11.2 illustrates how a ticket-sales database can be generated and how the data could be used.

Former NBA executive and marketing consultant Jon Spoelstra feels that the organization should attempt to secure the name, address, and phone number of everyone who purchases its products or services. He feels that building a database qualifies as a "quick-fix silver bullet" and should be one of the first things undertaken in any sport marketing effort.[12]

Management of the database is also a key element in the process. Each group or segment in the database should be tested and their responsiveness to certain appeals measured—ticket plans, telephone solicitation, direct mail, special offers. Responses should be measured to test ROI (return on investment) and should be documented in order to increase the targeting and hopefully the effectiveness of future efforts.

On the negative side, ROI obviously decreases if you waste your phone calls and have your mail returned—and also if the party repeatedly fails to respond to your offers. We recommend purging (removing) a name from the database in the absence of any sales activity (tickets, merchandise, subscriptions, membership renewals) in a 36-month period.

Many organizations construct databases and use them for periodic contact (special targeted mailings, newsletters, offers, and so forth) with their consumers. The previously mentioned San Diego Padres and their Compadres program represent a unique utilization of the database—namely, monitoring attendance and encouraging the registrants to increase their attendance through an incentive program.

Don Johnson, former San Diego Padres vice president of marketing, and Brook Govan can be credited with implementing the Compadres program—one of the first and most successful frequent-attender programs in professional sport. The intent of the program was to recognize and reward fans for their attendance at the ballpark. The program is similar to frequent-flier plans in which air travelers accumulate points that they can redeem for rewards. It is designed to move fans up the escalator by rewarding them for every game attended. The more games attended, the more points accumulated—redeemable for prizes (see reward system on page 232).

Club membership is free to any fan. To become a member, fans simply complete an application, which in actuality is a lifestyle survey (see application on page 233). This information then becomes part of the Padres' database. Upon completing the application, the fan receives an attractive bar-coded membership card that tracks his or her attendance and creates a record of points earned for every game attended. Each game is worth between three and five points depending on the date.

Upon arriving at the game, fans present their game ticket to enter, and once inside the gate they "swipe" their membership card at the Compadres kiosk. The Compadres member then receives a four-part coupon that has been printed inside the kiosk. The coupon contains three special offers for every game (from the Padres or from Compadres Club sponsors such as Oscar's Restaurant); the fourth part of the coupon shows the member's name and provides a cumulative point total.

According to Johnson, "The entire process of recognition and reward and creating a sense of privilege and exclusivity have allowed us to develop relationships with all of our fans—individual ticket buyers as well as ticket plan purchasers."[13]

TYPICAL SALES APPROACHES USED IN SPORT

One of the keys to successful sales is having a product that everyone wants. Another key is to have products that people can afford. Full-menu marketing is having something for everyone. A fan of the Chicago Bulls can wear a $500 leather jacket or $7 T-shirt. A New York Yankee fan can sit in the bleachers or in a luxury suite. The key is that the clubs or retailers recognize that demand for the product is present at dif-

Table 11.2   SAMPLE CONSTRUCTION AND UTILIZATION OF A TICKET DATABASE

Type of ticket purchaser	Source	Use
Season-ticket holders	Ticket applications	Renewals, upgrades, additional tickets, play-off tickets, PSLs, merchandise, special events, fantasy camps, youth clinics
Co-account holders (share season tickets)	Not usually listed on the application—provided by season ticket holders in exchange for an incentive (extra tickets, gift item, etc.)	New season tickets, partial plans, additional individual game tickets, play-off tickets, PSLs, merchandise, special events, fantasy camps, youth clinics
Corporate	Chamber of Commerce, vendor lists, Dun & Bradstreet, ticket applications	Season tickets, club seats, luxury suites, PSLs, sponsorships, groups, additional tickets, play-off tickets
Partial-plan holders (ticket plans less than a full season)	Ticket applications	Upgrades, renewals, additional tickets, play-off tickets, merchandise, special events, fantasy camps, youth clinics
Groups (usually defined as parties of 20 or more)	Group leader lists, surveys of group attendees, contest participants	Partial plans, group brochures, group leader packet, individual game tickets, merchandise, promotional schedule, special events, fantasy camps, youth clinics
Advance ticket purchasers (tickets purchased from the team or in-house box office	Credit card slips, ticket form	Partial plans, promotional schedule, single-game ticket brochure, play-off tickets, merchandise, special events, fantasy camps, youth clinics
Phone sales	Ticketmaster or other software phone sales list	Partial plans, promotional schedule, single-game ticket brochure, play-off tickets, merchandise, special events, fantasy camps, youth clinics
Outlet (walk-in other than the stadium/arena—department stores, grocery chains, etc.)	Point-of-sale record (voucher documenting the sale provided to the team), contest entries	Partial plans, promotional schedule, single-game ticket brochure, play-off tickets, merchandise, special events, fantasy camps, youth clinics
Day-of-the-game walk-up sales	No set format—many clubs use intern-run booths, kiosk computer terminals, and related formats	Partial plans, promotional schedule, single-game ticket brochure, play-off tickets, merchandise, special events, fantasy camps, youth clinics
Sweepstakes/contest entries	Entry forms	Merge/purge with other sources—promotional schedule, single-game ticket brochure, merchandise, special events

1999 COMPADRES CLUB REWARD SYSTEM

Point total	Prize
7 points	Voucher good for $5 off any purchase of $10 or more at all Padres Store locations. Plus, a free pack of Upper Deck Baseball Cards while supplies last.
10 points	Voucher good for $5 off any food purchase of $10 or more at Oscar's restaurants. Plus, three free breadsticks.
13 points	Voucher good for two Compadres "Day Tripper" passes for only $5 (save up to $10). Passes good for one day's travel on the SD Trolley, SD Transit Buses, Padres Express, all North County Transit Buses and the Coaster.
16 points	1998 National League Champion Frequent Friar Pin. *Compadres Club limited edition.*
20 points	New Compadres Upgrade Voucher. All available seats are just $8 for selected home games. *You may purchase up to four 1999 Padres $8 tickets with your voucher.
30 points	Tony Gwynn Poster. *Compadres Club limited edition.*
40 points	Trevor Hoffman Pin. *Compadres Club limited edition.*
50 points	National League Champion Baseball by Fotoball. *Compadres Club limited edition.*
60 points	Two free 1999 Padres Tickets.** Plus, Padres Season Ticket Holders will receive a Compadres 1999 Season Ticket Holder Pin.
70 points	Frequent Friar Cap. *Compadres Club limited edition.*
90 points	Lane Field Commemorative Pin. First in the annual series of "Padres Ballpark Collection" pins. Collect a new pin each season. *Compadres Club limited edition.*
120 points	Clubhouse and stadium tour for two or four free 1999 Padres tickets.** Plus, a Silver Star Member Padres 30th Anniversary Pin.
150 points	Two free AMC Movie Theatre passes and a Compadres Frequent Friar Key Chain. Use your Compadres Key Chain at AMC Theatres and get a free small popcorn throughout 1999.
180 points	Complimentary admission for one to the World-Famous San Diego Zoo. Make sure to visit Ituri Forest, a journey into the depths of the African Rainforest (opening Memorial Weekend).
200 points	You and a guest are invited to an exclusive Compadres Member workout on the field. Or choose four free 1999 Padres tickets.**
230 points	Compadres authentic Louisville Slugger Bat autographed by a Padres player and a Gold Star Member Pin. You will also be invited to a special pre-game ceremony.*

*, **, or *: See Official Rules for details.

ferent price points. Spoelstra feels that full-menu marketing is necessary not only because of price, but also because of time and one's level of interest and commitment as a fan.[14]

As the level of ability to pay, interest in the product or service, and availability of the product vary, so too must the approaches used to sell those products or services. A successful sport organization will employ a variety of sales approaches. And as the levels and types of products or services offered for sale within a sport organization vary, so should the sales approaches that aim to inform, persuade, and convince consumers of a product's value to them. Certain approaches are more appropriate and consequently more effective in selling types or volume of the sport product. In this section, we will examine the most common sales approaches used in sport.

TELEMARKETING

Telemarketing can be defined as a marketing approach that "utilizes telecommunications technology as part of a well-planned, organized, and managed marketing program that prominently features the use of personal selling, using non-face-to-face contacts."[15] Telemarketing via its telephone links can be used to complement, support, or substitute for a direct-sales force. Telemarketing can be one-dimensional—

Compadres Club Application

Fill this out. Turn it in. Receive your free card today.

For Compadres Use Only

☐ Mr. ☐ Mrs. ☐ Ms. ☐ Miss   Date of birth ☐☐ / ☐☐ / ☐☐☐☐
Mo   Da   Yr

First name ☐☐☐☐☐☐☐☐☐☐☐☐ Initial ☐ Last name ☐☐☐☐☐☐☐☐☐☐☐☐☐☐☐

Address ☐☐☐☐☐☐☐☐☐☐☐☐☐☐☐☐☐☐☐☐☐☐☐☐ Apt.# ☐☐☐☐☐

City ☐☐☐☐☐☐☐☐☐☐☐☐☐☐☐ State ☐☐☐ Zip code ☐☐☐☐☐ - ☐☐☐☐

Country ☐ US ☐ Mexico ☐ Canada ☐ Other

Day phone (☐☐☐) ☐☐☐ - ☐☐☐☐   Night phone (☐☐☐) ☐☐☐ - ☐☐☐☐

Fax (☐☐☐) ☐☐☐ - ☐☐☐☐ E-mail ☐☐☐☐☐☐☐☐☐☐☐☐☐☐☐☐☐☐☐☐☐☐☐

1. How many games do you expect to attend during this season?
   1. ☐ 3 or fewer 2. ☐ 4 to 6 3. ☐ 7 to 9 4. ☐ 10 to 19 5. ☐ 20 to 40 6. ☐ More than 40

2. What is your marital status?
   1. ☐ Married 2. ☐ Single

3. To measure the diversity of our fans, we invite you to identify your ethnic background. (optional)
   1. ☐ African American 2. ☐ Native American Indian 3. ☐ Asian/Pacific Islander
   4. ☐ Caucasian 5. ☐ Hispanic

4. Are there any children living in your home in any of the following age ranges? (Please check all that apply.)
   1. ☐ Under age 2 2. ☐ Age 3 to 4 3. ☐ Age 5 to 12 4. ☐ Age 13 to 18

5. What languages are spoken in your home?
   Primary: 1. ☐ English 2. ☐ Spanish 3. ☐ Other
   Secondary: 1. ☐ English 2. ☐ Spanish 3. ☐ Other 4. ☐ None

6. What level of education did you complete?
   1. ☐ Some high school 2. ☐ High school or equivalent 3. ☐ Some college 4. ☐ Associate's degree
   5. ☐ Bachelor's degree 6. ☐ Graduate student/degree

7. What is your occupation?
   1. ☐ Professional/Technical 2. ☐ Upper/Middle Management 3. ☐ Sales/Marketing 4. ☐ Clerical/Service Worker
   5. ☐ Skilled Laborer 6. ☐ Homemaker 7. ☐ Retired 8. ☐ Self-employed
   9. ☐ Student 10. ☐ Active Military 11. ☐ Retired Military

8. Which group describes your annual family income? (optional)
   1. ☐ Under $20,000 2. ☐ $20,000-$29,999 3. ☐ $30,000-$39,999 4. ☐ $40,000-$49,999
   5. ☐ $50,000-$74,999 6. ☐ $75,000-$99,999 7. ☐ $100,000 or over

9. For your primary residence, do you:
   1. ☐ Own 2. ☐ Rent

10. To help us understand how you spend your leisure time, please indicate the interests and activities in which you enjoy participating on a regular basis. (Please check all that apply.)
    1. ☐ Bicycling 2. ☐ Golf 3. ☐ Physical Fitness/Exercise
    4. ☐ Going to the Beach 5. ☐ Surfing 6. ☐ Tennis
    7. ☐ Volleyball 8. ☐ Foreign Travel 9. ☐ Fishing
    10. ☐ Travel in USA 11. ☐ Recreational Vehicles 12. ☐ Gourmet Cooking
    13. ☐ Wines 14. ☐ Stocks/Bonds 15. ☐ Entering Sweepstakes
    16. ☐ Electronics 17. ☐ Casino Gambling 18. ☐ Listening to Tapes/CDs
    19. ☐ Buying Pre-Recorded Videos 20. ☐ Avid Book Reading 21. ☐ Gardening
    22. ☐ Wildlife/Environmental Issues 23. ☐ Health/Natural Foods 24. ☐ Arts & Culture
    25. ☐ Fashion/Clothing

11. Please check all that apply to your household.
    1. ☐ Shop by Catalog/Mail Order 2. ☐ Support Health Charities 3. ☐ Fax Machine
    4. ☐ Have a dog/cat 5. ☐ Use a Computer PC__ Mac__ 6. ☐ Modem
    7. ☐ Internet access 8. ☐ Shop on-line 9. ☐ Cell phone
    10. ☐ Pager 11. ☐ Home Office

12. Do you share Padres season tickets?
    1. ☐ No, I don't. 2. ☐ Yes, I share with friends. 3. ☐ Yes, my family has Padres season tickets.

Correct address, phone number and date of birth are required for Compadres Club Membership.
All individual demographic information is confidential and will reside with San Diego Padres exclusively.

handling inbound calls from consumers inquiring as a response to a promotional campaign, catalogue, or other source. The Southwestern Conference, in cooperation with GTE and Sprint, established a toll-free number enabling fans to purchase available tickets to any game involving a team within the Southwestern Conference.[16]

The other approach is two-dimensional, as an outward-oriented vehicle to prospect for customers, follow up leads, or solicit existing customers for repeat or

- The Compadres Club is a highly successful direct data-based sales program that emphasizes purchasing frequency.

expanded business volume.[17] In 1996, American companies spent an estimated $57.8 billion on outbound telemarketing services; these services generated an estimated $412.9 billion[18] or an ROI of more than $7 for every $1 spent.

Telemarketing offers considerable possibilities for enhancing the productivity of the sales force by permitting more specialization by account type and better focus on high-yield accounts. Telemarketing is also valuable in terms of sales support: scheduling sales calls and deliveries, conducting surveys, checking the status of a customer, and providing customer service. The Boston Red Sox have taken such an approach in their telemarketing efforts. Utilizing software licensed through Advantix and maintained and programmed by NEXT ticketing, the Red Sox have implemented a system that can handle up to 90,000 incoming orders in one hour, operates 24 hours per day 7 days per week, and generates a database. The system can also be used to conduct surveys.[19]

However, the most compelling reason to adopt telemarketing is the cost savings.[20] The list that follows illustrates how the average outside salesperson (a salesperson making face-to-face sales calls) spends his or her time. The left column lists the various activities a salesperson engages in; the right column lists the percentage of time spent on each activity.[21] It is clear that only half of an outside salesperson's time is actually spent selling.

Selling	40 percent
Traveling	24 percent
Waiting	16 percent
Paperwork and meetings	20 percent

The Telemarketing Sales Process

Telemarketing involves training the sales personnel to "follow a script," become effective listeners, identify the objections to the sale (if any), and complete the sales process by countering the objection and selling the original offer or modifying the offer (by up-selling or down-selling) to better fit the needs of the consumer. All outbound telemarketing calls must take place after 8:00 A.M. and before 9 P.M. local time. The process looks like this:

1. Precall planning
   - Review client information
   - Plan the objective for the call
   - Psych up—get in the proper mental frame for the call
2. Approach/Positioning
   - Identify who you are and where you're from
   - Identify purpose of the call
   - Make interest-creating statement
   - Build rapport
   - Get through the gatekeeper (secretary or receptionist) and to the decision maker
3. Data gathering
   - Gain general understanding of the client or the client's business
   - Move from general to specific types of questions
   - Identify a personal or business need
4. Solution generation
   - Tailor communication to the specific client need
   - Ask in-depth questions to test the feasibility of the solution

➤ Gather data for cost/benefit analysis

➤ Prepare client for the recommendation

5. Solution presentation

➤ Get client agreement to area of need

➤ Present recommendation clearly and concisely

➤ Describe use benefits

6. Close

➤ Decide on timing—when to close

➤ Listen for buying signals

➤ Handle objections

➤ Use closing techniques

7. Wrap-up

➤ Discuss implementation issues

➤ Thank client for the business

➤ Confirm client commitment

➤ Position next call

Applying the Telemarketing Process

To see how this process works, let's imagine the following scenario. Jane Micelli is a telemarketer employed by the defending Stanley Cup Champion Detroit Red Wings. Jane has been given a list of leads, derived from people who used their credit card to purchase tickets to one or more games during the past season. Jane's goal is to sell a half-season plan (20 games), but she can also sell full-season tickets (40 games) or "6 packs"—a new product just being introduced.

1. *Precall planning.* Jane reviews the file on Mary Stuart, an attorney who purchased individual tickets to four games during the past season. Jane notices that Ms. Stuart purchased two tickets for each of the four games and attended once per month in January, February, March, and April. Jane reviews her script and places the call.

2. *Approach/Positioning.* "Hello. This is Jane Micelli from the Stanley Cup Champion Detroit Red Wings, may I please speak with Ms. Mary Stuart? Good evening, Ms. Stuart. As I stated, I'm calling from the Detroit Red Wings and we want to thank you for your support of the team during the past season. I'm sure you were happy with the outcome, and I'd like to talk to you about the upcoming season. We anticipate tickets being difficult to come by next season and we would like to provide loyal fans such as you the opportunity to purchase tickets before they go on sale to the general public. Do you have a few minutes?"

3. *Data gathering.* "According to our records, you purchased tickets to see the Avalanche, Rangers, Penguins, and Stars last season; is that correct? Did you attend any other games? How do you select the games that you will attend?"

4. *Solution generation.* "We have designed a ticket plan for people such as you that like to attend the *big* games against name opponents or teams with high-profile players. We also realize that these same games are great opportunities for business-women such as you to entertain clients. Would you be interested in a ticket plan that lets you see the best teams in the NHL yet requires a commitment of only six games?"

5. *Solution presentation.* "The Detroit Red Wings have designed a new ticket plan called the Big Game Plan. This plan lets you see the Avalanche, Stars, Penguins, Rangers, Devils, and Blackhawks. It also guarantees you the same seat for all six games and the opportunity to purchase tickets for some of the play-offs."

6. *Close.* "I'm sure that the Big Game Plan will meet your needs and be much more convenient than your current ticket-purchasing options. Can I reserve two Big Game Plans for you?"

7. *Wrap-up.* "I'm sure that you will be happy with your ticket plans. I will call you monthly in case you would like to purchase tickets to games that are not part of your plan and to make sure you are enjoying your seats."

Sport organizations are beginning to examine the benefits of expanding incoming phone-line capabilities to provide not only information, but also revenue opportunities. To better satisfy the desire of fans to stay abreast of team and player information and to increase sponsorship revenues, several teams are offering 24-hour-a-day interactive phone lines. Through this system a fan can get up-to-date team information and order a pizza all in the same phone call.

The Washington Capitals Fan Call system offers fans the following options: results and recap of the most recent game, messages from the Coaches Corner or from a player of the caller's choosing, ticket and merchandise information and ordering procedures, news from the minor league affiliates, schedule and fan club information, and a message describing sponsor Pizza Hut's specials—including the option to order pizza directly through the Fan Call line. This latter option generated $500,000 in sales for Pizza Hut on direct-line transfers during the hockey season.[22]

DIRECT MAIL

Like telemarketing and other forms of direct marketing, direct mail has distinct characteristics and advantages:

➤ *Direct mail is targeted.* The appeal is to certain groups of consumers that are measurable, reachable, and sizable enough to ensure meaningful sales volume.

➤ *It is personal.* Not only can the message be personalized according to the name and other demographic characteristics, but also with regard to lifestyle interests (football fan, Panther alumni, etc.).

➤ *It is measurable.* Because each message calls for some type of action or response, the organization mailing the message is able to measure the effectiveness of the marketing effort.

➤ *It is testable.* Because the effectiveness is measurable, marketers can devise accurate head-to-head tests of offers, formats, prices, terms, and so forth.

➤ *It is flexible.* There are few constraints (other than cost) with regard to size, color, timing, shape, and format of the mailing. Also, the marketer determines the mailing date.[23] In contrast, a face-to-face meeting takes place according to work schedules, travel commitments, family obligations, and the like.

As direct mail does not involve any personal contact (face-to-face, as in personal selling, or ear-to-ear, as in telemarketing), there is no opportunity to explain the program or the offer, nor an opportunity to counteract objections or even to answer questions. Thus the sender must clearly communicate the material, including the offer itself, so that the recipient can clearly understand it.

Developing the Direct-Mail Offer

In formulating the direct-mail offer the sport marketer should consider the following:

➤ *Differentiating the product to be offered from other products offered.* In other words, if one is mailing a ticket brochure to the target audience, is each ticket-plan option clearly distinguishable from the others? Can the reader easily assess the benefits of each, make a decision, and act accordingly?

➤ *Offering options or variations of the product to fit the price considerations and abilities of the marketplace.* This approach, sometimes referred to as the good, better, best scenario, was an essential part of Sears's catalogue marketing for decades. The Sears approach was to list three items in the catalogue with different features and at slightly increasing prices relative to the number of features. Each was then described (in ascending price order and feature order) as a good model, a better model, or the best model. The Golfsmith Store, a direct-mail merchandiser specializing in golf equipment and apparel, offers a range of options, from factory-closeout specials for the budget conscious to state-of-the-art equipment (to find out prices for the latter, the buyer calls the company). In one recent catalogue, a golfer looking for a new driver could choose from 27 different drivers and pay as little as $70 or more than $400.[24]

➤ *Providing an attractive range of benefits and/or exclusivity.* The 1990s have seen sport marketers appealing to consumers to "join them" in various direct-mail membership initiatives. These memberships, such as those offered by the National Baseball Hall of Fame and Museum, sometimes entail various levels that have different fees and a set of benefits—publications, admission privileges, and premium items that act as incentives to join a particular level.

In 1997, the PGA Tour introduced a membership club called the PGA TOUR Partners Club. Targeted to golfers, the PGA TOUR Partners Club offered the following membership benefits: (a) One free tournament pass per year, good for admission at more than 70 PGA Tour and Senior PGA Tour events; (b) The opportunity to become a golf-product tester; (c) Discounts on golf schools and lessons, and (d) A database of opportunities for members to trade a round of golf at their course with another member at that member's course.[25]

Affinity-type credit cards are another sport marketing venture utilizing direct mail and offering a set of well-targeted benefits. For example, MBNA offers a series of professional sport-related MasterCards that enable cardholders to accumulate points redeemable for merchandise from their favorite team. Citibank, targeting to the higher demographic profiles of golfers, introduced the Platinum Jack Nicklaus Visa card. This card enables golfers to earn points based on their spending. Cardholders can redeem the points for golf equipment and apparel (e.g., one dozen golf balls for 3500 points, which equate to having spent $3500), or they can let the points accumulate and redeem them for unique opportunities such as a golf trip to Palmilla/Cabo del Sol for two (for 187,000 points, equating to having spent $187,000).[26]

➤ *Utilizing discounts, sales, refunds, premium items, and other incentives to enhance the perceived value of the offer.* Direct mail seeks to cause an action, and the perception that in making the purchase "I'm getting a deal" is often the catalyst in producing the action. These "deals" can take many forms. One of the more popular forms of catalogue discounting allows a consumer to receive $10 off the order if the amount of the order exceeds $100. This offer is prevalent in apparel marketing, for manufacturers such as Eddie Bauer, but is also utilized by teams with their own catalogues or stores and by sport mass merchandisers, who may offer such deals as two New Era caps with team emblem for $25.

➤ *Flexible payment or deferred-payment terms.* Some consumers may be intrigued by the opportunity to purchase merchandise now and pay for it at a more convenient time.[27] This is a common retailing practice during the Christmas holidays, but it is also gaining momentum in the sport industry—particularly with regard to higher-priced items like season tickets. Some professional teams allow their season-ticket purchasers to agree to pay for season tickets and spread their payments over several months. The Pittsburgh Pirates have considered working with a bank sponsor to offer a direct-mail campaign for a Pittsburgh Pirates MasterCard/VISA; in this scenario, consumers who accept the bank affinity card can charge season tickets to the card and pay no interest on the purchase.

➤ *Money-back guarantee.* This type of offer permits the consumer to purchase (payment in full) the product and consume at least some portion of it. Consumers who are not satisfied with the product for a specified, or in some cases, an unspecified reason, may return it for a full refund of the purchase price. Los Angeles Kings President Tim Leiweke, during his term as president of the Denver Nuggets, offered such a guarantee, as did Jon Spoelstra during his term as president of the New Jersey Nets. Spoelstra's direct-mail piece even specified, "You can ask for a refund if you don't like my tie or the way I comb my hair." Both guarantees were effective; they not only sold tickets and motivated consumers to try the product, but also generated publicity.

The Appearance of the Mailing Piece

Today, when "junk mail" can fill the mailbox on a daily basis, the mailing piece must be not only unusual enough to gain attention, but also intriguing enough for the recipient to open. In the case of professional sport teams or collegiate athletic programs, the team logo on the envelope is usually enough to attract attention and motivate the addressee to open the envelope. Catalogues with the addressee's favorite team on the cover are usually effective; in other cases, it is desirable for the offer to appear on the outside of the envelope or on the cover. In any case, direct marketers must ensure that their mailing piece is sufficiently interesting to be opened, and hopefully acted upon.

Accompanying the offer should be a letter from a key individual associated with the product or service. If the direct-mail offer is from a team and concerns tickets, a personalized note or letter from the coaching staff or management should accompany it. The letter should express thanks for the individual's past support (if appropriate), explain that purchasing the tickets is a wise business or personal entertainment decision, and also present information or an opportunity that is not available to the general public.[28] Any direct-mail marketing efforts should involve similar letters and messages. Remember, the letter should provide any and all information pertinent to the offer. As we have discussed, the major limitation of direct mail is that the sender cannot talk with the recipient. Thus the mailing piece should enable the recipient to contact the sender to clarify the information, ask questions, or solicit additional information that will help in decision making regarding the offer.

Ticket-sales materials are among the most common types of mailing materials used in sport. From our experience, these materials should be tailored to specific groups; don't try and utilize one piece to reach all market segments. While each piece should have its own identity in terms of appearance, all should have the same general look so it is obvious they are from the same organization. A mailing piece should be colorful and if possible should contain photos, preferably of people enjoying themselves participating or spectating; remember that the goal is to attract a crowd. These are some of the more common mailing pieces that sport organizations use:

➤ *Full-season ticket brochure.* This type of brochure explains the locations of seats and the costs, levels and benefits of being a full-season ticket holder; includes order form.

➤ *Partial ticket-plan brochure.* This is similar to the full-season brochure, but must not confuse the reader with too many options; includes order form.

➤ *Group brochure.* The group brochure lists discounts, special promotional nights, schedule, fund-raising options, other area attractions, and special amenities; includes order form. Photos are essential.

➤ *Pocket schedules.* These schedules of all events and promotional activities include diagram of venue, price listing, all phone numbers, Internet addresses, and an order form for purchasing tickets.

➤ *Posters.* Posters list the schedule and promotional activities and identify contact sources—how and where to order.

➤ *Appeal letters.* Letters of appeal, on quality letterhead, clearly state what the sender is asking for and why; provide support materials, photos, brochures, and list payment options.

Direct Mail Can Be More Than an Offer

Organizations that use direct mail to do nothing more than initiate the sales process via an offer do not understand relationship marketing. As we discuss later in this chapter, the long-term goal of sales efforts is to develop relationships with the consumer. If the only time the consumer hears from the organization is at renewal time or when the aim is to sell more product, the relationship will never be expanded or strengthened. Regular communication via direct mail can also be used to enhance sales opportunities through several means:

➤ By providing a regular method of communication to keep the consumer informed (via letters, newsletters, and the like)

➤ By soliciting input and feedback via consumer questionnaires and surveys

➤ By showing accountability and expanding the knowledge of the consumer via an annual report

➤ Through thank-you letters, by acknowledging the support of the consumer over the past year and asking for continued support

A recent trend in the use of direct mail is the annual report. Much as it functions for shareholders, the annual report informs ticket holders about developments in the past year. Some teams produce an annual report in a brochure format, while others have utilized video. Shawn K. Hunter, president of the Phoenix Coyotes, has used the annual report format with great success.

As Spoelstra explains [or views] it, the annual report provides all the information that interests a particular sponsor and details how the sponsor has benefited.[29] However, given that vested individuals (ticket-plan owners) also have a stake in how the organization has performed and an interest in how the organization is doing (not only on the playing surface but in the community), an annual report for these stakeholders might be in order as well.

Hunter and his staff prepare an annual report that is mailed to the Coyotes' "stakeholders" at the end of every season. This annual report, described as updating the shareholders on the state of the franchise, contains the following elements:

➤ A letter from the ownership of the Coyotes

➤ An overview of the season and of what to look forward to next season

➤ A synopsis of charitable activities—Coyotes' Goals for Kids Foundation

➤ Past season attendance, percentage of capacity

➤ An explanation (and listing) of the benefits of being a season-ticket holder

➤ Thank-you quotes and notes from players to the fans

➤ A photograph montage of last season's highlights and activities[30]

The intent of such mailings is to make the purchaser feel special and informed. The annual report can take the form of a brochure or letter; it can even be on videotape or CD-ROM so that the message has a more multidimensional feel.

PERSONAL SELLING

"Face-to-face selling is the art of convincing, the use of learnable techniques to close a transaction and the application of basic rules to show a prospect or customer that you have something he or she needs."[31] While more costly than telemarketing, personal selling can be more precise, enabling marketers to closely target the most promising sales prospects.[32] Developing and maintaining a strong sales force can be the most expensive part of the promotional mix, and the management and motivation of this sales force require an experienced, gifted sales manager. However, the return on the investment in the sales force may be well worth the cost if one follows a few simple rules, as outlined in table 11.3.

Personal selling actually involves the integration of data-based marketing (previously discussed in chapter 5), relationship marketing, and benefit selling to effectively communicate to consumers. We will examine these individually in order to assess the contribution and importance of each to the personal selling process.

Relationship marketing. Implies finding a way to integrate the customer into the company, to create and sustain a relationship between the company and the customer.[36] Gronroos, an expert on relationship marketing, identifies three main conditions under which relationship marketing is a successful and productive marketing approach:

➤ The customer has an ongoing desire for service.

➤ The customer of the service controls selection of the service supplier.

➤ There are alternative service suppliers.[37]

These conditions are present in the sport marketplace, and they provide an excellent application forum for relationship marketing. In general, people who consume sport are highly involved consumers who have a desire for long-term association with a sport team or branded product. The sport marketplace is extremely competitive, and there are many providers for each sport product or service (not necessarily in the same sport type, but as a sport entertainment option), enabling the consumer to select his or her "provider" of sport entertainment.[38] Therefore, building a relationship with a customer is essential to retain that person as a repeat customer.

Table 11.3   RULES FOR EFFECTIVE PERSONAL SELLING

Rule	Rationale
Utilize data-based marketing	Generate leads with a high likelihood of interest and ability to purchase
Communicate to the consumer as you would with a friend[33]	You have something in common—some level of interest in the product
Follow the LIBK rule—let it be known that you are in sales and what you are selling[34]	Be proud and enthusiastic about what you do and what you are selling
Overcome objections and perceived barriers to the sale	Be familiar with the most common objections or barriers to the sale, and modify the product or provide examples showing that people with the same objections have enjoyed the product
Manage the conversation by being an effective listener as well as making your points	Consumers want to be heard—they want a reaction to what they perceive to be concerns
Try to develop a relationship as a consultant rather than just a salesperson[35]	In reality, you are consulting by proposing possible solutions to the various needs and wants of the consumer
Match the consumer with the appropriate product	A good sale "fits"—the budget and lifestyle of the consumer

Benefit selling. Involves the creation of new benefits to offset existing perceptions or assumed negatives related to the sport product or service.[39] For example, for consumers who state that they cannot commit to a ticket plan because they don't know where they will be in August, benefit selling may be the answer. The concept of benefit selling has been responsible for the creation of new products in the sport industry such as the Flex book. The Flex book, or Fan Flex as it is sometimes called, was developed in response to the frequent objection of potential consumers that they could not commit to a certain number of games on specific dates. The Flex book contains coupons for a specified number of games, usually 11 or 13 sold for the price of 10 or 12 game tickets. The coupons have no date and can be redeemed (exchanged for a ticket) either in advance or on game day. Purchasers can use the tickets in any way they choose—all at once, in multiples of two, or one game at a time. Consumers benefit in that they are not restricted to particular dates, and in some cases they receive an extra ticket as an incentive to buy. The incentive for the organization is that the tickets are presold, so filling the seats does not depend on team performance, weather, or any other factor. The only limitation is that the coupon does not guarantee admission; redemption is based on availability. If the game is sold out when the consumer arrives, he or she must use the ticket for another game. Thus for very attractive games, such as opening days or key promotions, consumers need to decide and redeem the coupon as soon as possible to guarantee admission. The Pittsburgh Pirates have been highly successful in selling Flex books. In addition, because of the low cost of this item, it is used in telemarketing, in direct mail, and in personal selling as a sell-down.

When these three approaches—data-based marketing, relationship marketing, and benefit selling—are integrated into the formulation of a personal selling campaign and fine-tuned into a sales style involving the personality and experiences of the salesperson, the results can be very effective.

When combined with concepts such as sampling, trial usage, and open houses, personal selling can be even more ef- fective, especially in certain segments of the sport industry such as fitness clubs, sporting goods sales, and the sale of high-end professional seating options such as club seats and luxury suites. Sampling, trial usage, and open houses are designed to put the product in the hands of consumers with the intent of letting them "experience" it. Personal selling complements the "experience" by educating consumers about what they are experiencing and the benefits thereof. The fitness industry, for example, is a proponent of trial visits—whereby a potential consumer takes a guided tour of the facilities and has an opportunity to work out—with professional instruction and attention. A sales presentation in the form of an interview between the salesperson and the consumer usually follows the workout. The topics of the interview usually include patterns of physical activity, fitness goals, and the benefits of the fitness club to the consumer's well-being.

Pittsburgh Pirates fans look at seat locations during a fan open house.

Professional sport teams such as the Pittsburgh Pirates conduct open houses in conjunction with their personal selling efforts. The "open house," which occurs in the preseason, consists of stadium tours and entertainment activities—mascots, clinics, autographs—and the opportunity for potential consumers to sit in the seats available for sale. Balloons often mark these seats so potential consumers can identify the existing inventory and "check out the view." Once they are seated (indicating at least some level of interest), sales staff introduce themselves and initiate the personal selling process.

One common misperception about personal selling is that it is nothing more than verbal interaction between parties. Remember the axiom: "Actions speak louder than words." The consumer often interprets the actions taken by an organization—or for that matter those not taken—as evidence of what to expect in the future. Thus hospitality management, staff interaction, and the way informational inquiries are handled are all key elements of the personal selling process. To paraphrase the Disney principle, an organization should take the approach "It's not doing one thing 100 percent better, it's doing one hundred things 1 percent better." Disney's involvement in the management of the Anaheim Angels resulted in several changes: a name change, to give the consumer a feeling of ownership; a logo change, to give the consumer a sense of identity; changes in the structure of the ballpark, to provide a "park-like" atmosphere that communicated a theme-park image; and changes in service, to make the customer feel wanted, appreciated, and comfortable. Thus Disney set the stage for personal selling efforts.

INNOVATIVE PROMOTIONAL APPROACHES FOR SELLING SPORT PRODUCTS AND SERVICES

The unique nature of sport allows us to become highly imaginative in the sale of the sport product. Here we list some additional reminders.

➤ *Education can sell the fan base.* Albert G. Spalding discovered more than 100 years ago that if people understood his products (at that point, baseball equipment), they would be more likely to play the game and have need to purchase his products.[40] Professional team sports, in particular hockey and football, have taken a similar approach and created "courses" like Hockey 101 and Football 101 to educate the fan on the nuances and complexities of the game by simplifying and explaining the terminology. Teams such as the Phoenix Coyotes have prepared printed materials to help fans become more aware—and hopefully to increase their interest in, and their consumption of, the product. Teams have also been known to offer clinics and demonstrations to help accomplish this educational process.

➤ *Remember your packaging.* Although we discussed promotions pertaining to sales in the previous chapter, one such promotion, tried by the New Jersey Nets, is relevant here because of its ability to attract trial users and because of its rather dramatic impact on sales. The Nets' speaker package was a three-game ticket plan targeted to New Jersey corporations and businesses as a way to enhance their companies. Lou Holtz, Tom Peters, and Harvey Mackay, packaged as motivational speakers, spoke for an hour prior to one of the three Nets games. Each speaker would appear on a particular date. The dates chosen were scheduled weeknight games against the three worst teams in the NBA, but all sold out through this package.[41] The Nets have since expanded the speaker series, and it has become part of the regular sales process.

➤ *Remember that fun is good.* The film *Field of Dreams* made famous the quote "If you build it, they will come." This quotation now epitomizes the emphasis and dependence on building new stadiums and arenas to generate new revenue streams. However, beginning in the 1940s with Bill Veeck's giveaways and continuing in the 1990s with his son Mike, "If it's fun, they will come" has been the rally cry. The Veecks believed, and rightly so, that to attract fans you can't just sell your win-loss record. You have to sell the experience of a good time and the possibility of winning.

Through their promotional flair, understanding of hospitality management (cleanliness and comfort), and their commitment to fun, they established attendance records at all levels. Veeck staples, such as giveaway days with promotional items such as bats, fireworks nights, and special theme nights, have become commonplace in baseball today.[42]

➢ *Couponing is not just for groceries and fast food.* One of the more common complaints about attending a sporting event is cost, particularly for families. The need for affordable family-entertainment options is critical, and it's one that creative packaging can answer. The Los Angeles Kings are among many sport organizations in both professional (major and minor league) and amateur sports (including those at colleges and universities) that have developed and implemented one-price tickets for families. The "package" is usually based on four admissions, parking, and refreshments. Some organizations elect to provide a souvenir (e.g., a cap) whereas others, such as the Kings, provide a sponsor's product. To take advantage of such offers, depending on how the redemption program is set up, the consumer redeems the coupon at the sponsor's place of business or at the team box office. Price usually varies by sport and can be as low as approximately $25.00.

➢ *Remember the profitability and impact of group sales.* As discussed earlier in this book, sport consumers usually do not attend a sporting event alone. Research has shown that less than 2 percent of fans attend a game by themselves. We also noted that for some fans, it is the social interaction that defines their evening's enjoyment, and that for others the social component may be the sole reason for attending. It is for these reasons that sport organizations should make every attempt to attract and sell tickets to large groups (25 or more). Discounts (ranging from $1 to $3 per ticket depending on the size of the group), special seating sections, menus, and dining options (from catered sit-down dinners to casual buffets) are all effective means to attract groups to a sporting event. Groups can be little league teams, scouts, employees, military units, college students—any collective that meets or exceeds the organizational minimum. The Pittsburgh Pirates are one of many sport organizations that offer birthday parties with their mascot (the Pirate Parrot) for groups of 10 or more.[43]

➢ *May the Force be with you: use volunteers and charitable groups as part of your sales force.* Being what it is, sport functions to attract people who want to do more than just watch events: they want to identify and be identified with the sport organization.[44] Organizations have recognized this and have created some unique opportunities for involving volunteers and charitable groups such as civic clubs in the sales process. The Baltimore Orioles were the first to capitalize on recruiting volunteers from the community and having them function as a volunteer sales force. The Designated Hitters, as the Orioles called them, function as unpaid sales representatives of the organization, calling on their friends, relatives, and business associates to purchase tickets. The Designated Hitters do not receive a commission or wage but compete for prizes such as merchandise and trips to spring training.

On a slightly different note is the use of community groups, such as civic clubs, church groups, and little league teams, in the sales process. These groups sell tickets and receive a percentage of the profits (via commission) to benefit their organizations. They usually buy the tickets or receive tickets on consignment at discounted prices. They then sell the tickets at face value, keeping the difference. The attraction

Many professional teams like the Phoenix Coyotes have developed innovative approaches to teach their fans the game.

Serious Hockey.

$75 Family Nights.
It's our way of encouraging Kings fans to multiply

The second of our popular new Family Nights. They're old time hockey at an old time price. 75 bucks gets you four tickets, four dogs, four sodas, parking and the infamous Chris Chelios. To order, send in the coupon below or call 1-888-KINGS-LA. Do it now. The biological clock is ticking. Kings vs. Chicago, Sat. Nov. 30, 7:30PM. Call 1-888-KINGS-LA.

For $75 you get:
Four $22 tickets.
Four hot dogs.
Four Pepsis.
Free parking.
A Sunday Times.

Los Angeles Times Family Night Coupon.
Redeem at Forum box office or mail to: Los Angeles Kings Family Night, PO Box 17013, Inglewood, CA 90308. Mail order must be received 7 days prior to Family Night. Late orders will be left at will call.
Total # of packages _____ x $75= _____
# of additional tickets _____ x $22= _____
Service Charge = $2
Total = _____

Name: _____
Address: _____
City: _____ State: ____ Zip: _____
Phone No: _____
I would like to pay by: __Check __Visa __MasterCard
Credit card # _____
Expiration date: _____
Signature _____ Date _____

Supported by: **K-BIG 104** **XTRA SPORTS 690**

> Coupons are a highly effective sales tool.

for the organization is that these are tickets sold in some cases to benefit the charity—they would not have been sold by the team. A second benefit is the publicity and the positive public relations value of being a good citizen and assisting the community.

A model called the "club sandwich" is an excellent ticket-marketing strategy. It represents an attempt to create a model with a recipe for successful, balanced sales distribution. The intent of the club sandwich model is to ensure a balance and thus minimize overdependence on any one ticket-purchasing segment. The model provides that there will always be consumers on all levels of the escalator (see chapter 10). In the club sandwich (see figure 11.3), the "meat" (our apologies to vegetarians), or main course, is the season-ticket holders.

As this group is the one that attends the highest percentage of games, it is the most important ingredient in the club sandwich. Partial plans (entailing some level of precommitment and a large volume of games) and groups (involving a large volume of tickets) are the next most important ingredients in our sandwich. Our final stage of sandwich construction consists of the "condiments," ingredients selected according to individual preference: a sport organization may prefer to use more than one condiment or to rely heavily on one condiment because the proverbial refrigerator is bare. Condiments include advance ticket sales (including those sold by in-house telemarketing, volunteers, and charitable groups), phone or outlet sales, walk-up/day-of-game sales, and complimentary tickets disbursed through community relations-based programs.

As the flavor of the club sandwich will change with changing ingredients or changing amounts of ingredients, so too will organizational profit margins (if there are too few season-ticket holders and too many groups or walk-ups). We recommend the following recipe for a good-tasting and profitable club sandwich:

Ingredient	Percentage
Season ticket equivalencies (full and partial plans)	50
Advance sales (telemarketing, volunteers, charitable, phone, and outlet)	25
Group sales	20
Day-of-game/Walk-up sales	5

AFTERMARKETING

The customer's lifetime value is defined as the present value of expected benefits (e.g., gross margin) less the burdens (e.g., direct cost of servicing and communicat-

The "Club" Sandwich

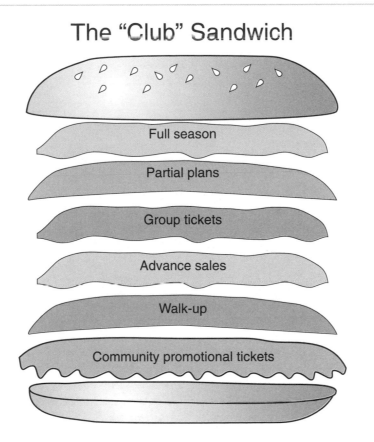

Full season

Partial plans

Group tickets

Advance sales

Walk-up

Community promotional tickets

Figure 11.3
The "club" sandwich: components of an effective ticket sales plan.

ing) associated with the customer.[45] Thus, for example, in terms of value, we should look at a season-ticket holder not as a $4000 per year purchaser but as someone who, depending on current age, could spend at least that amount and in addition pay for price increases, parking, and per capita items like concessions—possibly a total of somewhere in the neighborhood of $100,000 plus—over a 20-year period.

Obviously, customers have different value levels to an organization depending on the amount of revenue they contribute, the costs of serving them, and the estimated length of time they are projected to be with the organization: the more valuable the customer, the more effort on the part of the staff to retain that customer.[46] Figure 11.4 on page 246 illustrates how the value of a customer can be moderated.

Given the potential lifetime value of a customer, it becomes abundantly clear that certain activities and efforts must follow completion of the sale to ensure that the customer renews or becomes a repeat customer. The value of the fan as a customer is epitomized by San Francisco Giants' senior vice president of business affairs, Pat Gallagher, who developed an "upside-down organizational chart" (figure 11.5) to illustrate to the Giants' staff just how important fans really are.

Gale suggests that there are four principles to ensure long-term customer relationships. These principles address the following issues:

➤ *Quality as conformance.* The product or service must conform to a set of standards and requirements.

➤ *Customer satisfaction.* The organization must get close to the customer, understand the customer's needs and expectations, and become customer driven.

➤ *Market perceived quality versus that of competitors.* Understand the strengths and weaknesses of your product and the competitors' products through the eyes of the consumer—understand why sales are won and lost.

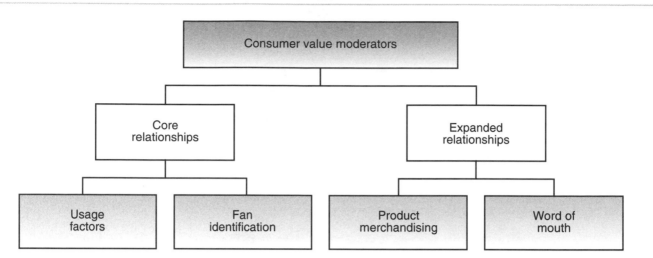

Figure 11.4
There are a variety of ways that the value of a customer can be increased by an organization.

➤ *Customer value management.* Monitor the competition, determine your business goals, and align the organization (people and processes) with the evolving needs of your targeted market.[47]

No matter how successful an organization is at servicing its clientele, there will always be some who discontinue their purchasing for one reason or another. Customers that leave an organization are often called defectors—because in effect they defect to another brand or organization. Defectors are costly to an organization, not only because the organization loses their lifetime value, but also because it is very expensive (in terms of time and resources) to replace them. According to some estimates, it costs up to five times as much to replace a customer as to service an existing customer.[48] To prevent defection, the sport organization must employ activities and services collectively referred to as aftermarketing.

Aftermarketing has been defined by Vavra as "the process of providing continued satisfaction and reinforcement to individuals or organizations who are past or current customers. Customers must be identified, acknowledged, communicated with, audited for satisfaction, and responded to. The goal of aftermarketing is to build lasting relationships with all customers."[49] Or, in the words of noted author Ken Blanchard, customers must become "raving fans"[50] so excited and pleased with your product that they not only remain loyal but also help attract new customers through word of mouth.

How can sport consumers become raving fans? Given the emotional nature of sport, sport consumers are already more emotional about their "product" than other consumers are about theirs. They have stronger feelings that elicit higher highs and lower lows. As sport marketers don't control product composition or performance, they must aggressively strive to ensure customer satisfaction as it relates to product extensions, which are often service oriented. All sport organizations should develop a customer service program in the hopes of retaining customers and attracting new ones through their overall service quality and their demonstrated interest in the well-being of their customers. Sport organizations should develop customer service approaches that encompass at least the following:

➤ Offer customized or personalized customer contact and treatment

➤ Conduct regular customer satisfaction surveys or audits

➤ Create and sponsor special events or activities for preferred customers

➤ Maintain a database of current customers and defectors

➤ Publish a proprietary magazine or newsletter for customers

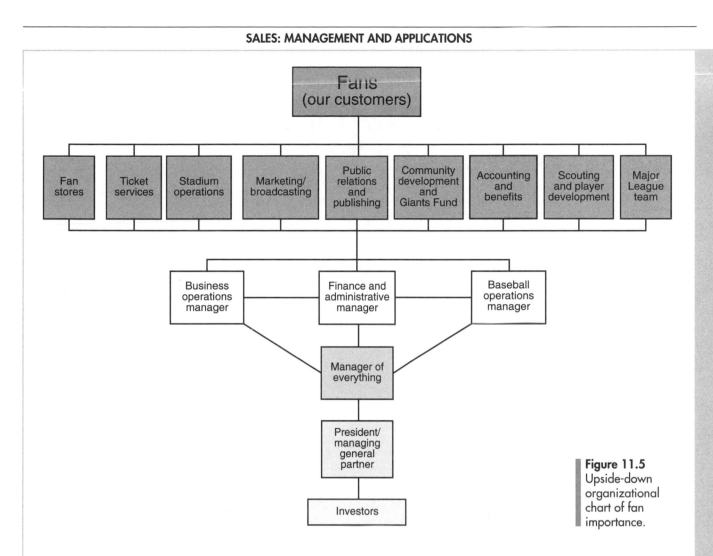

Figure 11.5
Upside-down organizational chart of fan importance.

➤ Offer an 800 telephone line, fax line, or e-mail address for customers

➤ Offer customers a frequency-incentive program

➤ Conduct stakeholder meetings or luncheons to gather feedback

➤ Provide shopping or purchasing services through a personal account representative[51]

Figure 11.6 on page 248 illustrates a very simple way in which an organization can gain immediate feedback with regard to the satisfaction of its consumers—in this case, group attendees. This simple survey yields names for the database as well as a follow-up methodology through which sales personnel can contact potential customers for future offers. In terms of satisfaction and lifetime value, it can also function as an intervention vehicle—permitting staff to contact people who have indicated that they might not attend again in order to determine why, and also to determine whether the organization can do anything to secure their continued patronage.

The NBA's Cleveland Cavs offer one of the better customer relations programs. Directed by MaryAnn Kellerman, the program utilizes personal account representatives who work with the sales personnel to service the account and ultimately to renew the ticket plan annually. According to Kellerman, "The customer service philosophy of the Cavs/Gund Arena organization is to create a vision of perfection centered on the customer. Our standards are based on providing the best service our guests will ever experience, nothing less. Quality and service are more than promises, they are a way of life. Our goal is to meet and exceed our guests' expectations and create lasting memories while providing exceptional value. We continually strive

---

College Athletic Department

Hey fans! We would like your feedback on tonight's event.
Please take a few moments to complete this card. Your name
will be entered to win team merchandise or tickets.

The best part of tonight's event was:_____

_____

The worst part of tonight's event was:_____

_____

Will you attend another athletic event?

     Yes ☐   Probably ☐   No ☐

Name _____

Address _____

City _____ State _____ Zip _____

Daytime Phone (_____)_____

If I win a prize you can find me in:

Section _____ Row _____ Seat_____

Figure 11.6
Group attendee
satisfaction survey
postcard.

to find ways to 'wow' our guests so that they become customers for life. We accomplish this through research programs that establishes forums for our guests to provide feedback regarding their satisfaction and perceptions."[52]

SELLING A NEW TEAM OR LEAGUE

One of the more interesting marketing/sales scenarios in recent years has been the WNBA. The WNBA, while a new product, had the advantage of being part of the NBA brand and utilizing the experienced sales staffs of the existing NBA teams in those respective markets. On the down side, the WNBA was positioned to play basketball in a nontraditional time (summer) and represented a concept (women's pro basketball) that had been attempted a number of times in the past with little success. Darrell Jenkins of the Cleveland Cavs and Rockers provides us with some insight regarding the strategic sales initiatives involved in launching that product.

TIPS FOR EFFECTIVE IMPLEMENTATION

The sales process is one of the most vital functions of a sport organization because it ensures the organization's growth and longevity. Sales campaigns must be clearly focused and have predetermined goals and objectives. To effectively implement a productive sales campaign, a sport organization must do the following:

➤ Hire and train a specialized sales force.

➤ Support this sales force through a well thought out management and development plan.

➤ Create and maintain an effective database that can be targeted in a variety of ways to reach the appropriate target market segments.

Selling a New Team or League

Darrell Jenkins, Director of Ticket Sales, Cleveland Cavs and Cleveland Rockers

The key to selling a new team (league, product, etc.) is to relate it to something the consumer already knows and to create a plan based upon that knowledge. A simple but well thought out marketing plan is always important, but when one is introducing a new product it becomes critical. One other factor absolutely will determine your level of sales success, namely data and research. These research data should always serve as a guiding light for introducing a new product into the marketplace.

In setting out to market the WNBA, the NBA had one major advantage, 29 experienced marketing staff personnel familiar with selling professional basketball in NBA markets. The NBA assembled key marketing personnel from those markets selected to host the WNBA in its initial season. This group of marketers analyzed the successful tour of the women's Olympic team as well as successful (in terms of attracting attendance) collegiate programs. The plans that emerged included soliciting corporate support, crossover from the cities' NBA fans, senior citizens, and, of course, women.

When corporations spend in order to be associated with sport, what they are really buying is affiliation and exposure. Therefore, the anticipated audience can dictate which corporations and which products are marketed to the new potential buyers. The corporate community accurately predicted that the new WNBA would attract large numbers of female fans. As research indicates that women are responsible for making many of the purchasing decisions for the family, many companies that typically had not utilized sport marketing took notice. For example, a national television deal was negotiated with the female-focused Lifetime Network, and grocery chains were a big part of the local corporate support in a number of WNBA cities.

In order to most successfully sell a new league to the corporate community, teams must package their least attractive events (such as Monday or Tuesday night games) and/or most readily available inventory with the highly sought-after commodities. For WNBA teams, this meant combining season and group tickets along with radio ads, television spots, and in-arena exposures. Corporate sponsorships were not the only deals that reflected the new league's need to sell tickets and attract spectators. Speaking engagements, skills camps, and even clinics required a minimum ticket purchase.

Teams in the WNBA anticipated that existing fans of their affiliated NBA teams would naturally have an interest and would support this brand of basketball by purchasing tickets. Each of the eight inaugural teams initially offered its best seats to the NBA season-ticket holders. However, the anticipated sales bonanza failed to materialize. According to team sales directors, no WNBA team sold as much as 10 percent of their inventory to this perceived target

Even with the NBA's vast marketing resources, the WNBA had a slow start. Sheryl Swoopes is one of the well-known athletes in the WNBA who has helped catapult the WNBA into widespread popularity.

market—a far cry from the anticipated 20-25 percent projected.

The marketing plan also missed the mark, although to a lesser extent, with regard to the level of interest and purchasing on the part of senior citizens. When WNBA league officials and team personnel had examined women's NCAA attendance leaders, they had found that the presence of senior citizens was a common denominator regardless of the location of the team. Further research showed that these statistics had a flaw, namely that for the most part the college arenas were not located downtown whereas the NBA arenas were. This caused a readjustment on the part of marketers to target senior citizens for day games only.

When selling a new team or league one is often forced to learn by trial and error. But to be successful, one must also learn to capitalize on success. A simple yet essential means to this end is to merely ask early customers why they are buying. If you find something that works, stay with it. Selling, as opposed to the more common (and much more annoying) telling, should always be solution based. *Telling* prospects what they should buy is not selling: *selling* involves listening and assessing what the prospect really needs. That is, what people buy is the solution to the problem or challenge. Therefore, good sales and marketing reps need to know what problem(s) their product solves or what challenge(s) their product overcomes.

In Cleveland, for example, the marketing plan anticipated that the women of the WNBA would fill a need among families and youngsters for positive role models. Bright professionals like Rockers stars Michelle Edwards and Janice Braxton spoke multiple languages, and Lynette Woodard (later obtained by the expansion Detroit Shock) held down an impressive position on Wall Street in addition to having gained international fame as the first female member of the Harlem Globetrotters. Affordable family entertainment was another solution the fledgling league offered. It seemed that dads brought kids and moms brought friends as more and more people passed through the WNBA turnstiles. One Rockers salesperson found a local politician who recognized the value of supporting and being associated with this new women's professional league. She and other Cleveland city officials purchased 24 tickets for the inaugural season, even though they knew little about basketball.

New leagues and teams often begin with limited resources. The WNBA was no exception. Thus we cannot overemphasize the importance of efficiency. If, for example, a nurse buys tickets, the team marketer might try to find a nurses' association meeting to attend and present the opportunity to dozens of nurses at once. Rockers tickets were particularly popular among groups of African American women to whom we gained access at an event called "Sisters: A Celebration of African-American Women." Female laborers whom we reached through an organization called "Hard Hatted Women" also showed support for the team by purchasing tickets.

Another way to gain efficiencies is to expand the sales staff, for free. The first buyers are usually the most enthusiastic. Capitalize on their excitement informally by asking for referrals and leads and also by formally offering incentives for finding actual buyers. Create an advisory committee; members can also assist in the selling process. This group may not only provide access to the companies and their constituents, but can also provide expertise, data, and the market feedback that is often critical at this stage.

The final piece of the marketing plan, particularly important when selling a new team, is the market itself, especially the competition. The WNBA was strategically positioned in the summer for this reason. In winter and fall, the rival American Basketball League competed for spectators and viewers with the NFL, NBA, NHL, and NCAA (football, basketball, and hockey) offerings. In the summer, the sport scene was much less crowded, with only baseball (and in limited cases, Arena Football) competing for spectators. For the four major sports, this challenge was far greater in some markets than in others. In New York, two baseball teams might pose a challenge; in Cleveland, the Indians had enjoyed two consecutive years of sellouts; finally, in Houston, the Astros, despite their success, had not been a hindrance to the WNBA Champion Comets.

However, summer provided another major form of competition—vacations. As this objection was anticipated, several teams offered some form of exchange program. In Cleveland, vacationing Rockers season-ticket holders had the opportunity to turn in tickets for games played during their vacations in exchange for tickets to games they were able to attend.

A good marketing plan, capitalizing on strengths and anticipating weaknesses, is essential in selling a new team. However, execution of the plan must provide room for flexibility when feedback from and conditions in the marketplace contradict the strategy.

As always, the key to selling is understanding what need your product meets and then asking questions to effectively identify similar people with that same need.

> ➤ Utilize the sales techniques and methodologies most appropriate to communicate with the target market and encourage them to perform.

> ➤ Produce and distribute sales materials that will effectively communicate the organization's offer to the target market.

> ➤ Emphasize relations with consumers and partnerships with sponsors—realize the long-term value of every relationship.

> ➤ Implement a customer relations program that is proactive rather than reactive in dealing with customers.

> ➤ Have a three-year plan: crawl in the first year, walk in the second, and run in the third. Increase the number of sellouts every year.

> ➤ Pick the dates that are the easiest to sell and concentrate your efforts on those dates. To create a sellout, use the power promotions approach: the best date, best opponent, and best promotions (events and/or giveaways).

> ➤ As total ticket-sales revenue is the critical factor, not just meat in the seats, don't discount season tickets.

> ➤ Put on an exciting sport entertainment product that encourages repeat business—"sell the sizzle *and* the steak."

> ➤ Develop a comprehensive ticket-sales plan and ensure that you have enough staff to implement it.

> ➤ Advertise, promote, and preach to the choir: utilize direct mail and telemarketing only to known fans and participants in your sport (from your database). Let your fans sell to nonfans through word of mouth, proclaiming the value and benefits of your sport or entertainment product.

> ➤ Develop loyalty programs for repeat purchasers.

> ➤ Use programs and promotions to increase the attendance frequency of existing fans.

> ➤ Whenever possible, use players and coaches (past and present) to contact every season-ticket holder, during the season if possible.

> ➤ Don't be afraid to try new and creative ideas even if some innovations fail.

WRAP-UP

Sales is the revenue-producing element of the marketing process. Marketing is communication, and as such, the sales process involves a high level of two-way communication. A salesperson must listen and assess as well as talk. Depending on the organization, some sales staffs specialize in selling some of the products that we have discussed, such as group tickets or season tickets. Other sales staffs sell a variety of products but might specialize in one type of methodology such as telemarketing or personal selling. As this chapter has pointed out, there are a variety of products to sell in the sport industry and a variety of methodologies with which to sell them. Because of this variety, effective training and management of sales personnel are necessary to ensure that they understand the products that they are selling, the prospective consumers to whom they are selling, and the appropriateness and benefits of each methodology that they might choose to employ to complete the sale.

The sales department of a sport organization contains the largest number of job positions and is responsible for the largest percentage of revenue. Marketing leadership in the organization usually comes from individuals who began as members of the sales staff. Therefore, we can make a correlation and state that success in marketing usually has some basis in sales—and that successful marketers understand and can manage the sales process of an organization.

ACTIVITIES

1. Identify someone you recognize as a leader in the area of sport marketing. Obtain the person's bio or profile (these can usually be found on the corporate or organizational Web site). How does the person's current position and/or past activities reflect sales experience?

2. Visit a stadium or arena in your town to conduct a sales inventory. What items constitute the inventory that has been sold? What items have not been sold?

3. Using the inventory that you prepared, analyze the inventory items that have not been sold. Select an appropriate sales methodology for each unsold inventory item.

4. Interview someone with sport marketing responsibilities in an athletic department, fitness facility, or pro sport organization, and ask about the person's duties. Ask what percentage of the person's time is devoted to sales activities. What methodologies does he or she employ? How does he or she train the sales staff? How did the individual begin in the business?

5. Assess your career plans. Is there a sales component in the job you envision? What will it require for you to attain this position? Begin compiling a roster of individuals in similar positions. You can use this roster to gather information and advice as you initiate your job search.

YOUR MARKETING PLAN

In the successful implementation of a marketing plan, objectives must be identified and achieved. Sales as a goal, revenue-production target, and methodology usually account for portions of the objectives and also serve as strategies and tactics in achieving these objectives. In reviewing your market plan, how do you see sales fitting in? Do you have an objective that might be stated in sales terms relating to increasing organizational revenue? For example, an objective like "Increase attendance (membership if you are interested in the fitness industry or other membership-based industry segments such as golf or tennis clubs) over last year's levels by 12 percent" implies that there are some sales strategies and tactics necessary to achieve the objective. Review your objectives and select sales methodologies and approaches that will help you reach your objectives.

CHAPTER 12

PROMOTIONAL LICENSING AND SPONSORSHIP

OBJECTIVES

1. To illustrate the relationship between the sport organization and the corporate sponsor.

2. To provide an understanding of the scope of sponsorship and promotional licensing.

3. To develop a comprehension of the motivations and rationale for the use of sponsorship by corporations and sport entities.

Sponsorship Fit: It Must Make Sense for Everyone

The Medalist Group, also known as the Senior Women's Golfing Tour, hoped to attract a $2 million title sponsor in 1999. The money was to be used to provide four $500,000 paydays at each of the tour events in 1999. The prize money, along with the commitment of the title sponsor, was expected to increase to $600,000 per event in 2000 and $750,000 in 2001. Experts felt that this payoff was too high, given that the LPGA had a number of events with prize money of $500,000 and thus a Medalist Group sponsor would be paying more for older players with declining skills. The most recognizable names on the Senior Tour were Nancy Lopez and Jan Stephenson, who were highly recognizable, but hardly enough to carry an entire tour event. And there was another obstacle to the sponsorship negotiations—lack of a television contract to provide exposure for the sponsor(s). This situation was hardly appealing to most potential sponsors.

Sometimes money and exposure are not the issues. Sometimes it comes down to fit. For instance,

Ford Motor Company entered into an estimated $5 million sponsorship of AmericaOne, the San Francisco yacht syndicate gearing up to challenge New Zealand for the America's Cup race in 2000. As the official automotive sponsor, Ford hoped to help AmericaOne design the fastest boat and to gain international exposure by aligning itself with a winning team. In exchange for its sponsorship, Ford would tack its logo on the sailboat and the crew clothing in addition to performing other branding, hospitality, and promotional activities.[1] Some critics complained that an automotive company should concentrate its efforts on its technology and design capabilities as they apply to the auto industry. But, if one thought more broadly about a marriage that would represent the best of technology, design, and handling, Ford's initiative made more sense. Sponsorship has to work for all the parties concerned. It must function as a partnership, with all parties receiving benefits and associations that can be leveraged to achieve their objectives.

In this chapter, we will examine the integrated nature of sponsorship. Sponsorship activities are more integrated than other promotional activities and contain a variety of marketing-mix elements. While a number of marketing-mix elements can function as stand-alones (e.g., an open house, discounts on tickets, community relations programs), a sponsorship usually involves two or more of the elements of the marketing mix to provide a sponsor with association, value, exposure, and opportunities to leverage this sponsorship to achieve its marketing objectives. In this chapter, we will examine those objectives and opportunities.

SPONSORSHIP DEFINED

Consider the following activities: Pizza Hut selling NCAA-logoed basketballs; Blockbuster Video obtaining the video rights to MLB[2]; *USA Today* sponsoring All-Star ballots for MLB; Target's entitlement of the LPGA's Fan Village; and Mattel's production of Barbie dolls in the cheerleading apparel of Oklahoma State University and other collegiate athletic programs. What do all these have in common? They represent the types of promotional licensing agreements that have become commonplace in sport and lifestyle marketing. Promotional licensing is really an umbrella term that encompasses sponsorship, but sponsorship has proven to be the accepted term throughout the world. Therefore, throughout this chapter and the text, we will use the term sponsorship to refer to the acquisition of rights to affiliate or directly associate with a product or event for the purpose of deriving benefits related to that affiliation or association. The sponsor then uses this relationship to achieve its promotional objectives or to facilitate and support its broader marketing objectives. The rights derived from this relationship may include retail opportunities, purchase of media time, entitlement (the inclusion of the sponsor name in the event or facility name, e.g., the

McDonald's LPGA Championship or the RCA Dome), or hospitality. Sponsorship agreements may include, but are not necessarily limited to, the following provisions and benefits:

> ➤ The right to use a logo, a name, a trademark, and graphic representations signifying the purchaser's connection with the product or event. These rights can be used in advertising, promotion, publicity, or other communication activities employed by the purchaser.

> ➤ The right to an exclusive association within a product or service category.

> ➤ The right of entitlement to an event or facility.

> ➤ The right to use various designations or phrases in connection with the product, event, or facility such as "official sponsor," "official supplier," "official product," or "presented by."

> ➤ The right of service (use of the product or exclusive use of the product) or the right to use the purchaser's product or service in conjunction with the event or facility.

> ➤ The right to conduct certain promotional activities, such as contests, advertising campaigns, or sales-driven activities, in conjunction with the sponsorship agreement. (See photo).

Events like the NCAA's Hoop City provide sponsors with unique opportunities to display their logo and state their message to their target markets.

Sponsorship, then, includes a wide array of activities associated with a communications process that is designed to utilize sport and lifestyle marketing to send messages to a targeted audience. The amount of money spent on sport and special-event sponsorships, as well as the number of sponsorships, has grown dramatically (figure 12.1).

Figure 12.1
Growth of sponsorship/promotional licensing.

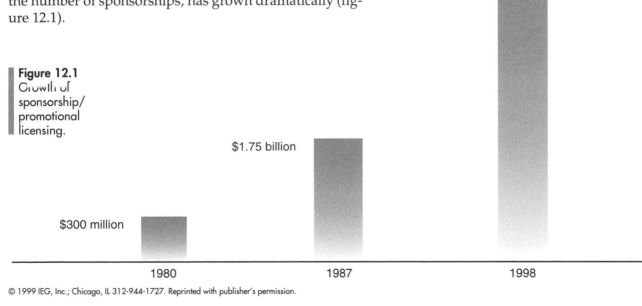

$300 million — 1980
$1.75 billion — 1987
$17.35 billion — 1998

SPONSORSHIP'S PLACE WITHIN THE MARKETING MIX

As previously discussed, the marketing mix comprises variables that fall into five broad categories: product, price, promotions, place (distribution), and public relations. The marketer's function is to manipulate these variables in order to meet the target market's needs in a continually changing environment (see figure 12.2).

As a key component of the marketing mix, promotions is often referred to by contemporary theorists as "communications mix."[3] (See figure 12.3.) In comparison to many other promotional activities, which are often stand-alones, sponsorship activities are more integrated and are composed of a variety of marketing and promotional components.

As discussed in chapter 10, the role of promotions is to inform and persuade the customer and thus influence the consumer's purchase decision. The elements of the promotions/communications mix are traditionally considered to be advertising, personal selling, publicity, and sales promotion. Combinations of some or all of these elements are inherent in sponsorship activities (see figure 12.4).

One sponsorship activity that combines personal selling and promotion is hospitality. Hospitality opportunities are a sponsor benefit commonly associated with premier events such as the Super Bowl, Daytona 500, or the NCAA Final Four. One can define hospitality as the provision of tickets, lodging, transportation, on-site entertainment, and special events to the sponsor. The sponsor can in turn use these benefits to entertain its own clients or to reward customers for their longtime support or volume of purchases. In this guise, the sponsorship acts as a form of personal selling, because it enables the sponsor to conduct activities through face-to-face contact with key customers. This sponsorship also functions as promotion, because it is promoting the company to current and potential clients (see photo).

Sponsorship benefits and relations could also be utilized in a combined advertising and sales promotion campaign. For example, Quaker State might utilize a relationship with NASCAR to conduct a national sales promotion that could include a sweepstakes for an all-expense-paid trip to the Daytona 500 and an opportunity to meet Richard Petty. Promotion of the contest could utilize special on-track signage, television advertising, and retail point-of-purchase displays. Thus, the sponsor has the opportunity to integrate a number of the elements of the promotional/communications mix in any sponsorship relationship.

One should realize that the costs the sponsor incurs to promote or leverage its affiliation or association with the sport organization come in addition to those costs—

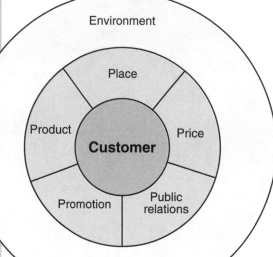

Figure 12.2
The marketing mix components.

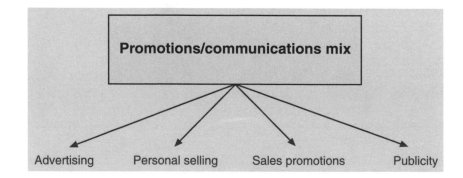

Figure 12.3
The traditional promotions/ communications mix.

usually referred to as licensing or partner-ship fees—that grant the sponsor the rela-tionship. For example, Pizza Hut is a sponsor, actually a corporate partner, of the NCAA. Pizza Hut pays an annual fee to the NCAA in exchange for the affiliation with the NCAA and receives certain benefits that include at least the following:

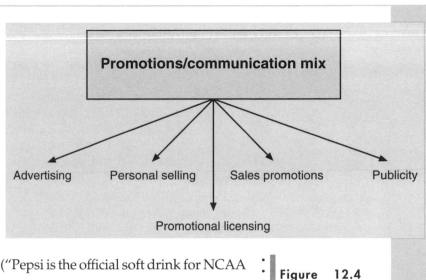

> Category exclusivity (no direct competitors, as Pizza Hut is a cor-porate partner; therefore Dominos cannot be)

> Use of NCAA registered trade-marks, official product designation ("Pepsi is the official soft drink for NCAA Championships")

> Preferred ticket packages to all NCAA Championship events

> The right to conduct in-store promotions

Figure 12.4
A broader promotions/ communications mix.

Thus when NCAA corporate-partner Pizza Hut engages in its annual March Mad-ness basketball promotion, which involves a free basketball with purchase of Pizza Hut products, all costs associated with the promotion are assumed by Pizza Hut and are in addition to the fee paid by Pizza Hut to be an NCAA corporate partner.

THE GROWTH OF SPONSORSHIP

Several factors contributed to the growth of sport sponsorship in the late 1970s and have continued to support this growth in the 1990s. The marketing literature shows some agreement that the emergence and growth of sponsorships coincided with the ban on tobacco and alcoholic drink advertising.[4] During that time, tobacco and alcoholic drink manufacturers were forced to look for ways of promoting their products other than through direct-advertising channels. Banning cigarette ads from the airways in 1971 was a tri-umph for anti-tobacco forces. However, as a result, these companies had to re-direct their massive advertising clout (and budgets) to sport sponsorships.[5] The *IEG Sponsorship Report* noted that in 1997, tobacco firms spent $195 mil-lion on sport sponsorships—95 percent of it in the area of motor sport, com-posing about 20 percent of the total sponsorship revenue for that sport segment.[6]

Special events are an integral aspect of corporate hospitality and entertainment programs.

Companies with substantial advertising budgets gradually discovered that there was too much "noise" in the print and electronic media. The average person is ex-posed to more than 5,000 selling messages each day, making separation and reten-tion of information difficult. Moreover, advertising costs, especially in television, continue to rise. For example, advertising costs for the NFL's 1998 Super Bowl amounted to $1.3 million for a 30-second ad spot, more than tripling the cost of the same sponsorship 10 years before.[7] By developing an alternative channel of communication via sport sponsorships, companies found that they could achieve new levels of exposure, in many cases at lower costs than through advertising campaigns. Figure 12.5 provides some insight into annual sponsorship spending by those corporations most vested in sponsorship activities.

Promotional licensing and sponsorship agreements skyrocketed as the public and the sport governing bodies increasingly accepted the commercialization of sport. See figure 12.6 to get an idea of the use of sponsorship, advertising, and sales promotion from 1994-1998. The 1984 Los Angeles Olympics were the first privately organized Olympics in history, and a landmark in the evolution of corporate sponsorship and promotional licensing through sport. The 1984 Olympic sponsors received significant media exposure and to some extent positive image building, while the games generated a profit for the Los Angeles Olympic Organizing Committee (LAOOC). Peter Ueberroth, president of the LAOOC, inaugurated his dream of a corporately subsidized Olympics by limiting the number of Olympic sponsors to 30 to avoid clutter and duplication—as well as to ensure category exclusivity.[9] Thus Ueberroth was able to increase the value of a sponsorship in relation to the increased cost of those same sponsorships. By demonstrating that as cost increased there was a subsequent increase in value, Ueberroth demonstrated that sponsorships actually became partnerships because they were mutually beneficial for both the sport (property) and the sponsor (corporations). Experiences such as the 1984 Olympics and other mutually beneficial relationships helped give rise to the term *corporate partners,* suggesting that sponsorships could be partnerships whereby partners who hope to achieve benefits work in harmony to create a desirable result.

Sponsorship has been effective, and logically, sponsorship costs have risen. To combat those costs and to retain control, some deep-pocketed companies are considering creating and owning their own events. In 1997, Nike announced the launch of Nike Sports Entertainment, a division of Nike that will initiate, produce, and control its own events. According to Ian B. Cambell, the manager of Nike's Sports Entertainment Division, "Asset acquisition is costing more, players and teams are more expensive than they were six months ago. I think if you are going to invest in an athlete or a team asset anywhere in the world, you've really got to justify what you're doing from an overall brand perspective and make sure it really is a total package. Why pay a third party to do that for you or interpret that for you or screw it up for you, when really you probably ought to do it for yourself."[10] Only time will tell whether this practice will become more widespread among the corporate community.

Figure 12.5
Top sports sponsors in the United States.

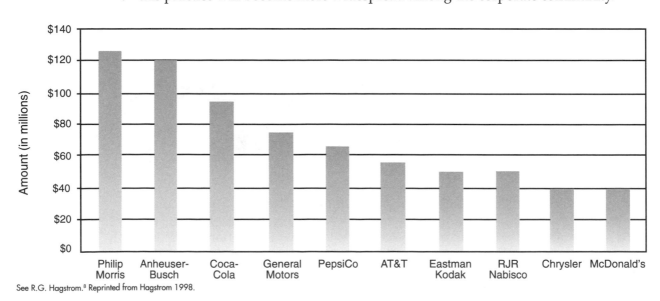

See R.G. Hagstrom.[8] Reprinted from Hagstrom 1998.

Annual Growth of Advertising, Sales Promotion, and Sponsoring

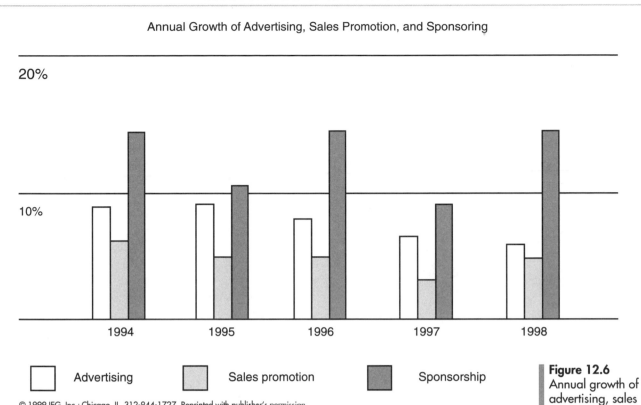

© 1999 IEG, Inc.; Chicago, IL. 312-944-1727. Reprinted with publisher's permission.

Figure 12.6
Annual growth of advertising, sales promotion, and sponsorship.

Another factor in the growth of sport sponsorship has been the increased media interest in sport programming, attributable mainly to the following:

> ➤ The general public's increased leisure time and interest in sport

> ➤ Increased commercialization of television through commercials and infomercials

> ➤ The fact that it is less costly for television networks to broadcast sporting events than to produce shows or documentaries

> ➤ The growth of new media sources, such as subscription services via cable or satellite transmissions and pay-per-view special events, which have increased the demand for live sport programming and provided additional channels of exposure for sport as well as sponsors

An example of a new media source is Direct TV, a satellite subscription service that offers a wide array of sport-viewing options for the sport enthusiast—and also for sponsors. Direct TV offers all its subscribers access to ESPN, ESPN2, and ESPNews as a basic benefit. In addition, the basic subscriber receives the local premium sport channel at no extra charge. Thus a subscriber in New England would receive the New England Sports Network for free as well. The next level of service gives the viewer an all-sports package, which includes all regional sport channels (including SportsChannel and FOX Sportsnet), the Golf Channel, and ESPN Classic—a total of 29 channels for a monthly charge of $10. This is also a great opportunity for sponsors, who can select regions of the country or individual cities in which to promote their products or events. Finally, Direct TV, which has agreements with the major sport leagues, can offer subscription-based packages ranging from a low of $60 per season to a high of $149 per season. These packages include the NFL Sunday Ticket, MLB Extra Innings, NBA League Pass, NHL Center Ice, and ESPN's "Game Plan" packages for NCAA football and basketball—once again, providing sponsors with a segmentation tool based on the demographics of the particular sport.

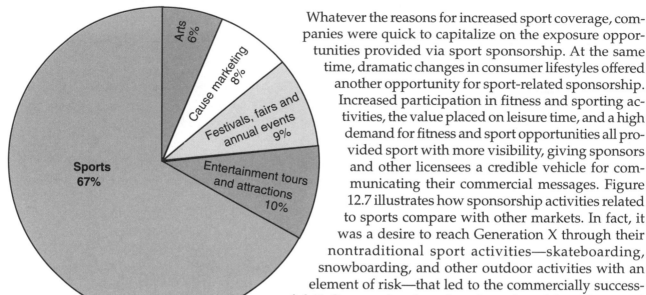

Figure 12.7
Projected 1999 North American sponsorship spending by type of property.

Whatever the reasons for increased sport coverage, companies were quick to capitalize on the exposure opportunities provided via sport sponsorship. At the same time, dramatic changes in consumer lifestyles offered another opportunity for sport-related sponsorship. Increased participation in fitness and sporting activities, the value placed on leisure time, and a high demand for fitness and sport opportunities all provided sport with more visibility, giving sponsors and other licensees a credible vehicle for communicating their commercial messages. Figure 12.7 illustrates how sponsorship activities related to sports compare with other markets. In fact, it was a desire to reach Generation X through their nontraditional sport activities—skateboarding, snowboarding, and other outdoor activities with an element of risk—that led to the commercially successful X Games, developed and produced by ESPN and warmly welcomed by sponsors such as Mountain Dew and Nike that wanted an opportunity to tap into this market.

Changes in governmental policies also contributed to the growth of sport sponsorship. Within the United States, sports have been, and continue to be, financed through the private sector. In Canada, Europe, and Asia, government funding was (and in many situations still is) the primary source. In economically difficult times, when governments reduced support for sport, corporations and industry felt pressure from the public to fill the gap. Social and environmental problems, coupled with increased awareness of corporate responsibilities to the local markets, led companies to pursue opportunities to improve perceptions of their corporate images, their activities, and their roles in society at large.

A final reason for the growth of sport sponsorship is that marketing has become increasingly global. Figure 12.8 depicts projections for the amount of money to be spent on sponsorship throughout the world in 1999.

Multinational companies have found it increasingly difficult to communicate with their target markets in so many different languages and cultures. Sport sponsorships and licensing programs offer a unique way to bridge language and cultural

Figure 12.8
Projected 1999 sponsorship spending worldwide.

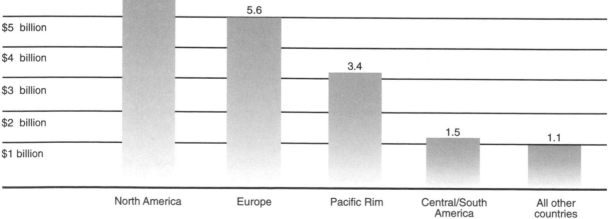

barriers; this is one of the reasons why the Olympics and other major international events such as the World Cup, McDonald's Challenge (basketball), and others receive such huge support from a broad range of corporate entities. In keeping with the global movement, professional teams have already begun to change their names or to incorporate the names of sponsors into their uniforms to accommodate the communication needs of companies operating in the now-unified European market.

Because of cultural, societal, and language barriers, companies that operate in Europe and throughout the world will probably use sport marketing programs increasingly to segment and effectively communicate with their target markets. Witness Nike's record 10-year, $400 million sponsorship of the Brazilian soccer team. The deal, which Nike made in hopes of growing its presence worldwide and establishing credibility in the area of soccer, grants the company not only merchandising rights, but also the rights to stage and broadcast five events per year with the team.[11] Such events may have a grassroots element that will provide exposure for Nike with emerging and developing players, as well as the opportunity to showcase and associate Nike with one of the most successful and respected soccer teams in the world.

WHAT DOES SPORT SPONSORSHIP HAVE TO OFFER?

During the 1970s, marketing through sport often served the personal interests of top executives or else served as a vehicle for charitable contributions. But beginning in the early 1980s, marketing through sport became a discipline involving serious research, large investments, and strategic planning. As the economic fortunes of companies changed, companies needed to prioritize their spending and justify the expenditures. They had to find a return on investment (ROI) and to allocate their sponsorship dollars wisely. What rationale and benefits can sport offer to its prospective corporate partners?

By marketing through sport, a company attempts to reach its target consumers through their lifestyles. According to Hanan, "life-styled" marketing is "a strategy for seizing the concept of a market according to its most meaningful recurrent patterns of attitudes and activities, and then tailoring products and their promotional strategies to fit these patterns."[12] Corporate marketing executives of both large and small companies have found that linking their messages to leisure pursuits conveys these messages immediately and credibly. The rationale is that leisure is a persuasive environment through which to relate a sales message to target consumers. The association of the company or product with the event is also important, because sporting events are well accepted by the public and have a strong fan following. By establishing a link with an event, a company shares the credibility of the event itself while delivering its message to a consumer who is apt to be relaxed and thus more receptive.

In addition, certain events enable the marketer to reach specific segments such as heavy users, shareholders, and investors, or specific groups that have been demographically, psychographically, or geographically segmented. Healthy Choice has become the official nutritional consultant to the U.S. ski team—the first sport sponsorship the company has undertaken. According to Mike Trautschold, president of ConAgra Brands, "Our goal is to create a deeper understanding of our message. Advising the team enables us to demonstrate our big strength to the consumer. Team members are young, vital people, who are not willing to compromise on nutrition or taste, so it's an exciting message for our consumers."[13]

Another example is Audi, which signed sponsorship agreements with equestrian events, ski races, and sailing after research indicated that participants in and followers of these events were typical Audi buyers. Jay Houghton, marketing manager for Audi, observed, "We try to reach consumers who understand and appreciate the integration of the driver and vehicle, pilot and vessel, rider and horse."[14]

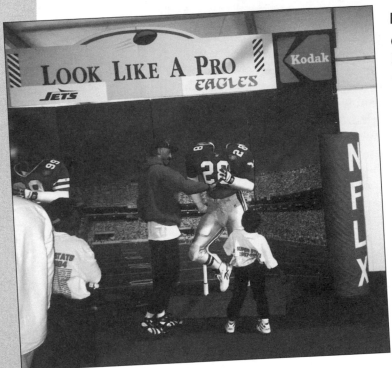

Some sponsorships provide an application to showcase the sponsor's product.

EXCLUSIVITY

Often a company will negotiate a sponsorship or licensing agreement that designates that company as the *exclusive* sponsor (see photo). The benefit of this type of sponsorship is a high level of exposure without the competition and clutter of traditional advertising. In other words, sponsorship can serve as a more subtle alternative to advertising; sponsorship may communicate the company's message in a "different," "new," and "less commercial" form. An example of exclusive sponsorship is the program developed by the International Olympic Committee (IOC) under the name TOP. For the first time, during the 1988 Seoul Olympics, the IOC designed worldwide exclusivity contracts that gave companies in various product categories exclusive rights to use the Olympic rings logo anywhere in the world. Exclusivity was a major factor in attracting sponsors to the WNBA. Lee Jeans, one of the four WNBA inaugural sponsors, entered into a three-year agreement with the league. Lee Jeans receives category exclusivity on all three WNBA television networks: NBC, ESPN, and Lifetime.[15]

HEIGHTENED COMMUNICATION

Communications through traditional advertising channels are often hit-or-miss. The targeted reader, viewer, or listener may or may not be exposed to the message. Sponsorship adds dimension to the product-audience communication; this communication can create experiences that appeal to all senses, encourage fan participation and feedback, provide opportunities for sampling and merchandising, and convey some of the excitement and drama inherent in sport. Most importantly, these experiences can be as memorable as the event itself.

PUBLICITY

Publicity is another integral benefit of sponsorship. The sponsored product (athlete, team, league, or event) is obligated by contract to credit the sponsor and, in entitlement agreements, to refer to the event as the XYZ Marathon or the Big City Marathon presented by XYZ. In the 1970s and 1980s, this gave tobacco companies an excellent opportunity to gain visibility via the media. Good examples of this type of sponsorship are the Winston Cup Racing Series and the Virginia Slims Tennis Tournament, commonly referred to as the Virginia Slims. Photographs as well as television coverage of the event often show boards and spots illustrating the corporate partner's name and logo. The benefit of such a sponsorship is that extensive media attention accrues to sport events and the personalities involved, and thus to their sponsors and licensees as well. Publicity via sport promotional agreements is delivered by the event or television broadcast, and this positions the company's messages more objectively in the eyes of the audience—messages that are more difficult for the audience to ignore than an advertisement is. Thus corporations, instead of paying for the news, have the chance to be the news, at a prime time and with a product for which the public has shown a strong affinity. For example, Goody's, manufacturer of a headache powder sold primarily in the South, becomes part of the national news when television broadcasts the Goody's Dash Series.

New media are another tool used by sponsors to publicize and promote themselves and their activities; they are also used by sport marketing agencies to make sponsor presentations. New media can be defined as newly created computer-based communication vehicles that allow the integration of audio, video, and animation. New media have rapidly become an integral part of the sponsorship process. Because this form of communication is often entertaining and because it holds an audience's attention, it is clearly more effective than traditional media that are viewed as flat—one-dimensional.

New Media: An Essential Tool in Sport Sponsorship

Alycen McAuley, General Manager (MAI)[2]

We consistently work with sport organizations to encourage the use of such new media tools as Internet Web sites, Intranets, Extranets, multimedia presentations, interactive kiosks, touch-screen technology, and interactive games. Sport organizations as well as corporate entities involved in sport sponsorship have realized the need to create personalized, tailored messages to capture key target audiences. Within the sport industry, one of the more effective tools for this type of communication is new media. New media allow sport organizations to improve revenue generation and create a sense of intimacy with the customer; they are also a tool for improving both internal and external communication processes. As a sport marketing agency with a new media division (MAI[2]), Marketing Associates International (MAI) consistently matches sport organizations with new media strategies and tools to supplement client goals.

The Chicago Bears enhanced their sponsorship sales efforts through the use of a multimedia presentation created by Marketing Associates International–Interactive MAI[2]. The goal of this "business-to-business" presentation was not only to communicate the history and tradition of the Bears' organization, but to effectively communicate the benefits of a sponsorship affiliation with the Bears. We structured the presentation to reflect these goals, creating four main categories (overview, marketing, case studies, and sponsorship), as well as a dynamic introduction that was emotive and nostalgic. Integrated throughout the presentation are video and audio segments that allow viewers to experience in-stadium promotions, television broadcasts, and community relations programs. Case study sections allow prospective sponsors to learn what other Bears sponsors are doing with their sponsorship: these sections include marketing collateral, advertising elements (in stadium and out of stadium), examples of television and radio advertisements, and in-stadium promotional elements. The Bears multimedia presentation was also designed for specific customization. Within the "sponsorship" category, MAI[2] designed the presentation to allow the Bears to insert graphics, video, audio, and text that are specific to the targeted prospect. In this way, the sponsorship sales process is carried through not only the Bears' profile, but also the attention given to the potential sponsor.

The St. Louis Rams provide another example of new media utilization. The Rams needed a way to reach two distinct audiences: new fans in St. Louis and old fans from Los Angeles who were still vested in the team. The solution? An interactive fan zone Web site. MAI[2] designed the Rams' Web site to capture all the major elements of a traditional team media guide: statistics, rosters, game schedules, ticket information, and other traditional sport information. In addition to having these traditional elements, the site needed to be fun and to allow for two-way communication between the fans and the Rams. A section entitled "The Edge" adds an interactive segment to the site: fans can play interactive football games that change on a regular basis. They can also take a virtual tour of the TransWorld Dome that presents three-dimensional images. Standing in the Dome on the Virtual Tour, fans can direct the computer to "look" at any other part of the Dome and can turn 360 degrees to see the entire stadium. The Virtual Tour also allows the viewer to zoom into any area in the stadium for an up-close look. Finally, a section called "Polls/Talkback," part of the Fan's Corner, not only provides fans the opportunity to talk to one another (through the posting of messages to the bulletin board) but also allows them to e-mail comments to the Rams directly.

The activities of Sprint present a final illustration of the use of new media. When Sprint's local telephone division wanted to capitalize on Sprint's sponsorship of the NFL within its markets, MAI and MAI² teamed up to create an integrated marketing campaign that utilized the Internet as an essential tool. MAI² designed a web page featuring Pittsburgh Steeler quarterback Kordell Stewart. Through an animated file, Kordell dropped back to pass, scrambled left, and then passed into the end zone, which was painted with the Sprint logo. On the field, a play was drawn out in Xs and Os, with the Os (representing Kordell's teammates) as hot buttons to aspects of the site; and in the end zone, the Os were replaced by Sprint phone products, thus creating the effect that you "score a touchdown" with Sprint products. Within the site, elements included e-commerce purchase ca-

pabilities, a weekly diary in which Kordell shared his thoughts on the season, an on line chat session during the season, an interactive trivia contest entitled "Who's calling Kordell?"—and finally, an interactive game entitled "You Make the Call!" The schedule of the trivia contest and diary created weekly "re-traffic" to the site; the games provided interactivity; and the integration of the phones with the football motif created a seamless link between Sprint and the NFL. In this instance, new media enhanced the value of corporate sponsorship by linking the sport organization with the corporate entity in a targeted marketing campaign.

We've been able to show sport organizations that effective marketing requires direct communication specific to the targeted group. Media like television and radio send broad messages to entire groups of people with little chance of personalizing the message to a particular person. New media, on the other hand, allow for frequent personalized messages directed at specifically defined target groups and markets. New media strategy allows sport organizations to succeed with respect to revenue generation, customer intimacy, and process improvement in a single integrated tool.

CORPORATE OBJECTIVES

Not every corporation has the resources and global reach of Nike. Therefore, every approach to sponsorship or promotional licensing should take into account the fact that it is difficult to classify corporate objectives in a clear-cut way. As they develop sponsorship objectives, corporations frequently have a number of objectives that overlap and interact. For example, MCI Corporation, a telecommunications company based in Washington, D.C., invests more than $5 million annually to sponsor the Heritage Golf Classic and a number of other sporting events. The company uses the Heritage Golf Classic as a reward/entertainment vehicle for customers who spend between $1 million and $3 million per month on telecommunication services. The MCI agreement serves a number of objectives: it targets a specific market (heavy users), builds goodwill among decision makers, and facilitates prospecting, that is, finding possible sales avenues or leads, for its salespeople.

According to Meenaghan, objectives in sponsorship range from assumption of social responsibility to the commercial objectives normally proposed for advertising.[16] Our review of academic writings and empirical research, as well as practical findings on the subjects of promotional licensing and sponsorship, indicates that there is no single corporate objective in the decision-making process about whether and what to sponsor. A study by Irwin, Asimakopoulos, and Sutton showed that company image and target market fit were the most important criteria in funding a sponsorship proposal.[17] Figure 12.9 on page 266 illustrates a tool that sponsors can use to screen potential sponsorship opportunities based upon corporate objectives.

According to the research, the following were the objectives that most often influenced the decision to enter sport sponsorship agreements:

- ➤ To increase public awareness of the company, the product, or both
- ➤ To alter or reinforce public perception of the company
- ➤ To identify the company with the particular market segments
- ➤ To involve the company in the community
- ➤ To build goodwill among decision makers
- ➤ To generate media benefits
- ➤ To achieve sales objectives
- ➤ To create an advantage over competitors, through association or exclusivity
- ➤ To gain unique opportunities in terms of hospitality and entertainment
- ➤ To secure entitlement or naming rights

Each objective should provide the sponsor with an ROI that might be in monetary form, but could also be measured through the media (number of impressions), the ability to exclude competitors, and so forth. In the next section, we will illustrate the importance of each objective, explain what it is and why it is important, and provide examples of how each objective can be utilized and achieved in the context of sport sponsorship. The Sponsorship Paradigm depicted in Figure 12.10 (page 267) illustrates a simple model of what the sponsor and the sport property hope to receive as a result of their partnership. Each party has expectations to be delivered and fulfilled by the other.

INCREASE PUBLIC AWARENESS

Sponsorship has sometimes been used with the sole aim of increasing awareness of a company or its products. Old Navy, the San Francisco-based division of the Gap, operates 265 clothing stores, primarily in metropolitan areas, in 41 states. To increase awareness of its product lines and to generate exposure, Old Navy has been actively pursuing sport sponsorship opportunities, particularly in relation to collegiate and minor league baseball apparel. To generate this awareness, Old Navy has secured sponsorships that have included in-store sweepstakes and even a fashion show. In the fashion show, the players on the Class A Kane County Cougars, dressed in Old Navy apparel, modeled the product in front of the fans.[18]

INFLUENCE PUBLIC PERCEPTION

The opportunity to capitalize on image association or image transfer makes sponsorship attractive to businesses as a marketing communications tool. The choice of a sport or event with particular attributes can help a company achieve a desired image that will reinforce or change consumers' perceptions of the company and its products. Choosing the sport or event becomes less formidable when there is an actual or logical link between the company and the sport or event. The potential for an effective sponsorship agreement is at its maximum when there is an association between the target group of the company and the target group of the sport or event, between the desired image of the company and the image of the sport or event, or between the product characteristics promoted and the credibility of the sport entity helping to promote the product.

As the popularity of in-line skating has skyrocketed over the past five years, competition among skate manufacturers has been fierce. One of the in-line skate manufacturers, Rollerblade, Inc., was looking to increase sales and also to generate

Criteria	WT	-4	-3	-2	-1	0	1	2	3	4	Total
Budget Consideration											
Affordability											
Cost effectiveness											
Management Issues											
Event profile											
Organizational committee status											
Media guarantees											
Legal status											
Regulatory policy											
Athletes' cooperation											
Governing body status											
Marketing agency profile											
Positioning Image											
Product/sport image fit											
Product utility fit											
Image/target market fit											
Targeting of Market											
Immediate audience											
Demographic fit											
Size											
Fan association strength											
Extended media coverage											
National coverage											
Local coverage											
Extended Audience Profile											
Demographics fit											
Size											
Public Relations											
Hospitality accommodation											
Community leader presence											
Customers presence											
Staff sport knowledge											
Event sales/retail tie-in											
New account opportunities											
Promotional Opportunities											
Promotional licensing											
Complementary advertising											
Signage opportunities											
Competition Consideration											
Competition's interest											
Ambush market avoidance											
Sponsorship Status											
Title sponsor											
Major sponsor											
Exclusivity											
Established											
Long-term involvement											
Alternative Sponsorship											
Co-sponsor											
In-kind supplier											
Sponsorship Type											
Team											
League/championship											
Event											
Facility											
Grand Total											

Figure 12.9
Revised sport sponsorship proposal evaluation model.

publicity for a new line of hockey-specific skates. So the company entered into an agreement with the Milwaukee Admirals of the International Hockey League. Rollerblade account executive John Smid commented, "Until now we haven't had an in-line product synonymous with hockey like many of the [ice] skate manufacturers do. Our hockey program will have credibility by being connected to the Admirals."[19]

Situation analysis
  • What clients want

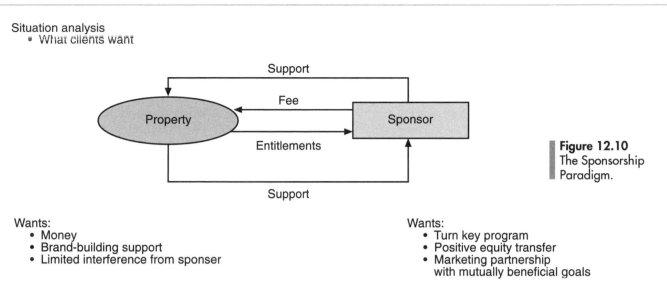

Figure 12.10
The Sponsorship
Paradigm.

Wants:
  • Money
  • Brand-building support
  • Limited interference from sponser

Wants:
  • Turn key program
  • Positive equity transfer
  • Marketing partnership
    with mutually beneficial goals

ESTABLISH ASSOCIATION WITH PARTICULAR MARKET SEGMENTS

Selecting a sponsorship agreement that matches the target has proven quite benefi-cial for sponsors. For example, Anheuser-Busch, the largest brewing company in the world, spends over $200 million (60 percent of its marketing budget) sponsoring a broad array of sporting events. In contrast, Coors, with a marketing budget of $20 million to $30 million, must be more selective in what it sponsors. Coors, using a demographic-lifestyle approach to sponsorship/licensing agreements, has turned down sponsorship of both tennis and golf events because fans of these sports gener-ally prefer wine and other alcohol products to beer. Thus, Coors has decided to be-come involved in auto racing and motorcross, noting that followers of these sports consume more beer than any other category of sport fan.[20]

We can see similar targeting efforts in Western Union's sponsorship of a College Night with the International Hockey League Indianapolis Ice. According to Todd Pierson, Western Union key accounts manager, the College Night was an attractive option because it allowed the company to target college students, whom the com-pany sees as a primary market for Western Union phone cards and the company's money transfers.[21]

But perhaps we see some of the best examples of appeal to an identified market segment in the relationship between the WNBA and Sears. Shortly after the WNBA concept and players were announced, Sears was lining up players to sign autographs among the appliances and clothes at its stores in WNBA cities. "These are high-achievement women who will have real relevance to our target customer, the middle-American woman and her family," according to John Costello, Sears's head of marketing.[22]

With regard to identifying with a global segment, Reebok has become involved with the World Cup as a way to encourage identification with its products in South America, in particular in Colombia, Paraguay, and Chile. According to Peter Moore, senior vice president of Reebok's global soccer division, "It [the World Cup] is a message that is giving us tremendous credibility in those countries and regions—and believe me, nothing engenders more passion in South America than soccer."[23]

BECOME INVOLVED IN THE COMMUNITY

Sponsorship has demonstrated more potential than any other promotion tool in terms of direct impact on the community. In this context, sponsorship often takes the form of public or community relations, and its objective is usually to position the com-pany as a concerned and interested citizen trying to put something back into the community. Companies may target community relations through sport sponsorship to specific communities, regional areas, or other geographic areas of influence as dictated by corporate objectives. Through licensing or sponsorships, the company demonstrates its awareness of local issues in an effort to influence potential customers and local social and governmental agencies. This is particularly true in cases in which the corporate partner provides financial or other support to an event that otherwise would not occur or could not continue. For example, a company could offer to help threatened local clubs or support interscholastic sport programs that cover a larger geographic area. Evidence supports the idea of using promotional programs designed to increase corporations' involvement with the community. Meenaghan cites a survey in which 72 percent of the respondents thought that business firms should sponsor more events and activities: 37 percent felt that companies should sponsor sport-related activities; 17 percent, children's activities; 11 percent, senior citizen programs; and 7 percent, charitable causes.[24]

An excellent example is the NBA's Cleveland Cavaliers' Minority Business Associates program. This is a program with two primary objectives: generating sponsorship and advertising revenue from nontraditional sources, and creating an effective way for community leaders to serve as role models for Cleveland schoolchildren. Ten African American business owners in Cleveland paid $6,500 each to join the program. They'll help support the Cavs' Stay in School Program—both financially and by speaking directly to kids—and provide free tickets for kids to attend games. In exchange, the business owners will receive arena signage and public service announcements during Cavs television broadcasts and the pregame coach's show.[25]

BUILD GOODWILL

Sport provides an excellent environment in which to conduct or influence business on a relaxed, personal basis. In recent years with the fast pace of market growth, the fight for increased market share among existing customers and the competition for new accounts (particularly in the international market) have been intense. Corporations that can deliver unique opportunities such as entertainment, tickets, and hospitality for key clients are also perceived to be corporations that will be good business partners and will always overdeliver goods and service. For example, Travelers Insurance Company is a sponsor of the prestigious Masters Tournament. The firm's director of corporate advertising and promotion, Ed Faruolo, notes that "the tournament is an upscale, prestigious event that provides a fit both demographically and psychographically." Each day of the tournament, a different group of executives from around the United States is flown to the event site. As Faruolo observes, "There are many golf enthusiasts in the trade, and a lot of our agents conduct business on the golf course. When you put those two factors together, the Masters makes good sense from a business standpoint."[26]

GENERATE MEDIA BENEFITS

Media benefits include advertising and publicity related to the promotional efforts surrounding the product or event. Media benefits are usually equated with ROI and measured in the numbers of impressions generated and the source of those impressions. Impressions are the number of viewers (television), readers (all print forms), and listeners (radio) exposed to the advertising message. The advertising message may be an actual advertisement, but it is often a logo or sign that appears during the television coverage or is evident in a newspaper photograph. In auto racing, for example, the driver often wears a cap with the name of a sponsor and sometimes changes the cap during a photo session or interview to provide exposure and impressions for the sponsor(s). The source of these impressions is also very important to the sponsor. A photograph in the *New York Times* is much more powerful in terms of impressions than a photo in the *Amherst Bulletin* (Massachusetts) because of the subscription base, the online value, and the regional editions of the paper that are sold nationally. In the following section, we examine some of the methods companies utilize to select events for sponsorship, some ways of evaluating media, and other benefits associated with the sponsorship opportunity.

Interest in sponsoring the World Cup is due in part to the global television audience, estimated at 37 billion people. Official sponsors of the World Cup receive advertising billboards at field level in every World Cup venue—and according to Marianne Fulgenzi, vice president for publicity at MasterCard, "During the World Cup we average 7 1/2 minutes per match when our logo is on camera."[27] Thus 37 billion people are exposed to MasterCard for 7 1/2 minutes during every match. When combined with the media coverage of the product or event, media benefits may be the most important objective for a number of companies involved in sponsorship agreements. This has been particularly true for companies in the tobacco and alcoholic drink industries, although other companies with access to direct-advertising channels have found the media exposure they get through sponsorship agreements to be cost effective.

For some sponsors, media benefits involving a variety of outlets or an association with an established entity may be the crucial element in determining whether or not to become involved as a sponsor. Clearly, this was the case for the WNBA. The WNBA, which premiered in the summer of 1997, attracted big-name sponsors, including Lee Jeans, Spalding, Anheuser-Busch, Champion, and Sears, in large part because of the league's unique broadcasting arrangement. In a singular marketing ploy, designed to appeal to several demographic segments, the WNBA entered into an agreement whereby three games per week are broadcast on national television, one each on NBC, ESPN, and Lifetime.[28]

Unfortunately for some sponsors, there are cases where they are promised the benefits of sponsorship, recognition, target market, and pay, but for one reason or another, those benefits fail to materialize. The media benefits for sponsors of the 1998 Winter Olympics were slim because of the ambush-marketing techniques (discussed later in this chapter) of several companies. On that occasion a sponsoring company expected media benefits, but nonsponsors actually gained more exposure.

A February 1998 telephone survey conducted by the Leo Burnett Agency and its Starcom media division revealed that television viewers had a difficult time identifying Olympic sponsors when provided with a list of companies that advertise heavily on television. *Of those surveyed, 73 percent incorrectly identified Nike as an official sponsor of the Olympics.* Among the actual sponsors who invested a minimum of $40 million to sponsor the games, only McDonald's scored better than Nike, attaining a recognition rate of 85 percent. VISA, an Olympic sponsor, had a 70 percent recognition rate, while competitor and nonsponsor MasterCard was misidentified as a sponsor by 49 percent of the respondents. In other sponsor-versus-nonsponsor recognition (sponsor listed first), Coke had 68 percent versus Pepsi's 55 percent, and United Parcel Service had 50 percent versus 40 percent for Federal Express. VISA's Becky Saeger felt that the sponsorship was worthwhile because VISA was the only card accepted at the Olympics and is the only card that can advertise during the games on CBS. Nevertheless, Saeger went on to say that advertisers face great difficulty in determining what is worth sponsoring and also in deciding how to leverage sponsorships. According to Saeger, all sponsors must face one question: How important is it that the people know you're an official sponsor?[29]

An excellent way to measure whether your company is receiving the media benefits is to ask for the help of a business like Joyce Julius and Associates, based in Ann Arbor, Michigan. Established in 1985, this company is the industry leader in the measurement and valuation of the benefits of sport sponsorship. Joyce Julius and Associates has two primary products—the *Sponsors Report* and the National

Television Impression Value (NTIV) Analysis. *Sponsors Report* provides complete exposure results stemming exclusively from national event broadcasts. These results assist brand and advertising managers in justifying budgetary expenditures, documenting impressions and exposure, and determining the value of the broadcast in comparison to other forms of sponsorship. For example, during the CBS coverage of the Masters Tournament, Joyce Julius and Associates found that the Nike-logoed hat and shirt worn by Tiger Woods were visible on screen for 16 minutes and 31 seconds. On the basis of an estimate of the cost of CBS's paid television ads, that loosely translates to $1,685,000 in on-air Nike exposure.[30]

The NTIV Analysis provides a comprehensive evaluation of the total sponsorship program. Thus, in addition to measuring the exposures and benefits of national television broadcasts, the NTIV examines responses generated from exposures, such as television news programming, national and event-market radio, event-site exhibits and displays, cross-corporate advertising, promotional efforts, and print media. This information is then entered into a formula and converted to a cost per impression and a corresponding value of the sponsorship. The success and acceptance of the NTIV instrument has led to the development of the NTIV Projection Analysis, which predicts the exposure return on proposed sponsorship programs.[31]

ACHIEVE SALES OBJECTIVES

The ultimate objective of marketing is to increase sales levels or profitability. Sponsorship, along with other elements of the communications mix, is usually viewed as an element that influences the buyer to purchase. In this sense, sponsorship constitutes an important stimulus within purchasing as a multi-stage, multi-influence process; but it can also influence sales in a more direct manner. To address the fact that a growing number of car buyers are women, BMW paid a mid-five-figure sponsorship fee to be a presenting sponsor of the Danskin Triathlon Series. In exchange, BMW received significant media benefits that were used to promote local dealerships, because the primary goal of the event was to boost showroom traffic by suitably affluent and aware women. The program was highly successful: in one market, 25 percent of the participants in the triathlon series visited BMW dealers.[32]

Another highly illustrative case is that of John Hancock Insurance. John Hancock is an Olympic sponsor, and according to David F. D'Alessandro, senior executive vice president, the sponsorship makes sense. "One of the reasons we are investing in the Olympics is what it's doing for us in Southeast Asia, where the insurance markets are growing at a double digit rate, and they're growing here at 1 percent or negative 1 percent. They have no idea who John Hancock is, or was, in Malaysia. But by marrying it with the Olympic marks, people know us more as an Olympic sponsor than a patriotic American company."[33] John Hancock hopes that this association with the Olympics and its global image will provide familiarity and an entry point for sales efforts in Malaysia.

Sales objectives can also relate to product utilization as a benefit of a sponsorship/licensing agreement. Sponsorship or licensing agreements with a venue such as an amusement park or arena may require the use of a particular product at all events or functions in the facility (i.e., the new Pepsi Center, scheduled to open in Denver in 1999 as the home of the Nuggets and Avalanche). For example, when the standard of comparison is supermarket sales, Coca-Cola wins the battle for market share by only a few percentage points over Pepsi. However, when it comes to park and recreation facilities, theaters, and sporting events, Coca-Cola is the clear winner. The strategy of Coca-Cola is to sign sponsorship/licensing agreements that ensure product exclusivity and utilization.

Another approach to sales-driven sponsorship agreements is the one VISA employed in its five-year (1995-2000) $40 million sponsorship agreement with the NFL.

"The bottom line reasoning at VISA is simple: Their experience with the Olympics since 1986 has shown that such activities significantly increase card use, help to retain existing cardholder accounts and generate significant numbers of new cardholder accounts. VISA saw a 28 percent jump in payment service to a total of $290.7 billion. VISA credits its sport marketing, particularly the Olympics, as well as non-sport promotions, as having a significant influence on those results. VISA believes the Olympic experience suggests that the NFL will also achieve these goals for them."[34]

CREATE EXCLUSIVITY

In some cases, particularly when the sponsorship fee is high or the commitment is long-term, an area integral to licensing agreements is product or category exclusivity. This assures, for example, that a particular soft drink will be the only soft drink or (in many cases) the only refreshment associated with the event/product or used at the venue. As stated previously, the great benefit is that this provides an opportunity

Utilizing Sport Marketing Agencies to Execute Sponsorship Elements

David Steffano and Hunter Lochman, Marketing Associates International

Corporate sponsorship marketing groups (CSMG) retain the services of sport marketing agencies for a wide variety of reasons. But the initial basis for a CSMG-agency relationship is the realization that an agency provides a method of allowing a CSMG to use its departmental resources efficiently by having access to agency personnel who can provide a complementary set of personalized expertise and experience.

Marketing Associates International is the sport marketing agency of record for Sprint's CSMG. Currently, Sprint sponsors a number of sport properties, including the largest professional sport sponsorship in history with the NFL and all its member teams. Sprint's CSMG hired MAI to help them implement and manage this sponsorship program. This CSMG consists of a director, four managers, and one support staffperson, while MAI's NFL account team has a project lead, one director, three managers, and support staff. In effect, utilizing MAI doubles the size of the CSMG's staff and provides accessibility, and a wide range of skills, to a geographically challenging program. The MAI staff members have backgrounds in advertising, corporate brand management, and league and team marketing.

Leading up to and during the season, the NFL account team (CSMG and MAI) is responsible for checklist details. Examples include ticket management, media management, Intranet updates, and integrated communication among the teams, MAI, and the CSMG. As the CSMG's days become increasingly busy during the NFL season, MAI becomes the day-to-day contact with the NFL clubs, handling those checklist details. When a situation arises that calls for CSMG involvement, MAI escalates the issue to the CSMG, providing all the details and offering recommendations. During the latter part of the NFL season, MAI assists the CSMG in developing a "play-off plan" that involves a new cycle of negotiation and implementation with the clubs.

Part of MAI's role is to evaluate the NFL program for the CSMG and to make recommendations for the following year. To that end, MAI has developed a proprietary valuation methodology that enables it to assign a value to every element and detail of the NFL sponsorship program and the individual club agreements.

A successful client-agency relationship occurs when—as in the case of MAI, NFL Properties, and the NFL clubs—the business units within Sprint see MAI as a seamless extension of Sprint's CSMG.

for sales-driven use of the sponsorship agreement and at the same time prohibits competitors from using the event, venue, product, or activity to transmit a message to the audience. This limitation of communication avenues can improve the ability of the marketing message to increase sales, and may impact the profitability of both the sponsor and the competitor. The exclusivity, in light of the strong emotional attachment and following that sport inspires, allows the marketer to position brands or products as supporting an event or the efforts of a particular team (while implying that the competitor's product does not), thereby encouraging consumer support where it counts most—at the cash register.

In its corporate-partner agreement with the NCAA, Gillette is guaranteed category exclusivity. As Gillette delineates it, the category consists of grooming/personal care, which includes the following products: blades/razors, shaving preparation, aftershave, cologne, deodorants, shampoo, conditioners, styling gel, mousse, hair spray, home permanents, styling aids, ethnic hair care products, and skin care products (hand and body lotion); toothbrushes, toothpaste, oral rinse, dental floss; electric shavers and electric hair care appliances. Gillette's two divisions, PaperMate and Braun, are also granted exclusivity for their respective products: stationery, pens, markers, highlighters, and correction fluid; coffee makers, clocks, toasters, and food processors. Thus Gillette can promote any or all of these items as it chooses while preventing any of its competitors from doing so via a relationship with the NCAA.

GAIN OPPORTUNITIES IN HOSPITALITY AND ENTERTAINMENT

Although hospitality and entertainment relate to a number of the other concepts, this function is worthy of examination on its own. Hospitality and entertainment play a critical role in the packaging of sponsorship and promotional licensing programs. These concepts enable the sponsor to construct certain benefits and opportunities that are often unique and unavailable in the marketplace. Such opportunities may include trips to the Super Bowl or the NCAA Final Four and on-site hospitality and special events. According to William Pate, vice president of advertising for BellSouth (which sponsors a NASCAR Winston Cup team, the Atlantic Coast Conference, and the Atlanta Braves), "Business people are more open to messages when they are at leisure than when they are working."[35]

Hospitality opportunities have become an integral part of sponsorship agreements for college athletic programs, which package hard-to-obtain tickets in prime locations along with tents, catering, and other amenities. There are similar hospitality programs on the professional golf tours and throughout professional football; such programs often form the basis for the sale of luxury suites and boxes in sporting venues throughout the world. The key to successful use of hospitality is to ensure that the hospitality is not available except as part of a comprehensive sponsorship or promotional licensing agreement.

Corporate partners use hospitality benefits to reward their own personnel, or, in the majority of cases, to induce their own clients to increase product utilization or consumption, renew agreements, or sign new ones. This is done through entertaining. For example, "IBM ponied up $2,500 each for twenty $20 passes to the 1997 Masters Tournament, and used them as a centerpiece for a week of entertainment for its top golf-nut clients to reward them for their continuous business."[36] Hospitality has long been an integral part of European sponsorship programs and accounts for as much as 25 percent of corporate-partner expenditures. Hospitality packaging is receiving more attention and has higher priority in the United States than ever before.

SECURE ENTITLEMENT OR NAMING RIGHTS

Corporations interested in purchasing naming rights to venues or in entitling events such as concert tours, auto racing events, and bowl games have an agenda in mind

Hospitality—A View From the Front Lines

Lisa Marie Weinzetl, Suite Manager, Pittsburgh Steelers

It's a common misconception that the person responsible for hospitality and client entertainment has the best job on the staff. After all, these people sit in luxury suites at sporting events, plan and give parties, and travel with clients on road trips. However, as sport has become more of a business, as opposed to simply a game, hospitality and client entertainment have taken on a different role.

Why Hospitality Is Important

Hospitality, be it an invitation to a pregame reception, a ticket to the owner's suite, or a seat on the team plane, has implications that last far beyond the end of the party, game, or trip. Although specific goals for each hospitality event vary, there are general themes that transcend all agreements. A hospitality event allows for the host's staff and their clients to develop a relationship beyond that of host and client. It provides a setting in which conversation can focus on family vacations and the team's chances for postseason play. The opportunity to develop this type of relationship should not be undervalued, as sport marketing is a business that depends on relationships. Often, when two competitors can provide the same products and services, the vendor who has developed a personal relationship with the client will get the account.

Hospitality also allows a company to bring its product or brand to life. Consumers form pictures in their minds when they hear of or see products or brands. Coppertone, for example, might convey an image of a young girl with a dog, while Miller Lite conveys images of unexpected moments. Hospitality can bring to life these images and the perceptions created in advertisements. For example, a Sprint reception might involve an appearance by spokesperson Kordell Stewart. Everyone has seen him on television, but now the invited guests can meet him, pose for a picture, and have a football autographed.

Hospitality also enables the hosts to give their guests something that otherwise might be inaccessible. It is impossible to buy a ticket on a team's charter jet, let alone accompany the team on a road trip, unless you are an invited guest or a member of the owner's family. A sponsorship agreement can provide this type of opportunity, and a sponsor can become part of the "family." Imagine traveling with Michael Jordan and the Chicago Bulls to an NBA play-off game. Out of the question? Not if your hospitality provider can arrange it.

Hospitality can also serve to thank a company's most important and often forgotten customers. In today's business climate, it is often difficult to reward people financially. In some cases, this type of financial thank-you would be inappropriate and ineffective. However, if you are able to provide tickets to a sold-out game to a "big fan" and his or her child, the thank-you will be remembered often and the story retold.

What the Client Wants From Hospitality

Frequently it is difficult to determine what clients hope to achieve because they are unsure of exactly what they want and what is possible. However, most clients want the hospitality provider to furnish the following:

➤ A "turn key" process in which the sponsor has nothing to do but "turn the key and open the door"—essentially just show up, as the provider has attended to every detail

➤ An environment conducive to personal interaction and the fostering of personal as well as business relationships

➤ A unique and memorable experience that capitalizes on the client's or the provider's exclusive relationships and that cannot be replicated by outside competitors

How Needs Are Met

How can these conditions be met? First, constant, open communication among all those involved, from the client, to the facility manager, to the operations crew, to the caterer, to the decorator, to the transportation company, and so on. Miscommunication can lead to disaster. For example, if security fails to hear about a time change, your guests might find themselves locked out of the venue. A second aspect is attention to detail and follow-through. Any detail—even the most minor one—that is not taken care of can result in a less-than-perfect event. And aside from the operational considerations of the event, don't overlook the creative aspect. Don't limit your event to what is typical. Look outside the normal and the expected. Don't be afraid to hold a reception in the storage area of a venue if it provides unique decorating or entertaining possibilities.

Although each hospitality provider wants every event to proceed precisely as planned on paper, at times this may not be possible, despite our best efforts, because of circumstances beyond our control. You are not and cannot be held responsible for severe weather or a team's on-field performance.

The important thing to remember is that only a few people know how an event looked on paper when it was being planned. The guests will judge the night's success on the basis of some or all of the following criteria:

➤ Was there a sufficient supply of appetizing food?

➤ Were the guests able to meet and perhaps get an autograph from their favorite player?

➤ Did lines move quickly and efficiently?

➤ Were all the logistical arrangements first-class?

➤ Was the event fun and memorable?

Hospitality is an aspect of sponsorship that one should never underestimate or undervalue. Hospitality can initiate, broaden, repair, or strengthen the relationships that impact the success of sport marketing endeavors.

---

when they consider such sponsorship possibilities. This agenda consists of the following elements and their value to the company in terms of cost and organizational priority:

➤ Number of impressions or exposures

➤ Sponsorship and cross-promotional activities

➤ Tax-deductible expenses

➤ Brand exclusivity

➤ Public relations and community image

➤ Related amenities (hospitality)[37]

Conseco (insurance and financial services company) recently agreed to pay a $40 million fee ($2 million per year for 20 years) for the naming rights to the new Indiana Pacers Conseco Fieldhouse.[38] Is this a good deal for the Pacers? For Conseco? For both? According to one national sport marketing expert, Alan Friedman of the *Sports Business Journal* and founder of *Team Marketing Report,* "Naming rights are the most expensive sport marketing investment in the current marketplace, the best dollar-for-impression sponsorship bargain, and one of the most underutilized promotional assets in a company's marketing arsenal."[39] Corporations that elect to become involved in securing naming rights or entitlements must have a strategic plan in place to leverage the opportunity and the additional financial resources to support it.

Entitlement and naming rights have a very high profile in NASCAR. In stock car racing, the corporate role, by tradition, has great prominence. If a company sponsors a racing event, the company's name is incorporated into the event name. For example, Mountain Dew, one of PepsiCo's many soft drinks, sponsors Darlington's Southern 500. Hence the race itself is known as the Mountain Dew 500. If a company becomes a racing team sponsor, the corporate name or brand is used in conjunction with the team name. Rick Hendrick owns a car sponsored by Kellogg's and Chevrolet and driven by Terry Labonte. In alluding to the team and its race car, commentators and fans refer to the car as Labonte's Kellogg's Chevrolet Monte Carlo.[40] An excellent opportunity for both Kellogg's and Chevrolet to leverage their sponsorship.

EVALUATING AND ENSURING SPONSORSHIP EFFECTIVENESS

This decade has seen an increase in research measuring the impact of sponsorship programs. A demand for fiscal accountability has been the driving force behind these research efforts—an attempt to insist that corporate decision makers be held accountable for the budget allocations and related spending. The majority of research throughout the 1980s and the mid-1990s centered on calculating the number of impressions generated or counting the number of coupons redeemed. A significant number of organizations either conduct their own proprietary research or engage a marketing research firm to do so for them.

The NBA's Toronto Raptors have developed a rather innovative approach to determine how effectively their sponsorships are working: they formed a research partnership with their sponsors to find out. The team offered all of its sponsors the opportunity to share the cost of a $50,000 survey to track consumer recall of, and reaction to, Raptors sponsorship programs every year. According to Michael Downey, Raptors vice president of sales and marketing, 11 of the team's major partners are participating. Mike Scarlett, communications manager for Ford Motor Company of Canada, has said that the company is "getting a lot of good feedback about the results of our sponsorship. . . . We very rarely track the performance [of a sponsorship] versus our objectives." Also according to Scarlett, in-stadium research indicated that a significant portion of Raptors attendees are potential buyers of sport utility vehicles and full-size pickup trucks. Despite Ford's good feedback, initial survey results have returned some less-than-flattering statistics regarding fans' recognition of the Raptors' sponsors. "We got some numbers back that weren't all rosy and we expected that and some of our partners expected that," said Downey. "Now we'll try and find out what's working and fix what's not."[41]

WHY SPONSORSHIPS WORK—AFFINITY MARKETING

Affinity marketing refers to "an individual's levels of cohesiveness, social bonding, identification, and conformity to the norms and standards of a particular reference group."[42] Affinity marketing comprises certain specific components and tactics such as *frequency marketing, loyalty marketing, relationship marketing,* and *database marketing.* The reference group, depending on its size and characteristics, can be an attractive market for sponsors. For example, MCI created an affinity marketing program through which collegiate athletic departments generate funds in exchange for sharing their database of supporters—alumni business owners, donors, sponsors, and advertisers. The company contacts the individuals and organizations on the list, and if they subscribe to MCI's services, the school receives 5 to 7 percent of their billings. The affinity with the university and its athletic programs is the key to initially securing and then retaining the customer. According to Gene Hooks, executive director of the Division IA Athletic Directors Association, "Because of loyalty to the University, once someone signs up for the service, they'll be reluctant to change." This feeling is confirmed by MCI's national program manager, Bill Browning, who stated, "The customers we gain wind up being long-term customers."[43]

Perhaps the best example of consumer loyalty and support of a sport product is illustrated in the relationship between NASCAR and its fans. According to a study conducted by Performance Research, NASCAR fans have a higher level of trust toward sponsors' products than other fan groups do—approximately 60 percent of NASCAR fans surveyed compared to only 30 percent of football fans. More importantly, over 40 percent of NASCAR fans purposely switched brands when a manufacturer became a NASCAR sponsor.[44]

In sport marketing, bank credit cards with the team logo, or special-purpose cards such as the Jack Nicklaus Platinum card, are the most common forms of affinity marketing. Both of these programs offer a low introductory interest rate and allow the cardholder to earn points for each purchase ($1 = 1 point) with points convertible to team merchandise, golf equipment, lessons, and so forth.

WHY SPONSORSHIPS DON'T ALWAYS WORK—AMBUSH MARKETING

Sandler and Shani defined ambush marketing as "a planned effort (campaign) by an organization to associate themselves indirectly with an event in order to gain at least some of the recognition and benefits that are associated with being an official sponsor."[45] This definition related directly to the issue of sponsors paying for an association with the product or event and "ambushers" not paying. Several years later, Meenaghan added to the definition, to include within ambush activities "a whole variety of wholly legitimate and morally correct methods of intruding upon public consciousness surrounding an event."[46] Including this broader scope of activities underscores the harm to the sponsor: namely, confusion in the mind of the consumer that denies the sponsor clear recognition of its role and support, resulting in less benefit than originally planned when the sponsorship agreement was enacted.

Most ambush marketing aims at major events (such as the Olympics, World Cup, Super Bowl, NCAA Final Four) and other events with high sponsorship price tags, limited partnership, or sponsorship opportunities. One of the more noteworthy examples of ambush marketing occurred at the 1992 Barcelona Olympic Games. Reebok International, Ltd. (Reebok) was the official Olympic sponsor and Nike, International (Nike) was the ambusher. Throughout the games, Nike conducted a highly visible advertising campaign featuring Olympic athletes who happened to be under Nike endorsement or personal-services contracts—without paying a penny in (Olympic) sponsorship fees. A common ambush tactic is to pass out spirit signs. See photo for an example. Nike also held press conferences for Olympic athletes under contract with Nike and additionally displayed large murals of U.S.A. basketball team members (aka Dream Team) on the sides of Barcelona buildings. As Nike explained its position, "We feel like in any major sporting event we have the right to come in and give our message as long as we don't interfere with the official proceedings."[47] It is also interesting to note that the biggest controversy regarding this ambush occurred when Michael Jordan, Charles Barkley, and other athletes under contract with Nike initially refused to take part in the medal ceremony because participation required them to wear a warm-up suit with the Reebok vector. The amount of free publicity surrounding this event was of great benefit and value to Nike.

SELLING THE SPONSORSHIP

Before beginning the sales process to locate a sponsor for your team or event, develop a strategic planning process for how to conduct the sales campaign. Strategic planning steps should include the following:

> ➤ Make a comprehensive list of all items in your inventory.
> ➤ Establish a list price for each item based upon cost per impression (usually 5 to 50 cents), demand, and the prestige of each item.

➢ Establish packaging discount policies.

➢ Total all inventory at list price; then set a sales goal based on these discount policies.

➢ Remember, you must determine the real cost of the sponsorship, which may include any or all of the following elements: tickets (full face value), promotions (premium items, shipping, fulfillment, and labor costs), print and point-of-sale pieces, staffing costs, dasherboards and program ads (production, design, and layout costs), and developmental costs.

➢ Establish your sales strategy. Which, if any, categories are exclusive? What sales do you expect from each category? In which order will you proceed?

➢ Initiate the six-step sales process (see next section) with the top three product and service categories, then the next three, and so on. Sell your best inventory first.

➢ The order in which you present categories and potential sponsors is critical: large categories first, major national sponsors first, easy closures first; gain momentum, use the recognition of "name sponsors" to attract lesser sponsors, and leverage the relationships to gain other relationships.

➢ Talk to competitors (Coke-Pepsi, Bud-Miller, VISA-MasterCard-American Express) simultaneously to ensure a decision at the same time.

➢ Remember—*All sponsor decision makers know each other; don't exaggerate and don't make special deals.*

> Seemingly innocent activities such as passing out free spirit signs can effectively enable a company who has not paid a sponsorship fee to "ambush" an official sponsor.

THE SIX-STEP SPONSORSHIP SALES PROCESS

Once your organization has agreed on and implemented the strategic planning process, you can initiate the sales process. The success of the sales process depends on adherence to the principles of the strategic planning process.

1. *Schedule a meeting with the sponsorship decision maker.* Meet only if the decision maker is present; remember, don't accept no from someone who is not empowered to say yes.

2. *At the first meeting, listen 80 percent of the time and sell only when you have to. You are there to observe and learn.* Where does the potential sponsor spend its marketing dollars right now? What is working? What isn't working? What other sport organizations or events does the company sponsor or support? What does the company like or dislike about these relationships?

3. *Arrange a follow-up meeting for the presentation of your proposal before leaving this initial meeting.* Try to schedule it within one week of this first meeting.

4. *Create a marketing partnership proposal.* Give the potential sponsor something unique (creative handles, program elements, or ownership). Act more like a marketing partner/agency than a salesperson.

5. *Present the proposal as a "draft" that you will gladly modify to meet the organization's needs.* Custom-tailored proposals are much more likely to succeed than generic proposals.

6. *Negotiate the final deal and get a signed agreement.* Close the deal when you have the opportunity; ensure that the final signed deal has agreed-upon deliverables, payment terms, and a mutually agreed-upon timetable.

CO-OP SPONSORSHIP OPPORTUNITIES

A co-op sponsorship agreement is the joining together of two or more entities to capitalize on a sponsorship or licensing opportunity. Co-op sponsorships are viable in today's marketplace for a number of reasons. Such agreements

> allow companies to share the total cost of the sponsorship;

> allow promotion of several product lines (with distinct organizational budgetary lines) within the same corporate structure (e.g., Budweiser and Eagle Snacks);

> enable corporations to utilize existing business relationships that make sense (e.g., Coca-Cola and McDonald's);

> enable a weaker corporation with something to offer to leverage the strength and position of another corporation to gain the sponsorship and a position of advantage over its competitors;

> allow testing of a relationship when future opportunities are under consideration; and

> create a pass-through opportunity, typically involving grocery chains that agree to a sponsorship and pass some or all of the costs (and benefits) to product vendors in their stores (e.g., Stop & Shop could agree to a sponsorship with the University of Connecticut and pass costs on to Pepsi, Frito-Lay, and Wonder Bread).

ETHICAL ISSUES IN SPONSORSHIP

As sponsorship has grown in scope and impact, sport organizations have become highly reliant on sponsorship income to make a profit, or in some cases to secure new facilities or balance their bottom line. This dependence on sponsorship revenue has in certain instances caused the sport organization to make decisions that the affected parties have viewed unfavorably. For example, an exclusive contract between Reebok International, Ltd. and the University of Wisconsin brought the university millions of dollars along with a great deal of criticism and protest. The contract, valued at $9.1 million over five years, provides shoes, uniforms, and other apparel for all 22 varsity sport teams. In addition, the contract provides $2.3 million in cash for scholarships, payments to coaches, recreational sport programs, and community service projects.[48] The contract engendered protests and campus debate about affiliating the university with Reebok, which was accused of "sweat shop" practices in the plants in the Far East that produce its athletic shoes. People felt that given the strong spirit of trade and unionism in the state of Wisconsin, there should have been input from a variety of sources and possibly public hearings before the university entered into the agreement.

Currently institutions are debating the issue of sponsorship by brewing companies of intercollegiate athletic programs or events. In the light of several well-publicized deaths of college students in alcohol-related incidents during the 1997-1998 academic year, current sponsorship agreements are being scrutinized and new proposals carefully studied and debated. Alcohol-related companies are currently involved in intercollegiate athletics through advertising in game programs, commercials during game broadcasts, and in some cases, sponsorship deals with individual institutions. Coors sponsored a Nebraska football commemorative championship can, has a sponsorship and contest with the Heisman Trophy committee, and provided a silver inflatable tunnel (resembling a Coors Light can) for the Fresno State basketball team's entrance onto and exit from the court.[49] Does the need for the money outweigh the requirement to be a good citizen and to refrain from promoting products that might harm the very students you seek to assist? What about sponsorships from lotteries? Are we inadvertently promoting gambling? These are some of the ethical issues that sport marketers face every day in their struggle to fund their organizations and remain competitive.

WRAP-UP

Sponsorships and licensing agreements should be positioned as partnerships. Partnerships imply a win-win situation for all parties. This is a progressive way of thinking, rooted in the principles of relationship marketing (as defined in chapter 11. Partnerships imply mutual interest, consideration, negotiation, and benefits.[50] For example, Nike, a noted ambush marketer, is very protective of its own agreements and relationships and never uses the word "sponsor" but always "partner," feeling that the term sponsor doesn't take into account the importance of partners working together to meet the needs and goals of each partner.

For sponsors to justify the ever increasing cost of sponsorships, there must be an ROI that is multifaceted. The ROI should contain multiple benefits, that is, more than one of the following: media/exposures, sales opportunities, image enhancement, effective communication with the target market, hospitality opportunities, and brand positioning.

The rationale for entering a sponsorship agreement varies according to the size, mission, vision, geographic scope, target market, and resources of an organization. Regardless of the particulars of the organization, all sponsorship decisions should be based on the suitability and fit of the opportunity with the organization and its priorities, as well as on how the sponsorship opportunity helps achieve organizational objectives.

ACTIVITIES

1. Select a prominent company involved in sport marketing sponsorship activity. Review the activities and events that the company sponsors and determine, based on the criteria listed in this chapter, whether that sponsorship is meeting objectives. Why or why not?

2. Sponsorships are often referred to as partnerships. Do you feel this is an appropriate term? Provide one sponsorship example to support your answer.

3. Nike is referred to as a company involved in ambush marketing. Explain ambush marketing and provide an example, other than Nike, of a company involved in such activities.

4. What is meant by the term exclusivity as it relates to sponsorship?

5. Imagine that you are employed by a marketing agency to provide hospitality for the clients of a large international courier service at an international sporting event viewed as very prestigious (e.g., Super Bowl, World Cup). What factors would you consider when planning your schedule of activities?

6. Why is sponsorship viewed as more beneficial than advertising?

YOUR MARKETING PLAN

In developing your marketing plan, you have generated a list of objectives, strategies, and tactics. Sponsorship can be instrumental in helping to achieve these elements of a marketing plan by providing the resources (not necessarily just financial) needed to be successful. Integrate one or more of the concepts of sponsorship discussed in this chapter into your marketing plan.

PLACE OR PRODUCT DISTRIBUTION

OBJECTIVES

1. To understand distribution as it relates to the marketing process and the place application of the five Ps.

2. To understand the theory of "place" as it relates to sport.

3. To recognize the importance of the venue and facility in sport marketing.

4. To understand the elements of marketing channels and their application to tickets and retail products.

A Real "Racket" in Grand Central Station

In early June 1995, many New York City train commuters contended with more than the usual urban "racket." The Professional Squash Association was holding one of its premier events—the New York Sports Club's Tournament of Champions—in the middle of Grand Central Station. Sound bizarre? Not really. Construction crews had set up a portable, one-way-glass squash court, in which the world's 64 best softball squash pros would compete for $65,000 in cash prizes. The six-day event sold a total of 3500 tickets for seats around the "Fishbowl." More important, however, an estimated 20,000 commuters caught a glimpse of the action, which included the exploits of the reigning champ, Jansher Khan of Pakistan. According to *Sports Illustrated*, this one train stop had "exposed the sport to more people than had ever before seen it live."[1]

Just think; in one week, the squash industry had exposed its product to over 20,000 customers, most of whom had never seen the game played at a high level of skill, if at all. Further, the commuters in Grand Central Station were likely to fit the perfect demographics for growing squash as a popular sport—urban professionals with discretionary time and income, who might be persuaded to pursue a game that combined skill, exercise, and a limited time commitment. It was a simple matter of "taking the game to the people," because the people were unlikely to stumble across squash on their own.

In this chapter, we discuss a number of facets related to effective distribution of the sport product—both the core event and its extensions. We begin with a look at the facility, its location, its layout, and its image. Next we consider other types of distribution channels related to sport, including retail distribution of sporting goods. Finally, after outlining some features of effective ticket distribution, we discuss some creative approaches to product distribution in sport. Chapter 14 addresses the related topics of print, broadcast, and Internet distribution.

PLACING CORE PRODUCTS AND THEIR EXTENSIONS

In many respects, "place" or distribution decisions may be the most important ones a marketer makes, because they have long-range implications and are harder to change than product, price, promotion, and public relations decisions. Think just briefly about the range of product elements that require distribution by a typical sport team:

➤ The live event itself

➤ Tickets to the live event

➤ Concessions

➤ The image of the live event, via media

➤ Players and coaches via personal appearances

➤ Merchandise and memorabilia

These elements require an integrated strategy with long-term commitments of assets. Take the game form itself. In a competitive marketplace, most sport governing bodies are looking to "grow their game" by introducing it into new markets. The Professional Squash Association had a good idea, and it was not a costly risk. Ice hockey, however, has higher stakes because the game requires a large surface of ice—an expensive proposition in most parts of the world. The NHL has recognized its own stake in "growing" the game, so it has developed an integrated distribution strategy with many elements, including the following:

Expanding grassroots hockey activity. Both the NHL and USA Hockey have realized that "ice" hockey might actually develop on a base of interest in "street" hockey played on in-line roller skates. To this end, for example, the NHL has had a multiyear partnership with Streetball Partners International to conduct a traveling street hockey tournament called NHL Breakout. In 1998, the tour expanded from 9 to 22 cities, including Anaheim, Nashville, and Tampa.[2]

Building ice rinks in expanding markets. In 1998, the NHL formed a partnership with a real estate development firm to begin building a series of ice and in-line rinks around the United States called NHL Skate. The first rinks were targeted in Exeter, New Hampshire, and St. John, Indiana; a total of 100 were planned. Regulation ice surfaces, seating for modest crowds, and NHL-themed restaurants and retail stores were to be among the design amenities. More important, each rink would emphasize not only NHL products but also basic instruction in skating and hockey skills, especially for girls.[3]

Team exhibitions in new world markets. In the fall of 1997, the Anaheim Mighty Ducks and the Vancouver Canucks played two games in Tokyo's Yayogi national gymnasium. Hockey interest is growing in Japan, so a visit by some of the world's top players made sense. Capacity crowds of over 10,000 paid up to $400 for a ticket, $50 for hats and T-shirts, and $25 for a program. Outside the rink, the NHL's interactive "Hockey Fest" exhibit was free to the public. Players made appearances around the city. By all accounts the visit succeeded. Said NHL Executive Vice President Brian Burke: "We came to pour a big load of fertilizer on the sport in a great market. . . . It's not just about selling T-shirts. This is a huge broadcast market with a professional hockey league already here. This is a market where we want to be active and popular from a marketing standpoint and a broadcasting standpoint."[4]

In these examples alone, the NHL is consciously and carefully distributing almost all the critical components of its product, from basic game knowledge to specialized team merchandise.

THEORY OF SPORT AND "PLACE"

One could argue that sports are no different from fast foods—it's all location, location, location. Because the core sport product is a game form, simultaneously produced and consumed, it makes sense that the venue of that game form should maximize exposure. For the New York Sports Club's Tournament of Champions, that meant setting up a "fishbowl" in Grand Central Station. Many sports, however, require less controllable topographic or geographic factors, such as a mountain, beach, or white-water river, where it is impossible to guarantee high levels of exposure. McDonald's or Safeway does not operate under such constraints. As we discussed in chapter 7, however, the "core experience" of the game or the event can be extended in many creative ways, through media distribution, videotapes, merchandise, and apparel—which is exactly the approach the NHL is taking to "grow" its game.

Location is critical to the experience of every sport consumer, whether participant or spectator. At the University of Massachusetts, the lacrosse field is located near the middle of campus, where more than 6500 students walk each day. The men's lacrosse team has enjoyed tremendous student support with crowds in excess of 8000 for big games. By contrast, the baseball team plays "America's game" in an out-of-the-way location where crowds have rarely exceeded 100, even for teams stocked with future Cy Young Award winners! But the difference goes beyond sheer proximity to the campus center. The lacrosse field is bounded in part by a long bank of grass that is perfectly sloped for students seeking a spot in the warm spring sun, where they can relax, kibitz, root for the home team, and maybe even crack open a book. The grassy embankment is part of an ensemble of elements that make this lacrosse field a special "place" in the campus life.

The NHL's "Breakout 98" brought the product into new markets.

The notion of the ensemble—developed by geographers—is important for sport marketers who work with core events. They must recognize the elements that enhance or diminish the attractiveness of their venue and surroundings. Take Boston's historic Fenway Park, one of the few North American sport venues that is truly cherished. Fenway's ensemble includes the following elements:

Landscapes. Fenway Park's surrounding landscapes include both the urban rhythms of Kenmore Square and the rural serenity of the nearby Back Bay Fens, the first park in Frederick Law Olmsted's "Emerald Necklace."

Artifacts. Fenway Park enjoys two noteworthy artifacts: the "Green Monster" (the left-field wall) inside the park and the giant neon "CITGO" sign outside.

History and memories. While Fenway Park is full of memories, none stands out more than Carlton Fisk's game-winning home run in the 1975 World Series.

Ideologies. Fenway Park may not conjure up serious political or social ideologies, but it does evoke notions (true or not) that baseball was somehow a better game when ballparks were simple and quaint, like Fenway.

Experiences. As baseball's premier writer, Peter Gammons, put it, "Fans know the soul of baseball is its atmosphere—the sights, smells, sounds, the very feel of the game."

Aesthetics. Besides the Green Monster, Fenway Park has irregular dimensions around the outfield, with various nooks and crannies that not only look interesting but also create havoc for visiting fielders and delight the home fans.

Problems. Fenway has plenty of problems, including traffic jams, limited and outrageously expensive parking, and all too many seats with views obstructed by support columns.

As Fenway Park slowly sags and creaks with age, the Red Sox must undertake a relocation or a massive renovation. In either case, however, the Red Sox recognize the wisdom of retaining as much of the historic Fenway ensemble as they can. They realize that Fenway's ensemble creates the emotional attachment that they want to retain and build upon.[5]

THE FACILITY

The facility is a central element of any sport "place" ensemble. An essential part of the marketing mix, it includes a number of ingredients that influence the attractiveness of the events held within—from accessibility and other transportation-related issues, to design and layout, to amenities, to personnel.

ACCESSIBILITY

Most sport marketers and consultants believe in the "Location, Location, Location" school of thought. Placement is paramount in retail sport products and services such as sporting goods stores, as well as in single-purpose health and fitness facilities. Where high levels of impulse business are to be expected, a high-traffic location is crucial. For the majority of sport products, the high level of visibility gained through media coverage can often overcome a less exposed site as long as the product is in demand and is getting good media coverage. Nonetheless, remember that up to 90 percent of a sport facility's customers (court or health club, retail sporting goods store, etc.) can be expected to live within 20 minutes' traveling time. Placement on the periphery of a market area leaves the door open for competition and results in inconvenience for the consumer.[6]

The facility should be readily accessible by major highways and mass transit. The latter is especially important when the facility aims to attract senior citizens, youth, or lower economic groups. Baseball magnates very early recognized the importance of access, and they linked their early "modern ballparks" (Comiskey Park, Fenway Park, Ebbets Field) to the paths of new trolley lines. The last five decades have demanded access by automobile. This caused problems in the 1980s for urban stadiums, situated as they were amid decaying infrastructures in need of repair. For example, the White Sox had long benefited from Comiskey Park's proximity to the Dan Ryan Expressway, which Mayor Richard Daley had allegedly routed near his beloved ballpark. Necessary repairs in 1988, however, had shut down the highway, adding to the White Sox' attendance woes.[7]

THE TRADE AREA OR "DRAWING RADIUS"

Accessibility influences the size of a facility's "drawing radius." Good highways and mass transit allow more people to travel farther in less time, and time is the critical cost factor in the consumer's mind. People will endure more or less traveling or "drive time" depending on the nature of their destination. For instance, most people expect to travel only 10 minutes to their local shopping center or strip mall. They will, however, drive 30 minutes to a "super" center that houses a few mass merchandisers, and it appears they will happily drive an hour or more to a new "megamall" that features many "big-box" discounters like Best Buy or Circuit City. Bostonians make regular two-and-one-half hour trips to Freeport, Maine—a manufacturer's outlet mecca and the home of L.L. Bean.[8]

As introduced in chapter 5, facility directors used to simply draw concentric circles around a facility, usually at five-mile intervals, as if mileage alone dictated a market. Figure 13.1 illustrates the modern methodology of drawing radii based upon drive or traveling time. At multipurpose facilities, the drawing radii change markedly for various events. The traveling-time drawing radii are much better predictors as each radius becomes elongated along major arterial and transit systems, providing a more accurate reflection of equal traveling-time segments.

Although the specific dynamics of the sport drawing radius demands much more rigorous consumer research, it appears that the following factors are critical:

Demographics. Discretionary time varies with income, occupation, and stage in the life cycle.

Duration and frequency of the event. Most people will travel much longer for an infrequent event (a concert by a favorite artist) than they will for a twice-weekly activity (a game of tennis).

Emotional commitment. Parents will travel hours to watch their children play; casual high school fans may never leave town.

Perception of quality. The "big" game or the "big" star will typically expand the drawing radius.[9]

The drive-time methodology has several applications:

➤ When locating a new facility and performing market feasibility studies, it is possible to make accurate market assessments of facility drawing power in the various market segments. Vision regarding drive time has been the key to opening southern markets. For instance, Max Muhleman sold the NBA on a Charlotte, North Carolina, franchise by demonstrating that 5 million people lived within a two-hour drive of a proposed facility—two hours being a perceived maximum for events of NBA quality and frequency. Likewise, "Big Bill" France expanded NASCAR by building facilities with expansive drive-time markets. Jim Foster, France's longtime

Figure 13.1
United Center area map showing drive time as well as mileage.

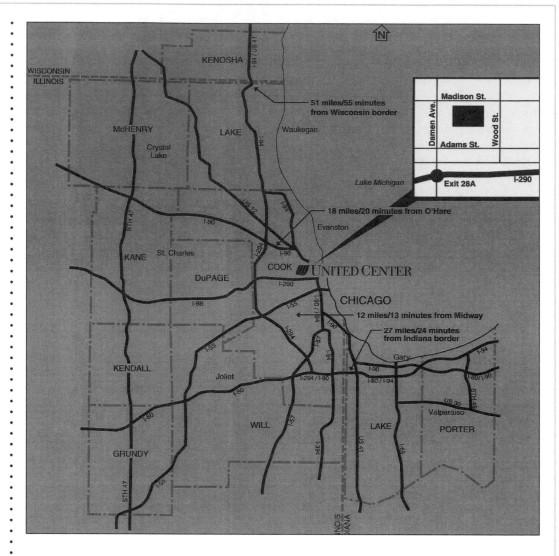

assistant, recalled the trips to Alabama, when France was negotiating to build a track in Talladega: "Alabama might seem in the middle of nowhere, but if you draw a 300-mile circle around Talladega—that is the distance race fans come from—they can drive down, see the race, and drive home in one day. There were 28 million people inside the circle." By overlaying radii for competing facilities, it is also possible to determine areas of competition and even probabilities of facility success.[10]

➤ Analysis of how drawing radii change for various events offered at a multi-purpose facility permits adjustments in event mix to satisfy all market segments. It also permits segmentation of the promotional media in direct response to the drawing radii. At the Springfield Civic Center in Springfield, Massachusetts, the analysis of drawing radii revealed a totally different drawing pattern for Ice Capades than for professional wrestling, yet remarkably similar media had been used to promote both events.

➤ Analysis of drawing radii will change due to scheduling of events at different times and on different days. Many sport marketers have scheduled their events at the same time every day. (Most baseball games start at 7:30 P.M. Monday through Saturday.) However, the New York Yankees, having long recognized that their market is different, have started their weekday games later, and have varied the starting time on Friday evenings. When setting starting times, a facility manager should account for "traveling lead time." Is the market primarily suburbanites who

work in the city and stay in town up to the starting time? Or do these people attempt to commute
home, then return to the event? Is the market
primarily city dwellers? Or is it a mix of the two?

PARKING

The facility should offer ample parking spaces.
For sport facilities such as court and health clubs,
resorts, YMCAs, or recreation programs, four
parking spots for every court is an industry
guide. A rule of thumb for stadiums and arenas is one parking space for every four seats in
environments where mass transit is available
(see photo). In 1998, for instance, the San Francisco Giants decided to schedule only 13 weekday games at the new Pac Bell Park (scheduled
to open in 2000), largely because of limited parking. The Giants estimated

that they needed 12,000 to 13,000 parking spaces for each game at the 42,000-seat facility. This corresponded to about a 1 to 3.3 space/seat ratio. With only 5,000 off-street
spaces, the Giants will have a greater-than-normal dependence on mass transit.[11]

From a financial, security, and service perspective, the facility operator should
also own or at least operate the parking facilities. Parking revenues from a 50,000-
seat stadium may average $50,000 to $70,000 per game for football or baseball games
with over 70 percent of seats filled. Control of the parking also permits control of
pricing and hence reduces gouging and "patron defection" due to high cost of product extensions. Finally, it permits control of parking personnel, who are a crucial
part of the overall facility image-building process.

> A rule of thumb
> for stadiums and
> arenas is one
> parking space for
> every four seats
> where mass transit
> is available.

SURROUNDING AREA

A facility is—and must be—linked to its surroundings in several ways:

Design. New or renovated facilities must fit with the local landscape aesthetics.
As concluded in one recent study of urban ballpark design, "Ballparks must
build upon the character of surrounding structures. Otherwise, they appear
as intrusions in the urban fabric." New ballparks in Baltimore, Dayton, Cleveland, and Louisville have integrated seamlessly with each city's overall development plans. Whether or not the facilities yield the economic impact that
boosters anticipate, they will contribute to the aesthetics of their communities—no mean accomplishment, and nothing to take for granted. Baltimore's
Oriole Park at Camden Yards blends ultramodern features inside the park
with old buildings and alleys outside. Pittsburgh's PNC Park (scheduled to
open in 2001) will likewise be built with an eye on blending with nearby bridges
and buildings.[12]

Politics. Sport facilities have never been welcomed by everyone, especially nearby
residents, who care less about their own easy access to games than they do
about the regular infusion of hordes of fans, their cars, and their often unruly
behavior. No sport organization is wise to develop its venue without clear
"neighborly" dialogue. In the early 1990s, Boston College ran into a maelstrom of protest when it announced plans for expanding the football stadium.
Local residents claimed that the school had broken a promised moratorium
on facilities expansion. In little time, BC faced new legislative and regulatory
hurdles, as well as enormous ill will that might have been avoided with clearer,
early dialogue.[13]

Sense of safety. The immediate environment surrounding a sport facility is an extremely important factor in determining attendance frequency. When a facility is located in an area that customers feel is "unsafe," sales will suffer. The environment can also determine the pattern of attendance. A court club or health club located in an industrial park will draw well during the day; but after 5 P.M., few people will venture into an industrial park, so evening and weekend attendance levels will be extremely low. Contrasting with this situation is the court or health club located in the suburbs, where the heaviest demand occurs on weekday evenings and during the day on weekends.

DESIGN AND LAYOUT

Design and layout are crucial to consumer satisfaction. These are some of the key aspects of facility design:

➤ *Ease of access and exit to minimize length of lines.* Few things upset today's consumers more than waiting in long lines, especially if their intent had been to "get away from it all."

➤ *Access and sight lines for consumers who are physically disabled.* This is much more than simple conformity to legal requirements such as the Americans with Disabilities Act. It is even more than an ethical issue, although that should be a central consideration. With an aging population, and with technologies that facilitate a more active lifestyle for all persons with physical disabilities, facility designs should incorporate the needs of this growing and important market.[14]

➤ *Location and design of food services/bars, concession stands, and bathrooms,* with sufficient number of these amenities to reduce lines. Given the rising tide of female fans, sports venues will have to provide additional facilities for women. A recent study used by the designers of Seattle's new Safeco Field found that women spend an average of three minutes in a restroom; men spend about 82 seconds. These facilities should also be clean and well maintained and should be as close as possible to where the consumer participates or watches. The location of any concourse is critical to this equation. As noted in a recent article, "Today, architects, team owners, and vendors think the concourse is as vital to any venue as the circulatory system is to the human body."[15]

➤ *Provisions for crowd management and control.* Crowd-management provisions should allow ample screening on entrance and minimum use of stairways for exiting the facility (see photo). Ramps are a much safer form of access and exit. In court and health clubs and YMCAs, the location of the control desk is a major factor in the success or failure of the operation. The control desk needs to become a control center from which the management of the facility can completely regulate access and oversee all amenities.[16]

➤ *Flexible versus dedicated usage.* In the last decade, professional sport teams have moved away from multipurpose venues toward single-use facilities. A main reason has been to maximize sight lines and intimacy for fans. Baseball simply doesn't "play" well in a cavernous stadium meant for 70,000 football fans. Likewise for soccer—

Exits, entrances, and concourses should balance the needs for crowd screening and crowd flow. On this narrow concourse, the exit is blocked by only a few people.

America's Major League Soccer has averaged under 20,000 fans per game. On the other hand, few schools or colleges can afford specialized venues; flexibility is dictated by budgets and often by space. Further, such facilities must anticipate changes in consumer interest. The last two decades have seen volatile swings of interest in racquetball, soccer, and aerobics. Recent trends have turned court and health clubs into holistic health centers, complete with seminar rooms for stress management and educational classes, swimming pools, and basketball courts. What consumer interests will the next century bring?[17]

➤ *Aesthetics.* As with any piece of architecture, the sport facility design requires an appealing blend of form, scale, color, and light. In the late 1990s, consumer tastes have dictated more "retro" blends. Baltimore's Camden Yards was the prototype. In 1997, the Toronto Maple Leafs promised that their new arena would be the "Camden Yards of hockey." The Indiana Pacers planned a retro facility with a retro name— "Fieldhouse"—complete with "metal seat-section signs printed with an old-style font; vintage-looking advertising signs; a scoreboard with an old-fashioned nondigital clock; even a section with pullout bleachers." Marketers should keep abreast of the facility design literature, including the Architectural Showcase Awards presented annually by *Athletic Business,* one of the sport industry's most widely read trade magazines.[18]

AMENITIES: CONVERGENCE TOWARD THE "SPORTS MALL"

A "retro" look does not mean that a facility should lack the latest amenities—those employing technologies to expand the consumption experience to incorporate all five senses. Some examples of the latest amenities:

➤ *"Smart seats."* A firm called ChoiceSeat installs special screen units on armrests for $1500 apiece. Fans in these seats can request replays from various camera angles, check a rule, call up stats, order food or merchandise, even (gulp!) switch to another game or shop in an online fashion catalogue.

➤ *Upscale food and drink.* Luxury-suite patrons have been munching on shrimp and caviar for years. Bill Dorsey of the Association of Luxury Suite Directors estimates that suite patrons average $30 per capita per game on food and beverages, compared to $7 for the "average" fan. But if the highbrows demand their Alsatian noodles with kangaroo fillets, that doesn't mean the hoi polloi will settle for the same old stale hot dogs. Cleveland's Gund Arena offers an extensive array on the

Details always vary, but the model suite for the Pittsburgh Steelers new stadium captures the ambience of luxury.

concourse and in the food court, including Philly cheesesteak, jalapeno "poppers," pierogis, chef's salad, chicken fajitas, microbrews, Bacardi breezers, and Gretel's hand-dipped ice cream.

➤ *Elaborate (and ever more expensive) big screens, electronic message centers, and sound systems.* When arena managers think about fan comfort these days, their concerns go well beyond the older notions of sight lines, seat backs, and warm fannies (see photo). With music so much a part of any event, arenas must install sound systems with the right blend of high tech components such as "reverberation time," "ambient noise levels," and "sound levels." Fans want more replays and more intermission entertainment on high-resolution screens. Sponsors want more electronic signage in areas of high visibility.

➤ *Hot tubs and halls of fame.* In the fall of 1993, Washington State University began promoting a

"Hot Spot" hot tub for use by the first eight WSU basketball fans to reach its corner location in the Beasley Performing Arts Coliseum. Since then, the hot tub amenity has become almost commonplace. Phoenix's Bank One Ballpark offers much more than its well-publicized outfield hot tub. It also includes a Walk of Fame Museum, an interactive play area called Diamondtown, and a miniversion of baseball's Hall of Fame in Cooperstown.[19]

The quest for amenities drives more than ballparks and arenas. In some respects, athletic clubs led the way in the 1980s with the "full-concept club" offering a complete line of courts, supervised health programs, a social bar or lounge area, pro shop, pool, day care, sauna, whirlpool, and the like. Some of today's clubs even offer videotaping services so members can save (and learn from) their performances in lessons or in competition. The bowling industry has also started to transform some of its venues in an effort to attract a younger generation. In early 1999, the Brunswick Corporation announced that it was converting three Chicago-area bowling centers into youth-oriented "bowling zones," equipped with interactive video games, big-screen televisions, and food kiosks oriented to youthful appetites. Said Brunswick President Warren Hardie, "We're trying to upgrade and brand the product. Right now there is no Brunswick brand." In bowling, at least, the brand begins with the venue.[20]

It would be easy to get cynical about the merger of sport and a "mall mentality"—that is, every conceivable outlet to induce a consumer to part with hard-earned money. For instance, take the case of Atlanta's Turner Field, otherwise known as the "Chop House." When Peter Gammons asked Atlanta Braves executive Stan Kasten if the center-field open-air restaurant would ever be enclosed to avoid October's chilly air, Kasten replied "Chop House parkas, Chop House sweatshirts." On the other hand, no one requires a patron to buy more than a ticket, a court rental fee, or a membership. It appears that in the court club or the hometown arena, consumers want more than sport. Brad Clark, a senior designer at Ellerbe Becket, summed up these attitudes nicely to *Sports Business Journal*: "Yes, they want to see the Michael Jordans and the Troy Aikmans, but they also want to be able to get a microbrew, buy some designer clothes, and maybe play an interactive game or two. It's not just a sports arena anymore. It's a sports and entertainment center." The more serious issue may be that grassroots sport organizations, such as high school programs and town recreation facilities, simply can't afford to provide the amenities many welcome or demand.[21]

PERSONNEL

The people who work in a facility may be *the* major force in projecting a facility's image and in its ultimate success. The attitudes of "operations" personnel directly affect consumer satisfaction because these workers are the primary (and in many cases, the only) personnel that consumers contact. Yet such nonmanagement personnel are often the least trained among a facility's staff. A stark example of this phenomenon can be seen in court and health clubs, where desk personnel are usually college or high school students employed part-time. What is the logic of allowing such inexperienced staff to provide not only the primary contact with existing members, but also the primary contact in membership sales? Over 70 percent of club memberships are initiated by a phone call, yet few club owners ever provide their part-time personnel appropriate telephone sales training. Fewer still ever test an applicant's "telephone voice" prior to hiring. The same is true in stadiums and arenas, whose events staff are almost all part-timers. How often do patrons face an uncaring or even a surly usher? Too often. All of this is unnecessary, especially when professional trade associations such as the International Health, Racquet, and Sports Club Association (IHRSA) and the International Association of Assembly Managers

The Club Seat

Club seats have become a standard component in today's sport venues. The club-seat concept was clearly designed to offer the upscale consumer something between the skybox and the best box or loge season seat. Like the skybox, the club seat is clearly segregated from the crowd; it also offers exclusive amenities. Like the loge or box seat, the club seat can stand alone; it is not designed as a "group" deal. For a higher price, the club-seat patron gets special treatment, as the *1996-97 United Center Club Seating Handbook* makes clear:

➤ Special parking—"reserved parking in fenced, well-lit and clearly marked parking lots adjacent to the United Center for all Blackhawks or Bulls preseason, regular season and playoff games."

➤ Membership in the Chicago Stadium Club—a "spectacular 260 seat restaurant, 'for members only.'"

➤ Controlled seat access through gates reserved for club-seat ticket holders.

➤ Waiter/waitress service during the event.

➤ Concierge service from "special attendants located in the Club seating level."

➤ Coat check and parcel services."

➤ Fully furnished, hotel-style lounge areas complete with full bar service."

➤ Private telephone booths."

➤ Delayed postgame departure—up to one hour in lounge areas, "while traffic clears. . . . Of course, guests in the general seating areas of the United Center must depart the building immediately following the conclusion of the event."

➤ Priority access to purchase tickets to special events (e.g., concerts, ice shows).

Most of all, as the *Handbook* states clearly in an introduction, club seats offer the "privileges" of suite ownership—including "the ultimate in prestige and satisfaction"—"at a fraction of the cost." Clearly not for the working-class family, club seats have been a "deep well" for teams and venues precisely because they slake a thirst for more and more amenities, including the desire to be segregated.[22]

(IAAM) offer training manuals and videos. The IAAM's 1999 list of video training programs included the following titles:

➤ "Customer Service Begins with Me"
➤ "Building, Motivating, and Maintaining the Crowd Management Team"
➤ "Safety Awareness at Public Assembly Facilities"
➤ "Service Excellence: Dealing with Guests' Problems and the Problem Guest"
➤ "Service Excellence: Patrons with Disabilities"

Clubs, schools, colleges, and youth programs all run events in venues. Some of the events draw patrons into the tens of thousands. Staff training for such events is no longer a luxury; it is a necessity.[23]

SENSE OF SECURITY

The IAAM training videos include a healthy emphasis on safety and security, with good reason. Nothing drives consumers away faster than a fear for their safety. Rowdy, unruly, drunken fans can quickly ruin a rare, long-planned outing for a family with young children. That may be four or five consumers lost for a long time, and with the word-of-mouth multiplier, the effect could reach into the dozens. The Philadelphia Eagles had a growing concern about rowdy fans that finally reached crisis proportions at a Monday night game on November 10, 1997, punctuated by dozens of fights in the stands and a flare that a drunken fan rocketed across the field into the stands (luckily into an empty seat). The Eagles' answer to the crisis was to work with the city to increase security and run an on-site municipal court, which in the next few games heard 20 cases ranging from disorderly conduct (a drunk male was caught urinating in a women's room) to violating the city's open-container law (some fans tried to sneak in their own bottles of brew). Seventeen rowdies pleaded guilty and accepted fines up to $300. On their end, the Eagles promised to punish any offending season-ticket holders by revoking their tickets.[24]

EVALUATING CONSUMER OPINION

The facility is the initial "place" of most sport experiences. Other sport products are generally derivative. As such, the facility needs to do its own evaluation by asking consumers certain key questions, such as "How do you perceive the facility, its physical layout, location, amenities, surrounding area, personnel?" and "What amenities might increase your attendance or participation?"

Some more specific questions may help the consumer provide valuable information:

➤ What do you do before an event or a workout at this facility?

➤ What do you do during the event or a visit? (Buy a snack, read the program, check an information board?)

➤ What do you do after an event?

➤ Where do you reside?

➤ What are your modes of transport?

➤ How do these patterns change for different events and different starting or workout times?

Marketers should ask these questions regularly as part of the comprehensive marketing information system. The answers form basic data components for effective facility layout, design, and expansion and for productive promotional strategies.

MARKETING CHANNELS

Although the facility is the primary element in distributing the core sport product, there are other aspects to the concept of "place" in the sport marketing mix. These involve the various channels by which marketers can deliver the product, in this case beyond the facility. "Channels" are simply various sets or configurations of organizations linked together to deliver a product to consumers. Channel systems often vary by product line or sales territory within a company's distribution network. Channel systems can be complex; they may shift and share functions, as is often the case in sport marketing. Standard channel elements have included the following:

Manufacturers (M)

Wholesalers (W) and jobbers (J)

Retailers (R)

Is "Shopping the Venue" a Recipe for Extortion and Bribery?

The last four decades witnessed a fundamental shift in the economics of "big-time" sports. Professional team owners and event managers have always depended on some "inside" help in locating a new stadium or an event like an NCAA Championship (see photo). Urban business owners and politicians have championed sport for well over a century. But if an "inside deal" in the past meant a quick processing of a zoning variance or a tip on the plan for a new trolley line or street, the typical sport magnate still needed to summon the vast bulk of facility investment from private funds. Things changed dramatically in the 1960s and '70s. Sport historian Steven Riess calculated that by 1988, only 20.8 percent of big-league baseball parks and only 7.1 percent of NFL venues were privately controlled. Hockey and basketball venues tended toward more private ownership, but as leagues expanded and franchises shuffled from city to city, the trend was clear: "You [the public] build it and maybe we will come to play in it."

Cities fell over one another in the mad quest to build publicly financed stadiums and arenas, in hopes of luring or keeping professional sport franchises. But it didn't stop there. As the Olympics grew in stature, the bidding to host an Olympics required huge public investments in facilities and "infrastructure" like new roads, ramps, and parking. Sport management scholar Dennis Howard estimates that in the 1970s and 1980s, taxpayers "paid 90 percent of the construction costs" for new sport facilities. As early as the mid-1970s, economists began to warn that taxpayers got little if any financial return on their investments, despite the rhetoric of urban boosters and their hired consultants. Few listened at first, largely because the bottom line was emotion, not economics. In 1995, for instance, St. Louis boosters engineered a huge, public handout—including a giveaway lease on a new, $260 million stadium—to attract the NFL's Los Angeles Rams. Many disgruntled taxpayers felt compelled to support the sacrifice. Without an NFL team like the Rams, said one St. Louis resident, "we're a cow town."

As franchise demands and prices shot upward in the 1990s, however, some states, counties, and

Cities have vied for sports teams and events for over a century.

municipalities began to balk at the necessity of huge public investments that only made rich people richer. They began listening to the academic economists. In 1998 alone, taxpayers in Pittsburgh, Minneapolis, Columbus (Ohio), Greensboro (North Carolina), and Birmingham (Alabama) voted down referendums for publicly financed stadiums. The Massachusetts House of Representatives refused to consider excessive public subsidies for a new football stadium, clearly saving taxpayers millions of dollars.

In late 1998, the issue of public subsidy turned into a scandal of worldwide proportions. A longtime member of the International Olympic Committee (IOC) went public with allegations about "the systematic buying and selling of the Olympic Games." Mark Hodler, a Swiss IOC member, cited a "pattern of bribery"—with payoffs up to $5 million—in the bidding and site selection of the games at Atlanta, Nagano, Sydney, and Salt Lake City. As of early 1999, investigations by the IOC and by state and federal agencies had corroborated much of Hodler's complaint, and then some.

The Olympic scandal raises questions about the ethics of any bidding war over a valuable sport event or property. Ironically, only a few months before the Olympics scandal broke, the NCAA announced that it was imposing a $500,000 spending limit on promotions and hospitality associated with bids for the Final Four basketball tournament. The tournament selection committee had been subject to more and more lavish productions as it toured potential host cities. The NCAA is to be applauded for its efforts at restraint. At the same time, however, it shopped its office headquarters around the country as if it were a Super Bowl unto itself.

One might argue that this is only sound business practice—use the laws of supply and demand to your advantage. That is all well and good. But if sport organizations want to preach about the need to protect their products from the claws of drug and gambling interests, perhaps they also need to temper their embrace of the rapacious side of capitalism. Professional leagues might well remember Laura Nash's question: "To whom and to what do you give your loyalty?" Gouging fans with the "franchise shuffle game" is hardly a show of loyalty to their interests.[25]

A traditional channel for hard goods would look like this:

$$M \rightarrow W \rightarrow J \rightarrow R \rightarrow C$$

This made sense for much of the sporting goods industry. A manufacturer like Spalding made balls, sold them to wholesalers, who worked with "jobbers" to sell to local stores, where consumers (C) would buy the balls.

On the other hand, a family ski outing would look more like this:

$$M \leftarrow C$$

Here the consumers actually work backward in the standard channel by traveling to the place of production, then take part in the production, and then consume the product simultaneously. The Internet and direct mail have reconstructed traditional channels of equipment and apparel to look similar to the ski outing. Consumers can surf the Web to find manufacturers' sites, check the online catalogue, and order by direct mail, all without using wholesaler or retailers.

In the increasingly complex world of sport marketing channels, it is more typical to find the two types of systems operating in parallel, sometimes to reach the same consumer. Take a professional sport team. It has a traditional channel of on-site box offices (see photo) for event tickets:

$$M \longleftrightarrow C$$

But it also may televise the event and distribute it via television to a wider audience, where the channel looks like this:

$$M \longleftrightarrow C = Event \rightarrow MEDIA \rightarrow C$$

If the on-site consumer taped the game at home, he or she would be part of both the beginning and the end of the channel! As teams use Web sites for the redistribution of broadcast highlights and for direct sale of team merchandise, one can see how complicated the channel loops become.

As any sport organization considers channels for product distribution, it must weigh at least four factors in tandem:

- Expertise
- Cost

On-site box offices for selling event tickets is a standard marketing channel for professional sports teams.

Control

Adaptability

When the NHL, for instance, developed its partnership with Streetball Partners International to conduct the traveling street hockey tournament called NHL Breakout, it chose to trade off some product control for the benefit of Streetball's expertise in running local, grassroots programs. On the other hand, the PGA's recent move into PGA outlet stores (many located in airport malls) signals a desire for more direct control of product presentation at the retail level, even at some risk to adaptability. Finally, the great consumer embrace of the Internet is a double-edged sword. Although Internet sales certainly offer consumers more access and control, retailers are realizing that cost savings are not always as high as expected. While the Internet may reduce the payroll for a sales force, it also forces a retailer to expand distribution warehouses (with all the associated labor costs). In summary, there is no simple formula for determining the best marketing channels. It is a constant balancing act.[26]

RETAIL SPORT OPERATIONS

Despite the rise of the Internet, traditional retail outlets remain important elements for sport marketing channels. Specialized outlets for sport products grew rapidly in the 19th century, as entrepreneurs recognized—and promoted—an interest in fish-ing, cricket, baseball, hunting, and other activities among urban populations that could support their businesses. Today's big-box firms such as The Sports Authority and MVP Sports have a long list of ancestors that include hardware stores and retail chains such as Sears and Montgomery Ward. But today's sport marketplace has seen some new twists as well, especially the integration by teams, clubs, and governing bodies forward into the retail business.[27]

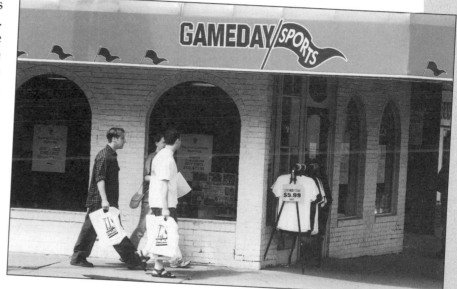

To some degree, college programs led the way. The University of Michigan was one of the first to realize the value of merchandizing. Offering a wide array of novelties, Michigan developed a range of retail outlets in the 1970s, including souvenir stands at Michigan Stadium, Crisler Arena, Yost Ice Arena, the tennis/track building, the golf course, and the ticket office. This was not all the outlets. Michigan had partnerships with high school booster clubs and cheerleader organizations, which sold Michigan novelties as part of their own fund-raising efforts. Finally, Michigan effectively used direct-mail sales to season-ticket holders and other targeted customers on mailing lists that the athletic department purchased. These practices are now fairly standard.[28]

Professional teams had long operated "pro shops" in arena lobbies, but the presence of these outlets was generally not part of a branding/distribution strategy. In 1997, by contrast, the NBA announced that it would open a retail store in Manhattan (see photo on page 296) complete with a "small court, with bleachers for special events." With three levels and 15,000 square feet of space, the NBA store would sell licensed NBA and WNBA products of any kind, from balls to "home furnishings." Patrons would also see videos of NBA and WNBA history as well as interviews with

Retail sporting goods stores continue to thrive.

The NBA store combines traditional retailing with interactive fan festival exhibits.

current players and coaches. The NBA stores were clearly part of a broad distribution strategy that included branded television shows, branded merchandise, and branded fan experiences. The NBA was not alone. By the summer of 1998, over 40 "big-league" professional teams had opened off-site retail outlets, including the Orlando Magic's 9800-square-foot Fan-Attic store in downtown Orlando.[29]

The trend of integrating entertainment backward into retail stores probably began with Disney, which opened its first store in 1987. Ten years later, Disney had 613 Disney stores that claimed to combine "retail and entertainment." In the world of the Disney store, a sales clerk was a "cast member." Sport would soon follow this path, led by Nike's first Niketown retail store in Portland, Oregon. By 1997, Nike had 10 of its "concept" stores in major U.S. urban markets, with plans to open two more in Australia, in time for the Sydney Olympics.[30]

The central concept behind the new sport retail outlets is a fusion of branded and licensed goods with the fan experience one would ordinarily associate with a big game. When all goes well, the consumer does not simply buy a shirt, a cap, or a pair of shoes. The consumer learns more about the team or the league, picks up a playing or coaching tip, and walks out of the store holding or wearing not a hat, but a touchstone of greater commitment and involvement. There is no reason why a high school athletic director or a soccer club manager could not develop similar marketing opportunities on a smaller scale. Network and cable television have not eliminated the need for grassroots education and grassroots heroes. Whether the retail outlet is a table in a gym corner or a multimillion dollar palace, however, the marketer must remember some tried-and-true "patronage motives" that help explain a consumer's choice of one store over another for repeat-purchase business:

> Convenience (proximity to the consumer's residence or place of employment)

> Variety or selection

> Quality of goods

> Courtesy of sales personnel

> Integrity—reputation for fairness in dealings

> Services offered (delivery, credit, returned-goods privileges)

> Value offered

The marketer must consider each factor on an ongoing basis to ensure continued retail success.[31]

THE TICKET DISTRIBUTION SYSTEM

Ticket distribution is a good example of the fast changing environment of sport marketing channels. The trend is clearly away from buying tickets at the gate, at least for the big-league teams with high demand on the part of suburban fans. For instance, the Boston Red Sox reported in February 1999 that they had already sold over a million tickets for the season, a pace that was 37 percent ahead of that for 1998. Only 10 percent of fans were buying tickets at the box office, however, compared with 90 percent a few years earlier. New electronic technologies, especially the computer, expanded the possibilities of ticket distribution, largely because computerized ticketing eliminated the problems of duplicate tickets, excess stock, and limited choice—

all of which had plagued earlier efforts to go beyond the box office. As with any decision on marketing channels, however, there is a balance to be struck among the aforementioned factors of expertise, cost, control, and adaptability.

The last decade has seen a few new standard distribution programs beyond the box office.[32] We will take a brief look at these.

Team Retail Outlets   Teams sell more than merchandise in their retail stores. In 1997, a survey of MLB clubs conducted by *Team Marketing Report* showed that 15 of 28 clubs were using team shops as a ticket outlet.[33]

Partnerships With Ticket Firms Such as Ticketmaster, BASS, and ETM   In 1968, Ticketron opened new worlds of ticket distribution for all kinds of events. Today's sport market is dominated by Ticketmaster (which bought Ticketron in 1991) and a few other firms, such as ETM and BASS. In 1997, 17 MLB clubs used Ticketmaster's services. Many of these deals include ticket kiosks at targeted retail outlets such as grocery stores, which can provide leverage for other forms of sponsorship. In 1998, for example, the Texas Rangers established electronic kiosks—provided by ETM Entertainment Network—at 60 Kroger supermarkets in north Texas. Ranger fans could use a credit card to buy the best tickets available for the games of their choice, with hard tickets printed on the spot.[34]

Partnerships With Other Consumer Retail Outlets   Ticket distribution often goes hand in hand with new sponsors and new promotions. In 1997, for instance, MLB's San Francisco Giants created a 10-year partnership with Chevron, whose corporate headquarters are local. Part of the estimated $15-20 million deal included the prospect of Chevron gas stations selling Giants tickets. A few years earlier, the Cleveland Lumberjacks had worked out a deal with northeastern Ohio Burger King stores in which BK purchased 15,000 tickets for each of two "Burger King Buyout Nights." Fans who wanted tickets to either game had to get them at a Burger King outlet, which enabled BK to create a number of promotional packages to drive store traffic.[35]

Payroll Deductions With Selected Companies   Colleges have for some time offered direct payroll deductions for employees who were also season-ticket holders, maximizing ease of access and payment. With the expansion of electronic banking systems, this possibility has extended to employees of any company that uses electronic payrolls. In the early 1990s, the Hamilton Canucks of the American Hockey League worked with the City of Hamilton to offer the city's 6000 public employees season tickets via payroll deduction. The city had an interest because the Canucks played in a city-owned rink, and a portion of ticket and concession revenues returned to the city.[36]

Television and Internet   In the 1980s, a number of teams began buying television time and running telethons to sell tickets. The Pittsburgh Penguins had an annual summer telethon, built around the movie *Slap Shot*. The NBA's Cleveland Cavs have transformed the concept into an infomercial, aired four times before Cleveland Indians games and once before an NFL game. The Cavs bought the time for a season preview show and used breaks to offer a television-only package of 16 games for the price of 15. Such deals could be an ongoing part of a team Web site, now a standard ticket sales outlet. In 1997, the MLB Giants reported that their Internet ticket sales had increased from about 20,000 in 1996 to 100,000 in 1997.[37]

Telephone Systems   In 1998, the Boston Red Sox began using the NEXT ticketing system, which is an automated, credit-card, phone-order system designed as an alternative to Ticketmaster. Unlike Ticketmaster, the NEXT system does not brand its own tickets. In the case of the Red Sox, for example, the consumer appears to be dealing directly with a Red Sox operation (even though it is all automated), and the tickets are issued on Red Sox stock. Better yet, there is no $6 surcharge. The NEXT system allows the Red Sox to handle 400 calls at a time and sell 75,000 tickets in an hour—a task that would be impossible for humans.[38]

CREATIVE DISTRIBUTION

As the previous examples suggest, the marketer must use creativity in planning and implementing new channels of distribution. Keeping abreast of the latest technologies and keeping an open mind are critical to success. The following are some simple questions marketers need to ponder continually:

> ➤ Who are my consumers and what are their needs?
>
> ➤ Where are my consumers?
>
> ➤ What are my products and their extensions?
>
> ➤ What vehicles—especially using new technologies—are available for distribution?

In the 1980s, for example, many sport teams developed "affinity" credit cards with banks. The New York Yankees were one of the first teams to do so, using the slogan "Get Credit For Being A Yankee Fan." Such VISA or MasterCards typically affixed a team logo or symbol. Purchases on the card brought the consumer points toward the purchase of tickets or team merchandise at reduced rates. Such cards extended market channels by building team allegiance and by making product purchase more attractive.[39] The 1990s saw sport organizations create new outlets for the consumer or the fan "experience": the NCAA's Hoop City, the LPGA's Fan Village, and the NHL's Breakout are but a few examples. The Internet continues to create whole new horizons for sport product distribution. We discuss the Internet and other electronic media in chapter 14.

THE PRODUCT-PLACE MATRIX

Ultimately, the marketer wants to ensure an effective and efficient use of all available distribution channels. A valuable analytical tool is the product-place matrix (see table 13.1), which helps to conceptualize both the array of products and the distribution channels. A simple start to a matrix for a collegiate sport program might look like this. Each row represents a product element (event, players, coach), and each column represents a distribution outlet (venues, media).

Table 13.1 PRODUCT-PLACE MATRIX

Product	Field-house, fields	Media	Place Retail outlets	Greeks/civic groups	Outer markets
Events	Games	Releases, TV, radiocasts, Internet	Game highlights on video kiosks in mall	Highlight films, pep rallies	Schedule a home game in a remote city
Players/coaches	Autograph sessions	Coach's corner on radio, TV, Internet	Clinics, autographs	Speeches on substance-free living	Clinics, press meetings
Tickets	Box office	Trade-outs with media	Schedule cards, posters, electronic kiosks	Group sales	Group sales
Merchandise	Concourse	Local cable, direct mail, Internet	Licensed outlets	Fund-raisers	Licensed outlets

The matrix simply provides a graphic representation of current or planned product distribution. In this example, the players and coaches are "distributed" in many ways beyond the game itself. They have autograph sessions after games; they offer clinics and talks to Greek houses and civic groups nearby or in "outer" markets. The coaches also are "distributed" via "Coaches Corner" shows on radio and television, or even in Internet chat rooms. Marketers can consider how best to fill each part of such a grid, using their imagination and creativity.

WRAP-UP

While the place function in sport marketing bears remote resemblance to the distribution function in consumer product marketing, its importance among the five Ps of sport marketing should not be minimized. The "place" in sport begins with the ensemble of elements comprising the venue or facility and its surroundings. The facility location is critical to the success of most sport businesses. Of equal importance is the facility image and operation, which are influenced by physical design, amenities, and the attitudes of facility personnel. The core event and its extensions must then be distributed by way of marketing channels that include retail outlets and the media (which we examine in detail in the next chapter). The marketing channels for sport products are limited only by budgets and imaginations, but the possibilities can be graphically illustrated by the use of a product-place matrix.

ACTIVITIES

1. Apply the theory of place to your favorite sport venue, the way we did to Fenway Park. What are the most important elements of the ensemble?

2. Analyze a local facility in terms of its accessibility, drawing radius, parking, surroundings, design and layout, and amenities.

3. Define distribution channels. Do all sport products and services have distribution channels? Why or why not? Give examples of various channels.

YOUR MARKETING PLAN

Create a product-place grid for your organization. Think carefully about alternative channels for your various products.

CHAPTER

14

ELECTRONIC
MEDIA

BY TIM ASHWELL

Vignette: Whither the Tube?

"No one in the television industry has enjoyed the past year," editorialized the *New York Times* as 1999 began.[1] "The networks—six of them now—preside over a steadily falling audience share," the *Times* proclaimed, and "digital television, perennially in the offing but now getting really close, will soon increase the number of channels to around 1500, fracturing the audience into ever smaller shards and enticing phone companies and Internet providers onto the tube."

The newspaper's dire prediction of the end of television as we know it was old news to the broadcasting industry. For a medium that exists to assemble mass audiences for advertisers, audience fragmentation has been a disturbing fact of life for years: new technologies have created new options for viewers. No longer does the audience choose among the offerings of three commercial networks. These days, there's something for everyone on television—and the Internet, radio, and pre-recorded digital audio and video provide even more alternatives. As network audiences shrink, advertisers grow reluctant to pay the hundreds of thousands of dollars networks demand for 30-second spots.

Programmers think there is one way to keep the audience intact, so they scramble to attract our attention with branded entertainment—programs that they know from experience we, the audience, will recognize and seek out. Their goal is to encourage appointment viewing. They want to put something on that we will make a point of sitting down and watching as it happens, rather than recording and watching weeks later.

Sports fit the bill. The NFL, University of Kentucky basketball, Wimbledon, the World Series, the Olympics—each is a proven brand that attracts a loyal and well-defined audience. And advertisers know those fans will watch the games as they happen, not weeks later, so time-sensitive advertising maintains its value. Not every sport guarantees a national audience, but for sport managers who understand how the electronic media work and how to take advantage of the rapidly changing media environment, these times can present great opportunities.

This chapter concentrates on today's competitive and rapidly changing media environment. Television, radio, and the Internet are powerful tools for marketing, promotion, and publicity. The chapter will familiarize readers with how the media are organized and addresses several ways in which sport organizations work with broadcasters to get their games on the air.

THE ELECTRONIC MEDIA LANDSCAPE

Television, despite the networks' troubles, remains the dominant medium, in terms of both market penetration and audience impact. Radio, often overlooked, can reach the local and regional sport audience efficiently. The Internet, the worldwide computer communications network first established as a tool for researchers, offers immediate, international reach; but despite the proliferation of computers, the medium has yet to approach either television or radio in terms of audience numbers or response. Television and radio broadcasters across the United States pay nearly $5 billion a year for rights to deliver games to loyal audiences of sport fans. In addition, the electronic media help motivate millions of consumer decisions to purchase such items as tickets, team merchandise, and memorabilia worth billions of dollars more. Sport, in turn, makes billions for broadcasters in advertising revenue and subscription fees while also allowing broadcasters to gain identity with consumers and burnish their images.

Although there are obvious differences among the electronic media, all follow a simple model: information—the sounds of a contest, pictures of an event, or textual accounts—is encoded as electromagnetic impulses and sent via satellite, wire, or over-the-air transmission to a receiving device that decodes the impulses and reproduces the information in usable form. The media also share a common business plan: television, radio, and the Web sites that populate the Internet rely on the audience to survive. Sport attracts audiences to Web sites and radio and television stations—audiences that advertisers pay to address or that pay to subscribe to the service.[2]

TELEVISION

Television has become our window on the world. The Television Bureau of Advertising, an industry trade association, estimates that 99.4 million of the approximately 100 million U.S. households own at least one television and that more than three quarters of all homes own two or more sets.[3] In the typical household, the television is on for more than seven hours every day. Women, on average, watch for four and a half hours a day; men, a half hour a day less. Advertisers paid $44.5 billion to reach those viewers in 1997, a $2 billion increase over the previous year.

While the financial pie is huge, the competition to capture desirable slices of the audience is becoming more intense as viewers' choices expand. More than 1200 commercial television stations are on the air today across the country, and viewers in the three quarters of American households wired for cable or equipped with home satellite dishes can choose among literally dozens of programming services designed to fit every fancy. ESPN capitalized on such niche programming with its debut on September 7, 1979. It marked the beginning of a new era in sports broadcasting by offering nothing but sports 24 hours a day (see photo).

Choice is good for television fans, but the fragmentation of the audience into ever smaller pieces has made life much more exciting and perilous for broadcasters. As the number of viewing options has increased, the audience for each individual program has dwindled. In an industry based on the belief that advertisers will pay to present their messages to mass audiences, that is big news.

KNOWING THE MARKET

Because television, radio, and the Internet are fundamentally advertising media, success or failure in the field is largely judged by audience size and composition. Just as the scoreboard tells us who won or lost on the playing field, audience measurements tell us who won or lost on the air. To play the media game effectively, sport marketers must be able to place their product in the right medium at the right time to reach the right audience. This requires us to understand whom we are trying to reach and how best to reach them. Astute sport marketers carry out research to define their audience. Media research organizations conduct the same kind of research to define and quantify the broadcast audience.

Thanks to satellite technology sports fans now have access to sporting events from around the world—and athletes can perform before a worldwide audience.

Sport marketers who want to use the electronic media should be as familiar with the substance and terminology of the media as they are with their own games.

Television audiences are scientifically measured and researched by both broadcasters and advertisers in hopes of discovering exactly who is watching what. Nielsen Media Research, since 1942 the leading audience analyst, judges audience size from data collected by electronic devices attached to televisions in a representative sample of about 5000 homes across the country.[4] Audience numbers are commonly expressed in terms of *ratings* and *shares.*

A program's rating represents the percentage of homes in the survey universe that are tuned to the program. For a nationally broadcast program available in every television home, one rating point represents 994,000 households, 1 percent of the national total. Nielsen calculated that the final game of the 1998 World Series earned a 16.6 rating, meaning it was viewed in 16,480,000 households. Ratings are also calculated locally. There are slightly more than 6.8 million television homes in the New York metropolitan area, the nation's largest single market, so a single local rating point represents about 68,000 homes, 1 percent of the total.

A program's share represents the percentage of those homes using television at the time that are tuned to the program. Research—and common sense—tells us that not every television set is on all the time. The viewing audience climbs gradually throughout the day and peaks during the evening hours before declining again. More people typically watch television on weeknights than on weekends. Accordingly, while ratings remain a constant measurement, shares fluctuate depending on the size of the total viewing audience. During the 1998 television season, for example, the network entertainment programs that aired at 10 o'clock Saturday night and 8 o'clock Sunday night each earned 9.7 ratings, indicating that nearly 7 million homes were tuned in. Because more homes use television on Sundays than on Saturdays, however, Sunday's rating represented a smaller percentage of homes using television. Accordingly, even though the two shows attracted audiences of the same size, the Sunday show's share was 14 while the Saturday program's share was 18.

When it comes to audiences, size matters, because broadcasters and advertisers calculate the cost and value of commercials by the number of people in the audience. The standard yardsticks are *cost per thousand,* often abbreviated CPM (because M represents one thousand in Roman numerals), or *cost per point* (CPP), which refers to the cost of reaching 1 percent of the audience, or one rating point. In addition to the size of the audience at any given time, broadcasters and advertisers look at the total number of households and viewers that a series of programs reaches over time. A single baseball broadcast, for example, may reach a relatively small audience; but over the course of a 162-game season, the total number of viewers will be much larger. The number of different viewers who tune in over time, usually termed the *reach* or *cume,* measures the true audience for sport broadcasts and is used to convince sponsors to sign on for season-long advertising contracts.

The size of the audience is vital, but the composition of the audience is equally important. Although women typically compose the majority of the television audience, sport programs traditionally attract a high percentage of male viewers. Compared to the typical prime-time television audience, sport viewers are older, better educated, wealthier, and overwhelmingly male—often two thirds are men. While sport audiences are typically older on average, they also contain a higher-than-usual concentration of younger male viewers and minority groups, target audiences that advertisers find notoriously hard to reach through traditional mass media. The sport audience is also intensely loyal. At a time when viewing options are expanding, sport fans will seek out and watch telecasts featuring their favorite teams and sports.

SPORT AND TELEVISION: A SYMBIOTIC RELATIONSHIP

The sport audience is attractive to advertisers. Television therefore is willing to pay for rights to broadcast games that produce audiences that can be sold to advertisers. Sport has also played an important role in driving new technology. Millions of fans bought radios in the 1920s and televisions in the 1950s in order to listen to and watch sporting events in their living rooms. The growth of both cable television in the 1980s and home satellite systems in the 1990s was also driven in large part by the lure of additional sport programming.

The growth of today's sport industry has also been driven by television exposure.[5] Televised games create new fans, increase interest among existing fans, and serve as powerful promotional and marketing tools. The explosive growth of the NFL can be credited in large part to the league's television policies in the 1960s, which rationed game broadcasts and emphasized the league as an entity rather than individual franchises. Following the NFL's lead, dozens of teams and leagues have used television to raise the profile of their product in the marketplace.

Sport can also create instant credibility for broadcasters. When the fledgling Fox Network in 1993 paid the NFL an astonishing $1.58 billion for rights to National Football Conference games, the network joined ABC, CBS, and NBC as a major player in the broadcasting business. The games attracted new viewers and new affiliates to the network. Fox, owned by Rupert Murdoch's News Corp., was following a proven game plan. The United Kingdom provides another example. News Corp.'s Sky cable and home satellite services now reach 16 million households there, thanks in large part to an aggressive campaign to secure rights to soccer, rugby, and cricket broadcasts. ABC used a similar sport strategy to climb out of the television basement in the 1960s and 1970s, and today ABC and ESPN, both owned by Disney, have used sport to promote cross-viewership on the two outlets.

Sport and television, then, rely on one another and enjoy a truly symbiotic relationship that benefits both sides. Broadcasters want sport to attract a proven audience and establish credibility within the industry. Teams, leagues, and events covet broadcast coverage because it expands their audience and revenue and helps establish them as significant "big-time" entities in the minds of fans. Cash forms the strongest bond between the industries; but, as observed by Dick Ebersol, president of NBC Sports, "Not far away is the marketing and promotion of those sports, and the people in the future who understand that best are the people who are going to succeed."[6]

Sport managers should understand how the broadcasting industry works so they can determine how their product fits in.[7] Proven commodities such as the NFL can demand huge payments from national networks because they have a track record of attracting huge national audiences. Established teams, leagues, and events usually auction their broadcast rights to the highest bidder. In exchange for a guaranteed payment, the winning bidder receives exclusive rights; pays production, distribution, and promotional expenses; and sells advertising time to cover its costs. Sport managers should understand that as they move down the television hierarchy, the rights fees that broadcasters are willing to pay rapidly dwindle. As audiences fragment, many teams find that they must accept lower guaranteed rights fees and share advertising revenue with their broadcast outlet. Indeed, it is not unusual for a local station or cable programmer to agree to broadcast your games only if you agree to subsidize the cost, either through cash payments or through production assistance.

The economic realities of today's media environment have changed the traditional relationship between sport organizations and broadcasters. In lieu of guaranteed fees, a growing number of broadcasters and sport organizations have agreed to base rights payments on advertising revenue. Revenue-sharing agreements protect broadcasters from fluctuations in the volatile advertising market and, by lessening

State-of-the-art production trucks are television studios on wheels. Fully loaded with the best equipment, a production truck can easily cost $5 million or more.

the broadcaster's risk, can make a team's games a more attractive package. Revenue sharing can also ultimately produce a higher return for the sport organization. The NBA was the first major sport league to sign a revenue-sharing contract with its primary network partners, NBC and TNT, but this type of arrangement is common in local broadcast agreements.

Many sport organizations will discover few broadcasters knocking at their door in search of broadcast rights to their games or events. Either the product is unproven or the broadcasters fear they will not be able to recoup the cost of production, let alone any rights payment, through advertising revenue. Often, inertia is an issue: a television or radio station has a successful program in place and sees no advantage in disrupting what works. In that case, sport managers must become even more aggressive and more involved in broadcast production. If the goal is to get on the air, it can be achieved by putting together a financial package that works for both the sport organization and the broadcaster.

One proven strategy is for a team to retain its broadcast rights, produce its own game broadcasts, line up sponsors, and offer broadcasters a complete package. Professionally producing a telecast of a football game or a tennis tournament sounds like a daunting task—and it is. Fortunately, sport managers can hire independent production firms to provide the equipment, personnel, and expertise needed to handle the technical details.[8] State-of-the-art production trucks are one such way to transmit a game. With an array of cameras, tape machines, and graphic design generators, directors and producers choose from a wall of monitors inside the truck what they want the audience to see (see photos). The cost of producing a game depends on numerous variables: transmission and travel costs, the amount and quality of equipment used, talent fees for popular announcers whose names will lend prestige to the broadcast, and the like. A television broadcast of a single football or basketball game might cost between $10,000 and $25,000, depending on those variables. Ideally, advertising sales will offset the costs associated with producing the game; but, should revenues fall short, sport managers should consider the return on that investment from a marketing and promotion perspective.

A three-hour college football game broadcast attracts viewers because it provides an "up close and personal" account of the game as it happens. Astute sport managers understand that the broadcast is much more than that. Television exposure allows a college to showcase its team, of course, but it is also an opportunity to display the beauty of the campus and generate interest and raise morale among potential fans, students, faculty, staff, and alumni. By making sure that the broadcast includes frequent announcements promoting upcoming games, giving ticket information, and noting the availability of licensed merchandise and the like, colleges can generate future revenue. A positive broadcast can also energize alumni to contribute to the annual fund and encourage high school students and their parents to consider the school at application time. College admissions officers across the country are well aware of the "Flutie spike" at Boston College, the sudden surge in freshman admissions applications that followed Doug Flutie's 1984 Heisman Trophy season. Television coverage of the Eagles' games, showcasing the attractive Chestnut Hill campus and the school's academic programs, raised the college's visibility among potential students.

Producing the game broadcast is only the first step. The sport organization has to find a station or group of stations willing to carry the game. That, not surprisingly, is a matter for negotiation.

In the broadcasting business, the term "syndicated programming" refers to programs that are neither provided by the local station's national network nor produced by the local station itself. Reruns of popular network series, game shows such as "Jeopardy," entertainment news programs, and original action dramas such as "Star Trek: The Next Generation" are all examples of syndicated programs. Contracts for syndicated programs may take several forms. The simplest arrangement is for the sport organization to purchase airtime from a station or stations for a negotiated fee. The broadcasters are guaranteed income, and the team gains positive exposure and retains all revenue from advertising sales. This is how those myriad infomercials for products and services find their way onto the air. Many television stations and cable services are only too glad to sell blocks of time for a guaranteed price rather than go through the trouble and risk of purchasing programming and selling advertising.

Depending on the demand for your organization's events and the state of the television market, syndication can take several other forms, usually involving an exchange of advertising time and sometimes cash. "Barter syndication" means that the producer of the program and the broadcaster are trading advertising time for the right to carry the program. The producer retains a portion of the advertising time to sell while making the rest available to the local station to sell. Each side keeps the revenue it receives from selling its allotment of time. "Cash syndication" represents the flip side of buying airtime. Rather than the producer's paying for airtime, the broadcaster pays for the program and gets to sell the advertising time. "Cash-barter" is a hybrid arrangement that includes both an exchange of advertising and a cash payment, either from the producer to the broadcaster or from the broadcaster to the producer.

Local television and radio contracts for MLB teams reflect the variety of broadcast arrangements in the industry and indicate how the most desirable commodities—successful teams in large media markets—command the best deals. The New York Yankees enjoyed the richest local television contract in 1999. The Yankees received $52.5 million in rights payments from Cablevision's MSG Network; MSG helped defray its costs by licensing 50 games to WNYW, an over-the-air New York station, for $17.5 million. In Kansas City, the Royals receive between $3 and $3.5 million for cable and broadcast television rights from Fox Sports Rocky Mountain, a regional sports channel. To ensure that fans without cable see some of the team's games, Fox pays KMBC, the local ABC affiliate, to air 50 games. KMBC, however, does not believe there is enough fan and advertiser interest in Royals baseball to warrant preempting its network programming, so KMBC places 35 of the 50 games on another Kansas City station, KCWE, which routinely garners lower ratings and less advertising revenue.[9]

Regardless of the financial arrangements, sport managers can and should insist that their games are broadcast so as to maximize interest and present their team or institution in a positive light. Standard broadcast agreements between sport organizations and broadcasters often include specific clauses reserving airtime for promotional announcements. Parties may also negotiate contracts that grant advertising time to the organization's corporate partners, or that bar or limit broadcasters from selling advertising time to businesses such as gaming casinos or breweries that might reflect unfavorably on the institution. Colleges and athletic conferences have negotiated contracts allowing coverage of popular sports such as basketball and football only if the broadcaster also agrees to broadcast emerging sports such as women's volleyball.

When the NCAA sold CBS exclusive broadcast rights to the men's Division I basketball tournament in 1989, the contract limited beer advertising to one minute per hour and banned any advertisement featuring professional basketball players. The NCAA also required CBS to set aside 90 seconds of airtime during each game for promotional announcements, produced by the NCAA, touting the organization's student-athlete and community services. Additionally, CBS agreed "to consult annually" with the NCAA before hiring announcers for the games and stipulated that it would not hire current NBA players, coaches, or team officials to broadcast the tournament. The NCAA also required CBS to telecast portions of a dozen other NCAA Championships in sports ranging from wrestling to track and field. For its part, the NCAA agreed to several conditions aimed at maximizing CBS's audience by staggering starting times of first- and second-round games and consulting with network programmers to ensure that attractive early-round match-ups were scheduled in prime time when they would attract the largest possible audience.[10]

Contract negotiations, of course, require give-and-take on both sides. Sport managers must realize, for instance, that limiting potential advertisers or holding back salable airtime for promotional use may reduce the amount of revenue that the broadcaster can generate and subsequently may mean a reduction in rights payments. The "cost" of lost revenue, however, can be offset by the benefits of positive exposure and future income. The NCAA's insistence in 1989 that CBS broadcast the Division I women's basketball Final Four made it possible for millions of new fans to see the sport, and helped pave the way for a 1995 agreement with ESPN that significantly expanded coverage of—and revenue from—the women's tournament.

If sport managers view television partnerships as promotional opportunities and as part of a well-designed marketing plan, rather than exclusively as sources of immediate revenue, the finances of getting games on television change. A bottom-line deficit may well be offset by the promotional value of several hours of positive exposure.

Sports fans loyal to a team will remain loyal to the "official" radio station of their team.

RADIO

If the television dial is crowded thanks to cable and satellites, radio is Times Square on New Year's Eve. Listeners in any community have dozens of radio options, and the audience is fragmented as stations seek to be heard amid the noise. By the fall of 1998, according to the Federal Communications Commission, 5639 commercial FM stations, 4734 commercial AM stations, and 2000 noncommercial FM stations were on the air in the United States; and in major metropolitan areas such as New York and Los Angeles, over a hundred local signals competed for listeners. Not surprisingly, although advertisers spent nearly $13.5 billion on radio in 1997, many stations are struggling to survive financially.

Radio Broadcast Basics

If you want your fans to be able to follow your team on the radio, you need to make sure that a station or a network of stations carries the games. That means the broadcast has to get from the arena to the network flagship station and then to the network affiliates. How does it work?

From the Press Box to the Flagship

A radio broadcast is much like a telephone call. The announcers connect equipment to a communications line at the game site, and their description of the game—along with the cheers of the crowd—is transmitted back to the station. While a growing number of major venues now boast fiber-optic links to satellite transmission facilities, most often the first leg of the broadcast is by land line, either POTS (plain old telephone service) or higher-quality ISDN (integrated services digital network). In either case, you will need a TA (terminal adapter) that links the announcers' microphones and tape decks with the communication line. Most broadcasters these days use a digital *codec* (coder/decoder) mixer that delivers a studio-quality signal to the station.

Meanwhile, Back at the Flagship

As the announcers describe the game, the engineer at the flagship station follows along on a prearranged *cue sheet* or *format*. When the announcer at the game says something like "We'll be back after this message," those words cue the engineer to play an advertisement. If the announcers follow the format, and the engineer at the station is paying attention, all the elements of the game broadcast fit neatly together. The flagship station will also frequently be the place where other announcers and producers prepare and broadcast pregame, halftime, and postgame programming to complement the actual game broadcast.

From Flagship to Affiliates

If the game is to be broadcast on a network of stations, the flagship station's signal must be transmitted to the other stations. For larger networks, *satellite* distribution has become the norm. Just as you rent the telephone company's facilities when you make a long-distance telephone call, you can rent the use of a satellite *transponder* to distribute a game broadcast. The game broadcast is bounced from an *uplink* transmitter to the satellite orbiting over the earth and then to each affiliate's receiver or *downlink*. For smaller networks, a network of ISDN or POTS lines can distribute the game. If the network stations are relatively close together, the signal can be passed from one station to the next over the air. This technique is most effective if the stations are FM (Frequency Modulation) broadcasters. While AM (Amplitude Modulation) signals often cover more territory, they are subject to atmospheric disturbance; FM offers a clear, static-free signal. As was the case with the flagship engineer, engineers at each affiliate follow along on the cue sheet and insert local advertisements at the appropriate times.

For many stations, sport programming offers help. The loyal sport audience will seek out on the dial the games and broadcasts that are dedicated to favorite teams, and many broadcasters believe that being identified as "the station of" the local team helps them stand out in the crowd. Sport managers should understand that although radio today lacks the raw audience numbers of prime-time television, the average American spends more than three hours a day listening to the radio, and over the course of a week, the medium reaches more than 95 percent of the population. Radio has also traditionally seen involvement with local organizations as an important tool in building audiences and creating alliances with local businesses. In suburban and rural areas especially, where television audiences watch programs from nearby major cities or national cable networks, the local radio station may be the principal local news, information, and advertising medium.

SPORT AND RADIO: AN ECONOMICAL CHOICE

Radio is also more economical than television. While television broadcasts require dozens of technicians and truckloads of expensive equipment, a radio broadcaster needs only a modest remote kit and a telephone line or low-power transmitter to get the signal back to the station. Whereas the cost of producing and transmitting a single football game, on a local or regional cable channel using four or five cameras, two or three tape machines, and a well-known local announcer, might be $25,000 or more, for example, that sum could easily pay for the equipment, transmission, and production costs of an entire season of radio broadcasts. Since the radio audience at any given time is typically smaller than the television audience, advertising rates are lower. Accordingly, the cost of purchasing blocks of airtime is also far lower than for television. Colleges, high schools, and minor league teams whose games cannot command a large audience often find that while television exposure is financially out of reach, radio time is both available and affordable.

As with television, rights to proven commodities such as NFL football, big-league baseball, and major college events will attract several eager broadcasters and are often auctioned off to the highest bidder. Many sport organizations, however, discover that the best way to market their team or event through radio is by producing their own broadcasts. A team or college, either on its own or with the help of a production company, obtains the necessary equipment, hires the talent, and produces the finished broadcast for airing by one or more stations. The stations agree to carry the games for either a cash payment or a combination of cash and commercial time that they can sell to local sponsors. The team or college covers its expenses, ideally, by selling commercial time to advertisers. By retaining the rights to its games and producing the broadcasts itself, the sport organization ensures that the broadcasts will project a positive image and that airtime can be used to market the organization's products and image.

RADIO: IT'S NOT JUST PLAY-BY-PLAY

Play-by-play game broadcasts are important marketing tools, but sport managers should not ignore other opportunities to promote their products on radio. To reinforce their identity as "the official station" of a team, broadcasters are often eager to air additional programming: interviews with coaches and players, daily reports from training camp or the practice facility, pregame broadcasts from the stadium parking lot, profiles of players, and the like. Programs such as these, as well as pregame and postgame interviews and scoreboard shows, are sometimes referred to in the radio business as "spot-hangers"—programming designed for the express purpose of creating additional advertising time to sell. The additional income from such advertising helps defray the cost of buying rights, or makes the idea of devoting blocks of airtime to game broadcasts more financially attractive. Many of these programming opportunities are also available on stations other than the one that broadcasts a team's games, and should not be overlooked.

Sport managers should remember that every radio and television exposure, whether it is a live game broadcast or a two-minute preview of an upcoming event, provides a marketing and promotional opportunity. A live radio station broadcast from the stadium parking lot on football game day may be designed by the broadcasters to promote the station and connect the station in the listeners' minds with the local college; but it also serves to remind listeners that there is a home game today and that the stadium is an exciting place to spend the afternoon. Many sport organizations routinely distribute free game tickets to local radio stations as prizes to be given away over the air. The local disk jockey gives the tickets to listeners who call in, creating excitement and a sense of value for the station. In the process of gifting the tickets, however, the deejay also reminds the audience that there is a game coming up that would be fun and exciting to attend—so much fun, in fact, that the station wants to give a loyal listener a chance to go for free!

Cross-promotional opportunities between sport organizations and broadcasters abound, and creative financing arrangements are plentiful. In the world of radio, time and money are interchangeable. This is especially true in smaller markets where broadcasters are struggling to make ends meet. Tickets, arena signage, and advertising space in game programs can be, and often are, exchanged for advertising time to promote ticket sales or licensed merchandise. Local radio stations, because of the relative flexibility of their daily broadcast schedule, are often much more willing than television stations to accept programming from outside producers. If the team's media relations staff is willing to prepare three- to five-minute game previews, post-game summaries, or daily features in a radio-friendly format that allow the station to sell a local commercial or two, a local broadcaster will likely find airtime to carry the programs.

As with television, radio can be a significant source of immediate revenue through rights fees. Sport managers, however, should also consider how they can use the medium to promote and market their products on the air during game broadcasts and other programming. Because of radio's lower production costs and typically smaller audiences, the medium may provide a lower-cost alternative than television. Radio is also the ideal medium for last-minute marketing efforts. If a block of tickets suddenly becomes available, if the weather forces a change in schedule, or if one last promotional effort seems needed, new advertising copy can be written and hand delivered or faxed to a radio station and be on the air immediately.

DIGITAL TECHNOLOGY

The electronic media are rapidly becoming a digital environment. Images and sounds are being recorded and transmitted in the bits and bytes of computer language and burned onto compact disks rather than recorded on magnetic tape. *Convergence* is the buzzword: soon we will no longer differentiate between radio, television, and computer technology. The game coverage, highlights, statistics, player biographies, and sport news fans now gather from radio, television, the Internet, and the daily sport page will all be electronically delivered to one device that will allow us to see, hear, and read what we want when we want.

Technology is racing ahead. Before too long, the experts say, we will be able to watch games on crystal-clear, wall-sized, high-definition television screens and hear the bands play and coaches shout in stereo sound. Fans will be able to choose what camera angle they prefer, summon instant replays on demand, and switch from game to game around the country to see how their team's rivals are doing. Need the latest statistical update for your fantasy league team? Want to purchase a replica game uniform just like the one on the player you are watching? Just click a button and connect to the press box computer or the team's licensed-merchandise cyberstore! Instantaneous, interactive communication on demand, experts say, is the future. Many of the nation's largest media corporations are betting billions of dollars that consumers want more information and entertainment and want it now. Television networks, cable services, telephone companies, and computer hardware and software providers have launched new television and Internet services that—they hope—will attract consumers willing to pay for the latest information, or at least enough consumers to make the new media attractive advertising buys.

Unfortunately, once the experts describe the latest technological bells and whistles, they begin to disagree. Research indicates that the Internet, and the World Wide Web, are rapidly joining the media mainstream. By the summer of 1998, according to one study, 79 million North Americans over the age of 16 were using the Internet. That number is expected to exceed 132 million by the turn of the century.[11] The vital

Building a Winning Web Site

Sport organizations—and everyone else, it sometimes seems—are setting up World Wide Web sites these days. Here are some ideas to keep in mind if you are developing a Web site:

➤ Use quick-hitting eye and ear appeal. Web surfers are impatient. If your home page doesn't grab their attention, they'll move on. Strive for a clean, colorful home page featuring eye-catching images. Put that award-winning action shot or the portrait of the star player up front. And don't ignore the possibilities of sound! The college fight song or an appropriate sound effect can be a positive addition.

➤ Aim for easy navigation. Make sure your visitors can move around the site easily. Include clear and easily understood icons and a navigation bar on each screen to allow browsers to access information. Arrange the navigation tools to guide visitors to where you want them to go.

➤ Remember, not everyone is state of the art. Although graphics and bells and whistles are important, avoid pages that take too long to load. Double-check your proposed design on an older, slower computer linked to the Internet by the local telephone company. Surfers want information now and won't wait patiently if it takes several minutes for your home page to appear.

➤ Make it interactive. The Internet is a two-way medium, so get the visitors to your Web site involved. Be sure to include contact information (including e-mail addresses) on the site so visitors can write to the organization, comment on last night's game, or send fan mail to their favorite players. Include a trivia contest or fan poll—how about an automated e-mail mailing list? Automated e-mail programs allow organizations to respond to e-mails with preprogrammed form letters.

➤ Don't get lost in the links. Be careful not to lose surfers in a maze of pages. Every screen on your site should have a clearly marked Home Page button to get visitors back to the beginning. Avoid links that take your visitor to another site with no way to return to yours, or links that place them several levels past your home page.

➤ Keep it current. The Internet means instant information, so don't let your site get old. If you include game-by-game results or updated standings on your site, make sure they are refreshed quickly and accurately. If your organization doesn't have the personnel to keep a site up to date, it's better not to include information that will soon turn into yesterday's news.

➤ Content is king. Don't let the technology divert your attention from the basic fact: visitors will return to your Web site only if you provide information, activities, and services that meet their needs.

Many sport Web sites also allow fans to listen to live radio broadcasts of events. Some analysts predict that the Internet will surpass traditional AM and FM transmitters as the preferred medium for radio within the next 20 years; others fear that if fans can listen to any game as it happens, the sport audience will splinter into fragments too small to attract significant advertising revenue, resulting in a sharp decline in broadcast rights fees. Many analysts doubt that subscription fees or per game payments can make up for lost advertising revenue, but no one is certain.

Computer technology offers sport managers an unparalleled opportunity to identify their audience. Radio and television are one-way media. The Internet is two-way. By offering electronic newsletters, giving away sweatshirts, or simply posting a brief questionnaire, a Web site operator can compile the names, addresses, and demographic data on fans who have visited the site. This information can be used to market future events and targeted products to fans with a demonstrated interest in the team or event.

question is whether or not the services made available by this new technology will survive in the marketplace. As one knowledgeable industry analyst observed, no one yet knows what consumers want and, more importantly, what they are willing to pay for—and "there is no way to find out except to 'build it and hope they will come.'"[12]

One thing does, however, seem likely: sport will play an important role in the new digital marketplace. Loyal fans will seek out their favorite sports, teams, and players; recognizable sport brands will attract an audience. Just as sport drove sales of radios, televisions, and cable and satellite services, some of the busiest sites on the Internet are sport related. Full-service sport sites such as ESPN's Sports Zone, CBS Sportsline, and CNN/SI (a joint venture of Time Warner's Cable News Network and *Sports Illustrated*) provide scores, news, and features to millions of fans every day. Virtually every professional sport league and major college boasts a World Wide Web site, and a growing number of consumers have begun to routinely purchase tickets and team gear via computer[13] (see Web page above).

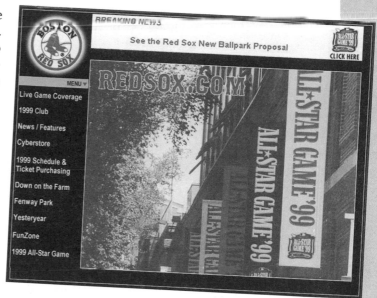

The Boston Red Sox home page at www.redsox.com welcomes visitors with a photograph of Fenway Park. Links in the left-hand column connect fans with further team information.

For most sport organizations, a well-designed, interactive World Wide Web site should be the first step into the digital future.[14] A colorful home page with links to up-to-date news releases, player biographies, statistics, and results can be an important promotional tool. A growing number of sport sites include recorded video and audio clips that allow fans to witness key plays or hear from a star player. As consumers grow more comfortable with encryption technology and secure servers, links to ticket offices and team stores or similar providers of licensed merchandise are becoming standard as well. Computer graphics allow marketers to utilize color, sound, and movement to sell products. Interactivity allows the consumer to play an active role in the transaction. A feature of many Web sites that demonstrates the marketing power of digital technology is a program allowing a potential ticket buyer to see the view from the seats he or she has chosen.

WRAP-UP

Broadcasters spend nearly $5 billion a year for the rights to bring sporting events to fans at home. That revenue has helped turn sport into a major industry. What has generated those billions, however, is advertising sales. New technology means more choices for fans, but it could mean trouble for advertisers. If audiences for individual sporting events decline, advertisers may no longer be willing to pay ever higher prices for commercials. If broadcasters can no longer generate revenues, rights fees to sport organizations will inevitably decline. Will fans be willing to make up the difference through pay-per-view or subscription fees?

While the financial future of the electronic media may be uncertain, new technology forges ahead. Digital technology makes it possible for fans to see more games, and allows sport managers to tailor and target their product to specific groups of consumers.

What remains constant is the loyalty of the sport audience and their willingness to use both new and old technology to find out about their favorites. According to a recent nationwide Nielsen Media Research survey, 44 percent of self-identified "avid sports fans" say they get most of their sport news from cable television, and 39 percent say they log on to the Internet at least once a week to access sport information.[15]

Sport managers should be familiar with the broad spectrum of electronic media options and should understand how each can reach potential consumers. Sport managers should also recognize the importance of taking an active role in using the electronic media. Organizations should investigate the relative cost and benefits of producing their own media products. Sport managers should also realize that they control valuable assets in today's hypercompetitive media environment and should exercise their bargaining power to make sure that their products are presented in a positive and creative manner.

ACTIVITIES

1. Television contracts mean money. But rights fees are not the only way sport organizations benefit from television coverage. What are some of the long- and short-term nonmonetary benefits of having your team's games televised?

2. To get a sense of today's "media-saturated" environment, examine the local broadcast market. How many television stations are on the air? Radio stations? What cable television and satellite services are available? How many information sources are competing for our attention?

3. Broadcasters are concerned about audience fragmentation. Analyze the television schedule on a given day and examine how many different types of programs are vying for the audience. What audiences are specific programs trying to attract? Why? How do sport broadcasts fit into the overall television schedule?

4. Suppose you are a college athletics director and are negotiating a new radio contract. What concessions might you seek from your broadcast partner to ensure a positive presentation of your college's team?

5. Explore the Internet. Visit and critique the World Wide Web sites of several sport organizations. What features make an interesting, easy-to-use site? Do the organizations maximize the marketing and promotion potential of the site?

YOUR MARKETING PLAN

How would you use radio, television, and the Internet to market your product or organization? Create a radio network, design a Web site, or strategize an advertising campaign that takes advantage of the electronic media.

C H A P T E R

15

PUBLIC RELATIONS

OBJECTIVES

1. To understand public relations and its role in positioning and in the formulation of the marketing mix.

2. To recognize the importance of effective community relations programming in product positioning and effective marketing efforts.

3. To understand the role, scope, and influence of the media and how that role can be used in conjunction with public and community relations programming to alter perceptions and influence public opinion and support.

Big Brother Not Only Is Watching, He Has Cable!

In this age of the media microscope, one can only wonder how shortsighted our sport executives, union leaders, and players are when they leave themselves open for negative media stories that greatly affect public opinion. While the exploits of Mark McGwire, Sammy Sosa, Cal Ripken, and others were positive sport stories throughout the 1998 baseball season, even a casual viewer noticed an abundance of negative stories in the sport world during 1998:

➢ Mike Tyson's continued disregard for how he acted and how he was perceived in the presence of the media.

➢ Latrell Sprewell's attempts to convince the average citizen he had done nothing wrong in physically attacking his coach.

➢ The questionable tactics (in terms of negotiation posturing) of both the NBA and the NBA Players Association in their inability to negotiate in good faith over a sport product that had made virtually everyone a millionaire.

➢ The failure of the Pittsburgh Pirates, Pittsburgh Steelers, and their supporting politicians to convey and explain how a proposed tax bill (which was defeated) contained much more than just two stadiums.

➢ The Women's Tennis Association and Association of Tennis Professionals requirement that media disclose the nature of a requested interview on a form so their stars could be better prepared. In some respects, this was seen as ensuring that the interview would fail to have any substance other than the spin being espoused by the organization and the player.

➢ The dismantling of the World Champion Florida Marlins and the disenfranchisement of their fans because their owner, a multimillionaire, feels he cannot compete financially.

All these stories have two sides, but unfortunately the other side is far less interesting than that receiving the bulk of attention in the media. Learning to build rapport, understanding, and comprehension is a key to successful marketing; public and community relations programming is the vehicle used to help build this infrastructure.[1]

The power of positive public relations to amplify a good marketing communications plan should never be underestimated. As we enter the new millennium, the media and public opinion continue to dominate how we perceive the world around us. The term "spin"—the ability to present an argument in several different ways, sometimes minimizing negative aspects and overstating positive attributes—was coined as a way of combating poor image perception. While "spin" evolved primarily in a political context, sport has seen similar efforts as they related to player behavior, franchise movement, the manufacture of athletic shoes, personnel problems such as coaching changes, and a variety of other situations. Thus, it has become critical in the sport setting to have effective public relations efforts and personnel that can function in times of crisis; it is crucial as well to promote local initiatives and positive actions occurring as a result of day-to-day operational activities and strategic planning.

Throughout this text we have discussed a variety of ways in which the sport marketer can use advertising and promotions to position the organization and its sport product(s) effectively in the marketplace. Unfortunately, these efforts can be undermined and rendered ineffective if the organization does not also have a good public relations program. In this chapter, we will examine the role of public relations in the sport context, where it consists primarily of community relations and media relations. We will also discuss and provide examples of three distinct forms of community relations—those initiated by players, those initiated by teams or institutions, and those initiated by leagues or governing bodies—and consider how they contribute to overall organizational marketing efforts.

PUBLIC RELATIONS DEFINED

Probably the most widely accepted definition of public relations, or PR as it is commonly called, is a practical definition developed by the *Public Relations News:* "Public Relations is the management function which evaluates public attitudes, identifies the policies and procedures of an individual or an organization with the public interest and executes a program of action to earn public understanding and acceptance."[2]

According to a more corporate definition, offered by Clarke L. Caywood, public relations is "the profitable integration of an organization's new and continuing relationship with stakeholders including customers by managing all communications contacts with the organization that create and protect the reputation of the organization."[3] Finally, Govoni, Eng, and Galper emphasize the relationship between the sender and the audience in terms of the credibility of the message. They define public relations as "a multifaceted form of communication, with the intent to foster a positive company or product image in a non-sponsored framework." A key aspect of this definition is its emphasis on nonsponsorship. The authors feel that nonsponsorship "enhances the credibility of the message and cloaks the company with the respectability of the source, which may be viewed by the audience as either the spokesperson or the medium."[4]

For the purposes of sport marketing, we will define public relations as an interactive marketing communications strategy that seeks to create a variety of mediums designed to convey the organizational philosophies, goals, and objectives to an identified group of publics for the purpose of establishing a relationship built upon comprehension, interest, and support. This communication strategy, which may take the form of activities as well as formal communication, may also involve players, media personnel, staff, mascots and other product extensions, sponsors, and other key components of the organization.

Public relations is a management function in that it reflects policies and programs developed at the top levels of management. Public relations systematically evaluates attitudes toward the organization and its products and hence depends on an effective and current marketing information system. Public relations identifies the impact of the public interest; this is clearly a consumer or marketing perspective that differentiates public relations from press agentry, propitiatory agenda, and advertising. What can be inferred from this impact? What consequences flow from a given course of action or inaction? How can the entity best disseminate messages or action to respond to this identified impact?

These and other questions, once identified and answered, form another function of public relations, namely that of executing a program of action. In this regard, public relations usually involves implementing specific marketing plans and tactics designed to alter or reinforce consumer perceptions, attitudes, or levels of awareness. The goal of this function is to earn public understanding and acceptance. Finally, the source, or more accurately the "perceived source," will in many cases lend credibility to the message or course of action. The use of consultants, market research firms, and other "third-party" sources lends the message an air of objectivity that in many cases might otherwise not be perceived.

In sport, public relations (PR) is often perceived to be synonymous with publicity or media relations (MR). Many people have developed this perception because public relations directors (especially those functioning as sport information directors) often deal largely with developing statistics and providing information to the media in order to gain increased media exposure for the sport organization.

Effective public relations programs (both media relations and community relations) usually create publicity—news stories, articles, interviews, and other activities. However, as this publicity is not paid media, it is not controllable. Thus activities can create both good and bad publicity.

Media relations is just one half of the public relations function. In the short term, media relations is probably the more important function. But in the long term, community relations (CR) can often be more or at least equally significant in impacting sales, generating positive public sentiment, and building a long-term relationship (and base) with the community.

Public relations then has two components, both of which must be developed and pursued if the public relations function is to reach its full potential and impact. In short, public relations can be expressed in the form of an equation, PR = MR + CR. An examination of these components will illustrate their importance individually and collectively.

MEDIA RELATIONS

Public opinion is one of the most powerful forces in our society, and media relations is designed to formulate and shape favorable opinion via the mass media. Media relations—communicating with the news media verbally or through other vehicles—must also balance public opinion with business strategy. Depending upon its role within the organization, media relations takes one or more of the following approaches: reactive, proactive, or interactive.[5]

Reactive media relations fields and responds to inquiries. Personnel respond to questions, queries, and requests from the media and other interested parties. In a sport setting, such requests may concern player interviews, appearances, autographs, photos, biographies, or profiles. In addition to these simple requests, the reactive function might also relate to requests for statements about or reactions to situations involving organizational policy.

Collegiate sport information offices or media relations departments perform many roles that are classified as reactive. The following overview of the University of Massachusetts Media Relations Office is an excellent illustration of the reactive functions of public relations.

In *proactive* media relations, the point of initiation is the organization rather than some external entity. For example, sport organizations could choose to contact

Case Study

Sport Information Functions at the University of Massachusetts

Kathy Connors, Assistant Sport Information Director, UMass Sports Info

Overview. The Sport Information Department (SID) is one of the most vital offices in any athletic department. The SID staff perform a variety of tasks within the athletic department, including all public relations functions such as writing press releases, producing media guides and game programs, providing game results and statistics, and coordinating interviews, as well as serving as the news bureau and maintaining department archives. The primary function of the SID is to disseminate information about the athletic department that will help promote the accomplishments and success of its athletes and teams.

The SID staff works closely with coaches and student athletes to build a relationship that allows the office to actively promote the accomplishments of each sport and the athletes and coaches in those sports.

The most vital function of the office is fostering a relationship with local, regional, and national media (both print and electronic) to enhance the image of the university, the athletic department, the coaches, and the student athletes.

Publications. The SID is responsible for all athletic department publications including media guides, press releases, schedule cards, posters, and promotional flyers. Most college athletic departments produce media guides for each sport offered at the varsity level. These publications serve a dual function for the department. They are helpful to the media not only as a source of player, school, and historical information and records, but also as a recruiting tool for the coaching staff of that particular sport.

Press releases, game notes, and promotional flyers are also the responsibility of the SID. Press releases, written after any newsworthy occurrence, announce game results, staffing changes, awards, and so on. These releases are distributed to local, regional, and national media that may have an interest in the topic of the release. Game notes are prepared for sports such as football and basketball that attract a large media following, especially if the games are televised. These packets contain detailed notes, statistics, comparisons, and other interesting facts that will help the media prepare their stories or enhance their broadcasts. Promotional flyers that generate publicity and create awareness and appreciation of athletes' accomplishments assist athletes in earning conference and All-America honors, as well as promoting athletes for national awards.

The SID has recently joined the information superhighway. The SID is responsible for upkeep of the university's Web site, which contains detailed information on every team. Some schools elect to maintain and update their web pages in-house, while others have decided to outsource these functions to an Internet provider or agency.

Archives, Records, and Statistics. The SID maintains the archives for the athletic department. The SID staff is responsible for keeping game and seasonal statistics as well as maintaining game, season, and all-time records. The SID is also responsible for coordinating all photography and maintaining all photo files. The SID archives all records, statistics, photos, biographies, results, and publications, along with clipping files (primarily newspaper based).

Building Rapport With the Media. The most important function of the SID is to build and maintain a strong relationship with the media. Because the SID office serves as the liaison between the athletic department and the media, it often functions as the university spokesperson in a sport context. It is the role of the SID to generate as much positive publicity as possible regarding the school's athletic teams and its athletes, and to present this information to the media in a prompt and useful manner. It is important to create and maintain an honest and open relationship with the media and to encourage a level of trust between the two parties.

Unfortunately, this "trust" is impacted when the SID must function as a damage-control officer in situations that portray athletes in an unfavorable light. It is the responsibility of the SID to diffuse potentially damaging situations between the university and the press, and hopefully to play a role in controlling or solving the crisis.

Marketing Role. The SID also serves a marketing function, assisting the marketing department by providing information and photos for sales brochures and by scheduling the athletes and coaches for personal appearances. In some cases, the SID also assists in providing media training classes or clinics to help prepare coaches and athletes for the media spotlight.

---

media outlets with possible stories or could distribute packages of player bios, media guides, or highlight films to a preselected audience without having been requested to do so. We see an excellent example of a proactive approach in a 1907 correspondence between Mr. R.J. Hellawell of Spalding & Bros. to James E. Sullivan, the Amateur Athletic Union driving force, whose real job was president of the American Sports Publishing Co., a firm owned by Spalding. In his letter, Hellawell writes:

"We should have articles in the newspapers praising and telling of the decrease in accidents (in football). We could have these in the shape of interviews with head Coaches, Trainers and others prominent in Foot Ball. Of course, it would add weight to them. You no doubt will see some way to work out this matter and perhaps you have something in mind that will be better than this suggestion, but I really think that we should do all we could to turn sentiment in favor of Foot Ball."[6]

Although media relations will always have reactive functions, the primary mode will be proactive—to take the initiative in providing information and creating publicity as a marketing function.

Interactive media relations involves developing mutually beneficial relationships with the media and assisting the media on a variety of issues. This function relates closely to relationship marketing and focuses on building lasting long-term relationships rather than accomplishing short-term public relations objectives. While these short-term public relations objectives might be part of the "mix," they are just a component of a larger mission designed to facilitate relationships and the essentials of a media relations program. In interactive media relations, either party can initiate the action or activity knowing that the other will cooperate fully because doing so is in the best interests of both.

COMMUNITY RELATIONS

Once viewed as an afterthought or as a "funding-permits" budget item, community relations has become an integral part of the marketing efforts of sport organizations. Community relations programs have emerged as a stratagem that sport organizations (particularly those at the professional level) use to deliver outreach-type programs. The aim of such programs is to achieve corporate public relations objectives related to enhancing public understanding and gaining public approval and acceptance, and hopefully leading to public support.[7]

Community relations programs usually are implemented in one of three ways. These efforts can be player initiated, team initiated, or league initiated. Within recent years, sport organizations have acknowledged the importance of community relations programs and have added staff to execute these programs, or have added community relations responsibilities to the job descriptions of existing staff. These community relations staff help to implement leaguewide initiatives (e.g., the NBA's Stay in School Program or the NCAA's clinics), team-based initiatives (e.g., the Cleveland Cavs' Read to Succeed program or the Pittsburgh Pirates' Major League Math program), and on occasion, player-based programs (e.g., Shaquille O'Neal's Shaqsgiving Program).

Players are an integral part of all three types of community relations initiatives. Almost all community relations programs have some element of player involvement because it is the presence of the players and their involvement that attract funding to the program via sponsorship, that garner media interest and coverage, and that finally attract an audience of participants and observers to the programs. Kathy Guy, director of community and player relations for the Pittsburgh Pirates, explains the role of players in such programs.

Community relations programs complement media relations programs and their goal of raising awareness levels among consumers and the general public. In addition to raising awareness by being visible in the community, community relations programs attempt to create goodwill. While the intent of both efforts is to generate publicity for the organization, media relations yields greater immediate results; com-

Case Study

The Role of Player Relations in a Comprehensive Community Relations Program

Kathy Guy, Director of Community and Player Relations, Pittsburgh Pirates

The director of community and player relations for the Pittsburgh Pirates functions as a bridge connecting the players and the organization to Pirate fans and the Pittsburgh community.

It is the responsibility and privilege of a professional sport franchise to "give back" to the community. The goal of our franchise is to reach as many fans as possible, most notably youth, and to service organizations that provide for people in need in our community. It is crucial to our survival as a small-market team that the Pirates reach beyond the city of Pittsburgh and into the outlying areas of western Pennsylvania, West Virginia, and Ohio. Our community relations activities serve to cultivate our fan base and promote the ball club, as well as the sport of baseball, throughout our region.

Since the baseball season is very long and includes few "off days," most of the community relations programs during the season take place in the Pittsburgh area. Our goal for in-season events is to give fans an opportunity to get to know the players they cheer for and perhaps to receive an autograph or other souvenir. Making this personal connection with the fans is extremely important to the franchise. In addition to reaching these specific fans, efforts such as conducting youth baseball clinics and refurbishing ball fields serve to demonstrate the Pirates' commitment to improving the quality of life throughout our marketplace.

During the off-season, the Pirates have two traveling programs designed to reach out to fans throughout the tri-state area. "Pirates in the Community" and the annual "Winter Caravan" provide venues where our fans can meet the Pittsburgh Pirates up close and personal. Through these programs, Pirate players, coaches, and other team personnel travel to a variety of schools, community groups, and charitable events to lend our unique resources to the region.

Under the umbrella of "Pirate Partners," the franchise utilizes these in-season and off-season programs

Pirates Partners

Your Team. Our Town.®

to thank our fans for their support—and at the same time to attempt to reach and develop new fans who are vital to our future growth and success.

In the scope of our community relations efforts, we work with area charities, non-profit organizations, schools, and special programs. We work directly with the charity in fundraising efforts and often provide autographs, memorabilia, or spokespersons to help promote the organization's aims. Autographs are among the most significant sources of support our players can provide. Sometimes players may shy away from autographing because of the sport memorabilia craze, but establishing a commitment from the players to sign autographs for charitable purposes, and for fans in general, is crucial to our long-term marketing efforts and relationship building in the community. Signing autographs yields many good results. Not only does the ball club begin to turn children into baseball fans, but the autographed items can be valuable for fund-raising by charitable and nonprofit groups. Each season the players and the overall organization donate more than 2,000 such items.

Many charities also receive financial contributions from either individual Pirate players, corporate sponsors, or a combination of players and sponsors. In some cases these donations are tied to a specific player's on-field performance or perhaps a cumulative team statistic. The Pirates also have a donations budget to provide financial support to a large number of nonprofit groups. The estimated annual value of financial (cash) and in-kind contributions by the Pirates to the community is in excess of $1 million.

In terms of player relations, it is important for the club to help each player find a match with a local charity or nonprofit group. This involves an education process: we educate the player on the benefits of this worthwhile relationship, and educate the organization on how to best utilize the player and his time. Our approach is to help the player connect, not only with the organization itself, but also with the fans of both the team and the organization. Making this connection is an effective win-win situation for all concerned.

Through the activities just described, the Pirates accomplish two very important goals. First, we demonstrate our commitment to the growth and development of our region and the lives of its residents by forming important partnerships within the community and reaching out to fans on an individual basis. Second, we continue to cultivate a long-term fan base to ensure the success of the Pittsburgh Pirates, a proud franchise in its second century of on-field competition and off-field enrichment.

---

munity relations programs, on the other hand, often have objectives—such as fan development—that are very long-term. However, while the long-term value and effectiveness of community relations programs can be measured in the goodwill and publicity generated, they should also be measured in terms of fan building. Fan building leads to not only ticket sales, but also broadcast ratings, merchandise sales, and sponsor interest and value. Fan building through community relations programs is a key ingredient in creating fan identification—the emotional involvement customers have with a sport organization and the basis for creating relationships with long-term value[8] (e.g., ticket sales, broadcast ratings, merchandise sales, positive word-of-mouth advertising) that we have previously discussed.

In terms of professional sport organizations, community relations may involve designating certain games as community nights so that marketing efforts are directed specifically at a geographic target market. In fact, this concept has been so successful that certain professional sport teams, most notably the New York Yankees and Pittsburgh Pirates, have defined community as ethnic groups and have set aside certain themed days for ethnic celebrations with special food, music, and player appearances (when players from that particular ethnic background are team members).

Community relations can also take the form of corporate philanthropy. Like sales promotion, advertising, event marketing, and sponsorship activities, corporate philanthropy is intended to position the company in the mind of the stakeholder. However, unlike these activities, which are budget-line items in an operating budget, corporate philanthropy activities come from a company's profits.[9] Corporations such as Yankee Candle Company (Deerfield, Massachusetts), McDonald's, and Coca-Cola use philanthropy not only to position themselves as good neighbors, but also to challenge their employees and other businesses to match their efforts and provide contributions to the selected beneficiaries.

Effective community relations programs can be structured so that they are profitable for the organization even in the short term, without regard to the long-term increase in sales. An excellent example of a program that had both short- and long-term benefits was an activity the Pittsburgh Pirates conducted in May of 1997. Called "Meet the Pirates

Most fans get excited when a player greets them at the stadium, as Pirates' Al Martin does here.

Night," it gave fans the opportunity to actually meet the players who greeted fans as they entered Three Rivers Stadium. According to Pirate Vice President Steve Greenberg, "More important than the ticket count last night or any one night is that people feel good about this team. I tell Kevin [Pirate owner Kevin McClatchy], be patient, the fans will come."[10]

Numerous activities can generate goodwill and revenue for an organization. The key is that both long- and short-term benefits derive from the development of a balanced, strategically designed community relations program. The three examples that follow, the Orlando Magic Youth Foundation, the Cleveland Cavs' programs, and the Cam Neely Foundation, all possess distinct elements that can be part of any effective community relations programming. The Orlando Magic Youth Foundation illustrates a bigger, more inclusive approach designed to help the community help itself. The Cleveland Cavs' efforts illustrate that these programs, if effective, can generate self-sustaining support from local businesses and corporations. Finally, the Cam Neely Foundation illustrates how an individual player, through commitment and involvement, can make a difference in the community.

The Orlando Magic Youth Foundation

The Orlando Magic have taken a foundation approach to community relations. The Orlando Magic Youth Foundation was founded in 1988 to raise funds and community awareness to help combat the many physical, emotional, and social challenges facing the children of Central Florida. OMYF is part of RDV Sports Team Charities, the non-profit, private foundations representing the company's three professional sports teams.

In 10 years of giving, the OMYF has positively impacted more than one million kids. Through private donations, fund-raising events, and contributions, more than $5.7 million has been raised and distributed to non-profit organizations that support the mission statement of OMYF. It is truly a team effort by Magic players, coaches, staff, and the DeVos Family, in partnership with season ticket holders, corporate sponsors, fans, and the community.

In addition to receiving a 60-cent match from its funding partner, the Robert R. McCormick Tribune Foundation, 100 percent of every donation to OMYF goes back into the community with an even greater impact. It's a winning combination for everyone.

OMYF fund-raising events and programs include: Outback Steakhouse/Orlando Magic Down Under Gold Scramble; Black Tie and Tennis Charity Gala; State Magic License Plate Program; SunTrust Magic Checks; Games Autographed Auction; the Outback Steakhouse 25 Point Program; and the Game 50/50 Raffle.

If you would like more information about OMYF or volunteer opportunities with various OMYF fund-raising events, please call the RDV Sports Teams Charities Department at (407) 916-2641, or send an e-mail to omyf@rdvsports.com.

The Cleveland Cavs

The Cleveland Cavs' community relations programs strongly emphasize the importance of education. The Cavs accomplish these educational objectives through their support of league-based (NBA) programs as well as team-initiated local programs. For example, like all other NBA teams, the Cavs participate in the NBA's Stay in School Program, which encourages students to remain in school and not drop out, as well as the Team Up Program, which encourages middle school students and local youth organizations to "team up" by giving time and service to their communities. NBA Team Up spokesperson Bob Lanier states that the main challenge in these types of community relations programs is to get the attention of the students. "You have to sell the student on it a little more now than maybe nine years ago. You have to make them understand the what's-in-it-for-them kind of deal."[12] What's in it for them is usually a concert or other NBA-related activity, a reward for those students who have participated.

In addition to these league-based initiatives, the Cavs have several of their own initiatives, such as the Cleveland Schools Conflict Resolution Program. This program teaches youngsters how to avoid violence in working out their disputes, culminating in a festival and celebration at Gund Arena during which the participants meet Cav players, attend presentations, and enjoy a Cavs game. Another successful program that exists in some form in almost all cities with professional sport franchises is the Read to Succeed program, a partnership between the Cavs, in this case, and seven library systems to encourage reading skills and interests.[13]

The Cavs have also developed a program called Minority Business Associates (referred to in chapter 12) that was designed to accomplish two primary objectives: generating sponsorship and advertising revenue from nontraditional sources and creating an effective way for community leaders to serve as role models for Cleveland schoolchildren. The program involves 10 African American businessmen who have each paid $6,500 to participate. These businessmen are in actuality helping support the Cavs' Stay in School initiative, both financially and by speaking directly to kids, and providing tickets for kids to attend games. In exchange, the business owners will receive arena signage, public service announcements during Cavs broadcasts, and ads during the pregame coach's show. In addition, each participant will be the subject of two features during the Cavs' "Fast Break Show" (which airs before televised games) and will travel with the team to a game in Chicago.[14] A win-win situation for all concerned.

One Player's Approach to Giving Back—the Cam Neely Foundation

The Cam Neely Foundation is dedicated to one specific cause—cancer and its devastating impact on families. Cam Neely of the Boston Bruins lost both of his parents to cancer, and that experience left him with a deep understanding of cancer's toll on families, and of the support families need and should have while struggling to help loved ones through treatment. The result was Neely house, a home away from home for the families of patients undergoing cancer treatment at New England Medical Center or its pediatric facility, the Floating Hospital for Children.

While he was with the Boston Bruins, Neely supported the foundation with a number of sport-related activities, including memorabilia auctions and other hockey-related events; but he is best known for his relationship with comic and Boston native Dennis Leary and their annual Comic Festival (and HBO special). Neely has been, and continues to be, extremely successful in raising funds for this project and drawing attention to the cause.[15]

PUBLIC RELATIONS FUNCTIONS

This section covers public relations functions and outlines a sport application for each, with the aim of clarifying the variety of roles public relations can play and the value of the various roles. To illustrate these roles and their value, we will consider the following list of functions:

> Provision of information and general communication (to consumers, shareholders, suppliers, competitors, government agencies, and the general public)

> Image shaping or enhancement via organizational publicity

> Community relations (previously discussed)

> Employee relations

> Educational efforts for the purpose of gaining political or popular support for the organizational agenda

➤ Recruiting/Business development

➤ Launching new products or innovations

➤ Obtaining feedback and reaction

➤ Coping with crisis[16]

INFORM AND COMMUNICATE

This function of a public relations program serves to maintain contact with the grassroots support of the organization. Sport organizations are acutely aware that a good community relations program can result in positive perceptions and, ultimately, financial or other benefits. For example, in intercollegiate athletics, community relations often takes the form of stories about "hometown heroes" that are written by sport information staffers at the university and disseminated to local papers. According to a former sport information director and award winner, Howard Davis, the "hometown" feature is one of the most important functions of a sport information office.[17] This information is important for several reasons: (a) it provides a "common denominator" for residents of the athlete's hometown and the university; (b) it may prompt residents of the area to attend an athletic contest at the university or to apply for admission; and (c) it may assist the athletic department in recruiting future athletes from that town or region.

Public relations departments communicate with consumers, shareholders, suppliers, competitors, government agencies, and the general public. Clearly, this is the aspect of a public relations program that is best understood (by the general public) and most utilized. This function involves the compilation, presentation, and dissemination of product or organizational information to the general public and/or to special segments of the population (alumni, sportswriters, newspapers, electronic media, web browsers, and so on). The process may be as simple as compiling statistics from basketball games; it may be as complex as providing statisticians, spotters, and other personnel for national broadcasts of games and events in order to give the broadcast "breadth, depth, and color" and make it informative and entertaining.

The communications function also involves publishing programs, brochures, sales support materials, and manuals; working with special-interest groups to ensure the accuracy of information (e.g., Baseball Writers' Association); maintaining and regularly updating a Web site and the appropriate linkages; and answering mail and other inquiries from the general public. Although informing and communicating constitute only one of the functions essential to developing and managing an effective public relations program, organizations often allocate resources and energies almost exclusively to this function at the expense of a strategically sound holistic program. Figure 15.1 illustrates the variety of publics with which a collegiate sport information director or media relations director must correspond and interact.

SHAPE AND ENHANCE IMAGE

Image shaping and enhancement constitute a complex function through which the organization attempts to demonstrate to the public that its products are well made, that its services are first-rate and vital to the industry, and that the organization itself is a responsible citizen and contributor to the community. Corporations, institutions, teams, leagues, and individuals may engage in this function.

In a corporate context, McDonald's represents an excellent example of how to shape and enhance your image. McDonald's has long been a leader in this image-building, enhancement, and protection approach to business. McDonald's has advertised the value of its meals, the friendliness and warmth of its staff, and the idea of taking a "break" from routine by visiting its restaurants. However, McDonald's has complemented these advertising efforts with charitable activities that have

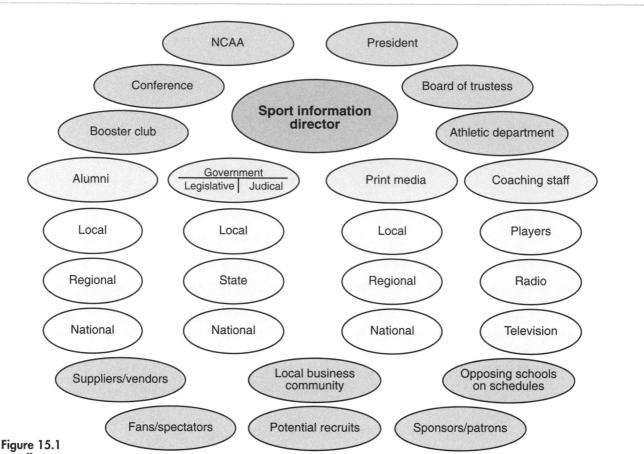

Figure 15.1
An effective sports information director works with a variety of publics.

enhanced the image of the corporation, portraying it as a vital member of the community. These efforts have been mostly local, taking such forms as donations to high schools to purchase band uniforms and involvement with local charities, particularly those sponsored by newspapers. Supporting a visible charity was not just an inexpensive form of advertising for the company; it was better, because it provided a visible association with an important element of community life.

For a drive-in restaurant chain looking to appeal to a family market and seeking respectability in an industry burdened with a questionable reputation, community involvement on the part of local operators produced the type of image boosting that McDonald's needed. This sponsorship of community programs became widespread, and it was logical that some type of national effort would evolve as the corporation grew. The Ronald McDonald House movement, long an integral part of NFL Charities' fiscal allocations, began in Philadelphia in 1974 and now includes over 100 houses nationwide. Located adjacent to children's hospitals, these houses provide free or low-cost room and board for families with children who require extended hospital care.[18]

Similar to the growth of McDonald's charity involvement and image building was the development and growth of NFL Charities, the official leaguewide charitable effort that disburses profits generated by NFL Properties. This endeavor began simply enough. At the time of the merger agreement (with the American Football League), NFL Properties was the league's independent marketing and promotional company; and as a condition of the agreement, all member teams were required to grant it control of NFL copyright privileges. The organization also printed all of the league's game programs and developed other self-liquidating premium items, which it worked out with advertisers and sponsors, that were designed to promote the league. This included the NFL's fledgling licensing program, which is now one of the largest in sport. At that time (around 1970), NFL Properties generated a relatively small income, and NFL Charities was designed to distribute those revenues. It was, one NFL executive commented, a good public relations gesture.[19]

While NFL Properties and its licensing and sponsorship agreements have been under attack recently by some owners (particularly Jerry Jones of the Dallas Cowboys), NFL Charities has established itself as an excellent image-enhancement tool for the NFL. This organization provides funds for community centers, minority scholarships, and educational assistance and also contributes to medical research and social service agencies.

Image shaping and enhancement make up a function closely associated with marketing, because public relations personnel work jointly with marketing personnel to introduce new programs, themes, campaigns, sales approaches, and promotional efforts. For example, the public relations staff might assist the marketing department in developing and implementing a new theme for season-ticket sales, a tennis tournament, or a campaign for a new stadium. Recently, the Continental Basketball Association signed filmmaker Spike Lee and his advertising agency (Spike DDB), according to Commissioner Gary Hunter, to "create a new look and give the league an edge."[20] The goal is for Lee to create a new logo, image, and theme for the league which has struggled to establish a clearly defined identity and position in the marketplace and is continually being challenged by other start-up basketball ventures.

Generating publicity about new programs or products, affiliating with "cause" programs or organizations, and reaching the public are essential public relations functions for sport organizations. For example, in 1997, the LPGA announced a partnership with the United States Golf Association (USGA) and the Girl Scouts of America in hopes of expanding its LPGA Junior Girls Golf Club. The goal of the program is to provide a network through which girls learn to play golf, build friendships, and sample competition in a fun and nonthreatening environment.[21] The partnership made it possible to promote and publicize this program through three organizations; additionally, it allowed the LPGA to associate with the values and traditions of the USGA and the Girl Scouts of America to attain its organizational and, in particular, its public relations and publicity goals.

Effective sport organizations such as the LPGA are able to integrate the marketing function (or other functions such as membership or development) with the public relations or media relations function to reach the target markets more effectively and efficiently.

PROMOTE EMPLOYEE RELATIONS

Most corporations recognize that an open flow between management and employees is essential. It is essential not only for purposes of morale, but also so that employees, who are often the public's first line of contact and communication with the organization, are capable of positive and favorable interaction. Because of the widespread public interest and involvement in sport, which has been documented by the *Miller Lite Report on American Attitudes Toward Sport*, the *Sports Illustrated Sports Poll '86*[22], and regular polling and measurement by services such as the ESPN/Chilton Sports Poll, all employees of a sport organization should understand management's position on a variety of issues and be able to convey this position to the public and especially the media. Players fall into this category of employees, and a number of universities and professional organizations provide formal training for these "player/employees" in the areas of public speaking and dealing with the media.

For "non-player/employees," organizations can use a number of effective vehicles to disseminate information from management to employees and vice versa. These include employee newsletters, brochures, and documents explaining organizational policies; an effective ongoing employee-orientation program; in-service training programs and seminars; and regularly scheduled staff meetings and special-topic luncheons that work like the "town meeting" in political election campaigns. Pat Williams, senior executive vice president of the Orlando Magic and a talented author and motivational speaker, is part of an Orlando Magic initiative called Magic University. This ongoing program is designed to educate and inform all employees with regard to the goals, objectives, and functioning of the Orlando Magic. According to Williams, "Sharing and openness erase barriers and distinctions within the team so that there is no perception of an inner circle or an outer circle. Nobody's in, nobody's out, everyone's together. If people feel that they are in the outer circle, that they are benchwarmers, they soon begin feeling expendable and powerless—and you lose valuable contributors to the team effort."[23] Lack of information can turn players into benchwarmers; thus the sport organization must ensure that everyone is informed and feeling part of the "team."

GAIN POLITICAL OR POPULAR SUPPORT

Clearly, a critical function of public relations is to educate as well as inform. Providing information is not necessarily the same as educating. Education, as defined in public relations, includes developing comprehension, understanding information, and applying information in the appropriate context. Publications such as the *IEG Sponsorship Report* and the *NCAA News* provide information on industry trends, educating their readerships on the implications of legislation and tax laws and promoting conferences and meetings that will increase understanding and promote growth.

Because of failure to understand, the 1990s have been a decade of "franchise free agency" in professional sport. For the most part, this movement of professional sport teams, which essentially began when the Brooklyn Dodgers left after the 1957 season to become the Los Angeles Dodgers[24], has been the product of consumer perception with regard to the value and costs of providing a "home" for a professional sport franchise. When we looked at consumers as voters we saw that some consumers felt that a sport franchise was a vital part of the community at any cost (Indianapolis, Nashville, and Baltimore), while others felt that it was not the community's responsibility to pay the costs (of stadiums, practice facilities, and revenue subsidies) (Baltimore, Houston, and Cleveland).

As the owners of the Pittsburgh Pirates and Pittsburgh Steelers learned, effective public relations efforts—both in the community and through the media—can be vital to ensuring that voters understand the consequences, advantages, and liabilities of the referendum or decision process. This educational process is not a short-term public relations campaign, but an ongoing public relations program. The following case study suggests the problems and difficulties faced by the Pittsburgh Pirates and Steelers, who failed to implement an effective educational public relations program in their community.

RECRUIT AND DEVELOP BUSINESS

Because of their need to continuously recruit new athletes, intercollegiate athletic programs—particularly high-profile Division IA programs—have provided some of the most fertile opportunities for public relations personnel to apply their skills. Public relations in this context essentially involves image construction (and reconstruction) and refinement. College life must be effectively portrayed to a variety of potential "recruits" who are looking to ensure that their visions of college, in terms of the educational and athletic experience, are compatible with the image of college presented during the recruiting visit. The function of public relations then is to ensure that questions are answered; that facilities are portrayed in their best light; that coaches and faculty are prepared to respond properly to questions and provide

Case Study

What Could Have Been—The Pittsburgh Stadium Tax

This case study exemplifies the lack of an effective proactive media relations/community relations. It also illustrates the powerful link between a media relations plan and public perception.

In 1996, the Pittsburgh Pirates and Pittsburgh Steelers, in conjunction with their local state legislative representatives, conceived a plan that would provide for two new stadiums and also provide dollars to 10 western Pennsylvania counties to construct roads; industrial parks; or recreational, tourist, or cultural attractions aimed at aiding economic development. The plan, called the Renaissance Initiative Act, would have increased the sales tax in those counties by 0.5 percent for a period of seven years and would generate $700 million. The bill provided that counties would keep 75 percent of the revenue raised in their counties, with 25 percent being earmarked for "regional attractions" such as the stadiums and convention center in Pittsburgh.[25]

Opponents of the tax plan nicknamed the initiative the "Stadium Tax"—a nickname that public relations efforts failed to counteract and one that identified a sore point for the voters. Criticism of the initiative was aimed at not only the stadiums—with citizens perceiving that tax dollars would be going to wealthy club owners—but also at the reality of the half-cent increase (it's only a half cent if you spend a dollar per year) and the possibility that the seven-year length of the tax could be extended.[26]

The "Stadium Tax" came under heavy fire in the counties surrounding Pittsburgh, where the focus was not on the 75 percent of revenues the county would retain but on the 25 percent viewed as "corporate welfare for downtown Pittsburgh." Critics also explained that the 75 percent of revenues would not be automatically returned to the counties; it would have to be applied for and might have to be matched with other funds, raising the possibility of additional tax hikes in the counties involved. One critic stated that new stadiums were not needed to stop the Pirates or Steelers from moving and that new stadiums would

not generate significant tourism, job growth, or economic development.[27]

United States Senator Rick Santorum recognized that the Renaissance Initiative was under heavy attack and urged the backers of the tax to speak out on the issues and controversies surrounding it. Santorum said that "Stadium Tax" was a misnomer, that in reality the tax was an economic development tax to rebuild and reenergize southwestern Pennsylvania. Further, according to Santorum, the media were at fault for publicizing the initiative as a stadium tax. Santorum was joined by Steve Greenberg of the Pirates, who said that a private-sector group composed of the Pirates, Steelers, Pittsburgh Cultural Trust, and the Pittsburgh Convention and Visitors Bureau was orchestrating a pro-tax publicity campaign.[28] Unfortunately, in addition to coming into play almost one year after introduction of the initial concept, this campaign appeared to be reactionary rather than proactive.

At the time when the new pro-tax group, the Community Alliance for Economic Development and Jobs, was introduced (less than two months before the referendum), polling indicated that the initiative trailed by about a 2 to 1 margin. Critics had launched a David Letterman parody called the "Top 10 Reasons to Vote NO on the Stadium Tax."[29] Both sides presented experts and consultants who proclaimed the benefits or decried the costs and lack of benefits associated with such a tax initiative. When experts criticized the stadium deals implemented in Denver (Coors Field) and Baltimore (replacing the Colts with the Browns, soon to be Ravens), Pirate owner Kevin McClatchy explained that a new stadium was vital to the Pirates. McClatchy promised $35 million toward the cost of the projected $200 million baseball park; he stated that the Pirates were the lowest-revenue team in all of baseball and that he needed a new stadium in order to put a consistently competitive team on the field. His partner in this stadium-related initiative, Steeler owner Dan Rooney, stated that every team in the division had built or was building a new stadium, and that to compete for players he needed luxury suites and additional stadium-related revenue. Rooney pledged $50 million toward a stadium cost of about $185 million.[30]

Critics including Peter Eisinger, a public policy professor specializing in stadium issues, countered with arguments regarding the proposed economic impact of a stadium. Eisinger explained that the majority of jobs created would be part-time and seasonal and would pay at a very low rate. He presented statistics showing that taxpayers in Denver had paid for the majority of Coors Field and that every new job created cost the taxpayers about $185,000. He closed his argument by stating what the opponents of the Renaissance Initiative (which they had successfully repositioned as the Stadium Tax) viewed as the bottom line: funding stadiums is subsidizing wealthy people.[31]

In the November referendum, the Renaissance Initiative or Stadium Tax, depending upon your view, failed to pass in any of the counties and was even voted down by a significant margin in Allegheny County, home of the Steelers and Pirates, which was perceived to be the county with the most to gain. There is no way of knowing, but a public relations campaign—one initiated at the inception of the idea and designed to educate the voters on the benefits and to explain the tax—might have led to a different result. Failure of the referendum led to Plan B: a public-private partnership that would fund the new stadium without involving the outlying counties or relying on a sales tax. Plan B was approved in January of 1999.

needed information; that the image presented is within conference and NCAA rules and regulations; that well-meaning alums and boosters comprehend what they can and cannot do; and that the recruit becomes aware of the entertainment, cultural, and growth opportunities as well as the educational benefits and athletic promises.

The public relations staff (media relations personnel, recruiting coordinator, institutional public relations officer) can accomplish all this by using a variety of media that we discuss in chapters 10, 11, 12, and 16. The primary medium is personal selling (chapter 11), which involves one-to-one discussions between the recruit and the recruiter that take place at the recruit's home and high school and later on the campus itself.

Prior to this visit to campus, and in many cases again during or after the visit, the recruit may receive a variety of brochures and printed material describing the college, the athletic program, and the opportunities available. This printed material is often augmented by video, CD-ROM, and other multimedia presentations designed to help the recruit "picture" the realities and also the possibilities. Since the mid-1970s, these multimedia presentations have sometimes taken a fantasy or "what if" approach and are often highly emotionally charged. For example, the recruit may sit in the fieldhouse or stadium and watch or listen to a scripted hypothetical broadcast of his or her future exploits and contributions at State University. Another approach is to use films depicting the tradition and stature of the university and its storied athletic program. These films usually feature famous alumni and past athletes endorsing the program and urging the recruit to make the right decision.

The term *recruiting*, not limited to intercollegiate athletics, can refer to any or all of the following:

> ➤ At the professional level, convincing draft choices and free agents to sign with a team, promoting the community, and offering various incentives in addition to the financial package. In a similar professional sport context, recruiting would entail describing the activities of agents seeking to enter into representation agreements with future and current professional athletes.

> ➤ The efforts by cities and sport commissions to attract professional franchises, amateur sporting events, and special events.
> ➤ The efforts of sport marketing agencies to secure sponsorship and corporate involvement for products, concepts, athletes, and events.

In terms of soliciting business opportunities, public relations programs help the organization attract corporate sponsorships by informing the potential corporate partner of the history and tradition of the product, event, or athlete and by helping to build a case to justify the pending financial agreement. One can determine what information is most influential by means of a little research. This may involve generating a basis of comparison with other teams by examining demographic factors or calculating numbers of impressions and the value of those impressions.

LAUNCH NEW PRODUCTS OR INNOVATIONS

If new products (or services) or product innovations are going to attract interest and gain market share, an effective public relations campaign is necessary to ensure that the people in the target market are aware of the product, understand the benefits of the product, and most importantly, understand why the product is important to them and how it can become part of their lifestyle. The public relations campaign to introduce and launch the WNBA is an excellent example.

According to marketing consultants Al Ries and Jack Trout, the easiest way to get into a person's mind is to be first, and if you can't be first you must find some way to position yourself against the product that did get there first.[32] The now defunct American Basketball League preceded the WNBA into women's professional basketball by one full season and signed significantly more "star" players than the WNBA did during that first year. The WNBA was not first, so why was it perceived to be the more successful of the two leagues and generally considered most likely to endure (a belief that proved to be correct.)? Simple. The NBA preceded the American Basketball League, and the WNBA was able to capitalize on the recognition and brand equity of the NBA to introduce itself and launch its marketing initiatives. The NBA brand provided an entree to television and print sources to publicize and promote the league, and owners and sponsors to help sell it. "Even before it had signed up all 80 players to do the passing and shooting, the WNBA brought in a host of ringers—three television networks (NBC, ESPN, and Lifetime) and a mighty roster of corporate sponsors, to do the selling. No other league in the history of American sport has made its debut with huge, glossy advertising spreads in *Glamour* and *Self* magazines." The goal of the launch? "Developing the players into household names" according to NBA marketing chief Rick Welts.[33]

The WNBA launch and ultimate success provide a case study in utilizing existing platforms (arenas, teams, owners, contracts [television], sponsorships, and broadcasts) to launch a new product; the case also illustrates how to use media and public relations to capture the imagination of the public even if you didn't introduce the product first.

This positioning can be effective in getting consumers to think about your products and services in a different way. Take, for instance, the case of a municipal parks and recreation department wishing to justify current levels of funding or perhaps to seek a budget increase. Some type of media and community relations program is essential, but what is the best approach? An open house? An annual report? Both might be effective, but the Needham (Massachusetts) Park and Recreation Department came up with a rather innovative way to create attention and stand out. The department created a campaign that featured the following information:

It costs $30,000 to incarcerate a juvenile offender for one year. If that money were available to the Park and Recreation Department, we could:

> *Train him to be an American Red Cross certified lifeguard in six weeks and*
> *Give him 36 weeks of archery lessons and*
> *Give him six weeks of lacrosse lessons and*
> *Give him 8 weeks of tennis lessons and*
> *Take him on two ski trips and*
> *Take him swimming every day for 11 weeks and*
> *Give him 8 weeks of skating lessons and*
> *Provide him with 22 weeks of after school activities and*
> *Let him play volleyball every week for 21 weeks and*
> *Let him learn the value of volunteering for a whole summer and*
> *Let him visit the Town Forest whenever he wanted, and*
> *Give him space to grow his own fruits and vegetables*

After which, we would return to you $28,582 and one exhausted, but much happier kid.[34]

GENERATE AND COLLECT FEEDBACK

Feedback is essential in the strategic planning process and critical to determining the acceptance and effectiveness of organizational policies and procedures. Public relations personnel play an integral role in monitoring the pulse of the public with regard to their interest in and acceptance and rejection of organizational products, concepts, and practices. Public relations people gather data on public attitudes, economic indicators, consumer preferences and behavior, and political and societal events in which the organization functions. Feedback may be generated by request (survey, poll, etc.) or simply as a result of past action or inaction, without an official request (unsolicited and uninitiated letters, phone calls, etc.).

For example, consider developments with regard to the NCAA. In recent years, the NCAA has solicited feedback on recruitment, retention, academic performance, and graduation rate of athletes; on issues relating to Title IX and gender equity; and on a variety of other issues. For the most part, the NCAA has used this feedback to monitor progress and assess public perception, and in some cases to initiate reforms or modify regulations. While the majority of feedback has been positive, there have also been negative feedback and criticism. As a result, the NCAA began to alter the structure of intercollegiate athletics. The most notable changes have included the formation of a presidents' council and a shift of power to these presidents; higher standards for student athletes' academic performance; fewer scholarships; increased opportunities for women (see photo); fewer coaches (full- and part-time) in particular sports; a football national championship; equipment redesign (baseball); and the right of student athletes to be employed during the academic year. Some of the changes have elicited a positive response, some have aroused criticism, and still others have resulted in litigation. Although some of this feedback was solicited, a portion was generated as a result of a lack of attentiveness and control in practices within the system. When the outcry and interest became great enough, the feedback, both solicited and unsolicited, spurred reform.

COPE WITH CRISIS

One of the most visible roles that a public relations professional performs is coping with crisis. Because the majority of these cases elicit media interest, the words and actions of the public relations department and its professionals are often in the news and engender as much interest as the incident that precipitated the crisis. The annals of sport are rife with the results of both crisis and "spin"—attempts to change the way people are interpreting the actions and words of the principals involved in the crisis. The following are some notable examples:

➤ *Reebok International Limited and the resultant furor in 1997 surrounding a women's running shoe named the Incubus.* In doing its due diligence, the marketing team concentrated on a name that did not exist in the marketplace and did not infringe on any existing trademarks. Thus the shoe was named Incubus, which according to the dictionary is an "evil spirit that has sexual intercourse with women while they are sleeping." Damage control became essential for obvious reasons, and also because the mistake was large enough to merit coverage on the front page of the *Boston Globe* as well as mention in *USA Today* and numerous newspapers throughout the country. Reebok Vice President of Public Relations Dave Fogelson acknowledged that a mistake had been made and that steps had been implemented to ensure that such a gaffe didn't happen again.[35]

There is an ever-increasing variety of athletics available for women at the college level.

➤ *In 1995, remarks about women golfers by CBS golf commentator Ben Wright at the McDonald's LPGA Championship.* Wright commented that "lesbians in the sport hurt women's golf" and that "women golfers are handicapped by having breasts because their boobs get in the way of their swing."[36] Not only the quotes, but also attempts by Wright and others to attack the credibility and integrity of the reporter, Valerie Helmbreck, kept this story in the news for an extended period of time; ultimately, Wright, admitting that he had made the remarks, received a suspension and underwent counseling. The Wright incident was even more infamous because it was not the first time that callous and flip opinions and remarks had damaged a segment of society and also hurt the reputations and careers of notable sport personages, like Al Campanis and Jimmy "the Greek" Snyder.

➤ *The 1997 sex scandals in Canadian hockey.* The scandals involved a noted junior hockey league coach, Graham James, as well as separate incidents pertaining to workers at Toronto's Maple Leaf Gardens in which young men were promised tickets and autographs in exchange for participation in group sex. These scandals served to tarnish the image of Canada's beloved national sport.

➤ *The NFL's New England Patriots and their drafting and termination of Christian Peter.* Peter, who had a checkered past at the University of Nebraska (with eight arrests for charges ranging from trespassing and disturbing the peace to third-degree sexual assault), was drafted by the Patriots in the fifth round of the 1996 NFL draft. After criticism in the media and through phone calls from fans protesting his presence on the Patriots' roster, Peter was dumped by the Patriots, who claimed that they had not investigated his background thoroughly—a contention that Peter disputed.[37]

Situations such as these have caused certain organizations to demonstrate that they can be proactive by implementing procedures to be followed in the event of a crisis. The NFL has developed an internal 10-point crisis-control plan for addressing volatile situations. As presented and discussed on ESPN's "Outside the Lines," components of the plan included the following:

> ➤ "First response should be 'no comment.'"
> ➤ "Convene an immediate meeting of the crisis team."
> ➤ "Formulate a statement that can be distributed to the media."
> ➤ "Develop talking points and send them to allies who will be speaking to the media."[38]

MEDIA IMPACT ON SPORT PUBLIC RELATIONS

The media's impact on the daily lives of people throughout the world cannot be underestimated. The death and funeral of Princess Diana, the Clinton-Lewinsky "Interngate" fiasco, and terrorist activities such as the Oklahoma City bombing illustrated the "magnifying glass" that media coverage can become. Daily, if not hourly, the media were providing not only coverage of the events taking place, but also global reaction and interpretation of those events.

Sport is not immune to this magnifying-glass effect, as we can see in the coverage of the 1998 pursuit of the baseball one-season home run record by Mark McGwire and Sammy Sosa. In fact, because of our levels of interest and involvement, sport has become one of the most interesting specimens for examination by the media. The late James Michener stated that "sport, and in particular baseball (during its professional infancy), prospered, because it received, at no cost, reams of publicity in daily and Sunday papers."[39] Michener explained that this coverage, which any other business would have had to pay for, was given freely because of its entertainment value and because a newspaper that contained information about sport would sell more copies, creating both higher circulation and higher advertising rates. In his classic *Sportsworld: An American Dreamland*, Robert Lipsyte echoed this sentiment: "Without the aid and abetment of sportswriters, Judge Kenesaw Mountain Landis would never have been able to revirginize baseball after the 1919 Black Sox scandal, Tex Rickard would never have been able to introduce the million-dollar boxing gate, and college football would never have been able to grow into America's grandest monument to hypocrisy."[40]

In addition to the contribution of the print media to the growth of sport, the electronic media—initially radio, later television, and now the Internet—have also publicized sports heavily, particularly golf and football, and created the mechanism responsible for their popularity today.

Three factors, namely the publication of Jim Bouton's *Ball Four*[41], the creation and success of Monday Night Football, and the founding and emergence of ESPN, changed the way sports were presented and accepted in American households, subsequently altering the role of public relations in sport from reactive to proactive. In other words, whereas the role had once been to maintain a protected image, free from the restraints and constraints of society, the new aim was to create an image of sport as a segment of American life, "mirroring" the larger context in which it operates. This image, reflecting all that is good and bad in society, placed sport in the "daily mix" of our lives—off the pedestal it had previously occupied. Public relations personnel were quick to capitalize on this new image, and community relations personnel began to plan how to rebuild and reshape it.

ATHLETES GET REAL

For decades, the press (as an unofficial public relations area of sport), as well as public relations directors of sport teams or organizations, had taken great pains to

Jim Bouton, author of *Ball Four*, was a catalyst in helping the media view athletes not only in terms of their on-field accomplishments but also in terms of their human nature.

ensure that the only sport stories were about athletes' on-field performances, or about athletes visiting children in hospitals and otherwise functioning as ideal role models and pillars of the community. With *Ball Four* (followed by *I'm Glad You Didn't Take It Personally*—the satirical title referred to the reaction to *Ball Four*), Bouton changed the face of sport reporting in terms of the scope of material covered and the way it would be covered. This change in sport reporting directly changed the role of public relations in sport.

After the publication of *Ball Four* in 1970, sport and its collective heroes were "set on their collective ear." Bouton had shown that many activities and behaviors that are part of the lives of ordinary people are an integral part of the lives of professional athletes as well. In other words, he explained that "role models" and superstars were, for the most part, like everyone else and that they had the same likes, dislikes, problems, and dreams. Interestingly enough, one person Bouton discussed in his book was the late Mickey Mantle, his contemporary and teammate. Bouton wrote about Mantle's "problem" with alcohol—a subject that was responsible for much of the negative reaction to the book. Before his death, and more than 25 years after the publication of Bouton's book, Mantle acknowledged his "problem," became a spokesperson for organ donations, and in a sense justified and recaptured his identity and value as a role model—because of his humanity and personal situation, apart from his baseball immortality.

Ball Four was the first book to deal with the off-field exploits of athletes; if Bouton set out to illustrate that sport is truly a microcosm of society, he could not have selected better subject material. But as the mystery and glamour were removed from our sport heroes and some of the luster was dulled, public perception of sport was altered. We were no longer interested solely in box scores and heroic exploits; we were also interested in the problems and pitfalls encountered along the way. We wanted, perhaps needed, to know the behind-the-scenes stories about Mike Tyson, Tonya Harding, the Dallas Cowboys, Lawrence Phillips, babies fathered out of wedlock by NBA superstars, Bob Davie and Notre Dame football, Frank Gifford's marriage to Kathie Lee, and so forth. Sport organizations now had to determine how much of this new information, in the best interests of the sport (including financial interests), they could present to the public and how they should present it. This is among the many problems that the public relations professional has had to face in the continuing "glass house" that sport has become.

FOCUS ON ENTERTAINMENT

The positioning of ABC's "Monday Night Football," now about to enter its third decade—as not just sport but as entertainment—marked a change in the public perception regarding sport that greatly aided the work of public relations professionals. These professionals no longer treated sport as though it existed in a cathedral, but could use techniques common in business and the entertainment industry to promote and publicize sport. Bill Gunther and Marc Carter chronicled the development of Monday Night Football through the vision of its executive producer, Roone Arledge, and his belief that "Monday Night Football would be as much entertainment as football. It would be a spectacle that people would watch whether or not they cared about the game, and would appeal to women as well as men."[42] Monday Night Football and future sport television such as ESPN's SportsCenter would provide intriguing opportunities for the public to see athletes in a variety of roles from performer to entertainer to spokesperson to humanitarian.

The two-decade-plus history of ESPN as the ultimate sport broadcasting network began in 1978. The success of ESPN (the first station to broadcast 24 hours a day, seven days a week, 365 days a year), besides giving birth to ESPN 2 ("the deuce") and ESPNews, has given rise to FOX Sportsnet, a satellite of regional sport networks located throughout the country, and several similar ventures. In addition to live programming, ESPN has initiated a series of programs called "Outside the Lines" that probe issues in sport such as homosexuality, gambling, and violence. These and similar issues and related situations may attract positive or negative attention, requiring a reactive response on the part of public relations or perhaps proactive planning to alleviate adverse effects. In addition to "Outside the Lines," ESPN offers a program called "Up Close" that presents interviews with players and leaders in sport. In terms of public relations, "Up Close," in a one-on-one format, gives the public an opportunity to learn more about the sport figure in a pleasant, conversational format.

The kind of information covered on ESPN sometimes necessitates a great deal of attention from public relations professionals. For instance, in "Outside the Lines: Sports Under Arrest" on September 2, 1997, ESPN examined athletes in trouble with the law. In his introduction, ESPN's Bob Ley said, "You can point to all the money, all the media or simply society, but there has never been such a time when so much of the sports news is right here in a court of law."

In a segment on managing a sport crisis, Ley explained how teams, leagues, agents, and corporate sponsors plan for and respond to arrests of players. After 76er Allen Iverson's recent arrest on weapons and marijuana charges, the response of his sponsor, Reebok, was quick and positive. Reebok Director of Public Relations Dave Fogelson stated, "Our first reaction is certainly going to be that we're going to support the athlete. And this is not a knee jerk reaction. . . . In the short term if there's some negativity, that's for the short term." Ley, who also interviewed executives at Advantage International, noted that crisis management by a player's agent is perhaps most critical immediately after an incident. According to Advantage International Senior Vice President Tom George, "They're looking for us to make things right. That's part of our job—to make those things go away so that they can concentrate on what they do best." Ley reported that in the wake of Warren Moon's arrest two years ago for domestic violence (Moon was later acquitted), Moon and his agents took the public relations offensive by holding two press conferences.[43]

Our interest in athletes has shifted because sport fills an entertainment role in our culture. On television, in particular on "Monday Night Football" and ESPN's SportsCenter, the entertainment has to be first-rate because it airs in and around prime time, affects network ratings, and influences advertising revenues. Howard Cosell and Chris Berman became premier sport broadcasters and personalities because they, like Bouton, shared information that was more than play-by-play or game summary, offering the information regardless of the consequences.

STRATEGIC PLANNING AND PUBLIC RELATIONS

"Strategic planning is a philosophy of management based on identifying purpose, objectives, and desired results, establishing a realistic program for obtaining these results, and evaluating the performance."[44] Too often, public relations personnel are not in the planning loop, and their role has been to react to the plan and create vehicles to support the objectives that others have identified for them. In truth, public relations personnel should help create the corporate mission and objectives. As discussed earlier in this chapter, publics and their individual and collective relationships dictate how successful an organization or corporation will be. A key function of public relations departments is to monitor, understand, and develop communication platforms with these publics. Establishing and maintaining this communication system is integral to defining objectives and projecting outcomes. For example, in the public relations office of a professional sport franchise or athletic department, community relations is an integral function. Such community relations efforts (as we have previously discussed) usually encompass the following functions:

> Speaker's bureau

> Clinics and player appearances

> Mascot, cheerleaders, and band appearances

> Correspondence (e.g., fan mail, photo requests)

By implementing and maintaining these functions, the public relations department can monitor the "pulse" of the community with regard to the organization. Monitoring provides significant feedback relating to program element performance, budgetary needs, selection of programs to be renewed, redefined, or terminated, and so forth. The public relations department should use this information in strategic planning as it formulates its short- and long-term objectives. This should result in a more focused and targeted strategic plan that serves the constituency adequately and that can play a key role in developing long-term relationships and growth.

INTEGRATING SALES, PROMOTION, SPONSORSHIP MEDIA, AND COMMUNITY RELATIONS

The former International Hockey League Denver Grizzlies (now the Salt Lake City Grizzlies) give us an excellent example of successful integration of the concepts discussed in this chapter. The Grizzlies set out to create a community relations program with multiple interrelated goals:

> To generate high awareness, visibility, and publicity for the Grizzlies in the community

> To generate goodwill and positive feelings about the Grizzlies throughout the community

> To develop new programs and support existing programs that encourage youth participation in hockey (ice and street)

> To identify quality organizations and provide them with Grizzlies tickets

Special features such as marching bands are an essential part of any athletic department's public relations efforts.

To accomplish these goals, the Grizzlies created a variety of activities and approaches that not only complemented each other but were fully integrated in order to capitalize on existing resources and generate income to pay for the programming. These activities and approaches included:

> *The Grizzlies Speaker's Bureau.* Bureau representatives speak once the group has contracted to purchase a group outing at a Grizzlies game. All honorariums and speakers' fees (if any) were payable to the Grizzlies Youth Foundation and used to purchase tickets for the Plus/Plus Club.

> *The Plus/Plus Club.* The name of the club was based on the idea that it was a win-win proposition. The Plus/Plus Club was an umbrella program that provided an opportunity for economically disadvantaged youth or at-risk youth to attend Grizzlies games. Tickets were complimentary but were funded by donations to the Grizzlies Youth Foundation or provided via corporate sponsors, player charitable

The presence of mascots at games entertain children and adults alike, connecting the average fan with the team in a tangible way—an effective community relations tool.

efforts, and donations of unused tickets by Grizzlies ticket holders. The organization hoped the program was building fans for the future.

➤ *Preseason Caravan.* Before training camp began, the Grizzlies hosted a preseason caravan consisting of players, coaches, and announcers. The caravan made stops at all the major towns and cities in the Grizzlies' market area (Colorado, Wyoming, and New Mexico). Clinics, shopping mall appearances, on-air interviews, and civic club appearances were integral because of the opportunity to sell tickets and merchandise as well as to maintain interest for radio and television broadcasts.

➤ *The School Assembly Program. Hockey is a great lesson for life.* This was a program of 50-minute presentations via school assemblies at area schools for children in kindergarten through fifth grade. Presentations included player and mascot appearances, skills demonstrations, video highlights, sponsor-provided gifts, and coupons for two youth tickets for that school district's night. Parents could buy tickets, and all tickets were upgradable (the upgrades alone paid for the cost of this program). Sponsors could, as part of their contracts and fees, provide free product to be distributed at the assemblies. Figure 15.2 illustrates the relationships that can be utilized in conducting this program.

➤ *"Bear Foot in the Park." Street Hockey and Roller Hockey Leagues.* A cooperative effort among the City of Denver Parks and Recreation Department, the YMCA of Denver, the Grizzlies, and their sponsors, this program was designed to increase interest in the sport of hockey and build long-term fans through these grassroots efforts.

➤ *Charitable Involvement.* The Grizzlies selected three youth-related local organizations for charitable involvement: Children's Hospital, the Make-A-Wish Foundation, and the YMCA of Denver. Although there were no cash contributions, the Grizzlies were active in serving on boards and committees; assisting in their respective fund-raising efforts; providing memorabilia items and donated tickets for the charity to use in its own fund-raising efforts; and targeting of one special event (season Face-off Luncheon, annual golf tourney, and annual awards banquet) to generate funds for each charity.

Figure 15.2
An example of a community outreach program.

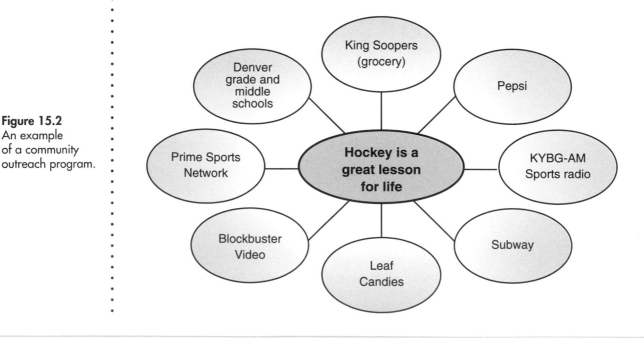

WRAP-UP

In order for public relations to be effective, the public relations specialist must not only react and respond to requests and situations, but must also actively initiate and develop media relations and community relations efforts in an integrated, proactive methodology. This methodology should focus on both short- and long-term objectives with attention to building and fostering relationships. These activities, and the public relations functions in general, must play an integral role in both the strategic planning process for the organization and the implementation and management of the strategic plan.

Public relations programs fulfill a variety of roles, including image shaping and enhancement, educational efforts, business development, recruiting, coping with crisis, and community relations. Community relations efforts can take many forms; they can be initiated by players, can be related to teams or institutions, and can be initiated by leagues or governing bodies. These programs must have reasonable organizational resources or receive corporate or philanthropic support to ensure their longevity and the credibility of the sponsoring organization.

In the sport setting, players have an integral role in the success of such programs, as they can attract media interest and coverage, corporate or philanthropic support, and participants and beneficiaries.

Finally, as media are their own muse, they may be influenced but are never controlled by the public relations department. Thus public relations professionals must build relationships with the various publics related to their particular sport industry segment. Again, these publics are best served if the public relations program is not only reactive, but also proactive and integrated.

ACTIVITIES

1. Set up an informational interview and visit the sport information/media relations entity on your campus. During your interview, discuss the concepts of reactive, proactive, and integrated media relations and identify an example of each function in that setting.

2. Begin a journal that you will keep for 30 days. The focus of the journal is to identify crises in sport (drugs, gambling, moral issues, and so on) that have required public relations efforts. Are there issues that seem to come up more frequently than others? Are there organizations that seem to be more adept than others at dealing with a crisis?

3. In reading sport-related periodicals (e.g., *USA Today, ESPN: The Magazine, Sports Illustrated, Sporting News*), identify controversial incidents or issues in which a "spin" factor is present. Identify the strengths and weaknesses of each argument.

4. Among the roles of a public relations professional in sport, what role and functions are the most common (present almost every day)? Which activities are only occasional?

5. Assume that you are a community relations director for the WNBA's Phoenix Mercury. Identify the various publics with whom you should communicate on a regular basis.

YOUR MARKETING PLAN

In any market plan (even those developed primarily for an internal audience), public relations is a critical function. Effective public relations can garner support for your concepts. A solid media relations component can ensure awareness and comprehension of your ideas and intent, while attention to community relations may generate acceptance of your ideas and programs. Review your marketing plan to determine how each of these elements should be addressed to achieve acceptance and support of your objectives either internally, externally, or both.

COORDINATING AND CONTROLLING THE MARKETING MIX

OBJECTIVES

1. To be able to compare and contrast the interaction and impact of the five Ps upon one another.

2. To understand how organizational structure, job descriptions, and staff training affect organizational control of the marketing function.

3. To understand the need for control in achieving marketing effectiveness and to recognize some standard benchmarks of marketing performance in sport.

Beer Promos Brew Trouble for Colleges

In 1997, the California State-Fresno men's basketball team had a standard pregame entry from their locker room to the court and the thundering applause of their ardent fans. They came through an inflated silver tunnel, provided by a local sponsor for free. You can imagine the scene—it happens all over the country, at all levels. The crowd is whipped into a frenzy of anticipation by an announcer until the home team makes its triumphant entrance though the tunnel, accompanied by smoke, lasers, and loud rock music. The same Fresno sponsor helped juice up the crowd by providing small, parachuted objects that fans could toss at a target for prizes. Neither was an unusual promotional gimmick; all elements were standard for today's carefully staged sport entertainment events.

There was, however, one major difference. The sponsor was a local Coors Light distributor. With the Coors name and the Coors colors, it was easy for most fans to perceive the tunnel as a giant beer can. What an image: a collegiate team projected out of a giant beer can for every home game! That is not what Fresno had had in mind. The beer promotion ran headlong against a rising awareness of alcohol abuse on the nation's campuses. A Harvard University survey had just found that 44 percent of responding college students had engaged in binge drinking in the two weeks prior to the survey. A Fresno administrator, John Zelezny, said the tunnel was not designed to look like a beer can, but in the face of withering criticism concluded, "If that was how people were perceiving it, then that was not appropriate." Fresno pulled the tunnel and stepped back to assess its engagement with the promotion of alcoholic beverages. "We need to find the line for our university," said Zelezny, "and decide what is acceptable and what is not."[1]

Beer promotions raise issues for college teams, while professional teams enjoy greater freedom.

Fresno State felt a backlash from an unanticipated and negative *cross-impact* of promotion and public relations. The potential synergies between and among the five Ps of sport marketing require constant evaluation. In this case, Fresno had a promotion that worked for the sponsor and, at one level anyway, worked for the fans. But the impact on public relations was clearly negative, largely because Fresno was an educational institution. The San Jose Sharks might never feel such pressure against a beer promotion because professional sport—rightly or wrongly—has been so historically entwined with beer sales that the public expects such promotions. Not so at the college level. To Fresno's credit, the university recognized the problem and stepped back to analyze its policies and its marketing.

In this chapter, we examine the range of cross-impacts among the five Ps—the sport marketing mix. We also consider some principles necessary for effective control of these elements and their related functions in the sport organization. As we noted in chapter 2, the marketing strategy, with its integration of product, price, place, promotion, and public relations, must be managed so as to move the organization toward its overall objectives.

CROSS-IMPACTS AMONG THE FIVE PS

Each element of the marketing mix has been treated thus far in somewhat isolated fashion, yet it is clear that these elements have a simultaneous cross-impact on the consumer. A potential buyer of a sport product does not view the price of a product in isolation from the promotional mix, the place function, or the nature of the product and product extensions. This impact can be assessed using a cross-impact matrix (see figure 16.1).

The figure summarizes the degree to which each element interacts with the others. In this section, we provide a more complete assessment of these interactions.

THE IMPACT OF PRODUCT AND PRICE

The impact of product and price is more truly the impact of price on product. Price, as we have discussed previously, is the most visible and most readily communicable variable of the marketing mix. The pervasive influence of price and its conveyance of perceived quality and value directly affect the product image. More often than not, consumers are balancing product and price in their minds as they consider purchasing a sport product. For instance, in spring 1998, the ESPN/Chilton poll surveyed 800 people who had purchased logoed sport merchandise within the past three months. The results (see tables 16.1 and 16.2), broken down by age groups, suggest that consumers under age 25 view product quality (in this case brand name) as slightly more important, while consumers 25-44 view price as slightly more important.

Consumers often view low-priced products as of low quality and high-priced products as high-quality/prestigious products. Price-product strategies based on such perceptions are dependent upon supply, demand, and market elasticity. They can also be tricky business. Nike was burned badly in 1997 when it misread the market for its new Tiger Woods line of apparel. The style and the supporting ads had Nike's usual hard edge, "in-your-face," antiestablishment look and feel. As *Sports Illustrated* reported, however, such products did not appeal to the core of golf's consumers. They appealed to kids, who could not afford the $75 shirts or the $225 shoes.

	Product	Price	Place	Promotion	Public relations
Product		Price = value	Images interact	Product position	Consumer receptivity
Price			Images interact	Choice of media	Sincerity of public relations
Place				Images interact	Images interact
Promotion					Completely interdependent
Public relations					

Figure 16.1 Cross-impact matrix for the five Ps of sport marketing.

Table 16.1 RESULTS OF ESPN/CHILTON POLL ASKING "HOW IMPORTANT IS BRAND NAME ON THE ITEM WHEN PURCHASING SPORTS LOGO CLOTHING?"

Importance	Age 12–17	18–24	25–34	35–44
Nat at all/Not so important	19.4%	25%	36.%	29.9%
Somewhat/Very important	80.5%	75%	63.9%	70.1%

Source: "ESPN CHILTON: are purchasing decisions based on brand?" *SBD*, 7/24/98:16.

Table 16.2 RESULTS OF ESPN/CHILTON POLL ASKING "HOW IMPORTANT IS THE PRICE OF THE ITEM WHEN PURCHASING SPORTS LOGO CLOTHING?"

Importance	Age 12–17	18–24	25–34	35–44
Nat at all/Not so important	17.3%	24.4%	16.3%	12%
Somewhat/Very important	82.7%	75.6%	83.8%	88%

Source: "ESPN CHILTON: are purchasing decisions based on brand?" *SBD*, 7/24/98:16.

Said one Oregon golf shop operator: "Young kids like it, but young kids don't have the money to buy it." Or as another golf executive put it, "Nike tries to use the different-is-cool theme that works well in sports. But in golf that formula doesn't work." Parents might part with $120 for a pair of Air Jordans, but a golf shirt or golf shoes?[2]

Marketers of women's athletics have faced the related conundrum of increasing the cost of their products at the same time that they seek increased attendance. They have hoped that fans perceive higher value in higher prices. For instance, in the late 1980s, as women's basketball began to draw a larger fan base, the Ohio State women's program recognized the need to charge admission to a "free" event but knew that the move would be a gamble. Their answer was to develop a promotion with local Big Bear supermarkets that focused on key games. Television, radio, and newspaper ads detailed the availability of coupons with any Big Bear purchase—coupons were redeemable, with a dollar, for a ticket with a face value of $2 or $3. This created a sense of value for the product and helped raise the team's average attendance by 1500.[3]

THE IMPACT OF PRODUCT AND PLACE

Consumers develop a product image based upon their perceptions of the product's attributes. Similarly, sport consumers develop perceptions of the place in which an event occurs, namely a facility image. These two images are interactive. When the New York Stars of the Women's Professional Basketball League (WBL) played their home games in the Iona College gymnasium in White Plains, New York, the image of playing in the gym of a small, remote college hurt the image of the product. It was almost impossible for the Stars to convince fans that their sport was big time when it was played in a minor facility. A move to Madison Square Garden helped; however, the increased overhead could not be borne by the severely underfinanced team. The Stars, who had been champions in 1980, folded, and a year later, so did the WBL. Consumers are convinced of one thing in sport: big-league products demand big-league places—a sentiment played out again in the WNBA's more recent "victory" over the American Basketball League. As we noted in chapters 7 and 13, the sport venue is part and parcel of the product. That immutable law helps drive the move to "techtainment" venues and sports malls with multiple screens and speakers and games that assault all senses simultaneously.

The smartest marketers, however, recognize that sport consumers seek multiple places for their product consumption. Michael Eisner recently described Disney's strategy as "operating on two tracks . . . yin and yang, the paradoxical pull of the opposites." "We're convinced," he said, "that people will seek more diverse entertainment in their homes, but also that they'll take advantage of familiar outdoor gathering spots and seek out new ones." In retrospect, Eisner's plan is clear—the careful placing of Disney's branded products in multiple strategic locations. Take ESPN. The ESPN consumer can stay home to watch SportsCenter, read ESPN's magazine, or surf through ESPN.com. When she tires of home, she can travel to the nearcst ESPN Zone restaurant to mingle with like-minded ESPNies, trading "Boomer" Berman imitations with a well-schooled waitstaff.[4]

THE IMPACT OF PRODUCT AND PROMOTION

Products define appropriate formats and media for promotions. For instance, Nike is unlikely to promote its Tiger Woods line via classified ads in the local paper; that is not the place to advertise high-priced golf apparel. Full-color ads in a golf magazine would make more sense. Similarly, the promotional mix defines the product position. As we saw earlier, Nike appeared to miss the mark in its first attempt to position the Woods line. The ad campaign influenced consumers who were not in a position to buy the product. We can see a more successful blend of promotion and position in the Utah Jazz's efforts to attract families. In February 1994, the Jazz ran a promotion with Continental Baking Co., the makers of Hostess Sno Balls. Continental distributed special packages of Sno Balls throughout the Jazz's market, in purple and green "Jazz" colors, complete with a special wraparound label that offered a family discount package for any of five designated games. What better way to project a product of family entertainment than through the family's favorite snack food?[5]

THE IMPACT OF PRODUCT AND PUBLIC RELATIONS

Public relations, a special part of promotions in sport, has an obvious effect on product image and position. But to a much greater extent than promotional efforts such as advertising, which the marketer controls, public relations efforts rely on the goodwill of the media. This is tricky business. While marketers hope to cultivate the media, they cannot expect a reporter to become a shill. When franchises exercise contractual rights to fire radio or television announcers they handpicked, the press and the public are usually outraged. Consumers expect spin control, but they have a sense of limits.

At a national level, leagues and corporations play the game with greater stakes on the table. For instance, Nike earned a well-deserved reputation in the late 1980s and early 1990s for its innovative advertisements and promotions, which created such high brand equity that most people didn't need a name to know what a "swoosh" stood for. But the very same aggressive, cocksure, antiestablishment image may have fueled a backlash in public relations. As Nike became the 500-pound gorilla of sport, the media focused on troubling aspects of Nike's labor practices in the Asian factories where its products were made. No matter what data Nike offered about the relative value of its wage scale, no matter how many celebrities returned satisfied from inspection tours, Nike could not seem to win on its own turf of media images. To make matters worse, in 1997, Nike was further burned by distribution of a new "Nike Air" model that outraged Muslims, who saw a resemblance between the flame-shaped image on the shoe and the Arabic word for Allah.[6]

If it is difficult to prevent public relations gaffes in developing athletic shoes, it is nearly impossible to develop a foolproof player who conforms to a sport's chosen image both in the venue and out. For most consumers, players *are* the game. When they misbehave in their personal lives, the whole product suffers. The NBA has walked a fine line on this since it carefully mapped its 1980s and '90s rejuvenation on the backs of star players. The plan worked, but the question for the next decade is, who will replace Michael? And despite taking a hard line in the bitter lockout of the 1998-1999 season, the NBA—and indeed, all its counterparts—must still convince fans that professional players are more than overpaid, ego-driven, undisciplined brats who will choke any coach who dresses them down. Even before the Latrell Sprewell incident, David Stern admitted that "we have to consider, in an honest way, what impact we have on society. We have to let our players know that we like their contributions but also that they have to behave themselves on and off the court." Amid the seamless components of the sport product, including players, venues, equipment, apparel, rules, and so on, any little action may have massive implications for public relations. As we outlined in chapter 15, a "crisis" plan is critical for handling the fires that continually erupt.[7]

THE IMPACT OF PRICE AND PLACE

There are two major impacts of price and place. First, sport consumers expect to pay higher prices for better facilities. Witness the growth in racquetball and fitness clubs in the 1970s. The YMCAs and YWCAs had offered such programs for years, yet the newer clubs with their sleek decor and sophisticated facilities charged higher prices and still captured the bigger share of the market. During the 1980s, Ys responded by building upscale facilities to capture the "yuppie" market; the

During the 1980s, YMCAs and YWCAs built new facilities that fostered an upscale image in order to appeal to the "yuppie" demographic.

private clubs then attacked the tax-exempt status of the Ys. The controversy focused on the interaction of price and place, because both sides recognized that in sophisticated markets the consumer will pay a higher price for a more prestigious facility. The same principle applies to spectators who line up to pay higher prices for the benefits of club seats, personal or permanent seat licenses, and skyboxes. The converse is also true, as the Boston Bruins discovered when their overpriced "upper-bowl" seats did not sell. Lower prices were a prerequisite to ticket sales in those remote locations.[8]

Another place-price principle is that consumers pay more for convenience (which is a benefit). Most people expect to pay a surcharge for tickets they purchase at a Ticketmaster outlet or a kiosk in a mall. They save time (another important benefit) if they don't have to drive to a central box office, and for the most part accept the additional convenience fee. Similarly, consumers have traditionally paid more for sporting goods that they purchase at local sporting goods stores. Although the larger discount houses may stock the same product, the local store's convenience (and often more personal service) often compensates for the additional cost. In summary, sport consumers will pay more to view a sport in a more attractive or convenient location, to play a sport at a more attractive (or more challenging, as in golf) facility, or to purchase sporting goods in a local store. The concept of place includes manifold benefits (or costs) that influence the consumer's perception of a fair price.

THE IMPACT OF PRICE AND PROMOTION

In the majority of cases, the price of a product dictates the media for advertising the product, for several reasons. First, the price determines the profit margin on the product, hence the promotional budget and in turn the media choice. Second, the price of a product reflects not only its nature and cost, but also the market to which the product is targeted. In both cost-plus and market-based pricing, the pricel reflects the target market's demographics and its media choices. Even a casual look at newspapers or television reveals this pattern. While the maker of a new, "foolproof" fishing lure might run a 30-second spot during a cable television fishing show (whose viewers match the product's target audience), a large chain like MVP Sports will prefer a multipage, multicolor insert for regional newspapers whose readers cross a wide range of demographics.

The last example suggests that size and scope influence price and promotion. With so much consolidation in ownership of "big-time" sports, we can expect to see interesting twists in strategies addressing price and promotion. For instance, in early 1998, the Texas Rangers (MLB) and the Dallas Stars (NHL), both owned by Tom Hicks, offered a special ticket package of 13 Rangers games and 6 Stars games, with play-off option guarantees for both teams. In the first hour and a half, 100 combo plans were sold, and after one week, 200 had been sold. What if Disney began a superticket promo that offered, for one price, access to a certain number of Ducks and Angels games, visits to Disneyland and Disney World, and dinner at an ESPN restaurant? Would Fox and Time Warner counter with their own "superticket" promo?[9]

THE IMPACT OF PRICE AND PUBLIC RELATIONS

Any superticket is promoted on the basis of value. Sport consumers keep value front and center when they make purchase decisions. In that respect, pricing strategies can have a strong effect on public relations, for better or worse. College and university athletics programs learned this lesson, sometimes the hard way, as they moved in the 1980s to required "donations" for the right to buy football or basketball tickets in preferred locations. This was the forerunner of the personal or permanent seat license, and some schools didn't handle things well. In 1987, Alabama could not keep ahead of a maelstrom of criticism as word spread about a surcharge. One administrator admitted, in words that have since echoed across the industry, "We didn't handle it right. We should have called a press conference and explained everything in great detail."[10]

A decade later, Coca-Cola walked away from its long-term sponsor relationship with the NFL, in part because it feared negative publicity from the "deep-well" pricing of concessions at NFL stadiums. Coke correctly felt that it did not need high-priced stadium signage to gain brand recognition. More importantly, exclusive "pouring rights" were backfiring. Consumer research showed Coke that 4 out of 10 people blamed Coke, at least partially, for the overpriced, watered-down stadium beverages. The question was simple for Coke executive Steve Koonin: "I'm going to pay for the privilege to upset people?"

Some player agents—to many the epitome of venality—have recently shown similar concern about image. In this case, the issue was high-priced autographs. Autograph-show promoters, recognizing the players' myopic greed, started contacting players directly rather than working through their agents, who might suggest to their clients that gouging an owner is one thing, but gouging a young fan is another. Said Wade Arnot, whose firm represented several Detroit Red Wings players, "It's not something we support."[11]

THE IMPACT OF PLACE AND PROMOTION

The ability to promote a facility's interior design, layout, or location parallels a tailor's ability to make "silk purses out of sows' ears." In other words, it is almost impossible. The sport facility image is a strong one, and it directly influences the product image, as we discussed in chapter 13. Take San Francisco's Candlestick Park. The cold, windy, wet environment might not affect 49er fortunes; even their most ardent fans make only a 10-game commitment for a sport filled with legends of "ice" and "mud" bowls. Not so with Giants fans, whose sport evokes images of lazy, sunny summer days. The Giants tried valiantly to overcome their location's liabilities, with clever promotions such as "glow glove" night and "ski cap" night, but the final answer was a new facility that promised more shelter from the chilly Bay elements.[12]

Some organizations have promoted special components of their venues. Take, for instance, ice hockey's penalty box—a place that conjures up images of tough

guys cooling off in the "sin bin" (see photo). The International Hockey League's San Antonio Dragons developed a clever promotion playing off this special "place." Once per period, the Dragons' mascot, Freddy the Fanatic, would move into the stands and haul an unsuspecting attendee (for being too quiet, for wearing the opponent's colors, whatever Freddy thought inappropriate) off to a "fan penalty box" (sponsored by Miller Brewing) behind one of the goals. Besides a close-up view, the fan got a small prize as part of the sentence. Fans seemed to love the promotion, cheering wildly whenever Freddy neared their sections. The Dragons even planned to make an inflatable version of the box for outside events.[13]

> Specific to hockey, the concept of the penalty box can be used as a promotional device.

THE IMPACT OF PLACE AND PUBLIC RELATIONS

Every cell in the product-place matrix (see table 13.1) has public relations implications. A coach who is an hour late for a Kiwanis Club appearance, and surly upon arrival, can undermine months of hard work by longtime or potential allies in group sales. Enlightened sport teams, on the other hand, have learned the prime public relations value of player clinics in outside venues, especially when the clinics help a worthy cause. The New York Rangers, for instance, have been longtime supporters of Ice Hockey in Harlem, a program that teaches not only hockey but also self-esteem and learning skills.

Ticket distribution systems can likewise help or hinder public relations. For instance, grassroots consumers are becoming more upset and impatient with mail-order, lottery approaches to ticket distribution for "big" events like the Olympics. In spring 1995, the Atlanta Games organizing committee began a massive campaign to solicit ticket orders for the 1996 Summer Games. In the first 60 days, consumers filed 314,000 ticket orders that included a $15 handling fee. More than 37,000 people got nothing for their efforts, and many of the "lucky" ones got less than their top choices for events. Media stories quickly mounted about how the choice seats were reserved for various Olympic sponsors and cronies. Or about how the family of Summer Sanders—a four-medal swimmer in Barcelona—could get no tickets for swimming, only volleyball and track. "We're treated like dog meat," complained Sanders's father to *Newsweek*. In the mid-1990s, the Olympic movement made no apologies for its high fees, early lottery, and massive interest from the advanced orders ($6 million by October 1995). Many speculated that in the wake of the 1999 bribery scandal, perhaps Olympic leaders would reconsider the effect of ticket distribution on public relations and public trust.[14]

THE IMPACT OF PROMOTION AND PUBLIC RELATIONS

Publicity is one of the four elements of promotion; therefore the two are interdependent. As stated previously, the impact of a favorable or unfavorable public relations image cannot be underestimated. It is conceivable that the public relations image can totally negate immense promotional efforts. The source credibility and high level of exposure from media coverage cannot be duplicated by promotional efforts. For example, Heavy Hands, a special dumbbell product designed for fitness walking and exercise, received considerable publicity in the 1988 presidential campaign because of the product's regular use by Democratic nominee Michael Dukakis. Although the product did not help Dukakis's campaign, the publicity for the product was incomparable. Heavy Hands could not have purchased more effective advertising at any price.[15]

CONTROLLING THE MARKETING FUNCTION

We have seen that each element of the marketing mix is interdependent, some to a larger extent than others. As each has the ability to influence the others, the only way to ensure marketing effectiveness is to control all parts of the marketing effort. In this section, we outline a comprehensive marketing control plan that has as its ultimate goal ensuring the creation and delivery of products that satisfy consumer wants and needs.

A sound control system can nurture and preserve the credibility of the image that consumers hold of both the product and the organization. Whether control involves the giant NFL's dictating specifications on player uniforms (shirts tucked in, socks pulled up and taped) or a local YMCA's training its staff to react courteously to member complaints, control is a central feature in successful marketing. Even the smallest item can create negative images that seriously undermine the overall organizational image. A small flaw may not affect all consumers or publics that interact with an organization, its personnel, products, services, or facilities; but it can affect enough people to cause damage. The athletic club that has cigarette machines in the lobby communicates inconsistency, insincerity, and a stronger adherence to the profit motive than to the health motive. Coaches who violate NCAA recruiting rules send a subtle but powerful message that their other promises cannot be believed. Maintaining consistency is important in a marketer's ability to communicate a clear and precise position. Inconsistencies blur images and project incoherent product positions.

The key to controlling the marketing mix lies in the ability to set a clear direction for all units and personnel. Employees need a road map to tell them where to go and how to get there. They need to know how they will be evaluated and how their efforts relate to those of others in the organization. An effective marketing control system, then, must be part of an ongoing planning system that has at least four components, as we outlined in chapter 2:

> Mission statements and objectives that have been established in light of current market position vis-a-vis desired position

> An organizational structure that marshals resources to meet objectives

> Employee performance standards and criteria that logically link performance to objectives

> Methods to adjust strategy, structure, and personnel in light of performance

In short, marketing control must be incorporated into an overall strategic plan.[16]

SETTING THE COURSE: MISSION STATEMENTS AND OBJECTIVES

Mission statements and objectives link strategic planning (which forces the organization to assess its relationship to its wider environment) with operational planning (which moves the organization toward its goals). One type of planning cannot succeed without the other. In other words, every piece of the marketing mix should be framed within a broader strategic vision. A good example of a broad strategic mission statement comes from Otterbein College, a Division III institution in Westerville, Ohio:

At Otterbein College, athletics are supported not for the purpose of training professional athletes, or for advertising the college, but as an educational activity in which participants may learn valuable lessons concerning sportsmanship, and the attainment and maintenance of a superior level of mental and physical health during the collegiate years and beyond.[17]

This statement makes it clear that, unlike its giant neighbor in nearby Columbus, Otterbein is not concerned with a potential bowl image or Heisman Trophy candidates. Its athletic administrators must instead market opportunities to play and learn. The same principles apply to the high school, the multinational equipment company, or the local racquet and fitness club: the mission statement is the touchstone for marketing strategy and tactics.

Clear, realistic, measurable objectives are the next step in setting the marketing course. Later in the chapter, we will consider some standard indexes of performance (e.g., attendance levels) that are often used in setting objectives. Leaders, however, should not wait until after the fact to consider objectives. Objectives must always be viewed as part of a continuous chain of ends and means, targets along the road to success. Vague or unrealistic objectives can be problematic, as Major League Soccer (MLS) found in 1997. Commissioner Doug Logan had set a public attendance objective of 20,000 fans per game for the 1997 season—a target that would bring owners close to the break-even point, but a good 30 percent increase over attendance averages in 1996, the premier season. Unfortunately for Logan, the final average for 1997 ended at 14,616 per game, almost a 10 percent decrease from year one. Did this mean that the MLS was in serious trouble? Not necessarily. But it required a reassessment and realignment of goals and strategies from short-term to long-term outlooks. As Logan put it, "A lot of people want to instantly assess you as a breakthrough or as a lack of a breakthrough." It was clear to him and the league owners that the MLS could no longer think in those terms.[18]

LINKING ORGANIZATIONAL STRUCTURE TO STRATEGY

In many organizations, marketing functions are not centralized, and this has caused problems. For instance, in professional and collegiate sport there is often minimal linkage between the public relations or sport information director (who is usually a journalist) and the director of promotions. At times, the units are antagonistic, vying for scarce resources or the ear of a higher executive. Such organizational conflict— usually the result of historical development—is illogical, since public relations and promotion should be part of an integrated marketing plan. A comprehensive marketing structure is needed to direct the efforts of marketing personnel and to ensure that these efforts are consistent with organizational goals and policies—and that they complement and do not duplicate one another.

As we noted in chapter 2, structure should evolve with organizational strategy. Take the Dallas Burn of MLS. In the fall of 1997, the Burn realized that their objective of building a stronger base of Hispanic fans required an alteration of their marketing structure. Andy Swift, who had served two seasons as Hispanic media liaison and community relations director, was promoted to director of the new Department of Hispanic Marketing and Community Development, with a staff of two account executives and a community liaison. The Dallas Burn had reconfigured structure to follow strategy.[19] We offer a sample design for a sport marketing function in figure 16.2. Although the sample is geared to high-performance spectator sports, the framework can be adjusted to the needs, resources, and products of other sport organizations. After outlining the basic positions, we provide indexes and measures for evaluating performance.

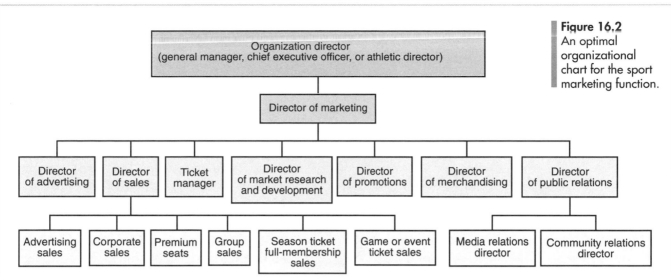

Figure 16.2
An optimal organizational chart for the sport marketing function.

Director of marketing: Responsible for all marketing efforts, reporting directly to the organization's chief executive. Oversees all other directors. Responsible for planning marketing activities and controlling their effectiveness. Determines budgets and resource allocations.

Director of advertising: Responsible for the design, layout, and media selection of all advertising materials. The advertising director is also responsible for all creative copy and illustrations in all print media published by the organization. (In small organizations this function is contracted out to an advertising agency. The coordination with the agency is the responsibility of the director of marketing.)

Director of sales: Coordinates all personal selling functions and is responsible for directing, training, and evaluating sales staff, who represent the following functions:

Advertising sales: The sale of all advertising space in programs, on the broadcast network, over the public address system, and on the electronic scoreboard, as well as all signage space in the venue that the organization controls.

Corporate sales: The sale of private boxes and group-rate plans or individual "company nights" to corporations, private businesses, and public institutions.

Premium seats: Sales of club or premium seats that combine box amenities with the lower cost of a single-season ticket

Group sales: Efforts (closely allied to corporate sales) to attract groups to events. Differs from corporate sales in that group-sales personnel target social groups, voluntary organizations, and clubs.

Season-ticket/full-membership sales: Sales to "heavy users" who have purchased season tickets or full memberships in the past or who are probable heavy users.

Game or event ticket sales: Function that falls under joint control with the ticket manager, who directs day-of-game sales by ticket salespeople.

Ticket manager: Directs the efforts of the ticket-office staff (and sales staff on day of game). Responsibilities include allocation of tickets to ticket outlets (distribution network); allocation of press or guest passes and media credentials; control of and accounting for tickets; and management of sales records broken down by location, ticket plan, game, or event day.

Director of market research and development: Provides primary and secondary market data, develops and maintains the marketing information system, identifies new markets, and creates preliminary penetration plans for new markets. Provides

Grassroots activities such as youth clinics are an excellent vehicle for college athletic programs to connect to their home communities.

service support to sales and public relations staff in terms of market research and intelligence. The person in this position is the logical person to oversee development and management of a Web site, since the Web serves and supports many interests (e.g., public relations, sales, promotions).

Director of promotions: Responsible for generating, planning, and implementing sales promotions. Role is coordinated with those of director of advertising, director of public relations, and director of community relations.

Director of merchandising: Responsible for marketing and merchandising the team logo and name and for any licensing activities. Controls and establishes production of souvenirs and programs that bear team name or logo. Responsible for marketing the athletes of the team and for endorsement contracts bearing team name or logo. Controls the concessions and souvenir stands and pro shops.

Director of public relations: Directs the media relations and community relations functions. In small organizations, the public relations director may be responsible for one of these two functions.

Media relations director: Responsible for all relations with the media. Disseminates information, distributes press releases, creates media guides, and organizes press conferences. Coordinates with ticket manager on press credentials and assignment of media to press box. Controls press box and develops game-day statistics.

Community relations director: Develops, coordinates, and executes all community relations activities (see photo). Responsible for activity development in the community and at the facility, including sport camps or clinics, community nights, athlete and personnel appearances, and relationships with general consumers other than the media. Also responds to fan mail.

Each of these functions is essential to an effective marketing effort. The failure to perform one of these functions substantially reduces marketing efficiency. Obviously, small organizations can subcontract these functions to sport marketing firms or advertising agencies. Organizations with limited resources or light workloads can combine some of the functions. When necessary, the directors of various functions can carry out the operational activities as well as maintain their primary responsibilities for planning and control. However, a small organizational structure can have a "collapsing effect," and combining roles can have the following counterproductive results:

➤ Lack of specialization results in lack of expertise. A manager hires either a person who is expert in one task and not good in the other, or someone who has general ability but no expertise in either task. This often happens in colleges that hire one person to direct both sport information and sport marketing.

➤ The emphasis becomes an operational emphasis (getting the job done), rather than a planning or control emphasis. Accomplishing the operational tasks precludes planning or reflecting on performance or strategies. The ability to effectively analyze staff performance and provide training rapidly diminishes. This latter effect can be visualized from figure 16.2. In small structures, the higher levels of management activity are lost and the degree of specialization is severely reduced; planning and control cease. Some might claim that the structure in figure 16.2 is unwieldy and too expensive. Obviously size and scope will vary with the organization's objectives and resources.

PERFORMANCE MEASURES FOR THE MARKETING UNITS

As noted earlier, the entire marketing unit needs clear objectives that move it closer to the organization's overall goals. A college athletic department, for instance, may have goals that include (a) improving the program image, (b) making a profit, and (c) obtaining a larger share of the entertainment market.

Such organizational goals can be translated into specific marketing objectives that clarify, for instance,

> ➤ the number of favorable stories the public relations staff should nurture in print or electronic media;

> ➤ improved results in consumer satisfaction surveys;

> ➤ the amount of revenue to be generated through various ticket packages, licensing agreements, or television contracts; or

> ➤ relative increases in television or radio ratings vis-a-vis those of competitors (e.g., regional professional teams).

Marketers must recognize and employ standard units of measurement to determine whether their goals are being reached. In the club industry, trade associations like the International Health, Racquet, and Sports Club Association (IHRSA) have prepared standard industry data reports that provide club averages on such items as revenue per member, revenue per square foot, and membership turnover.

Historically, the spectator sport industry lacked regular, rigorous surveys that established such benchmarks of performance. Leagues commissioned occasional surveys, but these did little to grab the attention of managers and marketers. In the last decade, however, trade publications such as *Team Marketing Report*, *Sports Business Daily*, and *Sports Business Journal* have created indexes of performance. In chapter 9, we discussed the *Team Marketing Report*'s "Fan Cost Index." In 1997, *Team Marketing Report* founder Alan Friedman and Paul Much created a "penetration index" to analyze the performance of professional sport teams. The penetration index simply took a team's "total attendance for the most recent season divided by the total population of the team's Metropolitan Statistical Area." Of course the penetration index must be analyzed with other data such as the number of competing franchises in other sports (given the spillover of seasons), but it offers a starting place for analysis. The rise of Internet commerce has resulted in greater efforts to measure success. Nielsen Media Research (of TV ratings fame) has recently added "net ratings" to its repertoire, calculating indexes like "page views" (the number of times a page is called up by users) and "click-throughs" (the number of times a consumer clicks on a button to go to an advertiser's Web site). Likewise, *Sports Business Daily* and *Sports Business Journal* offer regular features that analyze attendance as a function of special promotions (Beanie Babies) or star player (Mark McGwire).

Likewise, academic journals such as the *Sport Marketing Quarterly* and the *Journal of Sport Management* have fostered public dialogue on the strengths and weaknesses of measurements such as signage exposure, consumer recall and recognition, and economic impact studies. This is all to the good, both for the industry and for its marketers.[20]

General objectives must be refined for the people working in each unit. Following are some sample measures that can be adjusted for any overall plan.

Sales

- ➤ Sales dollar volume measured by actual sales
- ➤ Market share or increase in sales volume measured from year to year
- ➤ Number of prospects contacted from salesperson's "contact" records
- ➤ New business developed, measured from actual sales records

Public Relations

Each component of the public relations function can be monitored using appropriate criteria:

Media Relations

- ➤ Amount of media coverage (e.g., column inches, airtime) as evidenced by records such as clippings files
- ➤ Quality of coverage and media receptivity to the sport organization
- ➤ Quantity of legitimate media complaints received

Community Relations

- ➤ Number of community groups contacted
- ➤ Number of community projects held in the community or at the facility
- ➤ Sales revenues (e.g., merchandising) that result from the community relations effort
- ➤ Number of positive and negative letters received from the general public
- ➤ Number of children who participate in special programs (summer reading, student achievers)
- ➤ Hits, page views, and click-throughs on the organization's Web site

Ticket Manager

- ➤ Accuracy of financial records
- ➤ Minimization of errors, losses, or "unaccountables"
- ➤ Development of ticket distribution network and innovations in distribution policies

Promotions

- ➤ The number of promotions generated
- ➤ Sales response to promotions
- ➤ Overall image developed from promotions activities

Pro Shop or Team Store

- ➤ Revenue per square foot
- ➤ Stock turn

Market Research and Development

This function is perhaps one of the hardest to control because the output is the least subject to quantitative performance appraisal. However, some relationships can be computed as a basis of performance appraisal:

- ➤ Timeliness and accuracy of data collected (primary)
- ➤ Recency of secondary data supplied
- ➤ Ability of data and marketing information system to stimulate sales and marketing effectiveness
- ➤ Number of new markets developed and direct sales from these leads

Research and development is surely a creative process; a good marketing information system processes and analyzes consumer complaints as carefully as it does ticket sales. Likewise, the chief operating officer for the marketing functions must be creative in fashioning a system of appraisal criteria that is both fair and challenging. The effective manager is aware of all industry standards—from concession "per caps" to sponsor recognition rates, Web site page views, and attendance as a percentage of venue capacity. The manager is limited only by imagination and data availability.[21]

LINKING PERSONNEL PERFORMANCE TO STRATEGY

The marketing effort may be conceptualized as a series of goals and objectives, but nothing happens without a dedicated and competent staff. Someone or some group, then, must also lead and manage. We have discussed sales staff training in chapter 11, but we reiterate here some simple steps to follow to enhance staff performance across the marketing functions.

Step 1. Manager or director sits down with the staff, using a participative approach to setting performance goals and objectives. The manager or director clearly communicates expectations, performance goals, methods of evaluation, probable rewards for success, and negative reinforcements for failure.

Step 2. Performance is evaluated, initially at monthly intervals (intervals lengthening over time). Once satisfactory performance occurs, staff members are evaluated only once every 12 months.

Step 3. Where there are areas of weakness or areas showing room for improvement, the director or manager should outline the course for training, development, or corrective action.

Step 4. At each annual review, a new "contract" is developed that builds upon the experience of the previous evaluation period.

Through a systematic approach to managing the marketing function, the director can directly influence the organization's success. Each function is crucial to the marketing effort, whether performed by specialists or by individuals who generalize in two or more activities. To make a simple sport analogy, the marketing staff are the athletes out on the field, in the trenches, day after day. To ensure a coordinated, successful effort, they need intelligent, constructive coaching.

WRAP-UP

The notion of control moves the sport marketer from a land of wishful thinking to a realm of meaningful management. We have emphasized the need to control the marketing function, from research on potential consumers and their needs, to market segmentation, to product position, to the marketing mix, to sponsorships, and finally to evaluation of success. In today's sport marketplace, marketers must be managers and managers must be marketers.

As we have illustrated with countless examples throughout this textbook, the sport industry is evolving rapidly. As the century turns, the pressures will only increase for effective, innovative, and creative sport marketing techniques. The simple "selling-of-sport" approach—a giveaway here, some fireworks there—will not suffice. The market is more crowded and consumers more complex than was the case in 1928, when sport promoter Tex Rickard told a reporter, "By merely reading the newspapers, most anybody can tell what the public wants to see." The future Tex Rickard will be part scientist, armed with the latest techniques for research and development, and part artist, reshaping the product with creative inspiration that evokes passion and inspires colleagues and consumers alike. Whatever the game, the technique will be the same. A comprehensive and controlled marketing effort, coupled with creative ideas, will be the winning formula.

ACTIVITIES

1. As a simple review, find at least two examples of each cross-impact among the five Ps, either in this book or in some other resource.

2. Using an example from a current sport organization, illustrate the effects of price upon the remaining four Ps. Describe scenarios that demonstrate both positive and negative effects.

3. In your estimation, does one of the five Ps have greater cross-impact than the others? Price perhaps? Find examples to defend your position.

YOUR MARKETING PLAN

Lay out a clear diagram of the marketing structure for your organization. Be sure that the structure logically follows the direction and requirements of your overall strategy and its related plans. Include job descriptions and performance criteria for each position. Outline a process for evaluating each staffperson, each unit, and the marketing unit as a whole.

THE LEGAL ASPECTS OF SPORT MARKETING

OBJECTIVES

1. To alert sport marketers to the host of legal issues affecting the marketing of the sport product.

2. To teach sport marketers how to protect their own intellectual property associated with the creation of a sport product or with ideas developed out of sport sponsorship and licensing programs.

3. To examine the legal limits of sport marketing and promotion so sport marketers can avoid legal liability.

BY LISA PIKE MASTERALEXIS

Competition Begets Ambushing

Reebok paid $20 million for the right to advertise as an official Olympic sponsor during network Olympic coverage of the 1996 Centennial Olympics in Atlanta. Its competitor, Nike, blitzed the airways with its advertisements—outside of the official Olympic coverage. While Nike was forbidden from using the word "Olympics" or the trademark five rings in its advertisements, Nike did use in its advertisements the many top Olympians it sponsors. Nike also spent money creating billboards throughout Atlanta, especially those located on a warehouse overlooking Centennial Park. By entering into endorsement deals with individual Olympic athletes, Nike also had its trademark "Swoosh" strategically placed on the "hearts and soles" of many of the world's top Olympic athletes. According to analysts, this ambush by Nike confused much of the public into thinking that Nike, not Reebok, was the official sponsor of the 1996 Olympic Games in Atlanta.[1]

Competition is paramount to the proper functioning of our capitalist market. Viewed in its simplest terms, competition provides consumers with the best-quality products at the lowest prices. In a capitalist market, companies use sport marketing techniques to compete for consumers. As with competition in sport, market competition is not always fair. In a competitive market, a sport marketer may decide to engage in aggressive marketing tactics, such as ambush marketing (as in the case of Nike at the 1996 Olympic Games) or deceptive advertising, to get ahead. As with all competition, there is a fine line between that marketing behavior which is viewed as good, healthy competition and that which is unethical and illegal. To rid the market of the unethical and illegal conduct, state and federal governments have enacted laws to regulate anticompetitive business practices and unfair trade practices.

This chapter addresses the legal aspects of sport marketing by examining a host of legal issues that arise from sport marketing activities. These issues include the legal limits of sport-related promotions and the protection of intellectual property rights in sport products or sport sponsorship and licensing programs. Without attention to the legal aspects of sport marketing, those who market sport or market through sport risk losing their intellectual property and in turn their investments and financial return on their ideas. At the outset, we must recognize that many of these legal issues are complex and that they may often require assistance from an attorney specializing in intellectual property law. The issues are presented here to alert readers about how to protect intellectual property and how to avoid infringing on a competitor's intellectual property rights, as well as to point out those activities best handled by legal counsel.

WHAT IS INTELLECTUAL PROPERTY?

A capitalist market rewards invention, ingenuity, and creativity. To encourage this type of progress in science and the arts, the framers of the U.S. Constitution delegated to Congress the power to protect the intellectual property rights of artists, authors, and inventors by granting them "the exclusive right to their writings and discoveries."[2]

The law of intellectual property traditionally comprises three areas: copyrights, trademarks, and patents. Copyrights, trademarks, and patents are property rights granted to protect the products of one's intellect. Copyrights and patents grant property rights that have been valued in the United States since the drafting of the U.S. Constitution. Although people often see the symbols identifying intellectual property rights (© [copyright], ™ [trademark], and ® [patent]), most may not realize the exact nature of the legal protection provided to a copyright, trademark, or patent owner. We will examine these three areas that sport marketers need to be familiar with in order to protect themselves from intellectual property abuse and to ensure that they do not infringe upon another's intellectual property. The chapter, however, focuses more attention on trademark rights because this is the area sport marketers use most.

To decide the type of legal protection one should use to protect one's new ideas or products, one must first examine the character of the intellectual property. For example, copyrights protect original works of authorship; trademarks protect unique words, names, or symbols; and patents protect inventions (new products, processes, or plants). Ownership rights to trademarks may last forever, while rights to copyrights and patents have time limits. A copyright, trademark, or patent owner may grant permission for its use to others or may license that property to others for a fee. When another does not have permission or licensed rights to use the copyright, trademark, or patent, that person is infringing on the intellectual property owner's rights.

An injunction requires the intellectual property owner to prove in court, among other things, that he will be harmed by an infringement.

Before examining these laws, we will consider the initial step one should take if intellectual property abuse is suspected. When infringement is discovered, the property owner (or his or her attorney) should draft a letter to the alleged infringer asking the person to cease and desist infringing use of the protected intellectual property. Injunctive relief should also be sought. An injunction is a court order to stop the infringing activities prior to and during the trial for a copyright, trademark, or patent infringement case. To be granted an injunction against an alleged infringer, the intellectual property owner has to prove to the court that he/she will be irreparably harmed by the infringing activities; that the owner will be more harmed if the injunction is not granted than the defendant will be harmed if the injunction is granted; that the public interest favors the owner; and that the owner can prove a likelihood of winning the infringement case. Once the injunction is received, the owner seeks a trial on the merits of the copyright, trademark, or patent infringement case to receive a financial remedy for the infringement.

THE LAW OF COPYRIGHT

Original works of authorship appearing in any tangible medium of expression may be granted copyright protection. The copyright can be for something currently in existence or something to be developed later; but the work must be something that can be perceived, reproduced, or otherwise communicated. Works of authorship include the following:

➤ Literary works, such as books and stories

➤ Musical works, including any accompanying words

➤ Dramatic works, including any accompanying music

➤ Pantomimes and choreographic works

➤ Pictorial, graphic, and sculptural works

➤ Motion pictures and other audiovisual works

Books represent just one category of works of authorship that fall under the law of copyright.

> Sound recordings

> Architectural works[3]

Because of the large number of advances in technology, these protected works are defined in very broad terms. Copyright protection for an original work of authorship does not, however, extend to any idea, procedure, process, system, method of operation, concept, principle, or discovery, regardless of the form in which it is described, explained, or illustrated.[4]

The Copyright Act grants a copyright owner the right

> to reproduce and/or distribute copies or sound recordings of the copyrighted work to the public by sale, rental, lease, or lending;

> to prepare derivative works based upon the copyrighted work;

> to perform the copyrighted work publicly (literary, musical, dramatic, and choreographic works; pantomimes; motion pictures, and the like);

> to display the copyrighted work publicly (literary, musical, dramatic, and choreographic works; pantomimes; and pictorial, graphic, or sculptural works, including individual images of a motion picture or other audiovisual work); and

> to perform the copyrighted work publicly by means of a digital audio transmission (sound recordings).[5]

Under common law, copyright protection begins at the time the idea originates. To best protect a copyright, keep excellent records of your work as you are creating it; and place a copyright symbol, or write out the word "copyright," along with the origination date and the copyright owner's name, on the work. It is also a good idea to notarize the ideas expressed to prove that the date listed on the copyrighted work has been accurately reported.

Copyright protection for works created after January 1, 1978, exists for 50 years beyond the lifetime of the copyright owner; then the work of authorship falls into the public domain. If the work was created by more than one person, the protection extends for 50 years past the lifetime of the last surviving copyright holder. An employer holds the copyright on works created for an employer. For works made for an employer, the duration of the employer's copyright protection is 75 years from the time of publication or 100 years from the time of creation, whichever comes first.[6]

MISAPPROPRIATION AND COPYRIGHT INFRINGEMENT

Courts consider four factors when determining whether a copyright has been misappropriated and copyright infringement has occurred:

> The purpose of the use, including whether such use is of a commercial nature or is for nonprofit educational purposes

> The nature (character) of the copyrighted work

> The amount and substantiality of the portion used in relation to the copyrighted work as a whole

> The effect of the use upon the potential market for, or value of, the copyrighted work[7]

In a copyright infringement case, a defendant may challenge the copyright or may raise the defenses of the fair use doctrine. Later in this section, we will consider both defenses within the context of particular cases.

COPYRIGHTS AND ADVERTISING

Copyright protection is important for sport marketers who are involved in creating advertising or promotions that may be in the form of commercials and may use music, pictures, or graphic designs and/or audiovisual works. Copyright permission may need to be considered when one is contemplating the use of clips of athletic events that are protected.

Parodies are often used in advertising. A parody is a literary or musical work that imitates another work or imitates a person in a humorous or satirical way. When a creator of a parody imitates a copyrighted work, he or she may be accused of copyright infringement. When the parody focuses on an individual, the creator may be accused of misappropriating the person's name or likeness and violating the person's rights of privacy and publicity. We will consider these kinds of cases in more detail later in the chapter.

THE FAIR USE DOCTRINE

The fair use doctrine is a common defense to a copyright infringement claim. This doctrine allows for the fair use of a copyrighted work where the use is "for purposes such as criticism, comment, news reporting, teaching . . . , scholarship, or research."[8] The most recent U.S. Supreme Court opinion rejected the argument that the fair use doctrine does not apply to parodies created for a commercial use.[9] In *Campbell v. Acuff-Rose* (1994), U.S. Supreme Court Justice Souter noted that the fair use doctrine requires a case-by-case analysis and cannot be applied in such a manner that all parodies are considered copyright infringements.[10]

Film clips of Muhammad Ali fights appeared in the documentary *When They Were Kings* despite an attempted preliminary injunction by the copyright owner of the clips to bar their use. The court found that the defendant was likely to succeed on the fair use defense, thus allowing the film clips (between 9 and 14 clips, amounting to a total duration of 41 seconds to two minutes) to be used.[11] The key factors appeared to be that the work was a documentary and, although clearly commercial, it was also a combination of comment, criticism, scholarship, and research. In addition, public interest favored the production of Ali's biography; the use was quantitatively small; the clips were not the focus of the work; and use of the clips would have little or no impact on the market for the plaintiff's copyrighted fights.[12]

COPYRIGHTS AND SPORT EVENTS

The question whether sport events are copyrightable has yet to be fully answered. Currently, only broadcast or cable transmissions of sport events are copyrightable.[13] In 1976, Congress amended the Copyright Act to expressly ensure that simultaneously recorded broadcasts of live performances and sport events would be protected by copyright law.[14] Congress found authorship in the creative labor of the camera operators, director, and producer. On the other

> The jury is still out on whether sports events should be copyrighted. Currently, only the cable transmission or broadcast of a game is copyrightable.

hand, it would appear that the actual sporting events are not copyrightable because no authorship exists. In an event-related case, *Prod. Contractors, Inc. v. WGN Continental Broad. Co.*, the District Court for the Northern District of Illinois determined that a Christmas parade was not a work of authorship entitled to copyright protection.[15]

The issue recently arose in *N.B.A. v. Motorola and S.T.A.T.S.*,[16] when the Second Circuit Court of Appeals was asked to determine whether the NBA owns the statistics and scores of a game while the game is in progress. Motorola's SportsTrax pager system displays the following information on NBA games in progress:

- The teams playing

- Score changes

- The team in possession of the ball

- Whether the team is in the free-throw bonus

- The quarter of the game

- Time remaining in the quarter

The information is updated every two to three minutes, with more frequent updates near the end of the first half and the end of the game. There is a lag of approximately two to three minutes between events in the game and the information's appearance on the pager screen. SportsTrax's operation relies on a "data feed" supplied by S.T.A.T.S. reporters who watch games on television or listen to them on the radio. Using a personal computer, the reporters key in changes in the score and other information such as successful and missed shots, fouls, and clock updates. The information is relayed by modem to S.T.A.T.S.'s host computer, which compiles, analyzes, and formats the data for retransmission. The information is then sent via satellite to various FM radio networks that in turn emit a signal received by the individual SportsTrax pagers. On its America Online Web site, S.T.A.T.S. also provides slightly more comprehensive and detailed real-time game information. There, game scores are updated at intervals that are 15 seconds to a minute in length, and the player and team statistics are updated each minute. The court determined that Congress intended to protect the league's interest only in recorded broadcasts of games, not in the real-time data (scores, key plays, etc.) acquired by Motorola's employees and then broadcast on Motorola pagers.[17] Thus, the court found that Motorola and S.T.A.T.S. did not unlawfully misappropriate NBA's property by transmitting "real-time" NBA game scores and statistics taken from television and radio broadcasts of games in progress.

In *N.B.A. v. Motorola and S.T.A.T.S.*, Judge Winter also noted that sport events were not protected by copyright law because they were not authored. While he admitted that much preparation goes into participating in a game, there is no script. In fact, Judge Winter stated, what authorship did exist must be copied by opponents in order to attract fans. Competitors copy plays (team sports) or moves (i.e., gymnastics, figure skating). If players and coaches could copyright moves and plays, competition would be limited; play would be bogged down by the enforcement of copyrights; time would be wasted in seeking permission to use competitors' plays; and watching the competition would be boring. Copyrights for sporting events would also be bogged down by the joint ownership of all—leagues, teams, owners, players, umpires—who contributed to creating the event.[18]

Although the event may not be copyrightable, there are steps that event organizers may take to protect their proprietary interest in an event. Wall analyzed some of the steps taken by ESPN to protect its interest in its "Extreme Games."[19] The company used a trademark symbol for the name "Extreme Games" and for the "X" symbol, indicating that it had applied for trademark registration. A copyright notice was also affixed on all of ESPN's "Extreme Games" promotional materials. Publicity waivers were required from all athletes. Although these steps cannot protect ESPN from another organization's holding an event similar to the Extreme Games, it will protect ESPN from another's use of the name "Extreme Games" and the "X" symbol.[20] Reed suggests that additional steps, such as choosing a distinctive trademark as attractive as the event, establishing long-term contracts with participants, and prohibiting sponsors from sponsoring similar/competitor events, may protect event ideas.[21]

THE LANHAM TRADEMARK ACT

The Lanham Act governs the establishment and protection of trade, service, certification, and collective marks on the national level. Unlike copyrights and patents, which have expirations, trademarks can last indefinitely. Trademark registrations granted prior to November 16, 1989, have a 20-year term and may be renewed at 20-year intervals, whereas those granted after November 16, 1989, have 10-year terms and 10-year renewals.

The Lanham Act has become increasingly important for sport marketers involved in the marketing of sport products and sport events or exhibitions. The term trademark is often used to signify all types of marks, but technically four distinct marks are protected by the Lanham Act:

➤ *A trademark* is a word, name, symbol, or device used by a person, generally a manufacturer or merchant, to identify and distinguish its goods from those manufactured and sold by others.[22] Trade dress is a particular type of trademark that protects the distinctiveness of the appearance and image of a product or service. It involves the product's size, shape, color or color scheme, texture, graphics, and particular sales techniques.[23] Trade dress provides protection for the packaging of a product. Since sport marketers are often involved in the development of names and logos and the creative packaging of sport products, trademark and trade dress protection become important tools for protecting sport marketers' ideas.

➤ *A service mark* is a word, name, symbol, or device used to identify and distinguish a company's services, including a unique service, from those of another service provider.[24] Professional sport franchises' marks are registered as service marks that identify and represent the entertainment value of sport events. In many cases the marks may be the franchises' most valuable assets. In fact, it has become common for banks to accept the fair market value of minor league clubs' logos or marks as collateral.[25] As a result it is important to possess a keen awareness as to the marketability of a team's colors, logo, and identity.

➤ *A certification mark* is not as common as a trade or service mark. It is also a word, name, symbol, or device; it is used to certify a region or other area of origin; to certify a material, a mode of manufacture, quality, accuracy, or other characteristics of a person's goods or services; or to certify that the work or labor on the goods or services was performed by members of a union or other type of organization.[26]

➤ *A collective mark* is a trade or service mark used by the members of a cooperative, an association, or other group or organization; this type of mark includes marks indicating membership in a union, an association, or other organization.[27] A good example of a collective mark is the mark used by each of the players' associations in the professional sport industry.

The Lanham Act protects sport businesses engaged in interstate commerce, and state intellectual property laws protect those sport businesses operating locally, such as a community-based sport event. The Lanham Act is a federal law requiring that a mark be registered in order to be protected by the act. The Lanham Act does not preempt state laws. In many states, marks are protected as part of the common law of unfair competition, and often registration is not required. Thus, federal registration of a mark is not required in order to establish rights in a mark, but federal registration provides several benefits:

> Federal registration provides the ability to invoke the jurisdiction of the federal court system for any future legal action.

> Federal registration can be used as a basis for obtaining mark registration in foreign countries.

> Federal registration may be filed with the U.S. Customs Service to prevent the importation of infringing foreign goods.[28]

> By protecting its owner, a mark limits others from deceiving consumers by selling goods or offering services as the goods and services of the original source. This enables the consumer to distinguish between different producers of products or services.[29]

> Marks lower consumer costs because they provide a dependable guide to the quality of products or services a customer comes to expect from the trademark holder.[30]

> Marks symbolize and protect the goodwill of their holders.[31]

> Marks protect consumers from confusion and deception over the particular products or services they are purchasing.

> Marks provide public notice throughout the nation of an owner's claim. Evidence of trademark ownership creates an easier burden of proof of ownership.

From this point on, we will discuss trademarks, but keep in mind that the principles that apply to trademarks apply to other marks as well. Ownership of a trademark generally requires the holder to appropriate the mark and to use it for commercial purposes.[32] Since 1988, though, the Lanham Act has allowed an individual to apply for registration to the Patent and Trademark Office if one is able to establish "a bonafide intention" to use a trademark in commerce.[33] A person or organization registering under this "intention to use" provision must, however, show use in trade and commerce shortly thereafter or the trademark will be considered abandoned.

Trademarks are considered strong or weak with respect to their distinctiveness. Strong trademarks are legally entitled to a wide scope of protection; weak trademarks are entitled to more limited protection. Strong trademarks are inherently distinctive and completely distinguishable, and are characterized as fanciful and arbitrary.[34] Reed cites Exxon, Polaroid, and Kleenex as distinctive examples and Hoop-It-Up and Hoop-D-Do (outdoor three-on-three basketball tournaments) as good examples of fanciful, distinguishable event names.

On the other end of the spectrum are the weak trademarks, such as Music Fest, Fan Fest, or Art Expo, which are so literal, descriptive, and generic that they do not distinguish one event from another.[35] All use common words in their ordinary spelling and meanings. They are difficult, although not impossible, to protect. Weak trademarks may be protected if they possess secondary meaning. "[S]econdary meaning is a mental recognition in buyers' and potential buyers' minds that products connected with the symbol or device emanate from or are associated with the same source."[36] For example, in "World's Fair" the words are common and are used in their ordinary meaning, but the trademark is descriptive because of the amount of advertising and public exposure that the World's Fair, and its trademark, receive.

Since there is only one World's Fair, use of this trademark by others without permission may lead consumers to confuse the secondary use with the original trademark.[37]

When a trademark request is for a name that is merely the generic name of the good on which it is to be used, it cannot be registered. There are other common grounds that the U.S. Patent and Trademark Office cites for refusing to grant registrations. These include instances in which the proposed trademark

> possesses immoral, deceptive, or scandalous matter;

> disparages or falsely suggests a connection with persons (dead or alive), beliefs, institutions, or national symbols;

> possesses any insignia of the United States, any state or municipality, or a foreign nation;

> consists of a name, portrait, or signature of any living individual without the person's consent, or consists of the name, portrait, or signature of a deceased president during the life of his widow without her consent; or

> is merely a surname.[38]

It is under this provision that the Washington Redskins recently had their seven trademarks canceled by a three-judge trademark panel. The panel found that the Redskins' trademarks were disparaging to Native Americans. Similar challenges currently await the Atlanta Braves and Cleveland Indians.[39]

LICENSING

High schools, colleges, professional leagues, players' associations, and the Olympic movement protect their names, mottos, symbols, and goodwill through the Lanham Act. Once owners hold a trademark, they may license out its use to others (see chapter 8 on licensed merchandise). A license is a grant, permit, or contract that gives one the right to use or associate one's trademark with the licensee's business. In effect, the license is a contract that grants the licensee the right to use the trademark on its products. Licenses generate major revenues for the trademark holders in professional and collegiate sport. With the sale of licensed merchandise in North America alone totaling $73.8 billion in 1997,[40] professional leagues, collegiate programs, and major events such as the World Cup and the Olympic movement are increasingly licensing their "brands" to generate their portion of those sales. Others such as ESPN and the NBA are going one step further by creating products for the brand, namely theme restaurants. Professional athletes and celebrities are also viewed by themselves and by their agents and marketers as brands. They are taking steps to develop images and are using the Lanham Act and rights of publicity to protect their names and likenesses.

Professional sport leagues have created properties divisions that control and protect the various trademarks of teams. The properties division actually owns the trademarks of all team and league names, symbols, and logos and then licenses them back to the individual clubs.[41] Properties divisions are vigilant in enforcing trademark rights, even if this means resorting to a trademark infringement lawsuit against one of the owners in its own league, as occurred when Dallas Cowboys owner Jerry Jones attempted to market the Cowboys to competitors of the NFL's exclusive sponsors.[42]

TRADEMARK INFRINGEMENT

Trademark infringement is defined as the reproduction, counterfeiting, copying, or imitation in commerce of a registered mark. It requires simply proof that a valid and distinctive (strong) trademark exists and that the infringing trademark will cause a likelihood of confusion by the consuming public.[43] If the trademark (or trade dress) is inherently distinctive, there is no need for a plaintiff to establish the existence of secondary meaning.[44] If the trademark is descriptive or not distinctive (weak), the plaintiff must show that it possesses secondary meaning. A survey is often used to determine whether there is a likelihood of confusion, mistake, or deception as to the affiliation, connection, or association of the alleged infringer with the accuser as to the origin, sponsorship, or approval of its goods or services.[45] The plaintiff filing a trademark infringement case under a likelihood of confusion theory is the dominant trademark holder, who argues that the (defendant) junior user of the trademark is causing customer confusion and benefiting from the mark holder's strength in the market. These are the factors considered in the determination of whether a likelihood of confusion exists:

> The degree of similarity between the owner's trademark and the alleged infringing trademark

> The strength of the owner's trademark

> The price of the goods and other factors indicative of the care and attention expected of consumers when making a purchase

> The length of time the defendant has used the trademark without evidence of actual confusion

> The intent of the defendant in adopting the trademark

> The evidence of actual confusion[46]

In trademark infringement cases, a second theory, of reverse confusion, occasionally arises. A plaintiff filing a trademark infringement action on a reverse confusion theory is the original, although less recognizable party. *Illinois High School Association v. GTE Vantage, Inc.*[47] illustrates this theory. In that case, the Illinois High School Association had used the trademark March Madness since the early 1940s to designate its basketball tournament held every March. In 1982, CBS commentator Brent Musburger used the phrase "March Madness" to describe the NCAA's men's Final Four basketball tournament, and the media and public picked it up. Ten years later, in 1993 or 1994, the NCAA began to license the use of the phrase to sponsors who wished to associate their goods or services with the tournament. In 1996, the Illinois High School Association sued GTE Vantage, Inc. on a theory of reverse confusion, arguing that consumers would mistakenly believe that its trademark affixed to its merchandise referred to the NCAA tournament and in the end would hurt its ability to earn revenue by licensing its own trademark. (The Illinois High School Association sued GTE Vantage, Inc. rather than the NCAA, because GTE Vantage held a license for the March Madness trademark from the NCAA). The court found for the defendant, GTE Vantage, arguing that the trademark owner is not allowed to withdraw from the public domain a name that the public has adopted to denote someone else's good or service when there appears to be no culpable conduct on the part of the defendant.

A second reverse confusion case, *Harlem Wizard Entertainment v. NBA Properties*, also proved unsuccessful for the plaintiff.[48] This case involved changing the name Washington Bullets to Washington Wizards. The plaintiff, the Harlem Wizards, was a barnstorming theatrical basketball team founded in 1962 that operated in much the same way as the Harlem Globetrotters. The Harlem Wizards claimed that the infringement by the Washington NBA team would diminish the recognition consumers have with them and with the name Wizards, thereby diminishing their goodwill by giving people the impression that they had stolen the name Wizards from the dominant NBA team. The court disagreed, stating that the two organizations were not competing in the same market and thus the two names could coexist without causing consumer confusion. Although the Harlem Wizards argued that both plaintiff and defendant were in the business of basketball, the court narrowed the scope in which to compare the two.

False Designation of Origin

A third theory under which a trademark owner may sue is termed false designation of origin. Under this theory, the owner of the trademark must first establish that the public recognizes that the trademark identifies the owner's goods and services and distinguishes its goods or services from others. Once the plaintiff establishes public recognition, it must prove that the defendant's use of the trademark is likely to confuse or deceive the public into thinking that the plaintiff is the origin of the use.

The lead sport-related case is *Dallas Cowboys Cheerleaders, Inc. v. Pussycat Cinema, Ltd.* (1979).[49] In this case, the defendant owned and operated an X-rated cinema in which it showed a pornographic film entitled *Debbie Does Dallas*. According to the case, the plot in the film involved a high school cheerleader chosen to become a "Texas Cowgirl," but without the financial means to travel to Texas. To raise money, the character and eventually her entire team performed sexual favors. By the end of the film, she was shown wearing a uniform strikingly similar to that of the Dallas Cowboys Cheerleaders. The marquee posters advertising the film depicted Debbie in a Dallas Cowboys Cheerleader uniform and made references to Dallas and the Dallas Cowboys Cheerleaders. The appellate court affirmed the preliminary injunction granted to bar the defendant from distributing or exhibiting the film. The plaintiffs successfully established that they would face irreparable harm, that they would face greater hardship if the film was exhibited than the defendant would face if it was not exhibited, and that they had a likelihood of winning the trademark infringement case. The Cheerleaders established that they had a trademark in their uniform's white boots, white shorts, blue blouse, and star-studded white vest and belt. The Cheerleaders also established that they had a likelihood of proving that the public would associate them with the movie and would be confused into believing that the plaintiffs had sponsored the movie, had provided some of the actors, or had licensed the uniform to the defendants.[50]

While the defendants argued that no reasonable person would ever believe the Dallas Cowboys Cheerleaders would be involved with such a film, the court challenged such a reading of consumer confusion as too narrow. Instead the court stated that to evoke consumer confusion, the uniform depicted in the film need only bring to mind the Dallas Cowboys Cheerleaders, which the court stated it unquestionably did.[51]

Abandonment

Unlike copyrights and patents, which expire, trademarks registered under state or federal statutes last indefinitely, provided the holder continues to renew the registration and the trademark is not abandoned. When a trademark is abandoned, it returns to the public domain and is appropriable again by another potential trademark holder. In practice, because "subsequent use of [an] abandoned mark may well evoke a continuing association with the prior use, those who make subsequent use may be required to take reasonable precautions to prevent confusion."[52]

Under the Lanham Act, abandonment occurs when use has been discontinued and the holder has no intent to resume use or when the holder's own conduct causes the trademark to lose its significance.[53] Since the trademark is worth value, the court will require substantial proof of abandonment. An instructive case involving abandonment in professional sport is *Indianapolis Colts, National Football League Properties and National Football League v. Metropolitan Baltimore Football Club, Limited Partnership.*[54] The Indianapolis Colts and the NFL brought suit for trademark infringement against what was then the new Baltimore team of the Canadian Football League

(CFL), which sought to be called the "Baltimore CFL Colts." The plaintiffs obtained a preliminary injunction to stop the defendants from using the name "Colts," or "Baltimore Colts," or "Baltimore CFL Colts" in connection with the playing of professional football, the broadcast of football games, or the sale of merchandise to football fans and others. In this case, the former owner of the abandoned mark continued to market the same product or service under a similar name. It was clear that the Indianapolis Colts were the trademark NFL team that had previously been the NFL's Baltimore Colts. The court determined that a team named the Baltimore CFL Colts would be confusingly similar to the Indianapolis Colts by virtue of the history of the Indianapolis team and the overlapping product and geographical markets served by the Indianapolis Colts and by the new Baltimore CFL Colts. The Indianapolis Colts' abandonment of a trademark confusingly similar to their new trademark did not break the continuity of the team. The court declared that it was the same team—that the team was simply in a different home city and as a result had adopted a different geographical designation. Therefore, the CFL was not entitled to acquire and use the name, which would realistically confuse NFL Colts fans and other actual or potential consumers of products and services marketed by the Colts or by the NFL, with regard to the identity, sponsorship, or league affiliation of the new Baltimore team. The court agreed that the Indianapolis Colts owned the goodwill associated with the name "Baltimore Colts" and that the new Baltimore team was trying to acquire it from them.

Another case, *Abdul-Jabbar v. General Motors*,[55] raised the issue of abandonment of a birth name. During the time leading up to the 1993 NCAA men's Final Four, General Motors ran an advertisement for its Olds 88 that used trivia regarding Kareem Abdul-Jabbar's University of California-Los Angeles and NCAA records. When Abdul-Jabbar had set the records, his name was Lew Alcindor. Besides citing the trivia question, Abdul-Jabbar alleged that the advertisement compared the car to him. General Motors responded that when he had converted to Muslim he had abandoned the name Lew Alcindor and thus there was no infringement. In finding for Kareem Abdul-Jabbar, the judge stated, "One's birth name is an integral part of one's identity . . . it is not "kept alive" through commercial use . . . . An individual's decision to use a name other than the birth name . . . does not therefore, imply intent to set aside the birth name, or the identity associated with that name."[56]

THE POWER OF THE TRADEMARK

The following two examples portray the power of a trademark holder to block those whom it suspects or discovers may be misappropriating its trademark. Designer Ralph Lauren's corporation obtained a trademark for the term Polo and his ubiquitous logo of a polo player riding a house and swinging a polo mallet. The brand Polo Ralph Lauren produces cologne, clothing, furniture, and house paint.[57] Designer Ralph Lauren is aggressively pursuing the sport of polo for infringing upon his Polo products line.

In the first action, Ralph Lauren Corporation has filed a trademark infringement action against *POLO*, the 22-year-old magazine created by the U.S. Polo Association. The legal battle began in 1997 when the magazine was purchased by Westchester Media, which redesigned it from a sport magazine to a lifestyle publication. The new format includes features on polo-loving celebrities, articles on exotic vacation spots, and advertisements for luxury items. Ralph Lauren has received a preliminary injunction based on the contention that a likelihood of confusion exists due to the similarity of image being created by *POLO*'s new design, which the court found did suggest an identification with Polo Ralph Lauren products. The court further found that *POLO*'s target audience was no longer simply members of the U.S Polo Association, but "high-end retail" customers. The injunction requires disclaimers to appear on the magazine's cover, masthead, and table of contents to distance the publication from the Ralph Lauren Corporation.[58]

In a second action, Ralph Lauren recently sent a cease and desist order to the California Polo Club to stop its use of a circular logo created for its membership. Along the upper side of the circle were the words "California Polo Club," and rounding out the lower side was a silhouette of a polo player leaning down from his horse to strike a polo ball with his mallet. The club was to embroider the logo on shirts and/or other items to sell at its shop and to be worn by members. Ralph Lauren is arguing that the polo player too closely resembles the one in the logo used on his Polo signature products. The two silhouettes are somewhat similar, but a noticeable difference is the angle at which the polo player is sitting on the horse and using his mallet. When interviewed on ABC's "20/20," the California Polo Club's president complained of the uncertainty that the club will be able to use any silhouette of a player on a horse in its design. He also argued that the California Polo Club was a small club being blocked by a large international corporation, and that the club's logoed merchandise was intended for sale to its members and would neither create consumer confusion nor compete in a market with Ralph Lauren's Polo products.[59]

As a result of these two legal actions, polo participants and enthusiasts have argued that the power of the trademark goes too far: after all, polo is a generic term and the sport has been around for 2000 years. In fact, some fans have created a Web site on which people share opinions about designer Ralph Lauren's use of his trademark.

TRADEMARKS AND ADVERTISING: AMBUSH MARKETING

Trademarks have a love-hate relationship with advertising. Advertising is necessary to establish a trademark in the mind of the consumer and to establish a secondary meaning for a weak trademark. However, sport marketers working in the Olympic and event-management segments of the sport industry face challenges that result from a method of advertising called ambush or parasite marketing. Ambush or parasite marketing occurs when an advertiser capitalizes on the attention given to an event by using tactics to imply an official association with that sport event. The ambusher's tactics weaken a competitor's official association with the event acquired through the payment of sponsorship monies.[60] Ambushing also involves an organization's misappropriating the trademarks, logos, and goodwill of the event or its sponsoring organization.[61] It occurs when a company has not paid to be an official sponsor, but confuses the public into thinking it is a sponsor by indirectly associating itself with the event. A good majority of the ambush-marketing incidents occur at the Olympic Games because of the worldwide media attention and goodwill the games attract. McKelvey cites the following as the most prominent forms of ambush marketing:[62]

➤ Where the ambusher purchases advertising time in and around the event broadcasts, such as in 1992 American Express advertisements broadcast during the time leading up to the Winter Olympics. The advertisements told viewers, if you are going to the Olympics, you'll need a passport, but not a visa, just an American Express. At this same time VISA was paying $40 million for official sponsorship. In a study conducted shortly after the 1992 Olympic Games, 30 percent of the Americans surveyed thought that American Express, not VISA, was an official sponsor.[63]

➤ Where television rights holders create and offer to nonsponsors a composite logo combining a particular event and network logo to sell network sponsorship: for example, when the network recognizes non-Olympic sponsors in a broadcast billboard with the network's Olympic logo and a voice-over saying "Ambushing company, a proud sponsor of the Olympic Games broadcast." In this case, the ambushing company is not an official Olympic sponsor, but is an Olympic broadcast sponsor;

that is, it is paying television rights fees to the Olympic broadcaster, not sponsorship fees to the Olympic Committee. The ambushing company in this example is attempting to capitalize on the Olympic Games' public and media attention, and it counts on the public's not realizing the difference between official Olympic sponsor and Olympic broadcast sponsor.

➤ Where nonsponsors negotiate advertising directly with individual teams, athletes, or players' associations at a fraction of the cost of event sponsorship. There have been many instances of this in recent Olympic Games. For instance, Reebok officially sponsored the 1992 Barcelona Olympics, and those Dream Team members sponsored by Nike refused to wear the USA team uniform on the medal stand because it bore the logo of official sponsor Reebok. In Charles Barkley's words, Nike had given him "two million reasons not to wear Reebok."[64] The players chose instead to cover themselves with strategically placed American flags to hide the logos.

➤ Where corporations sponsor giveaways of event tickets designed to capitalize on an event's popularity.

➤ Where organizations use a good luck or congratulatory message or banner to associate with a special event, achievement, or athlete. Coca-Cola officially sponsored the 1992 Barcelona Olympics for $33 million. During the 1992 NBA All-Star Game, Pepsi ran advertisements wishing Earvin "Magic" Johnson good luck participating on the Dream Team—clearly a reference to the 1992 Olympic Games to build on their goodwill without sponsorship or direct mention of the games.

➤ Where nonsponsors market in, around, and above the event. Nike's advertising strategy for the 1996 Olympics in Atlanta, mentioned in the opening vignette, represents this form of ambush marketing. Nike did not pay the $40 million to be an official sponsor of the Olympics. Instead, it set up a massive display just outside of Centennial Park, individually sponsored some of the biggest-name athletes, and invested a great deal in advertising around the site of the Olympics and during Olympic broadcasts and media coverage. As a result, a majority of Americans believed Nike was a major sponsor of the 1996 Olympics.[65]

Although ambush marketing is difficult to combat, there are a few ways to help limit it. To prevent the type of ambushing represented by the television network's actions in the second example listed, the licensor (International Olympic Committee) can negotiate into the broadcasting contract a clause requiring the licensee (network) to monitor/police infringements. The official sponsor can also purchase the network advertising; however, given the expense of buying official sponsor rights, the sponsor may not have the financial wherewithal to purchase the additional advertising spots.

The licensor can negotiate with the host city and the event site to ban advertising that directly competes with official sponsors. For instance, the NCAA creates a "clean zone" for its Final Four whereby it imposes a ban on advertising in the area surrounding the facility hosting the event and at official Final Four hotels. To create the clean zone at the 1999 men's Final Four in St. Petersburg, 30 signs surrounding Tropicana Field that would be visible from the basketball court were covered up. Nonsponsors' promotional items were also banned from the area outside the arena and the official hotels.[66] This tactic is effective only if the host city, the host facility, the hotels, and others agree to the restriction on advertising. For instance, while the Atlanta Organizing Committee for the 1996 Olympics created an organization dedicated to sponsor protection, the city of Atlanta decided to allow companies such as Nike to sponsor the city itself.[67]

The local organizing committee of a major event, and the event itself, must also limit conflict when protecting sponsorship rights and prohibiting ambushing. To effectively block sponsorship conflicts or ambushing, there must be good communication between the two levels of governance. For example, during the 1994 World Cup, a conflict arose after MasterCard obtained the exclusive right to use World Cup '94 trademarks on all card-based payment and account-access devices. A few months later, the local organizing committee entered into a sponsorship agreement with Sprint to become an official partner of the 1994 World Cup. MasterCard sought and was granted an injunction to stop Sprint from using the World Cup trademark on any card issued by Sprint, despite Sprint's argument that its phone cards were distinguishable from the card-based payment and account-access devices intended in the MasterCard-World Cup '94 agreement.[68]

An official sponsor can also go on the offensive with a public relations campaign accusing the ambusher of ambush-marketing tactics. The official sponsor should explain the concept of ambush marketing, identify the ambushing tactics, and convince the media to tell the public the ambusher is not an official sponsor and did not pay for sponsorship.

An official sponsor or a licensor may bring a legal action against an ambusher. Ambush-marketing practices have the potential for violating the following laws: misrepresentation, misappropriation of one's name or likeness, defamation (libel and slander), and false advertising. Some of these actions are torts and may also violate state consumer-protection laws and other state laws such as the rights of privacy and publicity. There is not enough room in one chapter to discuss all of the potential legal actions to which ambushers may be subject.

On the other hand, some sport marketers may choose to employ ambushing as a marketing strategy. For those choosing this approach, Reed (1989) suggests the following guidelines for legal ambush marketing for the nonsponsor:

➤ Tie in with a related organization.

➤ Avoid using official symbols and trademarks of the main event.

➤ Do not use the main event's name in the headline of your advertisements or in the name of your promotion.

➤ Keep the period of the ambush short to minimize any serious damage (it takes time to prepare for and wage a legal battle).

➤ Consider adding a disclaimer to clarify the potential confusion.

➤ Where possible, use clearly geographic, rather than trademark-type names, that is, "the host city of the Olympics," not the name "Olympics."

➤ Congratulatory advertisements should not contain "sell" copy and should be one-time only.[69]

UNFAIR COMPETITION AND UNFAIR TRADE PRACTICES

Unfair competition and unfair trade practices encompass a large number of illegal actions and are bad business etiquette. These legal theories are based in common law and may be applied generally to all dishonest or fraudulent rivalries in trade or commerce, but they are specifically applied to the practice of "passing off" the goods or services of one party as those of another with a better-established reputation.[70] For example, in the Ralph Lauren Corporation's trademark infringement lawsuit brought against Westchester Media, the publisher of *POLO*, the plaintiff also sued under the theory of unfair competition. The argument was that *POLO* magazine was trying to capture the same market audience that Polo Ralph Lauren targets, and thus were attempting to capitalize on consumers' becoming confused into thinking the magazine was associated with Polo Ralph Lauren.[71]

Unfair competition and unfair trade practices may also give rise to lawsuits based in such torts as fraud, deceit, misrepresentation, and violations of rights of privacy and publicity, as well as violations of state consumer-protection laws and federal trademark-protection laws. We cannot consider all of the laws that may be violated in each state, so we will direct our attention to misappropriation of one's name or likeness and the protection provided by rights of privacy and publicity.

THE RIGHT OF PUBLICITY AND INVASION OF PRIVACY

The concept that one has a right to protect one's name or likeness is recognized in most jurisdictions. In a legal action arising from the misappropriation of one's name or likeness for a product, an advertisement, or any other commercial use, a plaintiff may choose to sue under invasion of privacy and/or the right of publicity. The key difference between the two is that the right of publicity is geared toward protecting one's financial stake in the commercial exploitation of one's name and likeness, whereas the right of privacy is geared toward protecting one's psyche.[72]

The right of publicity was originally intertwined with invasion of privacy, but courts soon separated the right to be left alone from the commercial right to control the use of one's likeness or identity.[73] Invasion of privacy arises out of the common law of torts or state statutes. Among other things, the right of privacy protects against intrusion upon one's seclusion, the misappropriation of one's name or likeness, unreasonable publicity, and placing one in a false light. The right of publicity prevents the unauthorized commercial use of an individual's name, likeness, or other recognizable aspects of his or her persona. It gives an individual the exclusive right to license the use of his or her identity for commercial promotion. More than half of all jurisdictions in the United States recognize the right of privacy, but nine of those states, including New York and Illinois, have rejected the right of publicity after death. However, Rosenthal suggests that the commercial reaction to the death of Princess Diana may cause states to revisit that ruling.[74]

Cases often arise on these two theories in the sport setting when a sport celebrity attempts to stop the misappropriation of his or her name and likeness. Athletes have discovered the commercial value in their names and likenesses, and thus the right of publicity and the enforcement of trademarks are crucial protections in this age of the "branding" of athletes. One of the initial cases in sport, *Haelan Laboratories v. Topps Chewing Gum,* involved a dispute over the right to market trading cards of professional baseball players.[75] In that case, the court established a property right in a person's identity, naming it the right of publicity.[76] The court recognized the right of the players to grant a license (or exclusive privilege) to merchandisers to their likenesses for the manufacture and sale of the cards.[77] This case opened the door for athletes and celebrities to enforce a right of publicity against those misappropriating their names and likenesses. In a similar case, *Uhlaender v. Henricksen,* the U.S. District Court for the District of Minnesota enjoined the maker of a table game from using MLB players' names without their consent because the players had a proprietary interest in their names, likenesses, and accomplishments.[78] Thus, the sport marketer should acquire written consent and provide proper payment for the use of the name or likeness of a star athlete or entertainer before using it for commercial gain.

An athlete might find himself seeking the advice of a lawyer to protect the use of his name and likeness.

The degree of consent that the sport marketer receives from the athlete or entertainer is also important and can provide a valid defense to a misappropriation lawsuit. For example, San Francisco Giants and St. Louis Cardinals player and Hall of Fame member Orlando Cepeda entered into a sponsorship agreement with Wilson to create a collection of baseballs bearing Cepeda's name. Swift and Company, a meat packaging company, entered into an advertising campaign with Wilson Sporting Goods Company. Under the terms of the promotion, Wilson's Orlando Cepeda baseballs could be purchased through the collection of wrappers for Swift meat products. Cepeda sued Swift for the unauthorized use of his name, likeness, photograph, and signature. The court found that Cepeda's agreement with Wilson Sporting Goods gave Wilson the exclusive right to "commercially exploit" the Cepeda name. This exclusive right allowed Wilson to create the promotion with Swift, thus leaving Cepeda with no claim against Swift.[79]

Because of the strength of the First Amendment protection of free speech or expression, permission is not needed to use a celebrity's name or likeness in a book, newspaper, magazine, television news show or documentary, or other news media outlet.[80] It is also allowable to use the name or likeness of an athlete or entertainer to advertise or promote media publications in which the athlete or entertainer once appeared. In both *Namath v. Sports Illustrated*[81] and *Montana v. San Jose Mercury News*,[82] courts allowed the defendants to use plaintiff's photos from prior editions of their publications in advertisements to sell their publications. The court stated that the photographs represented newsworthy events and that a newspaper had a constitutional right to promote itself by reproducing its news stories. These cases differ from the previously discussed *Abdul-Jabbar v. General Motors*,[83] in which Lew Alcindor's name and likeness were misappropriated in an advertisement for the Olds 88 automobile. While Lew Alcindor's record is in fact newsworthy, its use was to advertise an Oldsmobile and thus was not protected by the First Amendment.[84]

The First Amendment may also play a role in the appropriation of one's name or likeness in parodies. In a lead case on this issue, *Cardtoons v. Major League Baseball Players Association*, the Court of Appeals for the Tenth Circuit granted full protection to the parody cards created by the plaintiff on the basis of its First Amendment rights. The court determined that the parody cards provided social commentary on public figures, MLB players, who were involved in a significant commercial enterprise, Major League Baseball. The court stated that the cards were no less protected because they provided humorous rather than serious commentary. Thus, the plaintiff's First Amendment right to create the parody trading cards outweighed the MLB Players Association's right of publicity in their members' names and likenesses.[85]

Courts have also recognized a right of publicity and trademark protection for nicknames. In *Hirsch v. S.C. Johnson & Son, Inc.*,[86] the plaintiff, Elroy "Crazylegs" Hirsch, alleged that the nickname belonged to him, that it had commercial value, and that knowing this, the defendants marketed a shaving gel for women called "Crazylegs." In an action against S.C. Johnson & Son, Inc., Hirsch sought a remedy under two legal theories. Hirsch argued that the defendant violated his right to privacy by misappropriating his name and likeness for commercial use and infringed upon his trademark rights to the nickname "Crazylegs." The court determined that a celebrity's nickname had value and that Johnson could not use the name "Crazylegs" without permission from or payment to Hirsch for its use. The court found that all that is required to protect a nickname is that the nickname clearly identifies the wronged person.[87]

PATENTS

A patent may be granted to anyone who invents or discovers any new and useful process, machine, manufacture, or composition of matter, or any new and useful improvement.[88] A patent cannot be granted for a mere idea—only for the actual invention or complete description of it. A patent is not needed to make or sell a particular product. A patent does not grant the right to make, use, offer for sale, sell, or import the invention, but the right to exclude others from making, using, offering for sale, selling, or importing it.

To further delineate what is patentable, the law defines a process as an act or method, and it primarily includes industrial or technical processes. A machine does not need any further description. The term *manufacture* refers to all manufactured or made articles. Finally, the composition of matter relates to chemical compounds and may also include mixtures of ingredients.[89]

Like a copyright, a patent has a limited duration. Currently, its duration is 20 years from the date on which the application was filed with the Patent and Trademark Office.[90] During those 20 years, a patentee must not violate antitrust laws by virtue of having a patent, such as by unreasonably limiting the licensing of the patent or by using the patent to fix prices or restrain trade. Once the 20 years expires, anyone may make, use, sell, or import the invention without permission of the patentee.

Occasionally (about 1 percent of the time), inventors will file for patents simultaneously. Since a patent can be granted to only one applicant, the Patent and Trademark Office conducts a proceeding called an interference to discover which inventor first conceived of the invention and reduced it to practice (built it and used it). Thus, good record keeping, documentation, and notarizing are suggested for establishing conception of the idea and of when it was created and used for its purpose.[91]

Patent laws allow for joint ownership. Any joint owner may make, use, offer, sell, or import the invention for his or her own use or profit or may grant licenses to the patent without regard to the other owner(s) unless the joint owners enacted a contract governing their relations. Thus, clearly outlining each owner's rights and how the patent will be used between joint owners will help avoid legal disputes.[92]

Patent law is the most complex of the three areas of intellectual property. As a result, it is the area in which one will most likely need legal guidance for the patent registration process and patent protection.

In the sport context, inventors of sport equipment seek patents to protect their ideas. The invention of sport products is driven by consumer need. Sport equipment is invented and updated regularly in an effort to keep participants ahead of their competition and to keep them safe in sports of high contact or risk. As new materials are developed, new types of sport equipment and improvements on current equipment are also developed. These range from new types of bicycles, golf clubs, tennis racquets, and baseball bats to new protective gear, such as helmets and padding.

New methods or processes for playing sport are also patentable. For example, James Foster's Arena Football League (AFL) and its parent company, Gridiron Enterprises, Inc., have been issued patents in the United States and Mexico for Arena Football's game system and method of play.[93] The AFL has just sought an injunction barring the Professional Indoor Football League (PIFL) from play and has filed suit against the PIFL for infringing on its patent, arguing that the PIFL's game is virtually identical to the AFL's. The PIFL plays a similar game with the same number of players, but without play off the large nets characteristic of the AFL. The PIFL is located in smaller cities, and the salaries are lower.[94] Interestingly, the AFL has just created a new league, AFL 2, which is targeted toward smaller cities. It will be interesting to see whether the PIFL counterclaims that the patent infringement suit, coupled with the creation of the new league, anticompetitive acts, prohibited by the Sherman Antitrust Act. The two anticompetitive acts are 1) the lawsuit to keep PIFL from playing arena football and 2) the creation of AFL 2 to compete for PIFL's market in smaller cities.

EMERGING ISSUES

In this section, we consider some issues that have come to light as a result of an emphasis on global communication and global business ventures. This discussion is in no way intended to be inclusive, but rather to raise some issues that are emerging.

GLOBAL PROTECTION FOR INTELLECTUAL PROPERTY

As the world becomes smaller and a great deal of information is carried and commerce transacted through the World Wide Web and other modes of communication, it has become vital that owners of intellectual property consider registering copyrights, trademarks, and patents in foreign countries. The World Intellectual Property Organization Trademark Treaty promises to clean up trademark application and registration procedures. Of the 97 countries that have signed the treaty, 35 have agreed to standardize intellectual property procedures by October 2004. The new rules allow a single application for all signatory countries and 42 international registration classes, saving intellectual property owners time and money. Finally, multiple trademark registrations may be changed or amended via contact with one of the registration sites.

The second significant intellectual property system is the European Community Trademark System, which processes applications for European Community trademark registrations. European Community registrations are accepted and protected in all European Community member countries (currently 15). The trademarks are effective for 10 years and allow 10-year renewals. Additionally, Arena Football League patents through the European Community are currently pending.

THE WORLD WIDE WEB

Legal issues for sport marketers will emerge from the use of the Internet for commerce, communication, public relations, and advertising. The U.S. Copyright Office of the Library of Congress accepts registration for online works. The key factor in determining whether the online site is copyrightable is whether it possesses original authorship.[95] Garrote and Maher suggest that the trade dress of a Web site may be protected. They warn, though, that trade dress requires that the "packaging" create a distinctiveness that the public associates with that site. This may happen quickly if the site makes a swift, strong impact; but it is more likely to take time for the trade dress and site to create an association in the public's mind.[96]

The law of cyberspace is in its infancy. Numerous lawsuits have commenced nationwide to monitor and regulate Internet use and its impact on privacy and property rights, but few precedents have been established. To manage the risks involved in cybercommerce, sport businesses should consider insurance coverage for their Internet activities. One important source of protection may be advertising-injury coverage often sold under comprehensive or commercial general liability insurance policies. These policies often provide coverage for claims stemming from the policyholder's advertising activities that may lead to tort claims of libel, slander, defamation, or invasion of privacy, as well as for claims of violations of the right of privacy, piracy, unfair competition, or infringement of copyright or trademark rights. Advertising-injury insurance coverage should provide protection against many of the legal liabilities businesses face when doing business and communicating online.[97]

WRAP-UP

Copyrights, trademarks, and patents are property rights granted to protect the intangible products created by one's intellect. Intellectual property law is complex. As sport marketers seek to protect their own creativity and to avoid infringing upon others, a basic understanding of copyright, trademark, and patent law, as well as the torts of invasion of privacy and the right of publicity, is useful. When complex legal issues confront sport marketers, a good rule of thumb is to rely on legal counsel who are experts in this field to handle the situation.

ACTIVITIES

1. Describe the differences among the three forms of intellectual property. Give at least one sport example of each form.

2. Describe the six forms of ambush marketing listed in the chapter and develop some methods for challenging ambush marketers.

3. Watch or attend a major sporting event and track it for ambush marketing.

4. To get a sense of the pervasiveness of intellectual property in our society, track the number and types of items identified as copyrighted (©), trademarked (™), patented (®) or patent pending that you encounter in one day.

5. Add your marketing plan activities. Creative materials are an essential component of any marketing plan. In your plan, identify creative elements you have developed as well as those you have obtained from other sources. How do you protect your original ideas and concepts? How do you obtain permission to use materials from other outside entities?

CHAPTER

18

THE SHAPE OF THINGS TO COME

OBJECTIVES

1. To provide insight with regard to challenges facing sport marketers in the new millennium.

2. To learn about professional opinions regarding the future for sport marketers.

3. To consider projections about future developments in the sport industry and the ramifications of those developments.

In developing this chapter, we jokingly referred to it as the "Nostradamus chapter." Our intent was to provide our thoughts on what the future—the next 5 to 10 years—might hold for sport marketing. We have presented our thoughts, but we felt that it might be more effective also to include the thoughts and views of some of the leading experts in sport marketing. In Shakespeare's *Hamlet* (4.5.43), Ophelia sums it up best when she says, "We know what we are, but know not what we may be." What follows, then, is our attempt to "look beyond the veil" and see what may be. We gratefully acknowledge the contributions of our visionaries. We do ask you to remember only the things we predicted correctly and please to forget those items that we did not.

SHAWN HUNTER, CHIEF OPERATING OFFICER, PHOENIX COYOTES

While sport marketing has been around for a very long time, only in recent years has it become a big-time business—"big time" in the sense that it is becoming more sophisticated and more complex every day.

Today, more than ever, sport marketing is a vital form of communication and a common business practice. The major side effect of this overflow of marketers has been a departure from the roots of our industry—respect for the customer. And it is the customer, our average fan, who will determine our fate in the long run.

As sport marketers, we are not caretakers of our sports, but rather caretakers of the relationships that surround our sports—the relationships that will ultimately dictate success or failure. What does that mean? Today, more than ever, we have herculean responsibilities:

> ➤ A responsibility to our most important customers—the everyday fans. Without them we do not exist.

> ➤ A responsibility to our employers—the owners of professional sport teams, and on the collegiate side, athletic directors and presidents. For them, we must remain financially viable.

> ➤ A responsibility to the media. On a daily basis they help us tell our story.

> ➤ A responsibility to our marketing partners—sponsors. They help us generate the revenue and exposure necessary to stay competitive.

> ➤ And last but not least, a responsibility to our sports and the athletes who play them. Sport teams are community assets, and we must never let anyone forget that, especially the athletes.

As our business becomes more complicated, the margin for error gets closer to zero. As sport marketers, we must provide the vision and road map necessary for success in the decade ahead. So what does the future hold? What will sport marketing look like in 10 years? How will we thrive, let alone survive? A peek at the past might be the best guide for the future.

Let's start with the premise of our industry—*fun*. Simply stated, we are in the "fun business." If we are doing our jobs correctly, we are providing entertainment and escape for the everyday people of the world. It is these same everyday people who will measure us over time with regard to the job we have done.

With "fun" as our mission, we must never neglect our most precious products—our home games. These events are our lifeblood and represent our core connection to the fans. It is here that we must do our best work. Each home game and each event must be special. We must always strive to create *great moments of truth*—those first and everlasting impressions. Great moments of truth define an organization and represent the essence of our industry.

To make home games fun and special requires commitment. There is intense competition for both leisure time and the entertainment dollar. We battle not only the other teams and entertainment options in our markets but also the 500-channel television universe. Wouldn't it be easier to stay at home on some nights and watch the game on television? With this increasing galaxy of competition, we must work to make our events unique and ultimately in demand. If we lose our fans at the arena, we lose our most important core relationships.

A fun product is essential to our well-being, but that is only a start. We also need packaging that is fun and creative. This means being innovative in how we sell our games. Affordability and accessibility are paramount to growing and nurturing the next generation of fans: not everyone can afford season tickets. We must constantly challenge ourselves to package our products in a way that maximizes revenue yet does not construct barriers to entry, especially for families and children. So, returning to our roots, we discover a golden rule in sport marketing. We must preserve our most important relationship—the everyday fan. We must be fun; we must be affordable; and we must be accessible.

While fans represent our most important relationships, they are not our only relationships. As the industry becomes more competitive and more complex, we must strive to create great moments of truth for all of our customers.

Among the most important sport industry developments in recent years have been the efforts to create marketing partnerships between teams and corporations. This concept has required a radically different approach to what has traditionally been called sport sponsorship. By forging these partnerships, sport teams can create a powerful marketing environment, which ultimately impacts the marketing partner's bottom line. These exclusive and specially designed relationships service the individual business objectives of a company and help deliver its messages with powerful clarity.

Partnerships are exclusive by category (e.g., Coke would be the only partner in the soft-drink category) and are comprehensively designed to include all of the marketing elements that surround a team's brand: radio, television, print, signage, retail promotions in the marketplace, entertainment, and hospitality. In other words, we no longer just sell a single sign in the arena. We sell results—measurable results. Companies now demand a measured return on their sport investments, and we must be prepared to deliver if we desire to stay in business. Like the entertainment dollar, the marketing dollar is being stretched in all directions.

Key to developing these strategic partnerships is the ability to control all marketing inventory surrounding our core product. With control comes the ability to deliver exclusivity. Control also places quality and profitability in the hands of the sport marketer. Perhaps the most valuable inventory we will possess in the years ahead is our programming (radio and television). With a 500-channel universe, the ability to control and distribute programming provides wealth and stability.

The future of sport marketing is both exciting and scary. We have more opportunities than ever before, but we also have more pressures. These pressures attack us

Happy fans are a sport organization's lifeblood.

379

from all directions. It is our ability to preserve the integrity of our products and relationships that will make us successful.

Whether with the everyday fan or with the corporate marketing partner, relationships are the key to success for tomorrow's sport marketer. Our continual investment in relationships will help us avoid and in some cases overcome the problems that affect the bond between fan and sport.

So what will happen 10 years from now? Will sport still be the great common thread in our communities, bringing people together from different social and economic backgrounds? Will high ticket prices exclude families and younger fans? Will anyone go to the games in person, or will everyone be content to watch them on television? As sport marketers, you will play a critical role in answering those questions. Don't forget where you came from, and don't forget the basics:

> Have fun—that is ultimately our business.

> Create great moments of truth—those first and everlasting impressions.

> Create partnerships and relationships, always striving to deliver more than you promised.

JIM KAHLER, SENIOR VICE PRESIDENT, CLEVELAND CAVS

With a new millennium right around the corner, professional sports will face a number of challenges in the years to come. Rising ticket prices, accompanied by the NBA lockout of 1998, have helped to portray athletes as the bad guys. This image is causing many Americans to develop negative attitudes toward professional sport. Today's media cannot relate to athletes who are making tremendous amounts of money, and often the media expend considerable energy in pointing out the negative aspects of professional sport as opposed to the positive contributions that a pro athlete may be making. A star athlete found guilty of a drug conviction will sell more newspapers than one involved in helping a local charity in its efforts to aid children.

At the same time this negative attitude is developing, professional sports continue to enjoy tremendous growth. New arenas and stadiums have become major cornerstones for redevelopment in cities on the rebound. The major networks and cable stations are spending record amounts of money for broadcast rights to MLB, NBA, NFL, and NHL games. Emerging new leagues such as Major League Soccer and the WNBA, along with reenergized leagues like Arena Football and Roller Hockey International, are expanding the sport audience (spectators and viewers) both demographically and in terms of numbers. More and more corporations are involved in sport marketing and are successfully including sport as a major part of their overall strategy. Let's examine three critical challenges that face the sport marketer and organizations involved in sport marketing.

Increasing ticket prices. As player salaries continue to increase, fans have learned to accept the fact that ticket prices will also increase. While attendance at professional sporting events is at an all-time high, it is becoming more and more challenging for teams to sell tickets, whether season tickets, partial plans, or individual tickets. Chicago-based *Team Marketing Report* publishes an annual report on the cost for a family of four to attend a professional sporting event. The report factors in the average cost of four tickets, four hot dogs, four soft drinks, and parking. The latest research (1998) shows these average costs to attend games:

MLB $13.60   NBA $42.54

NFL $42.86   NHL $42.79

What the study doesn't indicate is that many families attend games on a complimentary basis, as the guests of companies that have made a major investment in professional sport. Corporate America has found that professional sport is a great way to entertain clients and reward employees. This is not to deny that there is still a large percentage of fans (30 to 50 percent depending upon the sport and the market) who are personally purchasing tickets. Teams cannot ignore this critical group of fans and must target marketing and promotional efforts to them. The Cavs have consistently offered a "Big Game Plan" with 16 games, featuring the most attractive teams and stars, for the price of 15 games. This plan has been in place for the past several years and has done extremely well in our marketplace.

A family attending a sports event can expect ticket and concessions prices to continue to rise.

Teams throughout the country offer "family fun packs" through their local newspapers that include tickets, refreshments, and sometimes parking for an all-inclusive price—discounted between 20 and 50 percent through the support of a corporate partner. In our case, the Cavs have maintained our lowest-priced ticket at $10 for seven years in a row; and to keep this ticket affordable for families, adults, or children wanting to see an NBA game, we do not offer it as a season ticket. It is critical that all professional franchises understand their markets and create ticket packages that work for both their corporate and individual fan bases.

Fan apathy. Remember the old saying that one bad apple can spoil the whole bushel? Similarly, attitudes about professional athletes are formed on the basis of a handful of players who have found themselves in trouble. This kind of bad press can lead to fan apathy. I am proud to work for an organization that values character as a key ingredient in our player-selection process. Over the past 15 years, Cavs owner Gordon Gund and General Manager Wayne Embry have done a wonderful job of drafting players with character. As a result, our team is very well respected in the community.

Dealing with fan apathy and negative attitudes toward professional athletes has become a challenge for the marketing departments of all teams in all leagues. When a professional athlete gets into trouble, there tends to be a rollover effect throughout the league, and in some cases into other sports as well. As marketers, it is our job to point out the public service that professional athletes perform and the millions of dollars that they help to raise every year.

Corporate sponsors are aware of the value of working with athletes on cause-related programs. A good example is the partnership that the Cavs have formed with the Fannie Mae Foundation. With the support of our players and the foundation, the Cavs organization has "rehabbed" more than 65 condemned houses in the inner city and made them available to first-time home buyers. This is a classic example of what professional athletes can do to heighten awareness for a sponsor and at the same time make a major contribution to a city. This is the direction that sport organizations have to take to generate a positive impact on their fans and to provide positive player stories for the media.

Recruiting tomorrow's sport marketing executives. One of the biggest challenges facing sport organizations is the recruitment of the next generation of sport marketers. We are fortunate to be in an exciting industry where there are many qualified candidates with master's degrees in sport administration. Typically, these individuals are willing to start out in entry-level positions to gain the experience necessary for developing their careers. The upside for the organization is the ability to place extra responsibilities on these individuals who are looking to make their mark in sport. The downside is simple—turnover. An organization with a number of talented young sport marketing executives will not be able to develop every individual internally because there are not enough promotion opportunities for all of these people. As a result, these organizations become the training ground for the recruiting efforts of other teams (both major and minor league). Thus employers and employees must be flexible. The employer must be prepared to lose potentially valuable marketers, and the employee must remain open to accepting new opportunities and challenges.

We, as sport marketers, must be focused on our constituencies—both external and internal—as we move into the next millennium. We must not lose track of who our consumers are, nor must we forget about our athletes and our staff. It is a delicate balance that must be maintained through constant attention and support.

JERRY SOLOMON, PRESIDENT, P.S. STARGAMES

The evolution of the sport business has been nothing short of dramatic over the past 20 years. This growth has been fueled, in large part, by the extraordinary developments in television and other forms of media distribution. The more recent creation of Internet technology and the coming ability to stream video and audio on the World Wide Web appear to be the next phase in this evolution.

Along with satellite technology, the Internet allows advanced communication to virtually every corner of the globe. The race to control the flow of distribution through these outlets has placed a premium on quality programming. Because of its universal appeal, sport has benefited from this need for such programming. Also, at this point, if you cannot attend the event in person, and sometimes even if you can and have a poor seat location, the drama of competition comes across best in the pictures that television is able to transmit.

Therefore, as a result of factors that to some extent have little to do with sport itself, the business of sport—meaning everything from contract negotiations to licensing to event creation to sponsorship sales—has evolved into a formidable worldwide industry. I see no signs that this industry growth will abate in the foreseeable future.

As with virtually every other industry, I expect that the sport business will go through certain traditional phases as it matures. Already we have seen a proliferation of sport marketing agencies and athlete representatives (agents) because of the barriers to entry. We are currently in the midst of a consolidation phase as the larger agencies seek to acquire some of the niche shops that have developed. Looking down the road, I suspect we will see new entities emerge, additional public offerings, business failures, and so on. Having said that, however, I believe some rules from other industries should govern, including these:

Location, location, location. While this is primarily a real estate rule of thumb, I believe it has implications for sport as well. Well-built arenas and stadiums in traditional and emerging markets will continue to attract leagues, teams, players (free agents), advertisers, and spectators. As a result, I think we will continue to see new stadiums built and continue to see teams and events—either through expansion or movement—seeking new markets and new and better facilities.

Immunity of entertainment to economic swings. While this may not always hold true, historically the entertainment industry has been largely unaffected by such economic conditions as inflation and recession. This is so because in good times people spend their disposable income on entertainment and in bad times, in order to escape reality, they do the same. With the lines between sport and entertainment virtually erased, sport will benefit from this same pattern. As a result, ownership of leagues, teams, and events will continue to be a big business and will be very attractive to entertainment- and media-based companies such as Fox and Disney.

Five hundred channels and nothing on. Ultimately, whether through cable, satellite, or digital delivery systems, we will have the 500-channel universe that has long been envisioned. Sport, which can attract and deliver (to its advertisers) a variety of demographic targets on a worldwide basis, will play an increasing role in this universe. The Golf Channel is merely the forerunner of a variety of niche channels based upon sport—so you can anticipate new networks devoted to auto racing, fishing, the Olympics, and so on.

I have had the good fortune to be involved in the sport business for the past 20 years. The changes that I have seen and experienced have been far reaching and powerful in their impact. However, I think the surface has just been scratched and that the next decade should be explosive.

LESA UKMAN, INTERNATIONAL EVENTS GROUP AND THE *IEG SPONSORSHIP REPORT*

One of the most significant ongoing changes that will continue is a move from signage forms of sponsorship to a new form called *hyperdimensional* sponsorships. Sponsors are no longer content to simply hang banners and air commercials during time-outs. They now want to entertain and interact. Whereas the soft-drink company used to just be there—its presence amounting to little more than a concession stand with advertising—companies like Coke and Pepsi want to interact with consumers and bring them fun experiences. Pepsi, for example, has created the "Pepsi Presence" as a way of getting the soft-drink marketer more directly involved with events through ownership and other forms of influence and control rather than merely advertising during events. The old ways of connecting with consumers are no longer enough. Activities such as the Pepsi Presence are telling us that we're about to usher in a new era in event marketing in which sponsors do not simply sign up properties as billboards, but indeed use the rights as the defining element of their brand.

Past marketing efforts that involved communicating to large numbers of people were initially conducted through advertising, a two-dimensional medium. But as clutter, audience fragmentation, and product parity became the norm, it became necessary to create an emotional connection with the customers. This brought sponsorship into the three-dimensional space it currently occupies, but as "sponsored by" has begun to mean nothing more than "check signed by," this level of interaction has come to be viewed as insufficient. This insufficiency drives the need to move to hyperspace, a place with more than three dimensions.

Hyperdimensional sponsorships embrace emotional, interactive, intellectual, and spatial dimensions all at once. The *emotional* dimension reflects a recognition that while technology will be an important part of marketing's future, it will be the ability to tap into a consumer's emotions that separates great marketers from everyone else. In this sense, hyperdimensional sponsorships are more about pull than push. They tap into consumers' own enthusiasm, rather than pushing enthusiasm for a brand onto them.

Next is the dimension of interactivity—the consumer, the company, and the product itself communicating with one another, relating to one another, even experiencing one another. The successful sponsorships will be those that do not seek simply to make people aware of a company's name but rather seek to win consumers over by involving them in the sponsorship. When a consumer actually experiences what a brand stands for, rather than just receiving a message, marketers are in a position to release that consumer's own energy into their promotions.

The intellectual dimension is propelled by the simple fact that to be believable, sponsorships must be built on substance. Sponsorship can indeed provide the trigger to buy, but the customer must understand the message and believe it.

Finally, there is the delivery of these dimensions—emotional, interactive, and intellectual—through the media and distribution channels. This is the packaging and presentation of the dimensions in some type of spatial dimension. Together these dimensions, in proper alignment, create hyperdimensional sponsorship opportunities. Examples of hyperdimensional sponsorship activities include:

> ➤ General Motors' relationship with Disney, which took the form of a $100 million investment in a new "Test Track Thrill Ride" at Epcot Center. Disney will use GM's 8400 dealerships to market its theme parks and merchandise while offering special privileges to GM customers.

> ➤ Nike's 10-year, $400 million sponsorship of the Brazilian soccer team. The sponsorship not only includes merchandising but creates mini-tournaments for all Nike-sponsored teams. In effect, this sponsorship links the attributes of the Brazilian team to the actual fabric of the Nike brand—the most storied team in soccer becomes, quite simply, *team Nike*.

Hyperdimensional sponsorships will take the industry to the next level. However, this means that sponsorship will also need a new means of measurement—one involving hyperdimensional components. This will entail shifting the center of sponsorship emphasis from an impressions environment to a world where interacting with your audience is more important than ubiquity. Thus sponsors will stop giving proposals to their ad agencies and media buyers just for quantitative evaluation and will start reviewing the proposals in qualitative terms—because targeted, quality encounters are where the equity is.

Over the next five years, the growth of sponsorship will dwarf anything we've seen to this point. Why? Because we're becoming consumers of messages, not products. In such a world, sponsorship is no longer just a marketing vehicle through which to communicate a message. In 1964, Marshall McLuhan electrified all communicators with his famous statement: "The medium is the message." I believe this statement needs to be updated: "The relationship is the message." Companies will increasingly be sponsoring not for the signage, sampling, or media spots, but for the borrowed imagery, "the soul," of a property. Hometown festivals and events and local teams are far more compelling to consumers than any brand. The unique selling proposition is defined in terms of supporting what the customer supports, his or her values, interests, and lifestyle. It's about staying personal and in tune with the consumers—about not getting lost in the mechanics of being a local, regional, national, or global marketer.

Thus we must think *vertically integrated, horizontally leveraged, and deeply connected.* Vertically integrated means interwoven in the fabric of the organization from top to bottom; horizontally leveraged means all departments across the organization are able to use and benefit from an association; and deeply connected means that sponsorship must be connected and rooted in the mission and vision of the company employing the sponsorship, not just purchased on a whim or because somebody thinks it might be a good idea. The image to hold in mind is that of a museum or a theme park filled with experiences and information coming at you in many forms, some scripted, others serendipitous. It may be intense, it may be ambient, but it works only when it provokes your participation. Niketown, the NBA Store, the All Star Cafe, and similar efforts are attempts at being hyperdimensional and at connecting with their respective markets. Look for this trend to continue and to be blended with technological innovations and effects to provide a form of connection provoking involvement and interaction.

ALAN FRIEDMAN, FOUNDER AND EXECUTIVE EDITOR, *TEAM MARKETING REPORT*

The most important target market in the future for team marketing executives will represent only about 20 percent of ticket buyers. This market, however, will account for a much larger percentage of ticket revenue, and in many ways is emerging as the key to a team's financial stability. Revenue from premium seating was the collateral that helped finance new buildings and now that a majority of teams play in newer venues or have plans to build them, this income has become arguably the most important in-house source of revenue.

Buyers of luxury suites and club seats may account for only 20 percent of the ticket buyers, but these high spenders can contribute upward of 40 percent of total ticket revenue. For example, for the 1998 NFL season, club seats represented only 6 percent of the total seat inventory but contributed 16 percent of ticket revenue, or about $136 million in sales. The growing importance of the premium-seating market is fueled by several factors:

> ➤ Arenas and stadiums opening during the next few years will aggressively price luxury-seating inventory.

> ➤ Purchasers of such seating have demonstrated little resistance to high prices. There will always be buyers willing to pay a premium for the best seats, and clubs are finding that the locations for those seats—the lowest levels or center court—can command ultra-premiums.

> ➤ There appears to be tremendous price elasticity for the best luxury seating.

> ➤ There is less chance for a public outcry about the price of luxury seating, so it is a safer public relations move for teams to raise the price of these seats than to raise the price of regular tickets.

> ➤ New designs and buildings will expand the number of premium seats available.

As the demand for and pricing of premium seating escalate, it is not out of the question to project a $500,000 per year luxury suite. With this type of revenue potential and the high rate of renewals—which for the most part are unaffected by team performance—it is easy to see why this predictable and stable source of revenue is a top priority for team marketers.

Another advantage of the premium-seating concept is the ability to sell the product in the form of a long-term lease, with preplanned annual increases. Fans can cancel season tickets, but locking in premium-seat buyers for 4-, 7-, or even 10-year commitments is money in the bank, even if the fortunes of the team turn dramatically as happened with the Florida Marlins. Many teams can then enter a season knowing that their most expensive and profitable seating is sold out for the entire year. The lure of such opportunity and profits will continue to drive the expansion of the premium-seating concept.

Arenas and stadiums developed during the building boom of the 1990s will institute large price increases as their luxury contracts come up for renewal. Marketers of premium seating at these newer arenas cannot expand their inventory dramatically, so pricing for this prime real estate will increase at a much higher rate than for other seating in the facility. At renewal time, marketers of premium seats at some venues will get a chance to repair a cardinal sin of sales—"leaving money on the table" by underpricing luxury seating. At renewal, average suite leases will increase 15-20 percent, with annual increases of 4-6 percent.

In the late 1990s, average suite prices were about $165,000 for new arenas that housed both NBA/NHL teams, $113,000 for new arenas that housed either a NBA or

NHL team , $81,000 for MLB-only stadiums, $77,000 for NHL-only arenas, and $76,000 for new NFL-only stadiums.

While a capacity crowd of non-premium ticket buyers looks good on television, on the balance sheet the revenue from premium seating now exceeds general ticket proceeds in many buildings. That is why premium seating, although it represents only about 20 percent of ticket buyers, will be the dominant focus in the future for team marketing executives.

ALYCEN C. McAULEY, HARRISON S. CAMPBELL, AND D. MITCHELL WHEELER, MARKETING ASSOCIATES INTERNATIONAL

Within an industry so complex as sport sponsorship, trends are difficult to predict, much less identify. In the past 10 years, sport sponsorship has grown into a multibillion-dollar business, with properties and corporate entities redefining the notions of sport sponsorship on both a daily basis (informally) and a yearly basis (in formal contract negotiations). Despite this redefinition, sport sponsorship spending continues to grow at a rate of almost 13 percent per year. Clearly, sport sponsorship has become a preferred vehicle for corporations seeking to reach their customers and prospects. Although this vehicle will play an increasingly important role in the market mix into the next millennium, the parameters of sponsorship will be continually redefined and redrawn.

The future of sponsorship will center on one global theme: sophistication. Sponsorship approaches will be more sophisticated. Elements within sponsorship will be more sophisticated. Information and information gathering will be more sophisticated. Marketers and decision makers will be more sophisticated. Fans will be more sophisticated. Much of this sophistication will center on the introduction of new technologies, but other elements will reflect the maturing nature of the sport sponsorship industry.

Measurement and measurement value have already become an area of greater sophistication. As the sport sponsorship industry continues to mature, corporate partners seek tools by which they can measure the effectiveness of their sponsorship dollars: exposure time, ratings, and impressions have all been the result of this need for measurable value. The sport sponsorship industry will continue to develop more innovative and acceptable methodologies to measure value. Use of improved tools will result from stronger definition within the industry, but also from the availability of improved technologies to measure value. In addition, as the media mix broadens (first radio, then television, and now the Internet), the need to measure results both within the individual media and across the various media will have greater importance.

Marketing in and around sport sponsorship will also become more sophisticated: relationship marketing, aided by the development of new technologies, will be the norm rather than the exception. Relationship marketing will take on a greater depth (the amount of information you know about a fan) and greater breadth (the amount of knowledge you have about the industry as a whole). This new, in-depth knowledge will generate a far more specific experience within sport sponsorship: properties will target smaller segments of the marketplace with more specific messages across tightly defined media choices.

Sophistication will most certainly change the relationship between sport properties and sponsors. Relationships like the Sprite-NBA agreement may become more prevalent as sport sponsorship becomes a more sharply defined marketing partnership between the property and the sponsor. As sport properties refine their marketing initiatives, the approach of having marketing partners (businesses that aggressively market the sport property while simultaneously marketing their brand) will become a necessity. Sponsorship fee structures may reflect this more evolved relationship, with a balance between fees and marketing expenditures, and perhaps an equity position for each party. While that may initially reduce the number of hard dollars committed to a property, the exchange in favor of co-marketing will bring greater value, and perhaps higher commitment and involvement, to the relationship.

In the future, communication channels between products and consumers will become more sophisticated. Today, sponsors must work to rise above the clutter that now exists in marketing and advertising. In order to emerge from the clutter, sponsors are using new, more discriminating tools: new advertising technology (virtual advertising), new relationship-marketing programs (frequent-fan identification swipe cards), and new sponsor programs (interactive fan zones). As technology continues to evolve and offer improvements in the way we communicate, sponsors will seize these opportunities to engage consumers in new and innovative ways.

Finally, the sophistication in the industry will demand a corresponding sophistication with regard to the individuals employed in the sport industry. Expectations concerning skill sets and abilities will be elevated to encompass greater demands for specific sport business expertise along with an understanding of the marketing parameters of sport products and the use of sport communication channels. Emphasis on business skills rather than sport participation will drive talent searches within sport properties. An expertise in sport marketing, as opposed to traditional marketing, will be required of individuals working for corporations involved in sport sponsorship. On both sides of the sponsorship, people will need to understand the unique aspects of sport marketing and of the sport industry in order to achieve success in a more sophisticated and industry-savvy marketing environment. If this can be accomplished, the mutually beneficial aspects of sponsorship and partnerships will be the impetus that continues to help the sport industry grow, expand, and evolve.

FROM OUR CRYSTAL BALL

On the basis of our research and consulting activities in the field, we have attempted to provide our vision of what we see happening in sport in the new millennium. As these events transpire, new marketing strategies and approaches will be necessary to capitalize on these opportunities.

Growth of international exhibitions will continue. Fueled by the success of the McDonald's Cup and regular-season NBA games played in Japan, NFL exhibition games, MLB games in Mexico and postseason all-star tours, the NHL All Star format, and a number of other events, current activities will expand and new international contests will develop. Given the need to grow new sources of income and expand international interest for the purposes of television programming and merchandise sales, we suggest two developments that could occur in the next decade.

First, we might look for sanctioned international competition in baseball. Teams, possibly the World Series champion but most probably a team like the Los Angeles Dodgers or an All-Star team, would represent the United States and play in an October-November series, initially competing against teams from Mexico, the Caribbean, Venezuela, and other Latin American countries. After this initial experiment and evaluation and adjustment, the competition could expand to include Japan, China, Korea, and other Pacific Rim countries, progressing toward a baseball World Cup format and tournament and providing a globally televised platform for the American pastime.

The second possibility we see is competition, sanctioned by the NBA and FIBA (International Basketball Federation), between the NBA and European teams—with the European teams possibly becoming a division of the NBA and ultimately competing against NBA teams in the regular season. Initially, the competition would entail some type of postseason activity similar to what we have envisioned for baseball, but because of a combination of factors: the NBA's need to increase revenue; the need for a new drawing card or factor in the post-Jordan era; the demonstrated success of interleague play in baseball (the importance of the opportunity to see new players for the first time); a spirit of national pride in European countries that are continually being prodded toward a continental identity rather than a national one; and the need for television networks to have something new to attract and retain viewers. The NBA Players Association will have critical input regarding how this will be implemented, but at some point in the first decade of the new millennium we will see it.

Women's professional team sports will continue to develop. The success of the WNBA, combined with the developing talents and increasing labor supply of elite women athletes, will provide the impetus for new leagues. Based upon interests, television ratings and corporate sponsor interest, expect to see women's soccer and perhaps a WNHL—if the sport continues to grow and attract fans and sponsorship as a result of the American victory in the 1999 World Cup. Other possibilities are volleyball and softball, structured in a new league format.

There will be a true national championship play-off format for NCAA football. We have continued to evolve in this direction over the past decade. Pressure on NCAA member schools from the media and sponsors, combining to create an unprecedented financial incentive that will be distributed to all teams, will finally close the deal. This financial incentive will allow most schools to comply with gender equity guidelines without eliminating other sports. Look for bowl games to begin as early as the second week of December with a national championship game held the second week of January.

College athletes will receive compensation. If the national championship play-off becomes a reality, look for compensation for college athletes to follow shortly. This will happen for a variety of reasons: the ever increasing number of players leaving college early to turn professional; the risk of injury that athletes assume every time they compete; the role of the athletes in revenue production and the amount of revenue they produce; and the dependence upon athletes to support the system that has been created. Decades after offering this suggestion, authors like James Michener and John F. Rooney will be validated.

There will be more mergers among sport marketing agencies and corporations involved in producing sport apparel and other merchandise. Absorption of smaller agencies or companies with attractive clients, licenses, relationships, contracts, or geographic presence will continue to be the rule. Such companies as the International Marketing Group, SFX, Nike, and Advantage will continue to grow by taking over smaller companies or agencies that have a desirable niche or characteristic.

Multiple ownership of sport teams in various leagues will continue, as will corporate ownership of those teams. Turner and the *Chicago Tribune*, once feared as owners because of their media capabilities, have been far overshadowed by Disney and Fox. The Disney empire owns an NHL team (Mighty Ducks) and an MLB team (Angels). Logic would suggest that an NFL and an NBA team are on the horizon. Currently, New York-based Cablevision has been in discussions with George Steinbrenner to purchase the Yankees to add to the NHL Rangers and NBA Knicks, which are featured on its Madison Square Garden (MSG) Network, while Turner (TNT/TBS) and NBC have been studying the concept of creating a new professional football league. With the current expansion fees and asking prices for existing teams, corporate ownership of some form will always be a factor in the next decade.

Player salaries will continue to escalate. Regardless of hard or soft salary caps, elite players will continue to receive unprecedented amounts of money and unique incentives to sign contracts. The recent signing of Kevin Brown by the Los Angeles

Dodgers for a record $100+ million contract will be eclipsed in the next decade by a long-term contract for perhaps as much as $200 million. In addition to the financial component, teams will be using unique assets and opportunities to entice players to sign with them. Fox can offer a player the possibility of a television career—not only as a sport anchor but also as an actor on a drama or sitcom. Disney could provide Disney World to players for charitable activities for their foundation or community relations efforts. The potential is limitless.

The unfolding soap opera of the haves and have-nots will continue and will become more pronounced. In baseball, it appears highly doubtful that teams with payrolls under $50 million (in 1999) will be able to seriously compete for postseason play. In the past five years, building new stadiums has played a key role in expanding the incomes of teams. Now, building a new stadium is a necessity for maintaining the status quo. Teams must continue to create luxury-seating options and more expensive sponsorship packages that force the team to direct their product to those that can afford it. This is a critical issue that must be addressed in baseball, and could also disrupt a number of other leagues with established revenue sharing.

Areas such as this one transform sports events into interactive experiences for children and families.

Facilities will continue to become complete entertainment palaces—much more than just a place to watch a game. Imagine sitting in your seat and having the ability to view replays at will, even to select the camera angle and to stop the action. How about participating in a virtual-reality football game while you are waiting for the NFL game to begin? Ever thought about making the stadium more children/family-friendly? The answer to this last might be interactive areas, playgrounds, and concession stands for children. (See photo.) These are not just possibilities; they're probabilities. Team owners and facilities designers are aware that they must add value to the ticket package to command the prices required. Adding value to the experience of attending has a multiplier effect: it keeps parties interested in attending, thus cutting down on the availability of tickets, and thus keeping the stands full, prices high, and demand in excess of supply. The end result of this equation—a full house—escalates sponsor interest and value, thus generating additional income just through the experience of attending.

Sports and activities with an increasing element of risk and challenge and inherent danger will continue to be developed. The success of the X Games (ESPN's Extreme Games) for both the participant and the spectator has led to a sport movement that can be called risk/adventure activities. These activities, initially seen as outside of the mainstream, have become increasingly mainstream due partly to their appeal to and acceptance by GenXers and the .com generation and their commercialization on television and through advertisers wanting to communicate with those market segments. Look for continued growth in this area, including travel and vacation programming that involves instruction and provides equipment for beginners as well as intense competitive experiences for more accomplished enthusiasts.

Enter the age of choice or on-demand television. The success of systems such as Primestar and Direct TV has revolutionized sport television viewing. We have the ability to select any NFL game via the NFL Sunday Ticket and have access to numerous NBA, NHL, MLB, Major League Soccer, and NCAA games through a variety of other subscription formats. Look for this trend to continue and expand. Consumers will be able to tailor their subscriptions to their specific wants. For instance, they may subscribe only to the games of their favorite teams or only to Friday night games. Unfortunately, this success may come at a price—the decline of sporting events on network television.

WRAP-UP

The new millennium holds many of the fears, expectations, and possibilities for sport that it holds for other businesses and activities. Perhaps rising costs will diminish the possibility of frequent spectator experiences; this could result in more experiences (accompanied by more technological innovations) as television/electronic viewers—or perhaps we will become more active as participants.

We can be assured that technology will continue to impact our sporting experience, whether we are electronic viewers, live spectators, or participants. Better facilities, better equipment, improved communication methods, virtual experiences, and who knows what else lie in store for us. As more opportunities develop and compete for our time, our ability to choose will dictate what is a fad, a complete failure, or a long-term success.

There are a number of developments that we may see in the next millennium: increased governmental regulation and control, more franchise movement, emphasis on environmental issues, 500 television channels, and so forth. While many of these things may be beneficial, they may also be detrimental—it's just too early to tell.

ACTIVITIES

1. Select the area of the sport industry most compatible with your career plans. Arrange an interview with a member of an organization in that industry segment. The focus of the interview should be on projecting future developments for that organization over the next 10 years.

2. Sport sociologists and other scholars have debated the future of sports. Some have argued that sports will be technologically driven while others suggest a movement away from spectatorship into a more personalized participatory experience. Identify several of these visions and contrast them with the components of your own vision. What do you feel sports will become in the next 10 years? 25 years? 50 years?

3. Identify the most critical issues that would need to be resolved if a professional sport league in the United States, for example the NBA, elected to expand overseas (Europe or Asia). How would these issues impact the job of a sport marketer?

APPENDIX A

SPORT INDUSTRY ORGANIZATIONS

This appendix has been created to provide the reader with a representative sample of organizations and contacts within the sport industry. It should serve as a "quick and dirty" directory to help the reader understand the breadth of the industry while providing some pertinent contact information along the way.

Please note that this directory is not meant to be a full listing of all sporting groups within the industry.

The items in this appendix are first grouped by category and then sorted alphabetically within each category. The categories are listed below. Each entry contains the name and address of the organization.

The categories listed are as follows:

> Single Sport Organizations and Publications

> Amateur Leagues and Teams (High School, College, and Olympic)

  High School

  College

  Olympic

> Multisport Media

  Electronic

  Multisport Magazines, Journals, Newsletters

  Newspapers

  Sport Business Directories

> Sport Sponsors

> Sport Sponsorship/Marketing/Event Agencies

> Professional Services

  Sports Agents

  Executive Search Services

  Market Research Services

> Sporting Goods (Equipment, Apparel, and footwear)

SINGLE-SPORT ORGANIZATIONS AND PUBLICATIONS

AUTO SPORTS

American Speed Association (ASA)
202 S. Main Street
Pendleton, IN 46064
317-778-4006

BASEBALL

Major League Baseball Properties
245 Park Ave
New York, NY 10167
212-931-7800

For more information on individual league teams, visit www.majorleaguebaseball.com.

BASKETBALL

National Basketball Association
645 Fifth Ave.
New York, NY 10022
212-826-0579

For more information on individual league teams, visit www.nba.com.

SOCCER

Major League Soccer
110 E. 42nd St., 10th Fl.
New York, NY 10017
212-450-1200

For more information on individual league teams, visit www.majorleaguesoccer.com.

FIELD HOCKEY

U.S. Field Hockey Association
One Olympic Plaza
Colorado Springs, CO 80909
719-578-4567

FOOTBALL

National Football League
410 Park Ave.
New York, NY 10022
212-758-1742

For more information on individual league teams, visit www.nfl.com.

GOLF

Ladies' Professional Golf Association
2570 W. International Speedway Blvd., Ste. B
Daytona Beach, FL 32114
904-254-8800

For more information on the association, visit www.lpga.com.

Professional Golfers' Association of America/ PGA of America
100 Avenue of Champions
P.O. Box 109601
Palm Beach Gardens, FL 33410
407-624-8400

For more information on the association, visit www.pga.com.

ICE HOCKEY

National Hockey League
1251 Avenue of the Americas
New York, NY 10020-1198
212-789-2000

For more information on each particular league team, visit www.nhl.com.

TENNIS

U.S. Tennis Association (USTA)
70 W. Red Oak Ln.
White Plains, NY 10604
914-696-7000

For more information on the association, visit www.usta.com.

TRACK AND FIELD

USA Track & Field
One RCA Dome, Ste. 140
Indianapolis, IN 46225
317-261-0500

AMATEUR LEAGUES AND TEAMS (HIGH SCHOOL, COLLEGE, AND OLYMPIC)

HIGH SCHOOL LEAGUES AND TEAMS

National Federation of State High School Associations
11724 N.W. Plaza Cir.
Kansas City, MO 64195-0626
816-464-5400

For information on a particular state association, please contact the national federation.

National Interscholastic Athletic Administrators Association (NIAAA)
11724 N.W. Plaza Cir.
Kansas City, MO 64195
816-464-5400

National High School Sports Hall of Fame
11724 N.W. Plaza Cir.
Kansas City, MO 64195
816-464-5400

COLLEGE LEAGUES AND TEAMS

National Collegiate Athletic Association (NCAA)
P.O. Box 6222
700 W. Washington St.
Indianapolis, IN 46206-6222
317-917-6222

For more information on a particular team or conference, please contact the NCAA directly.

National Junior College Athletic Association (NJCAA)
1825 Austin Bluffs Pkwy., Ste. 100
Colorado Springs, CO 80918
719-590-9788

For more information on a particular team or conference, please contact the NJCAA directly.

OLYMPIC ORGANIZATIONS AND TEAMS

ARCO Olympic Training Center
c/o San Diego National Sports Training Foundation
1650 Hotel Cir. N., Ste. 125
San Diego, CA 92108-2817

Sydney Olympic Organizing Committee
Level 14
The Maritime Center
207 Kent St.
Sydney, New South Wales, 2000
Australia
001 61 2 931 2000

U.S. Olympic Committee
One Olympic Plaza
Colorado Springs, CO 80909
719-632-5551

MULTISPORT MEDIA

ELECTRONIC

ABC Sports, Inc.
Subsidiary of Capital Cities/ABC Inc.
47 W. 66th St.
New York, NY 10023
212-456-7777

CBS Sports
51 W. 52nd St., 25th Fl.
New York, NY 10019
212-975-5230

ESPN—Entertainment & Sports Programming Network
Subsidiary of Capital Cities/ABC Inc.
ESPN Plaza
Bristol, CT 06010
860-585-2000

NBC Sports Division
Subsidiary of General Electric Company
30 Rockefeller Plaza
New York, NY 10112
212-664-4444

MULTISPORT MAGAZINES, JOURNALS, NEWSLETTERS

Athletic Business Magazine
1846 Hoffman St.
Madison, WI 53704
608-249-0186

NCAA News
P.O. Box 6222
700 W. Washington St.
Indianapolis, IN 46206-6222
317-917-6222

Sport Marketing Quarterly
P.O. Box 4425
Morgantown, WV 26504
304-599-3482

Sporting Goods Business
One Penn Plaza
New York, NY 10119-1198
212-714-1300

Sports Illustrated
1271 Avenue of the Americas
New York, NY 10020
212-522-1212

NEWSPAPERS

New York Daily News
450 W. 33rd St.
New York, NY 10001
212-210-2100

USA Today
1000 Wilson Blvd.
Arlington, VA 22229
703-276-3400

SPORT BUSINESS DIRECTORIES

IEG Sponsorship Sourcebook
213 W. Institute Pl., Ste. 303
Chicago, IL 60610-3175
312-944-1727

Sports Market Place
264 Wall St.
Princeton, NJ 08540
609-921-8599

Sports Sponsor FactBook
660 W. Grand Ave., Ste. 100E
Chicago, IL 60610
312-829-7060

For more information, please visit
www.teammarketing.com.

Western Sports Guide
3984 Doniphan Dr.
El Paso, TX 79922
915-584-7791

SPORT SPONSORS

American Express Company
American Express Tower
C 3 World Financial Center
New York, NY 10285
212-640-1494

For more information, please visit
www.americanexpress.com.

Anheuser-Busch Companies, Inc.
Sports Marketing Group/Bud Sports
701 Market St., Ste. 1290
St. Louis, MO 63101
314-259-3000

For more information, please visit
www.budweiser.com.

Arthur Andersen LLP
69 W. Washington St.
Chicago, IL 60602
312-580-0069

BellSouth Corporation
1155 Peachtree St. N.E.
Atlanta, GA 30309-3610
404-249-2000
For more information, please visit
www.bellsouth.com.

Benetton Sportsystem Active
997 Lenox Dr., Bldg. 3, Ste. 105
Lawrenceville, NJ 08648
609-896-3800

Blockbuster Entertainment Corp.
1 Blockbuster Plaza
Fort Lauderdale, FL 33301-1860
954-524-8200

Carquest Auto Parts
580 White Plains Rd.
Tarrytown, NY 10591
914-332-1515

For more information, please visit
www.cruzio.com.

Chase Manhattan Bank
One Chase Manhattan Plaza, 56th Fl.
New York, NY 10081
212-552-2818

For more information, please visit
www.chase.com.

Coca-Cola Company, The
One Coca-Cola Plaza
Atlanta, GA 30313
404-676-5577

For more information, please visit
www.cocacola.com.

Frito-Lay, Inc.
Subsidiary of PepsiCo, Inc.
7701 Legacy Dr.
Plano, TX 75024
214-334-7000

For more information, please visit
www.fritolay.com.

Gillette Company
One Gillette Park
Boston, MA 02127
617-463-2540

Goodyear Tire & Rubber Company, The
1144 E. Market St.
Akron, OH 44316-0001
216-796-2121

For more information, please visit
www.goodyear.com.

Goodyear Tire & Rubber Company, The
1144 E. Market St.
Akron, OH 44316-0001
216-796-2121

For more information, please visit
www.goodyear.com.

Home Depot, Inc., The
2727 Paces Ferry Rd.
Atlanta, GA 30339
770-433-8211

For more information, please visit
www.homedepot.com.

John Hancock Mutual Life Insurance Co.
John Hancock Pl.
200 Clarendon St.
Boston, MA 02117
617-572-6000

Kellogg Company
One Kellogg Square
Battle Creek, MI 49016
616-961-2000

For more information, please visit
www.kellogg.com.

Kraft USA/Oscar Mayer
One Kraft Court
Glenview, IL 60025
708-646-2000

For more information, please visit
www.kraftfoods.com.

Lipton, Inc., Thomas J.
Subsidiary of Unilever United States, Inc.
800 Sylvan Ave.
Englewood Cliffs, NJ 07632
201-871-8217

M&M/Mars
High St.
Hackettstown, NJ 07840
908-852-1000

MasterCard International, Inc.
200 Purchase St.
Purchase, NY 10577
914-249-5000

For more information, please visit
www.mastercard.com.

Mercedes-Benz of North America, Inc.
One Mercedes Dr.
Montvale, NJ 07645
201-573-0600

Miller Brewing Company
Subsidiary of Philip Morris Cos., Inc.
3939 W. Highland Blvd.
Milwaukee, WI 53208
414-931-2000

For more information, please visit
www.millerlite.com.

Motorola, Inc.
Corporate Advertising
1303 E. Algonquin Rd.
Schaumburg, IL 60196
708-576-4430

For more information, please visit
www.mot.com.

Ocean Spray Cranberries, Inc.
One Ocean Spray Dr.
Lakeville-Middleborough, MA 02349
508-946-1000

For more information, please visit www.ocean-spray.com.

Pennzoil Company
P.O. Box 2967
Houston, TX 77052-2967
713-546-4000

For more information, please visit
www.penzoil.com.

Quaker Oats Company/Gatorade Brand
321 N. Clark
P.O. Box 9004, Ste. 17-9
Chicago, IL 60604-9001
312-222-7111

For more information, please visit
www.quakeroats.com.

R.J. Reynolds Tobacco Company
Subsidiary of RJR/Nabisco, Inc.
P.O. Box 484
Winston-Salem, NC 27102
910-741-5000

Sara Lee Corporation
470 Hanes Mill Rd.
Winston-Salem, NC 27105
910-519-7162

For more information, please visit
www.saralee.com.

Shoprite
Subsidiary of Wakefern Food Corp.
Somers Manor, Ste. 202
599 Shore Rd.
Somers Point, NJ 08244
609-927-7888

3M Company
3M Center
St. Paul, MN 55144-1000
612-733-1110

Time Warner Inc./Sports Illustrated
1271 Avenue of the Americas
New York, NY 10020
212-522-0684

For more information, please visit
www.pathfinder.com.

Walt Disney World Company
1950 W. Magnolia Palm Dr.
Lake Buena Vista, FL 32830
407-824-2250

For more information, please visit
www.disney.com.

Xerox Corporation
101 Continental Blvd.
El Segundo, CA 90245
310-333-3469

For more information, please visit
www.xerox.com.

SPORT SPONSORSHIP/MARKETING/ EVENT AGENCIES

Advantage
1751 Pinnacle Dr., 15th Fl.
McLean, VA 22102
703-905-4495

Advantage Marketing Group
5215 N. O'Connor #770
Irving, TX 75039
214-869-2244

American Sports Marketing, Inc.
160 Fontaine Rd.
Mableton, GA 30059
770-941-9396

API Sponsorship
1633 Broadway, 27th Fl.
New York, NY 10019
212-841-1590

Centre Management
Division of Centre Group
One Harry S. Truman Dr.
Landover, MD 20785
301-499-6300

Champion Sports Group
5015-B West W.T. Harris Blvd.
Charlotte, NC 28269
704-596-9002

Championship Group Inc.
3690 N. Peachtree Rd.
Atlanta, GA 30341
404-457-5777

CMG Worldwide
1000 Waterway Blvd.
Indianapolis, IN 46202
317-633-2050

Coordinated Sports Management Group, Inc.
790 Frontage Rd.
Northfield, IL 60093-1210
708-441-4315

Event Marketing & Management Intl.
1322 N. Mills Ave.
Orlando, FL 32803
407-896-1160

Executive Sports Management
223 W. Jackson Blvd., Ste. 405
Chicago, IL 60606
312-322-1870

Host Communications Inc.
546 E. Main St.
Lexington, KY 40508
606-226-4678

International Management Group/IMG
One Erieview Plaza, Ste. 1300
Cleveland, OH 44114
216-522-1200

ISL Sports & Company
1281 E. Main St.
Stamford, CT 06902
203-324-6800

Lifestyle Marketing Group
345 Park Ave. South
New York, NY 10010
212-779-6600

Millsport Inc.
Stamford Towers, 750 Washington Blvd.
Stamford, CT 06901
203-977-0500

Ogden Entertainment Services
Subsidiary of Ogden Services Corp.
2 Penn Plaza, 25th Fl.
New York, NY 10121
212-868-6211

Proserv, Inc.
1101 Wilson Blvd., Ste. 1800
Arlington, VA 22209
703-276-3030

PSP Sports Marketing
355 Lexington Ave.
New York, NY 10017
212-697-1460

Russ Cline and Associates
2310 W. 75th St.
Prairie Village, KS 66208
913-384-8920

Sports Entertainment Group
25 E. Willow St.
Millburn, NJ 07041
201-467-1001

Triple Crown Sports
253 Linden St., Ste. 201
Fort Collins, CO 80524
303-224-2502

PROFESSIONAL SERVICES

SPORT AGENTS

Arthur Andersen & Co./Athlete Advisory Services
633 W. 5th St., 32nd Fl.
Los Angeles, CA 90071
213-614-6552

Bob Woolf Associates, Inc.
2475 Prudential Tower
Boston, MA 02199
617-437-1212

Falk Associates Management Enterprises/FAME
5335 Wisconsin Ave. NW, Ste. 850
Washington, DC 20015
202-686-2000

Golden Bear Sports Management
11780 U.S. Highway One
Palm Beach, FL 33408
407-626-3900

Pro Player Reps (PPR, Inc.)
2650 Royal Ln., Ste. 214
Dallas, TX 75229
214-247-4327

R.L.R. Associates, Ltd.
7 W. 51st St.
New York, NY 10019
212-541-8641

EXECUTIVE SEARCH SERVICES

Executive Career Options, Inc.
1125 Golfview Rd.
Glenview, IL 60025-3166
708-657-1073

Search Solutions, Inc.
P.O. Box 394
Harbert, MI 49115
616-469-6834

Sports Careers
Division of Stratford American Sports Corp.
2400 E. Arizona Biltmore Cir., Ste. 1270
Phoenix, AZ 85016
602-954-8106
800-776-7877

MARKET RESEARCH SERVICES

ESPN/CHILTON Sports Poll
Subsidiary of Capital Cities/ABC Inc.
201 King of Prussia Rd.
Radhor, PA 19089-0193
610-964-4285

Nielsen Co., A.C.
Subsidiary of Dun & Bradstreet
299 Park Ave.
New York, NY 10171-0074
212-708-7500

Sponsorship Research International USA
Subsidiary of Sponsorship Research International UK
1281 E. Main St.
Stamford, CT 06902
203-975-4450

Sports Information Resource Centre
1600 James Naismith Dr.
Gloucester, ON K1B 5N4
Canada
613-748-5658

SPORTING GOODS (EQUIPMENT, APPAREL, AND FOOTWEAR)

Adidas America
541 N.E. 20th St., Ste. 207
Portland, OR 97232
503-230-2920

For more information, please visit
www.adidas.com.

Brine, Inc.
47 Summer St.
Milford, MA 01757
508-478-3250

Callaway Golf
2285 Rutherford Rd.
Carlsbad, CA 92008
619-931-1771

Champion Products, Inc.
475 Corporate Square Dr.
Winston-Salem, NC 27105
910-519-6500

Danskin, Inc.
111 W. 40th St., 18th Fl.
New York, NY 10018
212-764-4630

Fila USA, Inc.
Executive Plaza 3, Ste. 1200
11350 McCormick Rd.
Hunt Valley, MD 21031
410-584-8196

New Balance Athletic Shoe, Inc.
61 N. Beacon St.
Boston, MA 02134
617-783-4000

For more information, please visit
www.newbalance.com.

Nike, Inc.
One Bowerman Dr.
Beaverton, OR 97005
503-671-6453

For more information, please visit
www.nike.com.

Precor, Inc.
20001 N. Creek Pkwy.
Bothell, WA 98011
206-486-9292

Rawlings Sporting Goods Co., Inc.
1859 Intertech Dr.
Fenton, MO 63026
314-349-3500

Reebok International Ltd.
100 Technology Center Dr.
Stoughton, MA 02072
617-341-5000

For more information, please visit
www.reebok.com.

Russell Athletic
Lee St.
Alexander City, AL 35010
205-329-4000

Spalding Sports Worldwide
425 Meadow St.
Chicopee, MA 01021-0901
413-536-1200

For more information, please visit
www.spalding.com.

Titleist and Foot-Joy Worldwide
P.O. Box 965
Fair Haven, MA 02719-0965
508-979-2000

SAMPLE SURVEYS

The following are examples of the surveys discussed in chapter 5.

NCAA Championship Patron Questionnaire

In an effort to continue providing championships, the NCAA would like to learn more about you and your interests. Your completion of the enclosed survey will provide valuable information instrumental for achieving this objective.

Please complete each item as accurately and as honestly as possible. While a limited number may require a brief written answer, most items will simply need the appropriate response to be (✔) as shown in the example below. The NCAA would like to thank you in advance for your willingness to assist with this project.

EXAMPLE:

When was your ticket for today's game purchased?
- ☐ Today
- ☐ More than two weeks ago
- ☐ Within last week
- ☑ When tickets first went on sale
- ☐ 1–2 weeks ago
- ☐ Tickets were given to me

1. How many times have you attended this NCAA championship? (including this year) _____

2. Are you here to specifically support a participating team?
   - ☐ **Yes****   ☐ **No**

3. **If yes to Item 2, please (✔) all descriptions that apply to your association with this team.
   - ☐ Alumnus of school   ☐ Currently enrolled student
   - ☐ Friend of participating player   ☐ Team booster club member
   - ☐ Relative of participating player   ☐ Former team participant
   - ☐ University employee   ☐ Other _____

4. Which of the following information sources do you recall seeing or hearing for this event?
   - ☐ College publication/schedule   ☐ Newspaper advertisement
   - ☐ TV advertisement   ☐ NCAA partner display
   - ☐ Direct mail/flier   ☐ Radio/news/TV coverage
   - ☐ Radio advertisement   ☐ Magazine/trade publication
   - ☐ Other _____

5. Which of the following was your **initial** information source for this event?
   - ☐ College publication/schedule   ☐ Newspaper advertisement
   - ☐ TV advertisement   ☐ NCAA partner display
   - ☐ Direct mail/flier   ☐ Radio/news/TV coverage
   - ☐ Radio advertisement   ☐ Magazine/trade publication
   - ☐ Word of mouth   ☐ Other _____

6. Your **decision to attend** today's event was made within the past:
   □ 24 hours □ 2–7 days □ 8–14 days □ 15–30 days □ 31+ days

7. How did you purchase/receive your ticket for today's event?
   □ Mail order □ Upon arriving today □ Telephone order □ College box office □ Ticket was given to me
   □ Other _____

8. You purchased/received your ticket for today's event within the past:
   □ 24 hours □ 2–7 days □ 8–14 days □ 15–30 days □ 31+ days

9. How would you rate the price of your ticket for this event?
   □ Very low □ Low □ Moderate □ High □ Very high

10. How likely are you to attend this event again next year?
    □ Very unlikely □ Probably not □ Maybe □ Probably □ Definitely

11. Excluding today's event, what NCAA championships have you attended in the past two years?
    _____
    _____
    _____
    _____

12. If the NCAA were to consider offering the following services to championship patrons please indicate all that would appeal to you.
    □ Special hotel rates
    □ Specially priced travel packages
    □ Pre-event merchandise purchases (e.g. mail order)
    □ Souvenir program included with advanced ticket purchase
    □ Fan Fest activities (e.g. games, contests, exhibits)
    □ NCAA Internet Web page purchasing for tickets and merchandise
    □ Championship club membership (priority seating, merchandise discounts, newsletter; approximately $25)
    □ Other (please provide recommendations and any details you would like to see)
    _____
    _____
    _____
    _____

13. Please check (✔) all existing NCAA programs and services with which you are familiar.
    □ NCAA Corporate Partner Program   □ Championship merchandise catalog
    □ Special car rental rates from National □ Championship travel packages

Economic Impact Analysis for **Non-Residents Only**

The following set of survey items are included for the sole purpose of assessing the impact of this NCAA Championship on the local economy. These items should only be completed by non-residents of the event host community.

If you reside less than 25 miles from the event site, please skip ahead to item 18.

14. Please indicate how much you anticipate spending *per day for yourself* in the host community while attending this event. (Please do not include expenses made by or for others).

    Average Personal Expenditures

Food and beverage	$ _____
Lodging (Your share of any overnight accommodations)	$ _____
Transportation (Your non-airfare expenses, including gas, rental car, parking, taxi/bus)	$ _____
Entertainment (Your non-event expenses for any amusement activities)	$ _____
Event-related (Your event-related expenses, including ticket, concessions, merchandise)	$ _____
Retail shopping (Your non-event expenses for any material purchases)	$ _____
Miscellaneous	$ _____

15. How many days will you spend in the host community while attending this event? _____

16. How did you travel to the event host community for this event?
    □ Airplane □ Bus □ Car □ Train □ Other

17. Who made your travel arrangements?
    □ Travel agent □ Myself □ University organization □ Companion □ Other

Spectator Profile

Please (✔) the response that applies to you.

18. Sex:
    □ Male   □ Female

19. Marital Status:
    □ Married   □ Unmarried   □ Living with significant other

20. Race
    □ African American   □ Asian   □ Hispanic   □ Native American   □ White   □ Other

21. Level of education:
    □ Enrolled in high school   □ High school graduate
    □ Trade/tech diploma   □ Some college
    □ College graduate   □ Graduate degree

22. Indicate the following that apply to your affiliation with the sport played at this event.
    □ Coach   □ Current competitive player
    □ Avid fan   □ Current recreational player
    □ Former player   □ Current governing body official
    □ Supporter of player   □ I have no direct affiliation
    □ Other _____

23. Age:
    □ Under 18   □ 18-24   □ 25-34   □ 35-44   □ 45-54   □ 55+

24. Annual household income:
    □ <$15,000
    □ $15,000-$24,999
    □ $25,000-$39,999
    □ $40,000-$59,999
    □ $60,000-$84,999
    □ $85,000+

25. Your residential zip code: _____

26. Which one of the following best describes the party attending with you today.
    □ Spouse only   □ Friend(s)   □ Teammates   □ Family   □ Team boosters   □ Alumni   □ Business associate(s)

If you would like to receive information on future NCAA championships, please provide your name and address:

_____

_____

_____

Thank you for your time.

Sample Mail Survey for Ticket Plan Holders

1. Which of the following best describes your ticket plan?
   A. Full season ticket holder
   B. Half season (20 games)
   C. 10 Pack
   D. 6 Game Plan
   E. 40 Game Flex Plan
   F. 20 Game Flex Plan

2. How many years have you been an Admirals' ticket-plan holder?
   A. This is the first year I have been a ticket-plan holder
   B. I have been an Admirals' ticket-plan holder for 2–4 seasons
   C. I have been an Admirals' ticket-plan holder for 5–10 seasons
   D. I have been an Admirals' ticket-plan holder for more than 10 seasons

3. How many Admirals' games did you attend last season (1996–97)? _____

4. How many Admirals' games will you attend this season (1997–98)? _____

5. Which of the following best describes the *primary* reason that you purchased your Admirals' ticket-plan holder?
   A. I purchased tickets to entertain clients and business contacts
   B. I purchased tickets for myself and other members of my family because we enjoy hockey
   C. I purchased tickets with a group of friends who enjoy hockey and the opportunity to socialize
   D. None of the above _____

Full season ticket holders skip to question 10

6. If you are a Half season, Flex Plan, 10 Pack, or Holiday Plan Holder, how do you feel about the number of games in your current plan? (Please circle your answer)
   A. There are not enough games in my current plan
   B. The number of games is just right
   C. There are too many games in my current plan

7. If you are a Half season, Flex Plan, 10 Pack, or Holiday Plan Holder, have you attended or are you planning to attend additional games that are not part of your plan?
   A. Yes
   B. No

IF YOU ANSWERED NO TO QUESTION 7 . . . . SKIP TO QUESTION 9.

8. Approximately how many more *regular season* games have you purchased or do you plan to purchase in addition to those games contained in your plan? _____ (Please fill in your answer.)

9. If you are a Half season, Flex Plan, 10 Pack, or Holiday Plan Holder, are you considering upgrading to full season tickets next season?
   A. Yes
   B. No

10. Do you currently share ownership of your season tickets or ticket plan?
    A. Yes
    B. No

11. Which is more important to you when purchasing season tickets or game plans?
    A. The location of the seat
    B. The price of the ticket

12. Based upon the location of your seat and the price you paid for your ticket, do you feel that your current seat is a/an:
    A. Excellent value
    B. Good value
    C. Fair value
    D. Poor value

13. Given that the game itself and the people with whom you are attending are the most important reasons for your attendance, which of the following factors would you consider to be the *second most important consideration* in your evening's entertainment?
    A. Concessions/restaurants at the Bradley Center
    B. Pre-game and timeout music
    C. Promotional contests and activities

    D.   Restaurants/other pre- and post-game activities not at the Bradley Center

    E.   Other _____

14. Please rate each of the Admirals' game elements listed below from 1 (poor) to 6 (excellent) when considering each of these elements based upon your personal standards of quality, quantity, variety, and performance.

Food at concession stands	1	2	3	4	5	6
Restrooms	1	2	3	4	5	6
Video screens and replays	1	2	3	4	5	6
Parking	1	2	3	4	5	6
Employees (vendors, ushers, etc.)	1	2	3	4	5	6
The overall experience of attending an Admirals' game	1	2	3	4	5	6
On-court contests	1	2	3	4	5	6
Music	1	2	3	4	5	6
In-game entertainment (contests, acts)	1	2	3	4	5	6
Level and quality of customer service	1	2	3	4	5	6

15. With regard to the music currently being played during the pre-game, timeouts, and halftime, which of the following statements best describes how you feel about the music selections and presentations:

    A.   I like the current music selections and presentations

    B.   I feel that the music played is too contemporary

    C.   I feel that the music played should be more contemporary

    D.   I like the current music but feel that the songs are too repetitive

    E.   I have no feeling whatsoever regarding the music selections and presentation

16. With regard to the volume of the music played, which of the following best describes your preference:

    A.   I like the volume at which the music is currently played

    B.   I would like the music played at a louder volume

    C.   I would like the music played at a softer volume

17. Which of the following area events have you attended in the past 12 months?
Please circle YES or NO for each of the listed events

Milwaukee Bucks	YES	NO
Green Bay Packers	YES	NO
Milwaukee Brewers	YES	NO
Marquette Basketball	YES	NO
Milwaukee Wave	YES	NO
Milwaukee Rampage	YES	NO
Milwaukee Mustangs	YES	NO
Badger Football	YES	NO
Badger Hockey	YES	NO
SummerFest	YES	NO

18. Which of the following is your preferred (the station you listen to most often) radio station?

    A.   WQFM 93.3

    B.   WKTI 94.5

    C.   WZTR 95.7

    D.   WKLH 96.5

    E.   WFMR 98.3

    F.   WMYX 99.1

    G.   WKKV 100.7

    H.   WLUM 102.1

    I.   WMIL 106.1

    J.   WLZR 102.9

    K.   WEZW 103.7

    L.   WTMJ 620

    M.   WOKY 920

    N.   WISN 1130

    O.   WEMP 1250

    P.   Other _____

19. My preferred television station for watching the local news is:

    A.   WTMJ 4 (NBC)

    B.   WITL 6 (FOX)

    C.   WISN 12 (ABC)

    D.   WVTV 18 (IND)

E.   WCGV 24 (UPN)
F.   WDJT 58 (CBS)
G.   Other _____

20. Which of the following companies are official sponsors of the Milwaukee Admirals:
(Circle YES or NO for each sponsor.)

Coca-Cola	YES	NO
Miller Brewing Company	YES	NO
Pizza Hut	YES	NO
Digital	YES	NO
Piggly Wiggly	YES	NO
M & I Bank	YES	NO
Budweiser	YES	NO
Target	YES	NO
Pepsi	YES	NO
Little Ceasars	YES	NO
Rollerblade/Play It Again Sports	YES	NO
Kmart	YES	NO

21. My favorite Milwaukee area professional sports team is the:
A.   Admirals
B.   Brewers
C.   Bucks
D.   Packers
E.   Other _____

22. In my opinion, the team that does the best job of providing quality entertainment at their games is the:
A.   Admirals
B.   Brewers
C.   Bucks
D.   Packers
E.   Other _____
F.   I'm not sure

23. In my opinion, the team that does the best job of providing value (in terms of the price paid for a ticket) for their fans is the:
A.   Admirals
B.   Brewers
C.   Bucks
D.   Packers
E.   Other _____
F.   I'm not sure

24. In my opinion, the team that does the best job of serving their customers (ushers and game related personnel) is the:
A.   Admirals
B.   Brewers
C.   Bucks
D.   Packers
E.   Other _____
F.   I'm not sure

25. In my opinion, the team that does the best job being active in the local community is the:
A.   Admirals
B.   Brewers
C.   Bucks
D.   Packers
E.   Other _____
F.   I'm not sure

26. If I was entertaining family or friends, my first choice as an entertainment option would be the:
A.   Admirals
B.   Brewers
C.   Bucks
D.   Packers
E.   Other _____
F.   I'm not sure

27. If I was entertaining clients or wanted to entertain guests from out of town, my first choice as an entertainment option would be the:
    A. Admirals
    B. Brewers
    C. Bucks
    D. Packers
    E. Other _____
    F. I'm not sure

28. Do you or your company own ticket plans for any of the following Milwaukee area sports teams:
    (Please circle YES or NO for each option.)

Brewers	YES	NO
Bucks	YES	NO
Packers	YES	NO
Marquette	YES	NO

29. When considering everything regarding my relationship with the Admirals (the team, Bradley Center, my experiences, servicing my account, the entertainment of the game and the cost), I would say that I am:
    A. Highly satisfied
    B. Moderately satisfied
    C. Somewhat satisfied
    D. Somewhat dissatisfied
    E. Moderately dissatisfied
    F. Highly dissatisfied

30. Which of the following best describes your intentions with regard to the Admirals' next season?
    A. I will renew my current plan
    B. I plan to upgrade to season tickets
    C. I plan to downgrade from season tickets to a partial plan
    D. I plan to upgrade from my current partial plan to a larger partial plan
    E. I plan to downgrade from my current partial plan to a smaller plan
    F. I will not be renewing my plan
    G. I am uncertain at this time

31. If you could make one suggestion to the Admirals that would increase your satisfaction or your enjoyment, what would it be:
    _____
    _____
    _____
    _____

32. Do you listen to Admirals' away games on radio (WISN 1130 AM)?
    A. Yes
    B. No

33. If available, would you be interested in watching Admirals' away games on television?
    A. Yes
    B. No

34. In your opinion, should the Admirals' create a mascot to entertain at games and make appearances at various community activities and at schools and hospitals?
    A. Yes
    B. No

35. My preferred weeknight (Monday thru Friday) starting time for Admirals' games is:
    A. 7:00 PM
    B. 7:30 PM

36. My preferred weekend (Saturday & Sunday) starting time for Admirals' games is:
    A. 1:30 PM
    B. 6:00 PM
    C. 7:00 PM

37. What is your age?
    (Please circle your answer.)
    A. 18-24 years of age
    B. 25-34
    C. 35-44
    D. 45-54
    E. 54 years of age or older

38. Your gender is:
    (Please circle your answer.)
    A.   Female
    B.   Male

39. Your marital status is:
    (Please circle your response.)
    A.   Unmarried
    B.   Married

40. Your highest level of education completed:
    A.   High school graduate
    B.   Trade/vocational program
    C.   Some college
    D.   Bachelors degree
    E.   Advanced degree
    F.   Other _____

41. Which of the following best describes your annual household income?
    (Please circle your answer.)
    A.   Less than $25,000
    B. $25,000 to $39,999
    C. $40,000 to $54,999
    D. $55,000 to $74,999
    E. $75,000 to $99,999
    F. $100,000 and over

42. Do you have children under the age of 18 in your household?
    (Please circle your answer.)
    A.   Yes
    B.   No

IF YOU ANSWERED NO TO QUESTION 42 . . . . SKIP TO QUESTION 45.

43. Which of the following best describes attending Admirals' games with your children?
    (Please circle your answer.)
    A.   I never bring my children to Admirals' games
    B.   I bring my children to about one Admirals' game per year
    C.   I bring my children to 2-4 Admirals' games per year
    D.   I bring my children to 5 or more Admirals' games

44. Would you be interested in an Admirals' sponsored Street/roller hockey program for your children?
    A.   Yes
    B.   No

45. What is your zip code?
    (Please write in your response.)
    _____

46. If you could speak directly to the owner of the Admirals about your experiences as a fan, what message would you provide?

Survey copyrighted by Audience Analysts, Amherst, MA and Mark Andrew Zwartynski.

406

1995 CAVS Akron/Cleveland Community Assessment

1. Who is your favorite Cleveland area sports team?
   - a. Browns
   - b. Cavs
   - c. Indians
   - d. Jacks
   - e. Crunch

2. Have you attended home games of the following Cleveland area sports teams in the past year?
   - a. Browns
   - b. Cavs
   - c. Indians
   - d. Jacks
   - e. Crunch

3. Which team do you think puts together the best entertainment package for its fans?
   - a. Browns
   - b. Cavs
   - c. Indians
   - d. Jacks
   - e. Crunch

   Please explain why _____

4. Have you attended any event at Gund Arena?
   - a. yes (continue)
   - b. no (skip to item 8)

   *_IF YES:_ What have you attended?

Jacks _____	CAVS game* _____
WWF _____	College BB _____
Concerts _____	HS BB _____
Disney _____	Circus _____
Other _____	Tennis _____
How many? _____	

   *If no CAVS game, why not?

Lack of interest _____	Distance _____
Cost _____	Surrounding area _____
Other _____	

5. Based on your visit to Gund Arena how would you rate each of the following on a scale of 1 (poor) to 6 (excellent)?

	NA						
Quality/variety of concessions	0	1	2	3	4	5	6
Ticket cost	0	1	2	3	4	5	6
Cost of parking	0	1	2	3	4	5	6
Parking availability	0	1	2	3	4	5	6
Parking accessibility	0	1	2	3	4	5	6
RTA convenience/accessibility	0	1	2	3	4	5	6
Scoreboard/statistics boards	0	1	2	3	4	5	6
Sound system	0	1	2	3	4	5	6
Comfort	0	1	2	3	4	5	6
Seat location	0	1	2	3	4	5	6
Overall appearance/enjoyment	0	1	2	3	4	5	6
Area surrounding the Arena	0	1	2	3	4	5	6

6. Has the Gund Arena lived up to your expectations?   Yes   No

7. Are you planning to attend/return to any events at Gund Arena in the next 6 months?   Yes   No

   SKIP TO ITEM #10

8. *_IF NO:_ Why not?

Lack of interest _____	Distance _____
Cost _____	Safety/location _____
Traffic _____	Work conflict _____
Other _____	

9. Have you read/heard anything about Gund Arena?

   Yes (was it +/–)**   No

   **Please explain _____

10. Prior to its closure how many events did you annually attend at the Richfield Coliseum? _____

11. What image comes to mind when I mention each of the following Cleveland area sports teams/organizations?
    Browns _____
       Why? _____
    CAVS _____
       Why? _____
    Indians _____
       Why? _____
    Lumberjacks _____
       Why? _____
    Crunch _____
       Why? _____

12. What team do you think does the best job of being involved in the local community?
    a. Browns   d. Jacks
    b. Cavs   e. Crunch
    c. Indians

13. Why? _____

14. Can you identify any of their community relations programs?
    Program _____

15. On a scale of 1 (poor) to 6 (excellent) how would you rate the Cavs community involvement? _____

16. Can you identify a CAVS community relations program?
    Program _____

17. What team has the most effective advertising?
    a. Browns   d. Jacks
    b. Cavs   e. Crunch
    c. Indians

18. Why? _____

19. What is the CAVS' 1994–95 advertising slogan?   Correct ID Incorrect ID?/Unknown**
    **Is it one of these?
       Get in the game _____   A jammin good time _____
       You gotta be there _____   Come Out & Play _____
       Still unsure _____

20. In an average month, how often do you get to downtown Cleveland for shopping/entertainment? _____

21. Gender:
    a. female   b. male

22. Marital Status:
    a. married   b. unmarried

23. Age:
    a. 18–24   d. 45–54
    b. 25–34   e. 55+
    c. 35–44

24. Your annual household income:
    a. under $25,000   d. $75,000–99,999`
    b. $25,000–49,999   e. $100,000–124,999
    c. $50,000–74,999   f. $125,000+

25. Highest level of education:
    a. high school graduate   d. bachelors degree
    b. some college   e. advanced degree
    c. trade/vocational program   f. other _____

26. Your residential zip code is: _____

If you would like to receive Cleveland CAVS information complete the following:

Name: _____

Address: _____

           _____

ENDNOTES

PREFACE

1. T. Jensen, "Tobacco Road paved with gold," Street and Smith's Sports Business Journal (18-24 May 1998): 19-20; Marc Goldin, "NHL to dabble in auto racing," Foster's Daily Democrat, 20 March 1997, 20.
2. "Shaq needs a new shoe," Sports Illustrated, 8 June 1998, 30.

CHAPTER 1

1. S. Rushin, "World domination," Sports Illustrated, 27 October 1997, 68-71.
2. M. Swift, "From corned beef to caviar," Sports Illustrated, 3 June 1991, 80.
3. Swift, "From corned beef to caviar," 83.
4. D. Higdon, "Basketball goes global," US Air Magazine, May 1996, 48-51, 68, 70; M. Gunther, "They all want to be like Mike," Fortune, 21 July 1997, 51-53; S. Fainaru, "Dominicans' hunger grows for NBA merchandise," Boston Globe, 4 June 1997, A1, 12; C. Desens and E. O'Reilly, "The NBA's fast break overseas," Business Week, 5 December 1994, 94; D. Filipov, "Hoop fanatics look to NBA, not the future," Boston Globe, 12 December 1994, 2; W. D'Orio, "Those things they do," Promo, November 1996, 28-31, 62-63; B. Ryan, "Profile: Hoop dreams," Sales and Marketing Management 146, no. 12 (December 1996): 48.
5. Rushin, "World domination," 71; Sports Business Daily (hereafter cited as SBD), 20 October 1997, 16.
6. Bozeman Bulger, "Twenty-five years in sports," Saturday Evening Post, 26 May 1928, 136.
7. A. Meek, "An Estimate of the Size and Supporting Economic Activity of the Sports Industry in the United States," Sport Marketing Quarterly, 6 December 1997, 15-22; K. Badenhausen et al., "More than a game," Financial World, 17 June 1997, 40-50; "NBC sells out," SBD, 25 November 1997, 3; Chronicle of Higher Education, 27 June 1997, 43; "Sidelines," Stephen Hardy, profile/interview with David Oprean, Sport Marketing Quarterly, 5 March 1996, 5-9; game televised on Lifetime, 17 December 1997; NFL fan statistics in SBD, 1 December 1997, 7; Richard Campbell, "Women's basketball attendance soars," NCAA News, 15 June 1998, 1, 14; New York Times, sports section reported in SBD, 15 September

1997, 6; video and television statistics reported in SBD, 5 June 1997, 7; SBD, 3, 4 December 1997, 6.
8. J. McCallum, "Foul trouble," Sports Illustrated, 15 December 1997, 68-69; J. Gotthelf and L. Brockinton, "It's damage-control time," Street and Smith's Sports Business Journal (hereafter cited as SSSBJ) (18-24 January 1999): 1, 9.
9. P. Taylor, "The race card," Sports Illustrated, 15 December 1997, 70-71; Parker quoted in SBD, 25 November 1997, 7.
10. For baseball's troubles, see T. Verducci, "Sign of the times," Sports Illustrated, 3 May 1993, 15-21; M. Starr et al., "Baseball's hardest sell," Newsweek, 12 December 1994, 84; Hall of Fame statistics in SBD, 1 August 1997, i. For 1997 statistics and polls, see SBD, 29 September 1997, 8; SBD, 30 September 1997, 7; W. Lester, "With excitement, fans returning," Foster's Sunday Citizen, 6 September 1998, 5B; minor league merchandise sales reported in SBD, 12 February 1998, 3.
11. See also "The future of spending" by the editors of American Demographics, January 1995, 12-19.
12. "McDonalds re-ups," SBD, 3 February 1998, 3; "Sign of the times," SBD, 3 August 1998, 3; R. Maloney, "Buffalo teams play on crowded field," SSSBJ (August 10-16): 17.
13. M. Grunwald, "No foothold in U.S.," Boston Globe, 16 June 1994, 45; CONCACAF crowd reported in SBD, 19 February 1998, 9.
14. L. Tye, "Boston's game plan: Get the children back," Boston Globe, 5 June 1997, A1, 19; L. Tye, Boston Globe, "City youths often lose the chance to play," 1 October 1997, A1, 18.
15. J. Larson, "The museum is open," American Demographics, November 1994, 32-38.
16. L. Kesler, "Man created ads in sport's own image," Advertising Age, 27 August 1979, 5-10.
17. The classic work on marketing is P. Kotler, Marketing management: Analysis, planning, implementation, and control, 9th ed. (Englewood Cliffs, NJ: Prentice Hall, 1997).
18. T. Levitt, "Marketing myopia," Harvard Business Review (July-August 1960): 45-56. See also J. Peterson, "20 marketing myths," Fitness Management, May 1992, 30-32; J. Peterson and C. Bryant, "Fifty nifty

marketing facts," *Fitness Management*, March 1998, 40-41; W. Weilbacher, "Yesterday's realities are today's myths," *Advertising Age*, 7 June 1993, 7.

19. D. Cooke, "Packaging for prestige: The tennis advantage," *IRSA Club Business*, July 1987, 62.

20. *SBD*, 22 August 1997, 11.

21. L. Bollig, "Professional marketing finds its way into college basketball," *NCAA News*, 6 December 1993, 12.

22. Stephen Hardy, "Profile/Interview with Matt Levine," *Sport Marketing Quarterly* 5 (September 1996): 5-12.

23. R. Stevens, et al., "Sport marketing among colleges and universities," *Sport Marketing Quarterly* 4 (March 1995): 41-47.

24. Jones quoted in *SBD*, 16 October 1997, 10; Stevens et al., "Sport marketing."

25. "Executive committee OKs stronger marketing program," *NCAA News*, 19 August 1996, 1, 24; M. Brunker, "Horse racing begins its run," *SSSBJ*, 27 April-3 May 1998: 1, 54-55; "National Girls and Women in Sports Day—community action kit," 1995, in author's possession; G. Brown, "Fanning the interest in soccer," *NCAA News*, 23 September 1996, 9; S. Hardy, "Profile/Interview with Vic Gregovits, VP, sales, Philadelphia Eagles," *Sport Marketing Quarterly* 6 (September 1997): 5-11; R. Burton and R. Cornilles, "Emerging theory in team sport sales: Selling tickets in a more competitive arena," *Sport Marketing Quarterly* 7 (March 1998): 29-37.

26. B. Enis and K. Roering, "Services marketing: Different products, similar strategy," in *Marketing of services*, ed. J.H. Donnelly and W.R. George (Chicago: American Marketing Association, 1981), 1. The classic definition of sport is that in J. Loy, "The nature of sport," *Quest* 10 (May 1968): 1-15. The human interaction renders sport more of a "service," in business terms. For the growing literature on marketing services, see S. Edgett and S. Parkinson, "Marketing for service industries," *Service Industries Journal* 13, no. 3 (July 1993): 19-39.

27. See the many works cited in Edgett and Parkinson, "Marketing for service industries."

28. B. Stavro, "It's a classic turnaround situation," *Forbes*, 1 July 1985, 70.

29. R. Poe, "The MBAs of summer," *Across the Board*, October 1985, 18-25.

30. T. Moroney, "Hopkinton finds itself in the winner's circle," *Boston Globe*, 3 April 1996, 1, 24.

31. Research and Forecasts, Inc., *Miller Lite report on American attitudes toward sports* (Milwaukee: Miller Brewing Co., 1985), 131-136.

32. C. Dickey and C. Power, "Soccer gets sexy," *Newsweek*, 11 May 1998, 42-43.

33. C. Sennott, "Glee over soccer signals a larger shift within Iran," *Boston Globe*, 8 December 1997, A1, 10.

34. D. Blum, "A $1.75 billion sports package," *Chronicle of Higher Education*, 14 December 1994, A37; "PGA Tour reports net income," *SBD*, 6 May 1998, 11.

35. "NBA news and notes," *SBD*, 20 February 1998, 5; "Marketplace roundup," *SBD*, 20 March 1998, 4.

36. K. Badenhausen, et al., "Sports: More than a game," "Disney wishes upon a starwave," *SBD*, 1 May 1998, 5; S. Schmid, "Sports, Disney style," *Athletic Business*, October 1996, 67-74; "Fox Sports set to enter magazine biz," *SBD*, 28 April 1998, 5.

37. T. Doyle, "Changes and trends in the retail segment of the sporting goods industry," *NSGA Report*, 1998, in sgrnet database: www.sgrnet.com.

38. S. Cohen, "It's not your father's ski business anymore," *Hemisphere*, January 1998, 62-66; "Let's hit the slopes," *SBD*, 24 April 1998, 11.

39. "The Marquee Group," *TV Sports File*, 17 November 1997, in sgrnet database: www.sgrnet.com; J. Gotthelf, "Sports agencies consolidating," *SSSBJ* (May 11-17 1998): 3.

40. "Family ties," *SBD*, 3 April 1998, 9.

CHAPTER 2

1. "Beach volleyball," *Sports Business Daily* (hereafter cited as SBD), 22 April 1998, 8.

2. For an excellent discussion of strategy in sport organizations, see T. Slack, *Understanding sport organizations* (Champaign, IL: Human Kinetics, 1997), 91-114.

3. A. Cohen, "Can the game return," *Athletic Business*, March 1996, 40; J. Burris, "Repairing the damage," *Boston Globe*, 24 June 1997, C1, 7; "State of the game," *SBD*, 25 August 1997, 7; "Troubles for tennis," *SBD*, 25 August 1997, 7; G. Faltin, "USTA offers programs," *Foster's Daily Democrat*, 10 May 1998, B8.

4. B. Kamenjar, "Trouble down the track?" *Athletic Management*, August-September 1994, 51-55; C. Mashback, "Back in the race," *Sports Illustrated*, 28 July 1997, 82; "Mashback runs through latest marketing endeavors for USATF," *SBD*, 3 June 1998, 5; P. Cooper, "The 'visible hand' on the footrace: Fred Lebow and the marketing of the marathon," *Journal of Sport History* 19 (winter 1992): 244-256.

5. "Golf's biggest supporters," *SBD*, 14 November 1998, 4.

6. P. Kotler, *Marketing management*, 9th ed. (Upper Saddle River, NJ: Prentice Hall, 1997); W.A. Sutton, "Developing an initial marketing plan for intercollegiate athletic programs," *Journal of Sport Management* 1 (1987): 146-158; S. Reese, "The very model of a modern marketing plan," *Marketing Tools*, January-February 1996, 56-65. For a larger look at sport organizations and strategy, see Slack, *Understanding sport organizations*. For a very detailed checklist for marketing planning see the 50-page appendix

in D.M. Carter, Keeping score: An inside look at sports marketing (Grant's Pass, OR: Oasis Press, 1996), 262-310.

7. P. Drucker, "The theory of the business," Harvard Business Review 72 (September-October 1994): 95-104; C. Hedden, "Build a better image," Marketing Tools, May 1996, 68-72.

8. S. Hardy, "Profile/Interview with Dick Lipsey," Sport Marketing Quarterly 7 (September 1998): 5-9; Charetz quoted in A. Disla, "Market-driven programming," Fitness Management, September 1994, 36-38; Aaron Conklin, "Paul Tagliabue is watching you," Athletic Business, June 1998, 9.

9. All quotes are from D. Fisher's excellent article, "The Rochester Royals and the transformation of professional basketball, 1945-57," International Journal of the History of Sport 10 (April 1993): 20-48. See also R.W. Peterson, Cages to jump shots: Pro basketball's early days (New York: Oxford, 1990), 150-166.

10. J. Mahaffie, "Why forecasts fail," American Demographics, March 1995, 34-40; P. Francese, "America at mid-decade," American Demographics, February 1995, 23-32. For a valuable assessment of some "growth markets" in sports, see R. Miller, J. Pursell, and T. Walker, 1998 Sports business market research handbook (Norcross, GA: Sports Business Market Research, 1998), 157-223.

11. G. Barnett and S. Rozin, "A lot of leagues of their own," Business Week, 3 March 1997, 54-55; "Women love the NHL," SBD, 7 May 1998, 9; "Can men's hockey ride on coattails?" SBD, 21 April 1998, 15; P. Hunt, "Gear," SI Womensport, fall 1997, 166-167.

12. "Wendy's inks $1 million deal," SBD, 20 April 1998, 3; "GM hopes to attract women consumers," SBD, 23 March 1998, 4.

13. "Big Blue connects with NFL," SBD, 24 November 1998, 4; Quokka quote in M. Meyer, "Taste the salt, feel the wind," Newsweek, 11 May 1998, 87-88.

14. J. George, "Pro teams seek backers for training facilities," Street and Smith's Sports Business Journal (18-24 May 1998): 16; J. Lombardo, "Hoping for an Rx for profits," Street and Smith's Sports Business Journal (15-21 June 1998): 24.

15. "Giants co-owner the point man on NFLX," SBD, 11 May 1998, 11.

16. "NASCAR aims to reach new markets," SBD, 27 May 1998, 3.

17. G. Krupa, "Betting on racing," Boston Globe, 12 June 1998, C1, 5.

18. P. Graham, "Ambush marketing," Sport Marketing Quarterly 6 (March 1997): 10-12; "Well, who does," SBD, 12 February 1998, 15.

19. M. Letscher, "How to tell fads from trends," American Demographics, December 1994, 38-44; M. Letscher, "Sports fads and trends," American Demographics, June 1997, 53-56; L.J. Wertheim, "Trout may jump for joy," Sports Illustrated, 23 March 1998, 22.

20. For a view of Nike at its height of power, see D. Katz, Just do it: The Nike spirit in the corporate world (Holbrook, MA: Adams, 1994).

21. P. Drucker, "The theory of the business"; Hedden, "Build a better image," 68-72. Bulleted list adapted from E. Pitts, "Imagination is better than knowledge," Fitness Management, March 1995, 33-35.

22. Denver Grizzlies Hockey Club, "Draft—community relations plan, 1994/1995 season," in authors' possession.

23. Kotler, Marketing management, 250-251; D. Shani, "A framework for implementing relationship marketing in the sport industry," Sport Marketing Quarterly 6 (June 1997): 9-15.

24. Hardy, "Profile/Interview with Dick Lipsey," 6. For a closer look at the fan escalator, see W. Sutton et al., "Escalating your fan base," Athletic Management, February-March 1997, 4-5.

25. A. Ries and J. Trout, Positioning: The battle for your mind (New York: Warner Books, 1982); M. Farber, "Is anyone watching?" Sports Illustrated, 15 June 1998, 46-55; William Sutton and Ian Parrett, "Marketing the core product in professional team sports in the United States," Sport Marketing Quarterly, 1 June 1992, 7-19.

26. B. King, "Drivers ever-mindful of their sponsors," Street and Smith's Sports Business Journal (18-24 May 1998): 26; "MLS faces tests," SBD, 24 March 1998, 12.

27. D. Cooke, "Packaging for prestige," IRSA Club Business, July 1987, 65.

28. R. Sherman, "Softball city," Athletic Business, July 1997, 28-29.

29. A. Chandler, Strategy and structure: Chapters in the history of industrial enterprise (Cambridge, MA: MIT Press, 1962); A. Friedman, "Coke agreement may leave NFL teams scrambling," Street and Smith's Sports Business Journal (8-14 June 1998): 6.

30. "Is there a spell over the MLS Wizards' marketing efforts?" SBD, 25 July 1998, 12.

31. L. Nash, "Ethics without the sermon," Harvard Business Review (November 1981): 79-90; E. Stavrowsky and S. Mosher, "Derogatory team names, logos have got to go," Street and Smiths Sports Business Journal, 31 May-6 June 1999, 29.

32. "Univ. of Memphis gambles on sponsorship," SBD, 23 April 1998, 3.

CHAPTER 3

1. R. Miller, J. Pursell, and T. Walker, 1998 Sports business market research handbook, 2nd ed. (Norcross, GA: Sports Business Market Research, 1998), 384-395.

2. All quotes and data from B. King, "NASCAR: It ain't just racin,'" Street and Smith's Sports Business Journal (18-24 May 1998): 1, 48.

3. "Creighton soccer audience profile"; "Economic impact study and demographic profile of the 1991 Volvo International," both in authors' possession.

4. Perrier Great Waters of France, Inc., The Perrier study: Fitness in America (New York: Perrier, 1979).

5. Many sponsor research firms are listed in Spring 1999 Sports market place, ed. K.J. Myers (Phoenix: Franklin Covey, 1999); W. Sutton, "Profile/Interview with Joyce Julius Cotman," Sport Marketing Quarterly 7 (June 1998): 6-7. See also data in Miller, Pursell, and Walker, 1998 Sports business market research handbook.

6. S. Hardy, "Profile/Interview with Richard Lipsey," Sport Marketing Quarterly 7 (September 1998): 5-9.

7. American Sports Data, Inc. brochure, in authors' possession.

8. J. Steinbreder, "Golf's boom figures to stay in bounds," Street and Smith's Sports Business Journal (4-10 May 1998): 1, 31.

9. For a valuable analysis of the U.S. soccer market, see "Special report: Soccer," Street and Smith's Sports Business Journal (1-7 June 1998): 19-33.

10. "The fans," Sports Business Daily, 19 August 1997, 8. For an example of clarifying participants, see J. Larson, "The bicycle market," American Demographics, March 1995, 42-50.

11. J. Adler, "The empty jogging suit," Newsweek, 1 March 1993, 74.

12. R. Thav, "Changes in magazine research," American Demographics, February 1995, 12-13. See the valuable caveats in M. Chubb and H. Chubb, One third of our time? An introduction to recreation behavior and resources (New York: Wiley, 1981), 261-263.

13. "ASD launches study on sporting goods industry," Sport Business 7 (June 1984): 3.

CHAPTER 4

1. C.F. Springwood, Cooperstown to Dyersville: A geography of baseball nostalgia (Boulder, CO: Westview Press, 1996).

2. Our general framework follows that found in most texts on marketing and consumer behavior. See, for instance, H. Berkman and C. Gilson, Consumer behavior: Concepts and strategies, 3rd ed. (Boston: Kent, 1986). We have tried to link the material on general consumers with that on sport consumers.

3. On sport socialization, involvement, and commitment, see J. Loy, B. McPherson, and G. Kenyon, Sport and social systems (Reading, MA: Addison-Wesley, 1978), 16-23, 215-248; R. Brustad, "Integrating socialization influences into the study of children's motivation in sport," Journal of Sport and Exercise Psychology 14 (1992): 59-77. For an interesting study of sport consumers, with implications about socialization, see A. Shohlan and L. Kahle, "Spectators, viewers, readers: Communication and consumption communities in sport marketing," Sport Marketing

Quarterly (hereafter cited as SMQ) 5 (March 1996): 11-20.

4. P. Graham, "A study of the demographic and economic characteristics of spectators attending the U.S. Men's Clay Court Championships," SMQ 1, no. 1 (March 1992): 25-30.

5. W. Gantz and L. Wenner, "Fanship and the television sports viewing experience," Sociology of Sport Journal 12 (1995): 56-74; T. Scanlon, "An introduction to the Sport Commitment Model," Journal of Sport and Exercise Psychology 15, no. 1 (March 1993): 1-15; C. Brooks, "Sport/Exercise identity theory and participation marketing," SMQ 7, no. 1 (March 1998): 38-47; W. Sutton, M. McDonald, G. Milne, and J. Cimperman, "Creating and fostering fan identification in professional sports," SMQ 6, no. 1 (March 1997): 15-22

6. P. Kotler, Marketing management, 9th ed. (Upper Saddle River, NJ: Prentice Hall, 1997).

7. Research and Forecasts, Inc., Miller Lite report on American attitudes toward sports (Milwaukee: Miller Brewing Co., 1983); D.S. Eitzen and G. Sage, Sociology of North American sport, 3rd ed. (Dubuque, IA: Brown, 1986); R. Brustad, "Integrating socialization influences."

8. Game Plan, Inc., Why people join: A market research study for racquet and fitness clubs (Boston: IRSA, 1985), 41-43; "The power of pals," Marketing Tools, March 1997, 39; C. Walker, "Word of mouth," American Demographics, July 1995, 38-44.

9. A. Lustigman, "Influences," Sporting Goods Business, February 1994, 56-60.

10. A. Cohen, "Power plays," Athletic Business, September 1995, 16-18; S. Hardy, How Boston played: Sport, recreation, and community 1865-1915 (Boston: Northeastern University Press, 1982), 59.

11. On the national "sports creed" see H. Edwards, Sociology of sport (Homewood, IL: The Dorsey Press, 1983), 334. For excellent history on the creed, see S.W. Pope, Patriotic games: Sporting traditions in the American imagination, 1876-1926 (New York: Oxford University Press, 1997); M. Dyreson, Inventing the sporting republic: American sport, political culture, and the Olympic experience, 1877-1919 (Urbana, IL: University of Illinois Press, 1997).

12. P. May, "Entertaining idea," Boston Globe, 26 May 1996, 49, 56; K. Kennedy, "Spice on the ice," Sports Illustrated, 1 April 1996, 3-4; "Is 'Hometown Stars' the breakfast of amateur champions?" Sports Business Daily (hereafter cited as SBD), 8 July 1997, 6. Contemporary "sports regions" are described in J. Rooney and R. Pillsbury, Atlas of American sport (New York: Maxwell Macmillan International, 1992).

13. R.P. Coleman, "The continuing significance of social class to marketing," Journal of Consumer Research 10 (December 1983): 265-280.

14. D. Booth and J. Loy, "Sport, Status, and Style," Sport History Review 30 (1999):1-26; T. Veblen, Theory of the leisure class (New York: New American Library,

1899); concerning "prole sports" see Eitzen and Sage, Sociology of North American sport, 244-245; G. Lipsitz, Class and culture in cold war America (South Hadley, MA: Bergin, 1982), 173-194; R. Gruneau, Class, sports, and social development (Amherst, MA: University of Massachusetts Press, 1984).

15. For a fine review of the historical literature, see J.T. Sammons, "'Race' and sport: A critical, historical explanation," Journal of Sport History 21 (fall 1994): 203-278; D. Wiggins, "'Great speed but little stamina': The historical debate over black athletic superiority," Journal of Sport History 16 (summer 1989): 158-185.

16. R. Brown and R.T. Jewell, "Is there customer discrimination in college basketball?" Social Science Quarterly 75, no. 2 (June 1994): 401-413; "Do NBA ratings increase with white athletes' playing time?" SBD, 20 April 1998, 4.

17. S. Hardy, Profile/Interview with Donna Lopiano, SMQ 5, no. 4 (December 1996): 5-8; S. Greendorfer, "Socialization into sport," in Women and sport: From myth to reality, ed. C. Oglesby (Philadelphia: Lea & Febiger, 1982), 115-142.

18. D. Branch, "Tapping new markets: Women as sport consumers," SMQ 4, no. 4 (December 1995): 9-12; S. Hofacre, "The women's audience in professional indoor soccer," SMQ 3, no. 2 (June 1994): 25-27.

19. W. Gantz and L. Wenner, "Men, women, and sports: Audience experience and effects," Journal of Broadcasting and Electronic Media 35, no. 2 (spring 1991): 233-243.

20. "Short shelf life," SBD, 25 July 1997, 6; W. Sutton, "Communicating with women in the 1990s," SMQ 3, no. 2 (June 1993): 9-14.

21. The literature on sport and gender is vast. For an introduction, see S. Cahn, Coming on strong: Gender and sexuality in twentieth century women's sport (Cambridge: Harvard University Press, 1995); M.B. Nelson, The stronger women get, the more men love football (New York: Avon, 1994).

22. M. Rossman, Multicultural marketing (New York: AMACOM Books, 1994), 33.

23. Contemporary sports regions are described in Rooney and Pillsbury, Atlas of American sport; B. Hunnicutt, "Sports," in Encyclopedia of southern culture, ed. C.R. Wilson and W. Ferris (Chapel Hill, NC: University of North Carolina Press, 1989), 1239. On the South and baseball, see K. Greenburg, Honor and slavery (Princeton: Princeton University Press, 1996). For a more expansive analysis of southern styles, see T. Ownby, Subduing Satan: Religion, recreation, and manhood in the rural South, 1865-1920 (Chapel Hill, NC: University of North Carolina Press, 1990).

24. T. Chamberlain, "A clash of cultures," Boston Globe, 23 December 1993, 61-63.

25. K.P. Dupont, "Carter scores big assist," Boston Globe, 23 September 1997, E1, 6; G.T. Brown, "Sudden impact," NCAA News, 31 March 1997, 1, 25.

26. Berkman and Gilson, Consumer behavior, 101-102; M.J. Sirgy, "Self concept in consumer behavior: A critical review," Journal of Consumer Behavior 1 (December 1982): 287-300.

27. "Why teenagers participate in sports," Fitness Management, March 1991, 15-16; T. Benson, "Copping an attitude," Sporting Goods Dealer, February 1995, 48-52; C. Brooks, "Promoting physical activity: A lifestyle approach," working paper no. 4, University of Michigan, Department of Sports Management and Communications, Ann Arbor, MI, 1987.

28. R. Burton, "Profile/Interview with Sara Levinson," SMQ 6, no. 4 (December 1997): 5-8; J.R. Kelly, Leisure (Englewood Cliffs, NJ: Prentice Hall, 1982), 133-156.

29. W. Gantz et al., "Televised sports and marital relationships," Sociology of Sport Journal 12 (1995): 306-323.

30. Berkman and Gilson, Consumer behavior, 273.

31. J.J. Zhang et al., "Spectator knowledge of hockey as a significant predictor of game attendance," SMQ 5 (September 1996): 41-48; S. Nottingham, "Juggling the learning curve," Fitness Management, August 1994, 40-43.

32. ESPN and ESPN2, "Guide to the X Games," insert in Rolling Stone, 25 June 1998.

33. R.F. Young, "The advertising of consumer services and the hierarchy of effects," in The marketing of services, ed. J.H. Donnelly and W. George (Chicago: American Marketing Association, 1981), 196-199; "Basketball according to me," insert in Sports Illustrated, 10 November 1997.

34. "Rollerblading looks to put the brakes on the competition," SBD, 5 June 1997, 6; "NCAA opens gates to Hoop City," NCAA News, 30 March 1998, 1, 28.

35. B. Berelson and G. Steiner, Human behavior: An inventory of scientific findings (New York: Harcourt Brace and World, 1964), 88; P. Kotler, Marketing management, 5th ed. (Englewood Cliffs, NJ: Prentice Hall, 1984), 140.

36. B. Enis and K. Roering, "Services marketing: Different products, similar strategy," in The marketing of services, 1-4; B. Veeck, Veeck as in wreck (New York: Signet, 1986); D. Kerstatter and G. Kovich, "An involvement profile of Division I women's basketball spectators," Journal of Sport Management 11 (1997): 234-249; A. Rohm, "The creation of consumer bonds within Reebok running," SMQ 6, no. 2 (June 1997): 18; SBD, 29 January 1998, 8.

37. Burton, "Profile/Interview with Sara Levinson," 5-8.

38. A. Korman, The psychology of motivation (Englewood Cliffs, NJ: Prentice Hall, 1974); G. Roberts, ed., Motivation in sport and exercise (Champaign, IL: Human Kinetics, 1992); S. Hardy, "Sport," Encyclopedia of social history, ed. P. Stearns (New York: Garland, 1994), 713-714; S. Hardy, "The material culture of sport," Yale-Smithsonian Symposium on Material Culture, May 1997; Why people play: A report on the sport of tennis (Lexington, MA: Game Plan, Inc., 1987); Research and Forecasts, Inc., Miller Lite report, 131-148; Game Plan, Inc., Why

people join; "Meeting friends," Team Marketing Report (October 1989): 5; L. Kahle, K. Kambara, and G. Rose, "A functional model of fan attendance motivations for college football," SMQ 5 (December 1996): 51-60; D. Wann and N. Brascombe, "Sports fans: Measuring degree of identification with their team," International Journal of Sport Psychology 24 (1993): 1-17; H. Hansen and R. Gauthier, "The professional golf product: Spectators' views," SMQ 3, no. 4 (December 1994): 9-16; M. Grunwald, "Taking funny business seriously," Boston Globe, 5 January 1998, A1, 12; A. Guttmann, The erotic in sports (New York: Columbia University Press, 1996); "Gator bait" ["Scorecard"], Sports Illustrated, 19 May 1997, 29-30; "Oh Oscar," SBD, 9 September 1997, 5.

39. Kotler, *Marketing management,* 9th ed., 188.

40. D. Zillman, J. Bryant, and B. Sapolsky, Enjoyment of watching sport contests, in Sport, games, and play: Social and psychological viewpoints, ed. J. Goldstein (Hillsdale, NJ: Erlbaum, 1979), 279-335; C. Lupton, N. Ostrove, and R. Bozzo, "Participation in leisure-time physical activity," Journal of Physical Education, Recreation and Dance 55 (November 1984): 20.

41. "Why not try playing a game that starts out love-love," press release from Brouillard Communications to authors, 4 May 1993.

42. T. Crossett, "Toward an understanding of on-site fan-athlete relations: A case study of the LPGA," *SMQ* 4 (June 1995): 31-38; W. Sutton, "Profile/Interview with Don Johnson," *SMQ* 6 (June 1997): 5-8; "Adoption program breeds early-season ticket sales," *Team Marketing Report* 8 (July 1996): 9; Sutton, et al., "Creating and fostering fan identification"; D. McGraw, "Big league troubles," *U.S. News and World Report,* 13 July 1998, 40-46.

43. For basic models see Berkman and Gilson, *Consumer behavior,* 472-511; Kotler, *Marketing management,* 9th ed., 192-198; J. O'Shaughnessy, *Why people buy* (New York: Oxford, 1987), 92-97; M. Chubb and H. Chubb, *One third of our time? An introduction to recreation behavior and resources* (New York: Wiley, 1981), 230-250.

44. Game Plan, Inc., *Why people join,* 42-44; D. Smith and N. Theberge, *Why people recreate* (Champaign, IL: Human Kinetics, 1987), 111-118.

45. Kotler, *Marketing management,* 5th ed., 464.

46. J. Faircloth et al., "An analysis of choice intentions of public golf courses," *SMQ* 4 (March 1995): 13-21; for a good introduction to factors influencing spectator choice, see J. Zhang et al., "Factors affecting the decision making of spectators to attend minor league hockey games," *International Sports Journal* 1 (summer 1997): 39-53.

47. Chubb and Chubb, *One third of our time?* 231-234.

48. Brooks, "Sport/Exercise identity theory," 38-47; Sutton, et al., "Creating and fostering fan identification."

49. L. Walczak and S. Forest, "Speed sells," *Business Week,* 11 August 1997, 86-90.

CHAPTER 5

1. W.A. Sutton, "SMQ profile/interview: Don Johnson," Sport Marketing Quarterly 6, no. 2 (1997): 5-8.

2. A.R. Andreasen, "Cost-conscious market research," Harvard Business Review (July-August 1983): 74-77.

3. We base the format of figure 5.1 on that in P.D. Boughton, "Marketing research and small business: Pitfalls and potential," Journal of Small Business Management (1983, July): 37. See also the questions in M. Levine, "Making market research hustle: The essential sweat of attendance building and fund raising" (paper presented at Athletic Business Conference, Las Vegas, NV, December 8, 1987).

4. For an approach to such data collecting, see J. Naisbitt, Megatrends: Ten new directions for transforming our lives (New York: Warner, 1982). For an analysis on how trends impact business and how to best prepare, see F. Popcorn, The Popcorn report (New York: Doubleday, 1991).

5. One short reference study to secondary material is the United States Small Business Administration (SBA) pamphlet entitled Marketing for small businesses, part of the Small business bibliography available from the SBA, P.O. Box 15434, Fort Worth, TX 76119.

6. G.R. Milne, W.A. Sutton, and M.A. McDonald, "Success with surveys," Athletic Management 9, no. 4 (1997): 12.

7. J. Johansson and I. Nonaka, "Market research the Japanese way," Harvard Business Review 65 (May-June 1967): 16-22.

8. W.A. Sutton, R.L. Irwin, and J.M. Gladden, "Tools of the trade: Practical research methods for events, teams and venues," Sport Marketing Quarterly 7, no. 2 (1998): 45-49.

9. R.P. Heath, "Seeing is believing," Marketing Tools, March 1997, 4-10.

10. For an actual example of how the results of such research can be utilized to increase marketing effectiveness and strategic planning, see "76ers community intercept surveys suggest new marketing tactics," Team Marketing Report 8, no. 9 (June 1996): 7.

11. J. O'Shaughnessey, Why people buy (New York: Oxford, 1987), 54; K. Ericsson and H. Simon, "Verbal report as data," Psychological Review 87 (May 1987): 215-251. The authors seem to call for protocol analysis in L. Fishwick and S. Greendorfer, "Socialization revisited: A critique of the sport-related research," Quest 39 (April 1987): 1-8.

12. G. Moeller and E. Shafer, "Use and misuse of Delphi forecasting," in Recreation planning and management, ed. S. Lieber and D. Fesenmaier (State College,

BA: Venture, 1983), 96-104. See the use of "experts" in the marketing research of the NHL in H.C. Mitchener, "The influence of selected changes, developments, and events on the promotion and marketing of National Hockey League teams" (master's thesis, University of Ottawa, 1983).

13. W. Sutton and R. Warnick, "LPGA panel survey on merchandising and attitudes related to golf" (consulting report, 1995). A study utilizing 417 consumers to solicit opinions and feedback regarding golf apparel-purchasing behavior documented the relationship between age and purchasing and the ways in which golf fashion is affected by age and apparel worn by LPGA golfers.

14. B. Edmondson, "The wired bunch," American Demographics/Marketing Tools home page, 1997.

15. B. Edmondson, "The wired bunch."

16. For an overview of the 1997 survey of Internet users by Nielsen and CommerceNet, contact Patrick Corman at CommerceNet (415-326-9648) or online at http://www.commerce.net. Also, CASRO's "Survey research quality guidelines" gives some information on how online surveys should be conducted. Contact Diane Bowers at 3 Upper Devon, Port Jefferson, NY 11777; or call 516-928-6954.

17. M.A. Wylde, "How to read an open letter," American Demographics, September 1994, 48-52.

18. J. Spoelstra, Ice to the Eskimos (New York: Harper Business, 1997).

19. P. Kephart, "The spy in aisle 3," Marketing Tools, May 1996, 16-21.

20. B. Veeck and E. Linn, Veeck as in wreck (New York: Putnam's, 1962); B. Veeck and E. Linn, The hustler's handbook (New York: Putnam's, 1965).

21. Sutton, Irwin, and Gladden, "Tools of the trade," 45-49.

22. Game Plan, Inc., Why people play: A report on the sport of tennis (Lexington, MA: Game Plan, Inc.).

23. L. Rea and R. Parker, Designing and conducting survey research: A comprehensive guide (San Francisco: Jossey-Bass, 1992), 107.

24. Modified from Rea and Parker, Designing and conducting research, 133.

25. For a useful guide for designing quantitative surveys, see Rea and Parker, Designing and conducting research; for assistance in developing a more qualitative instrument, see C. Marshall and G. Rossman, Designing qualitative research (Newbury Park, CA: Sage, 1989).

26. Rea and Parker, Designing and conducting research, 101.

CHAPTER 6

1. K. McCabe, "Lowering a gender handicap," Boston Sunday Globe, 27 July 1997, C1, 4; "Women golfers: By the numbers," Golf Market Today, September-October 1998, 4. The authors thank Melanie Bedrosian

of the Jane Blalock Company for research assistance on this vignette.

2. On the notion of global marketing, see T. Levitt, The marketing imagination (New York: Free Press, 1984).

3. "Golf Channel aims to up productions," Sports Business Daily (hereafter cited as SBD), 2 February 1998, 5.

4. For a general discussion of these criteria, see P. Kotler, Marketing management: Analysis, planning, and control, 5th ed. (Englewood Cliffs, NJ: Prentice Hall, 1984), 264-265.

5. P. Kotler, Marketing Management, 9th ed. (Upper Saddle River, NJ: Prentice Hall, 1997), 251; S. Ruibal, "Horwath seeks niche for snow skating," USA Today, 31 January 1997, 2C; G. Milne, W. Sutton, and M. McDonald, "Niche analysis: A strategic measurement tool for sport managers," Sport Marketing Quarterly (hereafter cited as SMQ) 5, no. 3 (29 September 1996): 15-22.

6. S. Mitchell, "Birds of a feather," American Demographics, February 1995, 40-48.

7. L. Mullen, "Chargers' new campaign will test drawing power in LA," Street and Smith's Sports Business Journal (hereafter cited as SSSBJ) (6-12 July 1998): 13; M. Levine, "Making marketing research hustle: The essential sweat of attendance building and fund raising" (paper presented at the annual Athletic Business Conference, Las Vegas, NV, December 1987).

8. M. Babineck, "Ralph Lauren's firm sues magazine to drop Polo name," Boston Globe, 27 May 1998, C3.

9. G. Meredith and C. Schewe, "The power of cohorts," American Demographics, December 1994, 22-31.

10. J. Gaines, "Generation Xercise" Boston Globe, 18 November 1995, 1, 17.

11. J. Rofe, "Angels push family values," SSSBJ (22-28 June 1998): 6.

12. C. Cox, "Rock 'n' bowl," Boston Herald, 20 August 1997, 37; "Youth interests in golf driving sales, new lines," SBD, 24 April 1998, 3; "Kid's stuff," SBD, 27 August 1997, 7; D. Turco, "The X factor: Marketing to generation X," SMQ 5, no. 1 (March 1996): 21-26.

13. "NASCAR targets kids, but must dance around RJR's sponsorship," SBD, 22 May 1998, 7.

14. J. Rude, "Making the mature decision," Athletic Business, January 1998, 31-37; C. Brooks, "The membership age wave," Fitness Management, March 1994, 38-40.

15. "NFL seminars targeting women big hit in Big D," SBD, 17 October 1997, 13; T. Cassidy, "Football 101," Sunday Globe, 26 October 1997, C1, 11; N. Kapsambelis, "Football 101," AP story run in Foster's Sunday Citizen, 16 November 1997, 9B.

16. S. Hardy, "Profile/Interview with Donna Lopiano," SMQ 5, no. 4 (December 1996): 5-8; B. Matson, "New target: Newsstands," Boston Globe, 11 February 1998, D8; "Female athlete publishes new edition," SBD, 28 March 1998, 4; D. Branch, "Tapping new markets:

Women as sport consumers," *SMQ* 4, no. 4 (December 1995): 9-12.

17. "A-B's Ponturo hopes NBC has more of an eye on young men," *SBD,* 24 February 1998, 12.

18. K. Armstrong, "Ten strategies to employ when marketing sport to black consumers," SMQ 7, no. 3 (September 1998): 11-19.

19. Armstrong, "Ten strategies"; L. McCarthy, "Marketing sport to Hispanic consumers," SMQ 7, no. 4 (December 1998): 19-24; M. Rossman, Multicultural marketing: Selling to a diverse America (New York: American Management Association, 1994). On World Cup ratings, see L. Mullen, "Univision scoring big," SSSBJ (29 June-5 July 1998): 4; "The Cup runneth over," SBD, 14 July 1998, 13.

20. R. Desloge, "Cards make pitch for blacks," SSSBJ (18-24 May 1998): 9.

21. "USA Today looks at MLS' target marketing of ethnic groups," SBD, 3 March 1998, 9; "Hockey team markets to Latin audience," Sports Business Update, no. 212, 23 February 1998, www.sgrnet.com.

22. Announcement in SSSBJ (6-12 July 1998): 15.

23. H. Kahan and D. Mulryan, "Out of the closet," American Demographics, May 1995, 40-47.

24. Kotler, Marketing management, 9th ed., 182-183.

25. C. Brooks, "Promoting physical activity: A lifestyle approach," working paper no. 4, University of Michigan, Department of Sports Management and Communications, Ann Arbor, MI, 1987; R. Piirto, "Cable TV," American Demographics, June 1995, 40-47.

26. M. Nowell, "The women's golf market," SMQ 4, no. 2 (June 1995): 40. See also the excellent usage-segmentation analysis in D. Howard, "Participation rates in selected sport and fitness activities," Journal of Sport Management 6 (September 1992): 191-205; "Seven ways to swing a club," American Demographics, July 1995, 16-18.

27. M. Levine, "Making marketing research hustle: The essential sweat of attendance building and fund raising" (paper presented at the annual Athletic Business Conference, Las Vegas, NV, December 1987).

28. J. Seabrook, "Tackling the competition," New Yorker, 18 (August 1997): 42-51.

29. WNBA fans discussed in SBD, 5 August 1997, 9. On women's team fans, see also D. Antonelli, "Marketing intercollegiate women's basketball," SMQ, 3, no. 2 (June 1994): 29-33; S. Hardy, "Profile/Interview with Donna Lopiano," 5-8. For some interesting data that relate to benefits segmentation, see C. Kim and S. Kim, "Segmentation of sport center members in Seoul based on attitudes toward service quality," Journal of Sport Management 12 (1998): 273-287.

30. J. Crompton, "Selecting target markets," Journal of Parks and Recreation Administration 1, no. 1 (1983): 7-26.

CHAPTER 7

1. S. Lainson, "Sports News You Can Use," e-mail newsletter, no. 3, 14 November 1996, 1-2; J. McPeek, "Football in a box," Sport, September 1998, 99-101; D. Kaplan, "This time around, NFL loves AFL," Street and Smith's Sports Business Journal (hereafter cited as SSSBJ) (3-9 August 1998): 16; Associated Press, "Arena Football hasn't reached its ceiling yet," Boston Globe, 25 April 1999, D2.

2. T. Levitt, "Marketing intangible products and product intangibles," Harvard Business Review (May-June 1981): 94-102.

3. "Adios Sports channel, hola Fox Sports Net," Sports Business Daily (hereafter cited as SBD), 29 January 1998, 6.

4. "Names in the News," SBD, 9 June 1998, 18.

5. For early voices in a "winning isn't everything" marketing philosophy, see F. Deford's profile of Don Canham in "No death for a salesman," Sports Illustrated, 28 July 1975, 56-65; and R. Kennedy's profile of Matt Levine in "More victories equals more fans equals more profits, right? Wrong, wrong, wrong!" Sports Illustrated, 28 April 1980, 34-45.

6. L. Nash, "Ethics without the sermon," Harvard Business Review (November 1981): 79-90; for historical tensions in the sport product, see S. Hardy, "Entrepreneurs, structures, and the sportgeist," in Sport history and sport mythology, ed. D. Kyle and G. Stark (College Station: Texas A&M Press, 1990), 45-82. For material on sporting behavior and fair play, see K. Hawes, "Sportsmanship: Why should anybody care?" NCAA News, 1 June 1998, 1, 18; "Strides in sportsmanship require first step from all," NCAA News, 15 June 1998, 1, 6, 7.

7. B. King, "Only Beanie Babies rival McGwire as a fan magnet," SSSBJ (6-12 July 1998): 17; "Hats off," SBD, 4 September 1998, 4.

8. "Sport's Pages," newsletter of Acme Mascots Inc., 1, no. 1 (winter 1994), in authors' possession.

9. A. Conklin, "Opening-round upset," Athletic Business, August 1998, 28-32.

10. Associated Press, "A new meaning to 'patented' move," Boston Globe, 16 June 1996, 74.

11. "She's Venus, she's on fire," SBD, 4 September 1997, 7; "Tuna helps boost ad sales," SBD, 1 August 1997, 9; "Lack of star power seen as major detriment to CART and IRL," SBD, 15 May 1998, 9.

12. L. Walczak, et al. "Speed Sells," Business Week, 11 August 1997: 86-90; "CNN's impact charts," SBD, 14 October 1997, 4; P. Speigel, "Heir Gordon," Forbes, 14 December 1998, 188-193.

13. "Top 25 female athlete endorsements," SSSBJ (11-17 May 1998): 25.

14. "Fortune says Jordan rules," SBD, 3 June 1998, 13; "On field popularity," SBD, 31 July 1998, 9; M. Starr, "The $16 million man," Newsweek, 1 May 1995, 72-75; on Shaq's 1997 movie image, see SBD, 18 August 1998, 14.

15. "At once," SBD, 2 April 1997

16. A. Meek, "An estimate of the size and supported economic activity of the sports industry in the United States," Sport Marketing Quarterly 6 (December 1997): 15-21. K.P. Dupont, "Auction is on tap for Garden," Boston Globe, 30 April 1998, 55; T. Grant, "Cold team, hot jersey," Boston Globe, 7 February 1995, 61; J. Marx, "It's a Babe-o-nanza," Sports Illustrated, 6 February 1995, 9, 10. For the importance of sporting goods in the development of the industry, see S. Hardy, "Adopted by all the leading clubs: Sporting goods and the shaping of leisure, 1800-1900," in For fun and profit: The transformation of leisure into consumption, ed. R. Butsch (Philadelphia: Temple University Press, 1990).

17. G. Krupa, "Golf firm opposes USGA's proposed club test," Boston Globe, 9 September 1998, F3; "Ski federation spins web control on itsy, bitsy spyder suits," SBD, 10 October 1997, 4; R. Glier, "Rawlings pitches ball with a speedometer," SSSBJ (3-8 August 1998): 48.

18. A. Bernstein, "Sports leagues get serious about toys," SSSBJ (10-16 August 1998): 9; B. King, "Owners, players agree: Beanies have it," SSSBJ (6-12 July 1998): 16; "One man gathers what another man spills," SBD, 4 December 1997, 4.

19. LPGA news release, 8 January 1997, in authors' possession; T. Cassidy, "A look at game plan," Boston Globe, 1 February 1997, F1, 2; "City planning: NCAA plans for Hoop City," NCAA News, 24 November 1997, A1, 10.

20. B. Kuklick, To everything a season: Shibe Park and urban Philadelphia, 1909-1976 (Princeton: Princeton University Press, 1991), 191, 193. See discussion of venues in S. Hardy, "The material culture of sport," Yale-Smithsonian Symposium on Material Culture, May 1997.

21. For a good look at a Super Bowl venue/spectacle/festival, see S. Orlean, "Super-duper," New Yorker, 13 February 1995, 42-51.

22. "Islanders ticket request: Look out below," Sports Illustrated, 14 September 1998, 23.

23. A.J. Magrath, "When marketing services, 4 Ps are not enough," Business Horizons, May-June 1986, 44-50.

24. C.L. Martin, "The employee-customer interface: An empirical investigation of employee behaviors and customer perceptions," Journal of Sport Management 4 (January 1990), 1-20; B. Mullin, "Applying Disney™ techniques to sport organizations," unpublished manuscript; R. Ross, "Creating the service experience," Fitness Management, September 1993, 32-33; J. Goldman, L. Delpy, The Ultimate Guide to Sport Event Management (Burr Ridge, IL: Irwin, 1996). The notion of customer service lies at the heart of T. Peters and R. Waterman, In search of excellence (New York: Warner Books, 1982), one of the best-selling business books of all time.

25. L. McCarthy and R. Irwin, "Permanent seat licenses as an emerging source of revenue production," Sport Marketing Quarterly 7 (September 1998): 41-46; SBD, 18 August 1997, 10.

26. R. Irwin and B. Fleger, "Reading between the lines," Athletic Management, May 1992, 15-18; S. Miller, "ESPN creates a rumble at the newsstand," SSSBJ (12-18 October 1998): 12.

27. R. Maloney, "Taking a shot at the 'virtual' dominator," SSSBJ (10-16 August 1998): 14.

28. G. Krupa, "Patriots keep on clicking," Boston Globe, 19 September 1998, F2, 3; "Trade a Clapton for a Piazza?"SBD, 9 July 1998, 3.

29. "NASCAR: Moving to the music," insert, Sports Illustrated, 3 August 1998; "Marquee Group's new team service," SBD, 24 June 1998, 3; "Alphabet city," SBD, 5 September, 1997.

30. L. Nash, "Ethics without the sermon," 79-80; "Selling violence with vulgarity," Sports Illustrated, 17 August 1998, 129-130.

31. L.J. Wertheim, "The sky's the limit," Sports Illustrated, 21 September 1998, 40, 42.

32. D. Cooke, "Packaging for prestige: The tennis advantage," IRSA Club Business, July 1987, 62-67.

33. G. Willigan, "High-performance marketing: An interview with Nike's Phil Knight," Harvard Business Review (July-August 1992): 92, 99; "Nike's Knight announces reforms," SBD, 13 May 1998, 3.

34. S.L. Price, "Spice and spite," Sports Illustrated, 14 September 1998, 90, 92.

35. M. Hiestand, "NBA puts clout to test," USA Today, 5 February 1997, 3C.

36. P. Kotler, Marketing management, 9th ed. (Englewood Cliffs, NJ: Prentice Hall, 1997), 282.

37. S. Hardy, "Profile/Interview with Matt Levine," Sport Marketing Quarterly 5 (September 1996): 5-12; D. Robson, "Sharks sink in sales rankings," SSSBJ (2-8 November 1998): 40.

38. S. Higgins and J. Martin, "Managing sport innovations: A diffusion theory perspective," Sport Marketing Quarterly 5 (March 1996): 43-48; E.M. Rogers, Diffusion of innovation, 3rd ed. (New York: Free Press, 1983).

39. P. Hemp, "In hockey, the goal is image," Boston Globe, 6 January 1993, 53, 55; K. Kennedy, "Twilight of the goons," Sports Illustrated, 8 March 1999, m29; "No competition," SBD, 30 July 1997, 12; "Are the Islanders' preseason ads too much for NHL office?" SBD, 4 September 1998, 5.

40. B. Mendel, "Up against the pros: Converting the community," Athletic Management, September 1993, 13.

41. For suggestions on the use of perceptual maps, see J. Martin, "Using a perceptual map of the consumer's sport schema to help make sponsorship decisions," Sport Marketing Quarterly 3, no. 3 (September 1994): 27-33.

42. "Out of style: Team marketers give insight on warning signs that a logo needs a makeover," Team Marketing Report (February 1998): 8; V. Abell, "What's in a name?" NCAA News, 28 September 1998, 9.

43. Willigan, "High-performance marketing," 91-101.

44. "ESPN's full-court press," Men's Journal, March 1998, 30; Kotler, Marketing management, 442-460; J. Gladden, G. Milne, and W.A. Sutton, "A conceptual framework for assessing brand equity in Division I college athletics," Journal of Sport Management 12, no. 1 (1998): 1-19; L.E. Boone, C.M. Kochunny, and D. Wilkins, "Applying the brand equity concept to major league baseball," Sport Marketing Quarterly 4 (September 1995): 33-42; D.A. Aaker, Building strong brands (New York: Free Press, 1996).

45. N. Dhalla and S. Yuspeh, "Forget the product lifecycle concept!" Harvard Business Review (January-February 1976): 102-112.

CHAPTER 8

1. "SGB retail registry 1997," Sporting Goods Business 30, no. 7, 12 May 1997, 27.

2. Ken Roberts, personal communication, 16 July 1997.

3. A.J. Sherman, Franchising and licensing: Two ways to build your business (New York: AMACOM Books, 1991).

4. R.C. Berry and G.M. Wong, Law and business of the sports industries: Common issues in amateur and professional sports, vol. 2, 2nd ed. (Westport, CT: Praeger, 1993), 620.

5. Basic facts about registering a trademark (Washington, DC: U.S. Government Printing Office, 1994).

6. W. Goldstein, Playing for keeps: A history of early baseball (Ithaca, NY: Cornell University Press, 1989), 109.

7. R.G. Hagstrom, The NASCAR way: The business that drives the sport (New York: Wiley, 1998), 8.

8. T. Lefton, "At age 50, Stern looks ahead," Brandweek 41 (28 October 1996): 35.

9. D. Van Meter, "Sales of licensed products and services," in Financing sport, ed. D.R. Howard and J.L. Crompton (Morgantown, WV: Fitness Information Technology, 1995), 171-185.

10. A. Bernstein, "Starter's bankruptcy sparks scrambling," Street and Smiths's Sports Business Journal, 2, no. 1 (1999): 1, 47.

11. Bernstein, "Starter's bankruptcy sparks scrambling," 47.

12. The ABC's of the NBA: A buyer's guide to NBA youth apparel (New York: National Basketball Association, 1997), 3.

13. W.A. Sutton, M.A. McDonald, G.R. Milne, and J. Ciperman, "Creating and fostering fan identification in professional sports," Sport Marketing Quarterly 6, no. 1 (1997): 15-22.

14. J. Helyar, Lords of the realm: The real history of baseball (New York: Ballantine Books), 70.

15. "Licensed sports products market expects moderate growth," Team Licensing Business 9, no. 3 (March-April 1997): 20-27.

16. "Logoed sports apparel tops $3 billion," Team Licensing Business 49, no. 6 (September-October 1997): 12.

17. "ESPN Chilton sports poll," Team Licensing Business 9, no. 6 (September-October 1997): 17.

18. "Licensed sports products market."

19. Basic facts about registering a trademark.

20. B.R. Sugar, Hit the sign and win a free suit of clothes from Harry Finklestein (Chicago: Contemporary Books, 1978).

21. "Sports merchandising industry loses its creator, David Warsaw," Team Licensing Business 8, no. 5 (July-August 1996): 18.

22. Sugar, Hit the sign, 129.

23. T. Jones, "Bridge over lucrative waters," Team Licensing Business 7, no. 8 (August 1995): 28.

24. R. Lipsey, ed., Sports marketplace (Princeton, NJ: Sportsguide, 1996).

25. William Marshall, personal communication, 27 May 1997.

26. "Baseball gets tough on All-Star goods," USA Today, 1 July 1997, 5C.

27. Collegiate Licensing Company buyer's guide (Phoenix: Virgo, 1997).

28. R. Burton, "A case study on sports property servicing excellence: National Football League Properties," Sport Marketing Quarterly 5, no. 3 (1996): 23.

29. "Unsuitable behavior," Boston Globe, 20 March 1997, D2.

30. R.H. Alexander, "The economic impact of licensing logos, emblems and mascots," Journal of Legal Aspects of Sport 5, no. 1 (spring 1995): 28-34.

31. A. Bernstein, "Eye on licensing," Sporting Goods Business 30, no. 3, 10 February 1997, 22.

32. G. Mihoces, "Franchises have vested interest in new clothes lines," USA Today, 26 August 1997, 10C.

33. T. Lefton, "Category wars: Nike uber alles," Brandweek 47 (9 December 1996): 25.

34. T. Lowry, "Sports shoemaker goes for rebound," USA Today, 21 October 1996, 1B-2B.

35. A. Bernstein, "That's business," Sporting Goods Business 30, no. 1, 6 January 1997, 41.

36. J. Cohen, "The elegance of flannel," in Hornsby hit one over my head: A fan's oral history of baseball, ed. D. Cataneo (New York: Harcourt Brace, 1997), 206.

37. Helyar, Lords of the realm, 90-91.

38. Licensing (Washington, DC: National Football League Players Association, 1995).

39. B. Horovitz, "Jocks don pay apparel," USA Today, 3 January 1997, 1C.

40. Licensing.

41. Hagstrom, The NASCAR way, 143-144.

42. M. Sperber, Shake down the thunder: The creation of Notre Dame football (New York: Holt, 1993).

43. C. Plata, "Ducks & dollars," Team Licensing Business 8, no. 6 (September-October 1996): 38.

44. "Budget supports new NCAA structure," NCAA News, 34, no. 31, 1 September 1997, 1.

45. Kevin Kelley, personal communication, 11 August 1997.

46. Alexander, "Economic impact."

47. M.E. Mazzeo, J. Cuneen, and C.L. Claussen, "Retail licensing procedures used by selected NCAA Division I institutions: Implications for licensees of collegiate memorabilia," Sport Marketing Quarterly 5, no. 1 (1997): 41-46.

48. R.L. Irwin and D.K. Stotlar, "Operational protocol analysis of sport and collegiate licensing programs," Sport Marketing Quarterly 2, no. 1 (1993): 7-16.

49. Kelley.

50. Irwin and Stotlar, "Operational protocol analysis."

51. Collegiate Licensing Company buyer's guide.

52. Players, Inc. (Washington, DC: National Football League Players Association, January 1997).

53. "Tar (swoosh) heels," USA Today, 10 July 1997, 1C.

54. K.B. Blackistone, "With Colorado deal, Nike swoosh sign of the times," Dallas Morning News, 12 July 1997, 1B.

55. E. Neuborn, "Nike to take a hit in labor report," USA Today, 27 March 1997, 1A.

56. J. Naughton, "Exclusive deal with Reebok brings U. of Wisconsin millions of dollars and unexpected criticism," Chronicle of Higher Education 43, no. 2, A65.

57. Code of conduct for University of Notre Dame licensees (Notre Dame, IN: University of Notre Dame, 19 February 1997).

58. A. Bernstein, "Vertical impact," Sporting Goods Business 30, no. 3, 10 February 1997, 58.

59. "Sports apparel monitor 1996," Team Licensing Business 9, no. 1 (January 1997): 38-39.

60. A. Nickell, "Delving into the women's market," Team Licensing Business 9, no. 4 (July-August 1997): 28-30.

61. ABC's of the NBA, 3.

62. J. Seabrook, "Tackling the competition," New Yorker, 73, no. 24, 13 August 1997, 50.

63. C. McKendry, producer, "The NBA today," Entertainment and Sports Broadcasting Network, Bristol, CT, 12 August 1997.

64. T. Bullington, "What a concept!" Team Licensing Business 7, no. 10 (October 1995): 22.

65. M. Nichols, "A look at some of the issues affecting collegiate licensing," Team Licensing Business 7, no. 4 (April 1995): 18.

66. "Annual industry report 1997," Team Licensing Business 9, no. 4 (May-June 1997): 22-27.

67. "Retail barometers," Team Licensing Business 9, no. 6 (September-October 1997): 23.

68. Burton, "A case study."

69. "Licensed sports products market."

70. "Licensed sports products market."

71. "NHL establishes partnerships with Nagano in mind," Team Licensing Business 9, no. 4 (May-June 1997): 12.

72. T. Jones, "Fashion forward," Team Licensing Business 7, no. 9 (18 September 1995): 18.

73. "Russell extends licensing concept to Europe," Team Licensing Business 7, no. 4 (April 1995): 16.

74. Bob Schichli, personal communication, 24 October 1994.

75. W. Lingo, "Logo mania," Baseball America, 20 February-5 March 1995, 22-23.

76. Lingo, "Logo mania."

77. "Unsuitable behavior."

78. J.L. Nicklin, "Marketing by design," Chronicle of Higher Education, 42, no. 28, 22 March 1996, A34.

79. G. Mihoces, "Franchises have vested interest in new clothes lines," USA Today, 26 August 1997, 10C.

80. J. Santoloquito, "Villanova's wildcat is seeking new sales," Philadelphia Inquirer, 17 January 1995, D1, 4.

81. F. Davis, Fashion, culture, and identity (Chicago: University of Chicago Press, 1992).

CHAPTER 9

1. K.P. DuPont, "Bruins' price reduction is just the ticket to fans," Boston Globe, 23 April 1998, C1, 8; "The B's are back in business in the Hub," Sports Business Daily (hereafter cited as SBD), 23 July 1998, 12.

2. M. Nowell, "The women's golf market," Sport Marketing Quarterly 4, no. 2 (June 1995): 40; J. Faircloth, M. Richard, and V. Richard, "An analysis of choice intentions of public course golfers," Sport Marketing Quarterly 4 (March 1995): 13-21.

3. "Early snow boosts chances for strong winter sports season," SBD, 24 November 1997, 16.

4. "NHL is the first league to surpass the $40 marks," Team Marketing Report 10 (October 1997): 7.

5. "MBL clubs offer more seats at highest and lowest prices," Team Marketing Report 9 (April 1997): 6-7; G. Edes, "Club rebuts report on costs at Fenway," Boston Globe, 17 July 1997, D5; SBD, 3 June 1998, 10; J. Kasky, "The best buys for fans," Money, October 1994, 158-170.

6. S. Lainson, "Sports News You Can Use," e-mail newsletter, no. 6, 1996.

7. Kasky, "Best buys for fans"; D. Arnott, "Game tickets are like fruit; don't let them rot," Street and Smith's Sports Business Journal (hereafter cited as SSSBJ) (29 June-5 July 1998): 41; T. Chamberlain, "Family values still rule in this sport," Boston Globe, 27 February 1997, C10.

8. MCI club tickets explained in "Yeah, that's the ticket," Sports Illustrated, 6 October 1997, 18-19. List of objectives adapted from D.R. Howard and J.L. Crompton, Financing, managing and marketing recreation and park resources (Dubuque, IA: Brown,

1980); P. Kotler, Marketing management, 9th ed. (Englewood Cliffs, NJ: Prentice Hall, 1997), 494-497.

9. For helpful overviews on standard practices, see D. Toxin, "The membership pricing game," Club Industry, October 1990, 32-43; Kotler, Marketing management, 502-508; M. Campanelli, "The price to pay," Sales and Marketing Management (September 1994): 96-102; A. Magrath, "Ten timeless truths about pricing," Journal of Consumer Marketing 8 (winter 1991): 5-13.

10. We would like to thank Eric Krupa for pointing out some errors and omissions in our discussion and graphs on this topic in the first edition of Sport Marketing. Eric's kind help has made this edition much stronger.

11. Camp example adapted from Howard and Crompton, Financing, managing and marketing, 435-437.

12. For more applications, see J. Newkirk, "Break into profit," Fitness Management, March 1998, 36-38; T. Sattler and J. Mullen, "The particulars of pricing your product," Fitness Management, May 1996, 44-46.

13. C. Swayne, "Pricing memberships: What are you worth?" Club Industry, November 1986, 27-32.

14. "Sports marketing: The elusive event pricing formula," Athletic Business, May 1989, 18.

15. "Not out of the woods yet, Nike revamps Tiger line," SBD, 3 September 1998, 6.

16. M.S. Baker, "Public is hired to sell Seahawks," SSSBJ (6-12 July 1998): 13.

17. D. Howard and J. Crompton, Financing sport (Morgantown, WV: Fitness Information Technology, 1995), 139-150; L. McCarthy and R. Irwin, "Permanent seat licenses (PSLs) as an emerging source of revenue production," Sport Marketing Quarterly 7 (September 1997): 41-46. Wall Street Journal story outlined in "PSL concept gets ink in WSJ," Sports Business Journal, 20 July 1998, 13.

18. S. Hildreth, "The new corporate market," CBI—Club Business International, August 1995, 38. Our thanks also to Lee Seidel, Professor of Health Management and Policy at the University of New Hampshire for explaining the general use of capitation in the health care industry.

19. M.H. Spencer, Contemporary economics, 6th ed. (New York: Worth, 1986), 346-347.

20. Kotler, Marketing management, 499.

21. T. Layden, "The hustle," Sports Illustrated, 7 April 1997, 103-120; J. Keri and M. Sunnucks, "D.C.'s ticket pros getting skinned," SSSBJ (30 November 6 December 1998): 13.

22. L. Zepp, "UIC hockey season tix sales show 400% jump," Amusement Business, 28 November 1987, 1, 16.

23. "MPG: Octane for management," Sports Management Review, fall 1979, 20.

24. W.R. Zimmer, "Breaking the group ticket sales barrier," Athletic Purchasing and Facilities, November 1982, 28-32.

25. R. Waddell, "Students get breaks on tickets at most major football schools," Amusement Business, 12 September 1987, 1, 14.

26. Howard and Crompton, Financing, managing and marketing, 429.

27. Toxin, "Membership pricing game"; J. Wagner, "Pricing to demand," Fitness Management, March 1996, 38, 40.

28. J. Rofe, "Six tix deal is hot seller for San Francisco," SSSBJ (18-24 May 1998): 6.

29. "Knicks spike up ticket prices: Courtsides now $1,350 a game," SBD, 27 May 1998, 12; K.P. Dupont, "A glut of tickets at Fleet Center," Boston Globe, 24 September 1996, A1, E7.

30. "Dasherboard pricing strategy helps Avalanche shatter revenue goals," Team Marketing Report (July 1996): 4-5.

31. "Slow back-to-school sneaker sales has Venator cutting prices," SBD, 1 September 1998, 5.

32. Kotler, Marketing management, 521-522.

33. D. McGraw, "Big league troubles," U.S. News and World Report, 13 July 1998, 44; R. Burton, "Apocalypse soon: Pro sports teetering on the edge of an abyss," SSSBJ (2-8 November 1998): 30-31.

34. "Does PGA's fee for Ryder Cup tickets fall under 'gray area'?" SBD, 28 July 1998, 9.

35. "Ducks not laying golden eggs: Team to raise ticket prices," SBD, 17 April 1998, 11.

36. B. Mohl, "Cable rates could take a big jump," Boston Globe, 22 June 1998, A1, A7; "Are ESPN execs ready to hear an earful from cable operators?" SBD, 1 May 1998, 5.

37. C. Finder, "Penguin ticket prices up again," Pittsburgh Post-Gazette, 6 May 1987.

38. L.A. Gorsuch, "Pricing theory and ad strategy: How retailers compete," Sporting Goods Dealer, June 1982, 27-31; T. Sitek, "Consumers speak out," Sporting Goods Dealer, February 1987, 99-104.

39. "Hurricanes admit mistake in pricing and cut most ducats," SBD, 1 April 1998, 12.

CHAPTER 10

1. R. Reilly, "The no.1 draw in sports? I hate to tell you," Sports Illustrated 89, no. 3, 20 July 1998, 84.

2. B. King, "Teams line up for another Beanie boost to their bottom lines," Sports Business Journal 1, no. 50 (5-11 April 1999): 46.

3. B. King, "Teams add Beanie Babies to lineups," Sports Business Journal 1, no. 5 (25-31 May 1998): 1, 49.

4. "Coast to coast: Beanie Babies bring out Sox fans," Sports Business Journal 1, no. 13 (20-26 July 1998): 37.

5. For general overviews, see P. Kotler, Marketing management: Analysis, planning, and control, 5th ed. (Englewood Cliffs, NJ: Prentice Hall, 1984), 636-715. For an outstanding compilation of promotional activities used by sport organizations, see D. Wilkerson, The sport marketing encyclopedia (Champaign, IL: Human Kinetics, 1986). Chicago-based Team Marketing Report is the most current source of promotional ideas utilized in professional and collegiate sport. The NACMA Resource Book is another worthy source of promotional concepts.

6. N. Sylvester, "Marketing fitness: Sell the imagery not the agony," Athletic Business, July 1984, 8-16; "Producing a winning ad: Industry leaders reveal what counts," IRSA Club Business, May 1986, 28-31.

7. R. Batra, J.G. Myers, and D.A. Aaker, Advertising management, 5th ed. (Englewood Cliffs, NJ: Prentice Hall, 1996), 47.

8. "Target stores team with the LPGA to embrace more fans," LPGA news release, 100 International Golf Drive, Daytona Beach, Florida, 8 January 1997.

9. D.E. Schultz, S.I. Tannenbaum, and A. Allison, Essentials of advertising strategy, 3rd ed. (Lincolnwood, IL: NTC Business Books, 1996), 49.

10. D. Stotler and D. Johnson, "Assessing the impact and effectiveness of stadium advertising on sports spectators at Division I institutions," Journal of Sport Management 3 (July 1989): 90-102.

11. Batra, Myers, and Aaker, Advertising management, 12.

12. R.F. Gerson, "What to expect from your ad agency," Fitness Management, January 1994, 22-23.

13. Batra, Myers, and Aaker, Advertising management, 45.

14. Audience Analysts conducted proprietary research studies for MLB Properties and the Pittsburgh Pirates during the period of June 30 through July 7, 1998. The research for the Pirates was conducted by videotaping interviews with respondents prior to entering Three Rivers Stadium. The research regarding MLB's FanFest was conducted in Denver using an exit survey format with a self-administered survey.

15. A. Bernstein, "High-tech a (virtual) sign of the times," Sports Business Journal 1, no. 9 (22-28 June 1998): 24, 36.

16. Stotler and Johnson, "Assessing the impact," 14-20.

17. N.K. Pope and K.E. Voges, "Sponsorship evaluation: Does it match the motive and the mechanism?" Sport Marketing Quarterly 3, no. 4 (1994): 37-45.

18. D.M. Turco, "The effects of courtside advertising on product recognition and attitude change," Sport Marketing Quarterly 5, no. 4 (1996): 11-15.

19. "New signage positioning nets revenue source for hockey teams," Team Marketing Report 10, no. 9 (June 1998): 5.

20. "MLB initiative helps Cardinals land new sponsor; Shell dealers sign on for scorekeeping promotions," Team Marketing Report 9, no. 6 (March 1997). 1-2.

21. Ann Reynolds, personal interview, 15 August 1998.

22. Bernstein, "High-tech," 24.

23. C. Brooks and K. Harris, "Celebrity athlete endorsement: An overview of the key theoretical issues," Sport Marketing Quarterly 7, no. 2 (1998): 34-44. See also H. Friedman and L. Friedman, "Endorser effectiveness by product type," Journal of Advertising Research 19, no. 5 (1979): 63-71; and G. McCracken, "Who is the celebrity endorser? Cultural foundations of the endorsement process," Journal of Consumer Research 19 (December 1989): 310-321.

24. McCracken, "Who is the celebrity endorser?"

25. B. Sugar, Hit the sign and win a free suit of clothes from Harry Finklestein (Chicago: Contemporary Books, 1978), 327-329.

26. D.K. Stotler, F.R. Veltri, and R. Viswanathan, "Recognition of athlete-endorsed sport products," Sport Marketing Quarterly 7, no. 1 (1998): 48-56.

27. J. Sivulka, Soap, sex and cigarettes: A cultural history of American advertising (Belmont, CA: Wadsworth, 1998), 397.

28. Brooks and Harris, "Celebrity athlete endorsement."

29. "Top female endorsers," USA Today, 29 June 1998, C1.

30. "Rayovac taps Michael Jordan to recharge battery brand," Sports Marketing Letter 7, no. 4, April 1995, 1, 3.

31. G. Johnson, "Shoe makers sizing up performance of celebrity endorsements," Los Angeles Times, 11 September 1997, D5.

32. B. Meyers, "Shoemakers giving sports stars the boot," USA Today, 13 February 1998, B1-2.

33. M. Phillips, "Taking stock: Top sports pros find a new way to score: Getting equity stakes," Wall Street Journal, 18 April 1997, A1-A3.

34. D. Gellene, "Outlived by fame and fortunes," Los Angeles Times, 11 September 1997, D4.

35. S. Wollenberg, "Jackie Robinson a celebrity endorser again," Marketing News 31, no. 9 (28 April 1997): 1.

36. "Advertising practices," Sporting Goods Dealer, November 1982, 24-29.

37. Batra, Myers, and Aaker, Advertising management, 94-95.

38. For some interesting approaches by the University of Virginia, see "Virginia's marketing plans increase sales," Team Marketing Report (November 1989): 8.

39. Batra, Myers, and Aaker, Advertising management, 425.

40. M.J. Houston, T.L. Childers, and S.E. Heckler, "Picture-word consistency and the elaborative processing of advertisements," Journal of Marketing Research 24 (December 1987): 359-369.

41. Author's note: These systems are also used to recognize individuals for birthdays, anniversaries, and so forth; the actual practice varies from venue to venue.

42. "Advertising rates on 1998 MLB radio broadcasts," Team Marketing Report 10, no. 5 (February 1998): 7.

43. "Knicks and Padres use television to tune into Hispanic population," Team Marketing Report 10, no. 6 (March 1998): 3.

44. "Regional marketing effort drives Ford to multi-university radio deal," Team Marketing Report 9, no. 9 (June 1997): 6.

45. "Phillies radio network tunes in to kids with hopes to attract listeners for life," Team Marketing Report 10, no. 6 (March 1998): 9.

46. Batra, Myers, and Aaker, Advertising management, 438.

47. B. King, "Sonics' home movies are a hit," Sports Business Journal 1, no. 5 (25-31 May 1998): 8.

48. R. Alridge, "This movie's the real thing," Chicago Tribune, 16 October 1981, sec. 6, p. 16.

49. Material for this sidebar compiled from B. Sugar, Hit the sign, 369-374.

50. This material derived from M. Wells, "Ads featuring athletes: They shoot, they score," USA Today, 13 July 1998, 5B.

51. K. Kranhold, "Golf's high profile drives firms to take whack at big campaigns," Wall Street Journal, 28 July 1997, B6.

52. D. Enrico, "Heart-warming ad impresses consumer panel," USA Today, 5 August 1996, 1B-2B.

53. For an excellent, informative article dealing with Internet marketing see L. Delpy and H.A. Bosetti, "Sport management and marketing via the World Wide Web," Sport Marketing Quarterly 7, no. 1 (1998): 21-27.

54. "SuperSonics ready new pitch for Web site sponsors—team will include traditional media to bolster Internet," Team Marketing Report 8, no. 12 (September 1996): 1-2.

55. Material for this table derived from G.E. White, Creating the national pastime: Baseball transforms itself 1903-1953 (Princeton, NJ: Princeton University Press, 1996). B. Sugar, "Hit the sign."

56. J.R.B. Ritchie, "Assessing the impact of Hallmark events: Conceptual and research issues," Journal of Travel Research 3, no. 1 (1984): 2-11.

57. P. Kotler, D.H. Haider, and I. Rein, Marketing places (New York: Free Press, 1993), 173.

58. W.A. Sutton, M.A. McDonald, G.R. Milne, and J. Cimperman, "Creating and fostering fan identification in professional sports," Sport Marketing Quarterly 6, no. 1 (1997): 15-22.

59. For an example of such a linkage, see http://www.nba.com/.

60. For an example, see http://www.nba.com.–sonics/.

61. "Sun Drop on-can promotion could pop top for future sponsorships," Team Marketing Report 10, no. 5 (February 1998): 4.

62. D. Ziccardi, Masterminding the store (New York: Wiley, 1997), 214.

63. B. Veeck and E. Linn, Veeck as in wreck (New York: Putnam's, 1962), 104-118.

64. G. Collier, "Drunken fans can turn on a dime," Pittsburgh Post-Gazette, 4 June 1994, D1.

65. M. Sedlak and W. Suggs, "The list: Most effective major league baseball promotions," Street and Smith's Sports Business Journal 1, no. 25 (1998): 35.

66. Ziccardi, Masterminding the store, 215-235.

67. This table was adapted from Exhibit 5-2 in D.E. Schultz, S.I. Tannebaum, and A. Allison, Essentials of advertising strategy, 3rd ed. (Lincolnwood, IL: NTC Business Books, 1995), 62-63.

68. Phoenix Coyotes 1997 ticket brochure.

69. Cleveland Cavs sales brochure, Gund Arena, 1 Center Court, Cleveland, OH.

70. C. Finder, "Walk-up bonanza, giveaways boost gate," 2 June 1998, http://www.post-gazette.com/pirates/19980602bfans5.asp

71. L. Berling-Manual, "Family fun comes to the forefront," Ad Age, 2 August 1984, 11.

72. K. Higgins, "Play ball," Marketing News (26 April 1985): 8.

73. N. Martinez and R. Van Kleeck, "Neophytes making a name on Madison Avenue," USA Today, 30 March 1998, 3B.

74. J. Lopiano-Misdom and J. DeLucca, Street trends (New York: Harper Collins, 1997), 147.

75. Lopiano-Misdom and DeLucca, Street trends, 142.

76. B. Giles, "Special efforts needed to attract new fans," Athletic Purchasing and Facilities, October 1980, 16-19.

77. C. Rees, "Does sports marketing need a new offense?" Marketing and Media Decisions, February 1981, 66-67, 126-132.

78. W.A. Sutton, R.L. Irwin, and J.M. Gladden, "Tools of the trade: Practical research methods for events, teams and venues," Sport Marketing Quarterly 7, no. 2 (1998): 45-49.

79. S. Brenner, "76ers Community intercept survey suggests new marketing tactics," Team Marketing Report 8 (June 1996): 9.

CHAPTER 11

1. Material compiled from D. Kaplan, "Soccer worth watching," Street and Smith's Sports Business Journal 1, no. 21 (14-20 September 1998): 1, 45; D. Kaplan, "Price tag for Yankees could reach $1 billion," Street and Smith's Sports Business Journal 1, no. 22 (21-27 September 1998): 1, 43.

2. R. Burton and R.Y. Cornilles, "Emerging theory in team sport sales: Selling tickets in a more competitive arena," Sport Marketing Quarterly 7, no. 1 (1998): 33.

3. Y. Berra, The Yogi book (New York: Workman, 1998), 16.

4. T. Hopkins, Selling for dummies (Foster City, CA: IDG Books Worldwide, 1995), 9.

5. M. McCormack, On selling (West Hollywood, CA: Dove Books, 1996), 7.

6. P. Honebein, Strategies for effective customer education (Lincolnwood, IL: NTC Business Books, 1997), 25.

7. N.J. Stephens, Streetwise customer-focused selling (Holbrook, MA: Adams Media, 1998), 4.

8. McCormack, On selling, 9-10.

9. J. Mielke, "Specialization through departmentalization," That's the Ticket 1, no. 1 (May 1997): 5.

10. S.K. Jones, Creative strategy in direct marketing (Lincolnwood, IL: NTC Business Books, 1990), 4-5.

11. For an excellent discussion of the importance of building a database and clear-cut examples of how this has been done in professional sport, see J. Spoelstra, How to sell the last seat in the house (Portland, OR: SRO Partners, 1991), 72-94.

12. J. Spoelstra, Ice to the Eskimos: How to sell a product nobody wants (New York: Harper Business, 1997), 32-38.

13. W.A. Sutton, "SMQ profile/interview: Don Johnson," Sport Marketing Quarterly 6, no. 2 (1997): 5-8.

14. Spoelstra, How to sell the last seat, 40-42.

15. B. Stone and J. Wyman, Successful telemarketing: Opportunities and techniques for increasing sales and profits (Lincolnwood, IL: NTC Business Books), 1986, 6.

16. "Establish league-wide 800 number for ticket orders," in 500 Great promotion ideas (Chicago, IL: Team Marketing Report, 1996), 21.

17. G.S. Day, Market driven strategy: Processes for creating value (New York: Free Press, 1990), 234.

18. L. Hansen, "Dialing for dollars," Marketing Tools, January-February 1997, 47.

19. "Red Sox telephone ticket system dials up immediate sales results," Team Marketing Report 10, no. 5 (February 1998): 3.

20. R.T. Moriarity, G.S. Swartz, and C.A. Khuen, Managing hybrid marketing channels with automation (Cambridge, MA: Marketing Science Institute, 1988).

21. Stone and Wyman, Successful telemarketing, 102.

22. "Teams, sponsors use phone system to ring up results," Team Marketing Report 6, no. 8 (May 1994): 4-5.

23. Jones, Creative strategy in direct marketing, 7-9.

24. Golfsmith International, L.P., Golfsmith store catalogue, Austin, TX, August 1998.

25. PGA TOUR Partners Club, PGA TOUR Partners Club brochure, Minnetonka, MN, 1998, 4-10.

26. Jack Nicklaus rewards brochure, Citibank, 1997-1998.

27. Jones, Creative strategy in direct marketing, 101.

28. W.T. Knudsen, Kiro Direct sales and marketing materials, Seattle, WA, 1997.

29. Spoelstra, Ice to the Eskimos, 173.

30. Phoenix Coyotes, 1996-97 annual report, Phoenix, 1997.

31. B. Breighner, Face-to-face selling (Indianapolis: Park Avenue, 1995), x.

32. D. Ziccardi, Masterminding the store (New York: Wiley, 1997), 238.

33. Spoelstra, Ice to the Eskimos, 146-151.

34. Breighner, Face-to-face selling, 84-85.

35. Stephens, Streetwise customer-focused selling, 25.

36. R. McKenna, Relationship marketing: Successful strategies for the age of the consumer (Reading, MA: Addison-Wesley, 1991), 4.

37. C. Gronroos, Service management and marketing: Managing moments of truth in service competition (New York: Lexington Books, 1990).

38. D. Shani, "A framework for implementing relationship marketing in the sport industry," Sport Marketing Quarterly 6, no. 2 (1997): 9-15.

39. R. Burton and R.Y. Cornilles, "Emerging ticket theory in team sport sales: Selling tickets in a more competitive arena," Sport Marketing Quarterly 7, no. 1 (1998): 29-37.

40. For an excellent study of how to create a market, see P. Levine, A.G. Spalding and the rise of baseball (New York: Oxford Press, 1985).

41. Spoelstra, Ice to the Eskimos, 91-93.

42. For a truly enjoyable read and examples of how to sell, see B. Veeck and E. Linn, Veeck as in wreck (New York: Putnam's, 1962). Mike Veeck's successful exploits with the independent Northern League St. Paul Saints is chronicled in S. Perlstein, Rebel baseball: The summer the game was returned to the fans (New York: Holt, 1994).

43. Pittsburgh Pirates group sales brochure G, 1998.

44. For an explanation of this need, see W.A. Sutton, M.A. McDonald, G.R. Milne, and J. Cimperman, "Creating and fostering fan identification in team sports," Sport Marketing Quarterly 6, no. 1 (1997): 15-22.

45. F.R. Dwyer, "Customer lifetime valuation to support marketing decision making," Journal of Direct Marketing 3 (autumn 1989): 8-15.

46. M.A. McDonald and G.R. Milne, "A conceptual framework for evaluating marketing relationships in professional sport franchises," Sport Marketing Quarterly 6, no. 2 (1997): 27-32.

47. B.T. Gale, Managing customer value (New York: Free Press, 1994), 3-23.

48. Forum Consulting, Boston MA; Customer Service Institute, Silver Spring, MD.

49. T.G. Vavra, Aftermarketing: How to keep customers for life through relationship marketing (New York: Irwin, 1992), 22.

50. K. Blanchard and S. Bowles, Raving fans (New York: Morrow, 1993).

51. Created on the basis of materials from Vavra, Aftermarketing, 25.

52. Interview with MaryAnn Kellerman, Cleveland Cavs, 27 August 1998.

CHAPTER 12

1. Material on both the Medalist Group and Ford compiled from "Senior women golfers look for $2M sponsor and Ford joins America's Cup effort," Street and Smith's Sports Business Journal 1, no. 23 (28 September-4 October 1998): 12.

2. "Chain-specific promotions yielding new alliances among licensors, retailers, fast-food chains," Entertainment Marketing Letter, October 1990, 1.

3. J. Meenaghan, Commercial sponsorship (West Yorkshire, England: MCB University Press, 1984).

4. Meenaghan, Commercial sponsorship.

5. S.A. Wichmann and D.R. Martin, "Sports and tobacco—the smoke has yet to clear," Physician and Sports Medicine 19, no. 11 (1991): 125-131.

6. N. Meyers and L. Clarke, "No trouble foreseen in finding sponsors," USA Today, 23 June 1997, 3B.

7. B. Horovitz, "Pepsi ad refreshes; Coke's falls flat," USA Today, 26 January 1998, 1B.

8. R.G. Hagstrom, The NASCAR way: The business that drives the sport (New York: Wiley, 1998), 50.

9. P. Ueberroth, Made in America (New York: Morrow, 1985), 61.

10. W. D'Orio, "Just doing it," Promo 10, no. 4 (March 1997): 38.

11. L. Ukman, notes from Sponsorship Trends Workshop, Chicago, IL.

12. M. Hanan, Life-styled marketing (New York: AMACOM Books, 1980), 2-3.

13. "Healthy Choice creates integrated promotions around ski team deal," IEG Sponsorship Report 16, no. 16 (18 August 1997): 1-3.

14. D. Wilber, "Linking sports and sponsors," Journal of Business Strategy (July-August 1998): 8-10.

15. M. Littman, "Sponsors take to the court with the new women's NBA," Marketing News 31, no. 5 (1997): 1, 6.

16. Meenaghan, Commercial sponsorship.

17. R.L. Irwin, M. Asimakopolous, and W.A. Sutton, "A model for screening sponsorship opportunities," Journal of Promotional Management 2, no. 3-4 (1994): 53-69.

18. "Old Navy finds sports a perfect fit," Team Marketing Report 10, no. 2 (November 1997): 5.

19. "In-line manufacturer gets hockey marketing strategy rolling with IHL Milwaukee Admirals," Team Marketing Report 8, no. 3 (December 1995): 1-2.

20. S.C. Schafer, "How Coors picks its winners in sports," Business Week, 26 August 1985, 56, 61.

21. "Western Union's team marketing aimed at several different targets," Team Marketing Report 10, no. 2 (December 1995): 5.

22. R. Thurow, "Full-court press: Women's NBA pins hopes on clean play and hard marketing," Wall Street Journal, 12 June 1997, A1, A8.

23. G. Krupa, "Cup runneth over," Boston Sunday Globe, 7 June 1998, F1, F7.

24. Meenaghan, Commercial sponsorship.

25. "Cavalier's new community relations program draws new advertisers from local minority-owned businesses," Team Marketing Report 8, no. 2 (November 1995): 1-2.

26. J. Carlucci, "Linking sports sponsorship to the trade," Marketing Communications, November-December 1988, 42.

27. F. Coleman, "Major sponsors love World Cup's marketing power," USA Today, 9 June 1998, 7B.

28. C. Miller, "Marketers look to score with women's sports," Marketing News 31, no. 16 (4 August 1997): 1, 16.

29. S.G. Beatty, "Public is confused on Olympic sponsors," Wall Street Journal, 18 February 1998, B8.

30. M. Hiestand, "Woods gets Nike logo maximum exposure," USA Today, 17 April 1997, 9C.

31. W.A. Sutton, "SMQ profile/interview with Joyce Julius Cotman," Sport Marketing Quarterly 7, no. 2 (1998): 6-7.

32. A.L. Schreiber, Lifestyle and event marketing (New York: McGraw-Hill, 1994), 140.

33. D.M. Halbfinger, "D'Alessandro: To market, to market," Boston Globe, 10 April 1996, 55-56.

34. "VISA signs NFL sponsor pact for $40 million+," Sports Marketing Letter 7, no. 4 (April 1995): 1-2.

35. S. Lainson, "Client entertainment," Sports news you can use (1997), 12 pp 1-3, slainson@sportstrust.com.

36. C. Sampson, The Masters: Golf, money and power in Augusta, Georgia (New York: Villard, 1998), xxiv.

37. A. Friedman, exec. ed., Naming rights deals (Chicago: Team Marketing Report, 1997), 8.

38. "Pacers ink Conseco to naming rights deal for new fieldhouse," Sports Business Daily 4, no. 160 (27 May 1998): 13.

39. A. Friedman, "Naming rights may be bargain for companies going national," Street and Smith's Sports Business Journal 1, no. 3 (1998): 8.

40. Hagstrom, The NASCAR way, 52.

41. "Raptors arrange consumer research to show partners how their sponsorships are—or aren't working," Team Marketing Report 9, no. 9 (June 1997): 1-2.

42. B. Macchiette and R. Abhijit, "Affinity marketing: What is it and how does it work?" Journal of Services Marketing 6, no. 3 (1992): 47-57.

43. "MCI's affinity marketing program offers colleges the chance to ring up revenues," Team Marketing Report 7, no. 3 (December 1994): 1, 6.

44. Hagstrom, The NASCAR way, 59-60.

45. D.M. Sandler and D. Shani, "Olympic sponsorship vs. 'ambush' marketing: Who gets the gold?" Journal of Advertising Research 29, no. 4 (1989): 9-14.

46. T. Meenaghan, "Point of view: Ambush marketing: Immoral or imaginative practice?" Journal of Advertising Research 34, no. 5 (1994): 77-88.

47. R.N. Davis, "Ambushing the Olympic games," Villanova Sports Law and Entertainment Journal 3 (1996): 423-442.

48. J. Naughton, "Exclusive deal with Reebok brings U. of Wisconsin millions of dollars and unexpected criticism," Chronicle of Higher Education, 6 September 1996, A65-A66.

49. K. Hawes, "A brewing dilemma on campus," NCAA News 35, no. 14 (1998): 1, 6, 7, 20.

50. W.A Sutton and M.A. McDonald, "Building partnerships," Athletic Management 10, no. 4 (1998): 16-19.

CHAPTER 13

1. J. Fraiberg, "A racket at rush hour," Sports Illustrated, 9 October 1995, 16.

2. "NHL breaks out another three-year deal with Streetball," Sports Business Daily (hereafter cited as SBD), 7 May 1998, 4.

3. "NHL links with Family Ice Enterprises to develop NHL SKATE," SBD, 19 May 1998, 13.

4. "NHL's two-game stint in Japan concludes with all sides happy," SBD, 6 October 1997, 6.

5. P. Gammons, "The place is the thing," Boston Globe, 25 April 1995, 76, in special section, "No replacement for Fenway." The notion of ensemble is developed in J. Bale, Sport, space and the city (London: Routledge, 1993); J. Bale, Landscapes of modern sport (Leicester: University of Leicester, 1994); J. Raitz, ed., The theater of sport (Baltimore: Johns Hopkins University Press, 1995).

6. M. Leve, A nationwide study of court and health clubs (Champaign, IL: Department of Leisure and Recreation, 1980), 31; M. Levine, "Know your facility's drawing radius," Sport Marketing Review, Spring 1977, 1.

7. R. Sandomir, "Sox detour time," Sports Inc., 28 March 1988, 32-33. For an excellent historical analysis of ballpark placement, see S.A. Riess, Touching base: Professional baseball and American culture in the Progressive Era (Westport, CT: Greenwood Press, 1980).

8. E. Cohen, "Miles, minutes, and custom markets," Marketing Tools, July-August 1996, 18-21.

9. For more on the concept of drawing radius, see M. Levine, "Making marketing research hustle" (presentation at the Athletic Business Conference, Las Vegas, NV, December 8, 1987, in author's posession).

10. P. Gollenback, American Zoom. (New York: Macmillan, 1993) 87. On Charlotte, see E. Hinton, "Long way to go," Sports Illustrated, 18 December 1995, 59-62.

11. "Will there be a Giant parking problem at Pac Bell Ballpark?" SBD, 20 August 1998, 13. See also the parking ratio issue related to the L.A. Coliseum in L.

Mullen, "Coliseum parking could add $100M to cost," Street and Smith's Sports Business Journal (hereafter cited as SSSBJ) (26 April-2 May 1999): 5.

12. M. DiNitto, "Fields of vision," Athletic Business, January 1999, 38-45.

13. Z. Dowdy, "BC told to redo plan for parking," Boston Globe, 2 September 1993, 25, 30.

14. M. Conrad, "Blame the feds for chaos over handicap seating," SSSBJ (1-7 June 1998): 43.

15. "Head count," SBD, 22 June 1999: 15; A. Goldfisher, "Concourses designed to serve up profits," SSSBJ (24-30 August 1998): 22.

16. For a good account of changes in "flow" made at Stanford Stadium in anticipation of the 1985 Super Bowl, see J. Anderson, "Management by design," Athletic Business, August 1985, 28-34.

17. "Building for diverse consumer demands," Managed recreation research report, annual report published by Recreation, Sports and Leisure, July-August 1987, 36-43. On single-purpose sport facilities, see R. Berg, "Two scores for U.S. soccer," Athletic Business, June 1998, 9-10; A. Cohen, "A field of their own," Athletic Business, May 1995, 26.

18. "11th Annual Architectural Showcase," Athletic Business, June 1998, 44-176; "When it comes to arenas, we like that old time rock 'n roll," SBD, 10 October 1997, 15; W. Hughes, "Aesthetic effect," Athletic Business, August 1997, 69-72.

19. J. Rofe, "'Smart' seats nifty, but will fans byte?" SSSBJ (7-13 December 1998): 22; D. Schwartz, "You have the snapper, I'll have the veal," SSSBJ (24-30 August 1998): 20; D. Schwartz, "Good food, shops are good for business," SSSBJ (24-30 August 1998): 26; J. Long, "Faster service, larger variety spice fare," (Cleveland) Plain Dealer, 16 October 1994, 15G; High tech sound components discussed in I. Wolfe and B. Kubicki, "Sound theories," Athletic Business, July 1994, 35-40; "WSU courtside hot tub is the best seat in the house," Team Marketing Report (February 1994): 3; I. Ruber, "Next generation of stadiums touches down in Phoenix," SSSBJ (27 April-3 May 1998): 28.

20. S. Schmid, "Pool payoffs," Athletic Business, May 1993, 33-36; J. Lombardo, "This is not your father's bowling alley," SSSBJ (4-10 January 1999): 6.

21. P. Gammons, "Baseball," Boston Sunday Globe, 31 August 1997, C12; D. Schwartz, "Good food, shops," 26.

22. United Center, 1996-97 Club Seating Handbook, in author's possession.

23. See the IAAM Web site at www.iaam.org [7 May 1999].

24. "Courtside at the Eagles' game" ["Scorecard"], Sports Illustrated, 1 December 1997, 24.

25. E. Hinton, "Not so fast," Sports Illustrated, 13 March 1995, 44; D. Howard, "The changing fanscape of big-league sports: Implications for sport managers," Journal of Sport Management 13 (1999): 82; S. Riess, City games: The evolution of American urban society and

the rise of sports (Urbana, IL: Illinois University Press, 1989), 239-245. For the economics of stadium financing, see R. Noll and A. Zimbalist, eds., Sport, jobs, and taxes: The economic impact of sports teams and stadiums (Washington, DC: Brookings, 1997); M. Rosentraub, Major league losers: The real cost of sports and who's paying for it (New York: Basic Books, 1997); S. Wilson, "IOC member alleges selection bribes," Boston Globe, 13 December 1998, E2; L. Mullen, "NCAA shuts door on lavish Final Four bids," SSSBJ 27 July-2 August 1998: 10.

26. "The PGA TOUR's latest stop: New golf retail outlet to expand," SBD, 12 August 1998, 3; M.B. Grover, "Lost in cyberspace," Forbes, 8 March 1999, 124-128. For more on channel decision making, see Kotler, Marketing management, 9th edition, 541-544.

27. S. Hardy, "Adopted by all the leading clubs: Sporting goods and the shaping of leisure," in For fun and profit, ed. R. Butsch (Philadelphia: Temple University Press, 1990), 71-101; S. Lainson, "Sports News You Can Use," e-mail newsletter, no. 28, 1996.

28. M. Palmisano, "Merchandising can mean added revenue for you," Athletic Purchasing and Facilities, October 1980, 22-24.

29. "I love these stores? NBA to enter crowded retail market," SBD, 17 November 1997, 14; A. Bernstein, "Souvenirs no longer an afterthought," SSSBJ (10-16 August 1998): 20, 22.

30. C. Reidy, "Equal parts entertainer and vendor," Boston Globe, 20 July 1997, F1, 3; "Niketown in the middle of a worldwide growth spurt," SBD, 27 November 1997, 12.

31. D.S. Crowther, "How much inventory should you have on hand?" Sporting Goods Dealer, April 1987, 11, 73; G. Laird, "9 Questions, when answered, improve sales performances," Sporting Goods Business, July 1983, 22; J. McCarthy, Basic marketing (Homewood IL: Irwin, 1975), 320.

32. W. McDonough, "Jets sign Tupa," Boston Globe, 13 February 1999, D6.

33. "The convenience story: MLB clubs' ticket sales methods," Team Marketing Report (February 1997): 7.

34. "The convenience story," 7; "ETM remote locations and kiosks," SBD, 9 February 1998, 10. For an excellent article on issues related to electronic ticket distribution, see L. Miller and L. Fielding, "Ticket distribution agencies and professional sports franchises: The successful partnership," Sport Marketing Quarterly 6 (March 1997): 47-55.

35. "Chevron inks reported $15-20M pact with MLB grants," SBD, 4 December 1997, 3; "Burger King sells tickets their way—lots of them," Team Marketing Report (January 1994): 4, 7.

36. "Payroll deductions add up to Hamilton season tickets," Team Marketing Report (October 1992): 5.

37. "What are this year's tickets to success for NBA team marketers?" Team Marketing Report (December 1997): 8; "Cyber sales," SBD, 4 December 1997, 3.

38. W. Suggs, "Sox ticket system target Ticketmaster," SSSBJ (18-24 May 1998): 7.

39. L. Deckard, "Pro sports franchises, banks work together in promotion of team affinity credit cards," Amusement Business, 7 May 1988, 1, 14.

CHAPTER 14

1. "Whither the tube?" editorial, New York Times [Online], 4 January 1999, http://www.nytimes.com.

2. The standard survey of all forms of broadcasting in the United States is S.W. Head, C.H. Sterling, et al., Broadcasting in America, 8th ed. (Boston: Houghton Mifflin, 1998).

3. Industry statistics from Television Bureau of Advertising, TV basics: The Television Bureau of Advertising's report on the growth and scope of television (New York: Television Bureau of Advertising 1998). See www.tvb.org for updated statistics.

4. Nielsen Media Research maintains an excellent and informative Web site detailing the basics of audience research at www.nielsen-media.com.

5. See B. Rader, In its own image: How television has transformed sports (New York: Free Press, 1984).

6. "TV's battle royal," Broadcasting & Cable, 13 May 1996, 35.

7. The best way to keep up to the minute on the rapidly changing broadcasting industry is to regularly read the leading trade journals such as Broadcasting & Cable, Mediaweek, and Multichannel News, as well as the media columns of major newspapers.

8. For a primer on television production, see L. Shyles, Video production handbook (Boston: Houghton Mifflin, 1998) or R. Whittaker, Television production (Mountain View, CA: Mayfield, 1993), now available online in an updated version at www.internetcampus.com.

9. "Local TV and radio lineup," Broadcasting & Cable, 29 March 1999, 26-27.

10. "National Collegiate Basketball Championship Agreement" between the NCAA and CBS Sports, dated 21 November 1989.

11. CommerceNet, "Internet population," 1998, www.commerce.net./research/stats/wwwpop.html June 29, 1999.

12. K. Auletta, "The magic box," New Yorker, 11 April 1994, 45.

13. For a summary of the World Wide Web as a sport marketing tool, see L. Delpy and H.A. Bosetti, "Sport management and marketing via the World Wide Web," Sport Marketing Quarterly 7, no. 1 (1998): 21-27.

14. Bookstore and library shelves are groaning with "how to build a Web site" books. A good starting point, but certainly not the only one, is S. Fisher, Creating dynamic Web sites: A webmaster's guide to interactive multimedia (Reading, MA: Addison-Wesley, 1997).

15. Nielsen Media Research, "Nielsen Media Research strengthens sports research with SportsQuest," 22 September 1998, www.nielsenmedia.com/news/sportsquest.html.

CHAPTER 15

1. Material for this vignette compiled in part from B. Schoenfeld, "Talk about shortsighted," Street and Smith's Sports Business Journal 1, no. 22 (21-27 September 1998): 1, 45.

2. R.T. Bronzan, Public relations, promotions and fund raising for athletic and physical education programs (New York: Wiley, 1977), 4.

3. C.L. Caywood, "Twenty-first century public relations," in The handbook of strategic public relations and integrated communications, ed. C.L. Caywood (New York: McGraw-Hill, 1997), ix.

4. M. Govoni, R. Eng, and M. Galper, Promotional management (Englewood Cliffs, NJ: Prentice Hall, 1986), 15-16.

5. M.P. Gonring, "Global and local media relations," in Handbook of strategic public relations, ed. Caywood, 63.

6. R.J. Hellawell, letter to J.E. Sullivan, 14 February 1907, c/o American Sports Publishing Co.

7. R.L. Irwin and W.A. Sutton, "Roles, responsibilities and effectiveness of urban community relations programs within professional sport franchises." Presented at "Sport in the City: An International Symposium on Cultural, Economic, and Political Considerations," Memphis, TN, November 10, 1996.

8. W.A. Sutton, M.A. McDonald, G.R. Milne, and J. Cimperman, "Creating and fostering fan identification in professional sports," Sport Marketing Quarterly 6, no. 1 (1997): 15.

9. J.A. Koten, "The strategic uses of corporate philanthropy," in Handbook of strategic public relations, ed. Caywood, 150.

10. D.N. Jones, "Meet 'em, greet 'em, beat 'em Bucs," Pittsburgh Post-Gazette, 10 May 1997, A1, A12.

11. "The Magic touch," Orlando Magic Youth Foundation brochure, Orlando Magic, 1997.

12. V. Lister, "Lanier: Helping children lifetime reward," USA Today, 4 February 1997, D4.

13. Cleveland Cavaliers in the community brochure, Cleveland Cavaliers, 1998.

14. "Cavaliers' new community relations program draws new advertisers from local minority-owned businesses," Team Marketing Report 8, no. 2 (April 1995): 1-2.

15. The Cam Neely Foundation brochure, Cam Neely Foundation, Boston, MA, 1998.

16. Compiled from D. Ziccardi, Masterminding the store (New York: Wiley, 1997), 254-259; and D. Wilcox, P. Ault, and W. Agee, Public relations: Strategies and tactics (Philadelphia: Random House, 1986).

17. H.M. Davis, Basic concepts of sports information, 2nd ed. (East Longmeadow, MA: Jostc, 1990), 16.

18. J.F. Love, McDonald's: Behind the arches (New York: Bantam, 1986), 213-214.

19. D. Harris, The League: The rise and decline of the NFL (New York: Bantam, 1986), 67-68.

20. J. Lombardo, "CBA hires Spike to build its star power," Street and Smith's Business Journal 1, no. 18 (24-30 August 1998): 1, 43.

21. "LPGA Girls Golf Club announces additional expansion: Partnership with USGA and Girl Scouts of the U.S.A. fosters growth," LPGA press release, Daytona Beach, FL, 29 July 1997.

22. For an examination of America's interest in terms of both participation and spectatorship see the following: Research and Forecasts, Inc., Miller Lite report on American attitudes toward sport (New York: Miller Brewing Co., 1983); and Lieberman Research Inc., Sports Illustrated sports poll '86 (New York: Sports Illustrated, 1986). There are also proprietary studies such as those published by American Sports Demographics of Dallas, TX, that can be obtained for a fee.

23. P. Williams, The magic of teamwork (Nashville: Thomas Nelson, 1997), 159.

24. Although the St. Louis Browns moved to Baltimore and the Boston Braves moved to Milwaukee prior to the Dodgers' leaving Brooklyn for L.A., each of these teams was the least successful team in a two-team market. When they left, the Cardinals were still in St. Louis and the Red Sox remained in Boston. When the Dodgers left Brooklyn, there was no other franchise competing in that unique market. For a unique and compelling analysis of that move see N. Sullivan, The Dodgers Move West, (New York, Oxford University Press, 1987).

25. T. Barnes, "New tax bill gives counties more," Pittsburgh Post-Gazette, 30 May 1997, http://www.postgazette.com/newsroom/extras/19971009salestax3.asp.

26. T. Barnes, "TV ads tout the benefits of tax boost," Pittsburgh Post-Gazette, 12 June 1997, http://www.postgazette.com/newsroom/extras/19971009salestax5.asp.

27. E. Hoffman, "Officials from five counties tear into sales tax," Pittsburgh Post-Gazette, 13 June 1997, http://www.postgazette.com/newsroom/extras/19971009salestax6.asp.

28. T. Barnes, "Santorum tells backers of tax plan to speak out," Pittsburgh Post-Gazette, 6 September 1997, http://www.postgazette.com/newsroom/extras/19971009salestax8.asp.

29. T. Barnes, "Stadium advocates stepping forward," Pittsburgh Post-Gazette, 16 September 1997, http://www.postgazette.com/newsroom/extras/19971009salestax10.asp.

30. M. Simonich, "New stadiums are born without growth guarantee," Pittsburgh Post-Gazette,

30 September 1997, http://www.postgazette.com/newsroom/extras/19971009salestax12.asp.

31. Simonich, "New stadiums."

32. A. Ries and J. Trout, Positioning: The battle for your mind (New York: McGraw-Hill, 1986), 19-27.

33. R. Thurow, "Full court press: Women's NBA pins hopes on clean play and hard marketing," Wall Street Journal, 12 June 1997, A1, A8.

34. Needham Parks and Recreation Department brochure, Needham, MA, 1998.

35. C. Reidy, "Reebok kicks itself over name with bad fit," Boston Globe, 20 February 1997, A1, A16.

36. R. Martzke, "Wright: 'Lesbians hurt women's golf,'" USA Today, 12 May 1995, C1.

37. P. King, "Patriot games: New England fumbled when it drafted Christian Peter and tried to recover by cutting him loose," Sports Illustrated, 6 May 1996, 32-33.

38. ESPN broadcast, "Outside the Lines—Athletes in Trouble," produced/moderated by Bob Ley, 2 September 1997.

39. J.A. Michener, Sports in America (New York: Random House, 1976), 355.

40. R. Lipsyte, Sportsworld: An American dreamland (New York: Quadrangle, 1975), 170.

41. J. Bouton, Ball four (New York: Stein and Day, 1970).

42. M. Gunther and M. Carter, Monday night mayhem (New York: Morrow, 1988), 34.

43. "ESPN's Outside the Lines examines athletes in trouble," Sports Business Daily, 3 September 1997, 15.

44. W. Sutton and R.H. Migliore, "Strategic long range planning for intercollegiate athletic programs," Journal of Applied Research in Coaching and Athletics 3, no. 4 (1988): 233-261.

CHAPTER 16

1. Kay Hawes, "A brewing dilemma on campus," NCAA News, 6 April 1998, 1, 6, 7; L. Kinney and S. McDaniel, "Public says 'yes' to corporate role in sports," Street and Smith's Sports Business Journal (hereafter cited as SSSBJ) 1-7 March 1999, 33.

2. "SI says NIKE made 'vast miscalculation' on Tiger Woods line," Sports Business Daily (hereafter cited as SBD), 19 August 1997, 3.

3. L. Zepp, "Supermarket promo lifts attendance for Ohio State Lady Buckeyes games," Amusement Business, 6 February 1988, 13, 15.

4. Michael Eisner with Tony Schwartz, "Running the Mouse house," Newsweek, 28 September 1998, 58.

5. "Jazz and Hostess offer fans a colorful snackfood," Team Marketing Report (March 1994): 6.

6. "Nike pulls shoe offensive to Muslims," Boston Globe, 25 June 1997, C2.

7. "Stern says league needs to address player behavior issues," SBD, 2 June 1997, 13.

8. P. Amend and W. Tobin, "Tax exempts: A snake in the grass?" Club Business, November 1988, 34-38, 64-67.

9. "New Texas twister: Rangers/Stars combine ticket packages," SBD, 6 March 1998, 17; D. Kaplan, "Tom Hicks eyes profits—and wins—in his sports ventures," SSSBJ (8-14 February 1999): 1, 46.

10. B. Lumpkin and P. Finebaum, "Alabama weathers storm over priority ticket plan," NCAA News, 10 June 1987, 9.

11. A. Bernstein, "NFL's soft-drink, fast-food deals slow in coming," SSSBJ (15-21 June 1998): 9; "Are autograph and collectible shows worth it for athletes?" SBD, 1 September 1998, 5.

12. L. Berling-Manuel, "Giants weathering Bay City blues," Advertising Age, 2 August 1984, 10-11.

13. "IHL Dragons increase in-arena interaction by putting partisans in penalty box," Team Marketing Report 9 (January 1997): 9.

14. S. Schmid, "Inner-city ice," Athletic Business, November 1996, 18; M. Starr, "Ticketless in Atlanta," Newsweek, 23 October 1995, 51.

15. See, for instance, W. Stockton, "The hand weights gospel," New York Times, 1 August 1988, C10; this article was picked up through the Times wire service by newspapers around the country.

16. For excellent insight into strategy and control in sport organizations, see T. Slack, Understanding sport organizations: The application of organizational theory (Champaign, IL: Human Kinetics, 1997); D. Howard and J. Crompton, Financing Sport (Morgantown, WV: Fitness Information Technology, 1995).

17. Quoted in W. Sutton and H. Migliore, "Strategic long range planning for intercollegiate athletic programs," Journal of Applied Research in Coaching and Athletics 3 (1988): 238.

18. A. Bernstein, "Without a breakaway threat, MLS aims for steady, long-term growth," SSSBJ (13-19 July 1998): 14.

19. SBD, 27 November 1997, 8.

20. A. Friedman and P. Much, Inside the ownership of professional team sports (Chicago: Team Marketing Report, 1997); B. King, "Primo premiums," SSSBJ (12-18 October 1998): 34-35; A. Friedman, "Poor planning dooms even the best-designed sponsorship deal," SSSBJ (1-7 February 1999): 11; R. Cawley, "Bottom line blurry on impact studies," SSSBJ (3-9 August 1998): 24; N. Liberman, "Battle of ratings firms a good sign," SSSBJ (26 April-2 May 1999): 14.

21. G. Wren, "The sales behind the scowl," Marketing Tools, March-April 1996, 14-17.

CHAPTER 17

1. R. Schaffler, "Nike's Olympic ambush," 19 July 1996, http://cnnfn.com/hotstories/companies/9607/19/olympic_pkg/index.html.

2. U.S. Constitution, art. 1, sec. 8, states, "Congress shall have the power to promote the progress of science and useful arts, by securing for limited times to authors and inventors the exclusive right to their own writings and discoveries."

3. Copyrights, 17 United States Code Annotated (hereafter cited as U.S.C.A.) sec. 102 (1996).

4. Copyrights, 17 U.S.C.A. sec. 102 (1996).

5. Copyrights, 17 U.S.C.A. at sec. 106. Exclusive rights in copyrighted works.

6. Copyrights, 17 U.S.C.A. sec. 302 (1996).

7. Copyrights, 17 U.S.C.A. sec. 302 (1996).

8. Copyrights, 17 U.S.C.A. sec. 107 (1996).

9. F.H. Kent, "Two 'fair use' cases," New York Law Journal (21 August 1998), http://www.ljextra.com/cgi-bin/f_cat?prod/ljextra/data/texts/082198c4.html.

10. 510 U.S. 569 (1994).

11. Monster Communications, Inc. v. Turner Broadcasting System, Inc., 935 F. Supp. 490 (S.D.N.Y. 1996).

12. A. Hartwick, "Props and clips: A fair use analysis," New York Law Journal (12 June 1998), citing Rudell, "Denial of Ali film clip," New York Law Journal (27 June 1997): 3. http://www.nylj.com/

13. N.B.A. v. Motorola, Inc., 105 F. 3d 841 (1997).

14. Copyrights, 17 U.S.C.A. sec. 101 (1996).

15. 622 F. Supp. 1500 (N.D. Ill. 1985).

16. 105 F. 3d 841 (2d Cir. 1997).

17. 105 F. 3d 841 (2d Cir. 1997).

18. 105 F. 3d 841 (2d Cir. 1997).

19. A.M. Wall, "Sports marketing and the law: Protecting proprietary interests in sports entertainment events," Marquette Sports Law Journal 7 (1996): 77.

20. Wall, "Sports marketing and the law," 77.

21. M.H. Reed, IEG legal guide to sponsorship (Chicago: International Events Group, 1989), 180-182.

22. The Lanham Trade-Mark Act of 1946, 15 U.S.C.A. sec. 1127 (1996).

23. Two Pesos Inc. v. Taco Cabana, Inc. 505 U.S. 763, 765 (1992), citing John H. Harland Co. v. Clarke Checks, Inc., 711 F. 2d 966 (11th Cir. 1983).

24. The Lanham Trade-Mark Act of 1946, 15 U.S.C.A. sec. 1127 (1990)

25. T.S. Sharin, "Marketing is major league in the minors," National Law Journal (17 November 1997): B7. http://www.ljx.com/practice/sports/1117minors.html

26. The Lanham Trade-Mark Act of 1946, 15 U.S.C.A. sec. 1127 (1990).

27. The Lanham Trade-Mark Act of 1946, 15 U.S.C.A. sec. 1127 (1990).

28. U.S. Patent and Trademark Office, "Basic facts about registering a trademark," 31 July 1995, http://www.uspto.gov/web/offices/tac/doc/basic/basic_facts.html

29. Blue Bell, Inc. v. Farah Manufacturing Co. Inc., 508 F. 2d 1260 (5th Cir. 1975).

30. W.M. Landes and R.A. Posner, "Trademark law: An economic perspective," Journal of Law and Economics 30 (1987): 265.

31. Yale Electric Corp. v. Robertson, 26 F. 2d 972 (2d Cir. 1928).

32. Blue Bell, Inc. v. Farah Manufacturing Co. Inc., 508 F. 2d 1260 (5th Cir. 1975), citing United Drug Co. v. Theodore Rectanus Co., 248 U.S. 90 (1918).

33. The Lanham Trade-Mark Act of 1946, 15 U.S.C.A. sec. 1051 (1990).

34. AMF, Inc. v. Sleekcraft Boats, 599 F. 2d 341, 349 (9th Cir. 1979).

35. Reed, IEG legal guide to sponsorship, 117.

36. National Football League Properties, Inc. v. Wichita Falls Sportswear, Inc., 532 F. Supp. 651, 658 (1982), citing Levi Strauss & Co. v. Blue Bell, Inc., 632 F. 2d 817 (9th Cir. 1980).

37. Reed, IEG legal guide to sponsorship, discussing Louisiana World Exposition, Inc. v. R. Gordon-Logue, Jr., 221 U.S.P.Q. 589 (E.D. La. 1983) and New York World's Fair 1939, Inc. v. World's Fair News, Inc., 297 N.Y.S. 923 (Sup. Ct. 1937) aff'd 10 N.Y.S. 2d 56 (App. Div. 1939).

38. U.S. Patent and Trademark Office, "Basic facts about registering a trademark."

39. B.A. Masters, "Taking team names to court," Washington Post, 7 April 1999, B1.

40. S. Elliott, "Sales of licensed merchandise increase in 1997," 7 January 1998, http://archives.nytimes.com/.

41. National Football League Properties, Inc. v. Dallas Cowboys Football Club, Ltd., 922 F. Supp. 849 (S.D.N.Y. 1996).

42. National Football League Properties, Inc. v. Dallas Cowboys Football Club, Ltd., 922 F. Supp. 849 (S.D.N.Y. 1996).

43. Nike, Inc. v. Just Did It Enterprises, 6 F. 3d 1225, 1227 (7th Cir. 1993).

44. Two Pesos, Inc. v. Taco Cabana, Inc., 505 U.S. 763 (1992).

45. The Lanham Trade-Mark Act of 1946, 15 U.S.C.A. sec. 1125(a) (1996).

46. National Football League Properties, Inc. v. N.J. Giants, 637 F. Supp. 507 (D.N.J. 1986), citing Scott Paper Co. v. Scott's Liquid Gold, Inc., 589 F. 2d 1225 (3d Cir. 1978) rev'g 439 F. Supp. 1022, 1036-1037 (D.Del. 1977).

47. 99 F. 3d 244 (7th Cir. 1996) cert. denied 117 S.Ct. 1083 (1997).

48. 952 F. Supp. 1084 (D.N.J. 1997).

49. 604 F. 2d 200 (2d Cir. 1979).

50. 604 F. 2d 200 (2d Cir. 1979).

51. 604 F. 2d 200 (2d Cir. 1979).

52. The Lanham Trade-Mark Act of 1946, 15 U.S.C.A. sec. 1127 (1996).

53. The Lanham Trade-Mark Act of 1946, 15 U.S.C.A. sec. 1127 (1996).

54. Indianapolis Colts, National Football League Properties and National Football League v. Metropolitan Baltimore Football Club, Limited Partnership, 34 F. 3d 410 (7th Cir. 1994), citing T.J. McCarthy, McCarthy on trademarks and intellectual property, 3d ed. 1994), sec. 17.01[2], at p. 17-3.

55. 85 F. 3d 407 (9th Cir. 1996).

56. 85 F. 3d 407, 410 (9th Cir. 1996).

57. Staff, "Ralph Lauren sued Polo magazine for trademark infringement," Law Street Journal (3 June 1998): 1, http://www.lawstreet.com/journal/art980603polo.html.

58. Westchester Media Company, L.P. v. PRL UAQ Holdings, Inc., 1998 U.S. Dist. LEXIS 11735 (1998).

59. Feature on ABC television program "20/20," October 16, 1998.

60. S. McKelvey, "Atlanta '96: Olympic countdown to ambush Armageddon," Seton Hall Journal of Sport Law 4 (1994): 397.

61. Reed, IEG legal guide to sponsorship, 159.

62. McKelvey, "Atlanta '96," 401-409.

63. M.J. Greenberg, Sports law practice (Charlottesville, VA: Michie Company, 1993), 677, n. 266.

64. J.B. Strasser and L. Becklund, swoosh (New York: Harper Collins, 1993), 539.

65. E. Thomas Jr., "The bottom line," Wall Street Journal, 19 July 1996, A14.

66. J. Ostrowski, "Tourney 'clean zone' cuts down on glitz," Street and Smith's Sports Business Journal (22-28 March 1999): 23.

67. M.J. Greenberg, Sports law practice supplement (Charlottesville, VA: Michie Company, 1995), 350.

68. Mastercard International, Inc. v. Sprint Communications Company, 1994 U.S. Dist. LEXIS 3398 (S.D.N.Y. 1994).

69. Reed, IEG legal guide to sponsorship, 164.

70. H.C. Black, J.R. Nolan, and M.J. Connolly, Black's law dictionary, 5th ed. (St. Paul, MN: West Publishing Co., 1979), 1371.

71. Westchester Media Company, L.P. v. PRL USA Holdings, Inc., 1998 U.S. Dist. LEXIS 11735 (1998).

72. Allison v. Vintage Sports Plaques, 136 F. 3d 1443 (11th Cir. 1998).

73. Cardtoons v. Major League Baseball Players Association, 95 F. 3d 959, 967 (10th Cir. 1996), citing volume 1 J. Thomas McCarthy, The rights of publicity and privacy sec. 1.1[A][1] (1996).

74. E.H. Rosenthal, "Selling Princess Di: Legal limits on celebrity memorabilia," New York Law Journal (16 January 1998): http://www.nylj.com/

75. 202 F. 2d 866 (2d Cir. 1953), cert. denied, 346 U.S. 816 (1953).

76. 202 F. 2d 866 (2d Cir. 1953), cert. denied, 346 U.S. 816 (1953).

77. 202 F. 2d 866 (2d Cir. 1953), cert. denied, 346 U.S. 816 (1953).

78. 316 F. Supp. 1277 (D.Minn. 1970).

79. Cepeda v. Swift and Co., 415 F. 2d 1205 (8th Cir. 1969).

80. Rosenthal, "Selling Princess Di."

81. 363 N.Y.S. 2d 276 (1975).

82. 34 Cal. App. 4th 790, 40 Cal. Rptr. 2d 639 (1995).

83. 85 F. 3d 407 (9th Cir. 1996).

84. 85 F. 3d 407 (9th Cir. 1996).

85. 95 F. 3d 959 (10th Cir. 1996).

86. 280 N.W. 2d 129 (1979).

87. 280 N.W. 2d 129 (1979).

88. Patents, 35 U.S.C.A. sec. 101 (1996).

89. U.S. Patent and Trademark Office, "What are patents?" 31 July 1995, http://www.uspto.gov/web/offices/

90. Patents, 35 U.S.C. sec. 154 (a)(2) Term of patent.

91. U.S. Patent and Trademark Office, "What are patents?"

92. U.S. Patent and Trademark Office, "What are patents?"

93. See Storm Shelter Notice of Trademark, Copyrights, and Ownership, http://galeforce.simplenet.com/stormshelter/notice.html; L. Mullen, "Arena Football asks court to crack back on rival," Street and Smith's Sports Business Journal (1-7 June 1998): 13.

94. Mullen, "Arena Football," 13.

95. N.E. Garrote and K.C. Maher, "Protecting website's look and feel via copyright and trademark law," New York Law Journal (9 June 1998): http://www.nylj.com/

96. Garrote and Maher, "Protecting website's look."

97. J.B. Berringer and J. Gold, "Advertising injury insurance coverage here and throughout the universe," New York Law Journal (22 September 1998): http://www.nylj.com/

INDEX

ABOUT THE AUTHORS

Bernard J. Mullin

Stephen Hardy

William A. Sutton

Bernard J. Mullin, PhD, is a principal in the Aspire Group, a Denver-based sport marketing and consulting firm with a prestigious list of professional team, arena, and sport facility clients. His 10 years as an executive in professional team sport include President/General Manager of the Denver Grizzlies, Senior Vice President of Business Operations for the Pittsburgh Pirates from 1986-1990, and Senior Vice President of Business Operations for the Colorado Rockies from 1991-1993. In all capacities, he initiated an increase in attendance and profitability. He has been dubbed the "father of sport marketing theory" and the "guru of ticket sales."

Besides his experiences in professional sport, Dr. Mullin spent 12 years in higher education. As Vice Chancellor of Athletics at the University of Denver, he took a Division II program to NCAA Division I classification, significantly increased ticket sales, and more than tripled sponsorship revenues. As a professor of Sport Management at the University of Massachusetts, Dr. Mullin helped evolve the program to international prominence.

Stephen Hardy, PhD, is a Professor and Coordinator of the Sport Studies Program at the University of New Hampshire. A Fellow of the American Academy of Kinesiology and Physical Education, Dr. Hardy previously served as the Assistant Commissioner of the Eastern College Athletic Conference. In his 25 years in the field, he has supervised championships in venues such as the Boston Garden and Madison Square Garden, and he has conducted projects for and with teams in Seattle, Pittsburgh, Cleveland, and Boston. In 1997, he was appointed UNH's faculty representative to the NCAA.

William A. Sutton is an Associate Professor and Graduate Program Director in the Sports Studies department at the University of Massachusetts-Amherst. Prior to assuming his present position, Dr. Sutton served as Vice President for Information Services for Del Wilber and Associates, a sport and lifestyle marketing agency, served as Coordinator of the Sport Management program at Ohio State University, and was a member of the faculty of Robert Morris College. A past president of North American Society for Sport Management, Dr. Sutton also is a principal in the consulting firm Audience Analysts and has worked for such clients as the NBA, the NFL, the NHL, Major League Baseball Properties, the LPGA, the NCAA, Hoop-It-Up, IBM, Mazda, and Sprint. Dr. Sutton has served as coeditor of *Sport Marketing Quarterly* and serves on the editorial board of the *Journal of Sports Marketing & Sponsorship*. Dr. Sutton is widely published in the field and has made more than 75 national and international presentations. The *Cyber Journal of Sport Marketing* named him Sport Marketer of the Year in 1999.

OTHER BOOKS FROM HUMAN KINETICS

Human Resource Management in Sport and Recreation

Packianathan Chelladurai, PhD

1999 • Hardback • 312 pp • Item BCHE0973
ISBN 0-87322-973-8 • $39.00 ($58.50 Canadian)

The first text to take a comprehensive, nuanced look at the critical aspects of human resource management within sport and recreation organizations.

Contemporary Sport Management

Janet B. Parks, DA, Beverly R.K. Zanger, MEd,
Jerome Quarterman, PhD, Editors

1998 • Hardback • 360 pp • Item BPAR0836
ISBN 0-87322-836-7 • $45.00 ($67.50 Canadian)

An ideal text for students majoring in sport management, exercise, fitness management, or athletic training, and for those contemplating majors in these fields.

Sport Tourism

Joy Standeven, DPhil, and Paul De Knop, PhD

1999 • Hardback • 376 pp • Item BSTA0853
ISBN 0-87322-853-7 • $38.00 ($56.95 Canadian)

An ambitious text, which provides an in-depth analysis of the nature of sport, the nature of tourism, and the symbiotic relationship between the two.

To request more information or to order, U.S. customers call 1-800-747-4457, e-mail us at humank@hkusa.com, or visit our Web site at www.humankinetics.com. Persons outside the U.S. can contact us via our Web site or use the appropriate telephone number, postal address, or e-mail address shown in the front of this book.

HUMAN KINETICS
The Information Leader in Physical Activity
P.O. Box 5076, Champaign, IL 61825-5076
2335